Lecture Notes in Computer Science 12831

More information about this subseries at http://www.springer.com/series/7407

Chu-Min Li · Felip Manyà (Eds.)

Theory and Applications of Satisfiability Testing – SAT 2021

24th International Conference
Barcelona, Spain, July 5–9, 2021
Proceedings

 Springer

Editors
Chu-Min Li ⓘ
Laboratoire MIS
University of Picardie Jules Verne
Amiens, France

Felip Manyà ⓘ
IIIA-CSIC
Spanish National Research Council (CSIC)
Bellaterra, Barcelona, Spain

ISSN 0302-9743   ISSN 1611-3349   (electronic)
Lecture Notes in Computer Science
ISBN 978-3-030-80222-6   ISBN 978-3-030-80223-3   (eBook)
https://doi.org/10.1007/978-3-030-80223-3

LNCS Sublibrary: SL1 – Theoretical Computer Science and General Issues

This Springer imprint is published by the registered company Springer Nature Switzerland AG
The registered company address is: Gewerbestrasse 11, 6330 Cham, Switzerland

Preface

This volume contains the papers presented at the 24th International Conference on Theory and Applications of Satisfiability Testing (SAT 2021), held during July 5–9, 2021, in Barcelona. Because of the COVID-19 pandemic, SAT 2021 followed a hybrid format, with both in-person and virtual participation options.

The SAT conference is the premier annual meeting for researchers focusing on the theory and applications of the propositional satisfiability problem, broadly construed. Aside from plain propositional satisfiability, the scope of the meeting includes Boolean optimization, including MaxSAT and pseudo-Boolean (PB) constraints, quantified Boolean formulas (QBF), satisfiability modulo theories (SMT), and constraint programming (CP) for problems with clear connections to Boolean reasoning.

Many challenging combinatorial problems can be tackled using SAT-based techniques, including problems that arise in formal verification, artificial intelligence, operations research, computational biology, cryptology, data mining, machine learning, mathematics, etc. Indeed, the theoretical and practical advances in SAT research over the past 25 years have contributed to making SAT technology an indispensable tool in various domains.

SAT 2021 welcomed scientific contributions addressing different aspects of SAT interpreted in a broad sense, including theoretical advances (such as exact algorithms, proof complexity, and other complexity issues), practical search algorithms, knowledge compilation, implementation-level details of SAT solvers and SAT-based systems, problem encodings and reformulations, and applications (including both novel application domains and improvements to existing approaches), as well as case studies and reports on findings based on rigorous experimentation.

SAT 2021 received 73 submissions, comprising 44 long papers, 18 short papers, and 11 tool papers. At least three Program Committee members reviewed each paper. The reviewing process included an author response period, during which the authors were given the opportunity to respond to the initial reviews for their submissions. To reach a final decision, a Program Committee discussion period followed the author response period. External reviewers supporting the Program Committee were also invited to participate directly in the discussion for the papers they reviewed. This year, most submissions received a meta-review, summarizing the discussion that occurred after the author response and an explanation of the final recommendation. In the end, the Program Committee decided to accept a total of 37 papers: 25 long, 3 short, and 9 tool papers.

The Program Committee singled out the following two submissions for the Best Paper Award and the Best Student Paper Award, respectively:

- Shaowei Cai and Xindi Zhang: "Deep Cooperation of CDCL and Local Search for SAT".
- Alexis de Colnet and Stefan Mengel: "Characterizing Tseitin-Formulas with Short Regular Resolution Refutations".

In addition to presentations on the accepted papers, the scientific program of SAT included two invited talks by the following speakers:

- Carlos Ansótegui, University of Lleida, Spain.
- Adnan Darwiche, University of California, Los Angeles (UCLA), USA.

The conference hosted various associated events. In particular, the following three workshops, affiliated with SAT-2021, were held July 5–6, 2021:

- International Workshop on Model Counting and Sampling (MCW 2021), organized by Johannes K. Fichte, Kuldeep Meel, Markus Hecher, and Mate Soos.
- Pragmatics of SAT Workshop (PoS 2021), organized by Matti Järvisalo and Daniel Le Berre.
- Quantified Boolean Formulas and Beyond Workshop (QBF 2021), organized by Hubie Chen, Florian Lonsing, Martina Seidl, and Friedrich Slivovsky.

The results of several competitive events were also announced at SAT 2021:

- EDA Challenge 2021, organized by Armin Biere, Chu-Min Li, Felip Manyà, and Zhipeng Lü.
- MaxSAT Evaluation 2021, organized by Fahiem Bacchus, Jeremias Berg, Matti Järvisalo, and Ruben Martins.
- Model Counting Competition 2021 (MC 2021), organized by Johannes K. Fichte and Markus Hecher.
- SAT Competition 2021, organized by Tomáš Balyo, Nils Froleyks, Markus Iser, Marijn Heule, Matti Järvisalo, and Martin Suda.

We thank everyone who contributed to making SAT 2021 a success. In particular, we thank the Publicity Chair, Jesús Giráldez; the Workshop Chair, Djamal Habet; the Local Arrangements Chairs, Josep Argelich and Jordi Planes; and all the organizers of the SAT affiliated workshops and competitions.

We are indebted to the Program Committee members and the external reviewers, who dedicated their time to review and evaluate the submissions to the conference. We thank the authors of all submitted papers for their contributions, the SAT Association for their guidance and support in organizing the conference, and the EasyChair conference management system for facilitating the submission and selection of papers as well as the assembly of these proceedings.

We gratefully thank the sponsors of SAT 2021: The Artificial Intelligence journal and CAS Software AC for providing travel support to students attending the conference, Springer for sponsoring the best paper awards, and the University of Picardie Jules Verne and its Modelling, Information and Systems (MIS) laboratory, the Spanish National Research Council (CSIC) and its Artificial Intelligence Research Institute (IIIA), and the Spanish Network on Satisfiability and Constraint Programming for financial and organizational support. Finally, we thank Huawei for its support to SAT 2021.

May 2021

Chu-Min Li
Felip Manyà

Organization

Program Committee Chairs

Chu-Min Li   Université de Picardie Jules Verne, France
Felip Manyà   IIIA-CSIC, Spain

Program Committee

Gilles Audemard	CNRS-Université d'Artois, France
Fahiem Bacchus	University of Toronto, Canada
Jeremias Berg	University of Helsinki, Finland
Olaf Beyersdorff	Friedrich Schiller University Jena, Germany
Armin Biere	Johannes Kepler University Linz, Austria
Miquel Bofill	Universitat de Girona, Spain
Shaowei Cai	Chinese Academy of Sciences, China
Jordi Coll	Aix-Marseille Université, France
Gilles Dequen	Université de Picardie Jules Verne, France
Fei He	Tsinghua University, China
Marijn Heule	Carnegie Mellon University, USA
Alexey Ignatiev	Monash University, Australia
Mikoláš Janota	Czech Technical University in Prague, Czech Republic
Jie-Hong Roland Jiang	National Taiwan University, Taiwan
Matti Järvisalo	University of Helsinki, Finland
Oliver Kullmann	Swansea University, UK
Massimo Lauria	Sapienza University of Rome, Italy
Daniel Le Berre	CNRS - Université d'Artois, France
Jordi Levy	IIIA-CSIC, Spain
Zhipeng Lü	Huazhong University of Science and Technology, China
Inês Lynce	INESC-ID/IST, Universidade de Lisboa, Portugal
Meena Mahajan	The Institute of Mathematical Sciences, India
Vasco Manquinho	INESC-ID/IST, Universidade de Lisboa, Portugal
Joao Marques-Silva	IRIT, CNRS, France
Ruben Martins	Carnegie Mellon University, USA
Carlos Mencía	University of Oviedo, Spain
Stefan Mengel	CNRS, CRIL, France
Tomáš Peitl	Friedrich Schiller University Jena, Germany
Luca Pulina	University of Sassari, Italy
Lakhdar Sais	CNRS-Université d'Artois, France
Martina Seidl	Johannes Kepler University Linz, Austria
Laurent Simon	Bordeaux Institute of Technology, France
Carsten Sinz	Karlsruhe Institute of Technology, Germany

Takehide Soh	Kobe University, Japan
Ofer Strichman	Technion, Israel
Zhouxing Su	Huazhong University of Science and Technology, China
Stefan Szeider	TU Wien, Austria
Mateu Villaret	Universitat de Girona, Spain
Toby Walsh	University of New South Wales, Australia

Additional Reviewers

Balyo, Tomáš	Hůla, Jan	Rabe, Markus N.
Bonacina, Ilario	Iser, Markus	Scheder, Dominik
Böhm, Benjamin	Ivrii, Alexander	Schleitzer, Agnes
de Colnet, Alexis	Jabbour, Said	Semenov, Alexander
Dreier, Jan	Kochemazov, Stepan	Shukla, Ankit
Fleming, Noah	Korhonen, Tuukka	Slivovsky, Friedrich
Fleury, Mathias	Morgado, Antonio	Trimoska, Monika
Galesi, Nicola	Möhle, Sibylle	Xu, Ke
Gocht, Stephan	Nabeshima, Hidetomo	Zaikin, Oleg

Contents

OptiLog: A Framework for SAT-based Systems

Carlos Ansótegui$^{(\boxtimes)}$, Jesús Ojeda$^{(\boxtimes)}$, Antonio Pacheco$^{(\boxtimes)}$, Josep Pon$^{(\boxtimes)}$, Josep M. Salvia$^{(\boxtimes)}$, and Eduard Torres$^{(\boxtimes)}$

Logic and Optimization Group (LOG), University of Lleida, Lleida, Spain
{carlos.ansotegui,jesus.ojedacontreras,josep.pon,eduard.torres}@udl.cat,
jpacheco@alumnes.udl.cat

Abstract. We present OptiLog, a new Python framework for rapid prototyping of SAT-based systems. OptiLog allows to use and integrate SAT solvers currently developed in C/C++ just by implementing the iSAT C++ interface. It also provides a Python binding to the PBLib C++ toolkit for encoding Pseudo Boolean and Cardinality constraints. Finally, it leverages the power of automatic configurators by allowing to easily create configuration scenarios including multiple solvers and encoders.

1 Introduction

Python [33] has emerged as one of the most preferred programming languages for rapid prototyping of applications because of its straightforward syntax and the great amount of established libraries that provide common functionality for researchers to readily use. We can find several of these libraries into diverse Artificial Intelligence disciplines like, for example, Numpy [20], Pandas [29], scikit-learn [31], Pytorch [30] or Keras [12].

In terms of performance, the core of the critical components of these systems is implemented with more efficient languages such as C++, although their interconnection is commonly materialized through Python.

Within the area of Constraint Programming, Python has also become quite popular. CPLEX [23], Gurobi [19], OR-Tools [18], COIN-OR [13], SCIP [17], Z3 [14] and many others have Python bindings. In particular, in the SAT community there have also been several contributions. PySAT [24] was the first framework, to our best knowledge, to provide Python bindings for several SAT solvers.

Recently, there have been other contributions that can be queried from Python such as SAT Heritage [4], intended to serve as an archive and to easily compile and run all SAT solvers that have been released so far, or *cnfgen* [25], that produces *hard* SAT benchmarks coming from research in Proof Complexity.

Supported by MINECO-FEDER TASSAT3 (TIN2016-76573-C2-2-P), MICINNs PROOFS (PID2019-109137GB-C21) and FPU fellowship (FPU18/02929).

C.-M. Li and F. Manyà (Eds.): SAT 2021, LNCS 12831, pp. 1–10, 2021.
https://doi.org/10.1007/978-3-030-80223-3_1

Our contribution in OptiLog[1] is two-fold. First, we provide a Python binding [28] for the PBLib [32] that allows to encode Pseudo Boolean (PB) constraints into SAT. This binding is also currently integrated into PySAT.

Second, we take a step further, easing both the integration of new C++ SAT solvers in OptiLog and their end usage into practical environments.

We isolate the development of C++ SAT solvers so that by implementing the iSAT C++ interface OptiLog gently incorporates the new SAT solver. In contrast, PySAT requires the user to write some ad-hoc additional Python code plus the Python bindings. The iSAT interface is inspired by the C interface IPASIR (Reentrant Incremental Sat solver API, in reverse) [7] and the PySAT interface.

To optimize the end-SAT-based system, the end-user is commonly forced to play by hand with a non-negligible amount of adjustable parameters coming from the solvers or encoders it uses. Automatic configurators should have to be used in this context. Unfortunately, it takes a while to become familiar on how to create the configuration of the scenarios, which is usually a source of countless bugs. OptiLog get rids of all this complexity and automatically generates all the pieces needed for the configuration, delivering a ready-to-tune application.

There have been a number of methods developed for tuning parameters automatically, such as CALIBRA [1], ParamILS [22], I/F-Race [11], SMAC [21] and GGA [2,3]. OptiLog currently provides support for SMAC and GGA.

The paper is structured as follows: In Sect. 2 we present the OptiLog framework with detail about the most important modules implemented, and how a new SAT solver can be integrated into it. Section 3 will present a comprehensive example of the framework. Finally, we will end with Sect. 4, providing some closing thoughts and future work.

2   OptiLog Framework Architecture

The general architecture of OptiLog is described in Fig. 1. Four main modules compose the end-user OptiLog API, which we briefly describe in the following subsections: the Formula module, the SAT Solver module, the PB Encoder module and the Automatic Configuration (AC) module. Additionally, new C++ SAT solvers can be integrated into OptiLog by implementing the C++ iSAT interface. Full details can be found in the OptiLog manual accessible from [27].

2.1   Formula Module

The Formula module is designed to ease the implementation and manipulation of boolean formulas. As such, two specific classes are created: *CNF* (for the typical Conjunctive Normal Form) and *WCNF* (for the Weigthed CNF version). These

---

[1] *Opti* stands for Optimization and *LOG* stands for Logic Optimization Group at UdL (http://ulog.udl.cat/).

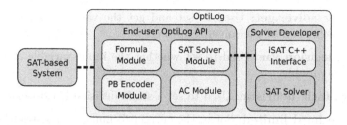

Fig. 1. OptiLog's architecture.

Formulas have the common functionality of setting new variables, adding clauses and exporting to the DIMACS file format.

CNF: The CNF class provides the traditional representation of a Conjunctive Normal Form fomula, a conjunction of clauses defined as disjunctions of literals. In code, clauses are provided as lists of integers.

WCNF: The WCNF class provides the interface for partial and weighted partial CNF formulas. In this case, clauses can be added with a weight. If this is the case, these clauses are considered *soft*. *Hard* clauses are added without weight or by specifying the weight INF_WEIGHT that represents ∞.

As an example, CNF Formula $(x_1 \vee x_2) \wedge (x_3 \vee \neg x_2)$ and WCNF Formula $(x_1 \vee x_2, 1) \wedge (x_3 \vee \neg x_2, \infty)$ would be implemented as follows

```
1 from optilog.sat import CNF, WCNF
2 cnf = CNF()
3 cnf.add_clauses([[1, 2], [3, -2]])
4 wcnf = WCNF()
5 wcnf.add_clause([1, 2], weight=1)
6 wcnf.add_clause([3, -2]) # equivalent to weight=WCNF.INF_WEIGHT
```

Aside from the typical formula manipulation methods, OptiLog provides additional methods. In particular, it provides explicit functions load_{cnf|wcnf} from the optilog.loaders Python module. These functions allow to load the formula directly into a SAT solver.

2.2   SAT Solver Module

OptiLog is inspired on the interfaces of IPASIR [7] and PySAT. The behaviour of some functions can slightly deviate, see the manual [27] for details. The solvers currently integrated in OptiLog are: Cadical [10], Glucose 4.1 and Glucose 3.0 [5], Picosat [8], Minisat [15] and Lingeling 18 [9]. Not all the solvers implement all the methods in the iSAT API, the only one that fully does is a modified version of Glucose 4.1. Here, we briefly describe some of the additional methods that we incorporated into the iSAT API and that are currently supported by the modified version of Glucose 4.1 delivered with the OptiLog tool.

solver.set & solver.get: Used to set and get the value of parameters that modify the behaviour of the solver.

solver.set_decision_var: Used to set whether the input variable can be used as a decision variable.

solver.set_static_heuristic: Used to set a static decision heuristic.

solver.solve_hard_limited: Solves the current formula with a strict budget in terms of conflicts or propagations.

solver.learnt_clauses: This method returns the learnt clauses that are currently in the solver including learnt unit clauses.

2.3 PB Encoder Module

The PB Encoder module currently integrates the Python binding for PBLib we developed for this project, which provides the access to PB and Card encoders, some of them incremental. It also incorporates the Totalizer incremental encoder implemented in Python in PySAT. The user can transparently create PB/Card constraints that are automatically encoded through PBLib and PySAT Card functions into a set of SAT clauses. If all coefficients (weights) in the constraint are equal to 1, Card constraint encoders are applied.

```
1 from optilog.sat.pbencoder import IncrementalEncoder
2 L = [1,2,-3]
3 W = [4,3,3]
4 encoder, max_var, C = IncrementalEncoder.init(
5     lits=L, bound=7, weights=W, max_var=3, encoding="seqcounter")
```

Lines 2–5 in the above example show how to encode the PB constraint $4 \cdot x + 3 \cdot y + 3 \cdot \neg z \le 7$ through an incremental encoder into SAT using OptiLog. Currently, we only support PB constraints with positive coefficients[2].

Function *IncrementalEncoder.init* takes as input the list of literals L, the bound, the list of weights W, the maximum variable and the encoding to be used. It returns an encoder object that can be used to refine the upper bound, the maximum variable used by the encoder and the list of clauses that encode the constraint C. In our example, to refine the upper bound to ≤ 6 we can use the command `max_var, C = encoder.extend(6)`, which returns the clauses C to force the new upper bound and the maximum variable used in C.

The possible encodings supported in PBLib for incremental encoding are *bdd* and *card* for cardinality constraints and *seqcounter* and *adder* for PB. PySAT Card supports *totalizer* for cardinality constraints. All these encodings are available in *IncrementalEncoder* through the parameter *encoding* in the *init* method. By default PBLib automatically overrides the user selected encoding when it detects it can generate too many clauses. In contrast, OptiLog always applies the encoding selected by the user.

---

[2] We will add in short a normalization step for general PB constraints.

2.4 Automatic Configuration (AC) Module

The AC module provides an API to generate configuration scenarios for AC tools. An AC tool searches for a setting, to the configurable parameters of a *target* function (algorithm), that optimizes some objective function or run time on a set of instances (data) under different seeds. We present the module features:

```
1  import random
2  from optilog.autocfg import ac, Bool, Int, Real, Categorical, CfgCall
3  from optilog.autocfg.configurators import SMACConfigurator
4  @ac
5  def func1(
6      x, data, p1: Bool() = True, p2: Real(-1.3, 2) = 0,
7      p3: Int(-5, 5) = 0, p4: Categorical("A", "B", "C") = "A"):
8      ...
9  @ac
10 def func2(
11     data, seed, l_func1: CfgCall(func1), n: Int(1, 10) = 1):
12     random.seed(seed)
13     res = n * l_func1(random.randint(20,30), data)
14     print("Result:", res)
15     return res
16
17 configurator = SMACConfigurator(
18     func2, global_cfgcalls=[func2], runsolver_path='./runsolver',
19     input_data=['path1', 'path2', 'path3'],
20     data_kwarg='data', seed_kwarg='seed',
21     run_obj='quality', cutoff=30, time_limit_sec=43200,
22     quality_regex=r"^Result: (\d+)$")
23 configurator.generate_scenario('./scenario')
```

Configurable Parameters: Leveraging Python's type hints we can specify the type, domain and default value of the parameters to configure. For example, the AC module will recognize four configurable parameters in *func1* $(p1, p2, p3, p4)$, where parameter $p3$ is of type `optilog.autocfg.Int`, and will collect the annotated information for creating the configuration scenario.

Configurable Functions: The AC module allows to gather the configurable parameters of a configurable function (decorated with *@ac*). All calls to the same *global* CfgCall function will share the same values for the configurable parameters, while calls to *local* CfgCall functions can have different values. In the example, *func2* is *global* while *l_func1* is a *local* call to *func1*.

Configuration Scenario: class *SMACConfigurator* is used to automatically generate the scenario for the SMAC configurator. It receives as parameters: (l. 18) the entry point *func2* (i.e., the function that SMAC will call), the list of *global* configurable functions [*func2*] (notice that in our example *func2* is itself configurable), the path to the *runsolver* tool, (l. 19) the list of input data (which is printed, item by item, to a text file and used by SMAC as the description of the set of instances where the function to be tuned will be evaluated), (l. 20) the parameters (*data_kwarg*, *seed_kwarg*) that will use the AC tool to send the data and seed to the entry point on which the current configuration will be evaluated, (l. 21) the objective is set to *quality* in order to minimize the result of the entry point (*runtime* is another possible objective), a set of parameters related to the automatic configuration process (*cutoff*, *time_limit_sec*), and (l. 22) the regular expression to extract the quality reported to the AC tool.

2.5 Adding SAT Solvers to OptiLog Through iSAT Interface

OptiLog automatically generates bindings to C++ SAT solvers that implement the iSAT abstract interface. In order to integrate a new SAT solver, the solver source code has to be included into the compilation pipeline and an implementation to the abstract iSAT interface has to be provided.

The `Extern/sat` directory contains the source code of the SAT solver. For example, in `Extern/sat/glucose41` we find the source code for Glucose 4.1.

The `Module/sat` directory contains the implementation for the iSAT interface. In particular, the files `solver.{cpp|hpp}` define the implementation of the iSAT abstract interface. These files contain macros that will be used to automatically generate Python bindings. In the Glucose 4.1 example, the implementation of the interface is located in `Module/sat/glucose41`.

All the process described above is automatically performed by executing the `new_solver` script provided by OptiLog.

3   Example: The Linear MaxSAT Algorithm with OptiLog

SAT-based MaxSAT algorithms reformulate the MaxSAT optimization problem into a sequence of SAT decision problems. Each SAT instance of the sequence encodes whether there exists an assignment with a cost $\leq k$, encoded as a PB or Card constraint depending on the weights of the soft constraints. SAT instances with a k less than the optimal cost are unsatisfiable, the others being satisfiable. In particular, the subclass of model-guided algorithms iteratively refine (decrease) the upper bound and guide the search with satisfying assignments (models) obtained from satisfiable SAT instances.

Left hand side of Program 1 shows an implementation of the Linear algorithm [16,26], a SAT-based model-guided algorithm for Weighted MaxSAT formulas, with OptiLog. The *linear* function takes as parameters the path to the Weighted MaxSAT instance in DIMACS format and the seed (lines 7, 8). Lines 10–12 create the incremental SAT solver, set its seed and load the hard clauses directly into the solver while the soft clauses are stored in the WCNF formula f.

Lines 15–19 make a relaxed copy of the soft clauses (adding a new blocking variable per clause) that is added to the SAT solver. Line 22 creates an incremental PB constraint on the blocking variables B that uses as coefficients W, the weights of the soft constraints, and the initial upper bound ub as the independent term. It retrieves the set of initial SAT clauses C for the PB encoding (added to the SAT solver in line 24), the max_var auxiliary variable used in

```
 1 from optilog.sat import Glucose41
 2 from optilog.sat.pbencoder import IncrementalEncoder
 3 from optilog.loaders import load_wcnf
 4
 5
 6 def linear(
 7     instance,
 8     seed
 9 ):
10     s = Glucose41()
11     s.set('seed', seed)
12     f = load_wcnf(instance, s)
13     B, W, max_var = [], [], f.max_var()
14
15     for w, c in f.soft_clauses:
16         max_var += 1
17         s.add_clause(c + [max_var])
18         B += [max_var]
19         W += [w]
20
21     res, ub = True, f.top_weight()
22     encoder, max_var, C = IncrementalEncoder
23                           .init(B, ub, W, max_var)
24     s.add_clauses(C)
25
26     while res is True and ub > 0:
27         max_var, C = encoder.extend(ub - 1)
28         s.add_clauses(C)
29         res = s.solve()
30         if res is True:
31             ub = f.cost(s.model())
32             print("o", ub)
33
34     return ub
```

```
 1 from optilog.autocfg import ac, Categorical, CfgCall
 2 from optilog.autocfg.sat import get_glucose41
 3 @ac
 4 def linear(
 5     instance,
 6     seed,
 7     init_solver_fn: CfgCall(get_glucose41),
 8     encoding: Categorical('best', 'adder', 'seqcounter') = 'best'
 9 ):
10     s = init_solver_fn(seed=seed)
11
12     f = load_wcnf(instance, s)
13     B, W, max_var = [], [], f.max_var()
14
15     for w, c in f.soft_clauses:
16         max_var += 1
17         s.add_clause(c + [max_var])
18         B += [max_var]
19         W += [w]
20
21     res, ub = True, f.top_weight()
22     encoder, max_var, C = IncrementalEncoder
23                           .init(B, ub, W, max_var, encoding)
24     s.add_clauses(C)
25
26     while res is True and ub > 0:
27         max_var, C = encoder.extend(ub - 1)
28         s.add_clauses(C)
29         res = s.solve()
30         if res is True:
31             ub = f.cost(s.model())
32             print("o", ub)
33
34     return ub
```

Program 1: Linear MaxSAT algorithm implemented with OptiLog (left) and modifications required to the same implementation to enable its automatic configuration (right). The imports for *IncrementalEncoder* and *load_wcnf* are omitted in the automatic configuration example.

the encoding and the object *encoder* through which we will be able to generate additional SAT clauses to further restrict the constraint (see line 27).

Lines 26–32 conform the main loop of the algorithm. The new clauses to extend the incremental PB constraints are generated and added (lines 27,28). Line 29 calls the SAT solver and, if the current SAT instance is satisfiable, the model is retrieved using its cost to refine the upper bound (lines 30,31).

Right hand side of Program 1 shows how the definition of the linear function has to be changed so that it can be automatically configured. There are, in particular, two main configurable aspects: the SAT solver and the PB encoder to be used plus their respective adjustable parameters.

Instead of initializing the SAT solver in line 10, we use the configurable function *get_glucose41* that returns a configured *Glucose41* solver[3].

The other aspect to be configured is the incremental encoder that we are using. We add a configurable categorical parameter called *encoding* (line 8), which is passed to the *init* method of *IncrementalEncoder* in line 22.

The following lines show how the SMACConfigurator object is created. Line 7 is used to report the quality to the AC tool and line 8 is used to specify the default quality when there is a *crash* such as a system timeout or memout.

```
 1 configurator = SMACConfigurator(
 2     linear, runsolver_path="./runsolver", global_cfgcalls=[linear],
 3     input_data=["inst1.wcnf", "inst2.wcnf", ..., "instN.wcnf"],
 4     data_kwarg="instance", seed_kwarg="seed",
 5     cutoff=30, memory_limit=6 * 1024,
 6     wallclock_limit=43200, run_obj="quality",
 7     quality_regex=r"^o (\d+)$",
 8     cost_for_crash=(2 << 64) - 1,    # Max sum WCNF weights
 9 )
10 configurator.generate_scenario("./scenario")
```

We experimented with the configurable version of the Linear algorithm on a computer cluster with 2.1 GHz cores. As benchmarks, we used the set of 600 instances from the complete weighted track of the MaxSAT 2020 evaluation [6].

We executed SMAC in parallel with 32 runs (one of them with the default configuration of Glucose41 and PB encoder). In 5 out of the 32 runs, SMAC was able to find a better configuration than the default. These 5 runs provide suboptimal values for 446, 445, 443, 443 and 424 instances, while the default only on 388. Curiously, 2 out of the 5 best runs (443, 424) set the PB encoder to *adder* (default value is *best*). The rest of the changes are applied on the Glucose41 parameters. This is a sign of the benefit of using AC tools even on systems that combine several pieces that already have good default parameters.

---

[3] A SAT solver developer can make his solver configurable providing a json describing all the parameters with their domain and default value. More details can be consulted in the online documentation [27].

4   Conclusions and Future Work

The SAT community has generated amazing tools that we need to make more accessible to our and other communities. OptiLog contributes in this sense, easing the access to solvers and encoders, providing the iSAT interface that could become the basis for an standard SAT API., and the AC module that can potentially be applied to tune any Python function.

As future work, we will add other solvers, like MaxSAT or PB solvers, adding support for more complex compilation flags. We will also provide support for callback functions as in Gurobi [19] to be applied on critical points: restarts, pick literal decision, conflict analysis, etc. Finally, we will integrate crafted and random instance generators and allow dynamic instance downloading from repositories.

References

1. Adenso-Diaz, B., Laguna, M.: Fine-tuning of algorithms using fractional experimental design and local search. Oper. Res. **54**(1), 99–114 (2006)
2. Ansotegui, C., Sellmann, M., Tierney, K.: A gender-based genetic algorithm for the automatic configuration of algorithms. In: Proceedings of the 15th International Conference on Principles and Practice of Constraint Programming, pp. 142–157 (2009)
3. Ansótegui, C., Malitsky, Y., Samulowitz, H., Sellmann, M., Tierney, K.: Model-based genetic algorithms for algorithm configuration. In: IJCAI, pp. 733–739 (2015)
4. Audemard, G., Paulevé, L., Simon, L.: SAT heritage: a community-driven effort for archiving, building and running more than thousand SAT solvers. In: Pulina, L., Seidl, M. (eds.) SAT 2020. LNCS, vol. 12178, pp. 107–113. Springer, Cham (2020). https://doi.org/10.1007/978-3-030-51825-7_8
5. Audemard, G., Simon, L.: Predicting learnt clauses quality in modern sat solvers. In: Proceedings of the 21st International Joint Conference on Artifical Intelligence, pp. 399–404. IJCAI 2009. Morgan Kaufmann Publishers Inc., San Francisco, CA, USA (2009)
6. Bacchus, F., Berg, J., Järvisalo, M., Martins, R.: MaxSAT evaluation 2020: solver and benchmark descriptions (2020)
7. Balyo, T., contributors: The standard interface for incremental satisfiability solving. https://github.com/biotomas/ipasir (2014)
8. Biere, A.: PicoSAT essentials. J. Satisfiability, Boolean Model. Comput. **4**(2–4), 75–97 (2008)
9. Biere, A.: Lingeling, plingeling and treengeling entering the sat competition 2013. Proc. SAT Competition **2013**, 1 (2013)
10. Biere, A., Fazekas, K., Fleury, M., Heisinger, M.: CaDiCaL, Kissat, Paracooba, Plingeling and Treengeling entering the SAT Competition 2020. In: Balyo, T., Froleyks, N., Heule, M., Iser, M., Järvisalo, M., Suda, M. (eds.) Proceedings of SAT Competition 2020 - Solver and Benchmark Descriptions. Department of Computer Science Report Series B, vol. B-2020-1, pp. 51–53. University of Helsinki (2020)
11. Birattari, M., Yuan, Z., Balaprakash, P., Stützle, T.: F-Race and iterated F-Race: an overview. In: Empirical Methods for the Analysis of Optimization Algorithms, pp. 311–336 (2010)
12. Chollet, F., et al.: Keras (2015). https://github.com/fchollet/keras

13. COIN-OR Foundation: Computational infrastructure for operations research. https://www.coin-or.org/ (2016)
14. de Moura, L., Bjørner, N.: Z3: an efficient SMT solver. In: Ramakrishnan, C.R., Rehof, J. (eds.) TACAS 2008. LNCS, vol. 4963, pp. 337–340. Springer, Heidelberg (2008). https://doi.org/10.1007/978-3-540-78800-3_24
15. Eén, N., Sörensson, N.: An extensible SAT-solver. In: Giunchiglia, E., Tacchella, A. (eds.) SAT 2003. LNCS, vol. 2919, pp. 502–518. Springer, Heidelberg (2004). https://doi.org/10.1007/978-3-540-24605-3_37
16. Eén, N., Sörensson, N.: Translating Pseudo-Boolean Constraints into SAT. J. Satisfiability, Boolean Model. Comput. 2(1–4), 1–26 (2006). IOS Press
17. Gamrath, G., et al.: The SCIP Optimization Suite 7.0. ZIB-Report 20–10, Zuse Institute Berlin, March 2020
18. Google: Google OR-Tools. https://developers.google.com/optimization (2021)
19. Gurobi Optimization: Gurobi. https://www.gurobi.com/ (2021)
20. Harris, C.R., et al.: Array programming with NumPy. Nature 585(7825), 357–362 (2020). https://doi.org/10.1038/s41586-020-2649-2
21. Hutter, F., Hoos, H.H., Leyton-Brown, K.: Sequential Model-Based Optimization for General Algorithm Configuration. In: Coello, C.A.C. (ed.) LION 2011. LNCS, vol. 6683, pp. 507–523. Springer, Heidelberg (2011). https://doi.org/10.1007/978-3-642-25566-3_40
22. Hutter, F., Hoos, H., Leyton-Brown, K., Stuetzle, T.: ParamILS: an automatic algorithm configuration framework. JAIR 36, 267–306 (2009)
23. IBM: IBM ILOG CPLEX. https://www.ibm.com/products/ilog-cplex-optimization-studio (2021)
24. Ignatiev, A., Morgado, A., Marques-Silva, J.: PySAT: a Python toolkit for prototyping with SAT oracles. In: SAT, pp. 428–437 (2018)
25. Lauria, M., Elffers, J., Nordström, J., Vinyals, M.: CNFgen: a generator of crafted benchmarks. In: Gaspers, S., Walsh, T. (eds.) SAT 2017. LNCS, vol. 10491, pp. 464–473. Springer, Cham (2017). https://doi.org/10.1007/978-3-319-66263-3_30
26. Le Berre, D., Parrain, A.: The Sat4j library, release 2.2. J. Satisfiability, Boolean Model. Comput. 7(2–3), 59–64 (2010). IOS Press
27. Logic and Optimization Group: Optilog official documentation (2021). http://ulog.udl.cat/static/doc/optilog/html/index.html
28. Logic Optimization Group: PyPBLib: PBLib Python3 bindings. https://pypi.org/project/pypblib/ (2019)
29. McKinney, W.: Data Structures for Statistical Computing in Python. In: van der Walt, S., Millman, J. (eds.) In: Proceedings of the 9th Python in Science Conference, pp. 56–61 (2010). https://doi.org/10.25080/Majora-92bf1922-00a
30. Paszke, A., et al.: Pytorch: an imperative style, high-performance deep learning library. In: Wallach, H., Larochelle, H., Beygelzimer, A., d' Alché-Buc, F., Fox, E., Garnett, R. (eds.) Advances in Neural Information Processing Systems 32, pp. 8024–8035. Curran Associates, Inc. (2019)
31. Pedregosa, F., et al.: Scikit-learn: machine learning in Python. J. Mach. Learn. Res. 12, 2825–2830 (2011)
32. Philipp, T., Steinke, P.: PBLib – a library for encoding pseudo-Boolean constraints into CNF. In: Heule, M., Weaver, S. (eds.) SAT 2015. LNCS, vol. 9340, pp. 9–16. Springer, Cham (2015). https://doi.org/10.1007/978-3-319-24318-4_2
33. Van Rossum, G., Drake, F.L.: Python 3 Reference Manual. CreateSpace, Scotts Valley, CA (2009)

PyDGGA: Distributed GGA
for Automatic Configuration

Carlos Ansótegui[1]([✉]), Josep Pon[1]([✉]), Meinolf Sellmann[2]([✉]),
and Kevin Tierney[3]([✉])

[1] LOG Group, University of Lleida, Lleida, Spain
`carlos.ansotegui@diei.udl.cat`, `josep.pon@udl.cat`
[2] General Electric, Boston, USA
`meinolf@ge.com`
[3] Decision and Operation Technologies Group, Bielefeld University,
Bielefeld, Germany
`kevin.tierney@uni-bielefeld.de`

Abstract. We present PyDGGA, a Python tool that implements a
distributed version of the automatic algorithm configurator GGA, which
is a specialized genetic algorithm to find high quality parameters for
solvers and algorithms. PyDGGA implements GGA using an event-
driven architecture and runs a simulation of future generations of the
genetic algorithm to maximize the usage of the available computing
resources. Overall, PyDGGA offers a friendly interface to deploy elastic
distributed AC scenarios on shared high-performance computing clusters.

Keywords: Automatic algorithm configuration · Satisfiability

1 Introduction

Automatic algorithm configuration (AAC) methods have become a critical tool
for solver developers and users to squeeze every last drop of performance out of
their approaches, as well as customize algorithms to perform well on a particular
set of instances. AAC tools do this by trying out different parameter settings
for solvers and returning the one that performs the best according to some
objective function, e.g., solver runtime or heuristic quality. Parameters range in
scope and can, for example, determine the type of heuristic an algorithm should
use, modify a learning rate, or decide whether to perform random restarts or not.
Regardless of what the parameters actually are, setting them to a specific value
can dramatically affect an algorithm's overall ability to solve problem instances
of a particular type. However, finding suitable parameters is difficult and time

This work was partially supported by the MINECO-FEDER project TASSAT3
(TIN2016-76573-C2-2-P) and the MICINNs project PROOFS (PID2019-109137GB-
C21).

© Springer Nature Switzerland AG 2021
C.-M. Li and F. Manyà (Eds.): SAT 2021, LNCS 12831, pp. 11–20, 2021.
https://doi.org/10.1007/978-3-030-80223-3_2

consuming because each evaluation of the algorithm being configured is very computationally expensive.

Setting parameters automatically dramatically reduces manual efforts and can result in orders of magnitude improvements in performance. Over the past decade there have been several methods developed for tuning parameters automatically, such as CALIBRA [1], ParamILS [13], I/F-Race [6], SMAC [12], ReACT/ReACTR [9,10] and CPPL [8]. We focus on the algorithm configurator GGA [3,4], which uses a gender-based genetic algorithm to search through the space of configurations on a set of instances to assign good values to parameters.

While previous work has explored parallel algorithm configuration in the context of ParamILS, SMAC [11] and grid search [18], we want to leverage the advantage of population-based approaches followed by GGA, and the inherent potential for parallelization [7] of genetic algorithms. We provide several novel enhancements of GGA that allow it to fully utilize parallel resources by simulating future generations even before the current generation is completely finished. Our experimental results show the effectiveness of our enhancements, leading to significant improvements on five different SAT benchmarks.

This paper is organized as follows. We first formalize AAC and provide some background information. Then we describe the PyDGGA architecture and novel components versus previous versions of GGA. We then provide brief instructions on how to use PyDGGA. Finally, we experiment on SAT problems and conclude.

2   Preliminaries

In this paper, we present a tool for AAC that extends the algorithm GGA [3], which we briefly present at the end of this section. Formally, in AAC, given a target algorithm A with parameter configuration space Θ, a set of instances Π and a cost metric $\hat{c} : \Theta \times \Pi \to \mathbb{R}$, the objective is to find a parameterization $\theta \in \Theta$ of A that minimizes $\hat{c}$ over Π. We refer to the combination of A, Θ, Π and the configuration of the AAC tool, including $\hat{c}$, as an *AAC scenario*. Since the behavior of A is determined by its parameterization, we could also state that AAC generates a specialized version of A to tackle the instances in Π and other instances with a similar structure more efficiently or effectively.

It is common for A to be a *black-box*, meaning it accepts some inputs (the parameters and a problem instance) and provides some output (e.g., $\hat{c}$), but we cannot see internal functionality. Practically speaking, A is implemented as a binary file that outputs its results in a format adequate for its domain, but likely not for the AAC tool. Moreover, it may also be necessary to limit the resources that A can use to solve an instance, such as memory or CPU time. The standard way of addressing these issues in AAC tools is for the user to replace A with a wrapper script that handles these and any other aspects that may be necessary.

The configuration space Θ is composed of categorical and numerical parameters. The former represent parameters with discrete domains whose values have no order, whereas the latter have an order and can be sub-classified as either integer or real parameters. Some AAC approaches, like GGA, support modeling Θ with dependencies or simple constraints.

GGA

GGA is a genetic algorithm-based approach to general AAC that has been used in practice for a wide array of applications, such as tuning solvers in SAT [15]/Max-SAT [2], machine reassignment [17], and mixed-integer programming [15]). As a genetic algorithm, it has the archetypal loop in which each iteration is referred to as a generation, and tries to improve the solution via recombination and mutation operators. In GGA, the population is partitioned into *competitive* and *non-competitive* groups. The former is evaluated on A, whereas the latter acts as a source of diversity to escape local optima. To conduct the evaluations of each generation, GGA uses a parallel racing scheme, called a tournament. If the entire population was placed into a single tournament, it would be too large for a single processor. Thus, the tournament is split into *mini-tournaments* that are run sequentially. This division yields one winner per mini-tournament, each of which is recombined with members of the non-competitive group to generate the offspring for the next generation.

In the first generations, we expect most individuals to perform rather poorly since they are generated at random. Thus, we do not wish to evaluate these individuals on the entire instance set Π. Instead, each tournament is evaluated using a randomly selected subset of Π. Initially, this subset is quite small (around 5 instances), but as further generations are expected to have better individuals, the size of the subset is increased linearly until roughly 75% of all generations have been carried out, and the subset becomes Π. For further details on GGA please refer to [3].

3   PyDGGA

PyDGGA is a distributed version of GGA written in Python that has been adapted to exploit the resources of High-Performance Computing (HPC) clusters. In this section, we first focus on the parts of the algorithm that have been modified to adapt GGA to HPC clusters. Then, we introduce a new instance selection policy and what we refer to as an *elite mini-tournament*, which are extensions to the original GGA introduced in PyDGGA. Finally, we comment on some practical enhancements that do not alter the original GGA approach.

3.1   Distributed Architecture

To adapt GGA to a distributed computing architecture while preserving the core algorithm as close as possible to the original description, PyDGGA is implemented using an event-driven architecture, which is known to be good for horizontal scalability. The events represent steps from the original GGA, such as the generation of new offspring or evaluation of a genome on an instance. Each event has the necessary information attached to it to perform its associated action and triggers the next event in a way to maintain the original GGA execution logic.

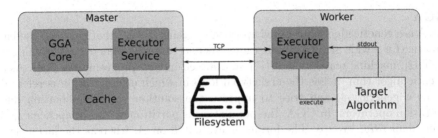

Fig. 1. Master-Worker architecture

To exploit the available computing resources to the fullest extent, PYDGGA uses a master-worker architecture, shown in Fig. 1 with just one worker for the sake of clarity, to distribute the genome-instance evaluations across several machines. The master runs the event-based core and the workers wait for parameters and instance data to evaluate and return the result. The workers have none of GGA's logic and can be added or removed at any time. The master will simply use the workers still available and rollback incomplete evaluations, if necessary. We use this approach instead of just relying on a batch-queuing system, such as SGE or SLURM, because these systems are used by multiple users concurrently and their tasks are interleaved, which adds a non-negligible delay when only a handful of tasks are to be executed. Since PYDGGA tries to run as many evaluations as possible, this delay ends up being a burden. The worker approach lets PYDGGA run on any distributed environment regardless of the batch-queuing system, as long as there is a shared file system. This ensures computing resources are reserved for a longer period and allows the user to terminate and re-submit more workers later to release resources for other jobs temporarily.

3.2   Simulation

Simply rewriting a sequential algorithm in a parallel or distributed fashion is no guarantee that it can exploit the full capacity of modern hardware. This holds for PYDGGA as well, thus we make some additions to the parallel logic to improve its performance. In PYDGGA, we run a simulation of the population's evolution, which creates a directed-graph that represents the dependencies between the different steps of the algorithm. In this graph, the nodes represent individuals and mini-tournaments, and the edges describe the action that they trigger on other individuals or mini-tournaments. For example, when a mini-tournament finishes it triggers a "create offspring" event on all those individuals that are to be children of the winner.

When coupling the simulator with the event-driven architecture, PYDGGA can exploit distributed environments even further by interlacing steps from different generations. For example, when a mini-tournament is done, the individuals of the next generation that depend on the winner of the mini-tournament can be generated and evaluated without waiting for the current generation to finish.

3.3   Scheduling and Canceling

A problem arises when we can run evaluations of different generations distributively at the same time. Which should be run first? It makes sense to run the evaluations in an order relative to the generation they belong to. This way we keep on fulfilling the dependencies of later generations, which trigger more evaluations, and thus the hardware rarely idles. However, this static order may break the efficiency of the original GGA racing scheme.

GGA uses mini-tournaments with size equal to the number of CPU cores on a single machine, and runs the evaluation of each individual on a different core. Then, as soon as an individual can be declared the winner it simply cancels the evaluations of the other individuals in the mini-tournament that have not been started yet.

PyDGGA can handle many more resources than GGA and can evaluate entire mini-tournaments at the same time, which means that it will waste time running evaluations that GGA would have skipped. To tackle this issue, PyDGGA keeps a dynamic priority value that determines the next evaluation to run. However, computing this value so as to maximize overall efficiency is still an open question. Our current approach tries to mimic the racing scheme behaviour. Finally, since the scheduling is not perfect, we know that PyDGGA will start some evaluations that will end up being unnecessary. To mitigate this, we also implement a way for PyDGGA to terminate running evaluations.

3.4   Instance Selection

As mentioned before, GGA randomly selects a subset of Π at each generation, meaning that two consecutive generations may be evaluated on completely different instances. Other approaches, such as IRACE [6] or SMAC [12], use a randomly augmented superset of the set used in the previous iteration. It seems likely that this type of instance selection would be beneficial for GGA in some scenarios, as many instances will have already been evaluated by the surviving individuals of a generation, and this will reduce the amount of work to determine the winner of the next generation.

We want to clarify, however, that using this strategy makes it easier to overfit the initial subset of instances, which may or may not be representative enough. For example, it may be a good approach to configure a solver for a specific family of SAT instances, but can lead to worse results if one wants a configuration that generalizes to all the instances in the crafted or industrial categories.

3.5   Elite Mini-Tournament

During the configuration process some genomes that used to be among the best of a generation end up being lost due to the changing subset of Π used to evaluate them. Nonetheless, we have observed that some of these would have become relevant again, or even the overall best genome as the subset of Π

becomes larger. To address this phenomenon we introduce an additional mini-tournament, the so-called "elite mini-tournament", to each generation in which only the best overall genomes of previous generations can compete. This gives a chance to these genomes to continue to be part of the recombination procedure and help drive the algorithm to their region of the search space should they become relevant again.

3.6   Other Tool Enhancements

On top of the more profound changes commented above, we also introduce some additional modifications to make PYDGGA more user-friendly.

- **Stop/Resume**: PYDGGA keeps a cache of all the evaluations performed so far inside the scenario directory. If the same scenario is used again it will reuse the cache whenever possible, which has the effect of resuming the search from wherever it was stopped as all the evaluations in the simulation graph up to that point are resolved instantly.
- **Enhanced configurations constraints**: GGA allows the user to specify combinations of forbidden values, but only can only express very simple constraints, such as $a = 10$ & $b = 5$ is forbidden, which forces the user to write the Cartesian product of all the forbidden parameter-value combinations. PYDGGA uses Python's abstract syntax tree module, which lets the user write Python logical expressions that must be satisfied (True) by all valid configurations, for example: $10 <= a < 20$ and b in $[5, 6, 7]$.
- **Abort Search**: GGA only supports two possible evaluation results: SUCCESS and CRASHED. The first denotes that the evaluation was successful and the second captures cases where A failed but are not critical, for example because it run out of memory. While CRASHED works fine in most situations, there are others that leave the user waiting for the algorithm to finish just to realize at the end that all the evaluations CRASHED. As an example, imagine that the instances or the target algorithm binary are moved while PYDGGA is running, or imagine that the user decides to abort if the program detects that the result it is computing is not correct and the same error may arise in the rest of the executions. For these situations, we add the evaluation result ABORT, which stops PYDGGA immediately.
- **Objective function**: GGA was designed with runtime tuning in mind. PYDGGA extends this to support a different type of objective function. Namely, the user can pass any value as the evaluation metric (including the runtime) and PYDGGA will try to configure the target algorithm for that metric.

4   Using PYDGGA

PYDGGA is available as a command-line tool from https://ulog.udl.cat/?page_id=30. There one can download a pre-built binary, the user manual and some examples. For the sake of brevity, we do not describe the details of the whole process. Instead, we explain what a scenario is and show that running PyDGGA locally or in a distributed environment is quite similar. We encourage the reader to follow the complete example on how to tune the SAT solver glucose 4 in the user manual.

A configuration scenario for PyDGGA is just a directory with some special files that contain the information required to configure the target algorithm. These files are:

- **conf.xml:** This file describes the parameter structure of A, as a tree. Additionally, it may also contain the so called seed genomes, i.e., the default solver parameter's values, and constraints to filter forbidden parameterizations.
- **instances.txt:** A simple text file that contains the instances that form Π. Each line of the file contains the path to an instance and the seed that the target algorithm should use to initialize the pseudo-random number generator of A when evaluating that instance.
- **settings.txt:** The configuration of PyDGGA itself, such as the number of generations, the size of the population, etc. It also contains the name of the wrapper file.
- **wrapper file:** This could be the target algorithm A or a script that acts as the interface between PyDGGA and A.

Once a scenario is set up, running or testing it is as simple as running the following command to start PyDGGA locally:

```
pydgga gga -s "/path/to/scenario_dir"
```

If the scenario works locally, it is almost ready for use in a distributed environment. The only additional element is a script that PyDGGA will invoke any time it needs to start a new worker. For example, to run it on an environment that uses **qsub** to submit jobs, the script could be:

```
1  #!/usr/bin/env sh
2
3  QUEUE="yourqueue.q"              # System specific configuration
4  PENV="smp"
5  MEM_LIMIT="35840M" # 35 GB
6  RT_LIMIT=172800 # 2 Days
7
8  name=${1}   # session name      | Extract fixed parameters
9  slots=${2} # number of slots    | passed by pydgga
10 shift 2     # remove 'name' and 'slots' from ${@}
11
12 olog="/path/to/stdout/directory"
13 elog="/path/to/stderr/directory"
14
15 echo "pydgga dggaw ${@}" | qsub -V -cwd -pe ${PENV} ${slots}\
16      -l h_vmem=${MEM_LIMIT} -l h_rt=${RT_LIMIT} -q ${QUEUE}   \
```

```
17     -N ${name} -o "${olog}" -e "${elog}"
18
19  exit 0
```

Then to run the same scenario distributed, one simply runs:

```
pydgga dgga -s "/path/to/scenario_dir" --worker-script "/path/to
    /script" --slots SLOTS_PER_WORKER --num-workers NUM_WORKERS
```

5 Experiments with SAT

In this section we conduct some experiments to showcase that PYDGGA can outperform the default parameters on several SAT scenarios. We focus on minimizing the runtime of a SAT solver. The experiments are conducted in a compute cluster with nodes equipped with two octo-core Intel Xeon Silver 4110 @ 2.10 GHz processors and 96 GB of RAM. The selected solver is the award-winning SparrowToRiss [5], which has a large configuration space with 222 parameters open for configuration. The instances come from the industrial and crafted benchmarks used in [16]: Bounded Model Checking (BMC), Circuit Fuzz (CF), IBM-Hardware Verification, Graph Isomorphism (GI), and N-Rooks, which are all available, including the train/test splits, in the AClib [14].

To configure the solver, we let PYDGGA run for 2 days. In both the training and test phases we use a time limit of 300 s and 5 GB per evaluation. We present the results of our evaluation in Table 1, which show that PyDGGA can find better parameteriztions than the defaults for SparrowToRiss on all the evaluated SAT benchmarks. The cost metric employed is PAR10, which is defined as the time needed to solve the instance if solved within the time limit, otherwise the run is penalized with a value 10 times the time limit. We report the results using the PAR10 metric as well as the number of solved instances. Finally, to make the PAR10 value more readable, we remove the constant value post hoc added by instances that are never solved by any configuration.

Table 1. PAR10 performance (# solved instances) on the test instances

	BMC	CF	IBM	GI	N-Rooks
Default	346 (262)	297 (276)	113 (232)	247 (307)	116 (348)
PYDGGA	**171 (267)**	**89 (283)**	**10 (232)**	**91 (317)**	**6.3 (351)**

6 Conclusions and Future Work

PyDGGA is able to exploit the resources of a distributed computing environment. Experiments using the SAT solver SparrowToRiss demonstrated that it can boost the performance of an algorithm by automatically finding a parameterization that yields better results than the default one. Additional performance

gains could be achieved by integrating surrogate models or by improving the
evaluations scheduling to utilize the computing resources more efficiently. Moreover, the usability of the tool could be improved by using zero-configuration
networking protocols on HPC clusters, and by providing an API that let the
users integrate PyDGGA in their pipelines using Python code.

References

1. Adenso-Diaz, B., Laguna, M.: Fine-tuning of algorithms using fractional experimental design and local search. Oper. Res. **54**(1), 99–114 (2006)
2. Ansótegui, C., Malitsky, Y., Sellmann, M.: MaxSAT by improved instance-specific
algorithm configuration. In: Twenty-Eighth AAAI Conference on Artificial Intelligence (2014)
3. Ansotegui, C., Sellmann, M., Tierney, K.: A gender-based genetic algorithm for the
automatic configuration of algorithms. In: Proceedings of the 15th International
Conference on Principles and Practice of Constraint Programming, pp. 142–157
(2009)
4. Ansótegui, C., Malitsky, Y., Samulowitz, H., Sellmann, M., Tierney, K.: Model-
based genetic algorithms for algorithm configuration. In: IJCAI, pp. 733–739 (2015)
5. Balint, A., Manthey, N.: Sparrowtoriss. In: Belov, A., Diepold, D., Heule, M.J.,
Järvisalo, M. (eds.) Proceedings of SAT Competition 2014. Department of Computer Science Series of Publications B, vol. B-2014-2, p. 77. University of Helsinki,
Helsinki, Finland (2014)
6. Birattari, M., Yuan, Z., Balaprakash, P., Stützle, T.: F-race and iterated f-race: an
overview. In: Empirical Methods for the Analysis of Optimization Algorithms, pp.
311–336 (2010)
7. Cantu-Paz, E.: A survey of parallel genetic algorithms. Calculateurs paralleles,
reseaux et systems repartis 10 (1998)
8. El Mesaoudi-Paul, A., Weiß, D., Bengs, V., Hüllermeier, E., Tierney, K.: Pool-based
realtime algorithm configuration: a preselection bandit approach. In: Kotsireas,
I.S., Pardalos, P.M. (eds.) LION 2020. LNCS, vol. 12096, pp. 216–232. Springer,
Cham (2020). https://doi.org/10.1007/978-3-030-53552-0_22
9. Fitzgerald, T., Malitsky, Y., O'Sullivan, B., Tierney, K.: ReACT: real-time algorithm configuration through tournaments. In: Proceedings of the Symposium on
Combinatorial Search (2014)
10. Fitzgerald, T., Malitsky, Y., O'Sullivan, B.: ReACTR: realtime algorithm configuration through tournament rankings. In: Twenty-Fourth International Joint
Conference on Artificial Intelligence. Citeseer (2015)
11. Hutter, F., Hoos, H.H., Leyton-Brown, K.: Parallel algorithm configuration. In:
Proceedings of LION-6, pp. 55–70 (2012)
12. Hutter, F., Hoos, H.H., Leyton-Brown, K.: Sequential model-based optimization
for general algorithm configuration. In: Coello, C.A.C. (ed.) LION 2011. LNCS,
vol. 6683, pp. 507–523. Springer, Heidelberg (2011). https://doi.org/10.1007/978-
3-642-25566-3_40
13. Hutter, F., Hoos, H., Leyton-Brown, K., Stuetzle, T.: ParamILS: an automatic
algorithm configuration framework. JAIR **36**, 267–306 (2009)
14. Hutter, F., et al.: AClib: a benchmark library for algorithm configuration. In:
Pardalos, P.M., Resende, M.G.C., Vogiatzis, C., Walteros, J.L. (eds.) LION 2014.
LNCS, vol. 8426, pp. 36–40. Springer, Cham (2014). https://doi.org/10.1007/978-
3-319-09584-4_4

15. Kadioglu, S., Malitsky, Y., Sellmann, M., Tierney, K.: ISAC-Instance-Specific Algorithm Configuration. In: Coelho, H., Studer, R., Wooldridge, M. (eds.) Proceedings of the 19th European Conference on Artificial Intelligence (ECAI). Frontiers in Artificial Intelligence and Applications, vol. 215, pp. 751–756. IOS Press (2010)
16. Lindauer, M., Hutter, F.: Warmstarting of model-based algorithm configuration. In: McIlraith, S.A., Weinberger, K.Q. (eds.) Proceedings of the Thirty-Second AAAI Conference on Artificial Intelligence, (AAAI-18), the 30th innovative Applications of Artificial Intelligence (IAAI-18), and the 8th AAAI Symposium on Educational Advances in Artificial Intelligence (EAAI-18), New Orleans, Louisiana, USA, February 2–7, 2018, pp. 1355–1362. AAAI Press (2018). https://www.aaai.org/ocs/index.php/AAAI/AAAI18/paper/view/17235
17. Malitsky, Y., Mehta, D., O'Sullivan, B., Simonis, H.: Tuning parameters of large neighborhood search for the machine reassignment problem. In: Gomes, C., Sellmann, M. (eds.) CPAIOR 2013. LNCS, vol. 7874, pp. 176–192. Springer, Heidelberg (2013). https://doi.org/10.1007/978-3-642-38171-3_12
18. Prettenhofer, P.: Parallel grid search for Sklearn Gradient Boosting. https://gist.github.com/pprett/3989337. Accessed May 2015

QBFFam: A Tool for Generating QBF Families from Proof Complexity

Olaf Beyersdorff[1] , Luca Pulina[2] , Martina Seidl[3] , and Ankit Shukla[3(✉)]

[1] Friedrich Schiller University Jena, Jena, Germany
olaf.beyersdorff@uni-jena.de
[2] University of Sassari, Sassari, Italy
lpulina@uniss.it
[3] Johannes Kepler University Linz, Linz, Austria
{martina.seidl,ankit.shukla}@jku.at

Abstract. We present QBFFam, a tool for the generation of formula families originating from the field of proof complexity. Such formula families are used to investigate the strength of proof systems and to show how they relate to each other in terms of simulations and separations. Furthermore, these proof systems underlie the reasoning power of QBF solvers. With our tool, it is possible to generate informative and scalable benchmarks that help to analyse the behavior of solvers. As we will see in this paper, runtime behavior predicted by proof complexity is indeed reflected by recent solver implementations.

Keywords: Quantified boolean formulas · Formula generator · Benchmarking

1 Introduction

In recent years, much progress has been achieved in the theory and practice of solving quantified Boolean formulas (QBF) [12], offering a rich solving infrastructure, ranging from preprocessing over solving to result validation, strategy extraction, and theoretical lower bounds. As the decision problem for QBF (QSAT) is PSPACE-complete, many practical application problems [35] from fields such as formal verification, artificial intelligence, and reactive synthesis can be efficiently encoded in QBF and handed over to a QBF solver. Because of the PSPACE-completeness of QSAT, however, solving a QBF is a difficult task.

To solve QBFs various solving approaches have been presented (see [12] for a description of recent QBF solving techniques). *Conflict-driven clause/cube learning* (QCDCL) generalizes the successful CDCL paradigm that is dominant in SAT solving. *Expansion-based techniques* that build propositional abstractions

This work has been supported by the Austrian Science Fund (FWF) under project W1255-N23, the LIT AI Lab funded by the State of Upper Austria, and a grant by the Carl Zeiss Foundation.

C.-M. Li and F. Manyà (Eds.): SAT 2021, LNCS 12831, pp. 21–29, 2021.
https://doi.org/10.1007/978-3-030-80223-3_3

and then exploit the power of SAT solvers have been extremely successful in the last QBFEval competitions [34].

Empirical observations indicated that different approaches have a different reasoning power, resulting in a more diverse solving technique landscape than present in SAT. These observations can be confirmed by proof complexity results, offering explanations how the different approaches relate to each other by establishing separation and simulation results of the proof systems underlying the solvers. In many cases, formula families play a crucial role to characterize what is easy/hard for a solver.

In this paper, we present QBFFam, a tool for generating prominent formula families from proof complexity. With this tool, we provide a diverse collection of benchmarks that can be arbitrarily scaled and that are used in proof complexity to compare those proof systems that underlie the behavior of the state-of-the-art solvers. In this way, it becomes possible to obtain an improved understanding of solver implementations and their behavior, because for the generated families many theoretical results with respect to lower and upper bounds have been established.

Our tool is available at

https://github.com/marseidl/qbffam.git

It is implemented in Python and is called via qbffam <family> <n> where n is the size of the generated formula according to the definition of the respective family and family is one of the following 12 formula families:

KBKF	KBKF_LD	KBKF_QU
Parity	LQParity	QUParity
EQ	EQ-Sq	BEQ
LONSING	TRAPDOOR	CR

Details on the formula families as well as an overview of their applications in proof complexity are given in Sect. 3. All of the generated formulas are false QBFs in prenex conjunctive normal form (PCNF) and have the structure $QX_1 \ldots QX_n.\phi$ where the prefix $Q_1X_1 \ldots Q_nX_n$ contains quantifiers $Q_i \in \{\forall, \exists\}$ and the matrix ϕ is a propositional formula in conjunctive normal form (CNF). As usual, a CNF is a conjunction of clauses, a clause is a disjunction of literals, and a literal is a variable or a negated variable. All formulas are closed, i.e., all variables are quantified. Formulas in PCNF are typically represented in the QDIMACS[1] format which is supported by the majority of modern QBF solvers.

Organisation. The rest of the paper is structured as follows. We first review related work in Sect. 2. In Sect. 3 we discuss the 12 formula families supported by QBFFam. Here we also give an overview of relevant results from proof complexity for these formulas in several QBF proof systems. In particular, we report which formula family has/does not have short proofs in what proof systems. In Sect. 4

---

[1] http://www.qbflib.org/qdimacs.html.

we describe a case study, where we evaluate modern QBFs solvers on two formula families. We conclude with an outlook to future work in Sect. 5.

2 Related Work

The tool most closely related to QBFFam is the tool CNFGen [29] which is a generator for crafted SAT instances from propositional proof complexity. Among others, it supports the generation of formula families such as the *pigeonhole formulas* or the *Tseitin formulas*. Many of the provided formula families are known to be exponentially hard for propositional resolution and therefore for plain resolution-based CDCL solvers, as propositional resolution and (non-deterministic) CDCL are known to be equivalent [3,33]. This is also underpinned by experimental evaluations. Together with the rigorous lower bounds obtained in proof complexity such experiments help to understand the solving behavior of SAT solvers, identify their limitations, and also point towards directions for improvement.

To the best of our knowledge, there is no similar generator in the context of QBF solving so far. There are tools and frameworks for generating hard *random formulas* with a CNF matrix [15] or non-CNF matrix [18]. These random generators are used to empirically support theoretical characterizations of random formulas (cf. for example [17]). On the practical side they form the foundation for fuzzing, a testing technique that aims to find defects in solvers by massively solving random instances, thus achieving high code coverage, which is important to detect conceptual errors and only sporadically triggered corner cases [14].

3 Formula Families

Currently, our tool QBFFam supports the generation of 12 different formula families which are summarized in Table 1 together with a characterization in terms of number of quantifier alternations, number of variables, and number of clauses. Additionally, we also provide information on their proof complexity indicating for which proof systems short proofs or lower bounds are known.

Q-resolution (QRes) is the simplest among the considered proof systems, providing rules for resolution over existential variables and universal reduction [28]. In QRes-QU [20] resolution over universals is allowed as well. In long-distance resolution QRes-LD [1] certain resolution steps, forbidden in Q-Resolution, generating tautologous clauses are allowed. The system QRes-LQU$^+$ [2] combines long-distance resolution with resolution over universals, yielding a very powerful proof system. Another extension of QRes is QRes-SYM [26] which is able to exploit symmetries of formulas [27].

The proof system ∀Exp-Res [25] is the formal basis for expansion-based QBF solving. In addition to the resolution rule it has a rule that captures the expansion of universal variables and the renaming of existential variables in terms of annotations. The more powerful proof systems IR-calc and IRM-calc provide more flexibility than ∀Exp-Res in the way how and when annotations are obtained [10].

Table 1. Characteristics of the families and overview of some results from proof theory.

Formula family	#alt	#vars	#cl	QRes	QRes-LD	QRes-QU	QRes-LQU⁺	∀Exp-Res	IR-calc	IRM-calc	QRes-SYM
KBKF	$n+1$	$4n$	$4n+1$	✗	✓	✓	✓	✗	✗	✓	✓
KBKF_LD	$n+1$	$4n$	$4n+1$	✗	✗	✓	✓	✗	✗	✗	✓
KBKF_QU	$n+1$	$5n$	$4n+1$	✗	✓	✗	✓	✗	✗	✓	✓
Parity	2	$2n$	$4n-2$	✗	✓	✗	✓	✓	✓	✓	✓
LQParity	2	$2n$	$8n-6$	✗	✗	✗	✓	✓	✓	✓	✓
QUParity	2	$2n+1$	$8n-6$	✗	✗	✗	✗	✓	✓	✓	✓
EQ	3	$3n$	$2n+1$	✗	✓	✗	✓	✗	✗	✓	✓
EQ-Sq	3	n^2+4n	$5n^2$	✗	✓	✗	✓	✗	✗	✓	✓
BEQ	4	$6n+2$	$5n+2$	✗	✓	✗	✓	✗	✗	✓	✗
CR	2	n^2	$2n$	✓	✓	✓	✓	✓	✓	✓	✓
TRAPDOOR	3	$O(n^2)$	$O(n^2)$	✓	✓	✓	✓	✓	✓	✓	✓
LONSING	2	$O(n^2)$	$O(n^2)$	✓	✓	✓	✓	✓	✓	✓	✓

✓ ... short proofs (poly size)   ✗ ... no short proofs (exponential lower bounds)

#alt ... number of quantifier alternations

#vars ... number of variables   #cl ... number of clauses

In the following, we briefly discuss the supported formula families.

KBKF Formulas and Extensions KBKF_LD, KBKF_QU. Already in their first paper on Q-resolution from 1995 [28] Kleine Büning, Karpinski, and Flögel introduced a formula family that is nowadays known as the KBKF formula family. Since their inception, the KBKF formulas have triggered lots of research in QBF proof complexity. The original motivation of [28] was to provide quantified extended Horn formulas that have no short QRes proofs. Interestingly, the formulas also provide exponential separations between QRes and QRes-QU [20] as well as between QRes and QRes-LD [19]. The formulas KBKF have unbounded quantifier complexity, and much later it became clear [7], that such formulas are indeed needed for separating QRes and QRes-QU. The KBKF formulas remain hard in expansion-based systems ∀Exp-Res and IR-calc, but become easy in IRM-calc [10].

Extensions of KBKF have been introduced to obtain hard formulas for more powerful proof systems. In particular, the formula family KBKF_QU duplicates universal variables in the prefix and in clauses and becomes hard for QRes-QU, but remains easy for QRes-LD [2]. Another modification KBKF_LD [2] adds variables from the innermost existential quantifier block to some clauses. These formulas are hard for the systems QRes-LD [2] and IRM-calc [10]. All three formula families exhibit many symmetries, making them simple if reasoning on symmetries is supported [26].

A simple self-contained proof of the hardness of KBKF in QRes is given in [5]. Most further hardness results mentioned above lift QRes hardness to stronger proof systems.

Parity Formulas Parity and Extensions LQParity, QUParity. The formulas of the parity family Parity are Tseitin-transformed CNF representations of QBFs with structure $\exists x_1, \ldots, x_n \forall z. (z \vee \phi_n) \wedge (\neg z \vee \neg \phi_n)$ where $\phi_n = x_1 \oplus \ldots \oplus x_n$. The unique strategy for falsifying the formula is to set the only universal variable z to $x_1 \oplus \ldots \oplus x_n$. Hence, the unique Herbrand function for z must compute the parity function, which is exponentially hard for bounded-depth circuits AC^0 [22]. As strategy extraction in QRes and QRes-QU is in AC^0 [1], the QRes and QRes-QU proofs of Parity must be of exponential size. An alternative proof of hardness for Parity in QRes, not relying on the complex machinery of AC^0 lower bounds, is given in [7].

In contrast, Parity is easy for QRes-LD [16] and $\forall$Exp-Res [10]. The extensions LQParity and QUParity are constructed to obtain hard formulas for QRes-LD and QRes-LQU$^+$, respectively [10].

Equality Formulas EQ and Extensions EQ–Sq and BEQ. The equality formulas [6] have a quantifier prefix of the form $\exists x_1 \ldots x_n \forall u_1 \ldots u_n \exists t_1 \ldots t_n$ and encode that $x_i \leftrightarrow u_i$ for $1 \leq i \leq n$. The t_i variables are Tseitin variables for obtaining a PCNF, collected in one clause of size n. Arguably, the equality formulas are the simplest formulas hard formulas for QRes. In [6] a semantic technique via cost is developed to show their hardness (as well as many more hardness results). A related technique [4] is applicable to show their hardness for the expansion systems $\forall$Exp-Res and IR-calc. However, they become easy in QRes-LD [8].

The EQ–Sq formulas [8] are a 'squared' version of the EQ formulas with n additional variables in each of the first two blocks and n^2 innermost Tseitin variables. They are used to show an exponential separation between QRes-LD without universal reduction (exponential lower bounds for EQ–Sq) and the proof system M-Res (short proofs for EQ–Sq) [8].

Finally the blocked equality formulas BEQ introduce a blocker such that symmetries are destroyed and cannot be exploited to find short proofs [13]. This technique does not only work for the equality formulas, but it is a general approach to eliminate symmetries from a formula without changing its meaning.

Completion Principle, Trapdoor, and Lonsing Formulas. The last block of formulas from Table 1 comprises of three formula families that are easy for all of the described proof systems. Though QCDCL is associated with the proof systems QRes and QRes-LD (QCDCL runs can be efficiently translated into QRes-LD refutations as clauses learned in QCDCL can be derived in QRes-LD), this correspondence is not an exact one as demonstrated by recent research [5,23]. In particular, [23] has shown that practical QCDCL does not simulate QRes. This builds on the completion principle formulas CR, first described in [25], which describe an easy 'completion' game, played on an $n \times n$ matrix by two players (cf. [25]). These formulas are easy for QRes, but hard for practical QCDCL using UIP learning [23].

This result was further strengthened in [9], where QRes and QCDCL (with arbitrary learning schemes) are shown to be incomparable. This is witnessed by the `Parity` formulas, which are hard in QRes, but easy in QCDCL (with the right heuristics, possibly difficult to find in practice).[2]

In the opposite direction, the `TRAPDOOR` and `LONSING` formulas (first defined in [9] and [30], respectively) are easy for QRes, but require exponential running time in QCDCL (even with arbitrary learning schemes). Both principles build QBFs that incorporate the well-known propositional pigeonhole principle (PHP). Using the right quantifier prefix, which needs to be obeyed by QCDCL decision heuristics, they 'trap' QCDCL into refuting the PHP formulas (which are exponentially hard for propositional resolution [21] and hence for (Q)CDCL), while easy (even constant size) QRes proofs of `TRAPDOOR` and `LONSING` exist.

4   Case Study

Our tool `QBFFam` opens up many possibilities to conduct interesting experiments. In particular, it can be used to investigate whether the solver implementations indeed follow the behavior predicted by proof complexity and to compare their strength.

As a first case study, we consider 30 formulas of the `KBKF` family as well as 30 formulas of the `LQParity` family. We selected those families because they are well investigated in proof complexity and correspond to incomparable proof systems as discussed above. In both cases we selected the values 10, 15–40, 50, 60, 70, 80 for n.

In our experiments, we considered five solvers in six configurations. The QCDCL solver DepQBF (version 6.1) [31] was run with and without long-distance enabled. We included the solver Qute [32] as a second QCDCL solver which supports dynamic dependency learning. As expansion-based solvers, we included Rareqs [24] which recursively processes the quantifier alternations to build the propositional abstraction of a formula as well as the non-recursive expansion-based solver Ijtihad. Finally, we included the solver Caqe that implements causal abstraction [36] and which dominated the QBFEval competitions [34][3] over the last years. All experiments were run on Intel Xeon E5-2620 v4 CPU machines with the timeout set to 300 s and the memory restricted to 7 GB.

The results of our experiments are shown in Fig. 1. The plot on the left shows the runtimes for the `KBKF` family. For four of the six solvers, the formulas are very hard, especially for the expansion-based solvers Rareqs, which does not solve any formula, and Ijtihad, which solves only one formula within the time limit. Also, for Qute and DepQBF the formulas get difficult with increasing n. Both get until $n = 20$. For this formula, DepQBF needs 167 s and Caqe needs 241 s. For DepQBF with long-distance resolution and Qute these formulas are very easy: all of them are solved in less than one second, confirming results from proof complexity.

The situation is different for the `LQParity` formulas (see Fig. 1 on the right). Here Caqe, Ijtihad, and Rareqs solve all of the formulas quickly. This is also in

---

[2] However, formulas hard for QRes-LD such as `LQParity` are hard for QCDCL (with arbitrary heuristics) from a theory point of view.

[3] http://www.qbfeval.org.

accordance with the results from proof complexity. The formulas are hard for the QCDL-based solvers, which could only solve 24 formulas (both configurations of DepQBF) and five formulas (Qute).

This also indicates that there is a close connection between the theoretical properties of the underlying proof systems and the practical implementations of the solvers.

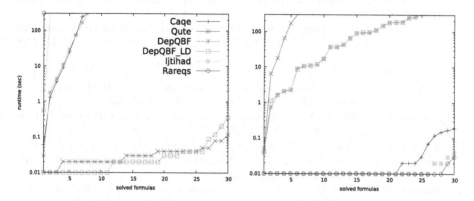

Fig. 1. Runtime comparison on KBKF formulas (left) and LQParity formulas (right).

5   Conclusion

We presented QBFFam, a tool for the generation of instances related to prominent formula families from proof complexity. We briefly described these families and surveyed recent results from proof complexity which help to understand the power of proof systems, and thus the power of QBF decision procedures and their implementations in QBF solvers. In a small case study we evaluated recent QBF solvers on two formula families and could indeed observe that the properties predicted by proof complexity are reflected by the solving runtimes. This opens the way to many further interesting experiments.

In future, QBFFam can be extended to support graph-based formulas [11] or random formulas [6]. Both also play an important role in the context of proof complexity. Another extension of QBFFam that seems to be of practical interest is the generation of true formulas. True QBFs are currently not investigated in proof complexity with the argument that in QBF, proof systems for satisfiability are dual to those of unsatisfiability. Having such formula families, however, seems to be useful for evaluating solver implementations as well.

References

1. Balabanov, V., Jiang, J.R.: Unified QBF certification and its applications. Formal Methods Syst. Des. **41**(1), 45–65 (2012)

2. Balabanov, V., Widl, M., Jiang, J.-H.R.: QBF resolution systems and their proof complexities. In: Sinz, C., Egly, U. (eds.) SAT 2014. LNCS, vol. 8561, pp. 154–169. Springer, Cham (2014). https://doi.org/10.1007/978-3-319-09284-3_12

3. Beame, P., Kautz, H.A., Sabharwal, A.: Towards understanding and harnessing the potential of clause learning. J. Artif. Intell. Res. (JAIR) **22**, 319–351 (2004)

4. Beyersdorff, O., Blinkhorn, J.: Dynamic QBF dependencies in reduction and expansion. ACM Trans. Comput. Log. **21**(2), 8:1–8:27 (2020)

5. Beyersdorff, O., Blinkhorn, J.: A simple proof of QBF hardness. Inf. Process. Lett. **168**, 106093 (2021)

6. Beyersdorff, O., Blinkhorn, J., Hinde, L.: Size, cost, and capacity: A semantic technique for hard random QBFS. Log. Methods Comput. Sci. **15**(1), 13:1–13:39 (2019)

7. Beyersdorff, O., Blinkhorn, J., Mahajan, M.: Hardness characterisations and size-width lower bounds for QBF resolution. In: Proceedings ACM/IEEE Symposium on Logic in Computer Science (LICS), pp. 209–223. ACM (2020)

8. Beyersdorff, O., Blinkhorn, J., Mahajan, M.: Building strategies into QBF proofs. J. Autom. Reasoning **65**(1), 125–154 (2021)

9. Beyersdorff, O., Böhm, B.: Understanding the relative strength of QBF CDCL solvers and QBF resolution. In: Proceedings of Innovations in Theoretical Computer Science (ITCS), pp. 12:1–12:20 (2021)

10. Beyersdorff, O., Chew, L., Janota, M.: New resolution-based QBF calculi and their proof complexity. ACM Trans. Comput. Theor. **11**(4), 26:1–26:42 (2019)

11. Beyersdorff, O., Chew, L., Mahajan, M., Shukla, A.: Feasible interpolation for QBF resolution calculi. Logical Methods Comput. Sci. **13**(2), 1–20 (2017)

12. Beyersdorff, O., Janota, M., Lonsing, F., Seidl, M.: Quantified Boolean formulas. In: Biere, A., Heule, M., van Maaren, H., Walsh, T. (eds.) Handbook of Satisfiability, 2nd edn. IOS press, Frontiers in Artificial Intelligence and Applications (2021)

13. Blinkhorn, J., Beyersdorff, O.: Proof complexity of QBF symmetry recomputation. In: Janota, M., Lynce, I. (eds.) SAT 2019. LNCS, vol. 11628, pp. 36–52. Springer, Cham (2019). https://doi.org/10.1007/978-3-030-24258-9_3

14. Brummayer, R., Lonsing, F., Biere, A.: Automated testing and debugging of SAT and QBF solvers. In: Strichman, O., Szeider, S. (eds.) SAT 2010. LNCS, vol. 6175, pp. 44–57. Springer, Heidelberg (2010). https://doi.org/10.1007/978-3-642-14186-7_6

15. Chen, H., Interian, Y.: A model for generating random quantified boolean formulas. In: Proc. of the 19th International Joint Conferences on Artificial Intelligence (IJCAI 2005), pp. 66–71. Professional Book Center (2005)

16. Chew, L.: QBF proof complexity. Ph.D. thesis, University of Leeds, Leeds (2017)

17. Creignou, N., Daudé, H., Egly, U., Rossignol, R.: New results on the phase transition for random quantified Boolean formulas. In: Kleine Büning, H., Zhao, X. (eds.) SAT 2008. LNCS, vol. 4996, pp. 34–47. Springer, Heidelberg (2008). https://doi.org/10.1007/978-3-540-79719-7_5

18. Creignou, N., Egly, U., Seidl, M.: A framework for the specification of random SAT and QSAT formulas. In: Brucker, A.D., Julliand, J. (eds.) TAP 2012. LNCS, vol. 7305, pp. 163–168. Springer, Heidelberg (2012). https://doi.org/10.1007/978-3-642-30473-6_14

19. Egly, U., Lonsing, F., Widl, M.: Long-distance resolution: proof generation and strategy extraction in search-based QBF solving. In: Proceedings of Logic for Programming, Artificial Intelligence, and Reasoning (LPAR), pp. 291–308 (2013)

20. Gelder, A.: Contributions to the theory of practical quantified Boolean formula solving. In: Milano, M. (ed.) CP 2012. LNCS, pp. 647–663. Springer, Heidelberg (2012). https://doi.org/10.1007/978-3-642-33558-7_47
21. Haken, A.: The intractability of resolution. Theor. Comput. Sci. **39**, 297–308 (1985)
22. Håstad, J.: Computational Limitations of Small Depth Circuits. MIT Press, Cambridge (1987)
23. Janota, M.: On Q-resolution and CDCL QBF solving. In: Proceedings of International Conference on Theory and Applications of Satisfiability Testing (SAT), pp. 402–418 (2016)
24. Janota, M., Klieber, W., Marques-Silva, J., Clarke, E.M.: Solving QBF with counterexample guided refinement. Artif. Intell. **234**, 1–25 (2016)
25. Janota, M., Marques-Silva, J.: Expansion-based QBF solving versus Q-resolution. Theor. Comput. Sci. **577**, 25–42 (2015)
26. Kauers, M., Seidl, M.: Short proofs for some symmetric quantified Boolean formulas. Inf. Process. Lett. **140**, 4–7 (2018)
27. Kauers, M., Seidl, M.: Symmetries of quantified Boolean formulas. In: Beyersdorff, O., Wintersteiger, C.M. (eds.) SAT 2018. LNCS, vol. 10929, pp. 199–216. Springer, Cham (2018). https://doi.org/10.1007/978-3-319-94144-8_13
28. Kleine Büning, H., Karpinski, M., Flögel, A.: Resolution for quantified Boolean formulas. Inf. Comput. **117**(1), 12–18 (1995)
29. Lauria, M., Elffers, J., Nordström, J., Vinyals, M.: CNFgen: a generator of crafted benchmarks. In: Gaspers, S., Walsh, T. (eds.) SAT 2017. LNCS, vol. 10491, pp. 464–473. Springer, Cham (2017). https://doi.org/10.1007/978-3-319-66263-3_30
30. Lonsing, F.: Dependency Schemes and Search-Based QBF Solving: Theory and Practice. Ph.D. thesis, Johannes Kepler University Linz (2012)
31. Lonsing, F., Egly, U.: DepQBF 6.0: a search-based QBF solver beyond traditional QCDCL. In: de Moura, L. (ed.) CADE 2017. LNCS (LNAI), vol. 10395, pp. 371–384. Springer, Cham (2017). https://doi.org/10.1007/978-3-319-63046-5_23
32. Peitl, T., Slivovsky, F., Szeider, S.: Qute in the QBF evaluation 2018. J. Satisf. Boolean Model. Comput. **11**(1), 261–272 (2019)
33. Pipatsrisawat, K., Darwiche, A.: On the power of clause-learning SAT solvers as resolution engines. Artif. Intell. **175**(2), 512–525 (2011)
34. Pulina, L., Seidl, M.: The 2016 and 2017 QBF solvers evaluations (qbfeval'16 and qbfeval'17). Artif. Intell. **274**, 224–248 (2019)
35. Shukla, A., Biere, A., Pulina, L., Seidl, M.: A survey on applications of quantified boolean formulas. In: Proceedings of the the 31st IEEE International Conferences on Tools with Artificial Intelligence, (ICTAI 2019), pp. 78–84. IEEE (2019)
36. Tentrup, L.: CAQE and quabs: Abstraction based QBF solvers. J. Satisf. Boolean Model. Comput. **11**(1), 155–210 (2019)

Davis and Putnam Meet Henkin: Solving DQBF with Resolution

Joshua Blinkhorn[1], Tomáš Peitl[1]([✉]), and Friedrich Slivovsky[2]

[1] Friedrich-Schiller-Universität Jena, Jena, Germany
{joshua.blinkhorn,tomas.peitl}@uni-jena.de
[2] TU Wien, Vienna, Austria
fslivovsky@ac.tuwien.ac.at

Abstract. Davis-Putnam resolution is one of the fundamental theoretical decision procedures for both propositional logic and quantified Boolean formulas.

Dependency quantified Boolean formulas (*DQBF*) are a generalisation of QBF in which dependencies of variables are listed explicitly rather than being implicit in the order of quantifiers. Since DQBFs can succinctly encode synthesis problems that ask for Boolean functions matching a given specification, efficient DQBF solvers have a wide range of potential applications. We present a new decision procedure for DQBF in the style of Davis-Putnam resolution. Based on the merge resolution proof system, it directly constructs partial strategy functions for derived clauses. The procedure requires DQBF in a normal form called H-Form. We prove that the problem of evaluating DQBF in H-Form is NEXP-complete. In fact, we show that any DQBF can be converted into H-Form in linear time.

1 Introduction

Continuing advances in the performance of propositional satisfiability (SAT) solvers are enabling a growing number of applications in the area of electronic design automation [28], such as model checking [6], synthesis [24], and symbolic execution [3]. In artificial intelligence, SAT solvers are a driving force behind recent progress in constrained sampling and counting [19], and they act as combinatorial search engines in competitive planning tools [10]. In most of these cases, SAT solvers deal with problems from complexity classes beyond NP and propositional encodings that grow super-polynomially in the size of the original instances. Clever techniques such as incremental solving can partly alleviate this issue, but ultimately the underlying asymptotics lead to formulas that are too large to be solved by even the most efficient SAT solvers.

This research was supported by the Vienna Science and Technology Fund (WWTF) under grant number ICT19-060, and by the Austrian Science Fund (FWF) under grant number J-4361N.

C.-M. Li and F. Manyà (Eds.): SAT 2021, LNCS 12831, pp. 30–46, 2021.
https://doi.org/10.1007/978-3-030-80223-3_4

This has prompted the development of decision procedures for more succinct generalizations of propositional logic such as Quantified Boolean Formulas (QBFs). Deciding satisfiability of QBFs is PSPACE-complete [25] and thus
believed to be much harder than SAT, but in practice the trade-off between
encoding size and tractability can be in favour of QBF [13]. Dependency QBF
(DQBF) in turn generalise QBF [1,2]. Whereas the nesting of quantifiers implicitly determines the arguments of Skolem (or Herbrand) functions of a QBF,
Henkin quantifiers explicitly specify the arguments of Skolem (or Herbrand)
functions in a DQBF. As a result, DQBFs can succinctly encode problems concerning the existence of Boolean functions subject to a set of constraints. For
instance, equivalence checking of partial circuit designs (PEC) can be naturally
encoded as DQBF [16].

Existing decision procedures for DQBF either use quantifier expansion to
obtain an equivalent propositional formula or QBF, or else adapt search-based
algorithms from QBF by introducing additional constraints to make sure the
search tree is consistent with the dependency sets of the input DQBF. Semantically, reasoning at the level of functions is more natural, but recent attempts
at lifting conflict-driven clause learning (CDCL) to the level of Skolem functions
are currently limited to 2QBF [21].

Our main contribution is a new decision algorithm for DQBF that operates directly at the level of functions. Based on the *merge resolution* (M-Res)
proof system [4], it maintains a set of clauses annotated with partial Herbrand
functions. Like the original Davis-Putnam procedure [12], it successively eliminates (existentially quantified) variables by creating all possible resolvents at
each step. Crucially, resolvents are created only for pairs of clauses with partial Herbrand functions that are consistent and can be combined into a larger
partial Herbrand function. Once all variables have been eliminated, either the
set of clauses is empty, in which case the input DQBF is true, or it contains
the empty clause, in which case the formula is false and the Herbrand functions
in the annotation form a countermodel. In contrast to variable elimination by
Q-resolution [5,18], where innermost existentially quantified variables must be
eliminated first, our algorithm may eliminate variables in any order. While this
is not surprising in DQBF, where there is no syntactic ordering of variables, it
means that our algorithm can be used to eliminate variables of a QBF in arbitrary order, too—possibly at the cost of increased computational complexity.

There is a surprising obstacle in the way of generalizing variable elimination
by resolution to DQBF—it is insufficient to resolve only clauses that contain the
current pivot variable being eliminated. In fact, we may need to resolve even pairs
of clauses neither of which contains the pivot variable. The requisite combination
of weakening and resolution has previously been studied under the name *w-
resolution* [8,9]. In turn, w-resolution paves the way for a seemingly absurd case:
a clause can now be resolved with itself—*self-resolution*. While self-resolution is
not essential, we show that it is a very natural explanation for why we keep
certain clauses between individual elimination steps. That understanding casts
the algorithm in a different light; as a series of transformations, which result in
a normal form where strategies are recorded explicitly.

Strictly speaking, our algorithm (as well as merge resolution) operates on *H-form* DQBF, where Henkin quantifiers specify the arguments of *universal* variables and the matrix is in conjunctive normal form [2]. NEXP-hardness of evaluating DQBF in this form does not immediately follow from known results [1, 23], and determining the complexity of this problem was recently stated as an open question [4]. As a further contribution, we show that it is in fact NEXP-complete, and that DQBF in H-form and the more frequently studied *S-form* (where Henkin quantifiers are used for *existential* variables) are interconvertible at a linear overhead while preserving strategies. Thus our variable elimination algorithm can be used to evaluate and construct (counter)models of arbitrary DQBFs.

The paper is structured as follows: after preliminaries in Sect. 2, we give our decision procedure in Sect. 3, and discuss NEXP-completeness of H-form DQBF in Sect. 4, concluding with a summary in Sect. 5.

2   Preliminaries

H-Form DQBF Intuition. The notion of H-form DQBF is arguably counter-intuitive, and so instead of a formal definition, we start informally. Consider an *S-form DQBF*, i.e. a formula of the form $\forall u_1 \cdots \forall u_m \exists x_1(S_{x_1}) \cdots \exists x_n(S_{x_n}) \cdot \phi$, where each existential variable x_i has a dependency set $S_{x_i} \subseteq \{u_1, \ldots, u_m\}$, and ϕ is a DNF. The goal with such a formula is to find a set of functions—called a *model*—for the existential variables respecting the dependencies so that after substitution into ϕ, the formula becomes a tautology in the universal variables. An example of such a formula is

$$\Psi = \forall u_1 \, \forall u_2 \, \exists x_1(u_1) \, \exists x_2(u_2) \quad (\overline{u_1} \wedge x_2) \vee (u_1 \wedge \overline{x_2}) \vee (\overline{u_2} \wedge x_1) \vee (u_2 \wedge \overline{x_1})$$

along with the model $x_1 = u_1, x_2 = \overline{u_2}$—whose substitution into Ψ indeed produces a tautology. An H-form DQBF with a CNF matrix is then simply a negation of an S-form DQBF with a DNF matrix, where strategies are sought for universal variables and the goal is to make the substituted formula unsatisfiable, rather than valid.

H-form DQBF Syntax. A *variable* is an element z of the countable set $\mathbb{V}$. A *literal* is a variable z or its *negation* $\overline{z}$. The negation of a literal a is denoted $\overline{a}$, where $\overline{\overline{z}} := z$ for any variable z. A *clause* is a disjunction of literals. A *conjunctive normal form formula* (CNF) is a conjunction of clauses. The set of variables appearing in a formula ψ is denoted vars(ψ). For ease, we often write clauses as sets of literals, and CNFs as sets of clauses.

An *H-form dependency quantified Boolean formula* (DQBF) is a sentence of the form $\Psi := \exists x_1 \cdots \exists x_n \forall u_1(H_{u_1}) \cdots \forall u_m(H_{u_m}) \cdot \psi$, where the part that holds quantification information is called the *prefix*, and the *matrix* ψ is a CNF. In the quantifier prefix, each universal variable u_i is associated with a *dependency set* H_{u_i}, which is a subset of the existential variables $\{x_1, \ldots, x_n\}$. With vars$_\exists$(Ψ)

and $\text{vars}_\forall(\Psi)$ we denote the existential and universal variable sets of Ψ, and with $\text{vars}(\Psi)$ their union. We deal only with DQBFs for which $\text{vars}(\psi) \subseteq \text{vars}(\Psi)$.

H-form DQBF Semantics. An *assignment* α to a set Z of Boolean variables is a function from Z into the set $\{0, 1, *\}$. An assignment whose range is $\{0, 1\}$ is called *total*. The set of all assignments to Z is denoted $\langle\!\langle Z \rangle\!\rangle$, and the set of all total assignments is denoted $\langle Z \rangle$. The *domain restriction* of α to a subset Z' of its domain is written $\alpha\!\restriction_{Z'}$. We say that α *extends* α', denoted by $\alpha' \subseteq \alpha$, when $\alpha(z) = \alpha'(z)$ for each $z \in \text{dom}(\alpha')$ with $\alpha'(z) \in \{0, 1\}$.

The *restriction* of a formula ψ by an assignment α, denoted $\psi[\alpha]$, is the result of substituting each variable z in the preimage $\alpha^{-1}(\{0, 1\})$ by $\alpha(z)$, followed by applying the standard simplifications for Boolean constants, i.e. $\overline{0} \mapsto 1$, $\overline{1} \mapsto 0$, $\phi \vee 0 \mapsto \phi$, $\phi \vee 1 \mapsto 1$, $\phi \wedge 1 \mapsto \phi$, and $\phi \wedge 0 \mapsto 0$. We say that α *satisfies* ψ when $\psi[\alpha] = 1$, and *falsifies* ψ when $\psi[\alpha] = 0$.

For a DQBF $\Psi := \exists x_1 \cdots \exists x_n \forall u_1(H_{u_1}) \cdots \forall u_m(H_{u_m}) \cdot \psi$, any set of functions $h := \{h_u : u \in \text{vars}_\forall(\Psi)\}$ of the form $h_u : \langle H_u \rangle \to \langle\!\langle \{u\} \rangle\!\rangle$ is called a *strategy* for Ψ. For convenience, we use the alias $h(\alpha) := \{h_u(\alpha\!\restriction_{H_u}) : u \in \text{vars}_\forall(\Psi)\}$. A strategy for Ψ is called *winning* when each combined assignment $\alpha \cup h(\alpha)$ falsifies ψ. The terms 'winning strategy' and '*countermodel*' are used interchangably. A DQBF is called *false* when it has a *countermodel*, otherwise it is called *true*.

3   Davis-Putnam Resolution for H-Form DQBF

In this section we describe a decision procedure for H-form DQBF in the style of Davis-Putnam resolution. We start by explaining the high-level idea by comparison to propositional DP-resolution.

In a nutshell, DP-resolution for propositional logic eliminates variables by exhaustive resolution—pick variables one at a time in arbitrary order, for every variable produce all resolvents, and then drop all clauses containing the eliminated variable.[1] If at the end the clause set is empty, the formula is satisfiable. If, on the other hand, we are left with the empty clause (we have eliminated all variables, so any clause must be empty), the formula is unsatisfiable, and we have constructed a resolution refutation.

For DQBF we adapt this process in three ways: First, we will only eliminate existential variables. We can still do so in arbitrary order.

Second, we treat universal variables in the spirit of the DQBF proof system M-Res [4]—by splitting clauses into the existential part and a partial-strategy part, initially constructed from universal literals. Strategies may prevent resolution steps if they mismatch; or they may be updated for variables that depend on the pivot—similarly to how it is done in M-Res—with a consistency check in place of the originally used and more strict isomorphism test. Consequently, at the end we obtain either the empty set, in which case the formula is true, or a

---

[1] The algorithm described by Davis and Putnam [12] also considers unit clauses and pure literals, but since these are neither necessary for completeness, nor complete on their own, we think of DP-resolution as consisting of variable elimination.

set containing clause-strategy pairs with empty existential parts, in which case the formula is false, and the partial strategies form a countermodel.

Third, when eliminating an existential variable x, we will need to *weaken* clauses that do not contain any literal on x with both x and $\overline{x}$ (separately), and such weakened clauses will enter the elimination step for x. M-Res is incomplete for DQBF without weakening, and the same issue forces us to include weakening in our algorithm as well. No such thing is necessary in the propositional case, intuitively because the only way how a variable can directly interact with a clause is if it occurs in the clause. In DQBF however, existential variables can affect dependent universal variables and thereby interact in complex ways with clauses where they do not occur at all. An elegant way of capturing this is by incorporating weakening directly into the resolution rule—resulting in a system known as *w-resolution* [8].

We begin the algorithm exposition by defining some relations and operations in Subsect. 3.1. The algorithm itself is described in Subsect. 3.2, and its correctness and completeness are shown in Subsect. 3.3. We discuss suitable data structures for the storage and manipulation of strategies in Subsect. 3.4.

3.1 Strategy Operations

We introduce a consistency relation and two operations for the manipulation of individual strategy functions.

Definition 1. *Let X be a set of variables and $\varepsilon, \delta \in \langle\!\langle X \rangle\!\rangle$. We say that ε and δ are* consistent, *denoted by $\varepsilon \simeq \delta$, if for every $x \in X$ for which $\varepsilon(x) \neq *$ and $\delta(x) \neq *$ we have $\varepsilon(x) = \delta(x)$.*

By abuse of notation, we treat (partial) assignments as both functions and sets of literals, i.e. an assignment ε corresponds to the set of literals it satisfies, namely $\{x : \varepsilon(x) = 1\} \cup \{\overline{x} : \varepsilon(x) = 0\}$. Through this correspondence we define the *union* of two assignments, and we say that δ *extends (is an extension of)* ε if $\varepsilon \subseteq \delta$.

Lemma 1. *Let X be a set of variables and $\varepsilon, \delta \in \langle\!\langle X \rangle\!\rangle$. The following conditions are equivalent:* (1) ε *and* δ *are consistent;* (2) *there is an assignment* $\gamma \in \langle\!\langle X \rangle\!\rangle$ *which extends both* ε *and* δ; (3) $\varepsilon \cup \delta$ *is an assignment.*

Furthermore, any assignment that extends both ε and δ also extends $\varepsilon \cup \delta$.

Let Ψ be a DQBF, let $u \in \text{vars}_\forall(\Psi)$ be a universal variable, and let h_u and h'_u be individual strategy functions for the variable u; that is, functions from $\langle H_u \rangle$ into $\langle\!\langle \{u\} \rangle\!\rangle$.

- *Consistency:* We say that h_u and h'_u are consistent (written $h_u \simeq h'_u$) when $h_u(\varepsilon) \simeq h'_u(\varepsilon)$ for each $\varepsilon \in \langle H_u \rangle$.
- *Union:* Provided $h_u \simeq h'_u$, their *union* is $(h_u \circ h'_u)(\varepsilon) := h_u(\varepsilon) \cup h'_u(\varepsilon)$.
- *If-then-else:* For each $x \in \text{vars}_\exists(\Psi)$, we define the *if x then h_u else h'_u* function

$$\left(h_u \overset{x}{\bowtie} h'_u\right)(\varepsilon) := \begin{cases} h_u(\varepsilon) & \text{if } \varepsilon(x) = 1, \\ h'_u(\varepsilon) & \text{if } \varepsilon(x) = 0, \end{cases} \quad \varepsilon \in \langle H_u \rangle.$$

3.2 Definition of the Construction

Given a DQBF $\exists x_1 \cdots \exists x_n \forall u_1(H_{u_1}) \cdots \forall u_m(H_{u_m}) \cdot \psi$, we define recursively a collection of sets $\mathsf{DP}(\Psi, i)$, for i in $\{0, \ldots, n\}$. Each $\mathsf{DP}(\Psi, i)$ is a set of *clause-strategy* pairs. A clause-strategy pair is of the form (C, h), where C is a clause with $\mathrm{vars}(C) \subseteq \mathrm{vars}_\exists(\Psi)$, and h is a strategy for Ψ.

We will obtain the set $\mathsf{DP}(\Psi, i)$ by applying *w-resolution*—resolution preceded by weakening—to $\mathsf{DP}(\Psi, i-1)$. The *w-resolvent* of C and D, over a *pivot* z with $z \notin C$ and $\bar{z} \notin D$, is defined as $C \cup_z D := (C \setminus \{\bar{z}\}) \cup (D \setminus \{z\})$ [8,9]. The w-resolvent is equal to the traditional resolvent if the pivot literals are present in the clauses, but it additionally extends resolution to cases when the pivot is absent from one or both premises—the condition $z \notin C$ and $\bar{z} \notin D$ ensures that weakening by the corresponding pivot literal does not create a tautology.

The recursive definition begins with $\mathsf{DP}(\Psi, 0) := \{(C_\exists, h^{C_\forall}) : C \in \psi\}$, where $C_\exists$ and $C_\forall$ are the existential and universal subclauses of C, and the strategy $h^{C_\forall}$ is the collection of constant functions

$$h_u^{C_\forall}(\varepsilon) := \begin{cases} u \mapsto 0 & \text{if } u \in C_\forall, \\ u \mapsto 1 & \text{if } \bar{u} \in C_\forall, \qquad \varepsilon \in \langle H_u \rangle, \\ u \mapsto * & \text{otherwise}, \end{cases}$$

over $u \in \mathrm{vars}_\forall(\Psi)$. Here, $\mathsf{DP}(\Psi, 0)$ is merely a representation of the matrix of Ψ as clause-strategy pairs. The universal subclauses are replaced by strategies, in which each individual literal is represented by the falsifying constant function.

For $i \geq 1$, we define the set $\mathsf{R}(\Psi, i)$ as consisting of all resolvent clause-strategy pairs $(C_0 \cup_{x_i} C_1, h^{1,0})$ for $(C_0, h^0) \neq (C_1, h^1) \in \mathsf{DP}(\Psi, i-1)$ satisfying (a) $x_i \notin C_0$ and $\overline{x_i} \notin C_1$, (b) $C_0 \cup_{x_i} C_1$ is not a tautology, and (c) $h_u^1 \simeq h_u^0$, for each u with $x_i \notin H_u$, where the strategy $h^{1,0}$ is the collection of functions

$$h_u^{1,0} := \begin{cases} h_u^1 \overset{x}{\bowtie} h_u^0 & \text{if } x_i \in H_u, \\ h_u^1 \circ h_u^0 & \text{if } x_i \notin H_u, \end{cases}$$

over $u \in \mathrm{vars}_\forall(\Psi)$. Finally we define $\mathsf{DP}(\Psi, i)$ as the set

$$\mathsf{R}(\Psi, i) \cup \{(C, h) \in \mathsf{DP}(\Psi, i-1) : x_i \notin \mathrm{vars}(C)\},$$

The set $\mathsf{R}(\Psi, i)$ consists of all possible w-resolvents with pivot x_i formed from clause-strategy pairs (C_1, h^1) and (C_0, h^0) in the previous set $\mathsf{DP}(\Psi, i-1)$, where the individual strategy functions h_u^1, h_u^0 must be consistent whenever u does not depend on x_i. The strategy for the resolvent is the union of h_u^1 and h_u^0 when u is indeed independent of x_i, otherwise it is 'if x_i then h_u^1 else h_u^0.' [2]

---

[2] Note that we still take the if-then-else even if the functions are compatible, and in particular also if one of the functions is undefined. This is slightly counter-intuitive at first because we could just take the union in those cases, but the if-then-else results in a more compatible strategy and is in fact necessary to ensure completeness.

Note that, for any clause-strategy pair $(C, h) \in \mathrm{DP}(\Psi, i)$, each individual function h_u depends only on the variables $\{x_1, \ldots, x_i\} \cap H_u$. This is an important observation, which we use later in our proof of completeness (Theorem 2).

We will be particularly interested in the final set of clause-strategy pairs generated by this process. Hence we write $\mathrm{DP}(\Psi) := \mathrm{DP}(\Psi, n)$. An immediate consequence of the construction is that each clause-strategy pair $(C, h) \in \mathrm{DP}(\Psi)$ has the empty clause $C = \square$. The construction is summarised in Aglorithm 1.

Algorithm 1. Davis-Putnam resolution for DQBF.

---

function $\mathrm{DP}(\Psi)$
    $\Psi^* = \mathrm{DP}(\Psi, 0)$
    for $x \in \mathrm{vars}_\exists(\Psi)$ **do**
        $\Psi^* = \Psi^* \cup \mathrm{WEAKEN\_AND\_RESOLVE}(x, \Psi^*)$
        $\Psi^* = \Psi^* \setminus \{(C, h) \in \Psi^* : x \in \mathrm{vars}(C)\}$
    end for
    return $\Psi^* \neq \emptyset$
end function

function $\mathrm{WEAKEN\_AND\_RESOLVE}(x, \Psi^*)$
    $\mathsf{R} = \emptyset$
    for all $(C_0, h^0) \neq (C_1, h^1) \in \Psi^* \times \Psi^*$ **do**
        if $x \notin C_0$, $\overline{x} \notin C_1$ **and** $h_u^0 \simeq h_u^1$ when $x \notin H_u$ **then**
            $h^{1,0} = \{h_u^1 \overset{x}{\bowtie} h_u^0 : x \in H_u\} \cup \{h_u^1 \circ h_u^0 : x \notin H_u\}$
            $\mathsf{R} = \mathsf{R} \cup \{(C_1 \cup_x C_0, h^{1,0})\}$
        end if
    end for
    return R
end function

There is a crucial difference compared to propositional or even QBF DP-resolution. While in those cases we only resolve pairs of clauses that do contain the pivot, here we need to resolve all pairs that have a w-resolvent (provided that the strategies are compatible where necessary). An interesting special case that arises out of this is *self-resolution*: when we take the w-resolvent of a clause with itself. It is readily verified that a clause C has a self-resolvent on a variable x if, and only if, $x \notin \mathrm{vars}(C)$. Self-resolving C on any variable simply produces C again. Moreover, since both the *self-union* and the *if-then-else* of any strategy function is equivalent to itself, self-resolving an entire clause-strategy pair makes no change to it. Thus, keeping the set $\{(C, h) \in \mathrm{DP}(\Psi, i-1) : x_i \notin \mathrm{vars}(C)\}$ for $\mathrm{DP}(\Psi, i)$ is tantamount to self-resolving each of those clauses and keeping only resolvents, discarding $\mathrm{DP}(\Psi, i-1)$ fully. This allows us to see the algorithm in a slightly different light; as a series of formula transformations. However, self-resolving clauses is not the most intuitive thing to do, and so for the sake of clarity and similarity to other versions of DP-resolution we assume we always resolve different clause-strategy pairs, as written in the pseudocode of Algorithm 1. We invite the reader to appreciate how adopting self-resolution and full discarding would eliminate case distinctions from some of the forthcoming proofs, arguably making them more elegant, if less humanly.

3.3   Correctness and Completeness

Now we show that the Davis-Putnam construction is both *correct* and *complete*, by which we mean that $\mathsf{DP}(\Psi)$ is non-empty if (*completeness*), and only if (*correctness*), Ψ is false.

Correctness. Our proof of correctness follows the same argument as the proof of soundness in the proof system M-Res [4].[3] For any pair $(C, h) \in \mathsf{DP}(\Psi, i)$, we show that h is a *partial countermodel* for Ψ with respect to C. This means that h behaves like a countermodel on input assignments that falsify C. The notion is captured formally in the statement of the following lemma.

Lemma 2. *Given a DQBF Ψ, an existential variable x_i, a clause-strategy pair $(C, h) \in \mathsf{DP}(\Psi, i)$, and an assignment $\gamma \in \langle vars_\exists(\Psi) \rangle$, the following holds:*

$$\gamma \text{ falsifies } C \quad \Rightarrow \quad \gamma \cup h(\gamma) \text{ falsifies } \psi.$$

Proof. We prove the theorem by induction on $i \in \{0, \ldots, n\}$. Let Ψ be the arbitrary DQBF $\Psi := \exists x_1 \cdots \exists x_n \forall u_1(H_{u_1}) \cdots \forall u_m(H_{u_m}) \cdot \psi$.

Base case $i = 0$. Let $(C_\exists, h^{C_\forall}) \in \mathsf{DP}(\Psi, 0)$. By definition, $h^{C_\forall}(\gamma)$ falsifies $C_\forall$ for each γ, and the lemma statement follows immediately.

Inductive Step $i \geq 1$. Let $(C, h) \in \mathsf{DP}(\Psi, i)$. Then, there are pairs (C_0, h^0) and (C_1, h^1) in $\mathsf{DP}(\Psi, i-1)$ such that $C = C_0 \uplus_{x_i} C_1$ and $h = h^{1,0}$. Aiming for contradiction, suppose that there exists some $\gamma \in \langle vars_\exists(\Psi) \rangle$ violating the lemma statement; that is, γ falsifies C, but $\gamma \cup h^{1,0}(\gamma)$ does not falsify ψ.

Now, let us assume for the moment that $\gamma(x_i) = 1$. For each u, let us consider the value of $h_u^{1,0}(\gamma \restriction_{H_u})$. If $x_i \in H_u$, then

$$h_u^{1,0}(\gamma \restriction_{H_u}) = \left(h_u^1 \overset{x_i}{\bowtie} h_u^0 \right)(\gamma \restriction_{H_u}) = h_u^1(\gamma \restriction_{H_u}). \tag{1}$$

Otherwise, if $x_i \notin H_u$, then $h_u^{1,0}(\gamma \restriction_{H_u}) = \left(h_u^1 \circ h_u^0 \right)(\gamma \restriction_{H_u})$, from which we get

$$h_u^1(\gamma \restriction_{H_u})(u) \neq * \quad \Rightarrow \quad h_u^{1,0}(\gamma \restriction_{H_u}) = h_u^1(\gamma \restriction_{H_u}), \tag{2}$$

by definition of $h_u^1 \circ h_u^0$.

From (1) and (2), we see that $h^{1,0}(\gamma)$ extends $h^1(\gamma)$. Together with the fact that $\gamma \cup h^{1,0}(\gamma)$ does not falsify ψ, we deduce that $\gamma \cup h^1(\gamma)$ does not falsify ψ. This contradicts the inductive hypothesis, which asserts the lemma statement for $(C_1, h^1) \in \mathsf{DP}(\Psi, i-1)$ and the assignment γ, which falsifies $C_1 \subseteq C \cup \{\overline{x_i}\}$.

The alternative case $\gamma(x_i) = 0$ follows the same lines, where the roles of C_1, h^1 and h_u^1 are played instead by C_0, h^0 and h_u^0. One shows that $\gamma \cup h^0(\gamma)$ does not falsify ψ, and a contradiction with the inductive hypothesis ensues.

---

[3] We cannot use soundness of M-Res, because our strategy compatibility notion is stronger.

The correctness of DP-resolution follows from Lemma 2.

Theorem 1. *Given a DQBF Ψ, if $\mathsf{DP}(\Psi)$ is non-empty, then Ψ is false.*

Proof. Suppose that $\mathsf{DP}(\Psi)$ is non-empty for some DQBF Ψ. Then there exists at least one pair $(\square, h) \in \mathsf{DP}(\Psi)$. Since every assignment falsifies $\square$, h is a countermodel for Ψ, by Lemma 2. Therefore Ψ is false.

Completeness. To demonstrate completeness, we must show that $\mathsf{DP}(\Psi)$ is non-empty whenever Ψ is false. A false DQBF must have at least one countermodel, h say. We show that h is 'represented' at each level of the DP construction; that is, for each $0 \leq i \leq n$ we can find a subset of $\mathsf{DP}(\Psi, i)$ whose strategies collectively describe h. Consequently the final set $\mathsf{DP}(\Psi)$ must be non-empty.

Lemma 3. *Let $\Psi := \exists x_1 \cdots \exists x_n \forall u_1(H_{u_1}) \cdots \forall u_m(H_{u_m}) \cdot \psi$, and let h be a countermodel for Ψ. For each $i \in \{0, \ldots, n\}$ and each ε in $\langle \{x_{i+1}, \ldots, x_n\} \rangle$, there exists some pair $(C, g) \in \mathsf{DP}(\Psi, i)$ such that (a) ε falsifies C, and (b) $g(\gamma) \subseteq h(\gamma)$ for every $\varepsilon \subseteq \gamma \in \langle \mathrm{vars}_\exists(\Psi) \rangle$.*

Proof. **Base case** $i = 0$. Let $\varepsilon \in \langle \{x_1, \ldots, x_n\} \rangle = \langle \mathrm{vars}_\exists(\Psi) \rangle$. Since ε is a full assignment, there is only one extension $\gamma = \varepsilon$. By definition of countermodel, $\gamma \cup h(\gamma)$ falsifies some $C \in \psi$. By definition of $\mathsf{DP}(\Psi, 0)$, there exists a clause-strategy pair $(C_\exists, g^{C_\forall}) \in \mathsf{DP}(\Psi, 0)$, where γ falsifies $C_\exists$ and $h(\gamma)$ extends $g^{C_\forall}(\gamma)$.

Inductive Step $i \geq 1$. Let $\varepsilon \in \langle \{x_{i+1}, \ldots, x_n\} \rangle$ be an assignment with extensions $\varepsilon_0 = \varepsilon \cup \{\overline{x_i}\}$ and $\varepsilon_1 = \varepsilon \cup \{x_i\}$. By the inductive hypothesis, there exists a pair $(C_0, g^0) \in \mathsf{DP}(\Psi, i-1)$ such that ε_0 falsifies C^0 and $h(\gamma_0)$ extends $g^0(\gamma_0)$ for every extension $\gamma_0 \supseteq \varepsilon_0$, and similarly $(C_1, g^1) \in \mathsf{DP}(\Psi, i-1)$ for ε_1. If $(C_0, g^0) = (C_1, g^1)$, we have $x_i \notin \mathrm{vars}(C_0)$, so $(C_0, g^0) \in \mathsf{DP}(\Psi, i)$, and it is the witness for ε.

Otherwise, we claim that the pairs (C_0, g^0) and (C_1, g^1) are resolvable. Firstly, $\overline{x_i} \notin C_0$ because C_0 is falsified by ε_0 and $x_i \notin C_1$ because C_1 is falsified by ε_1; hence the existential parts have an w-resolvent, and this resolvent cannot be a tautology because it is falsified by ε. Secondly, we need to show that the strategies g_u^0 and g_u^1 for variables u that do not depend on x_i are consistent. Consider $u \in \mathrm{vars}_\forall(\Psi)$ with $x_i \notin H_u$, and an assignment $\gamma \in \langle \mathrm{vars}_\exists(\Psi) \rangle$. We will show that $g_u^0(\gamma \lceil_{H_u}) \simeq g_u^1(\gamma \lceil_{H_u})$. For $j \in \{0, 1\}$:

- let γ_j be γ with values of the variables $x_i, \ldots, x_n$ overwritten to match ε_j. Since $x_i \notin H_u$, we have $\gamma_0 \lceil_{H_u} = \gamma_1 \lceil_{H_u}$.
- Because g_u^j only depends on $x_1, \ldots, x_{i-1}$ (because we have so far only resolved on those variables), we have $g_u^j(\gamma_j \lceil_{H_u}) = g_u^j(\gamma \lceil_{H_u})$.
- Because $\varepsilon_j \subseteq \gamma_j$, by the inductive hypothesis, $g_u^j(\gamma_j \lceil_{H_u})) \subseteq h_u(\gamma_j \lceil_{H_u})$.

Because $\gamma_0 \lceil_{H_u} = \gamma_1 \lceil_{H_u}$, we have $h_u(\gamma_0 \lceil_{H_u}) = h_u(\gamma_1 \lceil_{H_u})$, and by Lemma 1 $g_u^0(\gamma_0 \lceil_{H_u}) \simeq g_u^1(\gamma_1 \lceil_{H_u})$. Put together, we have

$$g_u^0(\gamma \lceil_{H_u}) = g_u^0(\gamma_0 \lceil_{H_u}) \simeq g_u^1(\gamma_1 \lceil_{H_u}) = g_u^1(\gamma \lceil_{H_u}).$$

Thus, $g_u^0 \simeq g_u^1$.

We claim that the resolvent $(C_1 \cup_{x_i} C_0, g^{1,0})$ of (C_0, g^0) and (C_1, g^1) is the witness for ε we are looking for. Clearly, ε falsifies $C_1 \cup_{x_i} C_0$. To verify the second condition, consider an extension $\gamma \supseteq \varepsilon$, and consider γ_0 and γ_1 with the values of x_i overwritten to 0 and 1, respectively.

Consider $u \in \text{vars}_\forall(\Psi)$ with $x_i \in H_u$. Without loss of generality assume $\gamma = \gamma_0 \supseteq \varepsilon_0$. Then, by definition of $g^{1,0}$, we have $g_u^{1,0}(\gamma\lceil_{H_u}) = g_u^0(\gamma\lceil_{H_u})$, and by the inductive hypothesis $g_u^0(\gamma\lceil_{H_u}) \subseteq h_u(\gamma\lceil_{H_u})$, as required.

On the other hand, consider $u \in \text{vars}_\forall(\Psi)$ with $x_i \notin H_u$, and observe that $\gamma_0\lceil_{H_u} = \gamma_1\lceil_{H_u} = \gamma\lceil_{H_u}$. Then, by definition of $g^{1,0}$, we have

$$g_u^{1,0}(\gamma\lceil_{H_u}) = g_u^0 \circ g_u^1(\gamma\lceil_{H_u}) = g_u^0(\gamma\lceil_{H_u}) \cup g_u^1(\gamma\lceil_{H_u}) = g_u^0(\gamma_0\lceil_{H_u}) \cup g_u^1(\gamma_1\lceil_{H_u}).$$

Because $\varepsilon_0 \subseteq \gamma_0$, we have $g_u^0(\gamma_0\lceil_{H_u}) \subseteq h_u(\gamma_0\lceil_{H_u}) = h_u(\gamma\lceil_{H_u})$, and similarly $g_u^1(\gamma_1\lceil_{H_u}) \subseteq h_u(\gamma\lceil_{H_u})$. Thus $g_u^0(\gamma\lceil_{H_u}) \cup g_u^1(\gamma\lceil_{H_u}) \subseteq h_u(\gamma\lceil_{H_u})$ by Lemma 1.

Theorem 2. *Given a DQBF Ψ, if Ψ is false, then $\mathsf{DP}(\Psi)$ is non-empty.*

Theorem 2 follows directly from Lemma 3 for $i = n$ since $\mathsf{DP}(\Psi) = \mathsf{DP}(\Psi, n)$. We will prove a slightly stronger version, which gives a finer lower bound on the size of $\mathsf{DP}(\Psi)$ based on the number of *minimal* countermodels.

Definition 2. *Let g, h be two strategies for a DQBF Ψ. We say that g extends h, denoted by $h \sqsubseteq g$, if for every total assignment $\gamma \in \langle\text{vars}_\exists(\Psi)\rangle$, $h(\gamma) \subseteq g(\gamma)$. A countermodel g is minimal, if for every countermodel h with $h \sqsubseteq g$, $g = h$. We denote the set of minimal countermodels of Ψ by $\mu(\Psi)$.*

Since the existential part of every pair in $\mathsf{DP}(\Psi)$ is the empty clause, we can afford to abuse our notation and treat $\mathsf{DP}(\Psi)$ as a set of strategies. This allows us to state the following theorem.

Theorem 3. *For a DQBF Ψ, $\mu(\Psi) \subseteq \mathsf{DP}(\Psi)$.*

Proof. By Lemma 3, every minimal countermodel g extends some strategy h in $\mathsf{DP}(\Psi)$. By Lemma 2, h is a countermodel, and by minimality of g, $h = g$.

Theorem 2 now follows from Theorem 3 as any false DQBF must have a minimal countermodel.

Example 1. Let us illustrate a run of Algorithm 1 on the following DQBF Ψ:

$$\exists x_1 \, \exists x_2 \, \forall u_1(x_1) \, \forall u_2(x_2) \quad (\overline{u_1} \vee x_2) \wedge (u_1 \vee \overline{x_2}) \wedge (\overline{u_2} \vee x_1) \wedge (u_2 \vee \overline{x_1})$$

Algorithm 1 first constructs the set $\mathsf{DP}(\Psi, 0)$, which is

$$\{ \, (x_2, \{u_1 = 1, u_2 = *\}), \, (\overline{x_2}, \{u_1 = 0, u_2 = *\}),$$
$$(x_1, \{u_1 = *, u_2 = 1\}), \, (\overline{x_1}, \{u_1 = *, u_2 = 0\}) \, \}.$$

We begin by eliminating x_1 (we could just as well start with x_2). Resolving the two clauses that contain literals on x_1 is impossible due to strategy mismatch on u_2, which is independent of x_1. Moving on to w-resolution, resolving (on x_1) the only two clauses that contain x_2 produces a tautology and so can be safely ignored. This leaves us with four w-resolution steps to take: clause pairs $(1,3); (1,4); (2,3); (2;4)$. Consequently, the set $\mathsf{DP}(\Psi,1)$ looks as follows:

$$\overbrace{\{ (x_2,\{u_1 = 1\}), (\overline{x_2},\{u_1 = 0\}),}^{\text{from } \mathsf{DP}(\Psi,0)}$$
$$(x_2,\{u_1 = 1 \overset{x_1}{\bowtie} *, u_2 = 1\}), (\overline{x_2},\{u_1 = 0 \overset{x_1}{\bowtie} *, u_2 = 1\}),$$
$$(x_2,\{u_1 = * \overset{x_1}{\bowtie} 1, u_2 = 0\}), (\overline{x_2},\{u_1 = * \overset{x_1}{\bowtie} 0, u_2 = 0\})\}.$$

In the next iteration we eliminate x_2. This time no weakening is necessary as all clauses contain a literal on x_2. Examining all pairs we find out that strategy mismatch on u_1 prevents resolving either of the original pairs with any of the new pairs, and that among the new pairs we can resolve only the first with the fourth and the second with the third. That finally gives us $\mathsf{DP}(\Psi,2) = \mathsf{DP}(\Psi)$:

$$(\square,\{u_1 = 1 \overset{x_1}{\bowtie} 0, u_2 = 0 \overset{x_2}{\bowtie} 1\}), \qquad (\square,\{u_1 = 0 \overset{x_1}{\bowtie} 1, u_2 = 1 \overset{x_2}{\bowtie} 0\}).$$

The strategy in the first pair can also be succinctly written as $u_1 = x_1, u_2 = \overline{x_2}$, and the one in the second pair is $u_1 = \overline{x_1}, u_2 = x_2$. It can easily be verified that both of them are indeed countermodels, in fact minimal ones. Moreover, since these strategies cannot be extended (they already assign a definitive value to all variables in all cases), and every countermodel must extend a strategy from some final pair, Ψ has no further countermodels. $\square$

A natural question is why and how much weakening do we need to make Algorithm 1 work. The fewer clauses to resolve, the better the performance of the algorithm, and while Algorithm 1 works as presented thanks to Theorems 1 and 2, it would be ideal if we could limit ourselves to resolving only clauses that contain the pivot, like in the propositional case. Example 1 shows that does not work—without weakening, resolving on both x_1 and x_2 would be impossible due to strategy mismatch, and hence the algorithm would finish with the empty set, wrongly concluding that Ψ is true. Example 2 goes a step further—it shows that already restricting the algorithm to resolving only pairs where at least one premise contains the pivot kills completeness.

Example 2. Consider the following DQBF Ψ:

$$\exists x_1 \exists x_2 \forall u_1(x_1) \forall u_2(x_2) \quad (\overline{x_2} \vee u_1 \vee \overline{u_2}) \wedge (\overline{x_2} \vee \overline{u_1} \vee \overline{u_2}) \wedge$$
$$(\overline{x_1} \vee x_2 \vee \overline{u_1} \vee u_2) \wedge (x_1 \vee x_2 \vee u_1 \vee u_2).$$

It is readily verified that Ψ is false, with the unique countermodel $u_1 = x_1$ and $u_2 = x_2$.

Imagine now that Algorithm 1 was modified to resolve only those pairs of clauses where the pivot is present in at least one clause. We will show that this variant would report the formula to be true. We start with $\mathsf{DP}(\Psi,0)$ as usual:

$$\{ \ (\overline{x_2}, \{u_1 = 0, u_2 = 1\}), \ (\overline{x_2}, \{u_1 = 1, u_2 = 1\}),$$
$$(\overline{x_1}, x_2, \{u_1 = 1, u_2 = 0\}), \ (x_1, x_2, \{u_1 = 0, u_2 = 0\}) \ \}.$$

Assume we first resolve on x_1. We can resolve the third and the fourth clause, the pivot is present in both premises. Tautologies on x_2 prevent all other resolution steps except with the first two clauses. But x_1 does not occur in either of those clauses, so that resolution is forbidden. Thus, $\mathsf{DP}(\Psi, 1)$ is

$$\{ \ (\overline{x_2}, \{u_1 = 0, u_2 = 1\}), \ (\overline{x_2}, \{u_1 = 1, u_2 = 0\}), \ (x_2, \{u_1 = 1 \overset{x_1}{\bowtie} 0, u_2 = 0\}) \ \}.$$

The u_1-strategies are now pairwise incompatible, and hence resolution on x_2 is impossible. Since all clauses contain a literal on x_2, they are all deleted, and the algorithm finishes with the empty set $\mathsf{DP}(\Psi)$, wrongly concluding that Ψ is true.

Had we resolved the first two clauses on x_1 as required, $\mathsf{DP}(\Psi, 1)$ would have instead been

$$\{ \ (\overline{x_2}, \{u_1 = 0, u_2 = 1\}), \ (\overline{x_2}, \{u_1 = 1, u_2 = 0\}), (x_2, \{u_1 = 1 \overset{x_1}{\bowtie} 0, u_2 = 0\}),$$
$$(\overline{x_2}, \{u_1 = 0 \overset{x_1}{\bowtie} 1, u_2 = 1\}), (\overline{x_2}, \{u_1 = 1 \overset{x_1}{\bowtie} 0, u_2 = 1\}) \ \},$$

and a further resolution step is possible, after which we arrive at the correct $\mathsf{DP}(\Psi) = \{(\square, \{u_1 = 1 \overset{x_1}{\bowtie} 0, u_2 = 1 \overset{x_2}{\bowtie} 0\}),$ containing the unique countermodel. Notice how we have to weaken each clause that does not contain x_1 in both possible ways, and take both resolvents—only one of them ends up being useful in the next iteration, but we cannot know which one it will be upfront.   □

3.4   Representing Strategies

In this subsection we discuss some details for a potential implementation of Algorithm 1. The most complicated component of the algorithm is the storage and reasoning with strategy functions, which can in general become exponentially large. Naturally, it is preferable to store strategies in such a way that consistency checking, union, and if-then-else are as fast as possible. We will show that *ordered binary decision diagrams (OBDDs)* with a fixed ordering, a well-studied target language in knowledge compilation, are a suitable data structure for all these tasks.

Definition 3 ([11,22])**.** *Let* $\mathbb{V}$ *be a countable set of propositional variables and* $\leq$ *a total order on* $\mathbb{V}$. *An* OBDD$_\leq$ *on* $\mathbb{V}$ *is a finite rooted labeled directed acyclic graph* $\mathcal{O}$ *whose each sink is labeled with either* 0 *or* 1, *whose non-sinks have outdegree* 2, *are labeled with variables from* $\mathbb{V}$, *and their outgoing edges are labeled with the two literals of the vertex label, and such that the vertex labels along any path are pairwise different and respect the order* $\leq$.

The order $\leq$ we use for the OBDD is the same as the order in which we eliminate variables in Algorithm 1, which can be arbitrary but fixed. However, since our strategy functions are 3-valued, we cannot simply write them down as an OBDD (which is 2-valued). Instead, we will rewrite each strategy g_u into a pair of Boolean strategy functions $(g_u^\top, g_u^\perp)$ defined as

$$g_u^\top(\gamma) = \begin{cases} 1 & \text{if } g_u(\gamma) = 1 \\ 0 & \text{otherwise} \end{cases}, \qquad g_u^\perp(\gamma) = \begin{cases} 1 & \text{if } g_u(\gamma) = 0 \\ 0 & \text{otherwise} \end{cases},$$

and we will represent $g_u^\top$ and $g_u^\perp$ as OBDDs. We refer to the pair $(g_u^\top, g_u^\perp)$ as the *Boolean basis* of g_u. Clearly, any strategy uniquely defines its Boolean basis, and for any Boolean basis it holds that $g_u^\top \wedge g_u^\perp$ is unsatisfiable. Conversely, from a Boolean basis, we can easily reconstruct the original function.

Lemma 4. *Let g^1, g^2 be two Boolean functions such that $g^1 \wedge g^2$ is unsatisfiable. Then, there is a unique 3-valued function g such that $g^1 = g^\top$ and $g^2 = g^\perp$.*

Proof. g is defined to output 1 when g^1 outputs 1, 0 when g^2 outputs 1, and $*$ otherwise. This is well defined thanks to $g^1 \wedge g^2$ being unsatisfiable, and clearly it is the only such g.

The following proposition, which is an easy consequence of the definition, shows how to answer consistency queries with Boolean bases, as well as how to perform union and if-then-else on them.

Proposition 1. *Let g_u, h_u be strategy functions for a universal variable u of a DQBF Ψ. Then*

- $g_u \simeq h_u \iff$ *both $g_u^\top \wedge h_u^\perp$ and $g_u^\perp \wedge h_u^\top$ are unsatisfiable;*
- $(g_u \circ h_u)^\top = g_u^\top \vee h_u^\top; \qquad (g_u \circ h_u)^\perp = g_u^\perp \vee h_u^\perp;$
- $(g_u \overset{x}{\bowtie} h_u)^\top = g_u^\top \overset{x}{\bowtie} h_u^\top; \qquad (g_u \overset{x}{\bowtie} h_u)^\perp = g_u^\perp \overset{x}{\bowtie} h_u^\perp;$

Proposition 1 requires satisfiability checking (also known as consistency checking), taking the conjunction and the disjunction of two functions (also known as bounded conjunction and disjunction), and the if-then-else. OBDDs support consistency checking and bounded conjunction and disjunction in polynomial time [11]. Since the variables on which we perform if-then-else come in a fixed order, it is clear we can compute $g \overset{x}{\bowtie} h$ simply by creating a new x-labeled vertex pointing to g and h. The constant functions in $\mathrm{DP}(\Psi, 0)$ can be represented with 1-node OBDDs, and thus we can perform all updates and all consistency checks in polynomial time.[4] At the end, the algorithm will produce the Boolean basis of a countermodel represented as a pair of OBDDs.

4   NEXP-completeness of CNF H-Form DQBF

For this section we recall an alternative syntactic form of DQBF: A DQBF in *S-form* is an expression of the form $\forall u_1 \cdots \forall u_m \exists x_1(S_{x_1}) \cdots \exists x_n(S_{x_n}) \cdot \psi$, where

---

[4] In the size of the functions, which may, inevitably, become exponential.

ψ is a propositional formula. The roles of universal and existential variables are swapped; we say that an S-form DQBF is *true* if there is a *model*, i.e. a set of functions for the existential variables with the right universal dependencies whose substitution in the matrix results in a propositional tautology. It is known that evaluating S-form DQBF is NEXP-complete, even if the matrix is restricted to a CNF [1,23].

It is easy to see that evaluating H-form DQBF, like evaluating S-form DQBF, is in NEXP. Additionally, any S-form DQBF can be translated, via negation, into an H-form DQBF, which shows that evaluating H-form DQBF with a DNF matrix is NEXP-complete. If we want the resulting matrix to be a CNF, we must start from an S-form DQBF in DNF. We therefore give a linear-time reduction from S-form DQBF in CNF, which is known to be NEXP-complete, into S-form DQBF in DNF, thereby establishing NEXP-hardness of the latter, and by extension of H-form DQBF in CNF. The reduction is in fact a direct generalization of the Tseitin translation known from propositional logic and QBF [27]—we add universal Tseitin variables and make no existential variable depend on them.

We say that two DQBFs Ψ and Ψ' are *logically equivalent* if they have the same set of models.

Theorem 4. *There is a linear-time algorithm that takes an input S-form DQBF with a CNF matrix and outputs a logically equivalent S-form DQBF with a DNF matrix.*

Proof. Let $\Psi = \forall u_1 \cdots \forall u_m \exists x_1(S_{x_1}) \cdots \exists x_n(S_{x_n}) \cdot \psi$ be an S-form DQBF where the matrix $\psi = C_1 \wedge \cdots \wedge C_r$ is a CNF. We define DNF(Ψ) as

$$\forall t_1 \cdots \forall t_r \forall u_1 \cdots \forall u_m \exists x_1(S_{x_1}) \cdots \exists x_n(S_{x_n}) \cdot \text{DNF}(\psi) \,,$$

where DNF(ψ) is the usual propositional Tseitin conversion into DNF applied to the matrix ψ, and whose auxiliary variables are $T := \{t_1, \ldots, t_r\}$, i.e.

$$\text{DNF}(\psi) := \text{DNF}(C_1) \vee \cdots \vee \text{DNF}(C_r) \vee (t_1 \wedge \cdots \wedge t_r) \,,$$

where $\text{DNF}(C_i) := T_i \bigvee_{a \in C_i} T_{i,a}$, $T_{i,a} := (\overline{t_i} \wedge a)$, and $T_i := (t_i \bigwedge_{a \in C_i} \overline{a})$. Note that this translation does indeed generalise QBF Tseitin translation.

Clearly, DNF(Ψ) can be computed in linear time. We now show that Ψ and DNF(Ψ) are logically equivalent. Since no existential variable depends on any T-variable, the dependency structure of both formulas is the same.

Let f model Ψ, and let $\alpha \in \langle \text{vars}_\forall(\text{DNF}(\Psi)) \rangle$. If $\alpha(t_1) = \cdots = \alpha(t_r) = 1$, then the top-level term $t_1 \wedge \cdots \wedge t_r$ is satisfied. Otherwise, let i be such that $\alpha(t_i) = 0$. Because f is a model for Ψ, there is a literal $a \in C_i$ for which the following holds: $\alpha\restriction_{\text{vars}_\forall(\Psi)} \cup f(\alpha\restriction_{\text{vars}_\forall(\Psi)})(a) = 1$. Hence, the term $T_{i,a}$ is satisfied. That means f is a model for DNF(Ψ) as well.

Conversely, let f be a model for DNF(Ψ). For an assignment $\alpha \in \langle \text{vars}_\forall(\Psi) \rangle$, let $\mathcal{Z}_\alpha := \{i : C_i[\alpha \cup f(\alpha)] = 0\}$ (we can write $f(\alpha)$ because no function in f depends on any variable in T, and so α contains full information for the application of f). We show that $\mathcal{Z}_\alpha = \emptyset$ for every $\alpha \in \langle \text{vars}_\forall(\Psi) \rangle$, which means

f is a model for Ψ. Let $\alpha \in \langle \text{vars}_\forall(\Psi) \rangle$. Consider the $\beta \in \langle T \rangle$ defined by $\beta(t_i) = 0 \iff i \in \mathcal{Z}_\alpha$. It is easy to see that, whether $i \in \mathcal{Z}_\alpha$ or not, $\alpha \cup \beta \cup f(\alpha \cup \beta)$ falsifies every term T_i and $T_{i,a}$, $a \in C_i$. But f is a model for DNF(Ψ), so $\alpha \cup \beta \cup f(\alpha \cup \beta)$ must satisfy some term—we conclude that it satisfies the top-level term $t_1 \wedge \cdots \wedge t_r$, and hence $\mathcal{Z}_\alpha = \emptyset$.

Corollary 1. *Evaluating S-form DQBF in DNF and H-form DQBF in CNF is* NEXP-*complete.*

Note that the proof of Theorem 4 goes through without modification even if we omit the terms T_i. Indeed, such a version would be a generalization of the Plaisted-Greenbaum translation for propositional logic and QBF [20].

The computational complexity of H-form DQBF manifests in an interesting way. Algorithm 1 proceeds in essentially the same way as QBF (and propositional) DP-resolution, eliminating variables one by one. In the QBF case, this process runs in at most single-exponential time, since there is only a single-exponential number of different clauses. In DQBF however, that would violate the hypothesis that EXP $\neq$ NEXP, and indeed, our algorithm can in general take double-exponential time and space. This is because our objects are clause-strategy pairs, and the number of different strategies is in general double-exponential. Every variable elimination step can asymptotically square the number of objects in the database, and this repeated squaring, unchecked by a bound on the total number of available objects, results in a double-exponential blow-up. Thus, in a sense, DQBF is 'one of the hardest' problems that can still be tackled with a DP-resolution-style algorithm—repeated squaring unfolds into its worst case here and, under standard complexity assumptions, cannot work for super-double-exponential problems anymore.

5   Conclusion

We presented a new decision procedure for DQBF in the style of Davis-Putnam resolution [12]. Based on the M-Res proof system [4], it constructs partial Herbrand functions along with derived clauses. The algorithm can thus be said to reason directly at the level of strategies. This is in contrast with known decision procedures for DQBF, which rely on quantifier expansion to reduce the problem to SAT/QBF [7,17], or adapt search-based algorithms for QBF by imposing additional constraints that enforce consistency with DQBF semantics [14,15,26]. Our decision procedure requires input DQBF in H-Form, as opposed to the more commonly used S-Form [2]. We presented a linear-time algorithm that converts S-Form DQBF into H-Form DQBF, thereby showing that this requirement can be easily met. As a corollary, we establish NEXP-completeness of evaluating DQBF in H-Form.

References

1. Azhar, S., Peterson, G., Reif, J.: Lower bounds for multiplayer non-cooperative games of incomplete information. J. Comput. Math. Appl. **41**, 957–992 (2001)
2. Balabanov, V., Chiang, H.K., Jiang, J.R.: Henkin quantifiers and Boolean formulae: a certification perspective of DQBF. Theor. Comput. Sci. **523**, 86–100 (2014)
3. Baldoni, R., Coppa, E., D'Elia, D.C., Demetrescu, C., Finocchi, I.: A survey of symbolic execution techniques. ACM Comput. Surv. **51**(3), 50:1–50:39 (2018)
4. Beyersdorff, O., Blinkhorn, J., Mahajan, M.: Building strategies into QBF proofs. J. Autom. Reasoning (2020). (in Press)
5. Giunchiglia, E., Tacchella, A. (eds.): SAT 2003. LNCS, vol. 2919. Springer, Heidelberg (2004). https://doi.org/10.1007/b95238
6. Biere, A., Cimatti, A., Clarke, E., Zhu, Y.: Symbolic model checking without BDDs. In: Cleaveland, W.R. (ed.) TACAS 1999. LNCS, vol. 1579, pp. 193–207. Springer, Heidelberg (1999). https://doi.org/10.1007/3-540-49059-0_14
7. Bubeck, U., Büning, H.K.: Dependency quantified horn formulas: models and complexity. In: Biere, A., Gomes, C.P. (eds.) SAT 2006. LNCS, vol. 4121, pp. 198–211. Springer, Heidelberg (2006). https://doi.org/10.1007/11814948_21
8. Buss, S.R., Hoffmann, J., Johannsen, J.: resolution trees with lemmas: resolution refinements that characterize DLL algorithms with clause learning. Logical Methods Comput. Sci. **4**, (4), (2008). https://doi.org/10.2168/LMCS-4(4:13)2008, https://lmcs.episciences.org/860
9. Buss, S.R., Kolodziejczyk, L.A.: Small stone in pool. Logical Methods Comput. Sci. **10**(2), (2014). https://doi.org/10.2168/LMCS-10(2:16)2014, https://lmcs.episciences.org/852
10. Cashmore, M., Fox, M., Long, D., Magazzeni, D.: A compilation of the full PDDL+ language into SMT. In: Coles, A.J., Coles, A., Edelkamp, S., Magazzeni, D., Sanner, S. (eds.) Proceedings of the Twenty-Sixth International Conference on Automated Planning and Scheduling, ICAPS 2016, pp. 79–87. AAAI Press (2016)
11. Darwiche, A., Marquis, P.: A knowledge compilation map. J. Artif. Intell. Res. **17**, 229–264 (2002) (electronic)
12. Davis, M., Putnam, H.: A computing procedure for quantification theory. J. ACM **7**(3), 201–215 (1960)
13. Faymonville, P., Finkbeiner, B., Rabe, M.N., Tentrup, L.: Encodings of bounded synthesis. In: Legay, A., Margaria, T. (eds.) TACAS 2017. LNCS, vol. 10205, pp. 354–370. Springer, Heidelberg (2017). https://doi.org/10.1007/978-3-662-54577-5_20
14. Fröhlich, A., Kovásznai, G., Biere, A.: A DPLL algorithm for solving DQBF, presented at Workshop on Pragmatics of SAT (POS) (2012). https://arise.or.at/pubpdf/Algorithm_for_Solving_DQBF_.pdf
15. Fröhlich, A., Kovásznai, G., Biere, A., Veith, H.: iDQ: instantiation-based DQBF solving. In: Berre, D.L. (ed.) Workshop on Pragmatics of SAT (POS). EPiC Series in Computing, vol. 27, pp. 103–116. EasyChair (2014)
16. Gitina, K., Reimer, S., Sauer, M., Wimmer, R., Scholl, C., Becker, B.: Equivalence checking of partial designs using dependency quantified boolean formulae. In: IEEE 31st International Conference on Computer Design, ICCD 2013, pp. 396–403. IEEE Computer Society (2013)
17. Gitina, K., Wimmer, R., Reimer, S., Sauer, M., Scholl, C., Becker, B.: Solving DQBF through quantifier elimination. In: Nebel, W., Atienza, D. (eds.) Design, Automation & Test in Europe Conference (DATE), pp. 1617–1622. ACM (2015)

18. Kleine Büning, H., Karpinski, M., Flögel, A.: Resolution for quantified Boolean formulas. Inf. Comput. **117**(1), 12–18 (1995)
19. Meel, K.S., et al.: constrained sampling and counting: universal hashing meets SAT solving. In: Darwiche, A. (ed.) Beyond NP. AAAI Workshops, vol. WS-16-05. AAAI Press (2016)
20. Plaisted, D.A., Greenbaum, S.: A structure-preserving clause form translation. J. Symbolic Comput. **2**(3), 293–304 (1986). https://doi.org/10.1016/S0747-7171(86)80028-1
21. Rabe, M.N., Seshia, S.A.: Incremental determinization. In: Creignou, N., Le Berre, D. (eds.) SAT 2016. LNCS, vol. 9710, pp. 375–392. Springer, Cham (2016). https://doi.org/10.1007/978-3-319-40970-2_23
22. Randal E. Bryant: Graph-based algorithms for boolean function manipulation. IEEE Trans. Comput. **C-35**(8), 677–691 (1986). https://doi.org/10.1109/TC.1986.1676819
23. Scholl, C., Jiang, J.R., Wimmer, R., Ge-Ernst, A.: A PSPACE subclass of dependency quantified Boolean formulas and its effective solving. In: The Thirty-Third AAAI Conference on Artificial Intelligence, AAAI 2019, pp. 1584–1591. AAAI Press (2019)
24. Solar-Lezama, A., Tancau, L., Bodík, R., Seshia, S.A., Saraswat, V.A.: Combinatorial sketching for finite programs. In: Shen, J.P., Martonosi, M. (eds.) Proceedings of the 12th International Conference on Architectural Support for Programming Languages and Operating Systems, ASPLOS 2006, pp. 404–415. ACM (2006)
25. Stockmeyer, L.J., Meyer, A.R.: Word problems requiring exponential time: Preliminary report. In: Aho, A.V., et al. (eds.) ACM Symposium on Theory of Computing (STOC), pp. 1–9. ACM (1973)
26. Tentrup, L., Rabe, M.N.: Clausal abstraction for DQBF. In: Janota, M., Lynce, I. (eds.) SAT 2019. LNCS, vol. 11628, pp. 388–405. Springer, Cham (2019). https://doi.org/10.1007/978-3-030-24258-9_27
27. Tseitin, G.S.: On the complexity of derivation in propositional calculus. Stud. Constructive Math. Math. Logic Part **2**, 115–125 (1968)
28. Vizel, Y., Weissenbacher, G., Malik, S.: Boolean satisfiability solvers and their applications in model checking. Proc. IEEE **103**(11), 2021–2035 (2015)

Lower Bounds for QCDCL
via Formula Gauge

Benjamin Böhm[(✉)] and Olaf Beyersdorff[(✉)]

Friedrich Schiller University Jena, Jena, Germany
{benjamin.boehm,olaf.beyersdorff}@uni-jena.de

Abstract. QCDCL is one of the main algorithmic paradigms for solving
quantified Boolean formulas (QBF). We design a new technique to show
lower bounds for the running time in QCDCL algorithms. For this we
model QCDCL by concisely defined proof systems and identify a new
width measure for formulas, which we call *gauge*. We show that for a
large class of QBFs, large (e.g. linear) gauge implies exponential lower
bounds for QCDCL proof size.

We illustrate our technique by computing the gauge for a number
of sample QBFs, thereby providing new exponential lower bounds for
QCDCL. Our technique is the first bespoke lower bound technique for
QCDCL.

Keywords: QBF · QCDCL · Proof complexity · Resolution · Lower
bounds

1 Introduction

The satisfiability problem for propositional formulas (SAT) is one of the central
problems of computer science. Traditionally perceived as a hard problem due to
its NP completeness, SAT is nowadays very efficiently tackled by SAT solvers,
building on the paradigm of conflict-driven clause learning (CDCL) [27], which
solve problems in even millions of variables on many industrial problems.

The success of SAT solving has been transferred to computationally even
more challenging settings, with quantified Boolean formulas (QBF) receiving key
attention during the last decade [14]. One of the main approaches to QBF solving
lifts CDCL to the quantified level, resulting in QCDCL [34]. In addition to
QCDCL there are a number of further competing approaches to QBF solving [20,
24,28]. Due to its PSPACE completeness, QBFs allow to encode many problems
more succinctly, thus allowing to tackle even further applications [31].

Understanding which formulas are hard for (Q)CDCL is one of the most
fascinating questions, both from a theoretical and a practical point of view.
The main approach to this problem is through interpreting runs of SAT and
QBF solvers on unsatisfiable formulas as formal proofs of their unsatisfiability.
Since learned clauses in CDCL are derivable in resolution, it was noted early on
that each run of a CDCL solver on an unsatisfiable formula can be efficiently

© Springer Nature Switzerland AG 2021
C.-M. Li and F. Manyà (Eds.): SAT 2021, LNCS 12831, pp. 47–63, 2021.
https://doi.org/10.1007/978-3-030-80223-3_5

translated into a resolution refutation [3]. Somewhat surprisingly, the converse holds as well, and when allowing arbitrary non-deterministic decision schemes, CDCL and propositional resolution are equivalent [29]. However, practical CDCL using decision schemes such as VSIDS [33] is exponentially weaker than the full resolution system [32].

Nevertheless, practical CDCL schemes are simulated by resolution and thus proof size lower bounds for resolution translate into lower bounds for CDCL running time. To obtain such lower bounds we can utilise the vast proof complexity machinery of resolution lower bound techniques [22] to show a plethora of lower bounds for combinatorial, random, and further formulas. Indeed, resolution is arguably the best-understood proof system, intensively studied long before the advent of SAT solving.

The situation is somewhat more intricate regarding the relation between QCDCL and Q-resolution, the latter being the simplest and most-studied analogue of propositional resolution for QBF [21]. The first result regarding their relative strength is due to Janota [19], who proved that practical QCDCL does *not* simulate Q-resolution. This can be interpreted as the QBF analogue of Vinyals result for practical CDCL vs resolution [32] (though [19] actually predates [32]). In contrast, the celebrated result on the equivalence of non-deterministic CDCL and resolution [29] does *not* lift to QBF as very recently shown in [7]: (non-deterministic) QCDCL and Q-resolution are incomparable, i.e., there exist formulas exponentially hard for Q-resolution, but easy for QCDCL, and vice versa.

This leaves us with the conundrum of how to show lower bounds for QCDCL. Though we understand Q-resolution fairly well and have a number of dedicated techniques for lower bounds in that system [5,6,8–10,12], unlike in the SAT case, these do not automatically apply to QCDCL.

The existing information on QCDCL lower bounds can be summarized as follows. In addition to the above-mentioned lower bound of [19] for practical QCDCL, we showed in [7] that under certain conditions, lower bounds from Q-resolution can be lifted to QCDCL. Also, while QCDCL runs on false QBFs cannot be efficiently transformed into Q-resolution proofs, they can be translated into long-distance Q-resolution proofs, an exponentially stronger proof system designed to model clause learning in QCDCL [1,16]. However, we only have very few examples of hard formulas for long-distance Q-resolution [2,9,10], which again are lifted from Q-resolution hardness.

In summary, it is fair to say that QCDCL is rather poorly understood from a theoretical point of view and in particular lower bound techniques that would allow to show exponential lower bounds for QCDCL are lacking.

Our Contributions. We devise the *first dedicated lower bound technique for QCDCL* (with arbitrary clause learning mechanisms including those used in practise). In contrast to previous lower bounds for QCDCL, our technique does not import Q-resolution hardness and thus applies to different formulas, regardless of whether they are hard for Q-resolution or not. We already mention at this point though, that our technique is not completely general, but is restricted to Σ_3^b-formulas that meet a certain XT-condition, considered already in [7].

Technically, our approach rests on interpreting QCDCL runs in a formal framework of proof systems, already used in [7]. Further, we define a property of long-distance Q-resolution proofs, which we call *quasi level-ordered*. This is inspired by the notion of level-ordered proofs, introduced in [20], where the order of resolution steps in proofs must follow the quantification order in the prefix. Quasi level-order proofs relax that condition (Definition 4).

Our lower bound technique then rests on two steps: (1) We show that for Σ_3^b-formulas with the XT-condition, QCDCL proofs can be efficiently translated into quasi level-ordered Q-resolution proofs. (2) We define a new measure called the *gauge* of a QBF and show that large (i.e. linear) gauge implies exponential size in quasi level-ordered Q-resolution. Together, (1) and (2) imply that formulas with the XT-property and large gauge are hard for QCDCL (our main Theorem 13).

We illustrate our technique on a couple of examples on which computing the gauge is fairly straightforward. Thus, though showing (1) and (2) above is rather technical, the lower bound technique itself is quite easily applicable.

It is also interesting to mention that our new notion of gauge is some kind of width measure on clauses. Showing proof size lower bounds via width lower bounds is a very well-explored theme in proof complexity, both propositionally [4] and in QBF [6,11]. We show, however, that gauge and proof width are not related in general.

Organisation. The remainder of this article is organised as follows. We start in Sect. 2 by reviewing notions from QBF, including Q-resolution and long-distance Q-resolution. In Sect. 3 we sketch QCDCL and explain how to model it as a formal proof system QCDCL. In Sect. 4 we introduce a new notion of quasi level-ordered proofs and give an algorithm to translate QCDCL proofs into quasi-level ordered Q-resolution. Section 5 introduces our lower bound method for quasi-level ordered proofs via the gauge measure, which we apply in Sect. 6 to a number of old and new QBF families. We conclude in Sect. 7 with some open questions.

2 Preliminaries

Propositional and Quantified Formulas. Variables and negated variables are called *literals*, i.e., for a variable x we can form two literals: x and its negation $\bar{x}$. We denote the corresponding variable as $\mathrm{var}(x) := \mathrm{var}(\bar{x}) := x$.

A *clause* is a disjunction of literals, sometimes also viewed as a set of literals. The *empty clause* is the clause consisting of zero literals, denoted ($\bot$). Terms are conjunctions of literals. Again, terms can be considered as sets of literals. A *CNF* (*conjunctive normal form*) is a conjunction of clauses. For $C = \ell_1 \vee \ldots \vee \ell_m$ we define $\mathrm{var}(C) := \{\mathrm{var}(\ell_1), \ldots, \mathrm{var}(\ell_m)\}$. For a CNF $\phi = C_1 \wedge \ldots \wedge C_n$ we define $\mathrm{var}(\phi) := \bigcup_{i=1}^{n} \mathrm{var}(C_i)$. A clause C is called *tautological*, if there is a variable x with $x, \bar{x} \in C$.

An *assignment* σ of a set of variables X is a non-tautological set of literals, such that for all $x \in X$ there is $\ell \in \sigma$ with $\mathrm{var}(\ell) = x$. The restriction of a clause C by an assignment σ is defined as $C|_\sigma := \top$ (true) if $C \cap \sigma \neq \varnothing$, and $\bigvee_{\ell \in C, \ell \notin \sigma} \ell$

otherwise. One can interpret σ as an operator that sets all literals from σ to the Boolean constant 1. We denote the set of assignments of X by $\langle X \rangle$.

A *QBF* (*quantified Boolean formula*) $\Phi = \mathcal{Q} \cdot \phi$ is a propositional formula ϕ (also called *matrix*) together with a *prefix* $\mathcal{Q}$. A prefix $Q_1 x_1 Q_2 x_2 \ldots Q_k x_k$ consists of variables $x_1, \ldots, x_k$ and quantifiers $Q_1, \ldots, Q_k \in \{\exists, \forall\}$. We obtain an equivalent formula if we unite adjacent quantifiers of the same type. Therefore we can always assume that our prefix is in the form of $\mathcal{Q} = Q'_1 X_1 Q'_2 X_2 \ldots Q'_s X_s$ with non-empty sets of variables $X_1, \ldots, X_s$ and quantifiers $Q'_1, \ldots, Q'_s \in \{\exists, \forall\}$ such that $Q'_i \neq Q'_{i+1}$ for $i \in [s-1]$. For a variable x in $\mathcal{Q}$ we denote the *quantifier level* with respect to $\mathcal{Q}$ by $\mathrm{lv}(x) = \mathrm{lv}_\Phi(x) = i$, if $x \in X_i$. Variables from Φ are called *existential*, if the corresponding quantifier is $\exists$, and *universal* if the quantifier is $\forall$.

A QBF with CNF matrix is called a *QCNF*. We require that all clauses from a matrix of a QCNF are non-tautological, otherwise we just delete these clauses. We further require that all variables in the matrix appear in the prefix. Since we will only discuss refutational proof systems, we only consider false QCNFs.

A QBF can be interpreted as a game between two players $\exists$ and $\forall$. These players have to assign the respective variables one by one along the quantifier order from left to right. The $\forall$-player wins the game if and only if the matrix of the QBF gets falsified by this assignment. It is well known that for every false QBF $\Phi = \mathcal{Q} \cdot \phi$ there exists a winning strategy for the $\forall$-player.

Q-resolution and Long-Distance Q-Resolution. Let C_1 and C_2 be two clauses of a QCNF Φ. Let also ℓ be an existential literal with $\mathrm{var}(\ell) \notin \mathrm{var}(C_1) \cup \mathrm{var}(C_2)$. Then the *resolvent* of $C_1 \vee \ell$ and $C_2 \vee \bar{\ell}$ over ℓ is defined as

$$(C_1 \vee \ell) \overset{\ell}{\bowtie} (C_2 \vee \bar{\ell}) := C_1 \vee C_2.$$

Let $C := u_1 \vee \ldots \vee u_m \vee x_1 \vee \ldots \vee x_n \vee v_1 \vee \ldots \vee v_s$ be a clause from Φ, where $u_1, \ldots, u_m, v_1, \ldots, v_s$ are universal literals, $x_1, \ldots, x_n$ are existential literals and $v_1, \ldots, v_s$ are exactly those literals $v \in C$ such that v is universal and $\mathrm{lv}(v) > \mathrm{lv}(x_i)$ for all $i \in [n]$. Then we can perform a reduction step and obtain

$$\mathrm{red}(C) := (u_1 \vee \ldots \vee u_m \vee x_1 \vee \ldots \vee x_n).$$

For a CNF $\phi = \{C_1, \ldots, C_k\}$ we define $\mathrm{red}(\phi) := \{\mathrm{red}(C_1), \ldots, \mathrm{red}(C_k)\}$.

Q-resolution [21] is a refutational proof system for false QCNFs. A Q-resolution proof π of a clause C from a QCNF $\Phi = \mathcal{Q} \cdot \phi$ is a sequence of clauses $\pi = C_1, \ldots, C_m$ with $C_m = C$. Each C_i has to be derived by one of the following three rules:

- *Axiom:* $C_i \in \phi$;
- *Resolution:* $C_i = C_j \overset{x}{\bowtie} C_k$ for some $j, k < i$ and $x \in \mathrm{var}_\exists(\Phi)$, and C_i is non-tautological;
- *Reduction:* $C_i = \mathrm{red}(C_j)$ for some $j < i$.

Note that none of our axioms are tautological by definition. A *refutation* of a QCNF Φ is a proof of the empty clause $(\bot)$.

To model clause learning in QCDCL, the proof system long-distance Q-resolution was introduced in [1,34]. This extension of Q-resolution allows to derive universal tautologies under specific conditions. As in Q-resolution, there are three rules by which a clause C_i can be derived. The axiom and reduction rules are identical to Q-resolution, but the resolution rule is changed to

- *Resolution (long-distance):* $C_i = C_j \overset{x}{\bowtie} C_k$ for some $j, k < i$ and $x \in \text{var}_\exists(\Phi)$. The resolvent C_i is allowed to contain a tautology $u \vee \bar{u}$ if u is a universal variable. If $u \in \text{var}(C_j) \cap \text{var}(C_k)$, then we additionally require $\text{lv}(u) > \text{lv}(x)$.

Note that a long-distance Q-resolution proof without tautologies is just a Q-resolution proof.

3   QCDCL as a Formal Proof System

In this section we review quantified conflict-driven clause learning (QCDCL) and its formalisation as a proof system from [7]. This provides the formal framework for our subsequent proof complexity analysis.

QCDCL is the quantified version of the well-known CDCL algorithm (see [27,33] for further details on CDCL, and [17,23,34] for QCDCL). Let $\Phi = \mathcal{Q} \cdot \phi$ be a false QCNF. Roughly speaking, QCDCL consists of two interleaved processes: *propagation* and *learning*.

In the *propagation process* we generate assignments with the goal to either find a satisfying assignment or to obtain a conflict. We start with clauses from ϕ that force us to assign literals such that we do not falsify these clauses (called unit clauses). The underlying idea of this process is *unit propagation*. One can think of a clause $x_1 \vee \ldots \vee x_n$ as an implication $(\bar{x}_1 \wedge \ldots \wedge \bar{x}_{n-1}) \rightarrow x_n$. That is, if we already assigned the literals $\bar{x}_1, \ldots, \bar{x}_{n-1}$, then we are forced to assign x_n in order to satisfy this clause. In QBF, we also insert reduction steps into this process, i.e., we are interested in clauses that become unit after reduction. For example, the clause $(\bar{x}_1 \wedge \ldots \wedge \bar{x}_{n-1}) \rightarrow (x_n \vee u)$ for an existential literal x_n and a universal literal u with $\text{lv}(x_n) < \text{lv}(u)$ can also be used as a ground clause for propagating x_n.

Performing unit propagation, the goal is to prevent a conflict for as long as possible. However, it is not guaranteed that we can even perform any unit propagations by just starting with the formula. Therefore we will make *decisions*, i.e., we assign literals without any solid reason. With the aid of these decisions (one can also think of assumptions) we can provoke further unit propagations. Since decision making is one of the non-deterministic components of the algorithm, we only make decisions if there are no more unit propagations available. In QCDCL these decisions follow the quantification order, i.e., we always decide a variable from the leftmost quantifier block.

After obtaining a conflict, i.e., falsifying a clause, we start the *clause learning process*. Here the underlying idea is to use Q-resolution resp. long-distance Q-resolution. We start with the clause that caused the conflict and resolve it with clauses that implied previous literals in the assignment in the reverse propagation order. At the end we get a clause such that is derived from existing clauses by long-distance Q-resolution. We add the learned clause to ϕ, backtrack to a state before we assigned all literals of this clause and restart the propagation process. The algorithm ends when we learn the empty clause ($\bot$) and therefore obtain a refutation of Φ.

QCDCL has to handle both refutations of false formulas as well as prove the validity of true formulas. Therefore one would additionally need to implement *cube learning* (or *term learning*) for satisfying assignments. Since we are only interested in refutations (otherwise we could not compare with Q-resolution), we will omit this aspect of QCDCL.

To prove rigorous lower bounds on the running time of QCDCL we cast QCDCL as a formal proof system. We recall the relevant details from [7], where we fully formalised all components of QCDCL. Each QCDCL run consists of backtracking steps and restarts. Between them we create *trails*, in which we store all information on decisions and unit propagations.

Definition 1 (trails, repeated from[7]). *Let $\Phi = \mathcal{Q} \cdot \phi$ be a QCNF in n variables. A trail $\mathcal{T}$ for Φ is a sequence of literals (or $\bot$) of variables from Φ with some specific properties. We distinguish two types of literals in $\mathcal{T}$: decision literals, that can be both existential and universal, and propagated literals, that are either existential or $\bot$. We write a trail $\mathcal{T}$ as*

$$\mathcal{T} = (p_{(0,1)}, \ldots, p_{(0,g_0)}; \mathbf{d_1}, p_{(1,1)}, \ldots, p_{(1,g_1)}; \ldots; \mathbf{d_r}, p_{(r,1)}, \ldots, p_{(r,g_r)}),$$

where we denote decision literals by d_i and propagated literals by $p_{(i,j)}$. We are not allowed to make a new decision unless there are no more propagations possible. Also, decision literals have to be level-ordered, i.e., we have to choose a leftmost quantified variable (still unassigned) as the next decision.

There are some further requirements on $\mathcal{T}$, for which we refer to [7].

For unit propagation we need the notion of *unit clauses* that allow us to assign a variable without making a decision. We call a clause C a *unit clause* if $\mathrm{red}(C) = (x)$ for an existential literal x or $x = \bot$.

The next definition presents the main framework for the analysis of QCDCL as a proof system. After having defined trails in a general way, we want to specify the way a trail can be generated during a QCDCL run.

Definition 2 (QCDCL proof systems[7]). *Let $\Phi = \mathcal{Q} \cdot \phi$ be a QCNF. We call a triple of sequences*

$$\iota = ((\mathcal{T}_1, \ldots, \mathcal{T}_m), (C_1, \ldots, C_m), (\pi_1, \ldots, \pi_m))$$

a QCDCL proof from Φ of a clause C, if for all $i \in [m]$ the trail $\mathcal{T}_i$ uses the QCNF $\mathcal{Q} \cdot (\phi \cup \{C_1, \ldots, C_{i-1}\})$, where C_j is a clause learnable from $\mathcal{T}_j$ and $C_m = C$. Each π_i is the long-distance Q-resolution derivation of the clause C_i from $\mathcal{Q} \cdot (\phi \cup \{C_1, \ldots, C_{i-1}\})$ that we learned from the trail $\mathcal{T}_i$.

Between two trails $\mathcal{T}_i$ and $\mathcal{T}_{i+1}$ we backtrack to some point which we can choose freely. Backtracking to the start (before any variable was assigned) is called restarting. If $C = (\bot)$ we call ι a refutation.

By sticking together $\pi_1, \ldots, \pi_m$, *we obtain a* long-distance Q-resolution *derivation* π *of* C *from* Φ. *We identify* QCDCL *proofs with this exact* π.

We require that all trails are naturally created, which means that we are not allowed to skip unit propagations if they are possible, as we explained before. A more detailed description of this condition is given in [7].

We remark that though QCDCL proofs are basically long-distance Q-resolution derivations (i.e., QCDCL is simulated by long-distance Q-resolution), these systems are not equal as QCDCL imposes a particular structure on long-distance Q-resolution proofs. Indeed, long-distance Q-resolution is exponentially stronger than QCDCL (cf. [7]).

4   Quasi Level-Ordered Proofs

For the remainder of this article we will entirely focus on Σ_3^b formulas and throughout fix the prefix $\exists X \forall U \exists T$, where X, U, and T are pairwise disjoint and non-empty sets of variables.

Our ultimate aim will be to develop a lower bound technique for such formulas for QCDCL. Conceptually, our technique is inspired by an approach for level-ordered proofs, which is why we recall that notion from [20].

Definition 3 ([20]). *A* long-distance Q-resolution *proof* π *from a QCNF* Φ *of a clause* C *is called* level-ordered *if for each path* P *in* π *and two resolution steps in* P *over variables* ℓ_1 *and* ℓ_2 *the following holds: if the resolution over* ℓ_1 *is closer to the root* C *than the resolution over* ℓ_2, *then* $lv(\ell_1) \leqslant lv(\ell_2)$.

For level-ordered proofs one can devise lower bounds as follows. A level-ordered long-distance Q-resolution refutation π of a Σ_3^b-formula $\Phi = \exists X \forall U \exists T \cdot \phi$ always starts with T-resolutions and ends with X-resolutions. We then count the clauses consisting only of X-literals at the transitions from a T-resolution to some X-resolution. For each $\tau \in \langle X \rangle$ we can find such a clause C_τ that is falsified by τ.

We will use this idea in a more general setting by introducing the notion of *quasi level-ordered* proofs where only the existence of these C_τ is required.

Definition 4. *A* long-distance Q-resolution *refutation* π *of a* Σ_3^b *formula with prefix* $\exists X \forall U \exists T$ *is called* quasi level-ordered, *if for each assignment* $\tau \in \langle X \rangle$ *there exists an* X-clause C_τ *which is falsified by* τ *and the subproof* $\pi_{C_\tau} \subseteq \pi$ *of* C_τ *is level-ordered.*

Clearly, level-ordered proofs are quasi level-ordered, but the converse does not hold in general.

In Sect. 5 we will devise a lower bound technique for quasi level-ordered proofs. To get the connection to QCDCL, we show that each QCDCL refutation of Σ_3^b formulas with a special property can be efficiently transformed into a quasi level-ordered Q-resolution refutation. The property needed is the *XT-property*, which we recall from [7].

Definition 5 ([7]). *Let Φ be a QCNF of the form $\exists X \forall U \exists T \cdot \phi$. We call a clause C in the variables of Φ*

- X-clause, *if* $var(C) \cap X \neq \varnothing$, $var(C) \cap U = \varnothing$ *and* $var(C) \cap T = \varnothing$,
- T-clause, *if* $var(C) \cap X = \varnothing$, $var(C) \cap U = \varnothing$ *and* $var(C) \cap T \neq \varnothing$,
- XT-clause, *if* $var(C) \cap X \neq \varnothing$, $var(C) \cap U = \varnothing$ *and* $var(C) \cap T \neq \varnothing$,
- XUT-clause, *if* $var(C) \cap X \neq \varnothing$, $var(C) \cap U \neq \varnothing$ *and* $var(C) \cap T \neq \varnothing$.

We say that Φ fulfils the XT-property if ϕ contains no XT-clauses as well as no unit T-clauses and there do not exist two T-clauses $C_1, C_2 \in \phi$ that are resolvable.

Intuitively, this says that there is no direct connection between the X- and T-variables, i.e., Φ does not contain clauses with X- and T-variables, but no U-variables. This XT-property allows us to prove several properties regarding QCDCL refutations.

Lemma 6 ([7]). *Let Φ be a QCNF that fulfils the XT-property. Then the following holds:*

(i) It is not possible to derive XT-clauses by long-distance Q-resolution.
(ii) It is not possible to resolve two XUT-clauses over an X-literal in a QCDCL *proof.*
(iii) Each QCDCL *refutation of Φ is a* Q-resolution *refutation (not just a long-distance Q-resolution refutation).*

Now we will work towards the transformation of QCDCL proofs into quasi level-ordered Q-resolution refutations. This transformation is described as an algorithm in the following theorem.

Theorem 7. *Let Φ be a Σ_3^b QCNF that fulfils the XT-property. Then each* QCDCL *refutation π of Φ can be efficiently transformed into a quasi level-ordered* Q-resolution *refutation π' of Φ with $|\pi'| \in \mathcal{O}(|\pi|^4)$.*

Proof. First, because of the XT-property each QCDCL refutation is also a Q-resolution refutation.

Let $\pi = C_1, \ldots, C_m = \perp$. Note that clauses could occur more than once in a proof since we cannot simply shorten a proof in QCDCL. Hence we will use indices to identify clauses in a proof. Each index not only determines the clause itself, but also its position in the proof. This is the reason why we will only use indices in the algorithm in order to store informations about a particular clause.

Technically, we define an order that will help us determine if a resolution $C_d \bowtie C_e$ takes place before or after another resolution $C_{d'} \bowtie C_{e'}$ in a given proof. For this we define a total order $\preccurlyeq$ on $\{\{d, e\} : d, e \in \mathbb{N}, d \neq e\}$ as follows:

$$A \preccurlyeq B \Leftrightarrow \max A < \max B \text{ or } (\max A = \max B \text{ and } \min A \leqslant \min B).$$

We use the notation $A \prec B$ for $A \preccurlyeq B$ and $A \neq B$.

Algorithm 1: The algorithm needs a QCDCL refutation π as input and outputs a quasi level-ordered long-distance Q-resolution refutation π'.

---

1 $M_X := \{m\}$; $M_{XUT} := \varnothing$; $L := \varnothing$; $\pi' := \pi$; $i := 1$;
2 **while** $M_X \neq \varnothing$ **do**
3   **while** $M_X \neq \varnothing$ **do**
4   choose $c \in M_X$ maximal;
5   **if** *subproof* π_{C_c} *of* C_c *is level-ordered* **then**
6 | add c to L;
7   **else**
8   **if** *last step in* π'_{C_c} *was a resolution over X, say* $C_c = C_d \overset{x}{\bowtie} C_e$
                then
9 | add d and e to M_X
10   **else**
11   Under all transitions from X-resolutions to T-resolutions in
                    π'_{C_c} of the form $C_d \overset{x}{\bowtie} C_e = C_f$ and $C_f \overset{t}{\bowtie} C_g = C_j$ let $\{d, e\}$
                    be maximal with respect to $\preccurlyeq$;
12   W.l.o.g. let C_d be the XUT-clause and C_e be the X-clause
                    (otherwise swap d and e);
13   add (d, e, c) to M_{XUT};
14   add e to M_X;
15   **end**
16   **end**
17   delete c from M_X;
18   **end**
19     $M_{XUT}^{(i)} := M_{XUT}$;
20     $i := i + 1$;
21   **while** $M_{XUT} \neq \varnothing$ **do**
22   Choose $(d, e, c) \in M_{XUT}$;
23   Let $C_d, C_{a_1}, C_{a_2}, \ldots, C_{a_k}, C_c$ be the path from C_d to C_c. Since C_c
            is an X-clause, all T-literals from C_d have to be resolved away. Let
            $C_{a_1} = C_d \overset{x}{\bowtie} C_e$, $C_{a_j} = C_{a_{j-1}} \overset{r_j}{\bowtie} C_{b_{j-1}}$ for T-variables r_j, some
            indices b_{j-1}, $j = 2, \ldots, k$ and $C_c = \mathrm{red}(C_{a_k})$;
24   Add the clauses $C_{a'_2} := C_d \overset{r_1}{\bowtie} C_{b_1}$, $C_{a'_j} := C_{a'_{j-1}} \overset{r_j}{\bowtie} C_{b_{j-1}}$ for
            $j = 3, \ldots, k$ and $C_{a'_{k+1}} := \mathrm{red}(C_{a'_k})$. If somewhere the resolution
            does not work due to a lacking literal r_j or x, we define the
            corresponding $C_{a'_j}$ as the clause that lacks this literal. The $C_{a'_j}$ are
            inserted at the end of the proof.;
25   add a'_{k+1} to M_X;
26   delete (d, e, c) from M_{XUT};
27   **end**
28 **end**

We sketch how the transformation (Algorithm 1) works: Throughout the whole process we work with two sets M_X and M_{XUT}. The set M_X contains indices of X-clauses, where initially we start with $M_X = \{m\}$ (remember that $C_m = (\bot)$). For each $c \in M_X$ we check whether the clause C_c has a level-ordered subproof. If the subproof is not level-ordered, and if the last step before C_c was an X-resolution, we just add the indices both parent clauses of C_c to M_X and delete c from it. Otherwise, if the subproof is not level-ordered, but the last step before C_c was no X-resolution, we search for the last transition that violates the level-order condition. This must be a transition from an X-resolution to a T-resolution. After this transition there will be only T-resolutions until we reach C_c. One of the parent clauses of this X-resolution, which we call C_d and C_e, is an X-clause and the other one is an XUT-clause due to the XT-property (Lemma 6). The index of the X-clause (either d or e) is again stored in M_X, while we delete c from M_X. However, for the XUT-clauses, which are stored as triples (d, e, c) in M_{XUT} (where C_d is the XUT-clause), we have to add several clauses to the proof, including a new X-clause $C_{a'}$. This clause $C_{a'}$ is then added to M_X as well, and the loop repeats until there are no more clauses in M_X left. Note that these added clauses will be part of a dead end in the proof and therefore are not necessary for the refutation itself. However, we need these new clauses for a counting argument in our lower bound technique.

We will show that at the end we return a proof that is quasi level-ordered. More specifically, the X-clauses we detect during the run whose subproofs are level-ordered will be exactly the clauses C_τ from the definition of quasi level-ordered proofs. This holds because, starting from the empty clause, whenever we detect an X-resolution we can choose which parent clause we will consider next. Hence we can choose the polarity of the X-variable we resolve over in the current step. At the end, this last X-clause (whose subproof is level-ordered) only consists of variables with the right polarity as previously chosen. Figure 1 depicts how the algorithm transforms a proof.

$\square$

Algorithm 1 can be easily modified to also transform long-distance Q-resolution refutations by adding more case distinctions to line 12. However, this might lead to an exponential blow up.

5   A Lower Bound Technique via Gauge

Now that we have proven that QCDCL is simulated by quasi level-ordered proofs, we continue by introducing a measure for Σ_3^b QCNFs that will provide an exponential lower bound for quasi level-ordered refutations of these formulas.

Definition 8. *For a Σ_3^b QCNF Φ with prefix $\exists X \forall U \exists T$ let W_Φ be the set of all Q-resolution derivations π from Φ of some X-clause such that π only contains T-resolution and reduction steps. We define the* gauge *of Φ as*

$$gauge(\Phi) := \min\{|C| : C \text{ is the root of some } \pi \in W_\Phi\}.$$

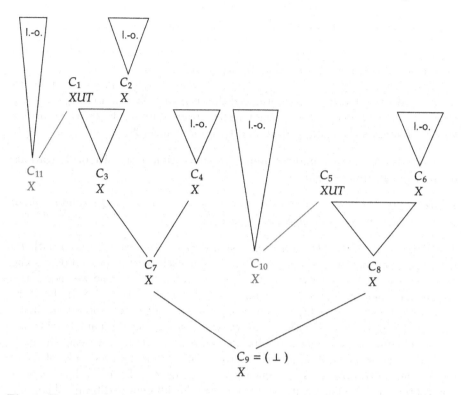

Fig. 1. Sketch of the functionality of the algorithm. Below each clause C_j we specify the type of clause (X- or XUT-clause). Newly added parts are coloured red. Triangles labeled with "l.-o." are level-ordered subproofs, otherwise they are not level-ordered and we can find a transition from an X-resolution to a T-resolution. The corresponding clause C_c is then one of the C_τ clauses for a particular τ. (Color figure online)

Intuitively, gauge(Φ) is the minimal number of X-literals that are necessarily piled up in a level-ordered Q-resolution derivation in which we want to get rid of all T-literals (hence we consider proofs of X-clauses).

Before showing how gauge lower bounds imply proof size lower bounds let us consider an example for which we recall the CR_n formulas from [20].

Definition 9 ([20]). *The QCNF* CR_n *consists of the quantifier prefix*

$$\exists x_{(1,1)}, \ldots, x_{(1,n)}, x_{(2,1)}, \ldots, x_{(2,n)}, \ldots, x_{(n,1)}, \ldots, x_{(n,n)} \forall u \exists s_1, \ldots, s_n, t_1, \ldots, t_n$$

and matrix clauses $(x_{(i,j)} \vee u \vee s_i)$, $(\bar{x}_{(i,j)} \vee \bar{u} \vee t_j)$ *for* $i, j \in [n]$ *as well as* $\bigvee_{i \in [n]} \bar{s}_i$ *and* $\bigvee_{i \in [n]} \bar{t}_i$.

The CR_n formulas describe a 'completion' game on an $(n \times n)$-matrix (cf. [20]). It is readily checked that the CR_n formulas fulfil the XT-property. We can now compute their gauge. Note that according to our convention, the T-variables comprise of all variables $s_1, \ldots, s_n, t_1, \ldots, t_n$.

Lemma 10. *We have gauge*(CR_n) $= n$.

Proof. Since there are no X-clauses as axioms, we necessarily need to resolve over T somehow. For this we need T-literals of negative polarity, hence each $\pi \in W_{\mathrm{CR}_n}$ contains $\bigvee_{i \in [n]} \bar{s}_i$ or $\bigvee_{i \in [n]} \bar{t}_i$. In each $\pi \in W_{\mathrm{CR}_n}$ every T-literal has to be resolved away. For this reason we need the corresponding clauses $x_{(i,j)} \vee u \vee s_i$ or $\bar{x}_{(i,j)} \vee \bar{u} \vee t_j$. Because we cannot resolve over X in $\pi \in W_{\mathrm{CR}_n}$, there are at least n X-literals that are piled up and therefore gauge(CR_n) $= n$.   □

Towards our lower bound technique we now estimate the size of derivations of X-clauses in terms of gauge.

Lemma 11. *Let Φ be a Σ_3^b QCNF. Let π be a level-ordered* Q-resolution *proof from Φ of a non-tautological X-clause D with $|D| = c$. Then $|\pi| \geqslant 2^{gauge(\Phi)-c}$.*

Proof. Let $V := X \backslash \mathrm{var}(D)$. For each assignment $\tau \in \langle V \rangle$ we will find a path P_τ in π_n by going backwards starting from D. For each resolution step over some $x \in V$ we choose the path whose literals are negated by τ, hence we choose the clause that contains x if $\tau(x) = 0$ and the other clause otherwise. If there are resolution steps over variables from var(D), then we will always choose the literal from D. If we reach a reduction step, we will just expand the path by this one parental clause. If we detect a resolution step over a T-literal, we stop there.

Let C_τ be the clause at which we stop. Clearly, the subproof π_{C_τ} of C_τ is one of the derivations in W_Φ, hence $|C_\tau| \geqslant$ gauge(Φ). Then C_τ has to be a non-tautological X-clause with at least gauge(Φ) different X-literals. Then C_τ contains at least gauge(Φ) $- c$ different X-literals whose variables are in V. These literals are negated by the assignment τ.

Now let a be the number of these clauses C_τ by summing over all τ. Since for each C_τ there are at most $|X|$ $-$ gauge(Φ) variables that are not contained as some literal in the clause, there are at most $2^{|X|-\mathrm{gauge}(\Phi)}$ paths that can lead to each C_τ. Multiplying with the number of C_τ gives us at least the number of paths $\tau \in \langle V \rangle$, hence

$$2^{|X|-\mathrm{gauge}(\Phi)} \cdot a \geqslant 2^{|X|-c}$$
$$\Leftrightarrow a \geqslant 2^{|X|-c}/2^{|X|-\mathrm{gauge}(\Phi)} = 2^{\mathrm{gauge}(\Phi)-c}.$$

Since each C_τ is a clause from π, we get $|\pi| \geqslant a \geqslant 2^{\mathrm{gauge}(\Phi)-c}$.   □

Note that the bound from Lemma 11 is an exact lower bound (no asymptotics involved). We will now use Lemma 11 to get a lower bound for quasi level-ordered Q-resolution refutations. We will do this with a similar counting argument as in Lemma 11 by counting the number of clauses C_τ in quasi level-ordered proofs.

Proposition 12. *Each quasi level-ordered* Q-resolution *refutation of a Σ_3^b QCNF Φ has size $2^{\Omega(gauge(\Phi))}$.*

Proof. Let π be the shortest quasi level-ordered refutation of Φ. By the definition of quasi level-ordered proofs we can find clauses C_τ for each $\tau \in \langle X \rangle$.

Let $h := \min_{\tau \in \langle X \rangle} |C_\tau|$. By Lemma 11 we get $|\pi| \geqslant 2^{\text{gauge}(\Phi)-h}$, hence $h \geqslant \text{gauge}(\Phi) - \log |\pi|$. Each clause C_τ can have at most $2^{|X|-h}$ assignments $\alpha \in \langle X \rangle$ such that $C_\alpha = C_\tau$. Let $a := |\{C_\tau : \tau \in \langle X \rangle\}|$, then $a \cdot 2^{|X|-h} \geqslant 2^{|X|}$ and thus

$$|\pi| \geqslant a \geqslant 2^h \geqslant 2^{\text{gauge}(\Phi)-\log|\pi|} = \frac{2^{\text{gauge}(\Phi)}}{|\pi|}.$$

We conclude that $|\pi|^2 \in 2^{\Omega(\text{gauge}(\Phi))}$. □

We combine Theorem 7 and Proposition 12 above and obtain a lower bound for QCDCL on formulas with the XT-property.

Theorem 13. *Each* QCDCL *refutation of a Σ_3^b QCNF Φ that fulfils the XT-property has size $2^{\Omega(gauge(\Phi))}$.*

6   Applications of the Lower Bound Technique

We now apply our new lower bound technique via gauge to show exponential lower bounds for QCDCL proof size (and thereby for QCDCL running time) for a number of QBF families. First, by combining Lemma 10 with Theorem 13 we obtain hardness for the CR_n formulas from [20].

Corollary 14. *The formulas CR_n require exponential-size proofs in* QCDCL.

With this result we gain an improved separation between Q-resolution and QCDCL. It was already shown in [7] that Q-resolution and QCDCL are incomparable. This involves constructing QBFs that are easy for QCDCL, but hard for Q-resolution, and vice versa. One direction is shown via the QParity formulas (Definition 18 below), which are hard for Q-resolution [9], but easy in QCDCL [7]. For the other direction, [7] used the Trapdoor [7] and Lonsing formulas [23], both of which are easy for Q-resolution, but hard for QCDCL. However, both QBF families incorporate the propositional pigeonhole principle (PHP) and the hardness of these formulas for QCDCL rests entirely on the hardness of PHP for propositional resolution [18]. This is somewhat unsatisfactory, as the hardness results do not refer to quantification and in particular do not hold in the presence of NP oracles (cf. [13,26] for a detailed formal account on how to equip QBF proofs with NP oracles or equivalently QBF solving with SAT calls).

Our improved separation is shown in Corollary 14 above, as these formulas are hard in QCDCL, but easy in Q-resolution [20]. Unlike the separations from [7], this hardness result does not make any reference to propositional hardness but also holds under NP oracles in the framework of [13].

We also note that Janota [19] already proved hardness of the QBFs CR_n for QCDCL with UIP learning. Corollary 14 improves on that result as well as our hardness result holds for arbitrary learning schemes in QCDCL.

As our second example we introduce the following formulas.

Definition 15. *Let* $\text{ENarrow}_n := \exists x_1, \ldots, x_{n+1} \forall u_1, \ldots, u_{n+1} \exists t_1, \ldots, t_n \cdot \psi_n$ *with the matrix* ψ_n *containing the clauses:*

$x_1 \vee u_1 \vee t_1, \quad \bar{x}_1 \vee \bar{u}_1 \vee t_1,$

$x_i \vee u_i \vee \bar{t}_{i-1} \vee t_i, \quad \bar{x}_i \vee \bar{u}_i \vee \bar{t}_{i-1} \vee t_i, \qquad for\ i = 2, \ldots, n$

$x_{n+1} \vee u_{n+1} \vee \bar{t}_n, \quad \bar{x}_{n+1} \vee \bar{u}_{n+1} \vee \bar{t}_n.$

It is easy to see that ENarrow_n fulfils the XT-property. Next we will show an exponential lower bound for ENarrow_n in QCDCL.

Lemma 16. *We have* $\text{gauge}(\text{ENarrow}_n) = n + 1$.

Proof. Let $\pi \in W_{\text{ENarrow}_n}$. Define the sets of clauses

$$Z_1 := \{x_1 \vee u_1 \vee t_1, \ \bar{x}_1 \vee \bar{u}_1 \vee t_1\}$$

$$Z_i := \{x_i \vee u_i \vee \bar{t}_{i-1} \vee t_i, \ \bar{x}_i \vee \bar{u}_i \vee \bar{t}_{i-1} \vee t_i\} \qquad \text{for } i = 2, \ldots, n$$

$$Z_{n+1} := \{x_{n+1} \vee u_{n+1} \vee \bar{t}_n, \ \bar{x}_{n+1} \vee \bar{u}_{n+1} \vee \bar{t}_n\}.$$

Let C be an axiom clause in π. Then C has to be contained in some set Z_i as above.

Case 1: $C \in Z_1$.

Then we have to get rid of $t_1 \in C$, hence we need a clause from Z_2. But then we have to get rid of t_2 and so on: $Z_1 \rightsquigarrow Z_2 \rightsquigarrow \ldots \rightsquigarrow Z_n \rightsquigarrow Z_{n+1}$. We conclude that π has to contain at least one clause from each Z_j, $j \in [n+1]$. Therefore we have to pile up $n + 1$ X-literals.

Case 2: $C \in Z_i$ for some $i \in \{2, \ldots, n\}$.

Then we have to get rid of $\bar{t}_{i-1}$ and $t_i \in C$, hence we need a clause from Z_{i-1} and Z_{i+1}. After this we have to resolve over $\bar{t}_{i-2}$ and t_{i+1} and so on, leading to a chain of resolutions $Z_1 \leftrightsquigarrow \ldots \leftrightsquigarrow Z_{i-1} \leftrightsquigarrow Z_i \rightsquigarrow Z_{i+1} \rightsquigarrow \ldots \rightsquigarrow Z_{n+1}$. Again, we conclude that π has to contain at least one clause from each Z_j, $j \in [n+1]$. Therefore we have to pile up $n + 1$ X-literals.

Case 3: $C \in Z_{n+1}$.

This works similarly to Case 1, except that we start at Z_{n+1} and go backwards: $Z_1 \leftrightsquigarrow Z_2 \leftrightsquigarrow \ldots \leftrightsquigarrow Z_n \leftrightsquigarrow Z_{n+1}$. □

Corollary 17. *The QBFs* ENarrow_n *require exponential-size proofs in* QCDCL.

The gauge of a formula is obviously some width measure and it seems natural to wonder how it relates to the notion of the existential proof width[1] of long-distance Q-resolution refutations of a formula as studied in [6,11,15]. However, it turns out that these two measures are not directly related. On the one hand, it is easy to see that ENarrow_n has long-distance Q-resolution refutations of constant existential clause width. Hence these formulas have small (constant) existential proof width, but linear gauge.

On the other hand, there are also formulas with constant gauge and linear proof width. For this we revisit the parity formula from [9].

---

[1] The existential width of a clause is defined as the number of existential literals in this clause. The existential proof width is defined as the maximal existential width over all clauses in this proof.

Definition 18 ([9]). QParity$_n$ *consists of the prefix* $\exists x_1 \ldots x_n \forall u \exists t_2 \ldots t_n$ *and the matrix*

$$x_1 \vee x_2 \vee \bar{t}_2, \ x_1 \vee \bar{x}_2 \vee t_2, \ \bar{x}_1 \vee x_2 \vee t_2, \ \bar{x}_1 \vee \bar{x}_2 \vee \bar{t}_2,$$
$$x_i \vee t_{i-1} \vee \bar{t}_i, \ x_i \vee \bar{t}_{i-1} \vee t_i, \ \bar{x}_i \vee t_{i-1} \vee t_i, \ \bar{x}_i \vee \bar{t}_{i-1} \vee \bar{t}_i \quad \text{for } i \in \{3, \ldots, n\}$$
$$u \vee t_n, \ \bar{u} \vee \bar{t}_n.$$

It was shown in [6,11] that QParity$_n$ requires linear proof width. Here we modify this formula such that proof width remains unaffected, but gauge is small. Let mQParity$_n$ be the modified variant of this formula that consists of the prefix $\exists x_1, \ldots, x_n, y \forall u \exists t_2, \ldots, t_n$ and the matrix $(\bar{y}) \wedge \bigwedge_{C \in \text{QParity}_n} (y \vee C)$. Obviously, because of the unit clause $(\bar{y})$, we have gauge(mQParity$_n$) = 1, but still linear proof width.

We can also use the QParity$_n$ formulas to show that large gauge alone is not sufficient to guarantee QCDCL hardness, but some further assumption such as the XT-condition is needed.

We continue with the equality formula from [5] as a further example of hard formulas for QCDCL. In [7] QCDCL hardness of Equality$_n$ was already proven by lifting Q-resolution hardness of these formulas to QCDCL. However, with our new lower bound technique it is possible to prove QCDCL hardness directly without importing Q-resolution lower bounds.

Definition 19 ([5]). *The formula* Equality$_n$ *is defined as the QCNF*

$$\exists x_1 \ldots x_n \forall u_1 \ldots u_n \exists t_1 \ldots t_n \cdot (\bar{t}_1 \vee \ldots \vee \bar{t}_n) \wedge \bigwedge_{i=1}^{n} ((\bar{x}_i \vee \bar{u}_i \vee t_i) \wedge (x_i \vee u_i \vee t_i)).$$

Proposition 20. *We have* gauge(Equality$_n$) = n. *Consequently the formulas are exponentially hard for* QCDCL.

Proof. Let $\pi \in W_{\text{Equality}_n}$. Since none of the axioms are X-clauses, we have to resolve over T somehow. For this we need the clause $\bar{t}_1 \vee \ldots \vee \bar{t}_n$. But that means we have to resolve over each t_i at least once in π, and therefore we will pile up all n X-variables. $\qquad\square$

7 Conclusion

We initiated the study of devising lower bound methods tailored to QCDCL. At the moment our techniques only applies to Σ_3^b-formulas. Though this is a quite relevant class of QBFs, also prominently represented in QBF benchmarks [25,30], it would be very interesting to extend the method to QBFs of higher quantifier complexity.

In another direction, future research should explore further conditions (besides the XT-condition considered here) that allow to efficiently translate QCDCL into quasi level-ordered proofs and thus enable to show lower bounds via gauge.

References

1. Balabanov, V., Jiang, J.H.R.: Unified QBF certification and its applications. Form. Methods Syst. Des. **41**(1), 45–65 (2012)
2. Balabanov, V., Widl, M., Jiang, J.H.R.: QBF resolution systems and their proof complexities. In: Proceedings of Theory and Applications of Satisfiability Testing (SAT), pp. 154–169 (2014)
3. Beame, P., Kautz, H.A., Sabharwal, A.: Towards understanding and harnessing the potential of clause learning. J. Artif. Intell. Res. (JAIR) **22**, 319–351 (2004)
4. Ben-Sasson, E., Wigderson, A.: Short proofs are narrow - resolution made simple. J. ACM **48**(2), 149–169 (2001)
5. Beyersdorff, O., Blinkhorn, J., Hinde, L.: Size, cost, and capacity: a semantic technique for hard random QBFs. Logical Methods Comput. Sci **15**(1), 13:1–13:39 (2019)
6. Beyersdorff, O., Blinkhorn, J., Mahajan, M.: Hardness characterisations and size-width lower bounds for QBF resolution. In: Proceedings of ACM/IEEE Symposium on Logic in Computer Science (LICS), pp. 209–223. ACM (2020)
7. Beyersdorff, O., Böhm, B.: Understanding the relative strength of QBF CDCL solvers and QBF resolution. In: Proceedings of Innovations in Theoretical Computer Science (ITCS), pp. 12:1–12:20 (2021)
8. Beyersdorff, O., Bonacina, I., Chew, L., Pich, J.: Frege systems for quantified Boolean logic. J. ACM **67**(2), 1–36 (2020)
9. Beyersdorff, O., Chew, L., Janota, M.: New resolution-based QBF calculi and their proof complexity. ACM Trans. Comput. Theor. **11**(4), 26:1–26:42 (2019)
10. Beyersdorff, O., Chew, L., Mahajan, M., Shukla, A.: Feasible interpolation for QBF resolution calculi. Logical Methods Comput. Sci. **13**, 7:1–7:20 (2017)
11. Beyersdorff, O., Chew, L., Mahajan, M., Shukla, A.: Are short proofs narrow? QBF resolution is not so simple. ACM Trans. Comput. Logic **19**, 1–26 (2018)
12. Beyersdorff, O., Chew, L., Sreenivasaiah, K.: A game characterisation of tree-like Q-resolution size. J. Comput. Syst. Sci. **104**, 82–101 (2019)
13. Beyersdorff, O., Hinde, L., Pich, J.: Reasons for hardness in QBF proof systems. ACM Trans. Comput. Theor. **12**(2), 1–27 (2020)
14. Beyersdorff, O., Janota, M., Lonsing, F., Seidl, M.: Quantified Boolean formulas. In: Biere, A., Heule, M., van Maaren, H., Walsh, T. (eds.) Handbook of Satisfiability, 2nd edn. IOS press, Frontiers in Artificial Intelligence and Applications (2021)
15. Clymo, J., Beyersdorff, O.: Relating size and width in variants of Q-resolution. Inf. Process. Lett. **138**, 1–6 (2018)
16. Egly, U., Lonsing, F., Widl, M.: Long-distance resolution: Proof generation and strategy extraction in search-based QBF solving. In: Proceedings of Logic for Programming, Artificial Intelligence, and Reasoning (LPAR), pp. 291–308 (2013)
17. Giunchiglia, E., Narizzano, M., Tacchella, A.: Clause/term resolution and learning in the evaluation of quantified Boolean formulas. J. Artif. Intell. Res. **26**, 371–416 (2006)
18. Haken, A.: The intractability of resolution. Theor. Comput. Sci. **39**, 297–308 (1985)
19. Janota, M.: On Q-Resolution and CDCL QBF solving. In: Proceedings of International Conference on Theory and Applications of Satisfiability Testing (SAT), pp. 402–418 (2016)
20. Janota, M., Marques-Silva, J.: Expansion-based QBF solving versus Q-resolution. Theor. Comput. Sci. **577**, 25–42 (2015)

21. Kleine Büning, H., Karpinski, M., Flögel, A.: Resolution for quantified Boolean formulas. Inf. Comput. **117**(1), 12–18 (1995)
22. Krajíček, J.: Proof complexity, Encyclopedia of Mathematics and Its Applications, vol. 170. Cambridge University Press (2019)
23. Lonsing, F.: Dependency Schemes and Search-Based QBF Solving: Theory and Practice. Ph.D. thesis, Johannes Kepler University Linz (2012)
24. Lonsing, F., Egly, U.: DepQBF 6.0: A search-based QBF solver beyond traditional QCDCL. In: Proceedings of International Conference on Automated Deduction (CADE), pp. 371–384 (2017)
25. Lonsing, F., Egly, U.: Evaluating QBF solvers: quantifier alternations matter. In: Hooker, J. (ed.) CP 2018. LNCS, vol. 11008, pp. 276–294. Springer, Cham (2018). https://doi.org/10.1007/978-3-319-98334-9_19
26. Lonsing, F., Egly, U., Seidl, M.: Q-resolution with generalized axioms. In: Creignou, N., Le Berre, D. (eds.) SAT 2016. LNCS, vol. 9710, pp. 435–452. Springer, Cham (2016). https://doi.org/10.1007/978-3-319-40970-2_27
27. Marques Silva, J.P., Lynce, I., Malik, S.: Conflict-driven clause learning SAT solvers. In: Handbook of Satisfiability. IOS Press (2009)
28. Peitl, T., Slivovsky, F., Szeider, S.: Dependency learning for QBF. J. Artif. Intell. Res. **65**, 180–208 (2019)
29. Pipatsrisawat, K., Darwiche, A.: On the power of clause-learning SAT solvers as resolution engines. Artif. Intell. **175**(2), 512–525 (2011)
30. Pulina, L., Seidl, M.: The 2016 and 2017 QBF solvers evaluations (QBFEVAL'16 and QBFEVAL'17). Artif. Intell. **274**, 224–248 (2019)
31. Shukla, A., Biere, A., Pulina, L., Seidl, M.: A survey on applications of quantified Boolean formulas. In: Proceedings of IEEE International Conference on Tools with Artificial Intelligence (ICTAI), pp. 78–84 (2019)
32. Vinyals, M.: Hard examples for common variable decision heuristics. In: Proceedings of the AAAI Conference on Artificial Intelligence (AAAI) (2020)
33. Zhang, L., Madigan, C.F., Moskewicz, M.W., Malik, S.: Efficient conflict driven learning in Boolean satisfiability solver. In: Proceedings of IEEE/ACM International Conference on Computer-Aided Design (ICCAD), pp. 279–285 (2001)
34. Zhang, L., Malik, S.: Conflict driven learning in a quantified Boolean satisfiability solver. In: Proceedings of IEEE/ACM International Conference on Computer-aided Design (ICCAD), pp. 442–449 (2002)

Deep Cooperation of CDCL and Local Search for SAT

Shaowei Cai[1,2(✉)] and Xindi Zhang[1,2]

[1] State Key Laboratory of Computer Science, Institute of Software,
Chinese Academy of Sciences, Beijing, China
{caisw,zhangxd}@ios.ac.cn
[2] School of Computer Science and Technology,
University of Chinese Academy of Sciences, Beijing, China

Abstract. Modern SAT solvers are based on a paradigm named conflict driven clause learning (CDCL), while local search is an important alternative. Although there have been attempts combining these two methods, this work proposes deeper cooperation techniques. First, we relax the CDCL framework by extending *promising* branches to complete assignments and calling a local search solver to search for a model nearby. More importantly, the local search assignments and the *conflict frequency* of variables in local search are exploited in the phase selection and branching heuristics of CDCL. We use our techniques to improve three typical CDCL solvers (glucose, MapleLCMDistChronoBT and Kissat). Experiments on benchmarks from the Main tracks of SAT Competitions 2017–2020 and a real world benchmark of spectrum allocation show that the techniques bring significant improvements, particularly on satisfiable instances. For example, the integration of our techniques allow the three CDCL solvers to solve 62, 67 and 10 more instances in the benchmark of SAT Competition 2020. A resulting solver won the Main Track SAT category in SAT Competition 2020 and also performs very well on the spectrum allocation benchmark. As far as we know, this is the first work that meets the standard of the challenge "Demonstrate the successful combination of stochastic search and systematic search techniques, by the creation of a new algorithm that outperforms the best previous examples of both approaches." [35] on standard application benchmarks.

Keywords: CDCL · Local search · Application benchmarks

1 Introduction

The Satisfiability problem (SAT) asks to determine whether a given propositional formula is satisfiable or not. In the SAT problem, propositional formulas are

---

S. Cai and X. Zhang—The authors are considered to have equal contributions. Cai contributes mostly on the ideas and partly on the implementations and writes the paper, while Zhang contributes mostly on the implementations and partly on the ideas.

© Springer Nature Switzerland AG 2021
C.-M. Li and F. Manyà (Eds.): SAT 2021, LNCS 12831, pp. 64–81, 2021.
https://doi.org/10.1007/978-3-030-80223-3_6

usually presented in Conjunctive Normal Form (CNF), i.e., $F = \bigwedge_i \vee_j \ell_{ij}$. A growing number of problem domains are successfully tackled by SAT solvers, including the electronic design automation (EDA) industry [37], mathematical theorem proving [20], AI planning [21], spectrum allocation [32], among others. Also, SAT solvers are often used as a core component of more complex tools such as solvers for Satisfiability Module Theory (SMT), which are indispensable for program analysis and software verification.

Many approaches have been proposed to solve SAT, among which conflict driven clause learning (CDCL) is the most popular one. Since their inception in the mid-90s, CDCL-based SAT solvers have been applied, in many cases with remarkable success, to a number of practical applications. Indeed, one of the main reasons of the widespread use of SAT is that CDCL solvers are so effective in practice. CDCL is evolved from the DPLL backtracking procedure [14], and usually involves a number of key techniques, mainly including 1) clause learning from conflicts [36], 2) exploiting the structure of conflicts during clause learning [36], 3) learnt clause management scheme [4], 4) lazy data structures for the representation of formulas [31], 5) effective branching heuristics, e.g., VSIDS [31], and 6) periodically restarting [18]. Additional techniques used in recent CDCL solvers include phase saving [34], switching between "stabilizing" mode (seldom-restart) and frequent-restart mode [33], clause veriification [29], among others.

On the other hand, there is another paradigm named local search, which is a main incomplete method biased towards the satisfiable side. Local search SAT solvers begin with a complete assignment and iteratively modify the assignment until a model is found or a resource limit (usually the time limit) is reached. Although local search solvers usually have poor performance on application instances, they may be competitive on certain types of instances [10,12,26].

There have been attempts combining CDCL and local search solvers. However, in previous hybrid solvers, CDCL and local search solvers usually see each other as a black box and the hybrid solver invokes the respective solver according to different situations [3,5,19,24,30]. This work is devoted to deeper cooperation of CDCL and local search for SAT, where CDCL is the main solver and local search is used as an aiding tool. We propose three ideas to use local search to help CDCL in different ways. The first idea is a method for plugging a local search solver into a CDCL solver, while the other two ideas concern with using information produced by the local search solver to enhance CDCL. We summarize the three techniques below.

- Explore promising branches by local search (Sect. 3)
  The first idea is to a novel method to plug a local search solver into a CDCL solver. We relax the backtrack process by allowing some promising branches to be extended to a complete assignment without backtracking, even if conflicts are met during extending the assignment. Then, a local search solver is called to find a model nearby. If the local search cannot find a model within a given time limit, the CDCL search process continues as normal from the node where the algorithm enters the non-backtracking phase.

- Phase selection with local search assignments (Sect. 4)
  Phase selection refers to pick a truth value (usually called phase) to assign the branching variable. Most modern CDCL solvers implement a phase selection heuristic named phase saving [34], which keeps the branching phase and uses the saved phase when a variable is picked to branch. Recent progress shows that using some other forms of *target phase*, e.g., the value under the largest conflict-free assignment in the solver, random value and the opposite of the saved phase, to reset the saved phase periodically could be beneficial [10]. We propose a phase resetting technique, which mainly relies on the assignments produced by the integrated local search solver.
- Branching with local search conflict information (Sect. 5)
  We use the variables' *conflict frequency*, i.e., the frequency appearing in unsatisfied clauses during local search, to enhance the branching heuristic in CDCL. Specifically, such information is used to modify the variables' *activity* in VSIDS heuristic and the variables' *learning rate* in LRB heuristic.

We apply our techniques to three state-of-the-art CDCL solvers, including the latest version of glucose [4], and the winner of the Main track of SAT Competition 2019 and 2020 namely MapleLCMDistChronoBT-DL [22] and Kissat_sat [10]. The experimental results show that our techniques allow them to solve a remarkable number of additional instances in the main track benchmark of SAT Competition 2017–2020. For example, the integration of our techniques allow the three CDCL solvers to solve 62, 67 and 10 more instances in the benchmark of SAT Competition 2020. Besides, the improved version of the three CDCL solvers also shows better results on a real world benchmark arising from a spectrum repacking problem in the context of bandwidth auction.

Seen from experiments, the promising branches exploration technique and the local search based phase resetting techniques are very helpful to solve satisfiable instances, with a price of slight degradation on unsatisfiable instances (usually solving 2 or 3 fewer unsatisfiable instances). The local search conflict frequency enhanced branching strategy can be positive to satisfiable and also saves back a few unsatisfiable instances. Overall, these techniques significantly improves the performance of the CDCL solvers, leading to a remarkable increase on the number of total solved instances.

2 Preliminaries

2.1 Preliminary Definitions and Notations

Let $V = \{x_1, x_2, ..., x_n\}$ be a set of Boolean variables, a *literal* is either a variable x or its negation $\neg x$. A *clause* is a disjunction of literals. A clause that contains only one single literal is called a *unit clause*. A Conjunctive Normal Form (CNF) formula $F = C_1 \wedge C_2 \wedge ... \wedge C_m$ is a conjunction of clauses.

A mapping $\alpha : V \rightarrow \{0, 1\}$ is called an *assignment*. If α maps all variables to a Boolean value, it is a *complete assignment*; otherwise, it is a *partial assignment*. The size of an assignment α, denoted as $|\alpha|$, is the number of assigned variables in it. The value of a variable x under an assignment α is denoted as $\alpha[x]$. An assignment α satisfies a clause iff at least one literal evaluates to true under α, and satisfies a CNF formula iff it satisfies all its clauses. A CNF formula F is satisfiable iff there is at least one satisfying assignment. The empty clause $\square$ is always unsatisfiable, and represents a conflict. SAT is the problem of deciding whether a given CNF formula is satisfiable.

The process of conditioning a CNF formula F on a literal ℓ amounts to removing the clauses containing an occurrence of ℓ and all occurrences of $\neg\ell$. A key procedure in CDCL solvers is *unit propagation*. For a unit clause, the variable is assigned to satisfy this unit clause, and then the formula is conditioned on this setting. The iterative execution of such steps until no more unit clause remains is called *unit propagation*.

2.2   CDCL Solvers

A CDCL solver performs a backtracking search (can be non-chronological) in the space of partial assignments, which is organized as a tree. Each node of the tree corresponds to a partial assignment, and the out edges represent the two *branching value* (also known as *branching phase*) for a variable. The root represents the empty assignment, while each leaf corresponds to a complete assignment. CDCL solvers can prune a large part of the tree thanks to reasoning techniques. A *branch* is a path from the root to an inner node. In this work, we use α_max to denote the largest conflict-free assignment that has been encountered by the solver so far.

Algorithm 1 shows the standard procedure of a CDCL solver, where α is the current assignment, dl is the current decision level and bl denotes the backtrack level. Arguments to the functions are assumed to be passed by reference, and thus F and α are supposed to be modified during the search. The functions are explained here. *PickBranchVar* consists of selecting a variable to assign and the respective phase. *UnitPropagation* performs unit propagation on the formula, and if a conflict is identified, then a conflict indication is returned. Once a conflict is derived, the reasons are analyzed and a clause is learnt (known as *learnt conflict clause*) and then added to the clause database. This is done by the *ConflictAnalysis* function. Finally, *BackTrack* backtracks to the decision level computed by ConflictAnalysis. Note that Algorithm 1 shows the skeleton of a typical CDCL algorithm, and does not describe a few often used techniques, including restarts, clause deletion polices, learnt clause simplification, among others.

We introduce two branching heuristics that are used to pick the variable to assign in CDCL, which are used in the studied solvers of this paper.

Algorithm 1: Typical CDCL algorithm: CDCL(F, α)

---

1   $dl \leftarrow 0$;   //decision level
2   **if** $UnitPropagation(F, \alpha)==CONFLICT$ **then return** UNSAT
3   **while** $\exists$ *unassigned variables* **do**
      /* PickBranchVar picks a variable to assign and picks the
        respective value   */
4       $(x, v) \leftarrow PickBranchVar(F, \alpha)$;
5       $dl \leftarrow dl + 1$;
6       $\alpha \leftarrow \alpha \cup \{(x, v)\}$;
7   **if** $UnitPropagation(F, \alpha)==CONFLICT$ **then**
8            $bl \leftarrow ConflictAnalysis(F, \alpha)$;
9   **if** $bl < 0$ **then**
10   **return** UNSAT;
11   **else**
12   BackTrack(F, α, bl);
13                $dl \leftarrow bl$;

14 **return** SAT;

Variable State Independent Decaying Sum (VSIDS) [31]: Here we describe the version used in MiniSAT [15] and most modern CDCL solvers. Each variable has an *activity* attached to it. Every time a variable occurs in a recorded conflict clause, its activity is increased. This is referred to as *bumping*. After the conflict, the activity of all the variables in the system are multiplied by a constant less than 1, thus decaying the activity of variables over time. When selecting a branching variable, VSIDS picks the variable with the maximum activity score.

Learning Rate Branching (LRB) [27]: It frames branching as an optimization problem that picks a variable to maximize a metric called *learning rate*. The learning rate of a variable x at interval I is defined as $\frac{P(x,I)}{L(I)}$, where I is the interval of time between the assignment of x until x transitions back to being unassigned, $P(x, I)$ is the number of learnt clauses x participates in interval I, and $L(I)$ is the number of learnt clauses generated in interval I. The authors of LRB proposed to solve the optimization problem via a Multi-Armed Bandit algorithm.

2.3 Local Search Solvers

For local search algorithms, we need to define the search space and a neighborhood relation. In the context of SAT, the search space is the set of complete assignments which can be characterized as the set of strings $\{0, 1\}^n$, where n is the number of variables in the formula. For SAT, the seemingly most natural neighborhood N maps candidate solutions to their set of Hamming neighbors, i.e., candidate solutions that differ in exactly one variable. A local search algorithm starts from a position of search space and then moves to one neighbor of the current position in each step, trying to find a position which represents a satisfying assignment.

2.4 Experiment Preliminaries

In this work, we use our methods to improve CDCL solvers and carry out extensive experiments to evaluate the effectiveness of the methods. In this subsection, we introduce the experiment setup including base solvers, benchmarks, running environment and reporting methodology.

Base Solvers: We choose three state of the art CDCL solvers as the base solvers for our studies, including glucose (v4.2.1)[1] [4], MapleLCMDistChronoBT-DL (v2.1)[2] [22], and Kissat_sat (2414b6d)[3] [10]. Glucose is a milestone of modern CDCL solvers and has won several gold medals in SAT Competitions. MapleLCMDistChronoBT-DL won the SAT Race 2019 and Kissat_sat won the Main Track of SAT Competition 2020.

We choose CCAnr [12] as the local search solver to integrate into the CDCL solvers glucose and MapleLCMDistChronoBT-DL, while Kissat_sat itself already includes a local search solver YalSAT [9]. CCAnr is a local search solver with the aim for solving structured SAT instances and has shown competitive results on various structured instances from SAT competitions and applications.

Benchmarks: The experiments are carried out with the main track benchmarks of the latest four SAT Competitions/Race (2017–2020). Additionally, we evaluate the solvers on an important application benchmark suite consisted of 10000 instances[4] from the spectrum repacking in the context of bandwidth auction which resulted in about 7 billion dollar revenue [32].

Experiment Setup: All experiments were conducted on a cluster of computers with Intel Xeon Platinum 8153 @2.00GHz CPUs and 1024G RAM under the operating system CentOS 7.7.1908. For each instance, each solver was performed one run, with a cutoff time of 5000 CPU seconds. For each solver for each benchmark, we report the number of solved SAT/UNSAT instances and total solved instances, denoted as '#SAT', '#UNSAT' and '#Solved', and the penalized run time 'PAR2' (as used in SAT Competitions), where the run time of a failed run is penalized as twice the cutoff time.

3 Exploring Promising Branches by Local Search

In this section, we present our method for plugging a local search solver into a CDCL solver. The method helps finding a model faster, by exploring promising branches via local search.

---

[1] http://sat-race-2019.ciirc.cvut.cz/solvers/glucose-4.2.1.zip.

[2] http://sat-race-2019.ciirc.cvut.cz/solvers/MapleLCMDistChronoBT-DL-v2.1.zip.

[3] https://github.com/arminbiere/kissat.git.

[4] https://www.cs.ubc.ca/labs/beta/www-projects/SATFC/cacm_cnfs.tar.gz.

First, we provide the motivation of our method. By using reasoning techniques, CDCL solvers are able to prune most of the branches of the search tree. This is useful for solving unsatisfiable instances—to prove a formula is unsatisfiable, a CDCL solver needs to examine the whole search space, and therefore the more of the search tree is pruned, the more efficient the solver is. However, when solving satisfiable formulas, some promising branches that are close to a satisfying assignment are also pruned without any exploitation. This would make CDCL solvers miss some opportunities of finding a solution. In our opinion, the exploration on promising branches may improve CDCL solvers on satisfiable formulas, and a natural way to do so is to employ local search at such branches.

Now, we present a method to explore promising branches during the search procedure of CDCL solvers, which can improve the ability to find solutions while keeping the completeness of the solvers. For this method, we need to identify which branches (i.e., partial assignments) deserve exploration. We propose two conditions below, and any assignment α satisfying at least one of them is considered as promising and will be explored:

- $\frac{|\alpha|}{|V|} > p$ and there is no conflict under α, where p is a parameter and is set to 0.4 according to preliminary experiments on a random sample of instances from recent SCs.
- $\frac{|\alpha|}{|\alpha\_max|} > q$ and there is no conflict under α, where q is set to 0.9 similarly.

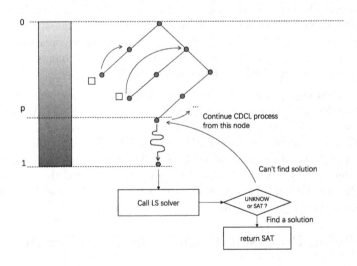

Fig. 1. Overall Procedure of Relaxed CDCL

With the conditions of promising assignments, the method is described as follows (depicted in Fig. 1). During the search of CDCL, whenever reaching a node corresponding to a promising assignment, the algorithm enters a non-backtracking mode, which uses unit propagation and heuristics in CDCL to assign the remaining variables without backtracking, even an empty clause is detected. At the end, this leads to a complete assignment β, which is fed to a local search solver to search for a model nearby. If the local search fails to find a model within a certain time budget, then the algorithm goes back to the normal CDCL search from the node where it was interrupted (we call this a breakpoint). The non-backtracking phase does not change the data structures used for CDCL search process. In this work, each call of the local search solver is cutoff when reaching a certain amount of memory accesses (5×10^7).

4   Phase Resetting with Local Search Assignments

In Sect. 3, we propose a method to plug a local search solver into boost CDCL solvers. Now, we propose a phase resetting heuristic based on the assignments obtained by the local search processes.

Phase selection is an important component of a CDCL solver. Most modern CDCL solvers utilize the phase saving heuristic [34], which returns the phase of a variable x corresponding to the last time x was assigned. This caching scheme reduces the repetition caused by non-chronological backtracking. Recently, Biere et al. proposed a phase resetting technique which overwrites all saved phases with some other information, based on the interval of number of conflicts encountered, which gives another boost to the performance [10].

Algorithm 2 describes a CDCL solver that implements the idea of exploring promising branches and phase resetting technique. After each time the CDCL solver is restarted, the technique overwrites the saved phases of all variables with assignments produced by local search. To this end, we record the best assignment (with the fewest unsatisfied clauses) in each run of the local search solver, and when we say the assignment of a local search procedure (run), we refer to the best assignment in this procedure.

For our phase resetting technique, we consider the following assignments, all of which come from the assignments of the local search procedures.

- α_max_LS. This refers to the assignment of the local search procedure in which the initial solution is extended based on α_max. Thus, whenever α_max is updated, the algorithm calls the local search solver and updates α_max_LS.
- α_latest_LS. This is the assignment of the latest local search procedure.
- α_best_LS. Among all local search assignments so far, we denote the best one (with the fewest unsatisfied clauses) as α_best_LS.

It is easy to see that α_max_LS and α_best_LS serve for the aim to maximize the depth of the branch, while α_latest_LS adds diversification in some sense, as different local search procedures start with initial assignments built upon different branches. Overall, it is expected this phase resetting technique with local search assignments would work well particularly for satisfiable instances, and our experiment results confirm this.

Phase Resetting Based on Local Search Assignment: Whenever the CDCL is restarted, we overwrites the saved phases. For each variable x, its phase is set according to the following probability distribution (Table 1).

Algorithm 2: Relaxed CDCL Algorithm with Phase Reset

---

1   $dl \leftarrow 0$, $\alpha \leftarrow \emptyset$, $\alpha\_max \leftarrow \emptyset$;
2   **if** $UnitPropagation(F,\alpha)==CONFLICT$ **then**
3     $\lfloor$ **return** UNSAT

4   **while** $\exists$ *unassigned variables* **do**
5     $(x,v) \leftarrow PickVariable(F,\alpha)$;
6     $dl \leftarrow dl + 1$;
7     $\alpha \leftarrow \alpha \cup \{(x,v)\}$;
8   **if** $UnitPropagation(F,\alpha)==CONFLICT$ **then**
9       $bl \leftarrow ConflictAnalysis(F,\alpha)$;
10   **if** $bl < 0$ **then**
11        $\lfloor$ **return** UNSAT

12   **else**
13        $\alpha\_max \leftarrow max(\alpha\_max,\alpha)$;
14        $BackTrack(F,\alpha,bl)$, $dl \leftarrow bl$;

     /* lines 15-22 corresponds to the technique in Section 3   */
15   **else if** $(|\alpha|/|V| > p$ **OR** $|\alpha|/|\alpha\_max| > q)$ **then**
16      $\beta \leftarrow \alpha$;
17   **while** β *is not complete* **do**
18        $(x,v) \leftarrow PickVariable(F,\beta)$;
19        $\beta \leftarrow \beta \cup \{(x,v)\}$;
20        $UnitPropagation(F,\beta)$;
21   **if** $LocalSearch(\beta, terminate\_condition)$ **then**
22        $\lfloor$ **return** SAT

23   **if** *Meet Restart Conditions* **then**
24      $BackTrack(F,\alpha,0)$;
25      $dl \leftarrow 0$;
26      $PhaseReset()$;   //corresponds to Section 4

27 **return** SAT;

Table 1. Probability of different phases in our phase resetting mechanism

Phase Name	$\alpha\_max\_LS[x]$	$\alpha\_latest\_LS[x]$	$\alpha\_best\_LS[x]$	no change
Probability	20%	65%	5%	10%

5 Branching with Conflict Frequency in Local Search

CDCL is a powerful framework owing largely to the utilization of the conflict information, and branching strategies aim to promote conflicts. In this section, we use a variable property which we refer to as *conflict frequency* in local search to improve the branching strategy of CDCL.

The best known branching strategy is VSIDS (Variable State Independent Decaying Sum) [31], which is surprisingly effective and also works well with restarts. Although variants [7, 8, 15–17] have been proposed over the years, they are similar in spirit to VSIDS in the sense that they prefer to pick variables participating in recent conflicts. Briefly speaking, the VSIDS heuristic maintains an activity score for each variable, and prefers to pick the variable with the maximum activity score. The activity score of a variable reflects the frequency that it occurs in conflicts, with emphasis on those in the recent period (please refer to [31] and [15] for more details).

Recently, a new branching strategy LRB (the learning rate based branching heuristic) [27] shows its effectiveness in the Maple series, which regularly won gold medals in main track of SAT Competitions since 2016. LRB is based on the concept called *learning rate*, which measures the portion of learnt clauses involving the variable among all learnt clauses in the period between the assignment of x until it transitions back to being unassigned (please refer to [27] for more details).

Intuitively, both VSIDS and LRB prefer to pick variables with higher frequencies occurring in conflicts, with an emphasis in a recent period. We propose to enhance the branching strategy by utilizing the conflict frequency of variables in the *latest* local search procedure.

Definition 1. *In a local search process for SAT, for a variable x, its conflict frequency, denoted as $ls\_confl\_freq(x)$, is the number of steps in which it appears in at least one unsatisfied clause divided by the total number of steps of the local search process.*

Now we describe how to use the *local search conflict frequency* in the branching strategies. As $ls\_confl\_freq(x)$ is a real number between 0 and 1, we first transfers it to an integer number so that it can be combined well with VSIDS and LRB. For each variable x, we multiply $ls\_confl\_freq(x)$ with a constant integer (100 in this work), and the resulting number is denoted as $ls\_conflict\_num(x)$. We use $ls\_conflict\_num(x)$ to enhance the branching strategies as follows. Note that $ls\_conflict\_num(x)$ is calculated according to the **latest** local search procedure. After each restart of the CDCL solver, $ls\_conflict\_num(x)$ is used to modify the activity score for VSIDS and learning rate for LRB.

- VSIDS: for each variable x, its activity score is increased by $ls\_conflict\_num(x)$.
- LRB: for each variable x, the number of learnt clause during its period I is increased by $ls\_conflict\_num(x)$. That is, both $P(x, I)$ and $L(I)$ are increased by $ls\_conflict\_num(x)$.

6   Experiments

We carry out extensive experiments to evaluate the effectiveness of our methods. The experiment setup is described in Sect. 2.4. For glucose and MapleLCMDistChronoBT-DL-v2.1, we implement all the three techniques in this work, including relaxed CDCL with local search (denoted as **rx**), phase resetting with local search (denoted as `rp`) and local search conflict frequency enhanced branching (denoted as `cf`). For Kissat_sat, we only implement the `cf` technique, as it is challenging to implement the relaxed CDCL framework in it, due to the difficulty of identifying all current clauses (which should be provided to local search) in the Kissat_sat solver. Nevertheless, it is easy to apply the `cf` technique to Kissat, which is what we do in this work. All the source codes, origin experiment statistics and the detailed data for Table 2 can be downloaded online.[5]

Evaluations on Benchmarks of SAT Competitions. The results of evaluations of all the base solvers and the different versions with our techniques are reported in Table 2. According to the results, we have some observations.

Table 2. Experiment results on benchmarks from SAT Competitions 2017–2020, where Maple-DL-v2.1 is short for MapleLCMDistChronoBT-DL-v2.1

solver	#SAT	#UNSAT	#Solved	PAR2	#SAT	#UNSAT	#Solved	PAR2
	SC2017(351)				SC2018(400)			
glucose_4.2.1	83	101	184	5220.0	95	95	190	5745.9
glucose+rx	88	95	183	5237.0	113	95	208	5283.4
glucose+rx+rp	112	94	206	4618.2	141	87	228	4698.3
glucose+rx+rp+cf	110	94	204	4668.5	150	91	241	4438.2
Maple-DL-v2.1	101	113	214	4531.0	133	102	235	4533.9
Maple-DL+rx	101	112	213	4520.3	149	101	250	4148.6
Maple-DL+rx+rp	111	103	214	4447.1	158	93	251	4147.2
Maple-DL+rx+rp+cf	116	107	223	4139.4	162	97	259	3927.6
Kissat_sat	115	114	229	3943.5	167	98	265	3786.4
Kissat_sat+cf	113	113	226	4001.0	178	104	282	3409.4
CCAnr	13	N/A	13	9629.9	56	N/A	56	8622.0
	SC2019(400)				SC2020(400)			
glucose_4.2.1	118	86	204	5437.6	68	91	159	6494.6
glucose+rx	120	84	204	5443.9	93	88	181	6018.1
glucose+rx+rp	134	85	219	5096.3	130	85	215	5123.7
glucose+rx+rp+cf	140	85	225	4923.6	134	87	221	4977.9
Maple-DL-v2.1	143	97	240	4601.8	86	104	190	5835.7
Maple-DL+rx	146	93	239	4602.1	121	105	226	4977.8
Maple-DL+rx+rp	155	94	249	4416.3	142	99	241	4589.2
Maple-DL+rx+rp+cf	154	95	249	4377.4	151	106	257	4171.1
Kissat_sat	159	88	247	4293.5	146	114	260	4048.8
Kissat_sat+cf	162	90	252	4211.7	157	113	270	3896.8
CCAnr	13	N/A	13	9678.3	45	N/A	45	8978.7

- The `rx` technique improves glucose and MapleLCMDistChronoBT-DL-v2.1 on solving satisfiable instances, particularly for the benchmarks of 2018 (increased by 18 and 16 for #SAT) and 2020 (increased by 25 and 35 for

[5] https://github.com/caiswgroup/relaxed-sat.

#SAT). On the other hand, the glucose+rx and Maple-DL+rx have slightly worse performance than the original versions on UNSAT instances, and the decrease on #UNSAT is only 2 on average, considering both solvers on all benchmarks.

- By adding the rp technique, glucose+rx+rp and Maple-DL+rx+rp gain further improvement on #SAT, which is significant for all benchmarks. Specifically, the #SAT number of glucose+rx+rp is greater than glucose+rx by 24, 28, 14 and 37 for benchmarks of 2017, 2018, 2019 and 2020 respectively, and the increment is 10, 9, 9 and 21 for Maple-DL+rx+rp over Maple-DL+rx. Similar to the rx technique, we observe slight degradation on solving UNSAT instances, and the decrease on #UNSAT is 3 on average for both solvers.
- The impact of the cf technique can be seen from the comparisons of glucose+rx+rp vs. Glucose+rx+rp+cf, Maple-DL+rx+rp vs. Maple-DL+rx+rp+cf, and Kissat_sat vs. Kissat_sat+cf. Overall, the cf technique is positive for solving both satisfiable and unsatisfiable instances on all benchmarks, with the exceptions of glucose+rx+rp+cf and Kissat_sat+cf on the 2017 benchmark (dropping 2 and 3 instances). For the benchmarks of 2018, 2019 and 2020, the cf technique leads to a remarkable increment on the #Solved number, which is (13, 6, 6) for glucose+rx+rp+cf, (8, 0, 7) for Maple-DL+rx+rp+cf, and (17, 5, 10) for Kissat_sat+cf. Particularly, noting that Kissat_sat is the winner of Main Track in SC 2020 and represents the latest state of the art, such improvements are remarkable by a single technique.
- By implementing all the three techniques, very large improvements are obtained for glucose and MapleLCMDistChronoBT-DL-v2.1 for all the benchmarks. Particularly, glucose+rx+rp+cf solves 62 additional instances than the original solver, and Maple-DL+rx+rp+cf solves 67 additional instances than its original solver for the SC2020 benchmark (which has 400 instances). We note that, Maple-DL+rx+rp+cf is a simplified and optimized version of our solver Relaxed_LCMDCBDL_newTech which won the gold medal of Main Track SAT category and the silver medal of the Main Track ALL category in SC 2020.

Evaluations on Benchmarks of Spectrum Repacking. We also carry out experiments on a suite of instances arising from an important real world project—the spectrum repacking project in US Federal Communication Commission (FCC). The instances from this project was available on line[6] [32]. This benchmark contains 10 000 instances, including both satisfiable and unsatisfiable instances. We compare each base CDCL solver with its final version using our techniques, as well as the underlying local search solver CCAnr.

The results on this benchmark suite are reported in Table 3. According to the results, for each of the base CDCL solvers, the improved version with our techniques has better performance than the base solver. Particularly, the Maple-

---

[6] https://www.cs.ubc.ca/labs/beta/www-projects/SATFC/cacm_cnfs.tar.gz.

DL+rx+rp+cf solver solves the most instances (8759+218=8977), significantly better than all the other solvers.

Table 3. Comparing with state-of-the-art solvers on FCC. glucose+ is short for glucose+rx+rp+cf, and malple+ is short for Maple-DL+rx+rp+cf.

Benchmark	glucose	glucose+	Maple	Maple+	kissat_sat	kissat_sat+cf	CCAnr
	#SAT	#SAT	#SAT	#SAT	#SAT	#SAT	#SAT
	#UNSAT	#UNSAT	#UNSAT	#UNSAT	#UNSAT	#UNSAT	#UNSAT
	#Solved	#Solved	#Solved	#Solved	#Solved	#Solved	#Solved
	PAR2	PAR2	PAR2	PAR2	PAR2	PAR2	PAR2
FCC (10000)	7330	8075	8084	8759	8192	8214	7853
	187	197	215	218	207	211	0
	7517	8272	8299	8977	8399	8425	7853
	2555.85	1850.58	1867.13	1243.66	1760.55	1734.61	2215.35

Further Analyses on the Cooperation. We perform more analyses to study the role of local search in the hybrid solvers based on glucose and MapleLCMDIstChronoBT-DL. This experiment does not include Kissat_sat as we do not apply the relaxed CDCL framework to it and the statistics in this experiment are not applicable to Kissat_sat+cf. Some important information is provided in Table 4.

We can see that the local search solver returns a solution for some instances, and this number varies considerably with the benchmarks. A natural question is: *Whether the improvements come mainly from the complementation of CDCL and local search solvers that they solve different instances?* If this were true, then a simple portfolio that runs both CDCL and local search solvers would work similarly to the hybrid solvers in this work. To answer this question, we compare the instances solved by the hybrid solvers with those by the base CDCL solver and the local search solver (both the CDCL and local search solver are given 5000 s for each instance). We observe that, there is a large number of instances (denoted by #SAT_bonus) that both CDCL and local search solvers fail to solve but can be solved by the hybrid solvers. For these instances, even a virtual best solver that picks the solver with the best result for each instance would fail. For glucose, this number reaches 29, 36, 26 and 37 for the four benchmarks respectively, while for MapleLCMDIstChronoBT-DL, this number reaches 16, 18, 15 and 36 respectively. This indicates the cooperation techniques have essential contributions to the good performance of the hybrid solvers.

We also calculate the number of calls of the local search solver in each run. This figure is usually from 10 to 25 for these benchmarks. As for the run time of local search, which can be seen as the price paid for the benefit of using local search, we calculate the portion of the time spent on local search. This figure is between 6% and 20% for the satisfiable instances, and it drops significantly on unsatisfiable instances, which is usually less than 7%. This is not inconsistent with the observations that the number of local search calls is not necessarily

Table 4. Analyses on the impact of Local Search on the CDCL solvers. Maple is short for Maple-DL to save space, #byLS is the number of instance for which the solution is given by the local search solver, #SAT_bonus is the number of instances for which both base CDCL solver and Local Search solver fail to solve but the hybrid solver finds a satisfiable solution. #LS_call is the average number of calls on Local Search, while LS_time is the average value of the proportion of time (in percentage %) spent on local search in the whole run, and these two figures are calculated for satisfiable and unsatisfiable instances respectively.

Solver	Analysis for SAT				Analysis for UNSAT	
	#byLS	#SAT_bonus	#LS_call	LS_time(%)	#LS_call	LS_time(%)
SC2017(351)						
glucose+rx	20	11	24.28	21.66	16.36	5.52
glucose+rx+rp	10	33	17.77	18.46	14.33	4.86
glucose+rx+rp+cf	17	29	22.7	22.19	15.3	5.81
Maple+rx	16	9	13.86	7.52	11.18	2.03
Maple+rx+rp	11	15	9.63	10.43	6.54	2.36
Maple+rx+rp+cf	6	16	12.59	7.49	8.59	2.12
SC2018(400)						
glucose+rx	50	4	11.27	20.66	29.62	4.94
glucose+rx+rp	47	31	9.46	18.4	21.66	5.64
glucose+rx+rp+cf	53	36	11.43	20.28	20.62	6.64
Maple+rx	52	7	4.8	13.02	11.69	2.81
Maple+rx+rp	56	13	4.84	15.21	8.7	3.04
Maple+rx+rp+cf	51	18	6.52	12.53	15.62	2.94
SC2019(400)						
glucose+rx	14	8	26.46	10.79	17.42	6.39
glucose+rx+rp	10	26	22.68	8.67	14.59	5.14
glucose+rx+rp+cf	11	26	20.39	11.82	15.51	5.95
Maple+rx	14	7	12.66	2.67	12.94	1.98
Maple+rx+rp	9	14	8.6	3.17	16.59	2.53
Maple+rx+rp+cf	12	15	11.21	3.05	17.23	2.22
SC2020(400)						
glucose+rx	30	9	14.94	11.75	14.67	10.27
glucose+rx+rp	23	37	13.17	10.79	9.4	9.71
glucose+rx+rp+cf	23	37	12.78	11.67	10.52	10.28
Maple+rx	19	13	14.21	6.69	10.24	5.25
Maple+rx+rp	30	29	8.53	6.62	11.7	6.18
Maple+rx+rp+cf	23	36	10.95	6.05	14.17	5.42

fewer on unsatisfiable instances, because the portion of the time on local search also depends on the total time of the hybrid solver. Our statistics show that the averaged time on solving UNSAT instances is about 1.5× to 2× that on SAT instances for both glucose+rx+rp+cf and Maple-DL+rx+rp+cf. In a nutshell, the price is acceptable and usually small for the UNSAT instances, which also partly explains that our techniques do not have obvious negative impact on solving UNSAT instances although they incline to the satisfiable side.

7   Related Works

There has been interest in combining systemic search and local search for solving SAT. Indeed, it was pointed as a challenge by Selman et al. [35]. Previous attempts can be categorized into two families according to the type (DPLL/CDCL or local search) of the main body solver.

A family of hybrid solvers use a local search solver as the main body solver. An incomplete hybrid solver hybridGM [5] calls CDCL search around local minima with only one unsatisfied clause. Audemard et al. proposed a hybrid solver named SATHYS [2,3]. Each time the local search solver reaches a local minimum, a CDCL solver is launched. Some reasoning techniques or information from CDCL solvers have been used to improve local search solvers. Resolution techniques were integrated to local search solvers [1,13]. Recently, Lorenz and Wörz developed a hybrid solver GapSAT [28], which used a CDCL solver as a preprocessor before running the local search solver ProbSAT. The experiments showed that, the learnt clauses produced by CDCL solver were useful to improve the local search solver on random instances.

The other family of hybrid solvers focus on boosting CDCL solvers by local search, and this work belongs to this line. A simple way for hybridizing local search and CDCL is to call local search before CDCL begins, trying to solve the instance or derive information such as variable ordering to be used in CDCL. The hyrid solvers Sparrow2Riss [6], CCAnr+glucose [11] and SGSeq [25] belong to this family.

Some works use local search to find a subformula for CDCL to solve. In [30], a local search solver is used to find a part of the formula which is satisfiable, which helps to divide the formula into two parts for the DPLL solver. In HINOTOS [24], a local search is used to identify a subset of clauses to be passed to a CDCL solver in an incremental way.

The most related works belong to those that call a local search solver during the CDCL procedure. WalkSatz [19] calls a local search solver WalkSAT at each node of a DPLL solver Satz. However, this is time consuming. This can be done in parallel with shared memory [23]. In CaDiCaL and Kissat [10], a local search solver is called when the solver resets the saved phases, and the phases produced by local search are used only once immediately after the local search process. However, the way CaDiCaL and Kissat use the local search assignments is different from our phase resetting method based on local search. CaDiCaL and Kissat only record the current local search assignment, which is used just for once right after the local search exists. They do not use information of previous local search processes. In fact, we also carry out experiments to see the impact of local search on the performance of Kissat_sat, which turns out to be limited. When Kissat_sat works without local search, #SAT drops by 5 on average over the SC benchmarks.

Although previous attempts have been made trying to combine the strength of CDCL and local search, they did not lead to hybrid solvers essentially better than CDCL solvers on application instances. This work, for the first, meets the standard of the challenge "create a new algorithm that outperforms the best previous examples of both approaches" [35] on standard application benchmarks from SAT Competitions.

8   Conclusions

This work took a large step towards deep cooperation of CDCL and local search. We proposed three techniques for using local search to improve CDCL solvers. The first idea is to protect promising branches from being pruned, and exploit them using a local search solver. The second idea is to utilize the assignments of the local search processes to reset the saved phases in the phase selection heuristic. Finally, we proposed to enhance the branching strategy of CDCL solvers by considering the conflict frequency of variables in the local search process. These techniques significantly improve the performance of state of the art CDCL solvers on application benchmarks. The proposed methods are generic and can be applied to improve other CDCL solvers.

This is the first time that the combination of stochastic search and systematic search techniques leads to essential improvements over the state of the art of both approaches on application benchmarks, thus answering Challenge 7 of the Ten Challenges in Propositional Reasoning and Search [35].

Acknowledgement. This work is supported by Beijing Academy of Artificial Intelligence (BAAI), and Youth Innovation Promotion Association, Chinese Academy of Sciences [No. 2017150].

References

1. Anbulagan, Pham, D.N., Slaney, J.K., Sattar, A.: Old resolution meets modern SLS. In: Proceedings of AAAI 2005, pp. 354–359 (2005)
2. Audemard, G., Lagniez, J., Mazure, B., Sais, L.: Integrating conflict driven clause learning to local search. In: Proceedings of LSCS 2009, pp. 55–68 (2009)
3. Audemard, G., Lagniez, J.-M., Mazure, B., Saïs, L.: Boosting local search thanks to CDCL. In: Fermüller, C.G., Voronkov, A. (eds.) LPAR 2010. LNCS, vol. 6397, pp. 474–488. Springer, Heidelberg (2010). https://doi.org/10.1007/978-3-642-16242-8_34
4. Audemard, G., Simon, L.: Predicting learnt clauses quality in modern SAT solvers. In: Proceedings of IJCAI 2009, pp. 399–404 (2009)
5. Balint, A., Henn, M., Gableske, O.: A novel approach to combine a SLS- and a DPLL-solver for the satisfiability problem. In: Kullmann, O. (ed.) SAT 2009. LNCS, vol. 5584, pp. 284–297. Springer, Heidelberg (2009). https://doi.org/10.1007/978-3-642-02777-2_28
6. Balint, A., Manthey, N.: SparrowToRiss 2018. In: Proceedings of SAT Competition 2018: Solver and Benchmark Descriptions, pp. 38–39 (2018)

7. Biere, A.: Adaptive restart strategies for conflict driven SAT solvers. In: Kleine Büning, H., Zhao, X. (eds.) SAT 2008. LNCS, vol. 4996, pp. 28–33. Springer, Heidelberg (2008). https://doi.org/10.1007/978-3-540-79719-7_4

8. Biere, A.: Pre, icosat@sc'09. In: SAT 2009 Competitive Event Booklet, pp. 42–43 (2009)

9. Biere, A.: Yet another local search solver and lingeling and friends entering the sat competition 2014. Sat Competition **2014**(2), 65 (2014)

10. Biere, A., Fazekas, K., Fleury, M., Heisinger, M.: CaDiCaL, Paracooba, Plingeling and Treengeling entering the SAT Competition, Kissat, pp. 51–53 (2020)

11. Cai, S., Luo, C., Su, K.: CCAnr+glucose in SAT Competition 2014. In: Proceedings of SAT Competition 2014: Solver and Benchmark Descriptions, p. 17 (2014)

12. Cai, S., Luo, C., Su, K.: CCAnr: a configuration checking based local search solver for non-random satisfiability. In: Proceedings of SAT 2015, pp. 1–8 (2015)

13. Cha, B., Iwama, K.: Adding new clauses for faster local search. In: Proceedings of AAAI, vol. 96, pp. 332–337 (1996)

14. Davis, M., Logemann, G., Loveland, D.W.: A machine program for theorem-proving. Commun. ACM **5**(7), 394–397 (1962)

15. Eén, N., Sörensson, N.: An extensible SAT-solver. In: Giunchiglia, E., Tacchella, A. (eds.) SAT 2003. LNCS, vol. 2919, pp. 502–518. Springer, Heidelberg (2004). https://doi.org/10.1007/978-3-540-24605-3_37

16. Gershman, R., Strichman, O.: Haifasat: a new robust SAT solver. In: Ur, S., Bin, E., Wolfsthal, Y. (eds.) Proceedings of Haifa Verification Conference 2005, pp. 76–89 (2005)

17. Goldberg, E.I., Novikov, Y.: Berkmin: a fast and robust sat-solver. In: Proceedings of DATE (2002), pp. 142–149 (2002)

18. Gomes, C.P., Selman, B., Kautz, H.A.: Boosting combinatorial search through randomization. In: Proceedings of AAAI/IAAI 1998, pp. 431–437 (1998)

19. Habet, D., Li, C.M., Devendeville, L., Vasquez, M.: A hybrid approach for SAT. In: Proceedings of CP 2002, pp. 172–184 (2002)

20. Heule, M.J.H., Kullmann, O., Marek, V.W.: Solving and verifying the boolean pythagorean triples problem via cube-and-conquer. In: Creignou, N., Le Berre, D. (eds.) SAT 2016. LNCS, vol. 9710, pp. 228–245. Springer, Cham (2016). https://doi.org/10.1007/978-3-319-40970-2_15

21. Kautz, H.A., Selman, B.: Planning as satisfiability. In: Proceedings of ECAI 1992, pp. 359–363 (1992)

22. Kochemazov, S., Zaikin, O., Kondratiev, V., Semenov, A.: Maplelcmdistchronobt-dl, duplicate learnts heuristic-aided solvers at the sat race 2019. In: Proceedings of SAT Race, pp. 24–24 (2019)

23. Kroc, L., Sabharwal, A., Gomes, C.P., Selman, B.: Integrating systematic and local search paradigms: a new strategy for maxsat. In: Proceedings of IJCAI 2009, pp. 544–551 (2009)

24. Letombe, F., Marques-Silva, J.: Improvements to hybrid incremental SAT algorithms. In: Kleine Büning, H., Zhao, X. (eds.) SAT 2008. LNCS, vol. 4996, pp. 168–181. Springer, Heidelberg (2008). https://doi.org/10.1007/978-3-540-79719-7_17

25. Li, C.M., Habet, D.: Description of RSeq2014. In: Proceedings of SAT Competition 2014: Solver and Benchmark Descriptions, p. 72 (2014)

26. Li, C.M., Li, Yu.: Satisfying versus falsifying in local search for satisfiability. In: Cimatti, A., Sebastiani, R. (eds.) SAT 2012. LNCS, vol. 7317, pp. 477–478. Springer, Heidelberg (2012). https://doi.org/10.1007/978-3-642-31612-8_43

27. Liang, J.H., Ganesh, V., Poupart, P., Czarnecki, K.: Learning rate based branching heuristic for SAT solvers. In: Creignou, N., Le Berre, D. (eds.) SAT 2016. LNCS, vol. 9710, pp. 123–140. Springer, Cham (2016). https://doi.org/10.1007/978-3-319-40970-2_9

28. Lorenz, J.-H., Wörz, F.: On the effect of learned clauses on stochastic local search. In: Pulina, L., Seidl, M. (eds.) SAT 2020. LNCS, vol. 12178, pp. 89–106. Springer, Cham (2020). https://doi.org/10.1007/978-3-030-51825-7_7

29. Luo, M., Li, C., Xiao, F., Manyà, F., Lü, Z.: An effective learnt clause minimization approach for CDCL SAT solvers. In: Proceedings of IJCAI 2017, pp. 703–711 (2017)

30. Mazure, B., Sais, L., Grégoire, É.: Boosting complete techniques thanks to local search methods. Ann. Math. Artif. Intell. **22**(3–4), 319–331 (1998)

31. Moskewicz, M.W., Madigan, C.F., Zhao, Y., Zhang, L., Malik, S.: Chaff: engineering an efficient SAT solver. In: Proceedings of the 38th Design Automation Conference, DAC 2001, pp. 530–535 (2001)

32. Newman, N., Fréchette, A., Leyton-Brown, K.: Deep optimization for spectrum repacking. Commun. ACM **61**(1), 97–104 (2018)

33. Oh, C.: Between SAT and UNSAT: the fundamental difference in CDCL SAT. In: Heule, M., Weaver, S. (eds.) SAT 2015. LNCS, vol. 9340, pp. 307–323. Springer, Cham (2015). https://doi.org/10.1007/978-3-319-24318-4_23

34. Pipatsrisawat, K., Darwiche, A.: A lightweight component caching scheme for satisfiability solvers. In: Marques-Silva, J., Sakallah, K.A. (eds.) SAT 2007. LNCS, vol. 4501, pp. 294–299. Springer, Heidelberg (2007). https://doi.org/10.1007/978-3-540-72788-0_28

35. Selman, B., Kautz, H.A., McAllester, D.A.: Ten challenges in propositional reasoning and search. In: Proceedings of IJCAI, vol. 97, pp. 50–54 (1997)

36. Silva, J.P.M., Sakallah, K.A.: GRASP - a new search algorithm for satisfiability. In: Proceedings of ICCAD 1996, pp. 220–227 (1996)

37. Silva, J.P.M., Sakallah, K.A.: Boolean satisfiability in electronic design automation. In: Proceedings of the DAC 2000, pp. 675–680 (2000)

Hash-Based Preprocessing and Inprocessing Techniques in SAT Solvers

Henrik Cao$^{(\boxtimes)}$ (iD)

Computer Science Department, Aalto University, Espoo, Finland
henrik.cao@aalto.fi

Abstract. Modern satisfiability solvers are interwoven with important simplification techniques as preprocessors and inprocessors. Implementations of these techniques are hampered by expensive memory accesses which result in a large number of cache misses. This paper explores the application of hash functions in encoding clause structures and bitwise operations for detecting relations between clauses. The evaluation showed a significant increase in performance for subsumption and Blocked Clause Elimination on the Main track benchmark of the 2020 SAT competition.

Keywords: SAT · CDCL · Preprocessing · Inprocessing · Hash

1   Introduction

Modern satisfiability (SAT) solvers are complemented with various simplification techniques before and during solving [4–7,18,19]. These techniques test important relational properties between clauses, the implementation of which requires expensive memory accesses. For example, in order to check whether $C \subseteq D$ for two clauses (i.e., C subsumes D), we typically have to access both the literals and their *signatures* (i.e., literal marks).

The use of hash functions in the context of simplification techniques was first documented in [19] and [4]. The authors proposed novel subsumption algorithms incorporating signature-based pre-checks for testing whether $C \not\subseteq D$. A similar pre-check is used in the MaxSAT preprocessor MaxPre to detect non-tautological clauses during variable elimination [9].

Signature-based approaches persist in some solvers and preprocessors today [2], but no formal analysis of these methods has been given. Also, as of this writing, I am unaware of literature documenting the use of similar methods in other simplification techniques. This is in spite of the extensive research on hash functions and their myriad applications in computer science [1,14,15]. Ironically, the use of SAT technology in encoding, testing and optimizing hash functions has become a hot topic of its own [8,10–13,16,17].

In this paper, I discuss the application of *clause signatures* in testing relational properties between clauses, especially those arising in simplification techniques on formulae in *conjunctive normal form* (CNF). In particular, I translate

© Springer Nature Switzerland AG 2021
C.-M. Li and F. Manyà (Eds.): SAT 2021, LNCS 12831, pp. 82–97, 2021.
https://doi.org/10.1007/978-3-030-80223-3_7

the contrary of four clause relations (subsumption, disjointness, membership and tautological resolvency) into their signature-based relations, which can then be tested using bitwise logical operators. The signature-based tests are constant-time and do not rely on accessing the underlying clause structure, thus introducing minimal computational overhead. Furthermore, the methods developed herein are auxiliary in nature and can be integrated into existing implementations. As a direct application, I demonstrate their use in three popular simplification techniques: Subsumption [3], Blocked Clause Elimination (BCE) [6] and Bounded Variable Elimination (BVE) [4]. I further provide a probabilistic analysis of signature-based methods, shedding light on their strengths and limitations.

Lastly, I offer full (C++) implementations of subsumption, BCE and BVE using signature-based techniques and a complete evaluation on the Main track benchmark dataset of the 2020 SAT competition [2].

2   Preliminaries

Let $\mathcal{V} = \{1, \ldots, N\}$ denote a set of propositional variables[1]. A *literal* l can be a variable v or its negation $\overline{v}$ and I will denote by $\mathcal{L}$ the set of literals on $\mathcal{V}$. A *clause* $C \subseteq \mathcal{L}$ will be any literal subset with its logical interpretation $C = l_1 \vee \cdots \vee l_n$. However, I have shunned references to the logical properties of clauses and you may think of C simply as a set of integers. Furthermore, to simplify notation, I have made C assume the dual role of C and $|C|$ (the number of literals in C).

Here are the main set-theoretic properties that I will consider.

Definition 1. *A clause C is tautological if both $l \in C$ and $\overline{l} \in C$.*

Definition 2. *A subset $C \subseteq D$ is said to subsume D.*

Definition 3. *Let $l \in C$ and $\overline{l} \in D$. The resolvent $C \otimes_l D$ on l is the set $C \setminus \{l\} \cup D \setminus \{\overline{l}\}$.*

Definition 4. *Let $l \in C$ and $\overline{l} \in D$. C strengthens D if $C \otimes_l D \subseteq D$.*

When querying properties in Definitions 1–4 over a set of clauses $\mathcal{C}$, simplification techniques rely on efficient data structures with constant-time access to certain subsets of clauses. The most common data structure is the *occurrence list*, $\mathcal{O}$, which is a list of sets $\mathcal{O}(l) = \{C \in \mathcal{C} \mid l \in C\}$ of all clauses with an occurrence of the literal l.

The methods I will discuss operate on *signatures* (or *words*), which are fixed-length natural numbers of m bits. A signature, then, is a number[2] in the range $[0, 2^m)$, but I encourage you to think of signatures as strings or vectors of m bits. The signature of zeroes, $0 \ldots 0$, like all zeros, is an abounding quantity and I will

---

[1] When there is a need to distinguish between a variable name and the numeral, e.g., the variable '17' and the number 17, we will explicitly write $(17)_{int}$ for the latter.

[2] The binary representation of an integer is indexed right to left, i.e., $01011 = 11$.

substitute it with the innocuous abbreviation 0. Analogous to the usual Boolean operators $\neg, \wedge, \vee, \oplus$ (negation, conjunction, disjunction, exclusive disjunction) on the Boolean values 0 and 1, signatures are subject to the bit-wise operators[3] $\sim, \&, |, \oplus$. For example, $01011 \,\&\, 11101 = 01001$ and $01011 \oplus 11101 = 10110$. Signatures are partially ordered by the relation $\leq$, where $a \leq b \implies a\&b = a$, and so $01100 \leq 01110$ but $01100 \not\leq 11001$.

A *hash function* is a mapping $h : \mathcal{U} \mapsto \mathbb{M}$ from some universe, $\mathcal{U}$, to the set of signatures or *hash values*, $\mathbb{M}$. I will consider hash functions exclusively on the subsets $C \subseteq \mathcal{L}$ and onto the domain $[0, 2^m)$. Unless explicitly mentioned, you may assume signatures to be 64-bit natural numbers (i.e., $m = 64$). When $C = \{l\}$, I like to write $h(l)$ instead of $h(\{l\})$.

A hash function that often occurs in practice is defined by element-wise division (modulo m):

$$h_a(C) = \sum_{v \in C} 2^{|v| \bmod m} \tag{1}$$

where $|v|$ is the absolute value of the variable, e.g., $|\overline{17}| = |17| = (17)_{int}$. The mapping h_a for $C_1 = \{7, \overline{10}, 13, 2, \overline{8}\}$ and $m = 8$ is illustrated in Fig. 1. Notice in particular the *collision* of indices corresponding to the literals $\overline{10}$ and 2. In general, h_a is not injective ($h_a(v) = h_a(u) \not\Longrightarrow v = u$) and collisions will occur even for prodigious values of m.

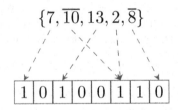

Fig. 1. A mapping of the hash function h_a.

Proofs in this paper involve the combinatorial quantities:

$$\left\{ {n \atop k} \right\} = \frac{1}{k!} \sum_{j=0}^{k} (-1)^j \binom{k}{j} (k-j)^n \tag{2}$$

and

$$\left\{ {n \atop k} \right\}_{\geq 2} = \sum_{i=0}^{k} (-1)^i \binom{n}{i} \sum_{j=0}^{k-i} \frac{(-1)^j (k-i-j)^{n-i}}{j!(k-i-j)!}, \tag{3}$$

which are the stirling number of the second kind and the 2-associated stirling number of the second kind respectively. $\left\{ {n \atop k} \right\}$ counts the number of unique surjective functions that map n elements into k bins, whereas $\left\{ {n \atop k} \right\}_{\geq 2}$ counts the

---

[3] In mixed symbol expressions, bit-wise operators take precedence, i.e., $p\&q = 0 \vee r \oplus s \neq 0$ evaluates as $((p\&q) = 0) \vee ((r \oplus s) \neq 0)$.

number of unique surjective functions that map n elements into k bins such that at least two elements are mapped into each bin. In order to simplify formulas arising in proofs, I adopt the convention $\left\{{n \atop 0}\right\}_{\geq 2} = 1$.

3 Hash-Based Methods

Simplification techniques rely on fast access to relevant data structures, especially clauses, literals and their respective properties. To expedite search, good implementations utilize efficient data structures (e.g., occurrence lists) and lookup tables (such as vector-based literal markers). Unfortunately the underlying data structures remain relatively expensive to access and tend to be scattered in memory, causing a large number of cache misses in practice.

For moderately sized clauses ($|C| < 10^3$), hash functions such as (1) provide a means to encode an abstraction of a clause C as an m-bit signature $h(C)$. This *clause signature* is a space-efficient abstraction of a set of literals and can be stored independently of the clause container, providing a compact means of querying properties of C in relation to other clauses. In particular, for a suitable family of hash functions $\mathcal{H}$, the signatures of two clauses can be used to assess (the contrary of) a number of important set relations.

Some common properties tested by simplification techniques are:

Definition 5. *Subsumption, $C \subseteq D$, for clauses C, D.*

Definition 6. *Disjointness, $C \cap D = \emptyset$, for clauses C, D.*

Definition 7. *Tautological resolvency, $C \otimes_l D = \top$, for clauses C, D with $l \in C$ and $\bar{l} \in D$.*

Definition 8. *Membership, $l \in C$, for a clause C and literal l.*

Due to collisions, the properties of Definitions 5–8 cannot be answered reliably; in other words, false positives may occur. However, failed queries are admissible (and tend to be more common anyhow). To show this, I will presume a family of hash functions, $\mathcal{H}$, with the following properties:

- $h \in \mathcal{H}$ maps variables independently and uniformly at random and

- $h(l) = h(\bar{l})$, i.e., l and $\bar{l}$ map to the same index.

Definition 9. *Let $h(C)$ be the m-bit hash value of a clause C. The collision signature $u(C)$ of $h(C)$ is the m-bit signature with the ith bit marked if there is a collision in the ith bit of $h(C)$.*

For example, the clause $C_2 = \{\bar{2}, 3, 5, \bar{8}\}$ (with $m = 5$) hashes to $h_a(C_2) = 01101$ and has the collision signature $u(C_2) = 01000$ with a collision on the literals 3 and $\bar{8}$.

Proposition 1. *Let $h \in \mathcal{H}$. If $h(C)\,\&\sim h(D) \neq 0$ or $u(C)\,\&\sim u(D) \neq 0$, then $C \not\subseteq D$.*

Proof. For suppose $h(C)\,\&\sim h(D) \neq 0$. Then $h(l)\,\&\sim h(D) \neq 0$ for some literal $l \in C$, which implies $l \notin D$ and therefore $C \not\subseteq D$. Now let $u(C)\,\&\sim u(D) \neq 0$. We must have $h(l)\,\&\sim u(D) \neq 0$ and $h(l) = h(o)$ for distinct literals $l, o \in C$. This implies that there is at most one literal $r \in D$ colliding with $l, o \in C$. Therefore either $l \notin D$ or $o \notin D$ and again $C \not\subseteq D$.

Proposition 2. *Let $h \in \mathcal{H}$. $h(C)\,\&\,h(D) = 0 \implies C \cap D = \emptyset$ for all $h \in \mathcal{H}$.*

Proof. If $h(C)\,\&\,h(D) = 0$, then $h(l)\,\&\,h(o) = 0$ for all literal pairs (l, o) with $l \in C$ and $o \in D$. We conclude that $C \cap D = \emptyset$.

Proposition 3. *Let $h \in \mathcal{H}$, $l \in C$ and $\bar{l} \in D$. If $u(C)\,\&\,u(D)\,\&\,h(l) = 0$ and $h(C)\,\&\,h(D) = h(l)$, then $C \otimes_l D$ is non-tautological.*

Proof. $h(C)\,\&\,h(D) = h(l)$ says that $h(l)$ is the only overlapping index (i.e., $o \in C \cap D \implies h(o) = h(l)$). If, in addition, $u(C)\,\&\,u(D)\,\&\,h(l) = 0$, then either l is the unique literal in C with $h(l) = h(\bar{l})$ or $\bar{l}$ is the unique literal in D with $h(\bar{l}) = h(l)$. Either way, the intersection $C \cap D = \emptyset$ and the resolvent $C \otimes_l D = (C \cup D) \setminus \{l, \bar{l}\}$ is non-tautological.

Proposition 4. *Let $h \in \mathcal{H}$. $h(C)\,\&\,h(l) = 0 \implies l \notin C$.*

Proof. Clearly, if $l \in C$ then $h(C)\,\&\,h(l) \neq 0$.

Through Propositions 1–4 we may now utilize the signature representation $(h(C), u(C))$ of a clause to test for the contrary of Definitions 5–8 respectively. As our first application, consider a typical subsumption routine (Algorithm 1) designed to remove all clauses $D \in \mathcal{F}$ (a set of clauses) for which there exists a subsuming clause $C \subseteq D$. Line 5 in Algorithm 1 applies Proposition 1 just before an explicit subsumption test on line 7. Importantly, Proposition 1 can be tested without accessing the clause structures of C or D; we only need their signatures and collision signatures.

As a second application, let us consider Proposition 3 for non-tautological resolvents. One of my favourite applications of tautological resolvent querying is in the detection of blocked clauses [6]. To this end, let $C \otimes_l \mathcal{O}(\bar{l}) = \{C \otimes_l D \mid D \in \mathcal{O}(\bar{l}\}$ and $\mathcal{O}(l) \otimes_l \mathcal{O}(\bar{l}) = \{C \otimes_l D \mid C \in \mathcal{O}(l), D \in \mathcal{O}(\bar{l})\}$ be the extensions of the resolvent operator to sets of clauses. A blocked clause is a clause C with some literal $l \in C$ whose resolvents $C \otimes_l D$ with *all* clauses $D \in \mathcal{O}(\bar{l})$ are tautological (and thus C is, in a sense, redundant). Indeed, to test whether C is blocked by a literal $l \in C$, we must check its resolvents $C \otimes_l \mathcal{O}(\bar{l})$, which is almost always too costly to verify for all clauses in a formula. What makes this routine so appealing to signature-based methods is that it suffices to provide just one clause $D \in \mathcal{O}(\bar{l})$ with a non-tautological resolvent $C \otimes_l D$ to show that C is *not* blocked by l.

I have sketched a typical BCE routine in Algorithm 2, where you will find Proposition 3 on line 6. Notice, again, how accessing the clause containers of C and D is deferred until an explicit check on line 11.

Algorithm 1. Subsumption

```
1: Input : F                                              // set of clauses
2: K = ∅                                                  // checked clauses
3: for C ∈ sorted (F, <) do                               // increasing size
4:     for D ∈ K do                                       // ensures |D| ≤ |C|
5:         if h(D) & ~h(C) ≠ 0 or u(D) & ~u(C) ≠ 0 then   // Proposition 1
6:             continue
7:         else if D ⊆ C then                             // explicit check
8:             F = F \ {C}                                // remove clause
9:             break
10:     if C ∈ F then
11:         K = K ∪ {C}                                    // keep clause
12: return F
```

Algorithm 2. Blocked clause elimination

```
1: Input : F                                              // set of clauses
2: for l ∈ L do
3:     for C ∈ O(l) do
4:         tautology = True
5:         for D ∈ O(l̄) do
6:             if h(C) & h(D) = h(l) and u(C) & u(D) & h(l) = 0 then // Prop. 3
7:                 tautology = False
8:                 break
9:         if tautology = True then
10:            for D ∈ O(l̄) do
11:                if C ⊗_v D ≠ ⊤ then                     // explicit check
12:                    tautology = False
13:                    break
14:        if tautology = True then
15:            F = F \ {C}                                 // remove clause
16: return F
```

Algorithm 3. Bounded variable elimination

```
1: Input : F, bound                                       // set of clauses
2: for v ∈ V do
3:     count = 0
4:     for (C, D) ∈ O(v) × O(v̄) do
5:         if h(C) & h(D) = h(v) ∧ u(C) & u(D) & h(v) = 0 then  // Proposition 3
6:             count = count + 1
7:     if count > |O(v) ∪ O(v̄)| + bound then              // bound exceeded
8:         continue
9:     for (C, D) ∈ O(v) × O(v̄) do
10:        if h(C) & h(D) ≠ h(v) ∨ u(C) & u(D) & h(v) ≠ 0 then  // Proposition 3
11:            if C ⊗_v D ≠ ⊤ then                         // explicit check
12:                count = count + 1
13:    if count ≤ |O(v) ∪ O(v̄)| + bound then
14:        F = (F \ (O(v) ∪ O(v̄))) ∪ (O(v) ⊗_v O(v̄))      // eliminate v
15: return F
```

Tautological resolvent querying also emerges in BVE [4], which eliminates variables $v \in \mathcal{V}$ by substituting the (satisfiability-equivalent) resolvents $\mathcal{O}(l) \otimes_l \mathcal{O}(\bar{l})$ for the clauses $\mathcal{O}(l) \cup \mathcal{O}(\bar{l})$. In particular, only variables with $|\mathcal{O}(l) \otimes_l \mathcal{O}(\bar{l})| \leq |\mathcal{O}(l) \cup \mathcal{O}(\bar{l})| + bound$ are eliminated, which amounts to counting the number of non-tautological resolvents (since tautological resolvents may be discarded after the substitution). Algorithm 3 sketches the routine with the application of Proposition 3 on line 5 and on line 10.

4   Probabilistic Analysis

On account of Propositions 1–4 derived in the previous section, we can test the complementary properties of Definitions 5–8 from the clause signatures $h(C)$ and $u(C)$. But how useful are these signatures in practice? From a practical point of view, we are interested in the probability that an arbitrary pair of clauses satisfies the premises corresponding to Propositions 1–4.

Clearly, if $m \ll |C|$, the signatures $h(C)$ and $u(C)$ tend to $1 \ldots 1$, and the comparisons $h(C) \& h(D) = 0$ and $u(C) \& u(D) = 0$ become vacuous. Therefore, the effectiveness of $h(C)$ and $u(C)$ is largely dependent on the number of collisions (overlaps) of literals in C under h. This relates to the size of C (fewer literals incur less collision) and how well h distributes C over m bits.

Notice that for a clause C whose literals are selected uniformly at random from $\mathcal{L}$ (and our assumption that $h \in \mathcal{H}$ distributes uniformly at random), we can model the mapping $h(C)$ as if C were drawn from the range $[0, m)$ instead. Let $\|w\|$ denote the *bit sum* of w (e.g., $\|01101\| = 3$).

Proposition 5. *Let $h \in \mathcal{H}$. $\mathbb{E}[\|h(C)\|] = m(1 - (\frac{m-1}{m})^C)$.*

Proof. We model the mapping $h(C)$ as C random and independent draws from $[0, m)$. Let $h(C)_i$ denote the ith index in $h(C)$. $\Pr[h(C)_i = 1] = 1 - (\frac{m-1}{m})^C$. By linearity of expectation, $\mathbb{E}[\|h(C)\|] = \sum_{i=0}^{m-1} \Pr[h(C)_i = 1] = m(1 - (\frac{m-1}{m})^C)$.

Proposition 6. *Let $h \in \mathcal{H}$. $\mathbb{E}[\|u(C)\|] = m(1 - (1 - \frac{C}{m-1})(\frac{m-1}{m})^C)$.*

Proof. We model the mapping $h(C)$ as C random and independent draws from $[0, m)$. Let $u(C)_i$ denote the ith index in $u(C)$. If $u(C)_i = 0$, then either one or zero literals in C are mapped to $h(C)_i$. The probability that $h(C)_i$ is zero is $p = (\frac{m-1}{m})^C$. The probability that exactly one literal is mapped to index i is $q = \frac{C}{m}(\frac{m-1}{m})^{C-1}$. Thus, $\Pr[u(C)_i = 1] = 1 - p - q = 1 - (1 - \frac{C}{m-1})(\frac{m-1}{m})^C$. By linearity of expectation, $\mathbb{E}[\|u(C)\|] = \sum_{i=0}^{m-1} \Pr[u(C)_i = 1] = m(1 - (1 - \frac{C}{m-1})(\frac{m-1}{m})^C)$.

Using Proposition 5, the expected number of collisions is $\mathbb{E}[\|collisions\|] = C - \mathbb{E}[\|h(C)\|]$. I have plotted this together with the results of Proposition 5 and Proposition 6 in Fig. 2 (left) for $m = 64$. You can see how the signature $h(C)$ is quickly populated after some 250 literals, beyond which all new literals collide with some previously populated index. The collision signature, $u(C)$, fills up more slowly and is expected to hit its capacity after ≈ 400 literals (which makes

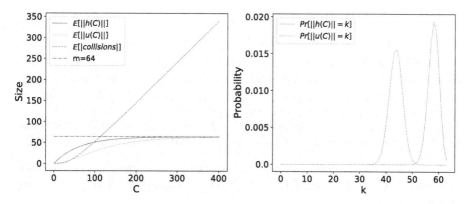

Fig. 2. (left) The expected size of $h(C)$ (blue), the expected size of $u(C)$ (orange) and the expected number of collisions (green) for $m = 64$ and clauses $2 \leq C \leq 400$. (right) The distributions of $\|h(C)\|$ (blue) and the distribution of $\|u(C)\|$ for $|C| = 150$ (orange). (Color figure online)

sense, as two literals corresponding to $h(l)_i$ are required to tick $u(l)_i)$. Moreover, from a SAT point of view, it is comforting to know that literal collisions are independent of the number of *overall* literals $|\mathcal{L}|$ in a formula.

We can also find expressions for the distributions of $Pr\left[\|h(C)\| = k\right]$ and $Pr\left[\|u(C)\| = k\right]$, which I have plotted in Fig. 2 for $C = 150$.

Lemma 1. *Let* $h \in \mathcal{H}$. *For* $k \leq |C|$,

$$Pr\left[\|h(C)\| = k\right] = \frac{1}{m^C}\begin{Bmatrix} C \\ k \end{Bmatrix}\binom{m}{k}k!$$

Proof. By counting the number of clauses C with $\|h(C)\| = k$. We model the mapping $h(C)$ as C random and independent draws from the range $[0, m)$. For $h \in \mathcal{H}$ there are m^C ways to sample C elements from $[0, m)$. There are $\binom{m}{k}$ k-element subsets in m bit indices, each having $k!$ permutations, and $\begin{Bmatrix} C \\ k \end{Bmatrix}$ ways to partition C into k disjoint subsets. Multiplying through and dividing by m^C gives the desired distribution.

Proposition 7. *Let* $h \in \mathcal{H}$. *For* $2k \leq |C|$,

$$Pr\left[\|u(C)\| = k\right] = \frac{1}{m^C}\sum_{j=0}^{\min\{m-k,C-2k\}}\begin{Bmatrix} C - j \\ k \end{Bmatrix}_{\geq 2}\binom{C}{C-j}\binom{m}{k+j}(k+j)!$$

Proof. By counting the number of clauses C with $\|u(C)\| = k$. We model the mappings $h(C)$ and $u(C)$ as C random and independent draws from $[0, m)$. Let $\|h(C)\| = k+j$, so that exactly $k+j$ of the m bit indices are set by literals in C. If $\|u(C)\| = k$, then j bit positions have exactly one literal mapped to them. The remaining $C - j$ literals are mapped to k bits, which can be done in $\begin{Bmatrix} C-j \\ k \end{Bmatrix}_{\geq 2}$

ways. The partition corresponding to $\|h(C)\| = k + j$ can be chosen in $\binom{m}{k+j}$ ways and from $(k+j)!$ permutations. Lastly, there are $\binom{C}{C-j}$ ways to choose the subset of $C - j$ elements from C. In total, there are $\left\{{C-j \atop k}\right\}_{\geq 2} \binom{C}{C-j} \binom{m}{k+j} (k+j)!$ clauses with $\|h(C)\| = k+j$ and $\|u(C)\| = k$. It remains to sum over all possible sizes $k + j$. Clearly, we must have $k \leq k + j \leq m$. If $C - 2k \leq m - k$, then we require $k + j \leq C - k$. Combining these two inequalities we have $k \leq k + j \leq \min\{m, C - k\}$ or $0 \leq j \leq \min\{m - k, C - 2k\}$. Summing over these limits and dividing by the total number of mappings m^C yields the desired distribution.

Let us now return to the premise of Proposition 2 and provide a probabilistic analysis; namely the probability that the clause signatures of two clauses are disjoint.

Proposition 8. *Let* $h \in \mathcal{H}$. *Then*

$$Pr\left[h(C) \& h(D) = 0\right] = \frac{1}{m^{C+D}} \sum_{k=1}^{\min\{C,m\}} \binom{C}{k} \left\{{C \atop k}\right\} k!(m-k)^D.$$

Proof. We model the mapping $h(C)$ as C random and independent draws from $[0, m)$. Let $E_C^D = (h(C) \& h(D) = 0)$ and consider the conditional formulation

$$\Pr\left[E_C^D\right] = \sum_{k=1}^{\min\{C,m\}} \Pr\left[E_C^D \mid \|h(C)\| = k\right] \Pr[\|h(C)\| = k] \qquad (4)$$

summed over all sizes of $\|h(C)\|$, i.e., the range $1 \leq k \leq \min(C, m)$. Notice that this defines a partition of the set of possible values for $h(C)$. For any particular $\|h(C)\| = k$, there are $m - k$ bits that can be mapped to by $h(D)$ without violating E_C^D and m^D choices in total, so that $\Pr[E_C^D \mid \|h(C)\| = k] = (m - k)^D/m^D$. Plugging this and the result of Lemma 1 into (4) yields the desired equation.

The probability distribution of Proposition 8 is depicted in Fig. 3 (left) for $m = 64$ and clauses of size $2 \leq C, D \leq 52$. It visualizes nicely how the disjointness of large clauses ($|C| > 10$ and $|D| > 10$) is difficult to certify from their signatures alone, which is to be expected unless $m \gg C + D$. On the other hand, if $h(C) \neq 1 \ldots 1$ (respectively $h(D) \neq 1 \ldots 1$) and $|D| < 10$ (respectively $|C| < 10$) then Proposition 8 still predicts a reasonable probability of success for signature-based disjointness querying.

Next, consider the signature-based subset relation from Proposition 1. The probability that the clause signatures of C and D detect the property $C \not\subseteq D$ is given as the following Proposition.

Proposition 9. *Let* $h \in \mathcal{H}$. $Pr[h(C) \& \sim h(D) \neq 0$ *or* $u(C) \& \sim u(D) \neq 0]$

$$= 1 - \frac{1}{m^{C+D}} \sum_{\substack{k_1=0 \\ r_1=\mathbb{I}[C \leq m]}}^{\substack{\min\{m,C\} \\ \min\{k_1,C-k_1\}}} \sum_{\substack{k_2=k_1 \\ r_2=\max\{r_1,\mathbb{I}[D>m]\}}}^{\substack{\min\{m,D\} \\ \min\{k_2,D-k_2\}}} S_{k_1,r_1}^C S_{k_2,r_2}^D \binom{m}{k_2} \binom{k_2}{k_1} \binom{k_1}{r_1} \binom{k_2 - r_1}{r_2 - r_1},$$

$$S_{k,r}^C = r!(k-r)!\binom{C}{k-r}\left\{{C-(k-r)}\atop{r}\right\}_{\geq 2}.$$

Proof. Let H_C^D and U_C^D be the events $h(C)\,\&\sim h(D) \neq 0$ and $u(C)\,\&\sim u(D) \neq 0$ respectively and denote their complements by $\overline{H_C^D}$ and $\overline{U_C^D}$ (i.e., $\overline{H_C^D}$ is the event $h(C)\,\&\sim h(D) = 0$). The union probability $\Pr[H_C^D \cup U_C^D]$ is equivalent to the complementary probability $1 - \Pr[\overline{H_C^D} \cap \overline{U_C^D}]$ and as there are m^{C+D} clause pairs in total, it remains to count the pairs satisfying $\overline{H_C^D} \cap \overline{U_C^D}$. Now, two clauses C, D satisfy $\overline{H_C^D}$ if $h(C) \leq h(D)$. Similarly, two clauses C, D satisfy $\overline{U_C^D}$ if $u(C) \leq u(D)$. Notice that $u(\cdot) \leq h(\cdot)$ holds in general. We can count the number of clauses C with $\|h(C)\| = k$ and $\|u(C)\| = r$ by distributing $k - r$ literals into $h(C)$ and distributing the remaining $C - (k-r)$ literals into r unset bits in $h(C)$. This can be done in $S_{k,r}^C = r!(k-r)!\binom{C}{C-(k-r)}\left\{{C-(k-r)}\atop{r}\right\}_{\geq 2}$ ways. If $r = 0$, we let $\left\{{p}\atop{r}\right\}_{\geq 2} = 1$. Let $\|h(C)\| = k_1, \|h(D)\| = k_2, \|u(C)\| = r_1$ and $\|u(D)\| = r_2$. There are $\binom{m}{k_2}$ choices for the subset $h(D)$ in an m-bit signature. For each choice, we can distribute the k_1 bits of $h(C)$ in $\binom{k_2}{k_1}$ ways such that $h(C) \leq h(D)$. There are then $\binom{k_1}{r_1}$ choices for $u(C) \leq h(C)$ and $\binom{k_2-r_1}{r_2-r_1}$ choices for distributing the remaining $r_2 - r_1$ bits of $u(D)$ to lie outside of $u(C)$. In summary, there are $S_{k_1,r_1}^C S_{k_2,r_2}^D \binom{m}{k_2}\binom{k_2}{k_1}\binom{k_1}{r_1}\binom{k_2-r_1}{r_2-r_1}$ pairs (C, D) with $\|h(C)\| = k_1, \|h(D)\| = k_2, \|u(C)\| = r_1$ and $\|u(D)\| = r_2$ satisfying $\overline{H_C^D} \cap \overline{U_C^D}$. It remains to establish the limits of the summation. Clearly, $k_1 \in [0, \min\{m, C\}]$ and $0 \leq r_1 \leq k_1$. When $r_1 = 0$, however, C must distribute into k_1 distinct bits, which can only happen if $C \leq m$. Furthermore, for $\|u(C)\| = r_1$ there must be at least $(k_1 - r_1) + 2r_1 = k_1 + r_1$ literals to distribute, and so $\mathbb{I}[C \leq m] \leq r_1 \leq \min\{k_1, C - k_1\}$. The limits for k_2 and r_2 are similar, except that $k_2 \geq k_1$ and $r_2 \geq r_1$. We have $k_1 \leq k_2 \leq \min\{m, D\}$ and $\max\{r_1, \mathbb{I}[D > m]\} \leq r_2 \leq \min\{k_2, D - k_2\}$. Summation over k_1, k_2, r_1 and r_2 yields the desired probability.

I plot the probability of Proposition 9 in Fig. 3 (right) for $m = 64$ and clauses in the range $2 \leq C, D \leq 800$. The diagonal line (white) shows the boundary where $|C| = |D|$ and in particular $C \not\subseteq D$ in the upper triangle, because $|C| > |D|$.

We see immediately that a signature-based test will most certainly fail if $|D| > 500$. As we discussed above, this is due to the clause signatures filling up for large clauses, i.e., $\|h(C)\| \to m$ and $\|u(C)\| \to m$ as $|C| \to 400$. This effect persists into the upper triangle, because although $Pr[C \not\subseteq D] = 1$ if $|C| > |D|$, the signature-based test fails for $|D| > 500$ (see the white area in the upper triangle of Fig. 3 (right)).

For clauses in the range $100 \leq |D| \leq 500$, Proposition 9 predicts that a signature-based test is indeed effective, unless $|C| \ll |D|$. This is within expectation, since the region $|C| \ll |D|$ houses most clauses with $C \subset D$.

For clauses in the range $|C| \leq 20$ and $|D| \leq 200$ (bottom left corner of Fig. 3 (right)), Proposition 9 predicts that most clauses with $C \not\subseteq D$ are detectable from their signatures.

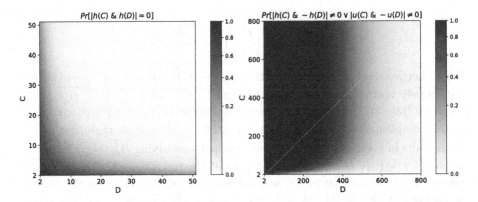

Fig. 3. The probabilities of Proposition 8 (**left**) and Proposition 9 (**right**).

Lastly, let us analyse the corresponding probability for non-tautological resolvent detection from Proposition 3.

Proposition 10. *Let $h \in \mathcal{H}$, $l \in C$ and $\bar{l} \in D$. Then*

$$Pr[u(C) \,\&\, u(D) \,\&\, h(l) = 0 \text{ and } h(C) \,\&\, h(D) = h(l)]$$

$$= \frac{1}{m^{C+D-2}} \sum_{k=1}^{\min\{C-1,m\}} \binom{C-1}{k} \left\{ \begin{matrix} C-1 \\ k \end{matrix} \right\} k!(m-k)^{D-1}.$$

Proof. Let U_C^D and H_C^D be the events $u(C) \,\&\, u(D) \,\&\, h(l) = 0$ and $h(C) \,\&\, h(D) = h(l)$ respectively. Since $l \in C$ and $\bar{l} \in D$ we have that $U_C^D \iff h(C \backslash \{l\}) \,\&\, h(D \backslash \{\bar{l}\}) \,\&\, h(l) = 0$. We also have $H_C^D \iff h(C) \,\&\, h(D) \,\&\, {\sim}h(l) = 0 \iff h(C \backslash \{l\}) \,\&\, h(D \backslash \{\bar{l}\}) \,\&\, {\sim}h(l) = 0$. Combining these, we find that $U_C^D \wedge H_C^D \iff h(C \backslash \{l\}) \,\&\, h(D \backslash \{\bar{l}\}) = 0$. Applying the results of Proposition 8 on the sets $C \backslash \{l\}$ and $D \backslash \{\bar{l}\}$ yields the desired probability. $\square$

The probability of Proposition 10 is two literals more forgiving than Proposition 8. Unfortunately, it still confirms that testing non-tautological resolvency from clause signatures is ineffective if $|C| > 10$ and $|D| > 10$ (see Fig. 4 (top-left)).

Verifying that C is *not* a blocked clause from the signatures $h(C), u(C)$ (lines 5–8 of Algorithm 2) amounts to finding a clause $D \in \mathcal{O}(\bar{l})$ satisfying Proposition 3. The probability that *at least one* non-tautological resolvent in the set $\mathcal{O}(\bar{l})$ is found can be computed as follows.

Proposition 11. *Let $h \in \mathcal{H}$ and $l \in C$. Then*

$$Pr[(u(C) \,\&\, u(D) \,\&\, h(l) = 0 \text{ and } h(C) \,\&\, h(D) = h(l)) \text{ for some } D \in \mathcal{O}(\bar{l})]$$

$$= 1 - \prod_{D \in \mathcal{O}(\bar{l})} \left[1 - \frac{1}{m^{C+D-2}} \sum_{k=1}^{\min\{C-1,m\}} \binom{C-1}{k} \left\{ \begin{matrix} C-1 \\ k \end{matrix} \right\} k!(m-k)^{D-1} \right].$$

Proof. Let E_C^D be the event $u(C) \,\&\, u(D) \,\&\, h(l) = 0$ and $h(C) \,\&\, h(D) = h(l)$.

$$\Pr\left[\exists_D E_C^D\right] = 1 - \Pr\left[\forall_D \overline{E_C^D}\right]$$

$$= 1 - \prod_{D \in \mathcal{O}(\bar{l})} \Pr\left[\overline{E_C^D}\right]$$

$$= 1 - \prod_{D \in \mathcal{O}(\bar{l})} (1 - \Pr[E_C^D]),$$

where $\exists$ and $\forall$ are the existential and universal quantifiers over the set $\mathcal{O}(\bar{l})$. Plugging in the probability from Proposition 10 gives the result.

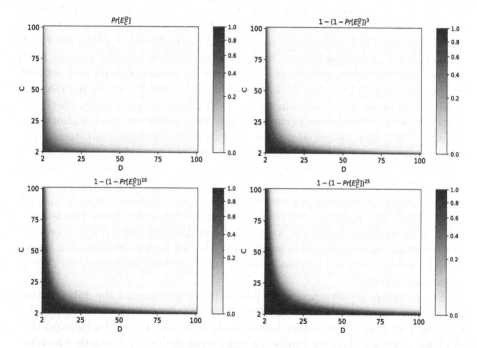

Fig. 4. Proposition 10 (**top-left**). Proposition 11 for $|\mathcal{O}(l)| = 3$ (**top-right**). Proposition 11 for $|\mathcal{O}(l)| = 10$ (**bottom-left**). Proposition 11 for $|\mathcal{O}(l)| = 25$ (**bottom-right**).

Figures 4 (top-right), (bottom-left) and (bottom-right), plot the probability of Proposition 11 for occurrence lists of size $|\mathcal{O}(\bar{l})| = 3, 10, 25$ respectively. This example is somewhat artificial, since every clause $C \in \mathcal{O}(\bar{l})$ is forced to be equal in size. The benefits of Proposition 11 compared to Proposition 10, however, should be apparent: Finding a counterexample in a larger list is more likely than finding one from a smaller one. In practice, the probability of certifying non-blockedness using clause signatures is greatly enhanced if at least one of the clauses in $C \cup \mathcal{O}(\bar{l})$ is small.

5 Evaluation

By way of demonstrating the effectiveness of the signature-based methods developed in Sect. 3, I implemented Algorithms 1–3 in the popular C++ programming language[4] and h_a as the underlying hash function. My subsumption algorithm (Algorithm 1) is based on a literal marking scheme and discussions in [3]. It seemed natural to test strengthening candidates in conjunction with subsumption, so I modified my implementation to test for both properties. My implementations of the BCE (Algorithm 2) and BVE procedures (Algorithm 3 with $bound = 16$) utilize the same literal marking scheme to test for tautological resolvents. To maintain the efficiency of these simplification techniques on large formulae, it was necessary to eliminate tests on gargantuan clauses and occurrence lists, so as to limit both memory and computational resources. I therefore chose to skip checks on clauses $|C| > 10^4$ and occurrence lists $|\mathcal{O}(l)| > 10^4$.

The benchmark I used comprises the full Main track dataset of the 2020 SAT competition [2], which includes a variety of formulae with $10^2 - 10^8$ clauses. Each method was run independently as a preprocessing technique, with and without a signature-based check, on all 400 formulae. No timeout or randomness was involved, so as to force the runs to be as identical as possible. Furthermore, no actual simplification was performed; only the number of simplifications was counted. The times measured are the total run-time (including construction of relevant data structures, e.g., occurrence lists), but excluding time spent on reading input formulae. Computation was done on an AMD Ryzen™ 9 3900X and 32 GB of RAM.

Figure 5 plots the resulting execution time gain $100(t_{base} - t_{hash})/t_{base}$ for Algorithms 1–3, where t_{hash} and t_{base} measure the total time spent by the algorithm with signature-based checks enabled and disabled respectively. I ordered the execution times in Fig. 5 in ascending order for better visualization, therefore the dataset indices between subplots (top),(middle) and (bottom) do not necessarily coincide.

Figure 5 (top) shows a promising gain in execution time for the Subsumption procedure (Algorithm 1) when signature-based checks were enabled. Especially for large formulae, the signature-based checks were able to avoid a large portion of clause accesses. The accumulative time spent on the benchmark was 601 s with signature-based tests enabled and 2451 s without.

Figure 5 (middle) shows that BCE (Algorithm 2) maintains an almost 20% gain in efficiency on the benchmark when signature-based methods were enabled. The difference in execution time was especially large for formulae with larger clause-to-variable ratios, which aligns with our analysis in Sect. 4 that clause-blockedness is easier to refute for large occurrence lists. The accumulative time spent on the benchmark was 154 s with signature-based tests enabled and 232 s without.

Figure 5 (bottom) verifies that BVE (Algorithm 3) does not consistently benefit from the signature-based approach. Upon closer analysis, this was in part

---

[4] Code available at www.github.com/incudine/sat2021.

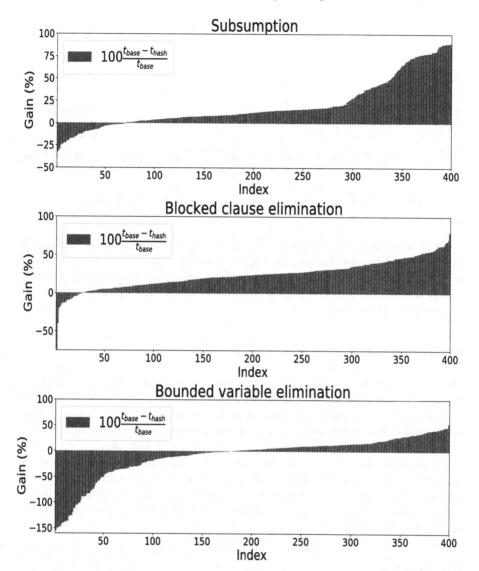

Fig. 5. The gain in execution time $100(t_{base} - t_{hash})/t_{base}$ for Algorithm 1 (**top**), Algorithm 2 (**middle**) and Algorithm 3 (**bottom**) for each formula.

due to the extra time spent constructing the larger occurrence lists to include the clause signatures. The accumulative time spent on the benchmark was 116 s with signature-based tests enabled and 96 s without.

Lastly, Fig. 6 plots the ratio of positive signature-based checks divided by the total number of checks for Algorithms 1–3 (note that I have once again ordered the ratios, wherefore indices between different algorithms do not necessarily coincide). Importantly, it shows the fraction of explicit checks which

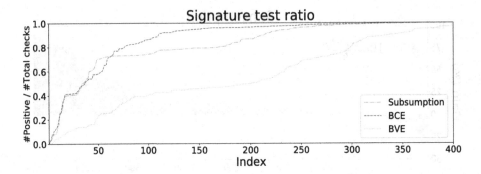

Fig. 6. The fraction of positive signature checks for Algorithms 1–3.

could be avoided by testing the clause signatures. Figure 6 is in close agreement with the experimental findings of Fig. 5, as well as the theoretical analysis of Sect. 4. In particular, explicit testing of subsumption/blockedness properties for a large number of clauses arising in practical applications can be avoided using signature-based methods.

6   Conclusions

I have discussed the use of hash-based methods using clause signatures and their application in Subsumption, BCE, and BVE. The theoretical findings of Sect. 4 promote their use in Subsumption and BCE, but not in BVE. This was verified in the evaluation, which shows a significant decrease in execution time for the Subsumption and BCE algorithms, especially on larger formulae.

In addition to fast pre-checking of clause relations, implementations of signature-based methods hold the advantage of not having to access clause containers. This seems to be the most salient factor in reducing runtime, although it comes at the cost of having to construct and maintain larger occurrence lists for storing clause signatures.

References

1. Bakhtiari, S., Safavi-Naini, R., Pieprzyk, J., et al.: Cryptographic hash functions: A survey. Technical Report, Citeseer (1995)
2. Balyo, T., Froleyks, N., Heule, M.J., Iser, M., Järvisalo, M., Suda, M.: Proceedings of sat competition 2020: Solver and benchmark descriptions (2020)
3. Bayardo, R.J., Panda, B.: Fast algorithms for finding extremal sets. In: Proceedings of the 2011 SIAM International Conference on Data Mining, pp. 25–34. SIAM (2011)
4. Eén, N., Biere, A.: Effective preprocessing in SAT through variable and clause elimination. In: Bacchus, F., Walsh, T. (eds.) SAT 2005. LNCS, vol. 3569, pp. 61–75. Springer, Heidelberg (2005). https://doi.org/10.1007/11499107_5

5. Han, H., Somenzi, F.: On-the-fly clause improvement. In: Kullmann, O. (ed.) SAT 2009. LNCS, vol. 5584, pp. 209–222. Springer, Heidelberg (2009). https://doi.org/10.1007/978-3-642-02777-2_21
6. Järvisalo, M., Biere, A., Heule, M.: Blocked clause elimination. In: Esparza, J., Majumdar, R. (eds.) TACAS 2010. LNCS, vol. 6015, pp. 129–144. Springer, Heidelberg (2010). https://doi.org/10.1007/978-3-642-12002-2_10
7. Järvisalo, M., Heule, M.J.H., Biere, A.: Inprocessing rules. In: Gramlich, B., Miller, D., Sattler, U. (eds.) IJCAR 2012. LNCS (LNAI), vol. 7364, pp. 355–370. Springer, Heidelberg (2012). https://doi.org/10.1007/978-3-642-31365-3_28
8. Jovanović, D., Janičić, P.: Logical analysis of hash functions. In: Gramlich, B. (ed.) FroCoS 2005. LNCS (LNAI), vol. 3717, pp. 200–215. Springer, Heidelberg (2005). https://doi.org/10.1007/11559306_11
9. Korhonen, T., Berg, J., Saikko, P., Järvisalo, M.: MaxPre: an extended MaxSAT preprocessor. In: Gaspers, S., Walsh, T. (eds.) SAT 2017. LNCS, vol. 10491, pp. 449–456. Springer, Cham (2017). https://doi.org/10.1007/978-3-319-66263-3_28
10. Legendre, F., Dequen, G., Krajecki, M.: Encoding hash functions as a sat problem. In: 2012 IEEE 24th International Conference on Tools with Artificial Intelligence, vol. 1, pp. 916–921. IEEE (2012)
11. de Mare, M., Wright, R.N.: Secure set membership using 3SAT. In: Ning, P., Qing, S., Li, N. (eds.) ICICS 2006. LNCS, vol. 4307, pp. 452–468. Springer, Heidelberg (2006). https://doi.org/10.1007/11935308_32
12. Mironov, I., Zhang, L.: Applications of SAT solvers to cryptanalysis of hash functions. In: Biere, A., Gomes, C.P. (eds.) SAT 2006. LNCS, vol. 4121, pp. 102–115. Springer, Heidelberg (2006). https://doi.org/10.1007/11814948_13
13. Nejati, S., Liang, J.H., Gebotys, C., Czarnecki, K., Ganesh, V.: Adaptive restart and CEGAR-based solver for inverting cryptographic hash functions. In: Paskevich, A., Wies, T. (eds.) VSTTE 2017. LNCS, vol. 10712, pp. 120–131. Springer, Cham (2017). https://doi.org/10.1007/978-3-319-72308-2_8
14. Wang, J., Shen, H.T., Song, J., Ji, J.: Hashing for similarity search: A survey. arXiv preprint arXiv:1408.2927 (2014)
15. Wang, J., Zhang, T., Sebe, N., Shen, H.T., et al.: A survey on learning to hash. IEEE Trans. Pattern Anal. Mach. intell. 40(4), 769–790 (2017)
16. Weaver, S., Heule, M.: Constructing minimal perfect hash functions using sat technology. In: Proceedings of the AAAI Conference on Artificial Intelligence, vol. 34, pp. 1668–1675 (2020)
17. Weaver, S.A., Ray, K.J., Marek, V.W., Mayer, A.J., Walker, A.K.: Satisfiability-based set membership filters. J. Satisfiability Boolean Model. Comput. 8(3–4), 129–148 (2012)
18. Wotzlaw, A., van der Grinten, A., Speckenmeyer, E.: Effectiveness of pre-and inprocessing for cdcl-based sat solving. arXiv preprint arXiv:1310.4756 (2013)
19. Zhang, L.: On subsumption removal and on-the-fly CNF simplification. In: Bacchus, F., Walsh, T. (eds.) SAT 2005. LNCS, vol. 3569, pp. 482–489. Springer, Heidelberg (2005). https://doi.org/10.1007/11499107_42

Hardness and Optimality in QBF Proof Systems Modulo NP

Leroy Chew$^{(\boxtimes)}$ (iD)

Technische Universität Wien, Vienna, Austria
lchew@ac.tuwien.ac.at
http://leroychew.wordpress.com/

Abstract. In this paper we show that extended Q-resolution is optimal among all QBF proof systems that allow strategy extraction modulo an NP oracle. In other words, for any QBF refutation system f where circuits witnessing the Herbrand functions can be extracted in polynomial time from f-refutations, f can be simulated by extended Q-resolution augmented with an NP oracle as described by Beyersdorff et al. We argue that using NP oracles and strategy extraction gives a natural framework to study QBF systems as they have relations to SAT calls and game instances, respectively, in QBF solving.

A weaker version of QBF extension variables also put forward by Jussila et al. does not have this optimality result, and we show that under an NP oracle there is no improvement of weak extended Q-Resolution compared to ordinary Q-Resolution.

Keywords: QBF · Proof complexity · Simulation · Resolution · Extended Frege · NP oracles · Optimal proof systems · Strategy extraction

1 Introduction

Quantified Boolean formulas (QBF) are an extension of propositional logic and extend the SAT problem from NP-complete to PSPACE-complete [31]. In the last decade the SAT community has developed a strong interest in QBF solving as a successor to SAT and the number of QBF solvers, benchmarks and proof systems has multiplied considerably. QBF solving employs a variety of new reasoning techniques not found in SAT in order to deal with quantification. However, universally verifying the results of these different solvers over incomparable techniques remains a difficult problem. Proof systems such as extended Q-Res [22] or the even stronger QRAT [18] have been put forward as candidates for universal checking formats but have not yet been put to significant use.

We show that extended Q-Res has theoretical properties that make it a good candidate for a QBF checking format under a reasonable set of assumptions, and through these results, we can conjecture that it can simulate the proof systems that underpin the most commonly used QBF solving techniques.

© Springer Nature Switzerland AG 2021
C.-M. Li and F. Manyà (Eds.): SAT 2021, LNCS 12831, pp. 98–115, 2021.
https://doi.org/10.1007/978-3-030-80223-3_8

Just as in the SAT case, proof complexity is the main theoretical framework for analysing the relative strengths of QBF solvers. To use proof complexity, solvers are classified by their underlying proof systems, which express the limits of that solver. Because there are a variety of QBF solving methods, there are also many different QBF proof systems. Expansion-based solvers such as RAReQS [19] use the definition of QBF and expand into potentially exponential size propositional formulas. Expansion solvers are captured by proof systems such as ∀Exp+Res [20]. Conflict-driven clause-learning (CDCL), from SAT solving, is another technique that can be adapted for a QBF setting. This deals with quantification via a reduction rule. Combining existential resolution and universal reduction in proof theory gives the refutationally complete system Q-resolution (Q-Res) [26]. More general CDCL solvers that can perform stronger unit propagations are better described by so-called long-distance Q-Resolution (LD-Q-Res), an exponentially more powerful system[2]. An example of a QBF solver using CDCL is Dep-QBF [29]. The "Dep" part of Dep-QBF actually indicates another quantification technique which uses the awareness of spurious dependencies in the ordered quantifier prefix. The theory of dependency is also hugely important for QBF solving and theory [9,28,32] and has given rise to other stronger variants of Q-Res that utilise the dependency schemes, such as the reflexive resolution scheme [32].

Solvers can be modified to output certificates that are used to verify their results. It is natural for these certificates to be valid proofs for the corresponding proof systems. As well as being able to output proofs of truth or falsity, solvers are often asked to provide the *strategies* that witness how each variable must be set. In some applications, the strategy is the whole point of using a QBF solver. In Feldman et al. [13], circuit design algorithms explicitly used the strategy circuits output by QBF solvers rather than the true/false results. If these strategies are circuits that are easy to compute from the proofs, that proof system is said to have *strategy extraction*, an often desirable property for proof systems corresponding to solvers. All proof systems in the previous paragraph have this property.

While the above proof systems are meant to correspond to particular solvers, there is no agreed upon universal checking format for certification for every known type of QBF solver. One approach is to incorporate as many techniques as possible into the proof system. The proof system IRM-calc [6] combines the main concepts from the expansion-based ∀Exp+Res and the CDCL-based LD-Q-Res into one sound system. While this is interesting in understanding how expansion and CDCL systems can interact, IRM-calc is somewhat ad hoc, and a new technique could easily emerge which IRM-calc is not designed to deal with. For example, IRM-calc can not deal with the resolution of universal variables [6].

Another approach is to pick one strong system and prove that each solving technique can be simulated. This approach can be seen in the QRAT system, where it was first shown that a number of QBF preprocessing techniques were simulated by it [18]. Later it was shown to simulate LD-Q-Res [23] and ∀Exp+Res

[24]. From these results, one could estimate that QRAT is indeed strong, but we would prefer a stronger theoretical reason for this.

If we want a QBF proof system suitable for universal certification, then the absolute ideal situation would be that it simulates every other QBF proof system. This is probably too ambitious as the existence of a theoretical optimal proof system remains a contested and open problem in propositional proof complexity, and it is an even stronger claim to suggest one exists for QBF. However, we can restrict our search to just proof systems with strategy extraction, and the problem becomes more manageable.

We find that with some extra help, extended Q-resolution is optimal among the proof systems with strategy extraction. Firstly we show in Theorem 1 that extended QU-Resolution (the 'U' in QU allows resolution on universal variables) is equivalent to the system eFrege + ∀red.

Theorem 1. *Extended* QU-Res *and* eFrege + ∀red *are p-equivalent.*

eFrege + ∀red has an important result where it can only have a lower bound if eFrege has a lower bound or PSPACE $\not\subseteq$ P/poly [5]. While this does not give us a simulation of another QBF proof system, it already indicates the strength of the system. With additional propositional power we show the next theorem.

Theorem 2. *For every refutational QBF Proof System S that has* P/poly-*strategy extraction, there is a set of polynomial-time verifiable propositional tautologies* $\|\Psi\|$ *such that* eFrege + ∀red + $\|\Psi\|$ *simulates S.*

For reasons that we discuss in Sect. 3, the extra propositional tautologies will not play a large role. Our main conjecture is that for the most interesting systems, the simulation requires no additional help.

Conjecture 1. ∀Exp+Res, IR-calc, LD-Q-Res, IRM-calc, QRAT(UR) and Q(D^{rrs})-Res are all simulated by eFrege + ∀red.

We saw that extra help needed for simulations can come in the form of propositional tautologies, but there is a second setting which achieves the same result- the use of NP oracles in a proof system.

This idea was first proposed by Chen [10] and refined by Beyersdorff, Hinde and Pich [8]. The Beyersdorff et al. NP derivation rule roughly allows one to make any propositional derivation in addition to the normal rules of whatever system we are adding the rule to. The motivation was to provide a theoretical framework that differentiated out genuine QBF hardness for QBF proof systems.

NP oracles model what happens in practice, as QBF solving algorithms often make black-box calls to SAT solvers. This usually does not affect strategy extraction as we see in Theorem 3.

Theorem 3. *The following strategy extraction theorems hold:*

- QU-Res ^{NP} *has depth-1 circuit decision list strategy extraction.*
- *For circuit class* C, C-Frege + ∀red ^{NP} *has* C-*decision list strategy extraction.*

NP oracles remove the need for the families of propositional tautologies, and we can express our simulation results in terms of optimality.

Theorem 4. *Extended* Q-Res[NP] *is optimal among all QBF proof systems with strategy extraction.*

The final three theorems examine a weaker form of extension in Q-Res and QU-Res under the lens of NP oracles.

Theorem 5. *Weak extended* QU-Res [NP] *does not simulate extended* Q-Res.

Theorem 6. *Weak extended* Q-Res *does not simulate* QU-Res.

Theorem 7. Q-Res $\equiv^{NP}$ QU-Res $\equiv^{NP}$ *Weak Ext.*Q-Res $\equiv^{NP}$ *Weak Ext.*QU-Res.

1.1 Organisation

In Sect. 2 we recap some essential definitions on QBF. In Sect. 3 we show Theorem 1 and 2 and discuss why this leads to Conjecture 1. Section 4 begins an analysis of proof systems under NP oracles with Theorems 3 and 4. This is finished in Sect. 5 where we prove Theorems 5, 6 and 7.

2 Preliminaries

2.1 Proof Complexity

Formally, a *proof system* [12] for a language $\mathcal{L}$ over alphabet Γ is a polynomial-time computable partial function $f : \Gamma^\star \rightarrow \Gamma^\star$ with $rng(f) = \mathcal{L}$, where rng denotes the range. A proof system maps *proofs* to *theorems*. A *refutation* is a proof system where the language $\mathcal{L}$ is of contradictions. The partial function f gives a proof checking function. Soundness and completeness are given by $rng(f) \subseteq \mathcal{L}$ and $rng(f) \supseteq \mathcal{L}$, respectively. The polynomial-time computability is an indication of feasibility.

Proof size is given by the number of characters appearing in a proof. Proof systems are compared by simulations. We say that a proof system f *simulates* g ($g \leq f$) if there exists a polynomial p such that for every g-proof π_g there is an f-proof π_f with $f(\pi_f) = g(\pi_g)$ and $|\pi_f| \leq p(|\pi_g|)$. If π_f can even be constructed from π_g in polynomial-time, then we say that f *p-simulates* g ($g \leq_p f$). Two proof systems f and g are *(p-)equivalent* ($g \equiv_{(p)} f$) if they mutually (p-)simulate each other.

Definition 1 (Messner, Toran [30]). *A proof system in language $\mathcal{L}$ is (p-)optimal if and only if it can (p-)simulate all other proof systems for $\mathcal{L}$.*

$$\frac{A_1 \dots A_n}{B} \ (r)$$

Here $A = \{A_1 \dots A_n\}$ and $r(A, B)$ holds.

Fig. 1. Example of rule r in a line-based proof system

Line-Based Proofs. A proof system is *line-based* if every proof consists of a sequence $L_1 \dots L_n$ of lines L_i. The data types of lines are dependent on the proof systems. A line-based system is verified by a set of rules R. Each rule is a relation between a set of lines, which are known as the premises, and a single conclusion line. Correct proofs have that for each line L_i, there is some rule r in R and a subset A of $\{L_j | 0 \le j < i\}$ such that $r(A, L_i)$ holds (see Fig. 1).

Given a line based proof system P with a set of rules R_P and a rule r, we can write $P + r$ to mean the proof system that consists of the rules of $R_P \cup \{r\}$ under the lines acceptable in P. If S is a set of propositional formulas, the proof system $P + S$ is the system $P + r$, where r is a rule that allows a conclusion s (with empty premises) if and only if $s \in S$. Note that rules and sets of lines have to be polynomial-time verifiable in order for the resulting system to be a proof system. While adding a rule r to a complete system P preserves completeness, soundness is not guaranteed and has to be reasoned for separately.

2.2   Propositional Logic

Propositional logic involves Boolean variables under operations $\neg, \wedge, \vee, 0, 1$. A literal is a variable or its negation, a clause is a disjunction of literals and a conjunctive normal form (CNF) is a conjunction of clauses. A formula is satisfiable if there is a $0, 1$ assignment to variables so that the formula evaluates to 1. Deciding whether a propositional formula is satisfiable is NP-complete.

Propositional Proof Systems. *Resolution* (Res) is a propositional refutation system that works on formulas in conjunctive normal form. Resolution is line-based, where every line is a clause. The axiom rule allows us to download any clause in our original CNF. The inference rule takes two premise clauses $C \vee x$ and $D \vee \neg x$ and outputs conclusion $C \vee D$.

Extended resolution (Ext. Res) for propositional logic [33], enables adding clauses expressing the equality $v \Leftrightarrow (\neg x \vee \neg y)$, for a fresh variable v. As NAND gates can be defined by new variables, subsequent new variables can represent more complicated functions.

Frege systems are line-based systems that work on propositional formulas. Frege systems consist of an implicationally complete finite set of sound rules, each of which is represented by a single example, which can be generalised by substitution. All Frege systems are known to be p-equivalent. While the lines of Frege systems are required to be formulas, a generalised version of Frege, denoted here by C-Frege, allows/restricts the lines to belong in circuit class C. For example, AC^0-Frege [3] is the Frege system where the lines are circuits with unbounded fan-in but have bounded-depth. NC^1-Frege is the Frege system where the lines have bounded fan-in and logarithmic depth, this is equivalent to the original Frege system [12] where lines are formulas. P/poly-Frege (defined as Circuit Frege by Jeřábek [21]) is the Frege system where general circuits have unbounded fan-in and depth. Extended Frege is known to be p-equivalent to P/poly-Frege, so we often use the notation eFrege to denote P/poly-Frege.

2.3   Quantified Boolean Formulas

Quantified Boolean Formulas extend propositional logic with quantifiers $\forall, \exists$ that work on propositional variables [25]. For formula (or circuit) A, we define $A[x/y]$ so that we replace all instances of y in A with x. The standard QBF semantics are that $\forall x\, \Psi$ is satisfied by the same truth assignments as $\Psi[0/x] \wedge \Psi[1/x]$, and $\exists x\, \Psi$ is satisfied by the same truth assignments as $\Psi[0/x] \vee \Psi[1/x]$.

A prenex QBF is a QBF where all quantification is done outside of the propositional connectives. A prenex QBF Ψ therefore consists of a propositional part ϕ called the matrix and a prefix of quantifiers Π and can be written as $\Psi = \Pi\phi$. Starting from left to right we give each bound variable a numerical level (lv) starting from 1 and increasing by one each time the quantifier changes (it stays the same whenever the quantifier is not changed). When the propositional matrix of a prenex QBF is a CNF, then we have a PCNF. We can feasibly transform any QBF into prenex form. A prenex QBF without any variables in the prefix is just a propositional formula.

A closed QBF is a QBF where all variables are bound in quantifiers. A closed QBF must be either true or false, since if we semantically expand all the quantifiers we have a Boolean connective structure on $0, 1$. TQBF and FQBF are used to denote the languages of true and false closed QBF, respectively.

QBF Game Semantics. Often it is useful to think of a closed prenex QBF $\mathcal{Q}_1 X_1 \ldots \mathcal{Q}_k X_k.\, \phi$, where X_i are blocks of variables, as a *game* between $\forall$ and $\exists$. In the i-th step of the game, the player $\mathcal{Q}_i$ assigns values to all the variables X_i. The existential player wins the game if and only if the matrix ϕ evaluates to 1 under the assignment constructed in the game. The universal player wins if and only if the matrix ϕ evaluates to 0. Given a universal variable u with index i, a *strategy for u* is a function, which maps the variables of lower index than u to $\{0,1\}$ (the intended response for u). A *strategy* for the universal player for QBF $\Pi\phi$ is a set which contains exactly one strategy for each universal variable in Π. A QBF is false if and only if there exists a *winning strategy* for the universal player, i.e. if the universal player has a strategy for all universal variables that wins any possible game [15][1, Sec. 4.2.2][31, Chap. 19]. Note that we differentiate between a universal strategy and what is known in the literature as a Herbrand function.

Strategies are allowed to depend on previous universal variables, whereas the input to Herbrand functions must be purely existential (this allows us to get Theorem 3 to work). Since strategies for each universal variable are Boolean functions, they can be expressed as circuits. In many QBF solvers, as well as evaluating the truth of a QBF, solvers output circuits expressing the strategies for each universal (existential) variable whenever the QBF is false (true).

QBF Proof Systems. QBFs extend propositional formulas, therefore it is natural that many QBF proof systems use rules from propositional inference. In addition, QBF systems have to include rules that keep quantification in mind.

Q-resolution (Q-Res) by Kleine Büning, Karpinski, and Flögel [26] is a QBF resolution system. It uses the propositional resolution rule on existential variables. In addition, Q-resolution has a universal reduction rule to locally assign universal variables in clauses (for Fig. 2 recall that $\neg\neg z = z$ for literals). QU-resolution (QU-Res) [34] removes the restriction from Q-Res that the resolved variable must be existential and also allows resolution of universal variables.

$$\frac{}{C}\;(\text{Ax}) \qquad\qquad \frac{C \vee x \qquad D \vee \neg x}{C \vee D}\;(\text{Res})$$

Ax: C is a clause in the propositional matrix.
Res: variable x is existential.

$$\frac{C \vee l}{C}\;(\forall\text{-Red})$$

literal l has variable u, which is universal and all other existential variables $x \in C$ are left of u in the quantifier prefix. Literal $\neg l$ does not appear in C.

Fig. 2. The rules of Q-Res [26]

Extended resolution for propositional resolution, enables adding clauses expressing the equality $v \Leftrightarrow (\neg x \vee \neg y)$, for a fresh variable v. We follow this idea in the context of Q-resolution. Here, we need to decide the position of the fresh variable in the prefix. Two versions are considered; a weak one and a general one. Both versions require extension variables to be existential. However, they differ in their placement of the existential quantifier. *Weak extended Q-resolution* [22] is the calculus of Q-Res enhanced with the extension rule in its weak form. Every extension variable appears at the end (innermost) of the prefix.

Extended Q-resolution is the calculus of Q-Res enhanced with the extension rule in general form (ext. Q-Res). Each extension variable is quantified after the variables it is defined from. Just as QU-Resolution introduces universal resolution to Q-Res, we can also get *extended QU-resolution* (ext. QU-Res) which adds universal resolution to extended Q-Res, the same can be done for *weak extended QU-resolution*.

C-Frege $+\forall$red uses circuit lines from the class C. It combines rules from Frege systems that operate on the circuit class C, with the reduction rule (See Fig. 3). While Frege systems are inferential, because we are using reduction, which is mainly used for refutation, C-Frege $+\forall$red is a refutational system.

$$\frac{}{D} \text{ (Ax)} \qquad\qquad \frac{C_1, \dots \qquad C_k}{D} \text{ (C-Frege)}$$

Ax: D is a circuit in the propositional matrix.
C-Frege: deriving circuit D from circuits $C_1, \dots C_k$ is compliant with an axiom or rule in the C-Frege proof system.

$$B \text{ is a C circuit in variables left of } u. \ \frac{D}{D[B/u]} \text{ ($\forall$-Red)}$$

Variable u is universal and all other variables $x \in D$ are left of u in the prefix.

Fig. 3. The rules of C-Frege $+ \forall$red [5]

In practice, we concentrate on a few special cases of C, particularly when C is AC^0 (bounded-depth), $AC^0[p]$ (bounded depth with mod p gates), NC^1 (the standard Frege systems) or P/poly (circuit Frege, equivalent to eFrege).

Definition 2 (Strategy Extraction). *A refutational proof system P has (circuit) strategy extraction if there is a polynomial-time algorithm that takes P refutations π of QBF Ψ and outputs a circuit D_u for each universal variable u in prenex QBF Ψ, where the input variables of D_u are quantified to the left of u in Ψ and playing every u according to the output of D_u constitutes a winning strategy for the universal player.*

We look at the strategy extraction lower-bound technique, using the circuit extracted from the proof. The technique depends on the proof systems having a strategy extraction property- that a circuit giving the winning strategy for the universal player can be efficiently extracted from the proof. If that circuit is large then the proof must also be large. For specific circuit class C, C-strategy extraction for a particular proof system P is the property that there is a polynomial-time way to extract from a P-proof of a false QBF, a winning universal strategy in circuit class C for the relevant false QBF. For example, the QBF proof system $AC^0[p]$-Frege $+\forall$red has $AC^0[p]$-strategy extraction [5]. Circuit lower bounds for $AC^0[p]$ can then be exploited to prove $AC^0[p]$-Frege $+\forall$red proof-size lower bounds.

One circuit model that is very useful when dealing with strategy extraction is the decision list. Below we define the C-decision list for circuit class C.

Definition 3 (C-decision list). *A C-decision list is a program of the following form*

$$\text{if } C_1(\boldsymbol{x}) \text{ then } u \leftarrow B_1(\boldsymbol{x});$$
$$\text{else if } C_2(\boldsymbol{x}) \text{ then } u \leftarrow B_2(\boldsymbol{x});$$
$$\vdots$$
$$\text{else if } C_{\ell-1}(\boldsymbol{x}) \text{ then } u \leftarrow B_{\ell-1}(\boldsymbol{x});$$
$$\text{else } u \leftarrow B_\ell(\boldsymbol{x}),$$

where $C_1, \ldots, C_{\ell-1}$ and $B_1, \ldots, B_\ell$ are circuits in the class C. Hence a decision list as above computes a Boolean function $u = g(\boldsymbol{x})$.

This comes from the original decision list where C_i is a term (conjunction of literals) and B_i is a Boolean constant. QU-Res has strategy extraction in these original depth-1 circuit decision lists, while other QBF systems have strategy extraction in C-decision lists where C depends on the system. Extended Q-Res and extended QU-Res have strategy extraction [7] in P/poly since they use the bounded-depth strategy extraction of Q-Res and QU-Res, but the extension variables disguise arbitrary circuits.

NP Oracles. In the above QBF proof systems, we take a propositional proof system and augment it with some rules in order for it to deal with genuine QBFs. This approach is mostly unavoidable as every QBF proof system also is a propositional system. The drawback is that when observing lower bounds every propositional lower bound is inherited for QBFs. We would like to separate lower bounds from propositional logic from "genuine" QBF hardness.

Recent work [8,10] has started to factor out the component of propositional hardness in QBF. Most work has been done on the QU-Res systems but generalise to other systems as well.

Definition 4 (NP Oracle derivations[8]). *For QBF proof system S, a S^{NP} proof of a QBF Ψ is a derivation of the empty clause by any of the S rules or the NP-derivation rule.*

$$\frac{C_1, \ldots \quad C_l}{D} \text{ (NP-derivation)}$$

For any l, where there is some Σ_1^b-relaxation Π' of the prefix Π such that $\Pi' \bigwedge_{i=1}^{l} C_i \vDash \Pi' \bigwedge_{i=1}^{l} C_i \wedge D$. D and C_i have to be lines permitted in S (e.g. clauses, formulas).

We will not here define a Σ_k^b-relaxation for every k we will just define for $k = 1$. We replace all universal quantifiers with existential ones. In other words, we can infer $\Pi D \wedge \bigwedge_{i=1}^{l} C_i$ from $\Pi \bigwedge_{i=1}^{l} C_i$ whenever $\bigwedge_{i=1}^{l} C_i \vDash D$ holds. When we do add D we do not change the prefix Π. Hence P^{NP} augments QBF proof system P with all propositional inference.

Notice that P^{NP} is not a proof system unless we can check the NP-derivation in polynomial-time. This cannot be done unless $\mathsf{P} = \mathsf{NP}$. However, it gives us a framework for analysing QBF proof systems ignoring propositional hardness, which would otherwise be pervasive in QBF proof complexity. A similar approach was made previously by Chen [10].

Definition 5. *Let P, Q be QBF proof systems, then we write $P \equiv^{\mathsf{NP}} Q$ whenever Q^{NP} and P^{NP} mutually p-simulate each other.*

3   Simulations with Extension Variables

In this section, we study the proof complexity of Ext QU-Resolution without NP oracles. NP oracles will be used in the next section. One may notice that in the definition of Beyersdorff et al. [5] eFrege + ∀red is actually P/poly-Frege + ∀red, and despite its name, it does not use extension variables in its definition. The fact that P/poly-Frege and Frege with extension variables are equivalent propositionally requires the proof of Jeřábek [21], and this has to be proven again for QBF versions. In fact, we prove an even stronger equivalence by using only resolution instead of Frege.

Theorem 1. *Extended QU-Res (with general extension variables) and P/poly-Frege + ∀red are p-equivalent.*

Proof. First, we show P/poly-Frege + ∀red p-simulates extended QU-Res. We take a proof π in extended QU-Res and convert it to a proof in P/poly-Frege + ∀red with the same structure. In order to do this we must convert the clausal lines in π to circuits without extension variables.

We replace every extension variable with the circuit it is describing (using the full circuit when an extension variable is based on others). The circuits introduced are only as large as π because they have to be defined using extension clauses. Hence the new proof is polynomial.

The resolution rule can be easily copied by P/poly-Frege steps. The extension rules are now tautologies that can be easily inferred (or taken as axioms). The reduction rule can be copied, but we have to verify that the new reduction instances are valid. The new clauses now have circuits in place of extension variables. Fortunately, the variables of the circuits are left of the extension variables, by definition. A clause $C \vee u$ in π where the variables in C are quantified before u is transformed into a circuit $D \vee u$ where the circuit D is in variables that are quantified before u. Hence reduction is valid.

We now show the converse- that extended QU-Res p-simulates P/poly-Frege + ∀red. Let π be a refutation in eFrege + ∀red of $\Pi\phi$. Π is a prefix where every universal is y_i for some $1 \le i \le n$ and $\mathrm{lv}(y_i) \le \mathrm{lv}(y_{i+1})$. We can (in polynomial time) change π into a normal form P/poly-Frege + ∀red proof π', which consists of two parts [5]. The first part contains a P/poly-Frege proof of $\bigvee_{i=1}^{n}(y_i \ne \sigma_{y_i})$, where σ_{y_i} are the extracted strategies from π. The second part is the QBF refutation of $\bigvee_{i=1}^{n}(y_i \neq \sigma_{y_i})$ where reduction rules are used.

Consider a CNF version of $\bigvee_{i=1}^{n}(y_i \neq \sigma_{y_i})$ with extension variables involved:

$$\bigwedge_{i=1}^{n} Def(s_i = \sigma_{y_i}) \wedge t_n \wedge \neg t_0 \wedge \bigwedge_{i=1}^{n}(\neg t_i \vee y_i \vee s_i \vee t_{i-1}) \wedge \bigwedge_{i=1}^{n}(\neg t_i \vee \neg y_i \vee \neg s_i \vee t_{i-1})$$

s_i are extensions variables that are defined as σ_{y_i} in $Def(s_i = \sigma_{y_i})$, possibly using more extension variables for the logic gates used in the circuits of σ_{y_i}. t_i are extra variables that allow us to split our large disjunction up, for $j \geq 0$, t_j is an extension variable defining $\bigvee_{i=1}^{j}(y_i \neq s_i)$. Since the gate variables in σ_{y_i} the s_i and t_{i-1} variables only depend on variables to the left of y_i we can place them in the quantifier prefix before y_i. As the CNF is a straightforward logical consequence from $\bigvee_{i=1}^{n}(y_i \neq \sigma_{y_i})$ it also has a short proof.

Induction Hypothesis: We can find short proofs of t_{n-k} using extended QU-Res with weakening (adding an extra literal to a clause) on $\Pi\phi$.

Base Case: The singleton clause (t_n) is a simple restatement of $\bigvee_{i=1}^{n}(y_i \neq \sigma_{y_i})$. We can derive (t_n) in extended resolution with weakening (adding an extra literal), as extended resolution with weakening simulates P/poly-Frege in propositional logic. Note that when we incorporate this into QBF, we have to use Ext. QU-Res, not Ext. Q-Res as Ext. Res. does not distinguish between $\exists$ and $\forall$. (Whether Ext. QU-Res and Ext. Q-Res are equivalent is still an open problem.)

Inductive Step: Suppose we have clause (t_i) with $i = n - k$, we can resolve it with both $(\neg t_i \vee y_i \vee s_i \vee t_{i-1})$ and $(\neg t_i \vee \neg y_i \vee \neg s_i \vee t_{i-1})$ to get $(y_i \vee s_i \vee t_{i-1})$ and $(\neg y_i \vee \neg s_i \vee t_{i-1})$. Since s_i and t_{i-1} variables occur before y_i in the prefix we can reduce y_i in both cases to get $(s_i \vee t_{i-1})$ and $(\neg s_i \vee t_{i-1})$ which we can resolve to get clause (t_{i-1}).

Once we derive t_0, we get a contradiction. In order to derive (t_n), we added extra literals to the clauses with weakening. These literals are not needed in a refutation. Therefore, we remove all of these clause weakening steps and end up with an extended QU-Res refutation. □

Theorem 1 gives us that our next results will hold for both extended QU-Res and P/poly-Frege which we will now refer to as eFrege + ∀red.

But the proof itself also tells us something important- it uses *strategy extraction for simulation*. Contrast this with how strategy extraction has been used previously for QBF lower bounds [5,6]. This idea has the potential to be used for other proof systems or even solvers. Say we have proof system f that has P/poly strategy extraction. If we have an f refutation of QBF $\Pi\phi$, we can use strategy extraction to gain circuits σ_{y_i} for each of the universal variables y_i and substitute each y_i for σ_{y_i} in ϕ, giving us a propositional contradiction. If we can confirm this contradiction in eFrege, we would be able to prove $\bigvee_{i=1}^{n}(y_i \neq \sigma_{y_i})$, and we can continue an eFrege + ∀red proof to get a refutation. This is *almost* a simulation of f by eFrege + ∀red. The thing that could go wrong is there is no guarantee that the substituted propositional matrix has a short eFrege proof. Nonetheless, eFrege is powerful enough for this problem not to occur very often. Theorems 2 and 4 give two different ways of clarifying what is meant by almost a simulation, but we need some technical lemmas on eFrege proofs.

Lemma 1. *For propositional circuits A, B and $\phi(X)$ any propositional tautology of the form $(A \leftrightarrow B) \rightarrow (\phi(A) \leftrightarrow \phi(B))$ has a polynomial-size proof in eFrege.*

Lemma 2. *Let Π be a QBF prefix where each $\forall$ variable is given as y_i for $1 \leq i \leq n$. Let ϕ and σ_{y_i} for $1 \leq i \leq n$ be propositional circuits. Now define $\phi_{\sigma,\Pi}$ to be the propositional circuit that replaces all occurrences of y_i with σ_{y_i}. The tautology $\phi \wedge \neg\phi_{\sigma,\Pi} \rightarrow \bigvee_{i=1}^{n}(y_i \neq \sigma_{y_i})$ has polynomial-size proofs in eFrege, (in the sizes of ϕ and σ_{y_i}).*

We can now talk about simulation by eFrege $+\forall$red. In the next theorem, we have the additional condition that we may need an infinite family of polynomially-recognisable tautologies added to eFrege$+\forall$red. Bear in mind these are only *propositional* tautologies, not QBF.

Theorem 2. *For every refutational QBF Proof System S that has P/poly-strategy extraction, there is a set of polynomial-time verifiable propositional tautologies $\|\Psi\|$ such that eFrege $+\forall$red $+\|\Psi\|$ simulates S.*

It is known [27] that any propositional proof system P is simulated by eFrege $+\|\mathrm{refl}(P)\|$ where $\|\mathrm{refl}(P)\|$ is a set of propositional tautologies that code arithmetic statements of P's correctness (the name "reflection principle" comes from the challenge of a system proving its own soundness). The idea is to use these propositional tautologies in a QBF setting, but we also need reduction and essentially strategy extraction.

Proof. Let S be our FQBF proof system which allows polynomial-time strategy extraction in circuits. Let $\Pi\phi$ be a closed QBF where Π is a quantifier prefix and ϕ is purely propositional. The strategy extraction means that from a refutation π of QBF $\Pi\phi$ we can extract in polynomial-time circuits σ_y that are strategies for each universal variable y. Let $\phi_{\sigma,\Pi}$ be the propositional formula that results from replacing every universal variable y with σ_y in ϕ. Since the strategy is correct, $\phi_{\sigma,\Pi}$ must be a propositional contradiction.

We can use this observation to design a propositional proof system $Strat(S)$. The idea is that this proof system verifies the proposition $(\neg\phi)_{\sigma,\Pi}$ instead of refuting the QBF $\Pi\phi$. Using the Cook-Reckhow definition of a proof system as a checking function (see Sect. 2.1) we define it as follows:

$$Strat(S)(\pi) = \begin{cases} \neg\phi_{\sigma,\Pi}, & \pi \text{ is an } S \text{ refutation of } \Pi\phi \\ & \text{and } \sigma \text{ is the strategy extracted from it,} \\ \mathrm{eFrege}(\pi), & \text{otherwise.} \end{cases}$$

Using information from [27] we know $Strat(S)$ is simulated by eFrege $+ \|\mathrm{refl}(Strat(S))\|$, where $\|\mathrm{refl}(Strat(S))\|$ is a polynomial-time recognisable set of propositions that encode an arithmetic statement of the correctness of $Strat(S)$. We will show that eFrege + $\forall$red + $\|\mathrm{refl}(Strat(S))\|$ simulates S, so we let π be a proof of $\Pi\phi$ in S with strategy extracted σ. Note that π is also a $Strat(S)$ proof.

We let π_1' be the eFrege + $\|\mathrm{refl}(Strat(S))\|$ proof that simulates π in $Strat(S)$. We know this is of polynomial-size in π. Likewise as we know the σ_y are polynomial-size, this means that by using Lemma 2 the circuit $\phi \wedge \neg\phi_{\sigma,\Pi} \rightarrow \bigvee_{i=1}^{n}(y_i \neq \sigma_{y_i})$ has a polynomial-size eFrege proof π_2', where y_i are the universal variables in Π in order (y_n being the innermost universal variable).

We show that eFrege + $\forall$red + $\|\mathrm{refl}(Strat(S))\|$ can refute $\Pi\phi$ in a short proof.

$$\frac{\dfrac{\phi \qquad \neg\phi_{\sigma,\Pi}}{\phi \wedge \neg\phi_{\sigma,\Pi}} \qquad \phi \wedge \neg\phi_{\sigma,\Pi} \rightarrow \bigvee_{i=1}^{n}(y_i \neq \sigma_{y_i})}{\bigvee_{i=1}^{n}(y_i \neq \sigma_{y_i})}$$

Similarly to Theorem 1, we show an inductive proof of $\bigvee_{i=1}^{n-k}(y_i \neq \sigma_{y_i})$ for increasing k eventually leaving us with the empty clause. This essentially is where we use the $\forall$-Red rule. Since we already have $\bigvee_{i=1}^{n}(y_i \neq \sigma_{y_i})$ we have the base case and we only need to show the inductive step.

We derive from $\bigvee_{i=1}^{n+1-k}(y_i \neq \sigma_{y_i})$ both $(0 \neq \sigma_{y_{n+1-k}}) \vee \bigvee_{i=1}^{n-k}(y_i \neq \sigma_{y_i})$ and $(1 \neq \sigma_{y_{n+1-k}}) \vee \bigvee_{i=1}^{n-k}(y_i \neq \sigma_{y_i})$ from reduction. We can resolve both with the easily proved tautology $(0 = \sigma_{y_{n+1-k}}) \vee (1 = \sigma_{y_{n+1-k}})$ which allows us to derive $\bigvee_{i=1}^{n-k}(y_i \neq \sigma_{y_i})$. We continue this until we reach the empty disjunction. $\qquad \square$

Conjecture 1. $\forall$Exp+Res, IR-calc, LD-Q-Res, IRM-calc, QRAT(UR) and Q(D^{rrs})-Res are all simulated by eFrege + $\forall$red.

Let us take one example, e.g. $\forall$Exp+Res and suppose it is not true. Then $\|\mathrm{refl}(Strat(\forall$Exp+Res$))\|$ would have to be an eFrege lower bound, an answer to a major open problem. Put another way, $Strat(\forall$Exp+Res$)$ would be a propositional proof system more powerful than eFrege on certain families. This would seem very unlikely. More likely would be that the steps of an $\forall$Exp+Res refutation of $\Pi\phi$ combined with formalised knowledge about the strategy extraction for $\forall$Exp+Res could help guide a short refutation of $\phi_{\sigma,\Pi}$ using extension variables and Frege. If so then we would get a simulation.

4   Extended Q-Res Modulo NP

We now analyse QBF proof systems with the NP oracle included. As it allows new derivations to occur immediately, this can change a system considerably. It is necessary to prove, where applicable, when strategy extraction remains.

Theorem 3. *The following strategy extraction theorems hold:*

- QU-Res ^{NP} *has depth-1 circuit decision list strategy extraction.*
- *For circuit class* C, *C-Frege + $\forall$red ^{NP} has C-decision list strategy extraction.*

Proof. The proof follows the line-based strategy extraction used by Balabanov et al. [2] and later generalised by Beyersdorff et al. [5]. Purely propositional rules make no changes to the extraction, and NP-derivations are purely propositional.   □

This is not an automatic result for any QBF proof system with strategy extraction; recent results [11] on strategy extraction indicate that expansion based systems may lose strategy extraction when equipped with NP oracles. It is also unclear whether variants of (Ext) Q(U)-Resolution that allow long-distance resolution steps have strategy extraction when NP oracles are allowed. Extended Q-Res^{NP} and extended QU-Res^{NP} are among the systems with strategy extraction. NP oracles allow us to remove $\|\mathrm{refl}(Strat(S))\|$ used in Theorem 2, but also collapses Q-Res and QU-Res into the same system.

Theorem 4. *Extended* Q-Res^{NP} *is optimal among all QBF proof systems with strategy extraction.*

By "optimal among all QBF proof systems with strategy extraction" we mean that it simulates all QBF proof systems with (circuit-)strategy extraction and has strategy extraction itself. The caveat is that neither extended Q-Res ^{NP} nor extended QU-Res ^{NP} are proof systems due to the NP oracle.

Proof. Ext. Q-Res ^{NP} simulates ext. QU-Res ^{NP} since universal resolution is subsumed by the NP-derivation rule. We know that ext. QU-Res ^{NP} has strategy extraction by the equivalence of extended QU-Res and P/Poly-Frege + ∀red, which when augmented with an NP-derivation rule has strategy extraction by Theorem 3.

Suppose we have QBF proof system S that has strategy extraction. We know from Theorem 2 we can simulate this by system eFrege + ∀red + $\|\mathrm{refl}(Strat(S))\|$, we can simulate this by ext. QU-Res ^{NP}, because $\|\mathrm{refl}(Strat(S))\|$ can be derived directly from the NP derivation and eFrege + ∀red rules can be simulated by extended QU-Res rules. Note that it does not matter here if S uses an NP derivation rule as this can be simulated by the NP derivation rule.   □

5   Weaker QBF Systems

So far we have only studied *extended* QU-Res and Q-Res with *general extensions*. There remains four weaker systems, *extended* QU-Res and Q-Res with *weak extensions* and standard QU-Res and Q-Res. We will analyse these four for the remainder of this paper, both with and without the NP oracle.

Theorem 5. *Weak extended QU-Resolution^{NP} does not simulate extended Q-Resolution.*

Proof. We take the QPARITY formulas [6] which are known to have short proofs in general extended Q-Res [7]. We will show that these are hard for weak extended

QU Resolution^{NP}. In fact, because of Theorem 7, we will only need to show these are hard for Q-Res^{NP}.

Let xor(o_1, o_2, o) be the CNF $(\neg o_1 \vee \neg o_2 \vee \neg o) \wedge (o_1 \vee o_2 \vee \neg o) \wedge (\neg o_1 \vee o_2 \vee o) \wedge (o_1 \vee \neg o_2 \vee o)$, which defines o to be equal to $o_1 \oplus o_2$. Define QPARITY$_n$ as

$$\exists x_1 \ldots x_n \,\forall z \exists t_2 \ldots t_n \, \text{xor}(x_1, x_2, t_2) \wedge \bigwedge_{i=3}^{N} \text{xor}(t_{i-1}, x_i, t_i) \wedge (z \vee t_n) \wedge (\neg z \vee \neg t_n).$$

While QPARITY is false, the only winning strategy of the universal player on the QPARITY formulas is to actually compute the PARITY function. However, PARITY is the classic example of a function hard for bounded-depth circuits and AC^0-decision lists [14,17]. Q-Res^{NP} has strategy extraction in AC^0-decision lists, but these must be exponential size, which means the proofs themselves are required to be of exponential size.   □

The separation between Q-Res and QU-Res comes from the formulas from Kleine Büning, Karpinski and Flögel [26,34]. QU-Res cannot simulate weak extended Q-Res due to propositional lower bounds like the pigeonhole principle [16]. We are only left to show one more separation, and we get the complete picture. Adapting the cost-capacity technique from [4], we can show that the KBKF formulas are also hard for weak ext. Q-Res, giving Theorem 6.

Theorem 6. *Weak extended* Q-Res *does not simulate* QU-Res.

Once we have that final lower bound, we prove the following complete simulation structure in Fig. 4. We then show in Theorem 7, that the opposite is true when using NP derivations.

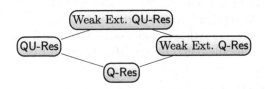

Fig. 4. The simulation structure of four variants of Q-Res, all pairwise simulations are given and are strictly one-way, and other pairs do not yield a simulation.

Theorem 7. Q-Res $\equiv^{NP}$ QU-Res $\equiv^{NP}$ *Weak Ext.*Q-Res $\equiv^{NP}$ *Weak Ext.*QU-Res.

Proof. Q-Res $\equiv^{NP}$ QU-Res and Weak Ext.Q-Res $\equiv^{NP}$ Weak Ext.QU-Res because NP derivations can be used to simulate universal resolution steps directly. We are left to show Q-Res $\equiv^{NP}$ Weak Ext.Q-Res.

The first observation is that every universal reduction step in Weak Ext. Q-Res has no extension variables, since these would always be quantified to the right of every universal variable (and thus block their reduction). This means the first lines we perform universal reduction on are just propositional implications of axioms. Likewise, any later lines we perform universal reduction on are propositional implications of the axioms plus the clauses that result from universal reduction (which are not inferred propositionally). So what we can do in Q-Res^{NP} to simulate Weak Ext. Q-Res^{NP} proofs is to use NP derivations to get to the lines that need universal reduction and then ∀red these clauses and continue to alternate between NP derivations steps and universal reduction steps.   □

6   Conclusion

We have shown that extended QU-Res and eFrege + ∀red are equivalent as long as the extension variables are defined generally. eFrege + ∀red has an important place among QBF proof systems, particularly among those with strategy extraction. This can be qualified with or without an NP oracle. This position allows us to conjecture that eFrege + ∀red will simulate the known QBF systems with strategy extraction and will be able to certify solvers that have strategy extraction.

These properties do not hold for weak extension variables even with the NP oracles. In fact, under the NP oracle, weak extended QU-Res has no more strength than regular Q-Res.

References

1. Arora, S., Barak, B.: Computational Complexity - A Modern Approach. Cambridge University Press, Cambridge (2009)
2. Balabanov, V., Jiang, J.H.R.: Unified QBF certification and its applications. Formal Methods Syst. Des. **41**(1), 45–65 (2012)
3. Bellatoni, S., Pitassi, T., Urquhart, A.: Approximation of small-depth Frege proofs. SIAM J. Comput. **21**, 1161–1179 (1992)
4. Beyersdorff, O., Blinkhorn, J., Hinde, L.: Size, cost, and capacity: a semantic technique for hard random QBFs. CoRR abs/1712.03626 (2017). http://arxiv.org/abs/1712.03626
5. Beyersdorff, O., Bonacina, I., Chew, L., Pich, J.: Frege systems for quantified boolean logic. J. ACM **67**(2), (2020). https://doi.org/10.1145/3381881
6. Beyersdorff, O., Chew, L., Janota, M.: New resolution-based QBF calculi and their proof complexity. ACM Trans. Comput. Theory **11**(4), 26:1–26:42 (2019). https://doi.org/10.1145/3352155
7. Beyersdorff, O., Chew, L., Janota, M.: Extension variables in QBF resolution. In: Beyond, N.P.: Papers from the 2016 AAAI Workshop (2016). http://www.aaai.org/ocs/index.php/WS/AAAIW16/paper/view/12612
8. Beyersdorff, O., Hinde, L., Pich, J.: Reasons for hardness in QBF proof systems. Electron. Colloquium Comput. Complexity (ECCC) **24**, 44 (2017). https://eccc.weizmann.ac.il/report/2017/044
9. Blinkhorn, J.L.: Quantified Boolean Formulas: Proof Complexity and Models of Solving. Ph.D. thesis, University of Leeds (2019)
10. Chen, H.: Proof complexity modulo the polynomial hierarchy: Understanding alternation as a source of hardness. In: ICALP, pp. 94:1–94:14 (2016)

11. Chew, L., Clymo, J.: How QBF expansion makes strategy extraction hard. In: Peltier, N., Sofronie-Stokkermans, V. (eds.) IJCAR 2020. LNCS (LNAI), vol. 12166, pp. 66–82. Springer, Cham (2020). https://doi.org/10.1007/978-3-030-51074-9_5

12. Cook, S.A., Reckhow, R.A.: The relative efficiency of propositional proof systems. J. Symbolic Logic **44**(1), 36–50 (1979)

13. Feldman, A., Kleer, J., Matei, I.: Design space exploration as quantified satisfaction (05 2019)

14. Furst, M.L., Saxe, J.B., Sipser, M.: Parity, circuits, and the polynomial-time hierarchy. Math. Syst. Theory **17**(1), 13–27 (1984)

15. Goultiaeva, A., Van Gelder, A., Bacchus, F.: A uniform approach for generating proofs and strategies for both true and false QBF formulas. In: Walsh, T. (ed.) International Joint Conference on Artificial Intelligence IJCAI, pp. 546–553. IJCAI/AAAI (2011)

16. Haken, A.: The intractability of resolution. Theor. Comput. Sci. **39**, 297–308 (1985)

17. Håstad, J.: One-way permutations in NC^0. Inf. Process. Lett. **26**(3), 153–155 (1987)

18. Heule, M., Seidl, M., Biere, A.: A unified proof system for QBF preprocessing. In: 7th International Joint Conference on Automated Reasoning (IJCAR), pp. 91–106 (2014)

19. Janota, M., Klieber, W., Marques-Silva, J., Clarke, E.: Solving QBF with counterexample guided refinement. In: Cimatti, A., Sebastiani, R. (eds.) SAT 2012. LNCS, vol. 7317, pp. 114–128. Springer, Heidelberg (2012). https://doi.org/10.1007/978-3-642-31612-8_10

20. Janota, M., Marques-Silva, J.: Expansion-based QBF solving versus Q-resolution. Theor. Comput. Sci. **577**, 25–42 (2015)

21. Jeřábek, E.: Dual weak pigeonhole principle, Boolean complexity, and derandomization. Ann. Pure Appl. Logic **129**, 1–37 (2004)

22. Jussila, T., Biere, A., Sinz, C., Kröning, D., Wintersteiger, C.M.: A first step towards a unified proof checker for QBF. In: Marques-Silva, J., Sakallah, K.A. (eds.) SAT 2007. LNCS, vol. 4501, pp. 201–214. Springer, Heidelberg (2007). https://doi.org/10.1007/978-3-540-72788-0_21

23. Kiesl, B., Heule, M.J.H., Seidl, M.: A little blocked literal goes a long way. In: Gaspers, S., Walsh, T. (eds.) SAT 2017. LNCS, vol. 10491, pp. 281–297. Springer, Cham (2017). https://doi.org/10.1007/978-3-319-66263-3_18

24. Kiesl, B., Seidl, M.: QRAT polynomially simulates ∀-Exp+Res. In: Janota, M., Lynce, I. (eds.) SAT 2019. LNCS, vol. 11628, pp. 193–202. Springer, Cham (2019). https://doi.org/10.1007/978-3-030-24258-9_13

25. Kleine Büning, H., Bubeck, U.: Theory of quantified Boolean formulas. In: Biere, A., Heule, M., van Maaren, H., Walsh, T. (eds.) Handbook of Satisfiability, Frontiers in Artificial Intelligence and Applications, vol. 185, pp. 735–760. IOS Press (2009)

26. Kleine Büning, H., Karpinski, M., Flögel, A.: Resolution for quantified Boolean formulas. Inf. Comput. **117**(1), 12–18 (1995)

27. Krajíček, J.: Bounded Arithmetic, Propositional Logic, and Complexity Theory, Encyclopedia of Mathematics and Its Applications, vol. 60. Cambridge University Press, Cambridge (1995)

28. Lonsing, F.: Dependency Schemes and Search-Based QBF Solving: Theory and Practice. Ph.D. thesis, Informatik, Johannes Kepler University Linz (2012)

29. Lonsing, F., Biere, A.: DepQBF: a dependency-aware QBF solver. JSAT **7**(2–3), 71–76 (2010)

30. Messner, J., Torán, J.: Optimal proof systems for propositional logic and complete sets. Technical Report, TR97-026, Electronic Colloquium on Computational Complexity, a revised version appears at STACS'98 (1997)
31. Papadimitriou, C.H.: Computational Complexity. Addison-Wesley, Boston (1994)
32. Slivovsky, F.: Structure in# SAT and QBF. Ph.D. thesis (2015)
33. Tseitin, G.S.: On the complexity of proof in prepositional calculus. Zapiski Nauchnykh Seminarov POMI **8**, 234–259 (1968)
34. Gelder, A.: Contributions to the theory of practical quantified Boolean formula solving. In: Milano, M. (ed.) CP 2012. LNCS, pp. 647–663. Springer, Heidelberg (2012). https://doi.org/10.1007/978-3-642-33558-7_47

Characterizing Tseitin-Formulas with Short Regular Resolution Refutations

Alexis de Colnet[1,2]($\boxtimes$) and Stefan Mengel[1,2]

[1] CNRS, UMR 8188, Centre de Recherche en Informatique de Lens (CRIL),
62300 Lens, France
{decolnet,mengel}@cril.fr
[2] Univ. Artois, UMR 8188, 62300 Lens, France

Abstract. Tseitin-formulas are systems of parity constraints whose structure is described by a graph. These formulas have been studied extensively in proof complexity as hard instances in many proof systems. In this paper, we prove that a class of unsatisfiable Tseitin-formulas of bounded degree has regular resolution refutations of polynomial length if and only if the treewidth of all underlying graphs G for that class is in $O(\log |V(G)|)$. To do so, we show that any regular resolution refutation of an unsatisfiable Tseitin-formula with graph G of bounded degree has length $2^{\Omega(tw(G))}/|V(G)|$, thus essentially matching the known $2^{O(tw(G))}\mathrm{poly}(|V(G)|)$ upper bound up. Our proof first connects the length of regular resolution refutations of unsatisfiable Tseitin-formulas to the size of representations of *satisfiable* Tseitin-formulas in decomposable negation normal form (DNNF). Then we prove that for every graph G of bounded degree, every DNNF-representation of every satisfiable Tseitin-formula with graph G must have size $2^{\Omega(tw(G))}$ which yields our lower bound for regular resolution.

Keywords: Proof complexity · Regular resolution · DNNF · Treewidth

1 Introduction

Resolution is one of the most studied propositional proof systems in proof complexity due to its naturality and it connections to practical SAT solving [9,22]. A refutation of a CNF-formula in this system (a resolution refutation) relies uniquely on clausal resolution: in a refutation, clauses are iteratively derived by resolutions on clauses from the formula or previously inferred clauses, until reaching the empty clause indicating unsatisfiability. In this paper, we consider regular resolution which is the restriction of resolution to proofs in which, intuitively, variables which have been resolved away from a clause cannot be reintroduced later on by additional resolution steps. This fragment of resolution is

This work has been partly supported by the PING/ACK project of the French National Agency for Research (ANR-18-CE40-0011).

C.-M. Li and F. Manyà (Eds.): SAT 2021, LNCS 12831, pp. 116–133, 2021.
https://doi.org/10.1007/978-3-030-80223-3_9

known to generally require exponentially longer refutations than general resolution [1,17,26,27] but is still interesting since it corresponds to DPLL-style algorithms [12,13]. Consequently, there is quite some work on regular resolution, see e.g. [3–5,25] for a very small sample.

Tseitin-formulas are encodings of certain systems of linear equations whose structure is given by a graph [24]. They have been studied extensively in proof complexity essentially since the creation of the field because they are hard instances in many settings, see e.g. [4,6,19,20,25]. It is known that different properties of the underlying graph characterize different parameters of their resolution refutations [2,15,19]. Extending this line of work, we here show that treewidth determines the length of regular resolution refutations of Tseitin-formulas: classes of Tseitin-formulas of bounded degree have polynomial length regular resolution refutations if and only if the treewidth of the underlying graphs is bounded logarithmically in their size. The upper bound for this result was already known from [2] where it is shown that, for every graph G, unsatisfiable Tseitin-formulas with the underlying graph G have regular resolution refutations of length at most $2^{O(tw(G))}|V(G)|^c$ where c is a constant. We provide a matching lower bound:

Theorem 1. *Let $T(G,c)$ be an unsatisfiable Tseitin-formula where G is a connected graph with maximum degree at most Δ. The length of the smallest regular resolution refutation of $T(G,c)$ is at least $2^{\Omega(tw(G)/\Delta)}|V(G)|^{-1}$.*

There were already known lower bounds for the length of resolution refutations of Tseitin-formulas based on treewidth before. For *general* resolution, a $2^{\Omega(tw(G)^2)/|V(G)|}$ lower bound can be inferred with the classical width-length relation of [6] and width bounds of [15]. This gives a tight $2^{\Omega(tw(G))}$ bound when the treewidth of G is linear in its number of vertices. For smaller treewidth, there are also bounds from [14] for the stronger proof system of depth-d Frege proofs which for resolution translate to bounds of size $2^{tw(G)^{\Omega(1)}}$, but since the top exponent is significantly less than 1, these results are incomparable to ours. Better bounds of $2^{\Omega(tw(G))/\log|V(G)|}$ for regular resolution that almost match the upper bound where shown in [20] for *regular* resolution refutations. Building on [20], we eliminate the division by $\log|V(G)|$ in the exponent and thus give a tight $2^{\Theta(tw(G))}$ dependence.

As in [20], our proof strategy follows two steps. First, we show that the problem of bounding the length of regular resolution refutations of an *unsatisfiable* Tseitin-formula can be reduced to lower bounding the size of certain representations of a *satisfiable* Tseitin-formula. Itsykson et al. in [20] used a similar reduction of lower bounds for regular resolution refutations to bounds on read-once branching programs (1-BP) for satisfiable Tseitin-formulas, using the classical connection between regular resolution and the search problem which, given an unsatisfiable CNF-formula and a truth assignment, returns a clause of the formula it falsifies [21]. Itsykson et al. showed that there is a transformation of a 1-BP solving the search problem for an unsatisfiable Tseitin-formula into a 1-BP of pseudopolynomial size computing a satisfiable Tseitin-formula with the same underlying graph. This yields lower bounds for regular resolution from lower bounds for 1-BP computing satisfiable Tseitin-formulas which [20] also shows. Our crucial insight here is that when more succinct representations are used to present the satisfiable formula, the transformation from the unsatisfiable instance can be changed to have only a polynomial instead of pseudopolynomial size increase. Concretely, the representations we use are so-called decomposable negation normal forms (DNNF) which are very prominent in the field of knowledge compilation [10] and generalize 1-BP. We show that every refutation of an unsatisfiable Tseitin-formula can be transformed into a DNNF-representation of a satisfiable Tseitin-formula with the same underlying graph with only polynomial overhead.

In a second step, we then show for every satisfiable Tseitin-formula with an underlying graph G a lower bound of $2^{\Omega(tw(G))}$ on the size of DNNF computing the formula. To this end, we adapt techniques developed in [8] to a parameterized setting. [8] uses rectangle covers of a function, a common tool from communication complexity, to lower bound the size of any DNNF computing the function. Our refinement takes the form of a two-player game in which the first player tries to cover the models of a function with few rectangles while the second player hinders this construction by adversarially choosing the variable partitions respected by the rectangles from a certain set of partitions. We show that this game gives lower bounds for DNNF, and consequently the aim is to show that the adversarial player can always force $2^{\Omega(tw(G))}$ rectangles in the game when playing on a Tseitin-formula with graph G. This is done by proving that any rectangle for a carefully chosen variable partition *splits* parity constraints of the formula in a way that bounds by a function of $tw(G)$ the number of models that can be covered. We show that, depending on the treewidth of G, the adversarial player can choose a partition to limit the number of models of every rectangle constructed in the game to the point that at least $2^{\Omega(tw(G))}$ of them will be needed to cover all models of the Tseitin-formula. As a consequence, we get the desired lower bound of $2^{\Omega(tw(G))}|V(G)|^{-1}$ for regular resolution refutations of Tseitin-formulas.

2   Preliminaries

Notions on Graphs. We assume the reader is familiar with the fundamentals of graph theory. For a graph G, we denote by $V(G)$ its vertices and by $E(G)$ its edges. For $v \in V(G)$, $E(v)$ denotes the edges incident to v and $N(v)$ its neighbors (v is not in $N(v)$). For a subset V' of $V(G)$ we denote by $G[V']$ the sub-graph of G induced by V'.

A binary tree whose leaves are in bijection with the edges of G is called a *branch decomposition*[1]. Each edge e of a branch decomposition T induces a partition of $E(G)$ into two parts as the edge sets that appear in the two connected components of T after deletion of e. The number of vertices of G that are incident to edges in both parts of this partition is the order of e, denoted

---

[1] We remark that often branch decompositions are defined as unrooted trees. However, it is easy to see that our definition is equivalent, so we use it here since it is more convenient in our setting.

by $order(e,T)$. The *branchwidth* of G, denoted by $bw(G)$, is defined as $bw(G) = \min_T \max_{e \in E(T)} order(e,T)$, where $\min_T$ is over all branch decompositions of G.

While it is convenient to work with branchwidth in our proofs, we state our main result with the more well-known *treewidth* $tw(G)$ of a graph G. This is justified by the following well-known connection between the two measures.

Lemma 2. [18, Lemma 12] *If $bw(G) \geq 2$, then $bw(G) - 1 \leq tw(G) \leq \frac{3}{2}bw(G)$.*

A *separator* S in a connected graph G is defined to be a vertex set such that $G \setminus S$ is non-empty and not connected. A graph G is called 3-connected if and only if it has at least 4 vertices and, for every $S \subseteq V(G)$, $|S| \leq 2$, the graph $G \setminus S$ is connected.

Variables, Assignments, v-trees. Boolean variables can have value 0 (*false*) or 1 (*true*). The notation ℓ_x refers to a literal for a variable x, that is, x or its negation $\overline{x}$. Given a set X of Boolean variables, $lit(X)$ denotes its set of literals. A truth assignment to X is a mapping $a : X \to \{0,1\}$. If a_X and a_Y are assignments to *disjoint* sets of variables X and Y, then $a_X \cup a_Y$ denotes the combined assignment to $X \cup Y$. The set of assignments to X is denoted by $\{0,1\}^X$. Let f be a Boolean function, we denote by $var(f)$ its variables and by $sat(f)$ its set of models, i.e., assignments to $var(f)$ on which f evaluates to 1. A v-tree of X is a binary tree T whose leaves are labeled bijectively with the variables in X. A v-tree T of X induces a set of partitions (X_1, X_2) of X as follows: choose a vertex v of T, setting X_1 to contain exactly the variables in T that appear below v and $X_2 := X \setminus X_1$.

Tseitin-Formulas. Tseitin formulas are systems of parity constraints whose structure is determined by a graph. Let $G = (V,E)$ be a graph and let $c : V \to \{0,1\}$ be a labeling of its vertices called a *charge function*. The Tseitin-formula $T(G,c)$ has for each edge $e \in E$ a Boolean variable x_e and for each vertex $v \in V$ a constraint $\chi_v : \sum_{e \in E(v)} x_e = c(v) \mod 2$. The Tseitin-formula $T(G,c)$ is then defined as $T(G,c) := \bigwedge_{v \in V} \chi_v$, i.e., the conjunction of the parity constraints for all $v \in V$. By $\overline{\chi_v}$ we denote the negation of χ_v, i.e., the parity constraint on $(x_e)_{e \in E(v)}$ with charge $1 - c(v)$.

Proposition 3. [25, Lemma 4.1] *The Tseitin-formula $T(G,c)$ is satisfiable if and only if for every connected component U of G we have $\sum_{v \in U} c(v) = 0 \mod 2$.*

Proposition 4. [16, Lemma 2] *Let G be a graph with K connected components. If the Tseitin-formula $T(G,c)$ is satisfiable, then it has $2^{|E(G)|-|V(G)|+K}$ models.*

When conditioning the formula $T(G,c)$ on a literal $\ell_e \in \{x_e, \overline{x_e}\}$ for $e = ab$ in $E(G)$, the resulting function is another Tseitin formula $T(G,c)|\ell_e = T(G',c')$ where G' is the graph G without the edge e (so $G' = G - e$) and c' depends on ℓ_e. If $\ell_e = \overline{x_e}$ then c' equals c. If $\ell_e = x_e$ then $c' = c + 1_a + 1_b \mod 2$, where 1_v denotes the charge function that assigns 1 to v and 0 to all other variables.

Since we consider Tseitin-formulas in the setting of proof systems for CNF-formulas, we will assume in the following that they are encoded as CNF-formulas. In this encoding, every individual parity constraint χ_v is expressed as a CNF-formula F_v and $T(G,c) := \bigwedge_{v \in V} F_v$. Since it takes $2^{|E(v)|-1}$ clauses to write the parity constraint χ_v, each clause containing $E(v)$ literals, we make the standard assumption that $E(v)$ is bounded, i.e., there is a constant upper bound Δ on the degree of all vertices in G.

DNNF. A circuit over X in *negation normal form* (NNF) is a directed acyclic graph whose leaves are labeled with literals in $lit(X)$ or $0/1$-constants, and whose internal nodes are labeled by $\vee$-gates or $\wedge$-gates. We use the usual semantics for the function computed by (gates of) Boolean circuits. Every NNF can be turned into an equivalent NNF whose nodes have at most two successors in polynomial time. So we assume that NNF in this paper have only binary gates and thus define the size $|D|$ as the number of gates, which is then at most half the number of wires. Given a gate g, we denote by $var(g)$ the variables for the literals appearing under g. When g is a literal input ℓ_x, we have $var(g) = \{x\}$, and when it is a $0/1$-input, we define $var(g) = \emptyset$. A gate with two children g_l and g_r is called *decomposable* when $var(g_l) \cap var(g_r) = \emptyset$, and it is called *complete* (or *smooth*) when $var(g_l) = var(g_r)$. An NNF whose $\wedge$-gates are all decomposable is called a *decomposable NNF (DNNF)*. We call a DNNF *complete* when all its $\vee$-gates are complete. Every DNNF can be made complete in polynomial time. For every Boolean function f on finitely many variables, there exists a DNNF computing f.

When representing Tseitin-formulas by DNNF, we will use the following:

Lemma 5. *Let G be a graph and let c and c' be two charge functions such that $T(G,c)$ and $T(G,c')$ are satisfiable Tseitin-formulas. Then $T(G,c)$ can be computed by a DNNF of size s if and only if this is true for $T(G,c')$.*

Proof (sketch). $T(G,c)$ can be transformed into $T(G,c')$ by substituting some variables by their negations, see [20, Proposition 26]. So every DNNF for $T(G,c)$ can be transformed into one for $T(G,c')$ by making the same substitutions. □

Branching Programs. A branching program (BP) B is a directed acyclic graph with a single source, sinks that uniquely correspond to the values of a finite set Y, and whose inner nodes, called *decision nodes* are each labeled by a Boolean variable $x \in X$ and have exactly two output wires called the 0- and 1-wire pointing to two nodes respectively called its 0- and the 1-child. The variable x appears on a path in B if there is a decision node v labeled by x on that path. A truth assignment a to X induces a path in B which starts at the source and, when encountering a decision node for a variable x, follows the 0-wire (resp. the 1-wire) if $a(x) = 0$ (resp. $a(x) = 1$). The BP B is defined to compute the value $y \in Y$ on an assignment a if and only if the path of a leads to the sink labeled with y. We denote this value y as $B(a)$. Let $f : X \to Y$ be a function where X is a finite set of Boolean variables and Y any finite set. Then we say that B computes f if for every assignment $a \in \{0,1\}^X$ we have $B(a) = f(a)$. We say that a node v in B computes a function g if the BP we get from B by deleting all nodes that are not reachable from v computes g.

Let $R \subseteq \{0,1\}^X \times Y$ be a relation where Y is again finite. Then we say that a BP B computes R if for every assignment a we have that $(a, B(a)) \in R$. Let $T(G,c)$ be an unsatisfiable Tseitin-formula for a graph $G = (V, E)$. Then we define the two following relations: $\mathrm{Search}_{T(G,c)}$ consists of the pairs (a, C) such that a is an assignment to $T(G,c)$ that does not satisfy the clause C of $T(G,c)$. The relation $\mathrm{SearchVertex}(G, c)$ consists of the pairs (a, v) such that a does not satisfy the parity constraint χ_v of a vertex $v \in V$. Note that $\mathrm{Search}_{T(G,c)}$ and $\mathrm{SearchVertex}(G, c)$ both give a reason why an assignment a does not satisfy $T(G,c)$ but the latter is more coarse: $\mathrm{SearchVertex}(G, c)$ only gives a constraint that is violated while $\mathrm{Search}_{T(G,c)}$ gives an exact clause that is not satisfied.

Regular Resolution. We only introduce some minimal notions of proof complexity here; for more details and references the reader is referred to the recent survey [9]. Let $C_1 = x \vee D_1$ and $C_2 = \overline{x} \vee D_2$ be two clauses such that D_1, D_2 contain neither x nor $\overline{x}$. Then the clause $D_1 \vee D_2$ is inferred by resolution of C_1 and C_2 on x. A resolution refutation of length s of a CNF-formula F is defined to be a sequence $C_1, \ldots, C_s$ such that C_s is the empty clause and for every $i \in [s]$ we have that C_i is a clause of F or it is inferred by resolution of two clauses C_j, C_ℓ such that $j, \ell < i$. It is well-known that F has a resolution refutation if and only if F is unsatisfiable.

To every resolution refutation $C_1, \ldots, C_s$ we assign a directed acyclic graph G as follows: the vertices of G are the clauses $\{C_i \mid i \in [s]\}$. Moreover, there is an edge $C_j C_i$ in G if and only if C_i is inferred by resolution of C_j and some other clause C_ℓ on a variable x in the refutation. We also label the edge $C_j C_i$ with the variable x. Note that there might be two pairs of clauses C_j, C_ℓ and $C_{j'}, C_{\ell'}$ such that resolution on both pairs leads to the same clause C_i. If this is the case, we simply choose one of them to make sure that all vertices in G have indegree at most 2. A resolution refutation is called *regular* if on every directed path in G every variable x appears at most once as a label of an edge. It is known that there is a resolution refutation of F if and only if a regular resolution refutation of F exists [13], but the latter are in general longer [1,26].

In this paper, we will not directly deal with regular resolution proofs thanks to the following well-known result.

Theorem 6. [21] *For every unsatisfiable CNF-formula F, the length of the shortest regular resolution refutation of F is the size of the smallest 1-BP computing Search_F.*

Since in our setting, from an unsatisfied clause we can directly inferred an unsatisfied parity constraint, we can use the following simple consequence.

Corollary 7. *For every unsatisfiable Tseitin-formula $T(G,c)$, the length of the shortest regular resolution refutation of $T(G,c)$ is at least the size of the smallest 1-BP computing $\mathrm{SearchVertex}(G, c)$.*

3   Reduction from Unsatisfiable to Satisfiable Formulas

To show our main result, we give a reduction from unsatisfiable to satisfiable Tseitin-formulas as in [20]. There it was shown that, given a 1-BP B computing SearchVertex(G, c) for an unsatisfiable Tseitin-formula $T(G, c)$, one can construct a 1-BP B' computing the function of a *satisfiable* Tseitin-formula $T(G, c^*)$ such that $|B'|$ is quasipolynomial in $|B|$. Then good lower bounds on the size of B' yield lower bounds for regular refutation by Corollary 7. To give tighter results, we give a version of the reduction from unsatisfiable to satisfiable Tseitin-formulas where the target representation for $T(G, c^*)$ is not 1-BP but the more succinct DNNF. This lets us decrease the size of the representation from pseudopolynomial to polynomial which, with tight lower bounds in the later parts of the paper, will yield Theorem 1.

Theorem 8. *Let $T(G, c)$ be an unsatisfiable Tseitin-formula where G is connected and let S be the length of its smallest resolution refutation. Then there exists for every satisfiable Tseitin-formula $T(G, c^*)$ a DNNF of size $O(S \times |V(G)|)$ computing it.*

In the proof of Theorem 8, we heavily rely on results from [20] in particular the notion of well-structuredness that we present in Sect. 3.1. In Sect. 3.2 we will then prove Theorem 8.

3.1   Well-Structured Branching Programs for SearchVertex(G, c)

In a well-structured 1-BP computing SearchVertex(G, c), every decision node u_k for a variable x_e will compute SearchVertex(G_k, c_k) where G_k is a *connected* sub-graph of G containing the edge $e := ab$, and c_k is a charge function such that $T(G_k, c_k)$ is unsatisfiable. Since u_k deals with $T(G_k, c_k)$, its 0- and 1-successors u_{k_0} and u_{k_1} will work on $T(G_k, c_k)|\ell_e$ for $\ell_e = \overline{x_e}$ and $\ell_e = x_e$, respectively. $T(G_k, c_k)|\ell_e$ is a Tseitin-formula whose underlying graph is $G_k - e$ and whose charge function is c_k or $c_k + 1_a + 1_b \mod 2$ depending on ℓ_e. For convenience, we introduce the notation $\gamma_k(x_e) = c_k + 1_a + 1_b \mod 2$ and $\gamma_k(\overline{x_e}) = c_k$. Since G_k is connected, $G_k - e$ has at most two connected components. Let G_k^a and G_k^b denote the components of $G_k - e$ containing a and b, respectively. Note that $G_k^a = G_k^b$ when e is not a bridge of G_k. Let $\gamma_k^a(\ell_e)$ and $\gamma_k^b(\ell_e)$ denote the restriction of $\gamma_k(\ell_e)$ to the vertices of G_k^a and G_k^b, respectively. While the graph for $T(G_k, c_k)|\ell_e$ has at most two connected components, exactly one of them holds an odd total charge, so only the Tseitin-formula corresponding to that component is unsatisfiable. Well-structuredness states that u_{k_0} and u_{k_1} each deal with that unique connected component.

Example 9. Consider the graph G_k shown on the left in Fig. 1. Black nodes have charge 0 and white nodes have charge 1. The corresponding Tseitin-formula $T(G_k, c_k)$ is unsatisfiable because there is an odd number of white nodes. Let $e := ab$. Then $T(G_k, c_k)|\overline{x_e}$ is the Tseitin-formula for the graph $G_k - e$ with charges as shown in the middle of Fig. 1. Note that $T(G_k, c_k)|\overline{x_e}$ is unsat-

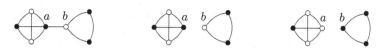

Fig. 1. The graphs of Example 9. On the left the graph G_k, in the middle the result after assigning 0 to x_e, on the right after assigning 1 to x_e.

isfiable because of the charges in the triangle component G_k^b. The repartition of charges for $T(G_k, c_k)|x_e$ illustrated on the right of Fig. 1 shows that $T(G_k, c_k)|x_e$ is unsatisfiable because of the charges in the rombus component G_k^a. Well-structuredness will ensure that, if u_k computes SearchVertex(G_k, c_k) and decides x_e, then u_{k_0} computes SearchVertex$(G_k^b, \gamma_k^b(\overline{x_e}))$ and u_{k_1} computes SearchVertex$(G_k^a, \gamma_k^a(x_e))$.

Definition 10. *Let $T(G, c)$ be an unsatisfiable Tseitin-formula where G is a connected graph. A branching program B computing SearchVertex(G, c) is well-structured when, for all nodes u_k of B, there exists a connected subgraph G_k of G and a charge function c_k such that $T(G_k, c_k)$ is unsatisfiable, u_k computes SearchVertex(G_k, c_k) and*

1. *if u_k is the source, then $G_k = G$ and $c_k = c$,*
2. *if u_k is a sink corresponding to $v \in V(G)$, then $G_k = (\{v\}, \emptyset)$ and $c_k = 1_v$,*
3. *if u_k is a decision node for x_{ab} with 0- and 1- successors u_{k_0} and u_{k_1}, set $\ell_0 = \overline{x_{ab}}$ and $\ell_1 = x_{ab}$, then for all $i \in \{0, 1\}$, $(G_{k_i}, c_{k_i}) = (G_k^a, \gamma_k^a(\ell_i))$ if $T(G_k^a, \gamma_k^a(\ell_i))$ is unsatisfiable, otherwise $(G_{k_i}, c_{k_i}) = (G_k^b, \gamma_k^b(\ell_i))$.*

We remark that our definition is a slight simplification of that given by Itsykson et al. [20]. It can easily be seen that ours is implied by theirs (see Definition 11 and Proposition 16 in [20]).

Lemma 11. [20, Lemma 17] *Let $T(G, c)$ be an unsatisfiable Tseitin-formula where G is connected and let B be a 1-BP of minimal size[2] computing the relation SearchVertex(G, c). Then B is well-structured.*

3.2 Constructing DNNF from Well-Structured Branching Programs

Similarly to Theorem 14 in [20], we give a reduction from a well-structured 1-BP for SearchVertex(G, c) to a DNNF computing a *satisfiable* formula $T(G, c^*)$.

Lemma 12. *Let G be a connected graph. Let $T(G, c^*)$ and $T(G, c)$ be Tseitin-formulas where $T(G, c^*)$ is satisfiable and $T(G, c)$ unsatisfiable. For every well-structured 1-BP B computing SearchVertex(G, c) there exists a DNNF of size $O(|B| \times |V(G)|)$ computing $T(G, c^*)$.*

Proof. Let $S = |B|$ and denote by $u_1, \dots, u_S$ the nodes of B such that if u_j is a successor of u_i, then $j < i$ (thus u_S is the source of B). For every $i \in [S]$, the

---

[2] [20, Lemma 17] is for *locally minimal* 1-BP, which encompass minimal size 1-BP.

node u_i computes SearchVertex(G_i, c_i). We will show how to iteratively construct
DNNF $D_1, \ldots, D_S$ such that, $D_1 \subseteq D_2 \subseteq \cdots \subseteq D_S$ and, for every $i \in [S]$,

$$\text{for all } v \in V(G_i), \text{ there is a gate } g_v \text{ in } D_i \text{ computing } T(G_i, c_i + 1_v). \quad (*)$$

Observe that, since $T(G_i, c_i)$ is unsatisfiable, $T(G_i, c_i + 1_v)$ is satisfiable for any
$v \in V(G_i)$. We show by induction on i how to construct D_i by extending D_{i-1}
while respecting $(*)$.

For the base case, u_1 is a sink of B, so it computes SearchVertex$(G_v, 1_v)$
where $G_v := (\{v\}, \emptyset)$ for a vertex $v \in V(G)$. Thus we define D_1 as a single
constant-1-node which indeed computes $T(G_v, 1_v + 1_v) = T(G_v, 0)$. So D_1 is a
DNNF respecting $(*)$.

Now for the inductive case, suppose we have the DNNF D_{k-1} satisfying $(*)$.
Consider the node u_k of B. If u_k is a sink of B, then we argue as for D_1 but
since we already have the constant-1-node in D_{k-1} we define $D_k := D_{k-1}$.

Now assume that u_k is a decision node for the variable x_e with 0- and 1-
successors u_{k_0} and u_{k_1}. Recall that u_k computes SearchVertex(G_k, c_k) and let
$e = ab$. There are two cases. If e is not a bridge in G_k then $G_k^a = G_k^b = G_k - e$ and,
by well-structuredness, u_{k_0} computes SearchVertex$(G_k - e, c_k)$ and u_{k_1} computes
SearchVertex$(G_k - e, c_k + 1_a + 1_b)$. For every $v \in V(G_k)$, since $k_0, k_1 < k$, by
induction there is a gate g_v^0 in D_{k_0} computing $T(G_k - e, c_k + 1_v)$ and a gate
g_v^1 in D_{k_1} computing $T(G_k - e, c_k + 1_a + 1_b + 1_v)$. So for every $v \in V(G_k)$ we
add to D_{k-1} an $\vee$-gate g_v whose left input is $\overline{x_e} \wedge g_v^0$ and whose right input is
$x_e \wedge g_v^1$. By construction, g_v computes $T(G_k, c_k + 1_v)$ and the new $\wedge$-gates are
decomposable since e is not an edge of $G_k - e$ and therefore x_e and $\overline{x_e}$ do not
appear in D_{k_0} and D_{k_1}.

Now if $e = ab$ is a bridge in G_k, by well-structuredness, there exist $i \in$
$\{0, 1\}$ and $\ell_e \in \{\overline{x_e}, x_e\}$ such that u_{k_i} computes SearchVertex$(G_k^a, \gamma_k^a(\ell_e))$ and
$u_{k_{1-i}}$ computes SearchVertex$(G_k^b, \gamma_k^b(\overline{\ell_e}))$. We construct a gate g_v computing
$T(G_k, c_k + 1_v)$ for each $v \in V(G_k)$. Assume, without loss of generality, that
$v \in V(G_k^a)$, then

- $T(G_k, c_k + 1_v)|\overline{\ell_e} \equiv T(G_k^a, \gamma_k^a(\overline{\ell_e}) + 1_v) \wedge T(G_k^b, \gamma_k^b(\overline{\ell_e})) \equiv 0$
  (because of the second conjunct which is known to be unsatisfiable), and
- $T(G_k, c_k + 1_v)|\ell_e \equiv T(G_k^a, \gamma_k^a(\ell_e) + 1_v) \wedge T(G_k^b, \gamma_k^b(\ell_e))$

For the second item, since $k_0, k_1 < k$, by induction there is a gate g_v^i in D_{k_i}
computing $T(G_k^a, \gamma_k^a(\ell_e) + 1_v)$ and there is a gate g_b^{1-i} in $D_{k_{1-i}}$ computing
$T(G_k^b, \gamma_k^b(\overline{\ell_e}) + 1_b)$. But $\gamma_k(\ell_e) = \gamma_k(\overline{\ell_e}) + 1_a + 1_b \mod 2$, so $\gamma_k^b(\ell_e) = \gamma_k^b(\overline{\ell_e}) + 1_b$
$\mod 2$, therefore g_b^{i-1} computes the formula $T(G_k^b, \gamma_k^b(\ell_e))$. So we add an $\wedge$-gate
g_v whose left input is ℓ_e and whose right input is $s_v^i \wedge s_b^{1-i}$ and add it to D_{k-1}.
Note that $\wedge$-gates are decomposable since G_k^a and G_k^b share no edge and therefore
D_{k_0} and D_{k_1} are on disjoint sets of variables.

Let D_k be the circuit after all g_v have been added to D_{k-1}. It is a DNNF
satisfying both $D_{k-1} \subseteq D_k$ and $(*)$.

It only remains to bound $|D_S|$. To this end, observe that when constructing
D_k from D_{k-1} we add at most $3 \times |V_k|$ gates, so $|D_S|$ is at most $3(|V_1| + \cdots +$

$|V_S|) = O(S \times |V(G)|)$. Finally, take any root of D_S and delete all gates not reached from it, the resulting circuit is a DNNF D computing a satisfiable Tseitin formula $T(G, c')$. We get a DNNF computing $T(G, c^*)$ using Lemma 5. □

Combining Corollary 7, Lemma 11 and Lemma 12 yields Theorem 8.

4   Adversarial Rectangle Bounds

In this section, we introduce the game we will use to show DNNF lower bounds for Tseitin formulas. It is based on combinatorial rectangles, a basic object of study from communication complexity.

Definition 13. *A (combinatorial) rectangle for a variable partition (X_1, X_2) of a variables set X is defined to be a set of assignments of the form $R = A \times B$ where $A \subseteq \{0,1\}^{X_1}$ and $B \subseteq \{0,1\}^{X_2}$. The rectangle is called balanced when $\frac{|X|}{3} \leq |X_1|, |X_2| \leq \frac{2|X|}{3}$.*

A rectangle on variables X may be seen as a function whose satisfying assignments are exactly the $a \cup b$ for $a \in A$ and $b \in B$, so we sometimes interpret rectangles as Boolean functions whenever it is convenient.

Definition 14. *Let f be a Boolean function. A balanced rectangle cover of f is a collection $\mathcal{R} = \{R_1, \ldots, R_K\}$ of balanced rectangles on $var(f)$, possibly for different partitions of $var(f)$, such that f is equivalent to $\bigvee_{i=1}^{K} R_i$. The minimum number of rectangles in a balanced cover of f is denoted by $R(f)$.*

Theorem 15. *[8] Let D be a DNNF computing a function f, then $R(f) \leq |D|$.*

When trying to show parameterized lower bounds with Theorem 15, one often runs into the problem that it is somewhat inflexible: the partitions of the rectangles in covers have to be balanced, but in parameterized applications this is often undesirable. Instead, to show good lower bounds, one wants to be able to partition in places that allow to cut in complicated subparts of the problem. This is e.g. the underlying technique in [23]. To make this part of the lower bound proofs more explicit and the technique more reusable, we here introduce a refinement of Theorem 15.

We define the adversarial multi-partition rectangle cover game for a function f on variables X and a set $S \subseteq sat(f)$ to be played as follows: two players, the cover player Charlotte and her adversary Adam, construct in several rounds a set $\mathcal{R}$ of combinatorial rectangles that cover the set S respecting f (that is, rectangles in $\mathcal{R}$ contain only models of f). The game starts with $\mathcal{R}$ as the empty set. Charlotte starts a round by choosing an input $a \in S$ and a v-tree T of X. Now Adam chooses a partition (X_1, X_2) of X induced by T. Charlotte ends the round by adding to $\mathcal{R}$ a combinatorial rectangle for this partition and respecting f that covers a. The game is over when S is covered by $\mathcal{R}$. The adversarial multi-partition rectangle complexity of f and S, denoted by $aR(f, S)$ is the minimum number of rounds in which Charlotte can finish the game, whatever the choices of Adam are. The following theorem gives the core technique for showing lower bounds later on. Due to space constraints, the proof is given in the full version.

Theorem 16. *Let D be a complete DNNF computing a function f and let $S \subseteq sat(f)$. Then $aR(f, S) \leq |D|$.*

5   Splitting Parity Constraints

In this section, we will see that rectangles *split* parity constraints in a certain sense and show how this is reflected in the underlying graph of Tseitin-formulas. This will be crucial in proving the DNNF lower bound in the next section with the adversarial multi-partition rectangle cover game.

5.1   Rectangles Induce Sub-constraints for Tseitin-Formulas

Let R be a rectangle for the partition (E_1, E_2) of $E(G)$ such that $R \subseteq sat(T(G, c))$. Assume that there is a vertex v of G incident to edges in E_1 and to edges in E_2, i.e., $E(v) = E_1(v) \cup E_2(v)$ where neither $E_1(v)$ not $E_2(v)$ is empty. We will show that R does not only respect χ_v, but it also respects a sub-constraint of χ_v.

Definition 17. *Let χ_v be a parity constraint on $(x_e)_{e \in E(v)}$. A sub-constraint of χ_v is a parity constraint χ'_v on a non-empty proper subset of the variables of χ_v.*

Lemma 18. *Let $T(G, c)$ be a satisfiable Tseitin-formula and let R be a rectangle for the partition (E_1, E_2) of $E(G)$ such that $R \subseteq sat(T(G, c))$. If $v \in V(G)$ is incident to edges in E_1 and to edges in E_2, then there exists a sub-constraint χ'_v of χ_v such that $R \subseteq sat(T(G, c) \wedge \chi'_v)$.*

Proof. Let $a_1 \cup a_2 \in R$ where a_1 is an assignment to E_1 and a_2 an assignment to E_2. Let $a_1(v)$ and $a_2(v)$ denote the restriction of a_1 and a_2 to $E_1(v)$ and $E_2(v)$, respectively. We claim that for all $a'_1 \cup a'_2 \in R$, we have that $a'_1(v)$ and $a_1(v)$ have the same parity, that is, $a_1(v)$ assigns an odd number of variables of $E_1(v)$ to 1 if and only if it is also the case for $a'_1(v)$. Indeed if $a_1(v)$ and $a'_1(v)$ have different parities, then so do $a_1(v) \cup a_2(v)$ and $a'_1(v) \cup a_2(v)$. So either $a_1 \cup a_2$ or $a'_1 \cup a_2$ falsifies χ_v, but both assignments are in R, so $a_1(v)$ and $a'_1(v)$ cannot have different parities as this contradicts $R \subseteq sat(T(G, c))$. Let c_1 be the parity of $a_1(v)$, then we have that assignments in R must satisfy $\chi'_v : \sum_{e \in E_1(v)} x_e = c_1$ mod 2, so $R \subseteq sat(T(G, c) \wedge \chi'_v)$. □

Renaming χ'_v as χ^1_v and adopting notations from the proof, one sees that $\chi^1_v \wedge \chi_v \equiv \chi^1_v \wedge \chi^2_v$ where $\chi^2_v : \sum_{e \in E_2(v)} x_e = c(v) + c_1$ mod 2. So R respects the formula $(T(G, c) - \chi_v) \wedge \chi^1_v \wedge \chi^2_v$ where $(T(G, c) - \chi_v)$ is the formula obtained by removing all clauses of χ_v from $T(G, c)$. In this sense, the rectangle is splitting the constraint χ_v into two subconstraints on disjoint variables. Since $\chi_v \equiv (\chi^1_v \wedge \chi^2_v) \vee (\overline{\chi^1_v} \wedge \overline{\chi^2_v})$ it is plausible that potentially many models of χ_v are not in R. We show that this is true in the next section.

5.2 Vertex Splitting and Sub-constraints for Tseitin-Formulas

Let $v \in V(G)$ and let (N_1, N_2) be a proper partition of $N(v)$, that is, neither N_1 nor N_2 is empty. The graph G' we get by *splitting* v along (N_1, N_2) is defined as the graph we get by deleting v, adding two vertices v^1 and v^2, and connecting v^1 to all vertices in N_1 and v^2 to all vertices in N_2. We now show that splitting a vertex v in a graph G has the same effect as adding a sub-constraint of χ_v.

Lemma 19. *Let $T(G, c)$ be a Tseitin-formula. Let $v \in V(G)$ and let (N_1, N_2) be a proper partition of $N(v)$. Let c_1 and c_2 be such that $c_1 + c_2 = c(v) \mod 2$ and let $\chi_v^i : \sum_{u \in N_i} x_{uv} = c_i \mod 2$ for $i \in \{1, 2\}$ be sub-constraints of χ_v. Call G' the result of splitting v along (N_1, N_2) and set*

$$c'(u) := \begin{cases} c(u), & \text{if } u \in V(G) \setminus \{v\} \\ c_i, & \text{if } u = v^i, i \in \{1, 2\} \end{cases}$$

There is a bijection $\rho : var(T(G, c)) \to var(T(G', c'))$ acting as a renaming of the variables such that $T(G', c') \equiv (T(G, c) \wedge \chi_v^1) \circ \rho$.

Proof. Denote by $T(G, c) - \chi_v$ the formula equivalent to the conjunction of all χ_u for $u \in V(G) \setminus \{v\}$. Then $T(G, c) \wedge \chi_v^1 \equiv (T(G, c) - \chi_v) \wedge \chi_v^1 \wedge \chi_v^2$. The constraints χ_u for $u \in V(G) \setminus \{v\}$ appear in both $T(G', c')$ and in $T(G, c) - \chi_v$ and the sub-constraints χ_v^1 and χ_v^2 are exactly the constraints for v^1 and v^2 in $T(G', c')$ modulo the variable renaming ρ defined by $\rho(x_{uv}) = x_{uv^1}$ when $u \in N_1$, $\rho(x_{uv}) = x_{uv^2}$ when $u \in N_2$, and $\rho(x_e) = x_e$ when v is not incident to e. □

Intuitely, Lemma 19 says that splitting a vertex in G and adding sub-constraint are essentially the same operation. This allows us to compute the number of models of a Tseitin-formula to which a sub-constraint was added.

Lemma 20. *Let $T(G, c)$ be a satisfiable Tseitin-formula where G is connected. Define $T(G', c')$ as in Lemma 19. If G' is connected then $T(G', c')$ has $2^{|E(G)| - |V(G)|}$ models.*

Proof. By Proposition 3, $T(G', c')$ is satisfiable since $T(G, c)$ is satisfiable and $\sum_{u \in V(G')} c'(u) = \sum_{u \in V(G)} c(u) = 0 \mod 2$. Using Proposition 4 yields that $T(G', c')$ has $2^{|E(G')| - |V(G')| + 1} = 2^{|E(G)| - |V(G)|}$ models. □

Lemma 21. *Let $T(G, c)$ be a satisfiable Tseitin-formula where G is connected. Let $\{v_1, \ldots, v_k\}$ be an independent set in G. For all $i \in [k]$ let (N_1^i, N_2^i) be a proper partition of $N(v_i)$ and let $\chi_{v_i}' : \sum_{u \in N_1^i} x_{uv_i} = c_i \mod 2$. If the graph obtained by splitting all v_i along (N_1^i, N_2^i) is connected, then the formula $T(G, c) \wedge \chi_{v_1}' \wedge \cdots \wedge \chi_{v_k}'$ has $2^{|E(G)| - |V(G)| - k + 1}$ models.*

Proof. An easy induction based on Lemma 19 and Lemma 20. The induction works since, $\{v_1, \ldots, v_k\}$ being an independant set, the edges to modify by splitting v_i are still in the graph where $v_1, \ldots, v_{i-1}$ have been split. □

5.3 Vertex Splitting in 3-Connected Graphs

When we want to apply the results of the last sections to bound the size of
rectangles, we require that the graph G remains connected after splitting vertices.
This is obviously not true for all choices of vertex splits, but here we will see
that if G is sufficiently connected, then we can always chose a large subset of
any set of potential splits such that, after applying the split for this subset, G
remains connected.

Lemma 22. *Let G be a 3-connected graph of and let $\{v_1, \ldots, v_k\}$ be an independent set in G. For every $i \in [k]$ let (N_1^i, N_2^i) be a proper partition of $N(v_i)$. Then there is a subset S of $\{v_1, \ldots, v_k\}$ of size at least $k/3$ such that the graph resulting from splitting all $v_i \in S$ along the corresponding (N_1^i, N_2^i) is connected.*

Proof. Let $C_1, \ldots, C_r$ be the connected components of the graph G_1 that we get
by splitting *all* v_i. If G_1 is connected, then we can set $S = \{v_1, \ldots, v_k\}$ and we
are done. So assume that $r > 1$ in the following. Now add for every $i \in [k]$ the
edge (v_i^1, v_i^2). Call this edge set L (for *links*) and the resulting graph G_2. Note
that G_2 is connected and for every edge set $E' \subseteq L$ we have that $G_2 \setminus E'$ is
connected if and only if G is connected after splitting the vertices corresponding
to the edges in E'. Denote by L_{in} the edges in L whose end points both lie in
some component C_j and let $L_{out} := L \setminus L_{in}$.

We claim that for every C_j, at least three edges in L_{out} are incident to a
vertex in C_j. Since G_2 is connected but the set C_j is a connected component of
$G_2 \setminus L = G_1$, there must be at least one edge in L incident to a vertex in C_j.
That vertex is by construction one of $v_1, \ldots, v_k$, say it is v_i. Since $N_1^i \neq \emptyset$ and
$N_2^i \neq \emptyset$, we have that v_i has a neighbor w in C_j and, $w \notin \{v_1, \ldots, v_k\}$ since
it is an independent set. Now let L_{out}^j be the edges in L_{out} that have an end
point in C_j. Note that if we delete the vertices $S^j \subseteq \{v_1, \ldots, v_k\}$ for which the
edges in L_{out}^j were introduced in the construction of G_2, then a subset of C_j
becomes disconnected from the rest of the graph (which is non-empty because
there is at least one component different from C_j in G_2 which also contains a
vertex not in $\{v_1, \ldots, v_k\}$ by the same reasoning as before). But then, because
G is 3-connected, there must be at least three edges in L_{out}^j. Let $k' := |L_{out}|$,
then since $|L_{out}| = \frac{1}{2} \sum_{j=1}^{r} |L_{out}^j|$, we have that

$$r \leq \frac{2}{3} k'.$$

Now contract all components C_i in G_2 and call the resulting graph G_3. Note
that G_3 is connected and that $E(G_3) = L_{out}$. Moreover, whenever $G_3 \setminus E^*$ is
connected for some $E^* \subseteq L_{out}$, then G is connected after splitting the corresponding vertices. Choose any spanning tree T of G_3. Then $|E(T)| = r - 1$ and
deleting $E^* := L_{out} \setminus E(T)$ leaves G_3 connected. Thus the graph G^* we get from
G after splitting the vertices corresponding to E^* is connected. We have

$$|E^*| = |L_{out}| - |E(T)| = k' - (r - 1) > \frac{k'}{3}.$$

Now observe that in G we can safely split all $k - k'$ vertices v_i that correspond to edges $v_i^1 v_i^2$ such that v_i^1 and v_i^2 lie in the same component of G_1 without disconnecting the graph. Thus, overall we can split a set of size

$$k - k' + |E^*| > k - k' + \frac{k'}{3} \geq \frac{k}{3}$$

in G such that the resulting graph remains connected.   □

6   DNNF Lower Bounds for Tseitin-Formulas

In this section, we use the results of the previous sections to show our lower bounds for DNNF computing Tseitin-formulas. To this end, we first show that we can restrict ourselves to the case of 3-connected graphs.

6.1   Reduction from Connected to 3-Connected Graphs

In [7], Bodlaender and Koster study how separators can be used in the context of treewidth. They call a separator S *safe for treewidth* if there exists a connected component of $G \setminus S$ whose vertex set V' is such that $tw(G[S \cup V'] + clique(S)) = tw(G)$, where $G[S \cup V'] + clique(S)$ is the graph induced on $S \cup V'$ with additional edges that pairwise connect all vertices in S.

Lemma 23. [7, Corollary 15] *Every separator of size 1 is safe for treewidth. When G has no separator of size 1, every separator of size 2 is safe for treewidth.*

Remember that a *topological minor* H of a G is a graph that can be constructed from G by iteratively applying the following operations:

- edge deletion,
- deletion of isolated vertices, or
- subdivision elimination: if $\deg(v) = 2$ delete v and connect its two neighbors.

Lemma 24. *Let H be a topological minor of G. If the satisfiable Tseitin-formula $T(G, 0)$ has a DNNF of size s, then so does $T(H, 0)$.*

Proof. Edge deletion corresponds to conditioning the variable by 0 so it cannot increase the size of a DNNF. Deletion of an isolated vertex does not change the Tseitin-formula. Finally, let e_1, e_2 be the edges incident to a vertex of degree 2. Since we assume that all charges $c(v)$ are 0, in every satisfying assignment, x_{e_1} and x_{e_2} take the same value. Thus we can simply forget the variable of x_{e_2} which does not increase the size of a DNNF [11].   □

Lemma 25. *Let G be a graph with treewidth at least 3. Then G has a 3-connected topological minor H with $tw(H) = tw(G)$.*

Proof (sketch). We use Lemma 23 to iteratively compute topological minors that have the same treewidth as the original graph. To this end, while there is a minimal size separator S of size at most 2, we choose a component of $G \setminus S$ on vertices V' such that $G[S \cup V'] + clique(S)$ has the same treewidth as G and iterate with that graph. When this process stops, the resulting graph H has no separator of size 2 anymore and it can be checked that H has more than 3 vertices, so it is 3-connected. It just has to be verified that H is a topological minor of G which one can do by checking that in every iteration one computes a topological minor. The details are given in the full version.   □

6.2   Proof of the DNNF Lower Bound and of the Main Result

Lemma 26. *Let $T(G,c)$ be a satisfiable Tseitin-formula where G is a connected graph with maximum degree at most Δ. Any complete DNNF computing $T(G,c)$ has size at least $2^{\Omega(tw(G)/\Delta)}$.*

Proof. By Lemma 5 we can set $c = 0$. By Lemmas 24 and 25 we can assume that G is 3-connected. We show that the adversarial multi-partition rectangle complexity is lower-bounded by 2^k for $k := \frac{2tw(G)}{9\Delta}$. To this end, we will show that the rectangles that Charlotte can construct after Adam's answer are never bigger than $2^{|E(G)|-|V(G)|-k+1}$. Since $T(G,c)$ has $2^{|E(G)|-|V(G)|+1}$ models, the claim then follows.

So let Charlotte choose an assignment a and a v-tree T. Note that since the variables of $T(G,0)$ are the edges of G, the v-tree T is also a branch decomposition of G. Now by the definition of branchwidth, Adam can choose a cut of T inducing a partition (E_1, E_2) of $E(G)$ for which there exists a set $V' \in V(G)$ of at least $bw(G) \geq \frac{2}{3}tw(G)$ vertices incident to edges in E_1 and to edges in E_2.

G has maximum degree Δ so there is an independent set $V'' \subset V'$ of size at least $\frac{|V'|}{\Delta}$. Since G is 3-connected, by Lemma 22 there is a subset $V^* \subseteq V''$ of size at least $\frac{|V''|}{3} \geq \frac{2tw(G)}{9\Delta} = k$ such that G remains connected after splitting of the nodes in V^* along the partition of their neighbors induced by the edges partition (E_1, E_2). Using Lemma 18, we find that any rectangle R for the partition (E_1, E_2) respects a sub-constraint χ'_v for each $v \in V^*$. So R respects $T(G,0) \wedge \bigwedge_{v \in V^*} \chi'_v$. Finally, Lemma 21 shows that $|R| \leq 2^{|E(G)|-|V(G)|-k+1}$, as required.   □

Theorem 1 is now a direct consequence of Theorem 8, Lemma 26 and Lemma 5

7   Conclusion

We have shown that the unsatisfiable Tseitin-formulas with polynomial length of regular resolution refutations are completely determined by the treewidth of their graphs. We did this by connecting lower bounds on these types of refutations to size bounds on DNNF representations of Tseitin-formulas. Moreover, we introduced a new two-player game that allowed us to show DNNF lower bounds.

Let us discuss some questions that we think are worth exploring in the future. First, it would be interesting to see if a $2^{\Omega(tw(G))}$ lower bound for the refutation of Tseitin-formulas can also be shown for general resolution. In that case the length of resolution refutations would essentially be the same as that regular resolution refutations for Tseitin formulas. Note that this is somewhat plausible since other measures like space and width are known to be the same for the two proof systems for these formulas [15].

Another question is the relation between knowledge compilation and proof complexity. As far as we are aware, our Theorem 8 is the first result that connects bounds on DNNF to such in proof complexity. It would be interesting to see if this connection can be strenghtened to other classes of instances, other proof systems, representations from knowledge compilation and measures on proofs and representations, respectively.

References

1. Alekhnovich, M., Johannsen, J., Pitassi, T., Urquhart, A.: An exponential separation between regular and general resolution. Theory Comput. **3**(1), 81–102 (2007). https://doi.org/10.4086/toc.2007.v003a005
2. Alekhnovich, M., Razborov, A.A.: Satisfiability, branch-width and tseitin tautologies. Comput. Complex. **20**(4), 649–678 (2011). https://doi.org/10.1007/s00037-011-0033-1
3. Atserias, A., Bonacina, I., de Rezende, S.F., Lauria, M., Nordström, J., Razborov, A.A.: Clique is hard on average for regular resolution. In: Diakonikolas, I., Kempe, D., Henzinger, M. (eds.) Proceedings of the 50th Annual ACM SIGACT Symposium on Theory of Computing, STOC 2018, Los Angeles, CA, USA, 25–29 June, 2018. pp. 866–877. ACM (2018). https://doi.org/10.1145/3188745.3188856
4. Beame, P., Beck, C., Impagliazzo, R.: Time-space tradeoffs in resolution: superpolynomial lower bounds for superlinear space. In: Karloff, H.J., Pitassi, T. (eds.) Proceedings of the 44th Symposium on Theory of Computing Conference, STOC 2012, New York, NY, USA, 19–22 May, 2012, pp. 213–232. ACM (2012). https://doi.org/10.1145/2213977.2213999
5. Beck, C., Impagliazzo, R.: Strong ETH holds for regular resolution. In: Boneh, D., Roughgarden, T., Feigenbaum, J. (eds.) Symposium on Theory of Computing Conference, STOC 2013, Palo Alto, CA, USA, 1–4 June, 2013. pp. 487–494. ACM (2013). https://doi.org/10.1145/2488608.2488669
6. Ben-Sasson, E.: Hard examples for the bounded depth frege proof system. Comput. Complex. **11**(3-4), 109–136 (2002). https://doi.org/10.1007/s00037-002-0172-5
7. Bodlaender, H.L., Koster, A.M.C.A.: Safe separators for treewidth. Discret. Math. **306**(3), 337–350 (2006). https://doi.org/10.1016/j.disc.2005.12.017
8. Bova, S., Capelli, F., Mengel, S., Slivovsky, F.: Knowledge compilation meets communication complexity. In: Kambhampati, S. (ed.) Proceedings of the Twenty-Fifth International Joint Conference on Artificial Intelligence, IJCAI 2016, New York, NY, USA, 9–15 July 2016, pp. 1008–1014. IJCAI/AAAI Press (2016). http://www.ijcai.org/Abstract/16/147

9. Buss, S., Nordström, J.: Proof complexity and sat solving. Chapter to appear in the 2nd edition of Handbook of Satisfiability, Draft version available at https://www.math.ucsd.edu/~sbuss/ResearchWeb/ProofComplexitySAT (2019)
10. Darwiche, A.: Decomposable negation normal form. J. ACM **48**(4), 608–647 (2001). https://doi.org/10.1145/502090.502091
11. Darwiche, A., Marquis, P.: A knowledge compilation map. J. Artif. Intell. Res. **17**, 229–264 (2002). https://doi.org/10.1613/jair.989
12. Davis, M., Logemann, G., Loveland, D.W.: A machine program for theorem-proving. Commun. ACM **5**(7), 394–397 (1962). https://doi.org/10.1145/368273.368557
13. Davis, M., Putnam, H.: A computing procedure for quantification theory. J. ACM **7**(3), 201–215 (1960). https://doi.org/10.1145/321033.321034
14. Galesi, N., Itsykson, D., Riazanov, A., Sofronova, A.: Bounded-depth frege complexity of tseitin formulas for all graphs. In: Rossmanith, P., Heggernes, P., Katoen, J. (eds.) 44th International Symposium on Mathematical Foundations of Computer Science, MFCS 2019, August 26–30, 2019, Aachen, Germany. LIPIcs, vol. 138, pp. 49:1–49:15. Schloss Dagstuhl - Leibniz-Zentrum für Informatik (2019). https://doi.org/10.4230/LIPIcs.MFCS.2019.49
15. Galesi, N., Talebanfard, N., Torán, J.: Cops-robber games and the resolution of tseitin formulas. ACM Trans. Comput. Theory **12**(2), 9:1–9:22 (2020). https://doi.org/10.1145/3378667
16. Glinskih, L., Itsykson, D.: Satisfiable tseitin formulas are hard for nondeterministic read-once branching programs. In: Larsen, K.G., Bodlaender, H.L., Raskin, J. (eds.) 42nd International Symposium on Mathematical Foundations of Computer Science, MFCS 2017, August 21–25, 2017 - Aalborg, Denmark. LIPIcs, vol. 83, pp. 26:1–26:12. Schloss Dagstuhl - Leibniz-Zentrum für Informatik (2017). https://doi.org/10.4230/LIPIcs.MFCS.2017.26
17. Goerdt, A.: Regular resolution versus unrestricted resolution. SIAM J. Comput. **22**(4), 661–683 (1993). https://doi.org/10.1137/0222044
18. Harvey, D.J., Wood, D.R.: Parameters tied to treewidth. J. Graph Theory **84**(4), 364–385 (2017). https://doi.org/10.1002/jgt.22030
19. Itsykson, D., Oparin, V.: Graph expansion, tseitin formulas and resolution proofs for CSP. In: Bulatov, A.A., Shur, A.M. (eds.) CSR 2013. LNCS, vol. 7913, pp. 162–173. Springer, Heidelberg (2013). https://doi.org/10.1007/978-3-642-38536-0_14
20. Itsykson, D., Riazanov, A., Sagunov, D., Smirnov, P.: Almost tight lower bounds on regular resolution refutations of tseitin formulas for all constant-degree graphs. Electron. Colloquium Comput. Complex. **26**, 178 (2019). https://eccc.weizmann.ac.il/report/2019/178
21. Lovász, L., Naor, M., Newman, I., Wigderson, A.: Search problems in the decision tree model. SIAM J. Discret. Math. **8**(1), 119–132 (1995). https://doi.org/10.1137/S0895480192233867
22. Nordström, J.: On the interplay between proof complexity and SAT solving. ACM SIGLOG News **2**(3), 19–44 (2015). https://dl.acm.org/citation.cfm?id=2815497
23. Razgon, I.: On the read-once property of branching programs and cnfs of bounded treewidth. Algorithmica **75**(2), 277–294 (2016). https://doi.org/10.1007/s00453-015-0059-x
24. Tseitin, G.: On the complexity of derivation in propositional calculus. Stud. Constructive Math. Math. Logic Part **2**, 115–125 (1968)
25. Urquhart, A.: Hard examples for resolution. J. ACM **34**(1), 209–219 (1987). https://doi.org/10.1145/7531.8928

26. Urquhart, A.: A near-optimal separation of regular and general resolution. SIAM J. Comput. **40**(1), 107–121 (2011). https://doi.org/10.1137/090772897
27. Vinyals, M., Elffers, J., Johannsen, J., Nordström, J.: Simplified and improved separations between regular and general resolution by lifting. In: Pulina, L., Seidl, M. (eds.) SAT 2020. LNCS, vol. 12178, pp. 182–200. Springer, Cham (2020). https://doi.org/10.1007/978-3-030-51825-7_14

Weighted Model Counting Without Parameter Variables

Paulius Dilkas[1]([⊠]) and Vaishak Belle[1,2]

[1] University of Edinburgh, Edinburgh, UK
p.dilkas@sms.ed.ac.uk, vaishak@ed.ac.uk
[2] Alan Turing Institute, London, UK

Abstract. Weighted model counting (WMC) is a powerful computational technique for a variety of problems, especially commonly used for probabilistic inference. However, the standard definition of WMC that puts weights on literals often necessitates WMC encodings to include additional variables and clauses just so each weight can be attached to a literal. This paper complements previous work by considering WMC instances in their full generality and using recent state-of-the-art WMC techniques based on pseudo-Boolean function manipulation, competitive with the more traditional WMC algorithms based on knowledge compilation and backtracking search. We present an algorithm that transforms WMC instances into a format based on pseudo-Boolean functions while eliminating around 43 % of variables on average across various Bayesian network encodings. Moreover, we identify sufficient conditions for such a variable removal to be possible. Our experiments show significant improvement in WMC-based Bayesian network inference, outperforming the current state of the art.

Keywords: Weighted model counting · Probabilistic inference · Bayesian networks

1 Introduction

Weighted model counting (WMC), i.e., a generalisation of propositional model counting that assigns weights to literals and computes the total weight of all models of a propositional formula [11], has emerged as a powerful computational framework for problems in many domains, e.g., probabilistic graphical models such as Bayesian networks and Markov networks [3,8,9,15,32], neuro-symbolic artificial intelligence [37], probabilistic programs [26], and probabilistic logic programs [21]. It has been extended to support continuous variables [6], infinite domains [4], first-order logic [24,36], and arbitrary semirings [5,27]. However, as the definition of WMC puts weights on literals, additional variables often need to be added for the sole purpose of holding a weight [3,8,9,15,32]. This can be particularly detrimental to WMC algorithms that rely on variable ordering heuristics.

© Springer Nature Switzerland AG 2021
C.-M. Li and F. Manyà (Eds.): SAT 2021, LNCS 12831, pp. 134–151, 2021.
https://doi.org/10.1007/978-3-030-80223-3_10

One approach to this problem considers weighted clauses and probabilistic semantics based on Markov networks [22]. However, with a new representation comes the need to invent new encodings and inference algorithms. Our work is similar in spirit in that it introduces a new representation for computational problems but can reuse recent WMC algorithms based on pseudo-Boolean function manipulation, namely, ADDMC [19] and DPMC [20]. Furthermore, we identify sufficient conditions for transforming a WMC instance into our new format. As many WMC inference algorithms [16,29] work by compilation to tractable representations such as arithmetic circuits, deterministic, decomposable negation normal form [14], and sentential decision diagrams (SDDs) [17], another way to avoid parameter variables could be via direct compilation to a more convenient representation. Direct compilation of Bayesian networks to SDDs has been investigated [13]. However, SDDs only support weights on literals, and so are not expressive enough to avoid the issue. To the best of the authors' knowledge, neither approach [13,22] has a publicly available implementation.

In this work, we introduce a way to transform WMC problems into a new format based on pseudo-Boolean functions—*pseudo-Boolean projection* (PBP). We formally show that every WMC problem instance has a corresponding PBP instance and identify conditions under which this transformation can remove parameter variables. Four out of the five known WMC encodings for Bayesian networks [3,8,9,15,32] can indeed be simplified in this manner. We are able to eliminate 43 % of variables on average and up to 99 % on some instances. This transformation enables two encodings that were previously incompatible with most WMC algorithms (due to using a different definition of WMC [8,9]) to be run with ADDMC and DPMC and results in a significant performance boost for one other encoding, making it about three times faster than the state of the art. Finally, our theoretical contributions result in a convenient algebraic way of reasoning about two-valued pseudo-Boolean functions and position WMC encodings on common ground, identifying their key properties and assumptions.

2   Weighted Model Counting

We begin with an overview of some notation and terminology. We use $\land$, $\lor$, $\neg$, $\Rightarrow$, and $\Leftrightarrow$ to denote conjunction, disjunction, negation, material implication, and material biconditional, respectively. Throughout the paper, we use set-theoretic notation for many concepts in logic. A *clause* is a set of literals that are part of an implicit disjunction. Similarly, a *formula* in CNF is a set of clauses that are part of an implicit conjunction. We identify a *model* with a set of variables that correspond to the positive literals in the model (and all other variables are the negative literals of the model). We can then define the *cardinality* of a model as the cardinality of this set. For example, let $\phi = (\neg a \lor b) \land a$ be a propositional formula over variables a and b. Then an equivalent set-theoretic representation of ϕ is $\{\{\neg a, b\}, \{a\}\}$. Any subset of $\{a, b\}$ is an interpretation of ϕ, e.g., $\{a, b\}$ is a model of ϕ (written $\{a, b\} \models \phi$) of cardinality two, while $\emptyset$ is an interpretation but not a model. We can now formally define WMC.

Definition 1 (WMC). *A WMC instance is a tuple* (ϕ, X_I, X_P, w), *where* X_I *is the set of* indicator variables, X_P *is the set of* parameter variables *(with* $X_I \cap X_P = \emptyset$*),* ϕ *is a propositional formula in CNF over* $X_I \cup X_P$, *and* $w \colon X_I \cup X_P \cup \{\neg x \mid x \in X_I \cup X_P\} \to \mathbb{R}$ *is a* weight function *such that* $w(x) = w(\neg x) = 1$ *for all* $x \in X_I$. *The* answer *of the instance is* $\sum_{Y \models \phi} \prod_{Y \models l} w(l)$.

That is, the answer to a WMC instance is the sum of the weights of all models of ϕ, where the weight of a model is defined as the product of the weights of all (positive and negative) literals in it. Our definition of WMC is largely based on the standard definition [11], but explicitly partitions variables into indicator and parameter variables. In practice, we identify this partition in one of two ways. If an encoding is generated by Ace[1], then variable types are explicitly identified in a file generated alongside the encoding. Otherwise, we take X_I to be the set of all variables x such that $w(x) = w(\neg x) = 1$. Next, we formally define a variation of the WMC problem used by some of the Bayesian network encodings [8,9].

Definition 2. *Let* ϕ *be a formula over a set of variables* X. *Then* $Y \subseteq X$ *is a* minimum-cardinality model *of* ϕ *if* $Y \models \phi$ *and* $|Y| \le |Z|$ *for all* $Z \models \phi$.

Definition 3 (Minimum-Cardinality WMC). *A* minimum-cardinality WMC *instance consists of the same tuple as a WMC instance, but its* answer *is defined to be* $\sum_{Y \models \phi, \, |Y|=k} \prod_{Y \models l} w(l)$ *(where* $k = \min_{Y \models \phi} |Y|$*) if* ϕ *is satisfiable, and zero otherwise.*

Example 1. Let $\phi = (x \lor y) \land (\neg x \lor \neg y) \land (\neg x \lor p) \land (\neg y \lor q) \land x$, $X_I = \{x, y\}$, $X_P = \{p, q\}$, $w(p) = 0.2$, $w(q) = 0.8$, and $w(\neg p) = w(\neg q) = 1$. Then ϕ has two models: $\{x, p\}$ and $\{x, p, q\}$ with weights 0.2 and $0.2 \times 0.8 = 0.16$, respectively. The WMC answer is then $0.2 + 0.16 = 0.36$, and the minimum-cardinality WMC answer is 0.2.

2.1 Bayesian Network Encodings

A *Bayesian network* is a directed acyclic graph with random variables as vertices and edges as conditional dependencies. As is common in related literature [15,32], we assume that each variable has a finite number of values. We call a Bayesian network *binary* if every variable has two values. If all variables have finite numbers of values, the probability function associated with each variable v can be represented as a *conditional probability table* (CPT), i.e., a table with a row for each combination of values that v and its parent vertices can take. Each row then also has a *probability*, i.e., a number in $[0, 1]$.

WMC is a well-established technique for Bayesian network inference, particularly effective on networks where most variables have only a few possible values [15]. Many ways of encoding a Bayesian network into a WMC instance have been proposed. We will refer to them based on the initials of the authors and

---

[1] Ace [11] implements most of the Bayesian network encodings and can also be used for compilation (and thus inference). It is available at http://reasoning.cs.ucla.edu/ace/.

the year of publication. Darwiche was the first to suggest the d02 [15] encoding that, in many ways, remains the foundation behind most other encodings. He also introduced the distinction between *indicator* and *parameter variables*; the former represent variable-value pairs in the Bayesian network, while the latter are associated with probabilities in the CPTs. The encoding sbk05 [32] is the only encoding that deviates from this arrangement: for each variable in the Bayesian network, one indicator variable acts simultaneously as a parameter variable. Chavira and Darwiche propose cd05 [8] where they shift from WMC to minimum-cardinality WMC because that allows the encoding to have fewer variables and clauses. In particular, they propose a way to use the same parameter variable to represent all probabilities in a CPT that are equal and keep only clauses that 'imply' parameter variables (i.e., omit clauses where a parameter variable implies indicator variables).[2] In their next encoding, cd06 [9], the same authors optimise the aforementioned implication clauses, choosing the smallest sufficient selection of indicator variables. A decade later, Bart et al. present bklm16 [3] that improves upon cd06 in two ways. First, they optimise the number of indicator variables used per Bayesian network variable from a linear to a logarithmic amount. Second, they introduce a scaling factor that can 'absorb' one probability per Bayesian network variable. However, for this work, we choose to disable the latter improvement since this scaling factor is often small enough to be indistinguishable from zero without the use of arbitrary precision arithmetic, making it completely unusable on realistic instances. Indeed, the reader is free to check that even a small Bayesian network with seven mutually independent binary variables, 0.1 and 0.9 probabilities each, is already big enough for the scaling factor to be exactly equal to zero (as produced by the bklm16 encoder[3]). We suspect that this issue was not identified during the original set of experiments because the authors never looked at numerical answers.

Example 2. Let $\mathcal{B}$ be a Bayesian network with one variable X which has two values x_1 and x_2 with probabilities $\Pr(X = x_1) = 0.2$ and $\Pr(X = x_2) = 0.8$. Let x, y be indicator variables, and p, q be parameter variables. Then Example 1 is both the cd05 and the cd06 encoding of $\mathcal{B}$. The bklm16 encoding is $(x \Rightarrow p) \land (\neg x \Rightarrow q) \land x$ with $w(p) = w(\neg q) = 0.2$, and $w(\neg p) = w(q) = 0.8$. And the d02 encoding is $(\neg x \Rightarrow p) \land (p \Rightarrow \neg x) \land (x \Rightarrow q) \land (q \Rightarrow x) \land \neg x$ with $w(p) = 0.2$, $w(q) = 0.8$, and $w(\neg p) = w(\neg q) = 1$. Note how all other encodings have fewer clauses than d02. While cd05 and cd06 require minimum-cardinality WMC to make this work, bklm16 achieves the same thing by adjusting weights.[4]

3 Pseudo-Boolean Functions

In this work, we propose a more expressive representation for WMC based on pseudo-Boolean functions. A *pseudo-Boolean function* is a function of the form

---

[2] Example 2 demonstrates what we mean by implication clauses.

[3] http://www.cril.univ-artois.fr/kc/bn2cnf.html.

[4] Note that since cd05 and cd06 are minimum-cardinality WMC encodings, they are not supported by most WMC algorithms.

$\{0,1\}^n \to \mathbb{R}$ [7]. Equivalently, let X denote a set with n elements (we will refer to them as *variables*), and 2^X denote its powerset. Then a pseudo-Boolean function can have 2^X as its domain (then it is also known as a *set function*).

Pseudo-Boolean functions, most commonly represented as algebraic decision diagrams (ADDs) [2] (although a tensor-based approach has also been suggested [18,20]), have seen extensive use in value iteration for Markov decision processes [25], both exact and approximate Bayesian network inference [10,23], and sum-product network [30] to Bayesian network conversion [38]. ADDs have been extended to compactly represent additive and multiplicative structure [35], sentences in first-order logic [33], and continuous variables [34], the last of which was also applied to weighted model integration, i.e., the WMC extension for continuous variables [6,28].

Since two-valued pseudo-Boolean functions will be used extensively henceforth, we introduce some new notation. For any propositional formula ϕ over X and $p, q \in \mathbb{R}$, let $[\phi]_q^p \colon 2^X \to \mathbb{R}$ be the pseudo-Boolean function defined as

$$[\phi]_q^p(Y) := \begin{cases} p & \text{if } Y \models \phi \\ q & \text{otherwise} \end{cases}$$

for any $Y \subseteq X$. Next, we define some useful operations on pseudo-Boolean functions. The definitions of multiplication and projection are equivalent to those in previous work [19,20].

Definition 4 (Operations). *Let $f, g \colon 2^X \to \mathbb{R}$ be pseudo-Boolean functions, $x, y \in X$, $Y = \{y_i\}_{i=1}^n \subseteq X$, and $r \in \mathbb{R}$. Operations such as addition and multiplication are defined pointwise, i.e., $(f+g)(Y) := f(Y)+g(Y)$, and likewise for multiplication. Note that properties such as associativity and commutativity are inherited from $\mathbb{R}$. By regarding a real number as a constant pseudo-Boolean function, we can reuse the same definitions to define* scalar *operations as $(r + f)(Y) = r + f(Y)$, and $(r \cdot f)(Y) = r \cdot f(Y)$.*

Restrictions $f|_{x=0}, f|_{x=1} \colon 2^X \to \mathbb{R}$ of f are defined as $f|_{x=0}(Y) := f(Y \setminus \{x\})$, and $f|_{x=1}(Y) := f(Y \cup \{x\})$ for all $Y \subseteq X$.

Projection $\exists_x$ is an endomorphism $\exists_x \colon \mathbb{R}^{2^X} \to \mathbb{R}^{2^X}$ defined as $\exists_x f := f|_{x=1} + f|_{x=0}$. Since projection is commutative (i.e., $\exists_x \exists_y f = \exists_y \exists_x f$) [19,20], we can define $\exists_Y \colon \mathbb{R}^{2^X} \to \mathbb{R}^{2^X}$ as $\exists_Y := \exists_{y_1} \exists_{y_2} \ldots \exists_{y_n}$. Throughout the paper, projection is assumed to have the lowest precedence (e.g., $\exists_x fg = \exists_x(fg)$).

Below we list some properties of the operations on pseudo-Boolean functions discussed in this section that can be conveniently represented using our syntax. The proofs of all these properties follow directly from the definitions.

Proposition 1 (Basic Properties). *For any propositional formulas ϕ and ψ, and $a, b, c, d \in \mathbb{R}$,*

- $[\phi]_b^a = [\neg\phi]_a^b$;
- $c + [\phi]_b^a = [\phi]_{b+c}^{a+c}$;
- $c \cdot [\phi]_b^a = [\phi]_{bc}^{ac}$;

- $[\phi]_b^a \cdot [\phi]_d^c = [\phi]_{bd}^{ac}$;
- $[\phi]_0^1 \cdot [\psi]_0^1 = [\phi \wedge \psi]_0^1$.

And for any pair of pseudo-Boolean functions $f, g: 2^X \to \mathbb{R}$ *and* $x \in X$, $(fg)|_{x=i} = f|_{x=i} \cdot g|_{x=i}$ *for* $i = 0, 1$.

Remark 1. Note that our definitions of binary operations assumed equal domains. For convenience, we can assume domains to shrink whenever a function is independent of some of the variables (i.e., $f|_{x=0} = f|_{x=1}$) and expand for binary operations to make the domains of both functions equal. For instance, let $[x]_0^1, [\neg x]_0^1: 2^{\{x\}} \to \mathbb{R}$ and $[y]_0^1: 2^{\{y\}} \to \mathbb{R}$ be pseudo-Boolean functions. Then $[x]_0^1 \cdot [\neg x]_0^1$ has $2^\emptyset$ as its domain. To multiply $[x]_0^1$ and $[y]_0^1$, we expand $[x]_0^1$ into $\left([x]_0^1\right)': 2^{\{x,y\}} \to \mathbb{R}$ which is defined as $\left([x]_0^1\right)'(Z) := [x]_0^1(Z \cap \{x\})$ for all $Z \subseteq \{x, y\}$ (and equivalently for $[y]_0^1$).

4   Pseudo-Boolean Projection

We introduce a new type of computational problem called *pseudo-Boolean projection* based on two-valued pseudo-Boolean functions. While the same computational framework can handle any pseudo-Boolean functions, two-valued functions are particularly convenient because DPMC can be easily adapted to use them as input. Since we will only encounter functions of the form $[\phi]_b^a$, where ϕ is a conjunction of literals, we can represent it in text as w $\langle\phi\rangle$ a b where $\langle\phi\rangle$ is a representation of ϕ analogous to the representation of a clause in the DIMACS CNF format.

Definition 5 (PBP Instance). *A PBP instance is a tuple* (F, X, ω), *where* X *is the set of variables,* F *is a set of two-valued pseudo-Boolean functions* $2^X \to \mathbb{R}$, *and* $\omega \in \mathbb{R}$ *is the scaling factor.*[5] *Its answer is* $\omega \cdot \left(\exists_X \prod_{f \in F} f\right)(\emptyset)$.

4.1   From WMC to PBP

In this section, we describe an algorithm for transforming WMC instances to the PBP format while removing all parameter variables. We chose to transform existing encodings instead of creating a new one to reuse already-existing techniques for encoding each CPT to its minimal logical representation such as prime implicants and limited forms of resolution [3,8,9]. The transformation algorithm works on four out of the five Bayesian network encodings: bklm16 [3], cd05 [8], cd06 [9], and d02 [15]. There is no obvious way to adjust it to work with sbk05 because the roles of indicator and parameter variables overlap [32].

---

[5]   Adding scaling factor ω to the definition allows us to remove clauses that consist entirely of a single parameter variable. The idea of extracting some of the structure of the WMC instance into an external multiplicative factor was loosely inspired by the bklm16 encoding, where it is used to subsume the most commonly occurring probability of each CPT [3].

Algorithm 1: WMC to PBP transformation

Data: WMC (or minimum-cardinality WMC) instance (ϕ, X_I, X_P, w)
Result: PBP instance (F, X_I, ω)

1 $F \leftarrow \emptyset$;
2 $\omega \leftarrow 1$;
3 **foreach** *clause* $c \in \phi$ **do**
4   **if** $c \cap X_P = \{p\}$ *for some* p *and* $w(p) \neq 1$ **then**
5   **if** $|c| = 1$ **then**
6              $\omega \leftarrow \omega \times w(p)$;
7   **else**
8              $F \leftarrow F \cup \left\{ \left[\bigwedge_{l \in c \setminus \{p\}} \neg l \right]_1^{w(p)} \right\}$;
9   **else if** $\{p \mid \neg p \in c\} \cap X_P = \emptyset$ **then**
10         $F \leftarrow F \cup \{[c]_0^1\}$;

11 **foreach** $v \in X_I$ *such that* $\{[v]_1^p, [\neg v]_1^q\} \subseteq F$ *for some* p *and* q **do**
12     $F \leftarrow F \setminus \{[v]_1^p, [\neg v]_1^q\} \cup \{[v]_q^p\}$;

The algorithm is based on several observations that will be made more precise in Sect. 4.2. First, all weights except for $\{w(p) \mid p \in X_P\}$ are redundant as they either duplicate an already-defined weight or are equal to one. Second, each clause has at most one parameter variable. Third, if the parameter variable is negated, we can ignore the clause (this idea first appears in the cd05 paper [8]). Note that while we formulate our algorithm as a sequel to the WMC encoding procedure primarily because the implementations of Bayesian network WMC encodings are all closed-source, as all transformations in the algorithm are local, it can be efficiently incorporated into a WMC encoding algorithm with no slowdown.

The algorithm is listed as Algorithm 1. The main part of the algorithms is the first loop that iterates over clauses. If a clause consists of a single parameter variable, we incorporate it into ω. If a clause is of the form $\alpha \Rightarrow p$, where $p \in X_P$, and α is a conjunction of literals over X_I, we transform it into a pseudo-Boolean function $[\alpha]_1^{w(p)}$. If a clause $c \in \phi$ has no parameter variables, we reformulate it into a pseudo-Boolean function $[c]_0^1$. Finally, clauses with negative parameter literals are omitted.

As all 'weighted' pseudo-Boolean functions produced by the first loop are of the form $[\alpha]_1^p$ (for some $p \in \mathbb{R}$ and formula α), the second loop merges two functions into one whenever α is a literal. Note that taking into account the order in which clauses are typically generated by encoding algorithms allows us to do this in linear time (i.e., the two mergeable functions will be generated one after the other).

4.2 Correctness Proofs

In this section, we outline key conditions that a (WMC or minimum-cardinality WMC) encoding has to satisfy for Algorithm 1 to output an equivalent PBP instance. We divide the correctness proof into two theorems: Theorem 2 for WMC encodings (i.e., `bklm16` and `d02`) and Theorem 3 for minimum-cardinality WMC encodings (i.e., `cd05` and `cd06`). We begin by listing some properties of pseudo-Boolean functions and establishing a canonical transformation from WMC to PBP.

Theorem 1 (Early Projection [19,20]**).** *Let X and Y be sets of variables. For all pseudo-Boolean functions $f\colon 2^X \to \mathbb{R}$ and $g\colon 2^Y \to \mathbb{R}$, if $x \in X \setminus Y$, then $\exists_x(f \cdot g) = (\exists_x f) \cdot g$.*

Lemma 1. *For any pseudo-Boolean function $f\colon 2^X \to \mathbb{R}$, we have that $(\exists_X f)(\emptyset) = \sum_{Y \subseteq X} f(Y)$.*

Proof. If $X = \{x\}$, then $(\exists_x f)(\emptyset) = (f|_{x=1} + f|_{x=0})(\emptyset) = f|_{x=1}(\emptyset) + f|_{x=0}(\emptyset) = \sum_{Y \subseteq \{x\}} f(Y)$. This easily extends to $|X| > 1$ by the definition of projection on sets of variables.

Proposition 2. *Let (ϕ, X_I, X_P, w) be a WMC instance. Then*

$$\left(\left\{ [c]_0^1 \mid c \in \phi \right\} \cup \left\{ [x]_{w(\neg x)}^{w(x)} \mid x \in X_I \cup X_P \right\}, X_I \cup X_P, 1 \right) \tag{1}$$

is a PBP instance with the same answer (as defined in Definitions 1 and 5).

Proof. Let $f = \prod_{c \in \phi} [c]_0^1$, and $g = \prod_{x \in X_I \cup X_P} [x]_{w(\neg x)}^{w(x)}$. Then the WMC answer of (1) is $(\exists_{X_I \cup X_P} fg)(\emptyset) = \sum_{Y \subseteq X_I \cup X_P} (fg)(Y) = \sum_{Y \subseteq X_I \cup X_P} f(Y)g(Y)$ by Lemma 1. Note that

$$f(Y) = \begin{cases} 1 & \text{if } Y \models \phi, \\ 0 & \text{otherwise,} \end{cases} \quad \text{and} \quad g(Y) = \prod_{Y \models l} w(l),$$

which means that $\sum_{Y \subseteq X_I \cup X_P} f(Y)g(Y) = \sum_{Y \models \phi} \prod_{Y \models l} w(l)$ as required.

Theorem 2 (Correctness for WMC). *Algorithm 1, when given a WMC instance (ϕ, X_I, X_P, w), returns a PBP instance with the same answer (as defined in Definitions 1 and 5), provided either of the two conditions is satisfied:*

1. *for all $p \in X_P$, there is a non-empty family of literals $(l_i)_{i=1}^n$ such that*
   (a) $w(\neg p) = 1$,
   (b) $l_i \in X_I$ or $\neg l_i \in X_I$ for all $i = 1, \ldots, n$,
   (c) and $\{c \in \phi \mid p \in c \text{ or } \neg p \in c\} = \{p \vee \bigvee_{i=1}^n \neg l_i\} \cup \{l_i \vee \neg p \mid i = 1, \ldots, n\}$;
2. *or for all $p \in X_P$,*
   (a) $w(p) + w(\neg p) = 1$,
   (b) for any clause $c \in \phi$, $|c \cap X_P| \leq 1$,
   (c) there is no clause $c \in \phi$ such that $\neg p \in c$,
   (d) if $\{p\} \in \phi$, then there is no clause $c \in \phi$ such that $c \neq \{p\}$ and $p \in c$,
   (e) and for any $c, d \in \phi$ such that $c \neq d$, $p \in c$ and $p \in d$, $\bigwedge_{l \in c \setminus \{p\}} \neg l \wedge \bigwedge_{l \in d \setminus \{p\}} \neg l$ is false.

Condition 1 (for d02) simply states that each parameter variable is equivalent to a conjunction of indicator literals. Condition 2 is for encodings that have implications rather than equivalences associated with parameter variables (which, in this case, is bklm16). It ensures that each clause has at most one positive parameter literal and no negative ones, and that at most one implication clause per any parameter variable $p \in X_P$ can 'force p to be positive'.

Proof. By Proposition 2,

$$\left(\left\{ [c]_0^1 \mid c \in \phi \right\} \cup \left\{ [x]_{w(\neg x)}^{w(x)} \mid x \in X_I \cup X_P \right\}, X_I \cup X_P, 1 \right) \tag{2}$$

is a PBP instance with the same answer as the given WMC instance. By Definition 5, its answer is $\left(\exists_{X_I \cup X_P} \left(\prod_{c \in \phi} [c]_0^1 \right) \prod_{x \in X_I \cup X_P} [x]_{w(\neg x)}^{w(x)} \right) (\emptyset)$. Since both Conditions 1 and 2 ensure that each clause in ϕ has at most one parameter variable, we can partition ϕ into $\phi_* := \{ c \in \phi \mid \mathtt{Vars}(c) \cap X_P = \emptyset \}$ and $\phi_p := \{ c \in \phi \mid \mathtt{Vars}(c) \cap X_P = \{p\} \}$ for all $p \in X_P$. We can then use Theorem 1 to reorder the answer into $\left(\exists_{X_I} \left(\prod_{x \in X_I} [x]_{w(\neg x)}^{w(x)} \right) \left(\prod_{c \in \phi_*} [c]_0^1 \right) \right.$
$\left. \prod_{p \in X_P} \exists_p [p]_{w(\neg p)}^{w(p)} \prod_{c \in \phi_p} [c]_0^1 \right) (\emptyset)$.

Let us first consider how the unfinished WMC instance (F, X_I, ω) after the loop on Lines 3 to 10 differs from (2). Note that Algorithm 1 leaves each $c \in \phi_*$ unchanged, i.e., adds $[c]_0^1$ to F. We can then fix an arbitrary $p \in X_P$ and let F_p be the set of functions added to F as a replacement of ϕ_p. It is sufficient to show that

$$\omega \prod_{f \in F_p} f = \exists_p [p]_{w(\neg p)}^{w(p)} \prod_{c \in \phi_p} [c]_0^1. \tag{3}$$

Note that under Condition 1, $\bigwedge_{c \in \phi_p} c \equiv p \Leftrightarrow \bigwedge_{i=1}^n l_i$ for some family of indicator variable literals $(l_i)_{i=1}^n$. Thus, $\exists_p [p]_{w(\neg p)}^{w(p)} \prod_{c \in \phi_p} [c]_0^1 = \exists_p [p]_1^{w(p)} [p \Leftrightarrow \bigwedge_{i=1}^n l_i]_0^1$. If $w(p) = 1$, then

$$\exists_p [p]_1^{w(p)} \left[p \Leftrightarrow \bigwedge_{i=1}^n l_i \right]_0^1 = \left[p \Leftrightarrow \bigwedge_{i=1}^n l_i \right]_0^1 \Big|_{p=1} + \left[p \Leftrightarrow \bigwedge_{i=1}^n l_i \right]_0^1 \Big|_{p=0}. \tag{4}$$

Since for any input, $\bigwedge_{i=1}^n l_i$ is either true or false, exactly one of the two summands in Eq. (4) will be equal to one, and the other will be equal to zero, and so $[p \Leftrightarrow \bigwedge_{i=1}^n l_i]_0^1 \big|_{p=1} + [p \Leftrightarrow \bigwedge_{i=1}^n l_i]_0^1 \big|_{p=0} = 1$, where 1 is a pseudo-Boolean function that always returns one. On the other side of Eq. (3), since $F_p = \emptyset$, and ω is unchanged, we get $\omega \prod_{f \in F_p} f = 1$, and so Eq. (3) is satisfied under Condition 1 when $w(p) = 1$.

If $w(p) \neq 1$, then $F_p = \left\{ [\bigwedge_{i=1}^n l_i]_1^{w(p)} \right\}$, and $\omega = 1$, and so we want to show that $[\bigwedge_{i=1}^n l_i]_1^{w(p)} = \exists_p [p]_1^{w(p)} [p \Leftrightarrow \bigwedge_{i=1}^n l_i]_0^1$. Indeed, $\exists_p [p]_1^{w(p)} [p \Leftrightarrow \bigwedge_{i=1}^n l_i]_0^1 = w(p) \cdot [\bigwedge_{i=1}^n l_i]_0^1 + [\bigwedge_{i=1}^n l_i]_1^0 = [\bigwedge_{i=1}^n l_i]_1^{w(p)}$. This finishes the proof of the correctness of the first loop under Condition 1.

Now let us assume Condition 2. We still want to prove Eq. (3). If $w(p) = 1$, then $F_p = \emptyset$, and $\omega = 1$, and so the left-hand side of Eq. (3) is equal to one. Then the right-hand side is $\exists_p [p]_0^1 \prod_{c \in \phi_p} [c]_0^1 = \exists_p \left[p \wedge \bigwedge_{c \in \phi_p} c \right]_0^1 = \exists_p [p]_0^1 = 0 + 1 = 1$ since $p \in c$ for every clause $c \in \phi_p$.

If $w(p) \neq 1$, and $\{p\} \in \phi_p$, then, by Condition 2d, $\phi_p = \{\{p\}\}$, and Algorithm 1 produces $F_p = \emptyset$, and $\omega = w(p)$, and so $\exists_p [p]_{w(\neg p)}^{w(p)} [p]_0^1 = \exists_p [p]_0^{w(p)} = w(p) = \omega \prod_{f \in F_p} f$. The only remaining case is when $w(p) \neq 1$ and $\{p\} \notin \phi_p$. Then $\omega = 1$, and $F_p = \left\{ \left[\bigwedge_{l \in c \setminus \{p\}} \neg l \right]_1^{w(p)} \;\middle|\; c \in \phi_p \right\}$, so we need to show that $\prod_{c \in \phi_p} \left[\bigwedge_{l \in c \setminus \{p\}} \neg l \right]_1^{w(p)} = \exists_p [p]_{1-w(p)}^{w(p)} \prod_{c \in \phi_p} [c]_0^1$. We can rearrange the right-hand side as

$$\exists_p [p]_{1-w(p)}^{w(p)} \prod_{c \in \phi_p} [c]_0^1 = \exists_p [p]_{1-w(p)}^{w(p)} \left[p \vee \bigwedge_{c \in \phi_p} c \setminus \{p\} \right]_0^1$$

$$= w(p) + (1 - w(p)) \left[\bigwedge_{c \in \phi_p} c \setminus \{p\} \right]_0^1$$

$$= \left[\bigwedge_{c \in \phi_p} c \setminus \{p\} \right]_{w(p)}^1 = \left[\bigvee_{c \in \phi_p} \bigwedge_{l \in c \setminus \{p\}} \neg l \right]_1^{w(p)} .$$

By Condition 2e, $\bigwedge_{l \in c \setminus \{p\}} \neg l$ can be true for at most one $c \in \phi_p$, and so $\left[\bigvee_{c \in \phi_p} \bigwedge_{l \in c \setminus \{p\}} \neg l \right]_1^{w(p)} = \prod_{c \in \phi_p} \left[\bigwedge_{l \in c \setminus \{p\}} \neg l \right]_1^{w(p)}$ which is exactly what we needed to show. This ends the proof that the first loop of Algorithm 1 preserves the answer under both Condition 1 and Condition 2. Finally, the loop on Lines 11 to 12 of Algorithm 1 replaces $[v]_1^p [\neg v]_1^q$ with $[v]_q^p$ (for some $v \in X_I$ and $p, q \in \mathbb{R}$), but, of course, $[v]_1^p [\neg v]_1^q = [v]_1^p [v]_q^1 = [v]_q^p$, i.e., the answer is unchanged.

Theorem 3 (Minimum-Cardinality Correctness). *Let (ϕ, X_I, X_P, w) be a minimum-cardinality WMC instance that satisfies Condition 2b to 2e of Theorem 2 as well as the following:*

1. *for all parameter variables $p \in X_P$, $w(\neg p) = 1$.*
2. *all models of $\{c \in \phi \mid c \cap X_P = \emptyset\}$ (as subsets of X_I) have the same cardinality;*
3. $\min_{Z \subseteq X_P} |Z|$ *such that $Y \cup Z \models \phi$ is the same for all $Y \models \{c \in \phi \mid c \cap X_P = \emptyset\}$.*

Then Algorithm 1, when applied to (ϕ, X_I, X_P, w), outputs a PBP instance with the same answer (as defined in Definitions 3 and 5).

In this case, we have to add some assumptions about the cardinality of models. Condition 2 states that all models of the indicator-only part of the formula have the same cardinality. Bayesian network encodings such as cd05 and cd06 satisfy this condition by assigning an indicator variable to each possible variable-value pair and requiring each random variable to be paired with exactly one value. Condition 3 then says that the smallest number of parameter variables needed to turn an indicator-only model into a full model is the same for all indicator-only models. As some ideas duplicate between the proofs of Theorems 2 and 3, the following proof is slightly less explicit and assumes that $\omega = 1$.

Proof. Let (F, X_I, ω) be the tuple returned by Algorithm 1 and note that $F = \left\{ [c]_0^1 \mid c \in \phi, c \cap X_P = \emptyset \right\} \cup \left\{ \left[\bigwedge_{l \in c \setminus \{p\}} \neg l \right]_1^{w(p)} \;\middle|\; p \in X_P, p \in c \in \phi, c \neq \{p\} \right\}$.
We split the proof into two parts. In the first part, we show that there is a bijection between minimum-cardinality models of ϕ and $Y \subseteq X_I$ such that $\left(\prod_{f \in F} f \right)(Y) \neq 0.$[6] Let $Y \subseteq X_I$ and $Z \subseteq X_I \cup X_P$ be related via this bijection. Then in the second part we will show that

$$\prod_{Z \models l} w(l) = \left(\prod_{f \in F} f \right)(Y). \tag{5}$$

On the one hand, if $Z \subseteq X_I \cup X_P$ is a minimum-cardinality model of ϕ, then $\left(\prod_{f \in F} \right)(Z \cap X_I) \neq 0$ under the given assumptions. On the other hand, if $Y \subseteq X_I$ is such that $\left(\prod_{f \in F} \right)(Y) \neq 0$, then $Y \models \{c \in \phi \mid c \cap X_P = \emptyset\}$. Let $Y \subseteq Z \subseteq X_I \cup X_P$ be the smallest superset of Y such that $Z \models \phi$ (it exists by Condition 2c of Theorem 2). We need to show that Z has minimum cardinality. Let Y' and Z' be defined equivalently to Y and Z. We will show that $|Z| = |Z'|$. Note that $|Y| = |Y'|$ by Condition 2, and $|Z \setminus Y| = |Z' \setminus Y'|$ by Condition 3. Combining that with the general property that $|Z| = |Y| + |Z \setminus Y|$ finishes the first part of the proof.

For the second part, let us consider the multiplicative influence of a single parameter variable $p \in X_P$ on Eq. (5). If the left-hand side is multiplied by $w(p)$ (i.e., $p \in Z$), then there must be some clause $c \in \phi$ such that $Z \setminus \{p\} \not\models c$. But then $Y \models \bigwedge_{l \in c \setminus \{p\}} \neg l$, and so the right-hand side is multiplied by $w(p)$ as well (exactly once because of Condition 2e of Theorem 2). This argument works in the other direction as well.

5   Experimental Evaluation

We run a set of experiments, comparing all five original Bayesian network encodings (bklm16, cd05, cd06, d02, sbk05) as well as the first four with Algorithm 1 applied afterwards.[7] For each encoding e, we write e++ to denote the combination of encoding a Bayesian network as a WMC instance using e and transforming it into a PBP instance using Algorithm 1. Along with DPMC[8], we also

---

[6] For convenience and without loss of generality we assume that $w(p) \neq 0$ for all $p \in X_P$.

[7] Recall that cd05 and cd06 are incompatible with DPMC.

[8] https://github.com/vardigroup/DPMC.

include WMC algorithms used in the papers that introduce each encoding: Ace for cd05, cd06, and d02; Cachet[9] [31] for sbk05; and c2d[10] [16] with query-dnnf[11] for bklm16. Ace is also used to encode Bayesian networks into WMC instances for all encodings except for bklm16 which uses another encoder mentioned previously. We focus on the following questions:

- Can parameter variable elimination improve inference speed?
- How does DPMC combined with encodings without (and with) parameter variables compare with other WMC algorithms and other encodings?
- Which instances is our approach particularly successful on (compared to other algorithms and encodings and to the same encoding before our transformation)?
- What proportion of variables is typically eliminated?
- Do some encodings benefit from this transformation more than others?

5.1 Setup

DPMC is run with tree decomposition-based planning and ADD-based execution—the best-performing combination in the original set of experiments [20]. We use a single iteration of htd [1] to generate approximately optimal tree decompositions—we found that this configuration is efficient enough to handle huge instances, and yet the width of the returned decomposition is unlikely to differ from optimal by more than one or two. We also enabled DPMC's greedy mode. This mode (which was not part of the original paper [20]) optimises the order in which ADDs are multiplied by prioritising those with small representations.

For experimental data, we use Bayesian networks available with Ace and Cachet. We split them into the following groups: – DQMR (390 instances) and – Grid networks (450 instances) as described by Sang et al. [32]; – Mastermind (144 instances) and – Random Blocks (256 instances) by Chavira et al. [12]; – other binary Bayesian networks (50 instances) including Plan Recognition [32], Friends and Smokers, Students and Professors [12], and tcc4f; – non-binary classic networks (176 instances): alarm, diabetes, hailfinder, mildew, munin1-4, pathfinder, pigs, and water.

To perform Bayesian network inference with DPMC (or with any other WMC algorithm not based on compilation such as Cachet), one needs to select a probability to compute [20,31]. If a network comes with an evidence file, we compute the probability of this evidence. Otherwise, let X be the variable last mentioned in the Bayesian network file. If true is one of the values of X, then we compute $\Pr(X = \text{true})$, otherwise we choose the first-mentioned value of X.

The experiments were run on a computing cluster with Intel Xeon E5-2630, Intel Xeon E7-4820, and Intel Xeon Gold 6138 processors with a 1000 s timeout separately on both encoding and inference, and a 32 GiB memory limit.[12]

---

[9] https://cs.rochester.edu/u/kautz/Cachet/.

[10] http://reasoning.cs.ucla.edu/c2d/.

[11] http://www.cril.univ-artois.fr/kc/d-DNNF-reasoner.html.

[12] Each instance was run on the same processor across all algorithms and encodings.

5.2   Results

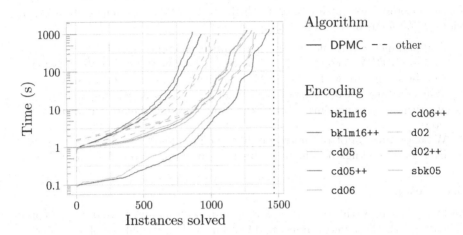

Fig. 1. Cactus plot of all algorithm-encoding pairs. The dotted line denotes the total number of instances used.

Figure 1 shows DPMC + bklm16++ to be the best-performing combination across all time limits up to 1000 s with Ace + cd06 and DPMC + bklm16 not far behind. Overall, DPMC + bklm16++ is 3.35 times faster than DPMC + bklm16 and 2.96 times faster than Ace + cd06. Table 1 further shows that DPMC + bklm16++ solves almost a hundred more instances than any other combination, and is the fastest in 69.1 s of them.

The scatter plots in Fig. 2 show that how DPMC + bklm16++ (and perhaps DPMC more generally) compares to Ace + cd06 depends significantly on the data set: the former is a clear winner on DQMR and Grid instances, while the latter performs well on Mastermind and Random Blocks. Perhaps because the underlying WMC algorithm remains the same, the difference between DPMC + bklm16 with and without applying Algorithm 1 is quite noisy, i.e., with most instances scattered around the line of equality. However, our transformation does enable DPMC to solve many instances that were previously beyond its reach.

We also record numbers of variables in each encoding before and after applying Algorithm 1. Figure 3 shows a significant reduction in the number of variables. For instance, the median number of variables in instances encoded with bklm16 was reduced four times: from 1499 to 376. While bklm16++ results in the overall lowest number of variables, the difference between bklm16++ and d02++ seems small. Indeed, the numbers of variables in these two encodings are equal for binary Bayesian networks (i.e., most of our data). Nonetheless, bklm16++ is still much faster than d02++ when run with DPMC.

It is also worth noting that there was no observable difference in the width of the project-join tree used by DPMC (which is equivalent to the treewidth of the primal/Gaifman graph of the input formula [20]) before and after applying

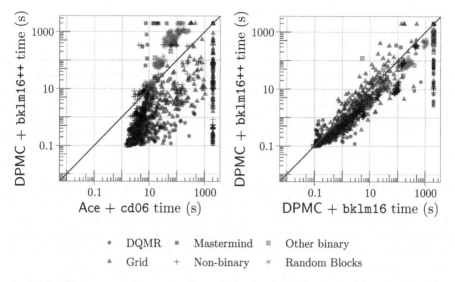

Fig. 2. An instance-by-instance comparison between DPMC+bklm16++ (the best combination according to Fig. 1) and the second and third best-performing combinations: Ace + cd06 and DPMC + bklm16.

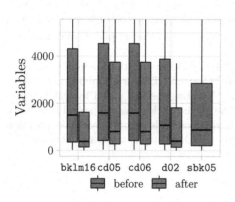

Fig. 3. Box plots of the numbers of variables in each encoding across all benchmark instances before and after applying Algorithm 1. Outliers and the top parts of some whiskers are omitted.

Table 1. The numbers of instances (out of 1466) that each algorithm and encoding combination solved faster than any other combination and in total.

Combination	Fastest	Solved
Ace + cd05	27	1247
Ace + cd06	135	1340
Ace + d02	56	1060
DPMC + bklm16	241	1327
DPMC + bklm16++	**992**	**1435**
DPMC + cd05++	0	867
DPMC + cd06++	0	932
DPMC + d02	1	1267
DPMC + d02++	7	1272
DPMC + sbk05	31	1308
c2d + bklm16	0	997
Cachet + sbk05	49	983

Algorithm 1—the observed performance improvement is more likely related to the variable ordering heuristic used by ADDs.[13]

Overall, transforming WMC instances to the PBP format allows us to significantly simplify each instance. This transformation is particularly effective on bklm16, allowing it to surpass cd06 and become the new state of the art. While there is a similarly significant reduction in the number of variables for d02, the performance of DPMC + d02 is virtually unaffected. Finally, while our transformation makes it possible to use cd05 and cd06 with DPMC, the two combinations remain inefficient.

6   Conclusion

In this paper, we showed how the number of variables in a WMC instance can be significantly reduced by transforming it into a representation based on two-valued pseudo-Boolean functions. In some cases, this led to significant improvements in inference speed, allowing DPMC + bklm16++ to overtake Ace + cd06 as the new state of the art WMC technique for Bayesian network inference. Moreover, we identified key properties of Bayesian network encodings that allow for parameter variable removal. However, these properties were rather different for each encoding, and so an interesting question for future work is whether they can be unified into a more abstract and coherent list of conditions.

Bayesian network inference was chosen as the example application of WMC because it is the first and the most studied one [3,8,9,15,32]. While the distinction between indicator and parameter variables is often not explicitly described in other WMC encodings [21,26,37], perhaps in some cases variables could still be partitioned in this way, allowing for not just faster inference with DPMC or ADDMC but also for well-established WMC encoding and inference techniques (such as in the cd05 and cd06 papers [8,9]) to be transferred to other application domains.

Acknowledgments. We thank the anonymous reviewers for their helpful comments. The first author was supported by the EPSRC Centre for Doctoral Training in Robotics and Autonomous Systems, funded by the UK Engineering and Physical Sciences Research Council (grant EP/L016834/1). The second author was supported by a Royal Society University Research Fellowship. This work has made use of the resources provided by the Edinburgh Compute and Data Facility (ECDF) (http://www.ecdf.ed.ac.uk/).

References

1. Abseher, M., Musliu, N., Woltran, S.: htd – a free, open-source framework for (customized) tree decompositions and beyond. In: Salvagnin, D., Lombardi, M. (eds.) CPAIOR 2017. LNCS, vol. 10335, pp. 376–386. Springer, Cham (2017). https://doi.org/10.1007/978-3-319-59776-8_30
2. Bahar, R.I., et al.: Algebraic decision diagrams and their applications. Formal Methods Syst. Des. **10**(2/3), 171–206 (1997). https://doi.org/10.1023/A:1008699807402

---

[13] The data on this (along with the implementation of Algorithm 1) is available at https://github.com/dilkas/wmc-without-parameters.

3. Bart, A., Koriche, F., Lagniez, J., Marquis, P.: An improved CNF encoding scheme for probabilistic inference. In: Kaminka, G.A., ET AL. (eds.) ECAI 2016–22nd European Conference on Artificial Intelligence, 29 August-2 September 2016, The Hague, The Netherlands - Including Prestigious Applications of Artificial Intelligence (PAIS 2016). Frontiers in Artificial Intelligence and Applications, vol. 285, pp. 613–621. IOS Press (2016). https://doi.org/10.3233/978-1-61499-672-9-613

4. Belle, V.: Open-universe weighted model counting. In: Singh, S.P., Markovitch, S. (eds.) Proceedings of the Thirty-First AAAI Conference on Artificial Intelligence, San Francisco, California, USA, 4–9 February 2017, pp. 3701–3708. AAAI Press (2017). http://aaai.org/ocs/index.php/AAAI/AAAI17/paper/view/15008

5. Belle, V., De Raedt, L.: Semiring programming: a semantic framework for generalized sum product problems. Int. J. Approx. Reason. **126**, 181–201 (2020). https://doi.org/10.1016/j.ijar.2020.08.001

6. Belle, V., Passerini, A., Van den Broeck, G.: Probabilistic inference in hybrid domains by weighted model integration. In: Yang, Q., Wooldridge, M.J. (eds.) Proceedings of the Twenty-Fourth International Joint Conference on Artificial Intelligence, IJCAI 2015, Buenos Aires, Argentina, 25–31 July 2015. pp. 2770–2776. AAAI Press (2015). http://ijcai.org/Abstract/15/392

7. Boros, E., Hammer, P.L.: Pseudo-Boolean optimization. Discret. Appl. Math. **123**(1–3), 155–225 (2002). https://doi.org/10.1016/S0166-218X(01)00341-9

8. Chavira, M., Darwiche, A.: Compiling Bayesian networks with local structure. In: Kaelbling, L.P., Saffiotti, A. (eds.) IJCAI-05, Proceedings of the Nineteenth International Joint Conference on Artificial Intelligence, Edinburgh, Scotland, UK, 30 July–5 August 2005, pp. 1306–1312. Professional Book Center (2005). http://ijcai.org/Proceedings/05/Papers/0931.pdf

9. Chavira, M., Darwiche, A.: Encoding CNFs to empower component analysis. In: Biere, A., Gomes, C.P. (eds.) SAT 2006. LNCS, vol. 4121, pp. 61–74. Springer, Heidelberg (2006). https://doi.org/10.1007/11814948_9

10. Chavira, M., Darwiche, A.: Compiling Bayesian networks using variable elimination. In: Veloso, M.M. (ed.) IJCAI 2007, Proceedings of the 20th International Joint Conference on Artificial Intelligence, Hyderabad, India, 6–12 January 2007, pp. 2443–2449 (2007). http://ijcai.org/Proceedings/07/Papers/393.pdf

11. Chavira, M., Darwiche, A.: On probabilistic inference by weighted model counting. Artif. Intell. **172**(6–7), 772–799 (2008). https://doi.org/10.1016/j.artint.2007.11.002

12. Chavira, M., Darwiche, A., Jaeger, M.: Compiling relational Bayesian networks for exact inference. Int. J. Approx. Reason. **42**(1–2), 4–20 (2006). https://doi.org/10.1016/j.ijar.2005.10.001

13. Choi, A., Kisa, D., Darwiche, A.: Compiling probabilistic graphical models using sentential decision diagrams. In: van der Gaag, L.C. (ed.) ECSQARU 2013. LNCS (LNAI), vol. 7958, pp. 121–132. Springer, Heidelberg (2013). https://doi.org/10.1007/978-3-642-39091-3_11

14. Darwiche, A.: On the tractable counting of theory models and its application to truth maintenance and belief revision. J. Appl. Non Class. Logics **11**(1–2), 11–34 (2001). https://doi.org/10.3166/jancl.11.11-34

15. Darwiche, A.: A logical approach to factoring belief networks. In: Fensel, D., Giunchiglia, F., McGuinness, D.L., Williams, M. (eds.) Proceedings of the Eights International Conference on Principles and Knowledge Representation and Reasoning (KR-02), Toulouse, France, 22–25 April 2002, pp. 409–420. Morgan Kaufmann (2002)

16. Darwiche, A.: New advances in compiling CNF into decomposable negation normal form. In: de Mántaras, R.L., Saitta, L. (eds.) Proceedings of the 16th Eureopean Conference on Artificial Intelligence, ECAI'2004, including Prestigious Applicants of Intelligent Systems, PAIS 2004, Valencia, Spain, 22–27 August 2004, pp. 328–332. IOS Press (2004)

17. Darwiche, A.: SDD: a new canonical representation of propositional knowledge bases. In: Walsh, T. (ed.) IJCAI 2011, Proceedings of the 22nd International Joint Conference on Artificial Intelligence, Barcelona, Catalonia, Spain, 16–22 July 2011, pp. 819–826. IJCAI/AAAI (2011). https://doi.org/10.5591/978-1-57735-516-8/IJCAI11-143

18. Dudek, J.M., Dueñas-Osorio, L., Vardi, M.Y.: Efficient contraction of large tensor networks for weighted model counting through graph decompositions (2019). CoRR abs/1908.04381

19. Dudek, J.M., Phan, V., Vardi, M.Y.: ADDMC: weighted model counting with algebraic decision diagrams. In: The Thirty-Fourth AAAI Conference on Artificial Intelligence, AAAI 2020, The Thirty-Second Innovative Applications of Artificial Intelligence Conference, IAAI 2020, The Tenth AAAI Symposium on Educational Advances in Artificial Intelligence, EAAI 2020, New York, NY, USA, 7–12 February 2020, pp. 1468–1476. AAAI Press (2020). https://aaai.org/ojs/index.php/AAAI/article/view/5505

20. Dudek, J.M., Phan, V.H.N., Vardi, M.Y.: DPMC: weighted model counting by dynamic programming on project-join trees. In: Simonis, H. (ed.) CP 2020. LNCS, vol. 12333, pp. 211–230. Springer, Cham (2020). https://doi.org/10.1007/978-3-030-58475-7_13

21. Fierens, D., et al.: Inference and learning in probabilistic logic programs using weighted Boolean formulas. Theory Pract. Log. Program. **15**(3), 358–401 (2015). https://doi.org/10.1017/S1471068414000076

22. Gogate, V., Domingos, P.M.: Formula-based probabilistic inference. In: Grünwald, P., Spirtes, P. (eds.) UAI 2010, Proceedings of the Twenty-Sixth Conference on Uncertainty in Artificial Intelligence, Catalina Island, CA, USA, 8–11 July 2010, pp. 210–219. AUAI Press (2010)

23. Gogate, V., Domingos, P.M.: Approximation by quantization. In: Cozman, F.G., Pfeffer, A. (eds.) UAI 2011, Proceedings of the Twenty-Seventh Conference on Uncertainty in Artificial Intelligence, Barcelona, Spain, 14–17 July 2011, pp. 247–255. AUAI Press (2011)

24. Gogate, V., Domingos, P.M.: Probabilistic theorem proving. Commun. ACM **59**(7), 107–115 (2016). https://doi.org/10.1145/2936726

25. Hoey, J., St-Aubin, R., Hu, A.J., Boutilier, C.: SPUDD: stochastic planning using decision diagrams. In: Laskey, K.B., Prade, H. (eds.) UAI '99: Proceedings of the Fifteenth Conference on Uncertainty in Artificial Intelligence, Stockholm, Sweden, 30 July–1 August 1999, pp. 279–288. Morgan Kaufmann (1999)

26. Holtzen, S., Van den Broeck, G., Millstein, T.D.: Scaling exact inference for discrete probabilistic programs. Proc. ACM Program. Lang. **4**(OOPSLA), 140:1-140:31 (2020). https://doi.org/10.1145/3428208

27. Kimmig, A., Van den Broeck, G., De Raedt, L.: Algebraic model counting. J. Appl. Log. **22**, 46–62 (2017). https://doi.org/10.1016/j.jal.2016.11.031

28. Kolb, S., Mladenov, M., Sanner, S., Belle, V., Kersting, K.: Efficient symbolic integration for probabilistic inference. In: Lang, J. (ed.) Proceedings of the Twenty-Seventh International Joint Conference on Artificial Intelligence, IJCAI 2018, Stockholm, Sweden, 13–19 July 2018, pp. 5031–5037. ijcai.org (2018). https://doi.org/10.24963/ijcai.2018/698

29. Oztok, U., Darwiche, A.: A top-down compiler for sentential decision diagrams. In: Yang, Q., Wooldridge, M.J. (eds.) Proceedings of the Twenty-Fourth International Joint Conference on Artificial Intelligence, IJCAI 2015, Buenos Aires, Argentina, 25–31 July 2015, pp. 3141–3148. AAAI Press (2015). http://ijcai.org/Abstract/15/443

30. Poon, H., Domingos, P.M.: Sum-product networks: a new deep architecture. In: Cozman, F.G., Pfeffer, A. (eds.) UAI 2011, Proceedings of the Twenty-Seventh Conference on Uncertainty in Artificial Intelligence, Barcelona, Spain, 14–17 July 2011, pp. 337–346. AUAI Press (2011)

31. Sang, T., Bacchus, F., Beame, P., Kautz, H.A., Pitassi, T.: Combining component caching and clause learning for effective model counting. In: SAT 2004 - The Seventh International Conference on Theory and Applications of Satisfiability Testing, Vancouver, BC, Canada, 10–13 May 2004, Online Proceedings (2004). http://www.satisfiability.org/SAT04/programme/21.pdf

32. Sang, T., Beame, P., Kautz, H.A.: Performing Bayesian inference by weighted model counting. In: Veloso, M.M., Kambhampati, S. (eds.) Proceedings, The Twentieth National Conference on Artificial Intelligence and the Seventeenth Innovative Applications of Artificial Intelligence Conference, Pittsburgh, Pennsylvania, USA, 9–13 July 2005, pp. 475–482. AAAI Press/The MIT Press (2005). http://www.aaai.org/Library/AAAI/2005/aaai05-075.php

33. Sanner, S., Boutilier, C.: Practical solution techniques for first-order MDPs. Artif. Intell. **173**(5–6), 748–788 (2009). https://doi.org/10.1016/j.artint.2008.11.003

34. Sanner, S., Delgado, K.V., de Barros, L.N.: Symbolic dynamic programming for discrete and continuous state MDPs. In: Cozman, F.G., Pfeffer, A. (eds.) UAI 2011, Proceedings of the Twenty-Seventh Conference on Uncertainty in Artificial Intelligence, Barcelona, Spain, 14–17 July 2011, pp. 643–652. AUAI Press (2011)

35. Sanner, S., McAllester, D.A.: Affine algebraic decision diagrams (AADDs) and their application to structured probabilistic inference. In: Kaelbling, L.P., Saffiotti, A. (eds.) IJCAI-05, Proceedings of the Nineteenth International Joint Conference on Artificial Intelligence, Edinburgh, Scotland, UK, 30 July–5 August 2005, pp. 1384–1390. Professional Book Center (2005). http://ijcai.org/Proceedings/05/Papers/1439.pdf

36. Van den Broeck, G., Taghipour, N., Meert, W., Davis, J., De Raedt, L.: Lifted probabilistic inference by first-order knowledge compilation. In: Walsh, T. (ed.) IJCAI 2011, Proceedings of the 22nd International Joint Conference on Artificial Intelligence, Barcelona, Catalonia, Spain, 16–22 July 2011, pp. 2178–2185. IJCAI/AAAI (2011). https://doi.org/10.5591/978-1-57735-516-8/IJCAI11-363

37. Xu, J., Zhang, Z., Friedman, T., Liang, Y., Van den Broeck, G.: A semantic loss function for deep learning with symbolic knowledge. In: Dy, J.G., Krause, A. (eds.) Proceedings of the 35th International Conference on Machine Learning, ICML 2018, Stockholmsmässan, Stockholm, Sweden, 10–15 July 2018. Proceedings of Machine Learning Research, vol. 80, pp. 5498–5507. PMLR (2018). http://proceedings.mlr.press/v80/xu18h.html

38. Zhao, H., Melibari, M., Poupart, P.: On the relationship between sum-product networks and Bayesian networks. In: Bach, F.R., Blei, D.M. (eds.) Proceedings of the 32nd International Conference on Machine Learning, ICML 2015, Lille, France, 6–11 July 2015. JMLR Workshop and Conference Proceedings, vol. 37, pp. 116–124. JMLR.org (2015). http://proceedings.mlr.press/v37/zhaoc15.html

ProCount: Weighted Projected Model Counting with Graded Project-Join Trees

Jeffrey M. Dudek, Vu H. N. Phan[(✉)], and Moshe Y. Vardi

Rice University, Houston, TX, USA
{jmd11,vhp1,vardi}@rice.edu

Abstract. Recent work in weighted model counting proposed a unifying framework for dynamic-programming algorithms. The core of this framework is a project-join tree: an execution plan that specifies how Boolean variables are eliminated. We adapt this framework to compute exact literal-weighted projected model counts of propositional formulas in conjunctive normal form. Our key conceptual contribution is to define *gradedness* on project-join trees, a novel condition requiring irrelevant variables to be eliminated before relevant variables. We prove that building graded project-join trees can be reduced to building standard project-join trees and that graded project-join trees can be used to compute projected model counts. The resulting tool `ProCount` is competitive with the state-of-the-art tools `D4ₚ`, `projMC`, and `reSSAT`, achieving the shortest solving time on 131 benchmarks of 390 benchmarks solved by at least one tool, from 849 benchmarks in total.

1 Introduction

Weighted projected model counting is a fundamental problem in artificial intelligence, with applications in planning [4], formal verification [34], and reliability estimation [20]. Counting is also closely connected to sampling [32], a problem of major interest in probabilistic reasoning [33]. The input is a set of constraints, whose variables are divided into *relevant variables* X and *irrelevant variables* Y. The goal is to compute the weighted number of assignments to X that, with some assignment to Y, satisfy the constraints. This problem is complete for the complexity class $\#P^{NP[1]}$ [63]. There are recent tools for weighted projected model counting [37,38].

Dynamic programming is a powerful technique that has been applied across computer science [7]. The key idea is to solve a large problem by solving many smaller subproblems then combining partial solutions into the final result. Dynamic programming is a natural framework to solve problems defined on

Work supported in part by NSF grants CCF-1704883, DMS-1547433, IIS-1527668, and IIS-1830549, DoD MURI grant N00014-20-1-2787, and an award from the Maryland Procurement Office.
Authors sorted alphabetically by surnames.

© Springer Nature Switzerland AG 2021
C.-M. Li and F. Manyà (Eds.): SAT 2021, LNCS 12831, pp. 152–170, 2021.
https://doi.org/10.1007/978-3-030-80223-3_11

sets of constraints, as subproblems can be formed by partitioning the constraints. This framework has been instantiated into algorithms for database-query optimization [41], SAT solving [3,45,59], QBF evaluation [10], model counting [5,17,25,31,49], and projected model counting [22,29].

Recently, a unifying framework based on *project-join trees* for dynamic-programming algorithms was proposed [17]. The key idea is to consider project-join trees as *execution plans* and decompose dynamic-programming algorithms into two phases: a *planning phase*, where a project-join tree is constructed from an input problem instance, and an *execution phase*, where the project-join tree is used to compute the result. The project-join-tree-based model counter DPMC [17] was found to be competitive with state-of-the-art exact weighted model counters [12,36,44,50]. Notably, DPMC subsumes ADDMC [18], which tied with D4 [36] for first place in the weighted track of the 2020 Model Counting Competition [23].

We adapt this framework for weighted projected model counting. The central challenge is that there are two kinds of variables: relevant and irrelevant. This contrasts with model counting, where all variables are relevant and can be treated similarly. This challenge also occurs for other problems. For example, in Boolean functional synthesis [56], some variables are *free* and must not be projected out. Our solution is to model multiple types of variables by requiring the project-join tree to be *graded*, meaning that irrelevant variables must be projected before relevant variables. Our main theoretical contribution is a novel algorithm to construct graded project-join trees from standard project-join trees. This has two primary advantages.

The first advantage is that graded project-join trees can be constructed using existing tools for standard project-join trees [17] in a black-box way. Tools exist to construct standard project-join trees with tree decompositions [48] or with constraint-satisfaction heuristics [8,13,14,35,58]. We can thus easily leverage all current and future work in tree-decomposition solvers [2,28,57] and constraint-satisfaction heuristics to produce graded project-join trees. This is crucial for the practical success of our tool.

The second advantage of our approach is in the simplicity of the algorithm. Given a project-join tree, its gradedness can be easily verified. Moreover, the algorithm to compute the projected model count from a graded project-join tree is straightforward. This gives us confidence in the correctness of our implementation. During our experimental evaluation, we found correctness errors in D4$_p$ [37], projMC [37], and reSSAT [38]. We reported these issues to the authors, who then fixed the tools. We believe that this work is a step towards certificates for the verification of projected model counters, similar to certificates produced by SAT solvers [60].

The primary contribution of this work is a dynamic-programming framework for weighted projected model counting based on project-join trees. In particular:

1. We show that graded project-join trees can be used to compute weighted projected model counts.
2. We prove that building graded project-join trees and project-join trees with free variables can be reduced to building standard project-join trees.

3. We find that project-join-tree-based algorithms make a significant contribution to the portfolio of exact weighted projected model counters (D4$_P$, projMC,
   and reSSAT). Our tool, ProCount, achieves the shortest solving time on 131
   benchmarks of 390 benchmarks solved by at least one tool, from 849 benchmarks in total.

2   Preliminaries

Pseudo-Boolean Functions and Projections. A *pseudo-Boolean function*
over a set X of variables is a function $f : 2^X \to \mathbb{R}$, where 2^X denotes the power
set of X. A Boolean formula φ over variables X represents a pseudo-Boolean
function over X, denoted $[\varphi] : 2^X \to \mathbb{R}$, where for all $\tau \in 2^X$, if τ satisfies φ
then $[\varphi](\tau) \equiv 1$ else $[\varphi](\tau) \equiv 0$. Operations on pseudo-Boolean functions include
product and *projections*. We define product as follows.

Definition 1 (Product). *Let X and Y be sets of Boolean variables. The* prod-
uct *of functions $f : 2^X \to \mathbb{R}$ and $g : 2^Y \to \mathbb{R}$ is the function $f \cdot g : 2^{X \cup Y} \to \mathbb{R}$
defined for all $\tau \in 2^{X \cup Y}$ by $(f \cdot g)(\tau) \equiv f(\tau \cap X) \cdot g(\tau \cap Y)$.*

   Product generalizes conjunction: if φ and ψ are propositional formulas, then
$[\varphi] \cdot [\psi] = [\varphi \wedge \psi]$.

Definition 2 (Projections). *Let X be a set of Boolean variables, x be a
variable in X, and $f : 2^X \to \mathbb{R}$ be a pseudo-Boolean function.*

- *The Σ-projection of f w.r.t. x is the function $\Sigma_x f : 2^{X \setminus \{x\}} \to \mathbb{R}$ defined for
  all $\tau \in 2^{X \setminus \{x\}}$ by $(\Sigma_x f)(\tau) \equiv f(\tau) + f(\tau \cup \{x\})$.*
- *The $\exists$-projection of f w.r.t. x is the function $\exists_x f : 2^{X \setminus \{x\}} \to \mathbb{R}$ defined for
  all $\tau \in 2^{X \setminus \{x\}}$ by $(\exists_x f)(\tau) \equiv \max (f(\tau), f(\tau \cup \{x\}))$.*

   Σ-projection is also called *additive projection* or *marginalization*. $\exists$-projection
is also called *disjunctive projection* and generalizes existential quantification: if
φ is a Boolean formula and $x \in \text{Vars}(\varphi)$, then $\exists_x [\varphi] = [\exists x. \varphi]$.
   Σ-projection and $\exists$-projection are each independently commutative. For-
mally, for all $x, y \in X$ and $f : 2^X \to \mathbb{R}$, we assert that $\Sigma_x \Sigma_y f = \Sigma_y \Sigma_x f$ and
$\exists_x \exists_y f = \exists_y \exists_x f$. For all sets $X = \{x_1, \dots, x_n\}$, we define $\Sigma_X f \equiv \Sigma_{x_1} \dots \Sigma_{x_n} f$
and $\exists_X f \equiv \exists_{x_1} \dots \exists_{x_n} f$. We also take the convention that $\Sigma_\varnothing f \equiv f$ and
$\exists_\varnothing f \equiv f$.
   In general, Σ-projection does not commute with $\exists$-projection. For example,
if $f(x, y) = x \oplus y$ (XOR), then $\Sigma_x \exists_y f \neq \exists_y \Sigma_x f$.

Weighted Projected Model Counting. We compute the total weight, subject
to a given weight function and a set of irrelevant variables, of all models of an
input Boolean formula. A formal definition follows.

Definition 3. *Let φ be a Boolean formula, $\{X, Y\}$ be a partition of $\text{Vars}(\varphi)$,
and $W : 2^X \to \mathbb{R}$ be a pseudo-Boolean function. We say that (X, Y, φ, W) is an
instance of* weighted projected model counting. *The W-weighted Y-projected
model count of φ is $\text{WPMC}(\varphi, W, Y) \equiv \sum_{\tau \in 2^X} (W(\tau) \cdot \max_{\alpha \in 2^Y} [\varphi](\tau \cup \alpha))$.*

Variables in X are called *relevant* or *additive*, and variables in Y are called *irrelevant* or *disjunctive*. For the special case of *unprojected model counting*, all variables are relevant, and the W-*weighted model count* is $\texttt{WPMC}(\varphi, W, \varnothing)$.

Weights are usually given by a *literal-weight function* $W \equiv \prod_{x \in X} W_x$, where the factors are functions $W_x : 2^{\{x\}} \to \mathbb{R}$. In detail, a positive literal x has weight $W_x(\{x\})$, and a negative literal $\neg x$ has weight $W_x(\varnothing)$.

Graphs. A *graph* G has a set $\mathcal{V}(G)$ of vertices, a set $\mathcal{E}(G)$ of undirected edges, a function $\delta_G : \mathcal{V}(G) \to 2^{\mathcal{E}(G)}$ that gives the set of edges incident to each vertex, and a function $\epsilon_G : \mathcal{E}(G) \to 2^{\mathcal{V}(G)}$ that gives the set of vertices incident to each edge. Each edge must be incident to exactly two vertices. A *tree* is a simple, connected, and acyclic graph. We often refer to a vertex of a tree as a *node*.

A *rooted tree* is a tree T together with a distinguished node $r \in \mathcal{V}(T)$ called the *root*. In a rooted tree (T, r), each node $n \in \mathcal{V}(T)$ has a (possibly empty) set of *children*, denoted $\mathcal{C}_{T,r}(n)$, which contains all nodes n' adjacent to n such that all paths from n' to r contain n. A *leaf* of a rooted tree T is a non-root node of degree one. We use $\mathcal{L}(T)$ to denote the set of leaves of T.

3 Using Project-Join Trees for Projected Model Counting

We first describe an existing framework for performing unprojected model counting [17]. We then adapt this framework for projected model counting.

3.1 Project-Join Trees for Model Counting

This framework leverages Boolean formulas given in a factored representation, *conjunctive normal form (CNF)*. A *clause* is a non-empty disjunction of literals, and a *CNF formula* is a non-empty set (conjunction) of clauses. The key idea is to represent the computation as a rooted tree, called a *project-join tree*, where leaves correspond to clauses, and internal nodes correspond to Σ-projections [17].

Definition 4 (Project-Join Tree). *Let φ be a CNF formula. A* project-join tree *of φ is a tuple $\mathcal{T} = (T, r, \gamma, \pi)$ where*

- *T is a tree with root $r \in \mathcal{V}(T)$,*
- *$\gamma : \mathcal{L}(T) \to \varphi$ is a bijection from the leaves of T to the clauses of φ, and*
- *$\pi : \mathcal{V}(T) \setminus \mathcal{L}(T) \to 2^{\texttt{Vars}(\varphi)}$ is a labeling function on internal nodes.*

Moreover, $\mathcal{T}$ must satisfy the following two properties.

1. *The set $\{\pi(n) : n \in \mathcal{V}(T) \setminus \mathcal{L}(T)\}$ is a partition of $\texttt{Vars}(\varphi)$.*
2. *Let $n \in \mathcal{V}(T)$ be an internal node, x be a variable in $\pi(n)$, and c be a clause of φ. If $x \in \texttt{Vars}(c)$, then the leaf node $\gamma^{-1}(c)$ is a descendant of n.*

A project-join tree of a CNF formula φ can be used to compute the weighted model count of φ. The algorithm traverses the project-join tree from leaves to root, multiplying clauses according to the tree structure and additively projecting out variables according to π. This is formalized with the following definition.

Definition 5. *Let $T = (T, r, \gamma, \pi)$ be a project-join tree and W be a literal-weight function over X. The W-valuation of a node n, denoted f_n^W, is*

$$
f_n^W \equiv \begin{cases} [\gamma(n)] & \text{if } n \in \mathcal{L}(T) \\ \displaystyle\sum_{\pi(n)} \left(\prod_{o \in \mathcal{C}_{T,r}(n)} f_o^W \cdot \prod_{x \in \pi(n)} W_x \right) & \text{if } n \in \mathcal{V}(T) \setminus \mathcal{L}(T) \end{cases}
$$

where $[\gamma(n)]$ is the pseudo-Boolean function represented by the clause $\gamma(n) \in \varphi$.

This leads to a two-phase algorithm for computing the weighted model count of a CNF formula φ. First, the *planning phase* builds a project-join tree (T, r, γ, π) of φ. Second, the *execution phase* computes f_r^W according to Definition 5. The following theorem asserts that f_r^W is the weighted model count of φ.

Theorem 1 ([17]). *Let φ be a CNF formula, $T = (T, r, \gamma, \pi)$ be a project-join tree of φ, and W be a literal-weight function over $\mathtt{Vars}(\varphi)$. Then $f_r^W(\varnothing)$ is the W-weighted model count of φ.*

When computing a W-valuation, the number of variables appearing in the intermediate pseudo-Boolean functions significantly influences the runtime. These variables are actually independent of W. For a node $n \in \mathcal{V}(T)$, define $\mathtt{Vars}(n)$ as follows.

$$
\mathtt{Vars}(n) \equiv \begin{cases} \mathtt{Vars}(\gamma(n)) & \text{if } n \in \mathcal{L}(T) \\ \left(\displaystyle\bigcup_{o \in \mathcal{C}_{T,r}(n)} \mathtt{Vars}(o) \right) \setminus \pi(n) & \text{if } n \in \mathcal{V}(T) \setminus \mathcal{L}(T) \end{cases}
$$

The W-valuation of a node n is then a pseudo-Boolean function over variables $\mathtt{Vars}(n)$. If $N \subseteq \mathcal{V}(T)$, for convenience, we define $\mathtt{Vars}(N) \equiv \bigcup_{n \in N} \mathtt{Vars}(n)$.

The difficulty of valuation scales with the maximum number of variables needed to compute each pseudo-Boolean function. The *size* of a node n, $\mathtt{size}(n)$, is defined as $|\mathtt{Vars}(n)|$ for leaf nodes and $|\mathtt{Vars}(n) \cup \pi(n)|$ for internal nodes. The *width* of a project-join tree $T = (T, r, \gamma, \pi)$ is $\mathtt{width}(T) \equiv \max_{n \in \mathcal{V}(T)} \mathtt{size}(n)$.

Two algorithms have been proposed to construct project-join trees [17]. The first, LG, uses *tree decompositions* [48], following similar work in join-query optimization [11,41]. The second, HTB, uses *bucket elimination* [13] and *Bouquet's Method* [8] with various constraint-satisfaction heuristics: *maximum-cardinality search* [58], *lexicographic search for perfect/minimal orders* [35], and *min-fill* [14].

3.2   Adaptations for Projected Model Counting

In order to adapt this framework for weighted projected model counting, we aim to modify the valuation of project-join trees to incorporate disjunctive as well as additive projections. In particular, we must perform ∃-projections with all disjunctive variables and Σ-projections with all additive variables.

$$n_{10} \overset{\pi}{\mapsto} \varnothing$$

$$n_8 \overset{\pi}{\mapsto} \{z_1\}$$

$$n_9 \overset{\pi}{\mapsto} \{z_3, z_5\}$$

$$n_6 \overset{\pi}{\mapsto} \{z_2, z_4\} \qquad n_1 \overset{\gamma}{\mapsto} z_2 \vee \neg z_4$$

$$n_7 \overset{\pi}{\mapsto} \{z_6\} \qquad n_2 \overset{\gamma}{\mapsto} z_1 \vee z_6$$

$$n_3 \overset{\gamma}{\mapsto} z_1$$

$$n_4 \overset{\gamma}{\mapsto} z_3 \vee z_5$$

$$n_5 \overset{\gamma}{\mapsto} \neg z_3 \vee \neg z_5$$

Fig. 1. A graded project-join tree $\mathcal{T} = (T, n_{10}, \gamma, \pi)$ of a CNF formula φ with relevant variables $X = \{z_1, z_3, z_5\}$ and irrelevant variables $Y = \{z_2, z_4, z_6\}$. Each leaf node corresponds to a clause of φ under γ. Each internal node is labeled by π with a set of variables of φ. Note that $\mathcal{T}$ is graded with grades $\mathcal{I}_X = \{n_8, n_9, n_{10}\}$ and $\mathcal{I}_Y = \{n_6, n_7\}$.

The challenge is that Σ-projections do not commute with $\exists$-projections. Since the $\exists$-projections appear on the inside of the expression for projected counting, we must ensure that all $\exists$-projections occur before all Σ-projections while traversing the project-join tree. We formalize this by requiring the project-join tree to be *graded*.

Definition 6 (Graded Project-Join Tree). *Let φ be a CNF formula with project-join tree $\mathcal{T} = (T, r, \gamma, \pi)$, and let $\{X, Y\}$ be a partition of $\mathtt{Vars}(\varphi)$. We say that $\mathcal{T}$ is (X, Y)-graded if there exist $\mathcal{I}_X, \mathcal{I}_Y \subseteq \mathcal{V}(T)$, called grades, that satisfy the following properties.*

1. *The set $\{\mathcal{I}_X, \mathcal{I}_Y\}$ is a partition of $\mathcal{V}(T) \setminus \mathcal{L}(T)$.*
2. *If $n_X \in \mathcal{I}_X$, then $\pi(n_X) \subseteq X$.*
3. *If $n_Y \in \mathcal{I}_Y$, then $\pi(n_Y) \subseteq Y$.*
4. *If $n_X \in \mathcal{I}_X$ and $n_Y \in \mathcal{I}_Y$, then n_X is not a descendant of n_Y in the rooted tree (T, r).*

Intuitively, a project-join tree is (X, Y)-graded if all X variables are projected (according to π) closer to the root than all Y variables in the tree. Figure 1 illustrates an exemplary graded project-join tree.

We now define a new valuation on graded project-join trees, which uses Σ-projections at nodes in $\mathcal{I}_X$ and $\exists$-projections at nodes in $\mathcal{I}_Y$.

Definition 7 (Projected Valuation). *Let (X, Y, φ, W) be a weighted projected model counting instance, and let $\mathcal{T} = (T, r, \gamma, \pi)$ be an (X, Y)-graded project-join tree of φ with grades $\mathcal{I}_X$ and $\mathcal{I}_Y$. The W-projected-valuation of each node $n \in \mathcal{V}(T)$, denoted g_n^W, is defined by*

$$g_n^W \equiv \begin{cases} [\gamma(n)] & \text{if } n \in \mathcal{L}(T) \\[2ex] \displaystyle\sum_{\pi(n)} \left(\prod_{o \in \mathcal{C}_{T,r}(n)} g_o^W \cdot \prod_{x \in \pi(n)} W_x \right) & \text{if } n \in \mathcal{I}_X \\[3ex] \displaystyle\exists_{\pi(n)} \left(\prod_{o \in \mathcal{C}_{T,r}(n)} g_o^W \right) & \text{if } n \in \mathcal{I}_Y \end{cases}$$

where $[\gamma(n)]$ is the pseudo-Boolean function represented by the clause $\gamma(n) \in \varphi$.

If the project-join tree is graded, then the projected valuation of the root node is the weighted projected model count.

Theorem 2. *Let (X, Y, φ, W) be an instance of weighted projected model counting, and let $\mathcal{T}$ be a project-join tree of φ with root r. If $\mathcal{T}$ is (X, Y)-graded, then $g_r^W(\varnothing) = \texttt{WPMC}(\varphi, W, Y)$.*

In the next section, we show how to build graded project-join trees.

4   Building Graded Project-Join Trees

We now show how building graded project-join trees can be reduced to building ungraded project-join trees. This allows us to use prior work on ungraded project-join trees [17] to compute graded project-join trees.

As a building block, we first show how constructing project-join trees with free variables can be reduced to constructing ungraded project-join trees. This both illustrates the key ideas of our approach and appears as a subroutine in the larger graded reduction.

4.1   Reducing Free Project-Join Trees to Ungraded Project-Join Trees

Project-join trees project out every variable in the set of corresponding clauses. This is desirable for applications where all variables are processed in the same way, e.g., model counting. In many other applications, however, it is desirable to process a set of clauses while leaving specified *free variables* untouched.

We model free variables by ensuring that they are projected in the project-join tree as late as possible, at the root node. Thus free variables must be "kept alive" throughout the entire tree.

Definition 8. *Let F be a set of variables, and let $\mathcal{T} = (T, r, \gamma, \pi)$ be a project-join tree. We say that $\mathcal{T}$ is F-free if $F = \pi(r)$.*

Note that Definition 8 is a much stronger restriction than Definition 6. In particular, if a project-join tree $\mathcal{T}$ of a CNF formula φ is F-free, then $\mathcal{T}$ is also $(F, \texttt{Vars}(\varphi) \setminus F)$-graded.

We now reduce the problem of building F-free project-join trees to building ungraded project-join trees. One approach is to build a project-join tree while ignoring all variables in F, then insert the variables in F as projections at the root. However, building minimal-width project-join trees while ignoring variables may not produce minimal-width F-free project-join trees for the full formula.

Instead, we adapt a similar reduction in the context of tensor networks [16] for the context of project-join trees. The key idea is to add to φ a *virtual clause* that contains all variables in F. For a set Z of variables, let $\texttt{virtual}(Z)$ denote a fresh clause with variables Z. Project-join trees of $\varphi \cup \{\texttt{virtual}(F)\}$ can then

---

Algorithm 1: Building an F-free project-join tree of a CNF formula

---

Input: φ: a CNF formula
Input: F: a subset of $\mathtt{Vars}(\varphi)$
Input: $\mathcal{T} = (T, r, \gamma, \pi)$: a project-join tree of $\varphi \cup \{C_F\}$, where
       $C_F = \mathtt{virtual}(F)$ is a fresh clause with variables F
Output: an F-free project-join tree of φ

1   $s \leftarrow \gamma^{-1}(C_F)$ // s will be the root node of the returned project-join tree
2   $\pi' \leftarrow$ a mapping where $\pi'(n) = \varnothing$ for all $n \in \mathcal{V}(T) \setminus \mathcal{L}(T)$ // π' will be the
    labeling function of the returned project-join tree
3   **for** $y \in \mathtt{Vars}(\varphi) \setminus F$
4      $\varphi_y = \{C \in \varphi : y \in \mathtt{Vars}(C)\}$
5      $i \leftarrow$ lowest common ancestor of $\{\gamma^{-1}(C) : C \in \varphi_y\}$ in the rooted tree (T, s)
6      $\pi'(i) \leftarrow \pi'(i) \cup \{y\}$ // project out y at the lowest allowable node
7   $\pi'(s) \leftarrow F$ // project out variables in F at the new root s
8   $\gamma' \leftarrow \gamma \setminus \{s \mapsto C_F\}$ // γ' is the bijection γ without the pair (s, C_F)
9   **return** (T, s, γ', π')

---

be used to find F-free project-join trees of φ. This virtual clause can be viewed as a goal atom in $\mathtt{DataLog}$ [39].

This reduction is presented as Algorithm 1. The input $\mathcal{T}$ is a project-join tree of $\varphi \cup \{C_F\}$, where C_F is a virtual clause with variables F. On lines 2-6, we rotate $\mathcal{T}$ so that the leaf node s corresponding to C_F becomes the root node. This rotation does not increase the width. Projecting F at the new root s still does not increase the width. Thus we obtain an F-free project-join tree of φ.

We state the correctness of Algorithm 1 in the following theorem. In particular, the width of the output F-free project-join tree is no worse than the width of the unrestricted input tree.

Theorem 3. *Let φ be a CNF formula, and let $F \subseteq \mathtt{Vars}(\varphi)$. If $\mathcal{T}$ is a project-join tree of $\varphi \cup \{\mathtt{virtual}(F)\}$, then Algorithm 1 returns an F-free project-join tree of φ of width at most $\mathtt{width}(\mathcal{T})$.*

We also prove that Algorithm 1 is optimal. That is, a minimal-width project-join tree for $\varphi \cup \{C_F\}$ produces a minimal-width F-free project-join tree for φ.

Theorem 4. *Let φ be a CNF formula, F be a subset of $\mathtt{Vars}(\varphi)$, and w be a positive integer. If there is an F-free project-join tree of φ of width w, then there is a project-join tree of $\varphi \cup \{\mathtt{virtual}(F)\}$ of width w.*

4.2   Reducing Graded Project-Join Trees to Free Project-Join Trees

In this section, we use free project-join trees as a building block to construct graded project-join trees. We present this framework as Algorithm 2. The key idea is to create a graded project-join tree by combining many free project-join trees for subformulas. We first combine clauses to remove Y variables, then we combine project-join-tree components to remove X variables.

Algorithm 2: Building a graded project-join tree of a CNF formula

---

Input: X: a set of Σ-variables
Input: Y: a set of $\exists$-variables where $X \cap Y = \varnothing$
Input: φ: a CNF formula where $\mathtt{Vars}(\varphi) = X \cup Y$
Output: T: an (X, Y)-graded project-join tree of φ

1   $partition \leftarrow \mathtt{GroupBy}(\varphi, Y)$ // group clauses that share Y variables
2   **for** $N \in partition$
3     $\big|$ $T_N \leftarrow \mathtt{BuildComponent}(N, \mathtt{Vars}(N) \cap X)$ // build a $(\mathtt{Vars}(N) \cap X)$-free project-join tree of N
4     $\big|$ $T_N \leftarrow T_N$ with all projections at the root of T_N removed
5     $\big|$ $C_N \leftarrow \mathtt{virtual}(\mathtt{Vars}(N) \cap X)$
6   $T \leftarrow \mathtt{BuildComponent}(\{C_N : N \in partition\}, \varnothing)$ // build a project-join tree from virtual clauses C_N
7   **for** $N \in partition$
8     $\big|$ $\ell_N \leftarrow$ leaf of T corresponding to C_N
9     $\big|$ $T \leftarrow T$ with ℓ_N replaced by T_N
10 **return** T

In detail, on line 1, we partition the clauses of φ into blocks that share Y variables. On line 3, we find a project-join tree T_N for each block N. This tree must keep all X variables free, i.e., must be $(\mathtt{Vars}(N) \cap X)$-free. The trees $\{T_N\}$ collectively project out all Y variables. On line 6, we construct a project-join tree T that will guide the combination of all trees in $\{T_N\}$ while projecting out all X variables, where each T_N is represented by the corresponding virtual clause C_N. On lines 7-9, we hook the trees in $\{T_N\}$ together as indicated by T.

The function $\mathtt{GroupBy}(\varphi, Y)$ in Algorithm 2 partitions the clauses of φ so that every pair of clauses that share a variable from Y appear together in the same block of the partition. A formal definition follows.

Definition 9. *Let φ be a set of clauses and Y be a subset of $\mathtt{Vars}(\varphi)$. Define $\sim_Y \subseteq \varphi \times \varphi$ to be the relation such that, for clauses $c, c' \in \varphi$, we have $c \sim_Y c'$ if and only if $\mathtt{Vars}(c) \cap \mathtt{Vars}(c') \cap Y \neq \varnothing$. Then $\mathtt{GroupBy}(\varphi, Y)$ is the set of equivalence classes of the reflexive transitive closure of $\sim_Y$.*

The intuition is that two clauses in the same block in $\mathtt{GroupBy}(\varphi, Y)$ must be combined to project out all variables in Y. Conversely, clauses that appear in separate blocks need not be combined in order to project out all variables in Y.

In Algorithm 2, each function call $\mathtt{BuildComponent}(\alpha, F)$ returns an F-free project-join tree of α, where α is a set of clauses and $F \subseteq \mathtt{Vars}(\alpha)$. $\mathtt{BuildComponent}$ can be implemented by implementing Algorithm 1 on top of an algorithm for building ungraded project-join trees. For example, in Sect. 5, we consider two implementations of Algorithm 2 built on top of the two algorithms to construct standard project-join trees [17] discussed at the end of Sect. 3.1.

We next state the correctness of Algorithm 2 and show that the width of the output graded project-join tree is no worse than the widths of the trees used for the components.

Theorem 5. *Let φ be a CNF formula, $\{X, Y\}$ be a partition of* Vars(φ), *and w be a positive integer. Assume each call to* BuildComponent(α, F) *returns an F-free project-join tree for α of width at most w. Then Algorithm 2 returns an (X, Y)-graded project-join tree for φ of width at most w.*

Although Algorithm 2 constructs a sequence of small ungraded project-join trees, it is sufficient to compute a single ungraded project-join tree from which all smaller trees can be extracted. This is demonstrated by the following theorem.

Theorem 6. *Let φ be a CNF formula, $\{X, Y\}$ be a partition of* Vars(φ), *and ψ be the CNF formula $\varphi \cup \{$*virtual*(Vars(N) $\cap X$) : $N \in$* GroupBy(φ, Y)$\}$. For every positive integer w, if there is a project-join tree $\mathcal{T}'$ for ψ of width w, then there is an (X, Y)-graded project-join tree for φ of width at most w.*

The key idea of the proof is to answer every BuildComponent call in Algorithm 2 by extracting a subtree of $\mathcal{T}'$ and applying Theorem 3.

We show in the following theorem that this approach is optimal. Thus (X, Y)-graded project-join trees of φ are equivalent to project-join trees of ψ.

Theorem 7. *Let φ be a CNF formula, $\{X, Y\}$ be a partition of* Vars(φ), *and ψ be the CNF formula $\varphi \cup \{$*virtual*(Vars(N) $\cap X$) : $N \in$* GroupBy(φ, Y)$\}$. For every positive integer w, if there is an (X, Y)-graded project-join tree for φ of width w, then there is a project-join tree for ψ of width w.*

Note that requiring the project-join tree to be graded may significantly increase the width of available project-join trees. Theorems 5 and 7 indicate that our algorithm for constructing a graded project-join tree pays no additional cost in width beyond what is required by gradedness.

5   Experimental Evaluation

To implement our projected model counter ProCount, we modify the unprojected model counter DPMC, which is based on ungraded project-join trees [17]. The DPMC framework includes: (1) the LG planner that uses tree-decomposition techniques, (2) the HTB planner that uses constraint-satisfaction heuristics, and (3) the DMC executor that uses *algebraic decision diagrams (ADDs)*. We generalize these three components to support graded project-join trees and projected model counting.

We conduct three experiments to address the following research questions.

(RQ1) In the planning phase (for constructing project-join trees), how do tree-decomposition techniques compare to constraint-satisfaction heuristics?

(RQ2) In the execution phase, how do different ADD variable orders compare?

(RQ3) How does ProCount compare to other exact weighted projected counters?

To answer RQ1, in Experiment 1, we compare the planner LG (which uses tree decompositions) and the planner HTB (which uses constraint-satisfaction heuristics). LG uses the tree decomposers FlowCutter [28], htd [2], and Tamaki [57]. HTB implements four heuristics for variable ordering: maximal-cardinality

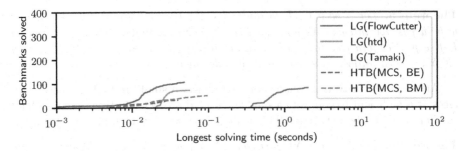

Fig. 2. Experiment 1 compares the tree-decomposition-based planner `LG` to the constraint-satisfaction-based planner `HTB`. A planner "solves" a benchmark when it finds a project-join tree of width 30 or lower. For `HTB`, we only show the variable-ordering heuristic `MCS`; the `LP`, `LM`, and `MF` curves are qualitatively similar.

search (`MCS`) [58], lexicographic search for perfect/minimal orders (`LP`/`LM`) [35], and min-fill (`MF`) [14]. `HTB` also implements two clause-ordering heuristics: bucket elimination (`BE`) [13] and Bouquet's Method (`BM`) [8].

To answer RQ2, in Experiment 2, we compare variable-ordering heuristics for the ADD-based executor `DMC`. An ADD [6] is a directed acyclic graph that compactly represents a pseudo-Boolean function. An ADD requires a variable order, which strongly influences the compactness of the ADD. `DMC` implements four aforementioned variable-ordering heuristics: `MCS`, `LP`, `LM`, and `MF`. Note that we use ADDs throughout the entire execution for consistency, although binary decision diagrams [9] or SAT solvers would suffice to valuate existential nodes.

To answer RQ3, in Experiment 3, we compare `ProCount` to state-of-the-art exact weighted projected model counters D4$_\mathrm{P}$ [37], `projMC` [37], and `reSSAT` [38].

We use 849 CNF benchmarks gathered from two families. The first family contains 90 formulas and was used for weighted projected sampling [27]. For each benchmark in this family, a positive literal x has weight $0 < W_x(\{x\}) < 1$, and a negative literal $\neg x$ has weight $W(\varnothing) = 1 - W_x(\{x\})$. The second family contains 759 formulas and was used for unweighted projected model counting [52]. We add weights to this family by randomly assigning $W_x(\{x\}) = 0.4$ and $W_x(\varnothing) = 0.6$ or vice versa to each variable x. All 849 benchmarks are satisfiable, as verified by the SAT solver `CryptoMiniSat` [53]. We run all experiments on single CPU cores of a Linux cluster with Intel Xeon E5-2650v2 processors (2.60-GHz) and 30 GB of RAM. All code and data are available (https://github.com/vardigroup/DPMC).

5.1   Experiment 1: Comparing Planners

In this experiment, we run all configurations of the planners `LG` and `HTB` on each CNF benchmark with a timeout of 100 s. We present results in Fig. 2. Each point (x, y) on a plotted curve indicates that: within x seconds, on each of y benchmarks, the first graded project-join tree produced by the corresponding planner

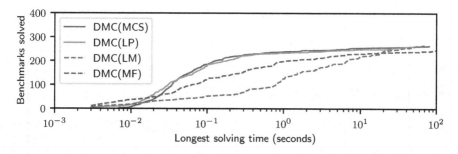

Fig. 3. Experiment 2 compares variable-ordering heuristics (MCS, LP, LM, and MF) for the ADD-based executor DMC. MCS and LP are significantly faster than LM and MF.

has width at most 30. We choose 30 because previous work shows that executors do not handle larger project-join trees well [16,17]. While LG is an *anytime* tool that produces several trees (of decreasing widths) for each benchmark, we only use the first tree. The tree-decomposition-based planner LG produces more low-width trees than the constraint-satisfaction-based planner HTB. Moreover, for LG, the tree decomposer FlowCutter is faster than htd and Tamaki. Thus we use LG with FlowCutter in ProCount for later experiments.

5.2 Experiment 2: Comparing Execution Heuristics

In this experiment, we take all 346 graded project-join trees produced by LG with FlowCutter in Experiment 1 and run DMC for 100 s with each ADD variable-ordering heuristic. We present the execution time of each heuristic (excluding planning time) in Fig. 3. We observe that MCS and LP outperform LM and MF. We use DMC with MCS in ProCount for Experiment 3.

5.3 Experiment 3: Comparing Weighted Projected Model Counters

Informed by Experiments 1 and 2, we choose LG with FlowCutter as the planner and DMC with MCS as the executor for our framework ProCount. We compare ProCount with the weighted projected model counters D4$_P$, projMC, and reSSAT. Since all benchmarks are satisfiable with positive literal weights, the model counts must be positive. Thus, for all tools, we exclude outputs that are zero (possible floating-point underflow). We are confident that the remaining results are correct. Differences in model counts among tools are less than 10^{-6}.

Figure 4 shows the performance of ProCount, D4$_P$, projMC, and reSSAT with a 1000-s timeout. Additional statistics are given in Table 1. Of 849 benchmarks, 390 are solved by at least one of four tools. ProCount achieves the shortest solving time on 131 benchmarks, including 44 solved by none of the other three tools. Between the two *virtual best solvers* in Fig. 4, VBS1 (all four tools) is significantly faster than VBS0 (three existing tools, without ProCount).

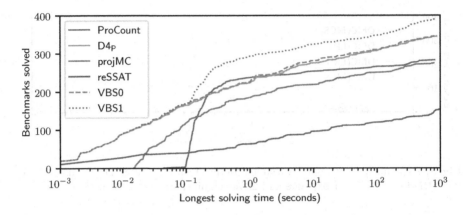

Fig. 4. Experiment 3 compares our framework ProCount to the state-of-the-art exact weighted projected model counters D4p, projMC, and reSSAT. VBS0 is the virtual best solver of the three existing tools, excluding ProCount. VBS1 includes all four tools. Adding ProCount significantly improves the portfolio of projected model counters.

Project-Join Tree Width and Computation Time. To identify which type of benchmarks can be solved efficiently by ProCount, we study how the performance of each projected model counter varies with the widths of graded project-join trees. In particular, for each benchmark, we consider the width of the first graded project-join tree produced by the planner LG (with FlowCutter) in Experiment 1. Figure 5 shows how these widths relate to mean PAR-2 scores of projected model counters. ProCount seems to be the fastest solver on instances for which there exist graded project-join trees of widths between 50 and 100.

6   Related Work

There are a number of recent tools for projected model counting. For example, D4p uses decision decomposable negation normal form [37], projMC leverages disjunctive decomposition [37], and reSSAT combines counting with SAT techniques [38]. While our focus in this work is on (deterministic) exact weighted projected model counting, it is worth mentioning that various relaxations have also been studied, e.g., probabilistic [51], approximate [21,26,52], or unweighted [4,29,42,63] projected model counting.

A recent framework for projected counting is nestHDB [29], a hybrid solver. Similar to our framework, nestHDB includes a planning phase (using the tree-decomposition tool htd [2]) and an execution phase (using the database engine Postgres [55] and the projected counter projMC [37], alongside other tools). We predict that nestHDB may benefit from switching the projected-counting component to ProCount, which was often faster than projMC in Experiment 3. While we were unable to run a full experimental comparison[1] with nestHDB,

---

[1] nestHDB is an unweighted tool, but the benchmarks in Sect. 5 are weighted. Moreover, the cluster used in Sect. 5 does not support database management systems.

Table 1. Experiment 3 compares our framework `ProCount` to the state-of-the-art exact weighted projected model counters `D4ₚ`, `projMC`, and `reSSAT`. There are 390 benchmarks solved by at least one of four tools. By including `ProCount`, the portfolio of tools solves 44 more benchmarks and achieves shorter solving time on 87 other benchmarks. For each tool-benchmark pair, the PAR-2 score is the runtime if the tool solves the benchmark (within time and space limits) or twice the 1000-s timeout otherwise.

Solver	Number of benchmarks solved (of 849)			Mean PAR-2 score
	Uniquely (solved by no other)	In shortest time	In total	
ProCount	44	131	283	1341
D4ₚ	50	235	345	1203
projMC	0	8	275	1362
reSSAT	1	16	154	1659
VBS0	NA	NA	346	1199
VBS1	NA	NA	390	1099

we evaluated `nestHDB` against `ProCount` on 90 benchmarks [27] (with weights removed) using a single CPU core of an Intel i7-7700HQ processor (2.80-GHz) with 30 GB of RAM. `ProCount` and `nestHDB` respectively solved 69 and 59 benchmarks, with a 100-s timeout. The mean PAR-2 scores for `ProCount` and `nestHDB` were 47 and 87. Further comparison is needed in future work.

Our proposed graded project-join trees can be seen as a specialization of *structure trees* [54] to the case of projected model counting. Sterns and Hunt [54] suggest constructing structure trees by manually modifying tree decomposers to consider only structure trees respecting the variable quantification order (i.e., to consider gradedness directly). In this work, we take a different approach by using existing tools for standard project-join trees (in particular, tree decomposers) in a black-box way. This is crucial for the practical success of our tool, as we can leverage continual progress in tree decomposition.

Projected model counting is also a special case of *functional aggregate queries (FAQs)* [1]. Our graded project-join trees can be seen as a specialization of FAQ variable orders. Theorem 7.5 of [1] gives an algorithm for constructing an FAQ variable order from a sequence of tree decompositions, which, in the context of projected model counting, is equivalent to the technique we discussed in Sect. 4.1 of ignoring relevant variables while planning to project irrelevant variables. In contrast, our approach may find lower-width graded project-join trees by incorporating relevant variables even when planning to project irrelevant variables. This improvement may be lifted to the FAQ framework in future work.

It is worth comparing our theoretical results to a different algorithm for projected counting [24], which runs on a formula φ in time $2^{2^{O(k)}} \cdot p(\varphi)$, where k is the *primal treewidth* [49] of φ, and p scales polynomially in the size of φ. Assuming the Exponential-Time Hypothesis [30], all FPT algorithms parameterized by

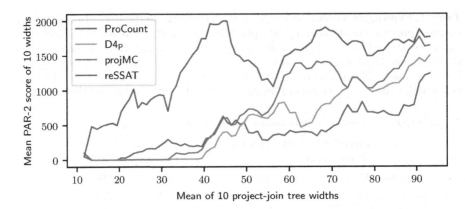

Fig. 5. We plot mean PAR-2 scores (in seconds) against mean project-join tree widths. Each projected counter in Experiment 3 corresponds to a plotted curve, on which a point (x, y) indicates that: x is the central moving average of 10 consecutive project-join tree widths $1 \leq w_1 < w_2 < \ldots < w_{10} \leq 99$, and y is the average PAR-2 score of the benchmarks whose project-join trees have widths w s.t. $w_1 \leq w \leq w_{10}$. We observe that the performance of ProCount degrades as the project-join tree width increases. However, ProCount tends to be the fastest solver on benchmarks whose graded project-join trees have widths roughly between 50 and 100.

primal treewidth must be double-exponential [24]. On the other hand, by Theorem 5 in [17] and Theorem 6 here, our algorithm, based on graded project-join trees, runs in time $2^{O(k')}$, where k' is the primal treewidth of ψ (which we call the $\{X, Y\}$-*graded treewidth* of φ). While k' is larger than k, we can see that k' is significantly smaller than 2^k on many benchmarks.

In some sense, projected model counting on Boolean formulas is a dual problem of *maximum a posteriori (MAP)* inference [40,43,62] on Bayesian networks [47]: a projected model count has the form $\sum_X \max_Y f(X, Y)$, while a MAP probability has the form $\max_Y \sum_X f(X, Y)$. Both problems can be solved using variable elimination, but an elimination order may not freely interleave X variables with Y variables. A valid variable order induces an *evaluation tree* (similar to a project-join tree) [46]. As mentioned in [46], exact MAP algorithms construct evaluation trees using constraint-satisfaction heuristics (similar to our planner HTB). Our work goes further by constructing low-width graded project-join trees using tree-decomposition techniques (with our planner LG) and by performing efficient computations using compact ADDs (with our executor DMC).

7   Discussion

We adapted an existing dynamic-programming framework [17] to perform projected model counting by requiring project-join trees to be graded. This framework decomposes projected model counting into two phases. First, the planning phase produces a graded project-join tree from a CNF formula. Second, the execution phase uses the this tree to guide the computation of the projected model count of the formula w.r.t. a literal-weight function. We proved that algorithms for building project-join trees can be used to build graded project-join trees. Our framework ProCount is competitive with the exact weighted projected model counters D4$_P$ [37], projMC [37], and reSSAT [38]. ProCount considerably improves the virtual best solver and thus is a valuable addition to the portfolio.

In future work, ProCount can be generalized for maximum model counting [26] and functional aggregate queries [1]. Another research direction is multicore programming. The planning tool LG can be improved to run tree decomposers in parallel [19] in a portfolio approach [61]. One can also make the execution tool DMC support multicore ADD packages (e.g., Sylvan [15]).

References

1. Abo Khamis, M., Ngo, H.Q., Rudra, A.: FAQ: questions asked frequently. In: PODS, pp. 13–28 (2016)
2. Abseher, M., Musliu, N., Woltran, S.: htd-a free, open-source framework for (customized) tree decompositions and beyond. In: CPAIOR, pp. 376–386 (2017). https://doi.org/10.1007/978-3-319-59776-8_30
3. Aguirre, A.S.M., Vardi, M.: Random 3-SAT and BDDs: the plot thickens further. In: CP, pp. 121–136 (2001). https://doi.org/10.1007/3-540-45578-7_9
4. Aziz, R.A., Chu, G., Muise, C., Stuckey, P.: Projected model counting. In: SAT, pp. 121–137 (2015)
5. Bacchus, F., Dalmao, S., Pitassi, T.: Solving #SAT and Bayesian inference with backtracking search. JAIR 34, 391–442 (2009). https://doi.org/10.1613/jair.2648
6. Bahar, R.I., et al.: Algebraic decision diagrams and their applications. Form. Method Syst. Des. 10(2–3), 171–206 (1997). https://doi.org/10.1023/A:1008699807402
7. Bellman, R.: Dynamic programming. Science 153(3731), 34–37 (1966). https://doi.org/10.1126/science.153.3731.34
8. Bouquet, F.: Gestion de la dynamicité et énumération d'impliquants premiers: une approche fondée sur les Diagrammes de Décision Binaire. Ph.D. thesis, Aix-Marseille 1 (1999). https://www.theses.fr/1999AIX11011
9. Bryant, R.E.: Graph-based algorithms for Boolean function manipulation. IEEE TC 100(8), 677–691 (1986). https://doi.org/10.1109/TC.1986.1676819
10. Charwat, G., Woltran, S.: BDD-based dynamic programming on tree decompositions. Technical report, Technische Universität Wien, Institut für Informationssysteme (2016). https://dbai.tuwien.ac.at/research/report/dbai-tr-2016-95.pdf
11. Dalmau, V., Kolaitis, P.G., Vardi, M.Y.: Constraint satisfaction, bounded treewidth, and finite-variable logics. In: CP, pp. 310–326 (2002). https://doi.org/10.1007/3-540-46135-3_21
12. Darwiche, A.: New advances in compiling CNF to decomposable negation normal form. In: ECAI, pp. 318–322 (2004). https://dl.acm.org/doi/10.5555/3000001.3000069
13. Dechter, R.: Bucket elimination: a unifying framework for reasoning. AIJ 113(1–2), 41–85 (1999). https://doi.org/10.1016/S0004-3702(99)00059-4
14. Dechter, R.: Constraint Processing. Morgan Kaufmann (2003). https://doi.org/10.1016/B978-1-55860-890-0.X5000-2

15. van Dijk, T., van de Pol, J.: Sylvan: multi-core decision diagrams. In: TACAS, pp. 677–691 (2015). https://doi.org/10.1007/978-3-662-46681-0_60
16. Dudek, J.M., Dueñas-Osorio, L., Vardi, M.Y.: Efficient contraction of large tensor networks for weighted model counting through graph decompositions (2019). arXiv preprint arXiv:1908.04381
17. Dudek, J.M., Phan, V.H.N., Vardi, M.Y.: DPMC: weighted model counting by dynamic programming on project-join trees. In: CP, pp. 211–230 (2020). arxiv.org/abs/2008.08748
18. Dudek, J.M., Phan, V.H., Vardi, M.Y.: ADDMC: weighted model counting with algebraic decision diagrams. AAAI **34**, 1468–1476 (2020). https://doi.org/10.1609/aaai.v34i02.5505
19. Dudek, J.M., Vardi, M.Y.: Parallel weighted model counting with tensor networks. In: MCW (2020). https://mccompetition.org/assets/files/2020/MCW_2020_paper_1.pdf
20. Duenas-Osorio, L., Meel, K.S., Paredes, R., Vardi, M.Y.: Counting-based reliability estimation for power-transmission grids. In: AAAI. pp. 4488–4494 (2017)
21. Ermon, S., Gomes, C., Sabharwal, A., Selman, B.: Taming the curse of dimensionality: discrete integration by hashing and optimization. In: ICML, pp. 334–342 (2013)
22. Fichte, J.K., Hecher, M.: Counting with bounded treewidth: meta algorithm and runtime guarantees. In: NMR, pp. 9–18 (2020)
23. Fichte, J.K., Hecher, M., Hamiti, F.: The Model Counting Competition 2020 (2020). arXiv preprint arXiv:2012.01323
24. Fichte, J.K., Hecher, M., Morak, M., Woltran, S.: Exploiting treewidth for projected model counting and its limits. In: SAT, pp. 165–184 (2018)
25. Fichte, J.K., Hecher, M., Thier, P., Woltran, S.: Exploiting database management systems and treewidth for counting. In: PADL, pp. 151–167 (2020). https://doi.org/10.1007/978-3-030-39197-3_10
26. Fremont, D.J., Rabe, M.N., Seshia, S.A.: Maximum model counting. In: AAAI, pp. 3885–3892 (2017)
27. Gupta, R., Sharma, S., Roy, S., Meel, K.S.: WAPS: weighted and projected sampling. In: TACAS, pp. 59–76 (2019)
28. Hamann, M., Strasser, B.: Graph bisection with pareto optimization. JEA **23**, 1–34 (2018)
29. Hecher, M., Thier, P., Woltran, S.: Taming high treewidth with abstraction, nested dynamic programming, and database technology. In: SAT, pp. 343–360 (2020)
30. Impagliazzo, R., Paturi, R., Zane, F.: Which problems have strongly exponential complexity? JCSS **63**(4), 512–530 (2001)
31. Jégou, P., Kanso, H., Terrioux, C.: Improving exact solution counting for decomposition methods. In: ICTAI, pp. 327–334 (2016). https://doi.org/10.1109/ICTAI.2016.0057
32. Jerrum, M.R., Valiant, L.G., Vazirani, V.V.: Random generation of combinatorial structures from a uniform distribution. Theor. Comput. Sci. **43**, 169–188 (1986)
33. Kelly, C., Sarkhel, S., Venugopal, D.: Adaptive Rao-Blackwellisation in Gibbs sampling for probabilistic graphical models. In: AISTATS, pp. 2907–2915 (2019)
34. Klebanov, V., Manthey, N., Muise, C.: SAT-based analysis and quantification of information flow in programs. In: QEST, pp. 177–192 (2013). https://doi.org/10.1007/978-3-642-40196-1_16
35. Koster, A.M., Bodlaender, H.L., Van Hoesel, S.P.: Treewidth: computational experiments. Electron. Notes Disc. Math. **8**, 54–57 (2001). https://doi.org/10.1016/S1571-0653(05)80078-2

36. Lagniez, J.M., Marquis, P.: An improved decision-DNNF compiler. In: IJCAI, pp. 667–673 (2017). https://doi.org/10.24963/ijcai.2017/93
37. Lagniez, J.M., Marquis, P.: A recursive algorithm for projected model counting. AAAI **33**, 1536–1543 (2019)
38. Lee, N.Z., Wang, Y.S., Jiang, J.H.R.: Solving stochastic Boolean satisfiability under random-exist quantification. In: IJCAI, pp. 688–694 (2017)
39. Lloyd, J.W.: Foundations of Logic Programming. Springer, Cham (2012). https://doi.org/10.1007/978-3-642-96826-6
40. Maua, D.D., de Campos, C.P., Cozman, F.G.: The complexity of MAP inference in Bayesian networks specified through logical languages. In: IJCAI, pp. 889–895 (2015)
41. McMahan, B.J., Pan, G., Porter, P., Vardi, M.Y.: Projection pushing revisited. In: EDBT, pp. 441–458 (2004). https://doi.org/10.1007/978-3-540-24741-8_26
42. Möhle, S., Biere, A.: Dualizing projected model counting. In: ICTAI, pp. 702–709 (2018)
43. Murphy, K.P.: Machine Learning: A Probabilistic Perspective. MIT press, Cambridge (2012)
44. Oztok, U., Darwiche, A.: A top-down compiler for sentential decision diagrams. In: IJCAI, pp. 3141–3148 (2015). https://dl.acm.org/doi/10.5555/2832581.2832687
45. Pan, G., Vardi, M.Y.: Symbolic techniques in satisfiability solving. J. Autom. Reas. **35**(1–3), 25–50 (2005). https://doi.org/10.1007/s10817-005-9009-7
46. Park, J.D., Darwiche, A.: Complexity results and approximation strategies for MAP explanations. JAIR **21**, 101–133 (2004)
47. Pearl, J.: Bayesian networks: a model cf self-activated memory for evidential reasoning. In: Proceedings of the 7th Conference of the Cognitive Science Society, University of California, Irvine, CA, USA, pp. 15–17 (1985)
48. Robertson, N., Seymour, P.D.: Graph minors. X. Obstructions to tree-decomposition. J. Comb. Theory B **52**(2), 153–190 (1991). https://doi.org/10.1016/0095-8956(91)90061-N
49. Samer, M., Szeider, S.: Algorithms for propositional model counting. J. Disc. Algor. **8**(1), 50–64 (2010). https://doi.org/10.1007/978-3-540-75560-9_35
50. Sang, T., Bacchus, F., Beame, P., Kautz, H.A., Pitassi, T.: Combining component caching and clause learning for effective model counting. SAT **4**, 20–28 (2004). http://www.satisfiability.org/SAT04/accepted/65.html
51. Sharma, S., Roy, S., Soos, M., Meel, K.S.: GANAK: a scalable probabilistic exact model counter. In: IJCAI, pp. 1169–1176 (2019)
52. Soos, M., Meel, K.S.: BIRD: engineering an efficient CNF-XOR SAT solver and its applications to approximate model counting. AAAI **33**, 1592–1599 (2019)
53. Soos, M., Nohl, K., Castelluccia, C.: Extending SAT solvers to cryptographic problems. In: SAT, pp. 244–257 (2009)
54. Stearns, R.E., Hunt, H.B., III.: Exploiting structure in quantified formulas. J. Algor. **43**(2), 220–263 (2002)
55. Stonebraker, M., Rowe, L.A.: The design of Postgres. ACM Sigmod Rec. **15**(2), 340–355 (1986)
56. Tabajara, L.M., Vardi, M.Y.: Factored Boolean functional synthesis. In: FMCAD, pp. 124–131 (2017). https://dl.acm.org/doi/10.5555/3168451.3168480
57. Tamaki, H.: Positive-instance-driven dynamic programming for treewidth. J. Comb. Optim. **37**(4), 1283–1311 (2019). https://doi.org/10.1007/s10878-018-0353-z

58. Tarjan, R.E., Yannakakis, M.: Simple linear-time algorithms to test chordality of graphs, test acyclicity of hypergraphs, and selectively reduce acyclic hypergraphs. SICOMP **13**(3), 566–579 (1984). https://doi.org/10.1137/0213035

59. Uribe, T.E., Stickel, M.E.: Ordered binary decision diagrams and the Davis-Putnam procedure. In: CCL, pp. 34–49 (1994). https://doi.org/10.1007/BFb0016843

60. Wetzler, N., Heule, M.J.H., Hunt, W.A.: DRAT-trim: efficient checking and trimming using expressive clausal proofs. In: Sinz, C., Egly, U. (eds.) SAT 2014. LNCS, vol. 8561, pp. 422–429. Springer, Cham (2014). https://doi.org/10.1007/978-3-319-09284-3_31

61. Xu, L., Hutter, F., Hoos, H.H., Leyton-Brown, K.: SATzilla: portfolio-based algorithm selection for SAT. JAIR **32**, 565–606 (2008)

62. Xue, Y., Li, Z., Ermon, S., Gomes, C.P., Selman, B.: Solving marginal MAP problems with NP oracles and parity constraints. In: NIPS, pp. 1127–1135 (2016)

63. Zawadzki, E.P., Platzer, A., Gordon, G.J.: A generalization of SAT and #SAT for robust policy evaluation. In: IJCAI, pp. 2583–2589 (2013)

Efficient All-UIP Learned Clause Minimization

Mathias Fleury$^{(\boxtimes)}$ (ID) and Armin Biere (ID)

Johannes Kepler University Linz, Linz, Austria
{mathias.fleury,armin.biere}@jku.at

Abstract. In 2020 Feng & Bacchus revisited variants of the all-UIP learning strategy, which considerably improved performance of their version of CaDiCaL submitted to the SAT Competition 2020, particularly on large planning instances. We improve on their algorithm by tightly integrating this idea with learned clause minimization. This yields a clean shrinking algorithm with complexity linear in the size of the implication graph. It is fast enough to unconditionally shrink learned clauses until completion. We further define trail redundancy and show that our version of shrinking removes all redundant literals. Independent experiments with the three SAT solvers CaDiCaL, Kissat, and Satch confirm the effectiveness of our approach.

1 Introduction

Learned clause minimization [18] is a standard feature in modern SAT solvers. It allows to learn shorter clauses which not only reduces memory usage but arguably also helps to prune the search space. However, completeness of minimization was never formalized nor proven. Using Horn SAT [9] we define trail redundancy through entailment with respect to the reasons in the trail and show that the standard minimization algorithm removes all redundant literals (Sect. 2).

Minimization, in its original form [18], only removes literals from the initial *deduced clause* during conflict analysis, i.e., the 1st-unique-implication-point clause [21]. In 2020 Feng & Bacchus [11] revisited the *all-UIP* heuristics with the goal to reduce the size of the deduced clause even further by allowing to add new literals. In this paper we call such advanced minimization techniques *shrinking*. In order to avoid spending too much time in such shrinking procedures the authors of [11] had to limit its effectiveness. They also described and implemented several variants in the SAT solver CaDiCaL [2]. One variant was winning the planning track of the SAT Competition 2020. The benchmarks in this track require to learn clauses with many literals on each decision level.

As Feng & Bacchus [11] consider minimization and all-UIP shrinking separately, they apply minimization first, then all-UIP shrinking, and finally again minimization (depending on the deployed strategy/variant), while we integrate both techniques into one simple algorithm. In contrast, their variants process

© Springer Nature Switzerland AG 2021
C.-M. Li and F. Manyà (Eds.): SAT 2021, LNCS 12831, pp. 171–187, 2021.
https://doi.org/10.1007/978-3-030-80223-3_12

literals of the deduced clause from highest to lowest decision level and eagerly introduce literals on lower levels. Thus their approach has to be guarded against actually producing larger clauses and can not be run unconditionally (Sect. 3).

We integrate minimization and shrinking in one procedure with linear complexity in the size of the implication graph (Sect. 4). Processing literals of the deduced clause from lowest to highest level allows us to reuse the minimization cache, without compromising on completeness, thus making it possible to run the shrinking algorithm unconditionally until completion. On the theoretical side we prove that our form of shrinking fulfills the trail redundancy criteria.

Experiments with our SAT solvers KISSAT, CADICAL, and SATCH show the effectiveness of our approach and all-UIP shrinking in general. Shrinking decreases the number of learned literals, particularly on the recent planning track. We also study the amount of time used by the different parts of the transformation from a conflicting clause to the shrunken learned clause (Sect. 5).

Regarding related work we refer to the *Handbook of Satisfiability* [7], particularly for an introduction to CDCL [17], the main algorithm used by state-of-the-art SAT solvers. This work is based on the classical minimization algorithm [18], which Van Gelder [19] improved by making it linear (in the number of literals) in the implication graph without changing the resulting minimized clause. The original all-UIP scheme [21] was never considered to be efficient enough to be part of SAT solvers, until the work by Feng & Bacchus [11]. We refer to their work for a detailed discussion on all-UIPs. Note that, Feng & Bacchus [11] consider their algorithm to be independent of minimization, more like a post-processing step, while we combine shrinking and minimization for improved efficiency. The technical report with the proofs of all theorems is available [13].

2 Minimization

We first present a formalization of what minimization actually achieves through the notion of "trail redundancy". Then the classical deduced clause minimization algorithm is revisited. It identifies literals that are removable and others literals called *poison* that are not. The algorithm uses a syntactic criterion, but removes exactly the trail redundant literals. We present five existing criteria to detect (ir)redundancy earlier and prove their correctness.

When a SAT solver identifies a conflicting clause, i.e., a clause in which all literals are assigned to false, it analyzes the clause and first deduces a 1st-unique-implication-point clause [17,21]. This *deduced clause* is the starting point for minimization and shrinking. The goal is to reduce the size of this clause by removing as many literals as possible. The following redundancy criterion specifies if a literal is removable from the deduced clause.

Definition 1 (Semantic Trail Redundancy). *Given the formula F_M composed only of the reason annotating propagated literals in the trail M and the conflicting clause D such that $M \vDash \neg D$. The literal $L \in \neg M$ is called redundant iff $F_M \vDash \neg L \vee (D \setminus \{L\})$.*

For this definition we only consider redundancy with respect to the reasons in the trail (ignoring other clauses in the formula). Note that, most SAT solvers only use the first clause in the watch lists to propagate, even though "better" clauses might trigger the same propagation. For instance PRECOSAT scans watch lists to find such cases [3]. However, due to potential cyclic dependencies, deducing the shortest learned clause is difficult [20].

Theorem 2 (Redundant Literals are Removable). *If $L \vee D$ is the deduced clause and L is redundant, then D is conflicting and entailed.*

Our next theorem states that the order of removal does not impact the outcome and that it is possible to cache whether a literal is (ir)redundant.

Theorem 3. *Literals stay (ir)redundant after removal of redundant literals.*

The reason $L \vee C$ annotates the propagation literal $L^{L \vee C}$ in the trail. Minimizing the deduced clause consists in recursively resolving with the reasons: If the clause becomes smaller, it is used. Duplicate literals are removed from the clause. Algorithm 1 shows a recursive implementation that resolve away the literal L without addition of literals. The minimization algorithm applies to every conflicting clause but is only applied to the *deduced clause* [21], namely the deduced clause after the first unique implication point was derived.

The minimization algorithm is standard in SAT solvers with several improvements. First, they use efficient data structures to efficiently check if a literal is in the deduced clause. Second, they use caching: if a literal was deemed (un)removable before, the same outcome is used again. Caching successes and failures [19] make the algorithm linear in the size of the implication graph. Literals that can not be removed are called *poison*.

Our definition of trail redundancy is semantic, while the minimization algorithm uses relies on syntactic criteria to determine if a literal is removable or not. We show that both criteria are equivalent by using a result of Horn satisfiability.

Definition 4 (Transition System by Dowling and Gallier [9]). *Consider the following rewriting system defined for Horn formulas, starting from the start symbol I*

1. *For every clause $L \vee \neg L_1 \vee \cdots \vee \neg L_n$, we consider the associated rewrite rule $\neg L \to \neg L_1 \cdots \neg L_n$ (where n can be zero).*
2. *For every clause $\neg L_1 \vee \cdots \vee \neg L_n$, we consider the rewrite rule $I \to \neg L_1 \cdots \neg L_n$.*

In Definition 4, given our SAT context the step $\neg L_1 \cdots \neg L_n$, represents the entailed clause $\neg L_1 \vee \cdots \vee \neg L_n$. One rewriting step is a resolution step.

Theorem 5 (Dowling and Gallier [9]). *Given a satisfiable Horn formula, a literal is true iff it can be rewritten to $\bot$.*

The transition system from Definition 4 is not linear. As far we are aware, this is the first description of minimization algorithm in terms of Horn SAT.

Function IsLiteralRedundant(L, d, C)

> **Input:** Literal L assigned to *true*, recursion depth d, deduced clause C
> **Output:** Whether L can be removed
>
> **if** L is a decision **then**
> | **return** *false*
> $D \vee L \longleftarrow$ reason(L);
> **foreach** *literal* $K \in D$ **do**
> | **if** $\neg$IsLiteralRedundant($\neg K$, $d+1$, C) **then**
> | | **return** *false*
> **return** *true*

Function MinimizeSlice(B, C)

> **Input:** A clause C (passed by reference) and a subset B of C to minimize
> **Output:** The minimized clause with redundant literals in B removed
>
> **foreach** $K \in B$ **do**
> | $R \longleftarrow \emptyset$
> | **if** IsLiteralRedundant($\neg K$, 0, C) **then**
> | | $R \longleftarrow R \cup \{K\}$
> $C \longleftarrow C \backslash R$

Algorithm 1: Basic recursive minimization algorithm similar to [18].

Theorem 6. *Algorithm 1 is the same as the transition system from Definition 4.*

Theorem 7 (Equivalence Syntactic and Semantic Redundancy). *Both notions of redundancy are equivalent. In particular, every redundant literal is also removable.*

In our formalization of learned clause minimization for our verified SAT solver IsaSAT [12], we use a different definition of redundancy, namely $F_M \vDash \neg L \vee D_{<_M L}$ where $D_{<_M L}$ are all the literals of D that appear before L in the trail M. This definition is equivalent but it makes more explicit that only literals that appear before L are relevant. We have not formalized completeness while working on IsaSAT since we only cared about correctness.

Theorem 8. *A literal L is redundant iff $F_M \vDash \neg L \vee D_{<_M L}$.*

Our implementation relies on the alternative definition: It sorts the literals in the clause by its position on the trail. Each literal, starting from the lowest position, is checked. If it is not redundant, it is marked as present in the deduced clause for efficient checking. This reduces the number of flags (like testing if a literal is present in the deduced clause) to reset. Instead we could use d: When $d = 0$, the condition "L is in the deduced clause" does not apply.

Thanks to caching both successes and failures, the complexity is linear in the number of literals of the trail. Compared to our simple break conditions, more advanced criteria are possible.

Function IsLiteralRedundantEfficient(*L*, *d*, *C*)

> **Input:** Literal *L* assigned to *true*, recursion depth *d*, deduced clause *C*
> **Output:** Whether *L* can be removed
>
> **if** status of *L* is cached in minimization cache **then**
> | **return** cached value
>
> **if** any advanced poison criterion from Theorem 9 applies (uses *d*) **then**
> | **return** *false*
>
> **if** *L* is root-level assigned (unit) or $\neg L \in C$ **then**
> | **return** *true*
>
> **if** *L* is a decision **then**
> | **return** *false*
>
> $D \vee L \longleftarrow$ reason(L)
> **foreach** $K \in D$ **do**
> | **if** ¬IsLiteralRedundantEfficient($\neg K$, *d* + 1, *C*) **then**
> | | Cache *false* for *L*
> | | **return** *false*
> Cache *true* for *L*
> **return** *true*

Algorithm 2: Advanced minimization algorithm equivalent to Algorithm 1.

Theorem 9 (Poison Criteria).

1. *If a literal appears on the trail before any other literal of the deduced clause on a decision level, then it is not redundant.*
2. *Literals with a decision level not in the deduced clause are not redundant.*
3. *Literals that are alone on a given decision level are not redundant (Knuth).*

The proof relies on the fact that the SAT solver propagates literals eagerly. This is not the case globally if the SAT solver uses chronological backtracking [15,16] but remains correct for the reason clauses. The second and third point are widely used (e.g., in MiniSAT and Glucose), whereas the first one is a novelty of CaDiCaL and is not described so far. Root-level assigned false literals can also appear in deduced clauses and be removed without recursing over their reasons.

Theorem 10. *Literals at level 0 are redundant.*

Algorithm 2 combines the two ideas that are described here, the caching and the advanced poison criteria. The ideas 1. and 3. from Theorem 9 require data structures that are not present in every SAT solver, namely the position τ of each literal in the trail. Doing so was not necessary until now, but it is required for shrinking. In our solvers, we also use the depth to limit the number of the recursive calls and avoid stack overflows. The implementation in MiniSAT [10] (and all derived solvers like Glucose [1]) uses a non-recursive version, but it requires two functions, one for depth zero and another for the recursive case.

3 Shrinking

After detecting conflicting clauses, the SAT solver analyzes them and deduces the first unique-implication point or 1-UIP [7], where only one literal remains on the current (largest) decision level. This is the first point where the clause is propagating, fixing the current search direction. The idea of 1-UIP can be applied on every level in order to produce shorter clauses. We call this process *shrinking*. It differs from minimization because it adds new literals to the deduced clause.

If fully applied, shrinking derives a subset of the decision-only clause. Therefore, it is limited. Feng & Bacchus [11] (abbreviated F&B from now on) have used various heuristics like not adding literals of low importance, without a clear winner across all implementations. We focus on their *min-alluip* variant. It applies the 1-UIP on every level. For each literal in the clause, the solver resolves with its reason unless a literals from a new level is added, thus making sure that the LBD or "glue" [1] is not increased, an important metric, which seems to relate well to the "quality" of learned clauses. In their implementation, if the clause becomes longer, the minimized clause would be used instead.

Algorithm 3 shows the implementation of *min-alluip*. It considers the set of all literals of the deduced clause on the same level, or *slice* (same as a block if no chronological backtracking [15,16] is allowed). Each slice is shrunken starting from the highest level. It resolves each literal of the slice with its reason or fails

---

Function MinAllUIPShrinkSlice(B, C)

> **Input:** Slice B of literals of the deduced clause C on the (slice) level
> **Output:** B unchanged or shrunken if *min-alluip* is successful
>
> $E \longleftarrow \emptyset$
> **while** $|B| > 1$ **do**
> > Remove from B last assigned literal $\neg L$
> > $D \vee L \longleftarrow$ reason(L)
> > **if** $\exists K \in D\backslash C$ assigned at lower level not already in C **then**
> > > $E \longleftarrow E \cup \{L\}$
> >
> > **else**
> > > $B \longleftarrow B \cup \{K \in D \mid K$ assigned on slice level$\}$
> >
> Replace in deduced clause C original B with $B \cup E$

Function MinAllUipShrinking(C)

> **Input:** The deduced clause C (passed by reference)
> **Output:** The shrunken clause using the *min-alluip* strategy
>
> $C' \longleftarrow C$
> **foreach** Level i of literals in the deduced clause – highest to lowest **do**
> > $B \longleftarrow \{L \in C \mid L$ assigned at level $i\}$
> > MinAllUIPShrinkSlice(B, C)
> Replace C with saved original deduced clause C' unless $|C| < |C'|$

Algorithm 3: Shrinking algorithm *min-alluip* from Feng&Bacchus [11].

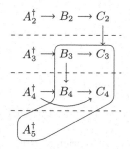

Fig. 1. Conflict example

when adding new literals on lower levels. Because SAT solvers propagate eagerly, $|B| \geq 1$ is an invariant of the while loop (and L cannot be a decision literal).

The key difference between shrinking and minimization is that reaching the UIP is a *global* property, namely of all literals on a level, and not of a single literal. This means that testing redundancy is a depth-first search algorithm while shrinking is a breadth-first search algorithm on the implication graph.

Example 11. Consider the implication graph from Fig. 1. The algorithm starts with the highest level, namely with B_4 and A_4. The level is reduced to A_4 introducing the already present B_3. On the next level, C_3 cannot be removed because it would import level 2. The resulting clause $\neg A_5 \vee \neg A_4 \vee \neg A_3$ is smaller and is used instead of the original clause.

F&B unfortunately do not provide source code nor binaries used in their experiments. Therefore we focus on their version of CADICAL submitted [14] to the SAT Competition 2020. It implements only one of their strategies, which, as far we can tell, matches the variant *min-alluip* [11] described above, while code for the other variants is incomplete or missing.

4   Minimizing and Shrinking

In contrast to F&B our algorithm minimizes literal slices of the deduced clause assigned on a certain level starting from the lowest to highest level. This enables us to remove all redundant literals on-the-fly. After presenting our algorithm we study its complexity and then discuss its implementation in our SAT solvers CADICAL, KISSAT, and SATCH.

The main loop of our Algorithm 4 interleaves shrinking and (if shrinking failed) minimization. For each slice of literals in the deduced clauses assigned on a certain level we then attempt to reach the 1-UIP, similarly to Algorithm 3. If this fails, we minimize the slice. This also allows to lift some restriction on shrinking: only non-redundant literals interrupt the search for the 1-UIP. We start from the lowest level to keep completeness of minimization.

Function ShrinkingSlice(B, C)

> **Input:** Slice B of literals of the deduced clause C on a single (slice) level
>
> **Output:** B unchanged or shrunken to UIP if our new method is successful
>
> **while** $|B| > 1$ **do**
>
> > Remove from B last assigned literal $\neg L$
> >
> > $D \vee L \longleftarrow$ reason(L)
> >
> > **if** $\exists K \in D \backslash C$ at lower level and $\neg$IsLiteralRedundant($\neg K$, 1, C)
> > **then**
> >
> > > | return with failure (keep original B in C)
> >
> > **else**
> >
> > > | $B \longleftarrow B \cup \{K \in D \mid K$ on slice level$\}$
>
> Replace in deduced clause C original B with the remaining UIP in B

Function Shrinking(C)

> **Input:** The deduced clause C (passed by reference)
>
> **Output:** The shrunken and minimized clause using our new strategy
>
> **foreach** Level i of literals in the deduced clause – lowest to highest **do**
>
> > $B \longleftarrow \{L \in C \mid L$ assigned at level $i\}$
> >
> > ShrinkingSlice(B, C)
> >
> > **if** shrinking the slice failed **then** MinimizeSlice(B, C);

Algorithm 4: Our new method for integrated shrinking with minimization.

Example 12. Consider the implication graph from Fig. 1. The algorithm starts with the slice of literals on the lowest decision level, namely with B_3 and C_3. No UIP can be found because it would import level 2. Level 1 is shrunken to A_4. The shrunken clause is $\neg A_5 \vee \neg A_4 \vee \neg B_3 \vee C_3$.

As mentioned before, for efficiency a cache is maintained during minimization to know whether a literal is redundant or not.

Theorem 13 (Shrinking and Redundancy). *Redundant literals remain redundant during shrinking.*

Theorem 13 ignores irredundant literals because new literals are added to the deduced clause, allowing for more removable literals. This explains why F&B propose (in one variant of shrinking) to minimize again after shrinking. For the same reason we do not check if literals are redundant on the current level, since added literals (e.g., new 1st UIPs) invalidate the literals marked as "poisoned". Instead, we check for redundancy of literals on lower levels and on current level only after shrinking them, when the literals on the slice level are fixed.

Example 14 (Minimization during shrinking). Consider the following trail

$$A_1^\dagger B_1^{B_1 \vee \neg A_1} \quad A_2^\dagger B_2^{B_2 \vee \neg B_1 \vee \neg A_2} \quad A_3^\dagger$$

where † marks a decision and the deduced clause is $\neg A_1 \vee \neg B_2 \vee \neg A_3$. Shrinking cannot remove B_2 because it would introduce the new literal B_1 on lower levels, unless it is determined to actually be redundant (A_1 is in the deduced clause).

To keep the complexity linear, when interleaving minimization with shrinking as shown in Algorithm 4, we maintain a global shared minimization cache, not reset between minimizing different slices. A more complicated solution consists in minimizing up-front (as in the implementation of F&B in [14]), followed by shrinking, and if shrinking succeeds, reset the poison literals on the current level.

Resetting only literals on the current level is important for reducing the runtime complexity from quadratic to linear in the size of the implication graph. As we are shrinking "in order" (from lowest to highest decision level) we can keep cached poisoned (and removable) literals from previous levels, thus matching the overall linear complexity of (advanced) minimization.

Our solution also avoids updating the minimization cache more than once during shrinking. When a slice is successfully reduced to a single literal, all shrunken literals are marked as redundant in the minimization cache. The process is complete in the sense that no redundant literals remain.

Theorem 15 (Completeness). *All redundant literals are removed.*

This result relies on the fact that during the outer loop no literal on a lower level is added to the deduced clause. If this would be allowed (as in Algorithm 3), the poisoned flag has to be reset and minimization redone, yielding a quadratic algorithm. However, the theorem says nothing about minimality of the shrunken clause if we allow to add new literals, as in the following example.

Example 16 (Smaller Deduced Clause). Consider the trail

$$A_1^\dagger B_1^{B_1 \vee \neg A_1} C_1^{C_1 \vee \neg B_1} \quad A_2^\dagger B_2^{B_2 \vee \neg A_2} C_2^{C_2 \vee \neg B_2 \vee \neg B_1} \quad A_3^\dagger$$

and the deduced clause $\neg C_1 \vee \neg B_2 \vee \neg C_2 \vee \neg A_3$. The clause is neither minimized nor shrunken by our algorithm, but can be shrunken to the smaller $\neg B_1 \vee \neg B_2 \vee \neg A_3$.

In Algorithm 4, on the one hand, shrinking could use a priority queue (implemented as binary heap) to determine the last assigned literal in B. Then for each slice, we have a complexity of $\mathcal{O}(n_b \log n_b)$ for shrinking where n_b is the number of literals at the slice level in the implication graph. On the other hand, minimization of all slices is linear in the size of the implication graph. Overall the complexity is $\mathcal{O}(\text{glue} \cdot n \log n)$ where the "glue" is the number of different slices (and a number that SAT solvers try to reduce heuristically) and n the maximum of the n_b. However, note that, bumping heuristics require sorting of the involved literals anyhow either implicitly or explicitly [6].

Instead of representing the slice B as a priority queue, implemented as binary heap, to iterate over its literals, it is also possible to iterate over the trail directly as it is common in conflict analysis to deduce the 1st-UIP clause. Without chronological backtracking, the slices on the trail are disjoint and iterating over the trail is efficient and gives linear complexity $\mathcal{O}(|\text{glue}| \times |\text{max\_trail\_slice\_length}|)$, i.e., linear in the size of the implication graph.

With chronological backtracking slices on the trail are not guaranteed to be disjoint. Therefore, in the worst case, iterating over a slice along the trail might require to iterate over the complete trail. In principle, this could give a quadratic complexity for chronological backtracking without using a priority queue for B. In our experiments both variants produced almost identical run-times and thus we argue that the simpler variant of going over the trail should be preferred.

We have implemented the algorithm from the previous section in our SAT solvers CaDiCaL [5], Kissat [5], and Satch [4]. The implementation is part of our latest release in the file shrink.c (shrink.cpp for CaDiCaL).[1] Note that, Satch is a simple implementation of the CDCL loop with restarts and was written to explain CDCL. It does not feature any in- nor preprocessing yet.

We either traverse the trail directly or use a radix heap [8] as priority queue. Unlike the implementation by F&B, our priority queue contains only the literals from the current slice until either shrinking fails or the 1-UIP is found. It allows for efficient popping and pushing trail positions. Note that, radix heaps require popped elements to be strictly decreasing, and as the analysis follows reverse trail order, we first compute the maximum trail position of literals in the considered slice and then index literals by their offsets on the tail from this maximum trail position. The literal position in the trail is not cached in every SAT solver, but was already maintained in Kissat and CaDiCaL.

5 Experiments

We have implemented our algorithm in the SAT solvers CaDiCaL, Kissat (the winner of the SAT Competition 2020), and Satch and evaluated them on benchmark instances from the SAT Competition 2020 on an 8-core Intel Xeon E5-2620 v4 CPUs running at 2.10 GHz (turbo-mode disabled). For both tracks we used a memory limit of 128 GB (as in the SAT Competition 2020). We tested 3 configurations, shrink (shrinking and minimizing), minimize, and no-minimize (neither shrinking nor minimizing). Due to space constraint we only give graphs for some solvers but findings are consistent across all of them.

Tables 1 for Kissat and Satch show that minimization is more important than shrinking, but the latter still improves performance for Kissat. In the planning track, running time decreases significantly, whereas the impact on the main track is smaller. Compared to the main track, the planning problems require much more memory and memory usage drops substantially with shrinking. For Satch, we observe a slight performance decrease. Figures 2 and 3 show that even if shrinking solves only a few more problems, the speedup is significant.

In all our SAT solvers we distinguish between *focused mode* (many restarts) and *stable mode* (few restarts). Note that CaDiCaL uses the number of conflicts to switch between these modes which is rather imprecise: in stable mode decision frequency is lower while the conflicts frequency is higher compared to focused mode and accordingly the fraction of running time spent in conflict analysis and thus minimization and shrinking increases in stable mode compared to focused mode. To improve precision both Kissat and Satch measure the time by estimating the number of possible cache misses instead, called "ticks" [5]. By default

---

[1] Source code and log files are available at http://fmv.jku.at/sat_shrinking.

Table 1. Results for new solvers on the SAT Competition 2020 benchmarks

Solver	Track	Configuration	Solved	PAR-2	Average clause size
KISSAT	Main track (400 problems)	Shrink	**270**	**1561735**	**46**
		Minimize	267	1566688	110
		No-minimize	235	1891872	183
	Planning track (200 problems)	Shrink	**85**	**1197799**	**5398**
		Minimize	83	1222535	13076
		No-minimize	74	1325957	16637
SATCH	Main track (400 problems)	Shrink	196	2271119	**46**
		Minimize	**203**	**2240351**	144
		No-minimize	159	2621070	370
	Planning track (200 problems)	Shrink	**85**	**1212977**	**5043**
		Minimize	80	1250861	11854
		No-minimize	72	1338592	15474
CADICAL 1.4.0	Main Track (400 problems)	Shrink	**240**	**1870484**	**90**
		Minimize	233	1939998	121
		No-minimize	194	2280897	153
	Planning track (200 problems)	Shrink	**73**	**1334718**	**4885**
		Minimize	64	1454186	7799
		No-minimize	42	1615676	11767

KISSAT also counts the number of such ticks during shrinking and minimization. To avoid the bias introduced by this technique in terms of influencing mode switching we deactivated this feature in our experiments (only for KISSAT).

We analyzed the results on the main track in more details over all instances (i.e., until timeout or memory out), not only over solved instances. The amount of time (in percentage of the total) more than doubles when activating shrinking: it goes from 6.3 % to 14.3 % of the total amount of time (Fig. 5). However, the size of the clauses is reduced with a similar ratio (Fig. 4): It drops from 110 to 46 (183 without minimization). On the planning track, it drops from 13 076 to 5 398 literals on average (16 637 without minimization).

To compare our method to the *min-alluip* implementation, which is based on CADICAL 1.2.1, we backported our *shrinking* algorithm to CADICAL 1.2.1 too. The results are in Table. 2. The only difference is the shrinking algorithm, hence there are not differences for the minimize and no-minimize configuration. The F&B version performs slightly better than our version. An interesting observation is that CADICAL 1.2.1 learns much larger clauses than KISSAT and SATCH but also larger than the latest CADICAL version. The effect can be partially explained by the stable mode that is much longer than on the other solvers. We have also experimented with minimizing separately from shrinking instead of combining them. As long as the cache is shared there is very little performance difference. Figure 7 shows the CDF for the main track.

Figure 6 shows percentages of removable literals on the planning track. Shrinking removes more literals than the subsequent minimization (and more than minimization alone).

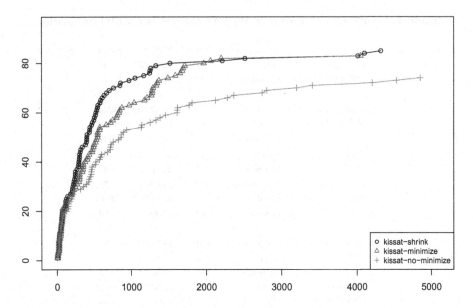

Fig. 2. KISSAT solving time on the planning track.

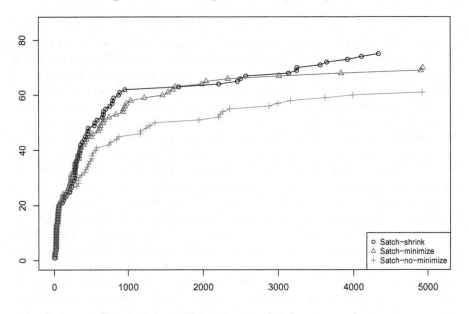

Fig. 3. SATCH solving time on the planning track.

We have mentioned the complexity difference between using a radix heap and iterating over the trail. We have implemented both versions in our three SAT solvers. We compare both version but could not observe any significant difference. We believe that this is due to the fact that finding the next literal is

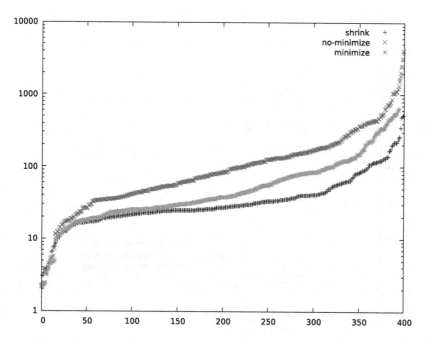

Fig. 4. Absolute sizes of learned clauses of KISSAT on main track.

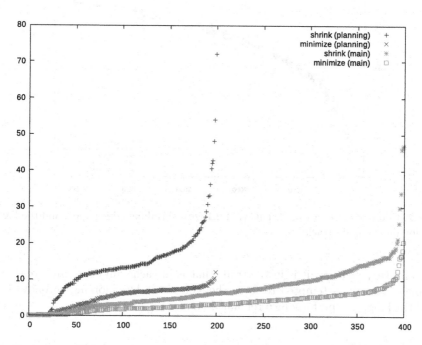

Fig. 5. Amount of time in percent spent during shrinking and minimization of KISSAT.

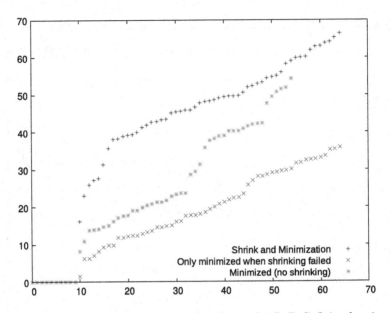

Fig. 6. Percentage removed literals in learned clauses for CADICAL in planning track.

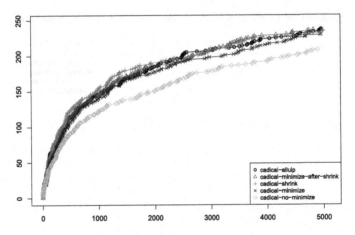

Fig. 7. Comparison between CADICAL-1.2.1 with shrinking (this paper) and the F&B version on the main track.

actually very efficient: it is in the trail (that is in cache anyways) and we check a single flag. We attempted to force the worst case by enforcing chronological backtracking, but performance remained similar.

Table 2. Results for solvers based on CADICAL 1.2.1 on the SAT Competition 2020 benchmarks with a memory limit of 128 GB, following the SAT Competition

Solver	Track	Configuration	Solved	PAR-2	Average clause size
shrinking (this paper)	Main track (400 problems)	Shrink	235	**1897387**	**92**
		Minimize	230	1972949	135
		No-minimize	208	2184920	187
	Planning track (200 problems)	Shrink	73	1351542	5373
		Minimize	63	1454871	6433
		No-minimize	39	1643665	9874
min-alluip [11,14]	Main track	Shrink	**237**	1904745	104
	Planning track	Shrink	**81**	**1271930**	**3261**

6 Conclusion

We presented a simple linear algorithm which integrates minimization and shrinking and is guaranteed to remove all redundant literals. In practice it can be run to completion unconditionally. Our implementation and evaluation with several SAT solvers show the benefit of our approach and confirm effectiveness of shrinking in general.

An open question is how to extend our notion of trail redundancy to capture that new literals can be added in order to reduce size. This would allow to formulate completeness of shrinking in the same way as we did for minimization.

Acknowledgment. This work is supported by Austrian Science Fund (FWF), NFN S11408-N23 (RiSE), and the LIT AI Lab funded by the State of Upper Austria. We also thank Sibylle Möhle and the anonymous reviewers for suggesting textual improvements.

References

1. Audemard, G., Simon, L.: Predicting learnt clauses quality in modern SAT solvers. In: IJCAI, pp. 399–404 (2009), http://ijcai.org/Proceedings/09/Papers/074.pdf
2. Biere, A.: CaDiCaL, Lingeling, Plingeling, Treengeling and YalSAT entering the SAT Competition 2018. In: Heule, M., Järvisalo, M., Suda, M. (eds.) Proceedings of of SAT Competition 2018 - Solver and Benchmark Descriptions. Department of Computer Science Series of Publications B, vol. B-2018-1, pp. 13–14. University of Helsinki (2018)
3. Biere, A.: Lingeling, Plingeling, PicoSAT and PrecoSAT at SAT Race 2010. Technical Report, FMV Reports Series, Institute for Formal Models and Verification, Johannes Kepler University (August 2021)
4. Biere, A.: The SAT solver Satch. Git repository (2021). https://github.com/arminbiere/satch Accessed 03 2021

5. Biere, A., Fazekas, K., Fleury, M., Heisinger, M.: CaDiCaL, Kissat, Paracooba, Plingeling and Treengeling entering the SAT Competition 2020. In: Balyo, T., Froleyks, N., Heule, M., Iser, M., Järvisalo, M., Suda, M. (eds.) Proceedings of SAT Competition 2020 - Solver and Benchmark Descriptions. Department of Computer Science Report Series B, vol. B-2020-1, pp. 51–53. University of Helsinki (2020)
6. Biere, A., Fröhlich, A.: Evaluating CDCL variable scoring schemes. In: Heule, M., Weaver, S. (eds.) SAT 2015. LNCS, vol. 9340, pp. 405–422. Springer, Cham (2015). https://doi.org/10.1007/978-3-319-24318-4_29
7. Biere, A., Heule, M.J.H., van Maaren, H., Walsh, T. (eds.): Handbook of Satisfiability, Frontiers in Artificial Intelligence and Applications, vol. 185. IOS Press, Amsterdam (2009)
8. Cherkassky, B.V., Goldberg, A.V., Silverstein, C.: Buckets, heaps, lists, and monotone priority queues. SIAM J. Comput. **28**(4), 1326–1346 (1999). https://doi.org/10.1137/S0097539796313490
9. Dowling, W.F., Gallier, J.H.: Linear-time algorithms for testing the satisfiability of propositional Horn formulae. J. Log. Program. **1**(3), 267–284 (1984). https://doi.org/10.1016/0743-1066(84)90014-1
10. Eén, N., Sörensson, N.: An extensible SAT-solver. In: Giunchiglia, E., Tacchella, A. (eds.) SAT 2003. LNCS, vol. 2919, pp. 502–518. Springer, Heidelberg (2004). https://doi.org/10.1007/978-3-540-24605-3_37
11. Feng, N., Bacchus, F.: Clause size reduction with all-UIP learning. In: Pulina, L., Seidl, M. (eds.) SAT 2020. LNCS, vol. 12178, pp. 28–45. Springer, Cham (2020). https://doi.org/10.1007/978-3-030-51825-7_3
12. Fleury, M.: Formalization of logical calculi in Isabelle/HOL. Ph.D. thesis, Saarland University, Saarbrücken, Germany (2020). https://tel.archives-ouvertes.fr/tel-02963301
13. Fleury, M., Biere, A.: Efficient all-UIP learned clause minimization (extended version). Technical Report. 21/3, Johannes Kepler University Linz, FMV Reports Series, Institute for Formal Models and Verification, Johannes Kepler University, Altenbergerstr. 69, 4040 Linz, Austria (2021). https://doi.org/10.350/fmvtr.2021-3
14. Hickey, R., Feng, N., Bacchus, F.: Cadical-trail, Cadical-alluip, Cadical-alluip-trail and maple-LCM-dist-alluip-trail at the SAT competition. In: Balyo, T., Froleyks, N., Heule, M., Iser, M., Järvisalo, M., Suda, M. (eds.) Proceedings of SAT Competition 2020 - Solver and Benchmark Descriptions. Department of Computer Science Report Series B, vol. B-2020-1, p. 10. University of Helsinki (2020)
15. Möhle, S., Biere, A.: Backing backtracking. In: Janota, M., Lynce, I. (eds.) SAT 2019. LNCS, vol. 11628, pp. 250–266. Springer, Cham (2019). https://doi.org/10.1007/978-3-030-24258-9_18
16. Nadel, A., Ryvchin, V.: Chronological backtracking. In: Beyersdorff, O., Wintersteiger, C.M. (eds.) SAT 2018. LNCS, vol. 10929, pp. 111–121. Springer, Cham (2018). https://doi.org/10.1007/978-3-319-94144-8_7
17. Silva, J.P.M., Lynce, I., Malik, S.: Conflict-driven clause learning SAT solvers. In: Biere, A., Heule, M., van Maaren, H., Walsh, T. (eds.) Handbook of Satisfiability, Frontiers in Artificial Intelligence and Applications, vol. 185, pp. 131–153. IOS Press (2009). https://doi.org/10.3233/978-1-58603-929-5-131
18. Sörensson, N., Biere, A.: Minimizing learned clauses. In: Kullmann, O. (ed.) SAT 2009. LNCS, vol. 5584, pp. 237–243. Springer, Heidelberg (2009). https://doi.org/10.1007/978-3-642-02777-2_23

19. Gelder, A.: Improved conflict-clause minimization leads to improved propositional proof traces. In: Kullmann, O. (ed.) SAT 2009. LNCS, vol. 5584, pp. 141–146. Springer, Heidelberg (2009). https://doi.org/10.1007/978-3-642-02777-2_15
20. Gelder, A.: Generalized conflict-clause strengthening for satisfiability solvers. In: Sakallah, K.A., Simon, L. (eds.) SAT 2011. LNCS, vol. 6695, pp. 329–342. Springer, Heidelberg (2011). https://doi.org/10.1007/978-3-642-21581-0_26
21. Zhang, L., Madigan, C.F., Moskewicz, M.W., Malik, S.: Efficient conflict driven learning in Boolean satisfiability solver. In: ICCAD, pp. 279–285. IEEE Computer Society (2001). https://doi.org/10.1109/ICCAD.2001.968634

Solving Non-uniform Planted and Filtered Random SAT Formulas Greedily

Tobias Friedrich[1], Frank Neumann[2], Ralf Rothenberger[1],
and Andrew M. Sutton[3]

[1] Hasso Plattner Institute, University of Potsdam, Potsdam, Germany
{tobias.friedrich,ralf.rothenberger}@hpi.de
[2] The University of Adelaide, Adelaide, Australia
frank.neumann@adelaide.edu.au
[3] University of Minnesota Duluth, Duluth, USA
amsutton@d.umn.edu

Abstract. Recently, there has been an interest in studying non-uniform random k-satisfiability (k-SAT) models in order to address the non-uniformity of formulas arising from real-world applications. While uniform random k-SAT has been extensively studied from both a theoretical and experimental perspective, understanding the algorithmic complexity of heterogeneous distributions is still an open challenge. When a sufficiently dense formula is guaranteed to be satisfiable by conditioning or a planted assignment, it is well-known that uniform random k-SAT is easy on average. We generalize this result to the broad class of non-uniform random k-SAT models that are characterized only by an ensemble of distributions over variables with a mild balancing condition. This balancing condition rules out extremely skewed distributions in which nearly half the variables occur less frequently than a small constant fraction of the most frequent variables, but generalizes recently studied non-uniform k-SAT distributions such as power-law and geometric formulas. We show that for all formulas generated from this model of at least logarithmic densities, a simple greedy algorithm can find a solution with high probability.

As a side result we show that the total variation distance between planted and filtered (conditioned on satisfiability) models is $o(1)$ once the planted model produces formulas with a unique solution with probability $1 - o(1)$. This holds for all random k-SAT models where the signs of variables are drawn uniformly and independently at random.

Keywords: Random k-SAT · Planted k-SAT · Non-uniform variable distribution · Greedy algorithm · Local search

Funded by the Deutsche Forschungsgemeinschaft (DFG, German Research Foundation) – 416061626.

C.-M. Li and F. Manyà (Eds.): SAT 2021, LNCS 12831, pp. 188–206, 2021.
https://doi.org/10.1007/978-3-030-80223-3_13

1 Introduction

Propositional satisfiability is one of the most intensively studied topics in theoretical computer science and artificial intelligence. Motivated by the desire to understand the hardness of typical propositional formulas, random satisfiability models were developed [23]. The archetype of these random structures is uniform random k-SAT: a family of distributions over formulas, parameterized by length, in conjunctive normal form with k literals in each clause. A vast number of compelling algorithmic hardness results both theoretical [13–16] and experimental [32,35] has developed from this field.

Despite bringing our understanding of the working principles of SAT solvers into sharper focus, a major drawback of the uniform random model is that it does not typically produce formulas that are similar to ones that come from applications. Thus it is not always clear how hardness results on the uniform random model might translate to other distributions. Recently, an effort has emerged to bridge this gap between the homogeneity of uniform random formulas and heterogeneous models of random satisfiability [2,9,10,17,34]. Moreover, specific properties of industrial instances have been identified, and non-uniform distributions have been subsequently introduced to produce such structures. Notable examples include the community attachment model [27] to address modularity, and the popularity-similarity model [28] to address locality.

Ansótegui et al. [5] studied the constraint graphs of industrial propositional formulas, and found that many reveal a *power law* degree distribution, while the variable degrees of formulas drawn from the uniform random k-SAT model are distributed binomially. To address this, they introduced a non-uniform random power law model that induces power law degree distributions. Other researcher have also noted that real-world formulas (especially those derived from bounded model checking) exhibit such heavy-tailed degree distributions [9]. Moreover, empirical results suggest that solvers specialized for industrial instances tend to perform better on formulas drawn from a power law model than on formulas drawn from a uniform model [3–6,8]. Non-uniform random k-SAT models for which the degree distribution follows a geometric law have also been introduced [6].

It is often difficult to understand how algorithmic results on uniform distributions translate to non-uniform models. We use a general variable distribution framework: random k-SAT models are described by an arbitrary ensemble of variable distributions $(\vec{p}_n)_{n \in \mathbb{N}}$ and the clauses are constructed by drawing variables from $\vec{p}_n$. This framework has recently gained interest in the SAT community. For example, it was shown that under some mild conditions on $\vec{p}_n$, the well-known sharpness result of Friedgut [24] generalizes to the non-planted version of this framework [26]. This line of work can help us understand if k-SAT instances with non-uniform variable distributions are easier to solve. If so, which distributions make them easier and why? If not, which other features of industrial instances are important to make them easily solvable?

Results. In this paper, we show that a result for uniform *planted SAT* models, in which a satisfying assignment is hidden, generalizes to a planted version of the non-uniform framework described earlier. In particular, we generalize an early result of Koutsoupias and Papadimitriou [30] to non-uniform planted SAT distributions. We also improve their lower bound on the density threshold by an $n/\log n$ factor. Distributions for which our results hold include recently introduced non-uniform random satisfiability models such as those with power law degree distributions and geometric degree distributions [6]. For those two models in particular only $\Omega(n \log n)$ clauses suffice to find a satisfying assignment with a simple greedy algorithm with high probability.

Furthermore, we investigate the relation between planted and filtered models. Here, filtered means any random SAT model, where we condition on the generated formulas to be satisfiable. We show a result for all k-SAT models in which the signs of variables are chosen uniformly and independently at random for each clause. This result states that, if the planted model asymptotically almost surely[1] generates formulas with a unique solution (the planted solution) at some constraint density m/n, then the total variation distance between the planted and the filtered model at that density is $o(1)$. This means, our results for non-uniform planted SAT transfer to the corresponding filtered models.

1.1   Planted *k*-SAT

Planted distributions are a common modification to average-case problem distributions for combinatorial problems in which instances are generated together with a solution. A motivation for studying planted distributions is that if no efficient algorithms exist for solving an instance, then the instance-solution pairs comprise a one-way function [22], which has important implications for cryptography.

The planted 3-SAT model has been studied in the context of the warning propagation algorithm, and noted for its similarity to low-density parity check codes [19]. The authors show that warning propagation can solve planted 3-SAT formulas with constant constraint density. Berthet [7] considers the problem of *detecting* whether a formula is drawn from the uniform or the planted distribution in the context of hypothesis testing.

Achlioptas, Jia, and Moore [1] analyze a 2-planted model, where two satisfying assignments are hidden at maximum distance from each other. They experimentally show that in their setting the runtime of local search algorithms is comparable to the runtime on completely random instances. Hu, Luo, and Wang introduce a planted version of community attachement [29] and study it experimentally. Feldman, Perkins, and Vempala [20] study planted k-SAT with different distributions on the signs of clauses.

We consider the greedy algorithm (Algorithm 1) originally introduced by Koutsoupias and Papadimitriou [30] who proved its success on uniform planted

---

[1] We say that an event $\mathcal{E}$ holds *asymptotically almost surely* (a. a. s.) if, over a sequence of sets, $\Pr(\mathcal{E}) = 1$. In the context of this paper, this means $\Pr(\mathcal{E}) = 1 - o(1)$.

formulas with at least linear constraint density, i.e., the ratio of clauses to variables is $\Omega(n)$. Bulatov and Skvortsov [11] proved a phase transition in the uniform model for this algorithm. In particular, for constraint densities above $\frac{7}{6}\ln n$, Algorithm 1 succeeds with high probability. On the other hand, the algorithm fails w.h.p. on formulas with uniformly positive constraint densities below this threshold. More sophisticated algorithms based on spectral techniques have been shown to be successful down to constant densities with high probability [21] and in expected polynomial time [31] on the uniform planted model.

Algorithm 1: Greedy algorithm [30]

1 $\alpha \leftarrow$ an assignment chosen uniformly at random;
2 **while** $\exists i \in [n]$ *such that changing* α_i *increases the number of satisfied clauses* **do**
3 $\quad \lfloor \;\; \alpha[i] \leftarrow 1 - \alpha[i];$
4 **return** α

---

2 Non-uniform Planted k-SAT

In this section we will introduce our model and relevant notation formally. We denote the Boolean variables by $x_1, \ldots, x_n$. A k-clause is a disjunction of k literals $\ell_1 \vee \ldots \vee \ell_k$, where each literal is a variable or its negation. For a literal ℓ_i let $|\ell_i|$ denote the index of its variable. A formula Φ in conjunctive normal form is a conjunction of clauses $C_1 \wedge \ldots \wedge C_m$. We interpret a clause C both as a Boolean formula and as a set of literals. We say that Φ is satisfiable if there exists an assignment of its variables such that the formula evaluates to 1.

Definition 1 (Non-Uniform Random k-SAT). *Let $(\vec{p}_n)_{n \in \mathbb{N}}$ be a set of probability distributions where $\vec{p}_n = (p_1, p_2, \ldots, p_n)$ is a probability distribution over n Boolean variables with $\Pr(X = x_i) = p_i$. The random model $\mathcal{D}(n, m, \vec{p}_n, k)$ can be described as follows.*

1. *for $j \leftarrow 1$ to m:*
   (a) *Sample k variables from the distribution $\vec{p}_n$ without repetition.*
   (b) *Choose one of the 2^k negation patterns uniformly at random.*

Definition 2 (Non-Uniform Planted k-SAT). *Let $(\vec{p}_n)_{n \in \mathbb{N}}$ be a set of probability distributions where $\vec{p}_n = (p_1, p_2, \ldots, p_n)$ is a probability distribution over n Boolean variables with $\Pr(X = x_i) = p_i$. The random planted model $\mathcal{F}(n, m, \vec{p}_n, k)$ can be described as follows.*

1. *Select a planted assignment $\alpha^\star \in \{0, 1\}^n$ uniformly at random*
2. *for $j \leftarrow 1$ to m:*
   (a) *Sample k variables from the distribution $\vec{p}_n$ without repetition.*
   (b) *Choose one of the $2^k - 1$ negation patterns that force the resulting j-th clause to evaluate to true under $\alpha^\star$ uniformly at random.*

We will show in Sect. 3 that the greedy algorithm is successful on non-uniform planted k-SAT if the clause-variable ratio is high enough and if the variable probability distribution is well-behaved in some sense. Moreover, we will relate the two models in Sect. 4, which allows us to conclude that the greedy algorithm also succeeds on satisfiable instances of non-uniform random k-SAT. Our results in Sect. 4 hold for more general versions of those models, which are defined as follows.

Definition 3 (Random k-SAT with Independent Signs). *Let $\mathcal{N}$ denote any random k-SAT model where m clauses are drawn and the signs of variables for each clause are drawn independently and uniformly at random among the 2^k possibilities. Let $F \sim \mathcal{N}$ denote a random formula F drawn in the model N. This means the probability to draw a certain k-CNF f is*

$$\Pr_{F \sim \mathcal{N}} (F = f) = p_f \cdot 2^{-k \cdot m},$$

where p_f denotes the probability to draw the sets of variables that the clauses of f consist of. We call such a model a random k-SAT model with independent signs.

Definition 4 (Corresponding Planted Model). *Let $\mathcal{N}$ be a random k SAT model with independent signs. Now let $\mathcal{P}$ be the following planted model: First draw a planted assignment with probability 2^{-n}, then we draw m clauses in the same way as in $\mathcal{N}$, and draw the signs of variables for each clause independently and uniformly at random among the $2^k - 1$ possibilities that make the planted assignment satisfy the clause. If $X(f)$ denotes the number of satisfying assignments of a k-CNF f, then the probability to draw f is*

$$\Pr_{F \sim \mathcal{P}} (F = f) = p_f \cdot \frac{X(f)}{2^n} \cdot \left(\frac{1}{2^k - 1} \right)^m.$$

We call $\mathcal{P}$ the corresponding planted model *of $\mathcal{N}$.*

Note that the definition of a random k-SAT model with independent signs is very general. It encompasses random k-SAT models where formulas with m clauses over n variables are drawn according to *any* distribution, as long as the sign of each literal is drawn independently at random with probability $1/2$. This includes the community attachment model by Giráldez-Cru and Levy [27] and the approach with given variable degrees of Omelchenko and Bulatov [33] and Levy [12]. Furthermore, it is easy to see that non-uniform random k-SAT is a random k-SAT model with independent signs and that non-uniform planted k-SAT is its corresponding planted model.

Throughout the paper, we will assume that $k \geq 3$ is a constant. Note that according to our models clauses can be drawn repeatedly. Furthermore, to simplify the proofs, we assume the variables are sampled with replacement. However, we remark that for k constant and p_n bounded away from 1 by a constant, this changes the clause probabilities by at most a constant factor (see, e.g., [25]).

In this setting, the probability to draw a legal clause $C = (\ell_1 \vee \ldots \vee \ell_k)$ is $\frac{k!}{2^k-1} \cdot \prod_{j=1}^{k} p_{|\ell_j|}$.

We denote $[n] := [1, n] \cap \mathbb{N}$. For a discrete probability distribution $\vec{p} = (p_1, \ldots, p_n)$ we assume $p_1 \leq p_2 \leq \cdots \leq p_n$. For a particular $\mathcal{F}(n, m, \vec{p}_n, k)$, we define the parameter $\gamma(\varepsilon) := \Pr(i \leq (1/2 - \varepsilon) \cdot n - (k-1))$. Here, i is a random variable with $\Pr(i = j) = p_j$ for $j \in [n]$. We will denote the Hamming distance between two assignments $\alpha, \beta \in \{0, 1\}^n$ by $d(\alpha, \beta)$ and simply refer to it as the "distance".

3   The Greedy Algorithm on Non-uniform Planted k-SAT

In this section, we will show that for sufficiently high constraint densities Algorithm 1 asymptotically almost surely finds a satisfying assignment of non-uniform planted k-SAT if a condition on the probability distribution of the model is fulfilled. The condition that has to be satisfied is that there are constants $\varepsilon \in (0, 1/2)$ and $\varepsilon' \in (0, \varepsilon)$ such that

$$\Pr\left(i \leq (1/2 - \varepsilon') \cdot n - (k-1)\right) > c + \Pr\left(i > (1/2 + \varepsilon) \cdot n\right) \tag{1}$$

for some $c = \Omega\left(\left(n \cdot p_1 \cdot \gamma(\varepsilon)^{3(k-1)}/\ln n\right)^{1/2k}\right)$. If a probability distribution $\vec{p}$ satisfies this condition, we call it "well-behaved". Formally, we show the following.

Theorem 11. *For a formula F drawn from $\mathcal{F}(m, n, \vec{p}, k)$ with a well-behaved probability distribution $\vec{p}$ with parameters ε and ε', and $m \geq \frac{C \ln n}{\gamma(\varepsilon)^{3(k-1)} p_1}$, where $k \geq 3$ is a constant and $C > 0$ is some sufficiently large constant, Algorithm 1 succeeds with high probability.*

Note that the choice of ε in the well-behavedness condition influences the value of $\gamma(\varepsilon)$ in the number of clauses necessary for the algorithm to succeed. It generally holds that the more uniform the probability distribution is, the smaller we can choose ε and a smaller ε results in a smaller lower bound on the number of clauses.

We call an assignment $\alpha \in \{0, 1\}^n$ *good* if it satisfies all clauses or if there is an assignment β with $|\{i : \alpha_i \neq \beta_i\}| = 1$ and β satisfies strictly more clauses than α. We will show that a. a. s. all assignments that Algorithm 1 finds are good. Thus, the assignment it returns must be satisfying. To this end we consider assignments at distances $(1/2 + \varepsilon') \cdot n$ and $(1/2 + \varepsilon) \cdot n$ from the planted assignment $\alpha^\star$. Here, ε' and ε are the parameters of the well-behavedness condition with $0 < \varepsilon' < \varepsilon < 1/2$. There are five ingredients to the proof: (1) two technical lemmas, Lemmas 6 and 7, (2) Lemma 8, which states that all assignments within distance $(1/2 + \varepsilon) \cdot n$ of $\alpha^\star$ are good, (3) Lemma 9, which states that the random starting assignment is at distance at most $(1/2 + \varepsilon') \cdot n$ from $\alpha^\star$, (4) Lemma 10, which states that any assignment at distance $(1/2 + \varepsilon') \cdot n$ from $\alpha^\star$ satisfies at least as many clauses as any assignment at distance $(1/2 + \varepsilon) \cdot n$ from $\alpha^\star$, and (5) Theorem 11, which puts these ingredients together.

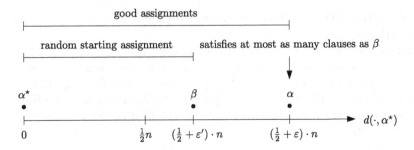

Fig. 1. Sketch of the assignment space with the planted assignment α^* and the properties we show. (2) Lemma 8: All assignments within distance $(1/2 + \varepsilon) \cdot n$ of α^* are good, (3) Lemma 9: The random starting assignment is at distance at most $(1/2+\varepsilon') \cdot n$ from α^*, (4) Lemma 10: any assignment at distance $(1/2 + \varepsilon') \cdot n$ from α^* satisfies at least as many clauses as any assignment at distance $(1/2 + \varepsilon) \cdot n$ from α^*

The argument now works as follows. Since the local search algorithm always picks an assignment that strictly increases the number of satisfied clauses, (4) implies that from an assignment at distance $(1/2 + \varepsilon') \cdot n$, it will never reach one at distance $(1/2 + \varepsilon) \cdot n$. Due to (3) the algorithm starts with an assignment within distance $(1/2+\varepsilon') \cdot n$ of α^*. Thus, all assignments found by the algorithm must remain within distance $(1/2+\varepsilon) \cdot n$ of α^*. Since all assignments within that distance to α^* are good due to (2), all assignments found by the algorithm are good and the final assignment must be satisfying. Figure 1 visualizes the idea of the proof. Furthermore, Corollary 12 shows that some natural probability distributions are well-behaved for certain constants $\varepsilon, \varepsilon'$, which result in a constant $\gamma(\varepsilon)$. For instances of non-uniform planted k-SAT with these input distributions Algorithm 1 already works for logarithmic densities.

The efficiency of the greedy algorithm depends on the probability of sampling clauses over certain subsets of variables. We capture the probability of sampling a certain subset of variables in the following definition.

Definition 5. *Given any index set $I \subseteq [n]$, let $\mathcal{P}_l(I) = \{J \subseteq I : |J| = l\}$ denote the cardinality-l elements of the power set of I and define $Q_l(I) := \sum_{J \in \mathcal{P}_l(I)} \prod_{j \in J} p_j$ to be the probability of selecting l elements of I over $\bar{p}$.*

$Q_l(I)$ is the probability of choosing l variables with indices only from I. Note that $Q_l(I) \geq Q_{l'}(I)$ for $l \leq l'$. We want to lower-bound the probability $Q_l(I)$ for $|I| \geq (1/2 - \varepsilon) \cdot n$. In the uniform planted model a lower bound would be roughly $(1/2 - \varepsilon)^l$, where $0 < \varepsilon < 1/2$ is a constant. However, in our setting, where variable probabilities are non-uniform, $Q_l(I)$ depends on the total probability mass of the $(1/2 - \varepsilon) \cdot n - (l - 1)$ least probable variables. We underestimate and capture this probability mass in the parameter $\gamma(\varepsilon) = \Pr(i \leq (1/2 - \varepsilon) \cdot n - (k - 1))$. The following lemma now provides us with a lower bound on $Q_l(I)$ depending on $\gamma(\varepsilon)$.

Lemma 6. *If $\gamma(\varepsilon) > 0$ for some constant $0 < \varepsilon < 1/2$, then for any index set I with $|I| \geq (1/2 - \varepsilon) \cdot n$ and any natural number $l \leq k$, we have $Q_l(I) \geq \frac{\gamma(\varepsilon)^l}{l!}$.*

Proof. We can express $Q_l(I)$ as the following nested sum

$$Q_l(I) = \frac{1}{l!} \sum_{i_1 \in I} \sum_{i_2 \in I \setminus \{i_1\}} \cdots \sum_{i_l \in I \setminus \{i_1, \ldots, i_{l-1}\}} \prod_{j=1}^{l} p_{i_j}$$

$$= \frac{1}{l!} \sum_{i_1 \in I} p_{i_1} \sum_{i_2 \in I \setminus \{i_1\}} p_{i_2} \cdots \sum_{i_l \in I \setminus \{i_1, \ldots, i_{l-1}\}} p_{i_l}.$$

This sum essentially captures the choices of elements we have for each term in $Q_l(I)$, where i_j is the j-th chosen element. Since we only forbid repetitions of elements, the j-th element can be anything from $I \setminus \{i_1, i_2, \ldots, i_{j-1}\}$. Since $|I| \geq (1/2 - \varepsilon) \cdot n$, we can always choose from at least $(1/2 - \varepsilon) \cdot n - (l-1)$ many elements. It holds that

$$Q_l(I) \geq \frac{1}{l!} \left(\sum_{i=1}^{(1/2-\varepsilon) \cdot n - (l-1)} p_i \right)^l = \frac{1}{l!} \Pr(i \leq (1/2 - \varepsilon) \cdot n - (l-1))^l \geq \frac{\gamma(\varepsilon)^l}{l!}.$$

as we assume the p_i to be in ascending order.   □

The following technical lemma bounds the probability of making a random clause satisfied or unsatisfied by decreasing the Hamming distance to the planted solution. These bounds especially hold if the distance is decreased by only one, i.e. we flip the assignment of a single variable. The statements of this lemma will be used in order to show that assignments close to the planted solution are good.

Lemma 7. *Fix an assignment $\alpha \in \{0,1\}^n$ at Hamming distance $d(\alpha, \alpha^\star) < (1/2+\varepsilon) \cdot n$ from the planted solution. For any assignment β with $\{i : \alpha_i = \alpha_i^\star\} \subseteq \{i : \beta_i = \alpha_i^\star\}$, denote $\pi_{\alpha\beta}$ as the probability over $\mathcal{F}(n, m, \vec{p}, k)$ that a clause is false under α and true under β. Analogously, we let $\pi_{\beta\alpha}$ denote the probability that a clause is false under β and true under α. With $I = \{i : \alpha_i \neq \beta_i \wedge \beta_i = \alpha_i^\star\}$ it holds that*

1. *$\pi_{\beta\alpha} \leq (1 - \frac{\gamma(\varepsilon)^{k-1}}{(k-1)!}) \cdot \pi_{\alpha\beta}$, and*
2. *$\pi_{\alpha\beta} \geq \frac{k \cdot \gamma(\varepsilon)^{k-1} \cdot |I| \cdot p_1}{2^k - 1}$.*

Proof. In addition to I, we will denote the set $J := \{i : \alpha_i = \alpha_i^\star\}$. Note that $|I| = d(\alpha, \beta) \leq d(\alpha, \alpha^\star)$ and that $d(\alpha, \alpha^\star) = n - |J|$. A clause changes from false to true between α and β if it (1) contains any variable indexed in I, and (2) the literals in the clause are set such that it evaluates to false under x. Note that the first condition implies $\alpha \neq \beta$ and $\alpha \neq \alpha^\star$. This is necessary in order for a clause to evaluate to false under α and to evaluate differently under β. The probability for these events to occur is

$$\pi_{\alpha\beta} = \frac{k!}{2^k - 1} \sum_{\ell=1}^{k} Q_\ell(I) \cdot Q_{k-\ell}([n] \setminus I)$$

We have the same for $\pi_{\beta\alpha}$. Again, the clause must contain a variable from I for α and β to be different and this time the literals must evaluate to false under β. Additionally, we must take care that clauses that are false under $\alpha^\star$ are not allowed. In particular, if a clause contains only variables from $I \cup J$, i.e. only variables where β and $\alpha^\star$ do not differ, then the clause cannot evaluate to false under β. Thus, we must exclude such clauses from the probability mass. In particular,

$$\pi_{\beta\alpha} = \frac{k!}{2^k - 1} \sum_{\ell=1}^{k} Q_\ell(I) \cdot (Q_{k-\ell}([n] \setminus I) - Q_{k-\ell}(J))$$

$$\leq \frac{k!}{2^k - 1} \sum_{\ell=1}^{k} Q_\ell(I) Q_{k-\ell}([n] \setminus I) - \frac{k!}{2^k - 1} \sum_{\ell=1}^{k} Q_\ell(I) Q_{k-\ell}([n] \setminus I) Q_{k-\ell}(J)$$

$$\leq \left(1 - \frac{\gamma^{k-1}}{(k-1)!}\right) \pi_{\alpha\beta}.$$

The final inequality comes from Lemma 6 and the fact that $|J| = n - d(\alpha, \alpha^\star) \geq (1/2 - \varepsilon) \cdot n$, which allows us to bound $Q_{k-\ell}(J) \geq Q_{k-1}(J) \geq \frac{\gamma(\varepsilon)^{k-1}}{(k-1)!}$.

The second statement holds since

$$\pi_{\alpha\beta} \geq \frac{k!}{2^k - 1} Q_1(I) \cdot Q_{k-1}([n] \setminus I) = \frac{k!}{2^k - 1} \sum_{i \in I} p_i \cdot Q_{k-1}([n] \setminus I)$$

$$\geq \frac{k! \cdot |I| \cdot p_1}{2^k - 1} \cdot Q_{k-1}([n] \setminus I) \geq \frac{k \cdot \gamma(\varepsilon)^{k-1} \cdot |I| \cdot p_1}{2^k - 1}.$$

The final inequality comes from Lemma 6 and the fact that $|[n] \setminus I| = n - d(\alpha, \beta) \geq (1/2 - \varepsilon) \cdot n$.   □

We will now show that w. h. p. assignments close to the planted assignment $\alpha^\star$ are good. This is the second ingredient of our argument. Remember that we call an assignment $\alpha \in \{0,1\}^n$ good if it satisfies all clauses or if there is an assignment β at distance one which satisfies strictly more clauses.

Lemma 8. *Let F be a formula drawn from $\mathcal{F}(m, n, \vec{p}, k)$, let $\varepsilon \in (0, 1/2)$ be a constant, and let $m \geq \frac{C \ln n}{\gamma(\varepsilon)^{3(k-1)} p_1}$, where $k \geq 3$ is a constant and $C > 0$ is some sufficiently large constant. Then all assignments α within distance $(1/2 + \varepsilon) \cdot n$ of the planted assignment $\alpha^\star$ are good with high probability.*

Proof. Fix an assignment α with $d(\alpha, \alpha^\star) < (1/2 + \varepsilon) \cdot n$. Denote the random variable X_{ij} that indicates that the j-th clause is false under α, but becomes true by flipping the i-th variable. Similarly, denote as Y_{ij} the random variable that indicates that the j-th clause is true under α but becomes false by flipping the i-th variable. Define $X = \sum_{i:\alpha_i \neq \alpha_i^*} \sum_{j=1}^m X_{ij}$ and $Y = \sum_{i:\alpha_i \neq \alpha_i^*} \sum_{j=1}^m Y_{ij}$. By Lemma 7, $E[X_{ij}] = \pi_{\alpha\beta}$ and $E[Y_{ij}] = \pi_{\beta\alpha}$, where α and β differ only on $I = \{i\}$. Thus, $E[Y] \leq (1 - \frac{\gamma(\varepsilon)^{k-1}}{(k-1)!})E[X]$.

We want to use Chernoff bounds to show that the values of X and Y are concentrated around their expected values. First, we argue why Chernoff bounds can be applied. X and Y only consider assignments β that differ from α in one variable and are closer to α^*. Let $X_j = \sum_{i:\ \alpha_i \neq \alpha_i^*} X_{ij}$ and $Y_j = \sum_{i:\ \alpha_i \neq \alpha_i^*} Y_{ij}$. X_j denotes the number of those assignments, which make a clause true that is false under α, while Y_j denotes the number of those assignments that make a clause false that is true under α. It holds that $Y_j \leq 1$. If a clause is false under one assignment β, it must be true under all assignments that differ on that clause's variables. We know that the clause is true under α and since all other assignments $\beta' \neq \beta$ we consider differ from α in exactly one variable, as soon as they differ from α on one of the clause's variables, they must also differ from β on the clause's variables. Thus, the clause must be satisfiable on all assignments $\beta \neq \beta'$ we consider. $Y_j \leq 1$ implies that we can use a Chernoff bound on $Y = \sum_{j=1}^m Y_j$, since the Y_j are independent random variables with values in $[0, 1]$. Similarly, $X_j \leq k$, because if a clause is false under α, then all assignments that differ on that clause's variables will make the clause true. Thus, this holds for all assignments β that differ on one of the clause's variables. However, since we only consider those assignments β that differ from α by at most one variable, there are at most k such assignments, one for each variable of the k-clause. $X_j \leq k$ implies that we can use a Chernoff bound after resizing the variables X_j with a factor of $1/k$. This yields random variables whose values are independently distributed in $[0, 1]$. However, it means that the expected value in the exponent also has to be multiplied with $1/k$.

Applying the Chernoff bounds as stated, for any $\delta \in (0, 1)$, we have $\Pr(X \leq (1 - \delta)E[X]) \leq e^{-\delta^2 E[X]/(2 \cdot k)}$. For Y we choose δ' such that $(1 + \delta')E[Y] = (1 + \delta)(1 - \frac{\gamma(\varepsilon)^{k-1}}{(k-1)!})E[X]$. Then, $\delta' \geq \delta$ and $\delta' \cdot E[Y] \geq \delta \cdot (1 - \frac{\gamma(\varepsilon)^{k-1}}{(k-1)!})E[X]$. We can now apply a Chernoff bound to get

$$\Pr\left(Y \geq (1 + \delta')E[Y]\right) \leq e^{-\delta'^2 E[Y]/(2+\delta')} \leq e^{-\delta^2(1-\frac{\gamma(\varepsilon)^{k-1}}{(k-1)!})E[X]/(2+\delta)}.$$

Taking a union bound, the probability of event $\{X \leq (1 - \delta)E[X]\} \cup \{Y \geq (1+\delta)\left(1 - \frac{\gamma(\varepsilon)^{k-1}}{(k-1)!}\right)E[X]\}$ is at most $\exp(-\delta^2 \left(1 - \frac{\gamma(\varepsilon)^{k-1}}{(k-1)!}\right)E[X]/(k \cdot ((2+\delta)) + \ln 2)$. Setting $\delta = \kappa/(2 - \kappa)$ with $\kappa = \frac{\gamma(\varepsilon)^{k-1}}{(k-1)!}$, the event $\{X > Y\}$ occurs with probability at least

$$1 - \exp\left(-\frac{(1 - \kappa) \cdot \kappa^2}{k \cdot (2 - \kappa)(4 - \kappa)}E[X] + \ln 2\right). \tag{2}$$

Remember that X only considers assignments which differ from α in one variable $\alpha_i \neq \alpha_i^*$. Hence, $|I| = 1$ for α and any such assignment β. Thus, according to Lemma 7,

$$E[X] \geq m \cdot d(\alpha, \alpha^\star) \cdot \frac{k \cdot \gamma(\varepsilon)^{k-1} \cdot p_1}{2^k - 1} = m \cdot d(\alpha, \alpha^\star) \cdot \frac{k! \cdot \kappa \cdot p_1}{2^k - 1}.$$

Substituting this into Eq. (2) and using $0 \leq \kappa = \frac{\gamma(\varepsilon)^{k-1}}{(k-1)!} \leq \frac{1}{(k-1)!}$ we get $\frac{(1-\kappa)\cdot\kappa^3}{(2-\kappa)(4-\kappa)} \geq (1 - 1/(k-1)!) \cdot \gamma(\varepsilon)^{3k-3}/(2 \cdot (k-1)!)^3 = \Omega(\gamma(\varepsilon)^{3(k-1)})$. Thus, the event $\{X > Y\}$ occurs for assignment α with probability at least

$$1 - \exp\left(-\Omega\left(\gamma(\varepsilon)^{3(k-1)} \cdot p_1 \cdot d(\alpha, \alpha^\star) \cdot m\right)\right).$$

This means the average count of clauses that go from false to true minus the count that go from true to false by flipping assignments in $\{i : \alpha_i \neq \alpha_i^\star\}$ is positive, and we can conclude that there exists at least one such flip that increases the total count of satisfied clauses. Hence, α is *good* with the above probability.

Taking a simple union bound over all $\binom{n}{d} \leq n^d$ assignments α at distance $d = d(\alpha, \alpha^\star)$, all assignments at this distance are good with probability at least

$$1 - n^d \exp\left(-\Omega\left(\gamma(\varepsilon)^{3(k-1)} \cdot p_1 \cdot d \cdot m\right)\right) \geq 1 - \exp(-\Omega(d \log n)) = 1 - n^{-C'd}$$

for some constant C' by choosing $m \geq \frac{C \cdot \ln n}{\gamma(\varepsilon)^{3(k-1)} \cdot p_1}$ with constant C large enough. A subsequent union bound over all such radius-d spheres yields that all assignments within distance $(1/2 + \varepsilon) \cdot n$ of the planted solution are good with probability at least $1 - \sum_{d=1}^{\lfloor (1/2+\varepsilon)n \rfloor} n^{-C'd} \geq 1 - 1/\left(n^{C'} - 1\right)$, i.e. with high probability. □

Now we are going to show the third ingredient of our argument, i.e. that the random starting assignment is close to the planted assignment with high probability.

Lemma 9. *For any constant $\varepsilon' \in (0, 1/2)$ the random starting assignment is within distance at most $(1/2 + \varepsilon') \cdot n$ of the planted assignment $\alpha^\star$ with high probability.*

Proof. Since the starting assignment $\alpha = (\alpha_1, \alpha_2, \ldots, \alpha_n)$ is generated uniformly at random, each α_i differs from $\alpha_i^\star$ with probability $1/2$ independently at random. Let X_i denote the random variable indicating that $\alpha_i \neq \alpha_i^\star$ and let $X = \sum_{i=1}^n X_i$. We can see that $d(\alpha, \alpha^\star) = X$. It holds that $E[X] = n/2$ and

$$\Pr(d(\alpha, \alpha^\star) > (1/2 + \varepsilon') \cdot n) = \Pr(X > (1 + 2 \cdot \varepsilon') \cdot E[X]) \leq e^{-\frac{2 \cdot \varepsilon'^2 \cdot n}{2 + 2 \cdot \varepsilon'}}$$

due to a Chernoff bound. □

The last ingredient of our argument is to show that any assignment β at distance $(1/2 + \varepsilon') \cdot n$ from $\alpha^\star$ satisfies at least as many clauses as any assignment α at distance $(1/2 + \varepsilon) \cdot n$ from $\alpha^\star$. In order to show this result, we require the variable probability distribution of our random model to be well-behaved. For β

and α well-behavedness essentially states that it is more probable to randomly sample a variable on which $\alpha^\star$ and β agree than it is to sample a variable on which $\alpha^\star$ and α agree. For a uniform probability distribution this is trivially true, since the number of those variables is much larger in β than it is in α due to β's smaller Hamming distance to $\alpha^\star$. However, for a non-uniform probability distribution, the property must be ensured. We will later see in Corollary 12 that uniform, power-law and geometric distributions are well-behaved.

Lemma 10. *Let $k \geq 3$ be a constant and let $\vec{p}$ be a probability distribution that is well-behaved for constants $\varepsilon \in (0, 1/2)$ and $\varepsilon' \in (0, \varepsilon)$. Further, let $m \geq \frac{C \ln n}{\gamma(\varepsilon)^{3(k-1)} p_1}$ for a sufficiently large constant $C > 0$, and let F be a formula drawn from $\mathcal{F}(m, n, \vec{p}, k)$. Then with high probability any assignment α with $d(\alpha, \alpha^\star) = (1/2 + \varepsilon) \cdot n$ satisfies at most as many clauses of F as any assignment β with $d(\beta, \alpha^\star) = (1/2 + \varepsilon') \cdot n$.*

Proof Sketch. The idea of the proof is to lower-bound the difference $\pi_{\alpha\beta} - \pi_{\beta\alpha}$, where $\pi_{\alpha\beta}$ is the probability that a random clause is not satisfied by α and satisfied by β. This difference depends on the probabilites of variables in I, the set of variables on which α and β differ. More precisely, it depends on the difference between the probability of sampling a variable from I for which α and $\alpha^\star$ disagree and the probability of sampling a variable from I for which α and $\alpha^\star$ agree. In the worst case the prior set of variables are those of minimal probabilities, while the latter are those of maximal probabilities according to the probability distribution $\vec{p}$. If we pessimistically assume this, the difference is minimized if I is of maximum size. Then, there are $(1/2 - \varepsilon') \cdot n$ variables in I on which α and $\alpha^\star$ disagree and $(1/2 - \varepsilon) \cdot n$ variables on which the assignments agree. However, the difference of the probabilites to sample those variables is lower bounded by $c = \Omega\left(\left(n \cdot p_1 \cdot \gamma(\varepsilon)^{3(k-1)} / \ln n\right)^{1/2k}\right)$ by the well-behavedness of $\vec{p}$ (Eq. 1).

By using a Chernoff bound, we can now show that the probability that α satisfies at least as many clauses as β is upper bounded by $\sim \exp(-m \cdot c^{2k}) \sim 2^{-\Omega(n)}$. Via a union bound we get that the probability is still exponentially small in n for all pairs of assignments α and β if C is sufficiently large. $\square$

We can now put the ingredients of our argument together to get our main theorem.

Theorem 11. *For a formula F drawn from $\mathcal{F}(m, n, \vec{p}, k)$ with a well-behaved probability distribution $\vec{p}$ with parameters ε and ε', and $m \geq \frac{C \ln n}{\gamma(\varepsilon)^{3(k-1)} p_1}$, where $k \geq 3$ is a constant and $C > 0$ is some sufficiently large constant, Algorithm 1 succeeds with high probability.*

Proof. All statements in the proof hold with high probability. Lemma 9 tells us that the random starting assignment is within distance $(1/2 + \varepsilon') \cdot n$ of the planted assignment $\alpha^\star$. The local search algorithm now considers assignments within Hamming distance one of the currently best assignment found. Furthermore, the algorithm only accepts a new best assignment if it satisfies strictly more clauses than the previous best assignment. Thus, to reach an assignment α at distance $(1/2 + \varepsilon) \cdot n$ from α^*, it first has to accept an assignment β at distance $(1/2 + \varepsilon') \cdot n$ from α^* and α has to satisfy strictly more clauses than β. However, Lemma 10 tells us that this is not possible. Therefore, any assignment found by the algorithm has to be within distance $(1/2 + \varepsilon) \cdot n$ of α^*. Lemma 8 states that all those assignments are good. Thus, all assignments found by the algorithm are good and the final assignment must be satisfying.   □

The $\gamma(\varepsilon)$ term in our proofs is a penalty incurred from having a potentially pathologically "light" tail in the variable distribution. If $\gamma(\varepsilon) = o(1)$, this means that most of the probability mass is concentrated around the $(1/2 + \varepsilon) \cdot n$ most frequent variables, and the tail vanishes very quickly. In some sense, if the tail is at least as heavy as the uniform distribution, then $\gamma = \Theta(1)$. This is the case for most proposed classes of non-uniform variable distributions, as we formalize in Corollary 12.

The well-behavedness of the variable distribution intuitively states something similar. It also requires that not too much probability mass is concentrated around the most frequent variables. Note that ε denotes the same value in both requirements. We can see that increasing ε and decreasing ε' makes it easier to satisfy this prerequisite. However, increasing ε decreases $\gamma(\varepsilon)$ and thus increases the lower bound on the clause-variable ratio for which our main theorem holds.

Theorem 11 implies that the greedy algorithm already works at some logarithmic density if the variables of the planted model follow three well-known probability distributions: uniform, power-law, or geometric. We show this in the following corollary.

Corollary 12. *The greedy algorithm is successful over a $1 - o(1)$ fraction of planted*

1. *uniform random k-SAT formulas,*
2. *power-law random k-SAT formulas with power-law exponent $\beta > 2$,*
3. *geometric random k-SAT formulas[2] with a base $b > 1$,*

with $\frac{m}{n} \geq C \ln n$, for constant $k \geq 3$ and a sufficiently large constant C.

Proof. The statement follows by application of Theorem 11, so it suffices to verify the minimum variable probability p_1, the γ term, and the well-behavedness of the distribution for each of the stated models.

1. Uniform: In the uniform k-SAT distribution, $p_1 = p_i = 1/n$ for all $i \in [n]$. Therefore, $\gamma(\varepsilon) = (1/2 - \varepsilon) - (k - 1)/n = \Theta(1)$ and

$$\Pr\left(i \leq (1/2 - \varepsilon') \cdot n - (k - 1)\right) = (1/2 - \varepsilon') - (k - 1)/n$$
$$\geq c + (1/2 - \varepsilon) = c + \Pr\left(i > (1/2 + \varepsilon) \cdot n\right)$$

for $c = \varepsilon - \varepsilon' - (k - 1)/n$. Thus, Algorithm 1 succeeds w. h. p. for clause-variable ratios $\frac{m}{n} \geq C \cdot \frac{\ln n}{n \cdot \gamma(\varepsilon)^{3(k-1)} \cdot p_1} = C \cdot \ln n$ for some sufficiently large constant $C > 0$.

---

[2] We refer to the geometric degree-distribution model introduced by Ansótegui et al. [6].

2. Power law: For the power-law distribution, $p_1 = (1/\sum_{i=1}^{n} (\frac{n}{i})^{\frac{1}{\beta-1}}) = \Omega(1/n)$ and $p_n = \Theta(n^{-(\beta-2)/(\beta-1)})$. Thus, $\gamma(\varepsilon) = \Pr(i \le (1/2-\varepsilon) \cdot n - (k-1)) = \Theta(1)$, since $\Pr(i \le (1/2-\varepsilon) \cdot n - (k-1)) \ge (1/2-\varepsilon) \cdot n \cdot p_1 - (k-1) \cdot p_n = \Omega(1)$. In order to validate the well-behavedness of the distribution, we can estimate $\Pr(i > (1/2+\varepsilon) \cdot n) \le (1/2-\varepsilon)^{(\beta-2)/(\beta-1)}$ and, equivalently

$$\Pr(i \le (1/2-\varepsilon') \cdot n - (k-1)) = 1 - \Pr(i > (1/2-\varepsilon') \cdot n - (k-1))$$
$$\ge 1 - (1/2+\varepsilon' + (k-1)/n)^{(\beta-2)/(\beta-1)}.$$

Thus, for any $\varepsilon' \in (0, 1/2)$ we can choose $\varepsilon > \max(\varepsilon', \varepsilon_0)$, where ε_0 is the solution of

$$1 - (1/2+\varepsilon' + (k-1)/n)^{(\beta-2)/(\beta-1)} = (1/2-\varepsilon)^{(\beta-2)/(\beta-1)}.$$

Note that this lower bound on ε is always in $(0, 1/2)$ and thus satisfies our requirements. As in the uniform case, this results in a lower bound of $\frac{m}{n} \ge C \cdot \ln n$ for some sufficiently large constant $C > 0$ in order for Algorithm 1 to succeed with high probability.

3. Geometric: In geometric random k-SAT, $p_i = \frac{1-b^{-1/n}}{b-1} \cdot b^{i/n}$. It now holds that $\sum_{i=1}^{(1/2-\varepsilon)n} p_i = \frac{b^{1/2-\varepsilon}-1}{b-1}$ and thus $\gamma(\varepsilon) = \frac{b^{1/2-\varepsilon-(k-1)/n}-1}{b-1} = \Theta(1)$. Furthermore,

$$p_1 = \frac{b^{1/n}-1}{b-1} = \frac{e^{\ln(b)/n}-1}{b-1} \ge \frac{1+\ln(b)/n-1}{b-1} = \frac{\ln(b)}{b-1} \cdot \frac{1}{n}.$$

For the requirement from Eq. 1, we get

$$\Pr(i > (1/2+\varepsilon) \cdot n) = 1 - \Pr(i \le (1/2+\varepsilon) \cdot n) = 1 - \frac{b^{1/2+\varepsilon}-1}{b-1}.$$

This means, we need to ensure $\frac{b^{1/2-\varepsilon'-(k-1)/n}-1}{b-1} > 1 - \frac{b^{1/2+\varepsilon}-1}{b-1}$ or, equivalently, $b^{1/2+\varepsilon} > b + 1 - b^{1/2-\varepsilon'-(k-1)/n}$. Note that $b^{1/2-\varepsilon'-(k-1)/n} > 1$. Thus, the right-hand side is a constant smaller than b. If we make $\varepsilon \in (0, 1/2)$ sufficiently large, we can make the left-hand side by a constant bigger than the right-hand side. This is sufficient for the requirement from inequality 1. Again, we get that the greedy algorithm succeeds w. h. p. for $\frac{m}{n} \ge C \cdot \ln n$ and $C > 0$ sufficiently large. $\square$

4   Relationship Between Planted and Filtered Instances

One interesting question is if the behavior of the greedy algorithm is an artifact of the instances being planted or if the same behavior emerges for satisfiable instances of the corresponding non-planted model. Thus, we now look at random k-SAT models with independent signs and their corresponding planted models. We show the following theorem, which is a generalization of a result by Doerr, Neumann, and Sutton [18].

Theorem 13. *Let $\mathcal{P} = \mathcal{F}(n, m, \vec{p}_n, k)$ be a non-uniform planted k-SAT model and let $\mathcal{N}$ be a non-uniform random k-SAT model on the same input parameters. Then for $m \geq \frac{(1+\varepsilon)\cdot(2^k - 1)}{p_1} \cdot \ln n$ with any constant $\varepsilon > 0$ and for any event $\mathcal{E}$ it holds that $\Pr_{F \sim \mathcal{N}} (\mathcal{E} \mid X(F) \geq 1) = \Pr_{F \sim \mathcal{P}} (\mathcal{E}) \pm o(1)$.*

Proof Sketch. The proof follows the same lines as the one in [18]. We first show that for a random k-SAT model with independent signs and its planted equivalent the conditional probability to sample a certain formula is the same in both models if we condition on there being exactly one satisfying assignment. Then, we show that the probability to have exactly one satisfying assignment in the filtered model (conditioned on formulas being satisfiable) is at least as high as in the planted model. These two statements already imply a total variation distance that tends to zero as soon as the probability to have a unique satisfying assignment tends to one in the planted model. The last step of the proof consists of finding a number of clauses m for which formulas generated with non-uniform planted k-SAT a. a. s. only have one satisfying assignment. A first oder bound shows that this is case if $m \geq \frac{(1+\varepsilon)\cdot(2^k - 1)}{p_1} \cdot \ln n$ for any constant $\varepsilon > 0$.   □

Theorem 13 asserts that Theorem 11 also holds for the filtered non-uniform random k-SAT model. That means, for satisfiable formulas drawn from the non-uniform random k-SAT model the greedy algorithm also succeeds with probability $1 - o(1)$.

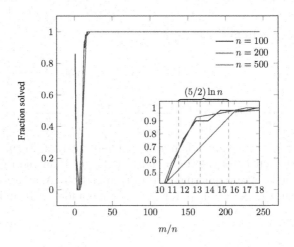

Fig. 2. Fraction of formulas solved by Algorithm 1 on the planted uniform 3-SAT distribution as a function of constraint density m/n for various n.

5 Experiments

We performed a number of experiments for the example distributions we consider in Corollary 12 to argue that the logarithmic lower bound in constraint density for Algorithm 1 is likely to be tight asymptotically, and that the leading constants are small. For the uniform planted 3-SAT model, we sampled formulas at $n \in \{100, 200, 500\}$ with densities $1 \leq m/n \leq n^2/2$. For each n and m, we sampled 100 formulas and determined whether they could be solved by the greedy algorithm. We report the results as the fraction of formulas solved depending on the constraint density in Fig. 2.

As expected, above constraint densities of roughly $\Theta(\log n)$, the proportion of formulas solved by Algorithm 1 quickly goes to one. We see success rates of 70–90% already at $(5/2) \ln n$ for each n, but a more detailed analysis would be needed to get an accurate estimate for the true leading constant.

Non-uniform distributions typically have more parameters, and we are interested in the influence of these parameters on the success of the greedy algorithm. In particular, other than the minimum variable probability p_1, and the γ term for tail lightness, no other distribution parameter appears in our bound. To quantify the effect of constraint density and distribution parameter on geometric random 3-SAT and power-law random 3-SAT, we sampled 100 formulas for each value of the parameters across a range. We measured the proportion of these formulas that were solved by the greedy algorithm, and display the results in heat maps in Fig. 3. On the left, the fraction solved is shown as a function of density and base parameter b for the geometric distribution. On the right, the fraction solved is shown as a function of density and power law exponent β for power-law formulas. As reflected in our theoretical bounds, for the most part there is little influence of the distribution parameters b and β on the constraint density above which Algorithm 1 is successful. In the power law model, there appears to be a regime of the power law exponent β near 2 that seems to be influencing the lower bound. This might be due to hidden constant factors which depend on the power law exponent β. However, it is not clear how or whether this effect scales with n, and this is an avenue for future work. Of course, we cannot claim that our lower bound on the constraint density is tight for all possible well-behaved distributions. As we stated before, our lower bound only considers the smallest

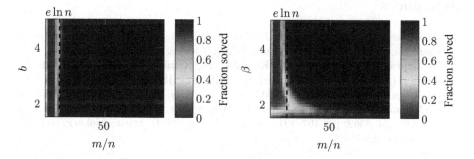

Fig. 3. Fraction of formulas solved by Algorithm 1 on geometric 3-SAT distribution as a function of constraint density m/n and base parameter b (left) and power law 3-SAT distribution as a function of constraint density m/n and power law exponent β (right) for $n = 200$ variables.

variable probability p_1, and the γ term, whereas the actual bound might have a more intricate relation to other distribution parameters.

6   Conclusions

Non-uniform k-SAT models have gained increased attention in recent years. With this paper, we contribute to the theoretical understanding of SAT problems with such non-uniform distributions by studying a greedy local search algorithm. We have shown that this algorithm is highly effective on planted SAT formulas drawn from k-SAT models realized by choosing variables from an arbitrary variable distribution, provided that the clauses are generated independently and that the variable distribution is not too skewed. Models with these properties include geometric and power-law random k-SAT [6].

Our experimental results reveal that for geometric and power-law distributions the exact parameters of the variable degree distribution have little influence on the success of the local search algorithm, at least in the planted setting. Moreover, our rigorous lower bounds on the clause-variable ratio necessary for the algorithm to succeed with high probability are asymptotically the same as for uniform planted k-SAT. This is somewhat surprising, as for state-of-the-art SAT solvers it is typically assumed that the non-uniform distributions we consider make instances easier to solve [5].

We also show that there is a correspondence between non-uniform planted k-SAT distributions and their *filtered* analogues, i.e., the non-planted distribution conditioned on satisfiability. We show that for large enough clause-variable ratios the total variation distance for events in filtered and their corresponding planted models vanishes in the limit. This result actually holds for all random k-SAT models, where the signs of literals are chosen independently at random without bias. It allows us to transfer our results for the greedy local search algorithm to filtered non-uniform models.

References

1. Achlioptas, D., Jia, H., Moore, C.: Hiding satisfying assignments: two are better than one. J. Art. Int. Res. 24 (2005). https://doi.org/10.1613/jair.1681
2. Achlioptas, D., Kirousis, L.M., Kranakis, E., Krizanc, D.: Rigorous results for random (2+p)-sat. Theor. Comput. Sci. **265**(1–2), 109–129 (2001)
3. Ansótegui, C., Bonet, M.L., Giráldez-Cru, J., Levy, J.: The fractal dimension of SAT formulas. In: Demri, S., Kapur, D., Weidenbach, C. (eds.) IJCAR 2014. LNCS (LNAI), vol. 8562, pp. 107–121. Springer, Cham (2014). https://doi.org/10.1007/978-3-319-08587-6_8
4. Ansótegui, C., Bonet, M.L., Giráldez-Cru, J., Levy, J.: On the classification of industrial SAT families. In: Armengol, E., Boixader, D., Grimaldo, F. (eds.) 18th International Conference Catalan Association for Artificial Intelligence. Frontiers in Artificial Intelligence and Applications, vol. 277, pp. 163–172. IOS Press (2015). https://doi.org/10.3233/978-1-61499-578-4-163

5. Ansótegui, C., Bonet, M.L., Levy, J.: On the structure of industrial SAT instances. In: Gent, I.P. (ed.) CP 2009. LNCS, vol. 5732, pp. 127–141. Springer, Heidelberg (2009). https://doi.org/10.1007/978-3-642-04244-7_13

6. Ansótegui, C., Bonet, M.L., Levy, J.: Towards industrial-like random SAT instances. In: Boutilier, C. (ed.) 21st International Joint Conference Artificial Intelligence (IJCAI), pp. 387–392 (2009). http://ijcai.org/Proceedings/09/Papers/072.pdf

7. Berthet, Q.: Optimal testing for planted satisfiability problems. CoRR abs/1401.2205http://arxiv.org/abs/1401.2205 (2014)

8. Bläsius, T., Friedrich, T., Sutton, A.M.: On the empirical time complexity of scale-free 3-SAT at the phase transition. In: Vojnar, T., Zhang, L. (eds.) TACAS 2019. LNCS, vol. 11427, pp. 117–134. Springer, Cham (2019). https://doi.org/10.1007/978-3-030-17462-0_7

9. Boufkhad, Y., Dubois, O., Interian, Y., Selman, B.: Regular random k-sat: Properties of balanced formulas. J. Autom. Reasoning 35(1–3), 181–200 (2005)

10. Bradonjic, M., Perkins, W.: On sharp thresholds in random geometric graphs. In: Jansen, K., Rolim, J.D.P., Devanur, N.R., Moore, C. (eds.) Approximation, Randomization, and Combinatorial Optimization. Algorithms and Techniques, APPROX/RANDOM 2014. LIPIcs, vol. 28, pp. 500–514. Schloss Dagstuhl - Leibniz-Zentrum fuer Informatik (2014). https://doi.org/10.4230/LIPIcs.APPROX-RANDOM.2014.500

11. Bulatov, A.A., Skvortsov, E.S.: Phase transition for local search on planted SAT. In: Italiano, G.F., Pighizzini, G., Sannella, D.T. (eds.) MFCS 2015. LNCS, vol. 9235, pp. 175–186. Springer, Heidelberg (2015). https://doi.org/10.1007/978-3-662-48054-0_15

12. Ansótegui, C., Maria Luisa Bonet, J.L.: Scale-free random SAT instances. CoRR abs/1708.06805http://arxiv.org/abs/1708.06805 (2017)

13. Chao, M., Franco, J.V.: Probabilistic analysis of two heuristics for the 3-satisfiability problem. SIAM J. Comput. 15(4), 1106–1118 (1986)

14. Chao, M., Franco, J.V.: Probabilistic analysis of a generalization of the unit-clause literal selection heuristics for the k satisfiability problem. Inf. Sci. 51(3), 289–314 (1990)

15. Chvátal, V., Reed, B.A.: Mick gets some (the odds are on his side). In: 33rd Symposium Foundations of Computer Science (FOCS), pp. 620–627. IEEE Computer Society (1992). https://doi.org/10.1109/SFCS.1992.267789

16. Chvátal, V., Szemerédi, E.: Many hard examples for resolution. J. ACM 35(4), 759–768 (1988)

17. Coja-Oghlan, A., Wormald, N.: The number of satisfying assignments of random regular k-SAT formulas. Comb. Prob. Comput. 27(4), 496–530 (2018)

18. Doerr, B., Neumann, F., Sutton, A.M.: Time complexity analysis of evolutionary algorithms on random satisfiable k-CNF formulas. Algorithmica 78(2), 561–586 (2017)

19. Feige, U., Mossel, E., Vilenchik, D.: Complete convergence of message passing algorithms for some satisfiability problems. Theor. Comput. 9, 617–651 (2013)

20. Feldman, V., Perkins, W., Vempala, S.S.: On the complexity of random satisfiability problems with planted solutions. SIAM J. Comput. 47(4), 1294–1338 (2018)

21. Flaxman, A.: A spectral technique for random satisfiable 3CNF formulas. Random Struct. Algorithms 32(4), 519–534 (2008)

22. Flaxman, A.D.: Average-case analysis for combinatorial problems. Ph.D. thesis, Carnegie Mellon University (May 2006)

23. Franco, J., Paull, M.C.: Probabilistic analysis of the davis putnam procedure for solving the satisfiability problem. Discrete Appl. Math. **5**(1), 77–87 (1983)
24. Friedgut, E.: Sharp thresholds of graph properties, and the k-SAT problem. J. Amer. Math. Soc. **12**(4), 1017–1054 (1999)
25. Friedrich, T., Krohmer, A., Rothenberger, R., Sauerwald, T., Sutton, A.M.: Bounds on the satisfiability threshold for power law distributed random SAT. In: Pruhs, K., Sohler, C. (eds.) 25th European Symposium on Algorithms (ESA). LIPIcs, vol. 87, pp. 37:1–37:15. Schloss Dagstuhl - Leibniz-Zentrum fuer Informatik (2017). https://doi.org/10.4230/LIPIcs.ESA.2017.37
26. Friedrich, T., Rothenberger, R.: Sharpness of the satisfiability threshold for non-uniform random k-SAT. In: Kraus, S. (ed.) 28th International Joint Conference Artificial Intelligence (IJCAI), pp. 6151–6155. ijcai.org (2019). https://doi.org/10.24963/ijcai.2019/853
27. Giráldez-Cru, J., Levy, J.: Generating SAT instances with community structure. Artif. Intell. **238**, 119–134 (2016)
28. Giráldez-Cru, J., Levy, J.: Locality in random SAT instances. In: Sierra, C. (ed.) 26th International Joint Conference Artificial Intelligence (IJCAI), pp. 638–644. ijcai.org (2017). https://doi.org/10.24963/ijcai.2017/89
29. Hu, Y., Luo, W., Wang, J.: Community-based 3-sat formulas with a predefined solution. CoRR **abs/1902.09706**, http://arxiv.org/abs/1902.09706 (2019)
30. Koutsoupias, E., Papadimitriou, C.H.: On the greedy algorithm for satisfiability. Inf. Process. Lett. **43**(1), 53–55 (1992)
31. Krivelevich, M., Vilenchik, D.: Solving random satisfiable 3CNF formulas in expected polynomial time. In: 17th Symposium Discrete Algorithms (SODA), pp. 454–463. ACM Press (2006). http://dl.acm.org/citation.cfm?id=1109557.1109608
32. Mitchell, D.G., Selman, B., Levesque, H.J.: Hard and easy distributions of SAT problems. In: Swartout, W.R. (ed.) 10th Conference Artificial Intelligence (AAAI), pp. 459–465. AAAI Press/The MIT Press (1992). http://www.aaai.org/Library/AAAI/1992/aaai92-071.php
33. Omelchenko, O., Bulatov, A.A.: Satisfiability threshold for power law random 2-SAT in configuration model. In: Janota, M., Lynce, I. (eds.) SAT 2019. LNCS, vol. 11628, pp. 53–70. Springer, Cham (2019). https://doi.org/10.1007/978-3-030-24258-9_4
34. Rathi, V., Aurell, E., Rasmussen, L., Skoglund, M.: Bounds on threshold of regular random k-SAT. In: Strichman, O., Szeider, S. (eds.) SAT 2010. LNCS, vol. 6175, pp. 264–277. Springer, Heidelberg (2010). https://doi.org/10.1007/978-3-642-14186-7_22
35. Selman, B., Kirkpatrick, S.: Critical behavior in the computational cost of satisfiability testing. Artif. Intell. **81**(1–2), 273–295 (1996)

MCP: Capturing Big Data by Satisfiability (Tool Description)

Miki Hermann[1] and Gernot Salzer[2]([✉])

[1] LIX, CNRS, École Polytechnique, Institut Polytechnique de Paris,
91120 Palaiseau, France
`hermann@lix.polytechnique.fr`
[2] Technische Universität Wien, Vienna, Austria
`gernot.salzer@tuwien.ac.at`

Abstract. Experimental data is often given as bit vectors, with vectors corresponding to observations, and coordinates to attributes, with a bit being true if the corresponding attribute was observed. Observations are usually grouped, e.g. into positive and negative samples. Among the essential tasks on such data, we have compression, the construction of classifiers for assigning new data, and information extraction.

Our system, MCP, approaches these tasks by propositional logic. For each group of observations, MCP constructs a (usually small) conjunctive formula that is true for the observations of the group, and false for the others. Depending on the settings, the formula consists of Horn, dual-Horn, bijunctive or general clauses. To reduce its size, only relevant subsets of the attributes are considered. The formula is a (lossy) representation of the original data and generalizes the observations, as it is usually satisfied by more bit vectors than just the observations. It thus may serve as a classifier for new data. Moreover, (dual-)Horn clauses, when read as if-then rules, make dependencies between attributes explicit. They can be regarded as an explanation for classification decisions.

Keywords: Data classification · Bit vectors · Information extraction · Explainable AI · Machine learning

1 Introduction and Related Work

Since several years, computer science applications are challenged by very large amounts of data, commonly referred to as *Big Data*, that must be understood, captured, treated, and transformed. There exist several approaches to cope with this challenge, mainly from the field of Artificial Intelligence. One of these approaches is *Logical Analysis of Data*. This document presents a tool called MCP, performing logical analysis of big data, producing a propositional formula. The basic idea behind this tool programmed in C++ is to describe a very large data set by a propositional formula.

Partially developed within the ACCA Project.

C.-M. Li and F. Manyà (Eds.): SAT 2021, LNCS 12831, pp. 207–215, 2021.
https://doi.org/10.1007/978-3-030-80223-3_14

Logical Analysis of Data is a part of Machine Learning, which has been developed by Hammer and his colleagues [5,9]. There also exists another approach through mechanized hypothesis formation, the GUHA Project developed in Prague by Hájek and his colleagues [12,14].

2   Preliminaries

We recall the main structures of Boolean algebra. A *literal* is either a variable, called positive literal, or its negation, called negative literal. A *clause* is a disjunction of literals. A *formula* in *conjunctive normal form* is a conjunction of clauses. A *Horn* clause is a clause with at most one positive literal. A *dual Horn* clause is a clause with at most one negative literal. A *bijunctive* clause is a clause consisting of at most two literals. An *affine* clause is a linear equation of the form $x_1 + \cdots + x_k = b$, where x_i are variables, $+$ is the exclusive-or operator, and $b \in \{0,1\}$ is a Boolean value. A Horn, dual Horn, bijunctive, or affine formula is a conjunction of only Horn, dual Horn, bijunctive, or affine clauses, respectively.

We will work with vectors, also called tuples, of finite arity over a domain D. This domain is either Boolean, i.e., $D = \{0,1\}$, or finite, i.e., $|D| = n$ for some natural number $n \geq 2$. Vectors $(a_1, \ldots, a_k)$ of arity k will be shortened to $a_1 \cdots a_k$ when the elements a_i are clear.

Let $\boldsymbol{a} = a_1 \cdots a_k$, $\boldsymbol{b} = b_1 \cdots b_k$, and $\boldsymbol{c} = c_1 \cdots c_k$ be Boolean vectors of the same arity k. There exist different closures of these Boolean vectors.

- *Horn closure* of $\boldsymbol{a}$ and $\boldsymbol{b}$ is the vector $\boldsymbol{d} = d_1 \cdots d_k$, such that $d_i = a_i \wedge b_i$;
- *Dual Horn closure* of $\boldsymbol{a}$ and $\boldsymbol{b}$ is the vector $\boldsymbol{d} = d_1 \cdots d_k$, such that $d_i = a_i \vee b_i$;
- *Bijunctive closure* of $\boldsymbol{a}$, $\boldsymbol{b}$, and $\boldsymbol{c}$ is the vector $\boldsymbol{d} = d_1 \cdots d_k$, such that $c_i = \mathrm{maj}(a_i, b_i, c_i)$, where maj is the associative-commutative majority operator;
- *Affine closure* of $\boldsymbol{a}$, $\boldsymbol{b}$, and $\boldsymbol{c}$ is the vector $\boldsymbol{d} = d_1 \cdots d_k$, such that $d_i = a_i + b_i + c_i$, where $+$ is the exclusive-or operator in the Boolean ring $\mathbb{Z}_2$;

all for each $i = 1, \ldots, k$. Given a set of Boolean vectors S of arity k, we denote by $\langle S \rangle_C$ the C-closure of S for C being Horn, dual Horn, bijunctive, or affine. A basic result from universal algebra states that for an arbitrary set of Boolean vectors S of the same arity k, the C-closure is the set of satisfying assignments for some C-formula φ [3,4].

3   Core of the MCP System

MCP has a modular architecture. It is composed of several modules, which perform designated tasks. The core of the system is composed of different variants of the module generating a propositional formula from sets of binary tuples. The main task of the MCP system, solved by its core modules, is defined as follows:

Problem 1 (MCP Problem). Given two sets of Boolean vectors (tuples) of arity k over the Boolean domain $D = \{0,1\}^k$, representing positive examples $T \subseteq D$ and negative examples $F \subseteq D$, **compute** a Horn, dual Horn, bijunctive, or general CNF formula φ, respectively, such that (1) $T \models \varphi$ and (2) for each $f \in F$, $f \not\models \varphi$.

There are several reasons why we focus on the aforementioned four subcases of propositional formulas. Horn, dual Horn, bijunctive, and affine formulas are the four families of Boolean formulas, whose satisfiability problem can be decided in polynomial time. Horn formulas represent a theoretical background of Prolog programs. Horn clauses (implications of the form antecedent $\rightarrow$ consequent) represent a natural explanation pattern—easy to explain also to a non-expert in computer science or logic. The posed problem is an instance of PAC-learning.

There are several caveats for this problem we must deal with, namely what to do if (1) $T \cap F \neq \emptyset$, (2) $\langle T \rangle_C \cap F \neq \emptyset$, (3) $\{0,1\}^k \setminus (\langle T \rangle_C \cup F) \neq \emptyset$. There is no solution for the first two cases, since we cannot satisfy the basic requirements of the MCP Problem. The third caveat is solved by means of **strategy**.

3.1 Strategies for Computing the Closure

Depending on how we want to treat the vectors absent from $\langle T \rangle_C \cup F$, we have two available *strategies*, depending on whether we consider the largest or the smallest closure of the set of positive examples T.

The **large** strategy, which is the default, computes the *largest* C-closure containing T that does not intersect with F. The computed formula φ satisfies the condition $f \not\models \varphi$ for each $f \in F$. The **exact** strategy computes the *smallest* C-closure containing T. It satisfies the conditions $\langle T \rangle_C \models \varphi$ and $f \not\models \varphi$ for each $f \in \{0,1\}^k \setminus \langle T \rangle_C$.

3.2 Minimal Section

We want to keep the sets $\langle T \rangle_C$ and F disjunct on the smallest number of coordinates, to keep the number of variables of the produced formula as small as possible. Given the sets of vectors $\langle T \rangle_C$ and F or T and F as binary codes, composed of codewords over Boolean domain, we want to compute their *minimal section*, i.e. their restriction to a maximal set of coordinates A, such that $\langle T \rangle_C|_A \cap F|_A = \emptyset$ or $T|_A \cap F|_A = \emptyset$. Computing the optimal minimal section is an NP-complete problem. Therefore we adopt several approximation approaches by means of **direction**, always skipping coordinates whose removal would render the problem unsolvable. Following directions are available:

begin: Prefer coordinates to the left (at the begin) of the codewords by removing coordinates from the right. This direction is the default.

end: Prefer coordinates to the right (at the end) of the codewords by removing coordinates from the left.

lowcard: Prefer coordinates with a lower Hamming weight, by removing coordinates with high Hamming weight.

highcard: Prefer coordinates with a higher Hamming weight, by removing coordinates with small Hamming weight.

random: Removing coordinates in random order.

There also exists the **nosect** option, where no minimal section is computed and all coordinates considered.

3.3   Effective Learning of Formulas

The MCP system learns *Horn* formulas by the following procedure. For each $f \in F$ it determines if $f \in \langle T \rangle_{\text{Horn}}$ efficiently, without computing the Horn closure. Then it computes the minimal section of $\langle T \rangle_{\text{Horn}}$ and F, followed by the computation of the corresponding Horn formula according to the chosen direction and strategy on the (approximate) minimal section of $\langle T \rangle_{\text{Horn}}$ and F. It uses different algorithms for the strategies: that of Angluin *et al.* [1] for the large strategy and another of Hébrard and Zanuttini [13] for the exact strategy.

Learning of *dual Horn* formulas is done very easily. MCP system first swaps the polarity of the Boolean vectors in T and F, producing the new sets T' and F', respectively. Then it computes the Horn formula φ' for T' and F', followed by swapping the polarity of literals in φ', producing the dual Horn formula φ.

There is no known possibility to determine if $f \in \langle T \rangle_{\text{bijunctive}}$ for each $f \in F$ without computing the bijunctive closure $\langle T \rangle_{\text{bijunctive}}$. Moreover, the bijunctive closure $\langle T \rangle_{\text{bijunctive}}$ can be (and usually also is) very much time and space consuming. We adopted the following solution to produce *bijunctive* formulas by MCP system: It computes the minimal section using an intersection test, followed by application of the *Baker-Pixley Theorem* [2] (projection on every pair of coordinates), which implicitly guarantees the bijunctive closure.

Learning a *general CNF* formula presents several challenges. Its advantage is that We get a propositional formula in any case, provided that $T \cap F = \emptyset$. Its drawback is that the produced formula is usually very big. We adopted two different approaches in the MCP system, depending on the applied strategy. In case of large strategy, for each false element $f \in F$ the MCP system produces the unique clause c_f which falsifies f. The resulting formula φ is the conjunction of all falsification clauses c_f. In case of exact strategy, the MCP system uses an algorithm producing a CNF formula in time $O(|T| k^2)$, where k is the arity of vectors in T, using a Boolean restriction of a larger algorithm from [11].

Learning *affine* formulas reveals more from linear computer algebra than from logic, therefore we did not implement it in the MCP system for the time being. We may implement it in a further version if there is demand.

3.4   First Postprocessing: Redundancy Elimination

The inferred formula φ can contain redundant literals and clauses, which can and must be eliminated to produce the smallest possible formula. There are several stages, which can be applied for *redundancy elimination*, called **cooking** inside the MCP system, with the following options: **raw** performs no redundancy elimination, **bleu** performs unit resolution, **medium** performs unit resolution and clause subsumption, and finally **well done**, which is the default, performs unit resolution, clause subsumption, and implied clause removal. Moreover, the *exact* strategy includes a **primality** step, reducing the clauses by elimination of unnecessary literals, using an algorithm from [11].

3.5 Second Postprocessing: Set Cover

In case of the *large* strategy, we are mainly interested in producing a formula φ falsified by each tuple $f \in F$. However, the inferred formula φ may contain more clauses than necessary, even after full redundancy elimination. Our task is to keep the smallest number of clauses in φ which are necessary to guarantee falsification by all tuples $f \in F$. For this purpose in the MCP system, we use *Set Cover* where a clause $c \in \varphi$ covers a vector $f \in F$ if f falsifies c. Set Cover is a well-known NP-complete problem, therefore we use Johnson's approximation algorithm (see e.g. [10]), where the measure of a clause is the number of covered tuples. Of course, this approach is inapplicable for the *exact* strategy.

3.6 Input Format and Action Possibilities

The input file of the MCP system core, is a Boolean matrix, one Boolean vector per row. Each vector is prefixed by a string g, identifying a group to which the vector belongs. The MCP system core collects first the vectors from the input matrix and distributes them into the identified groups. Each input file starts with an indication line, containing two boolean values. If both values are equal to 0, the following lines are the rows of the Boolean matrix with leading group indicators. If the first value is equal to 1, the following line contains the variable names ordered by coordinates. If the second value is equal to 1, there is one more line of supplementary information before the matrix. However, this supplementary information is unused by the MCP system, but it is still maintained for compatibility reasons with data sets used in [7,8].

Let G be the set of identified groups. The actual computation is determined by the **action**, which determines how the sets of positive examples T and negative examples F are constituted. The are two options, **one** and **all**.

The option *one* consecutively selects two groups $g, g' \in G$, determines the vectors belonging to the group g as the positive examples T and the vectors belonging to the group g' as the negative examples F, then starts the computation of the corresponding formula with minimal section. If there are n groups in the set G, this action proceeds with the computation of $n(n-1)$ formulas.

The option *all*, which is the default, consecutively selects a group $g \in G$, determines the vectors belonging to the group g as the positive examples T and all vectors belonging to any group from $G \setminus \{g\}$ as the negative examples F, then starts the computation of the corresponding formula with minimal section. For n groups in the set G, this action proceeds with the computation of n formulas.

3.7 Parallelization

For a set of n groups, the MCP system computes either n or $n(n-1)$ formulas. These computations are independent, therefore they can be performed in parallel. This is called *outer parallelism* in the MCP core.

In case of Horn closure of the positive examples T, the MCP core needs to determine if a given vector $f \in F$ from negative examples belongs to $\langle T \rangle_{\text{Horn}}$, without computing the closure itself. This procedure is quite time consuming when the set T is quite large. It can be computed in parallel, each time taking only a determined chunk of T. This is called *inner parallelism* in the MCP core.

We adopted three types of parallelization within the MCP core: the **Message Passing Interface** (MPI) [15], the **POSIX threads** (pthreads) [6], and a **hybrid** version combining both. These parallelizations are effective only on very large input data sets. The MPI version is applied only for outer parallelism, the pthreads version to both, and in the hybrid version MPI is applied for outer parallelism and pthreads for inner parallelism.

3.8 Invocation

MCP core is called by one of the following commands and options:

sequential version:	**mcp-seq**	-i *input-file*	-o *output-file*
MPI version:	**mcp-mpi**	-l *formula-prefix*	-c *closure*
POSIX threads version:	**mcp-pthread**	-d *direction*	-s *strategy*
hybrid version:	**mcp-hybrid**	--cook *cooking*	--setcover *y/n*

Each of these core modules produces files *formula-prefix_g*.log containing the learned formula for each group g inside *input-file*. Consult the manual pages for more detailed information.

4 Prequel and Sequel Modules

4.1 Data Binarization

The core of the MCP system accepts only Boolean vectors. However, data are usually spanning much larger domains: finite, or infinite but countable, or uncountable. In the latter two cases, every very large finite data set contains only a finite subset of the domain, but it can be intractable due to the amount of data to be treated. The MCP system copes with this situation by *binarization*.

Binarization is the process of transforming data of any domain into binary vectors to make classifier algorithms, in our case the MCP system core, more efficient. Its advantage is that we obtain the possibility to treat any data by propositional formulas. Its drawback is a possible exponential explosion. Binarization concerns both, particular values, especially for finite domains, as well as intervals, usually used for infinite ones. MCP system adopts both approaches.

Binarization in the MCP system is a two-step procedure. The first step consists of scanning of the CSV file and generating a meta-file template. This step is performed by the command

mcp-guess   -i *csv-file*   -o *meta-template*

where it is implicitly assumed that the *csv-file* contains one data vector per line, the vector elements are separated by commas or semicolons or space or tabs, vector element can be quoted, missing elements are denoted by a question mark.

The template generated by *mcp-guess* cannot be used directly by the next module, but it must be manually adapted to a proper meta-file. This command just creates indications if the values of a given coordinate are Boolean, enumerated strings, enumerated integers, integers in a range, or floats in a range.

The second step of the binarization process is performed by the command

mcp-trans   -i *data-file*   -m *meta-file*   -o *binarized-file*

which generates a *binarized-file*, ready to be treated by the MCP system core, from the original *data-file* using a *meta-file*. This meta file consists of transformation commands. Each transformation command has the following format:

$$identifier \quad = \quad coordinate \quad : \quad indicator \quad ; \quad \{\# \; comment\}$$

where # starts an optional comment stretching until end of line, the symbols = and : and ; are syntactic sugar, *identifier* will become the name of the variable for the given *coordinate* and the *indicator* has one of the following forms:

ident	group identifier
bool $[elem_0 \; elem_1]$	boolean 2-element set
enum $[elem_0 \ldots elem_\ell]$	enumerated set of $\ell + 1$ elements
up $[elem_0 \ldots elem_\ell]$	enumerated set of increasing $\ell + 1$ elements
down $[elem_0 \ldots elem_\ell]$	enumerated set of decreasing $\ell + 1$ elements
int $min \; max$	integers in the range between min and max
dj $n \; min \; max$	interval $[min, max)$ cut in n disjoint chunks
over $n \; min \; max \; \ell$	$[min, max)$ cut in n chunks with overlaps of length ℓ
span $\ell \; min \; max$	$[min, max)$ cut in disjoint chunks, each of length ℓ
warp $\ell_0 \; min \; max \; \ell_1$	$[min, max)$ cut in chunks of length ℓ_0, overlaps of ℓ_1

4.2 Formula Evaluation

If we are interested only in the produced formula, then the output file generated by the MCP core contains the satisfied formulas for each group of Boolean vectors. However, if we want to evaluate the accuracy of the produced formula, we must proceed further. The first prerequisite for a possibility to check the accuracy of a formula, is to have two sets of vectors: one for learning the formula, the other for checking its accuracy. Either we have these two sets of vectors already from the beginning or we need to split the original set of Boolean vectors into the learning part and the checking part before running the MCP core on the learning part. The latter is performed by the command

mcp-split   -i *input-file*   -l *learn-file*   -c *check-file*   -r *ratio*

that splits uniformly at random the *input-file* into a *learn-file* and *check-file*, where *ratio* is the percentage of vectors from the *input-file* populating the *check-file*. If the options -l or -c are not explicitly stated, the software deduces the file identifiers from the base name of the *input-file* and adding the suffix .lrn or .chk to it, respectively. The *ratio* default is 10.

The accuracy of the formula for a given group g is checked by the command

mcp-check   `-i` *check-file*   `-l` *formula-file*   `-o` *output-file*

where *formula-file* is the file *formula-prefix_g*.`log` produced by the MCP core. Its *output-file* reproduces the formula and reports the following statistical entities, measured on the vectors from *check-file*: true positives (tp), true negatives (tn), false positives (fp), false negatives (fn), sensitivity ($tp/(tp+fn)$), miss rate ($fn/(fn+tp)$), specificity ($tn/(tn+fp)$), and precision ($tp/(tp+fp)$). The optimal situation would be to have neither false positives nor false negatives. If, however, these values are non-zero, it can be either due to an insufficient cardinality of learning data, or a wrong binarization, or else the data itself are not precise.

5   System Distribution and Examples

The MCP system is available at the github.com/miki-hermann/mcp. Follow the instructions in **README.md** file at the root. It is indispensable to run the installation instructions described in that file to be able to run the MCP system properly.

The overall performance of the MCP system is very competitive, both in terms of time, as well as in terms of quality of the produced formulas. The performance of the system has been measured on a DELL computer with an Intel Core^{TM} i7-9700 CPU @ 3.00 GHz × 8 with 16 GB of memory, running under Linux Fedora 33. All examples from [7,8] run under one second.

We have been testing the MCP system on several examples from the UCI Machine Learning Repository (archive.ics.uci.edu/ml). All examples in the subdirectories are equipped by a **Makefile** simplifying the application of the MCP system on them. The directory *uci* contains the following treated examples: *abalone* identifying abalone with 27 rings, *balance-scale* identifying psychological experiments balancing a scale, *balloons*—a toy example, where specific formulas are required to be produced, *breast-cancer-wisconsin* identifying benign and malignant breast cancer cases in Wisconsin, *car* identifying very good cars, *forest-fire* predicting forest fires in July, August, and September, *iris* identifying three types of iris flowers, *mushroom* identifying edible and poisonous mushrooms, and *vote* identifying democrats and republicans in the House of Representatives according to the 1984 US Congressional Voting Records.

We would especially drive the readers attention to the *mushroom* example, which identifies the edible and poisonous mushrooms always with 100% accuracy. This illustrates very well the strength of the MCP system.

6   Concluding Remarks

The MCP system consists of more than 7000 lines of C++ code, using only the standard library. Parallel execution requires installation of the MPI software. Future versions of MCP will include a web GUI to enhance usability, as well as support for finite domains [11] to obviate the need for data binarization.

References

1. Angluin, D., Frazier, M., Pitt, L.: Learning conjunctions of Horn clauses. Mach. Learn. **9**(2–3), 147–164 (1992)
2. Baker, K.A., Pixley, A.F.: Polynomial interpolation and the Chinese remainder theorem for algebraic systems. Mathematische Zeitschrift **143**(2), 165–174 (1975)
3. Böhler, E., Creignou, N., Reith, S., Vollmer, H.: Playing with Boolean blocks, part I: post's lattice with applications to complexity theory. SIGACT News **34**(4), 38–52 (2003)
4. Böhler, E., Creignou, N., Reith, S., Vollmer, H.: Playing with Boolean blocks, part II: constraint satisfaction problems. SIGACT News **35**(1), 22–35 (2004)
5. Boros, E., Crama, Y., Hammer, P.L., Ibaraki, T., Kogan, A., Makino, K.: Logical analysis of data: classification with justification. Ann. Oper. Res. **188**(1), 33–61 (2011)
6. Butenhof, D.R.: Programming with POSIX threads. Addison-Wesley, Boston (1997)
7. Chambon, A., Boureau, T., Lardeux, F., Saubion, F.: Logical characterization of groups of data: a comparative study. Appl. Intell. **48**(8), 2284–2303 (2017). https://doi.org/10.1007/s10489-017-1080-3
8. Chambon, A., Lardeux, F., Saubion, F., Boureau, T.: Computing sets of patterns for logical analysis of data. Technical Report, Université d'Angers (2017)
9. Crama, Y., Hammer, P.L.: Boolean Functions - Theory, Algorithms, and Applications, Encyclopedia of Mathematics and its Applications, vol. 142. Cambridge University Press, Cambridge (2011)
10. Garey, M.R., Johnson, D.S.: Computers and intractability: A guide to the theory of NP-completeness. W.H, Freeman and Co (1979)
11. Gil, A., Hermann, M., Salzer, G., Zanuttini, B.: Efficient algorithms for constraint description problems over finite totally ordered domains. SIAM J. Comput. **38**(3), 922–945 (2008)
12. Hájek, P., Holena, M., Rauch, J.: The GUHA method and its meaning for data mining. J. Comput. Syst. Sci. **76**(1), 34–48 (2010)
13. Hébrard, J.J., Zanuttini, B.: An efficient algorithm for horn description. Inf. Proc. Lett. **88**(4), 177–182 (2003)
14. Hájek, P., Havránek, T.: Mechanizing Hypothesis Formation. Springer, Berlin (1978) https://doi.org/10.1007/978-3-642-66943-9
15. Snir, M., Otto, S.W., Huss-Lederman, S., Walker, D.W., Dongarra, J.: MPI: The Complete Reference. MIT Press, Cambridge (1995)

Chinese Remainder Encoding for Hamiltonian Cycles

Marijn J. H. Heule[(⊠)] [iD]

Computer Science Department, Carnegie Mellon University, Pittsburgh, PA, United States
marijn@cmu.edu

Abstract. The Hamiltonian Cycle Problem (HCP) consists of two constraints: i) each vertex contributes exactly two edges to the cycle; and ii) there is exactly one cycle. The former can be encoded naturally and compactly, while the encodings of the latter either lack arc consistency or require an exponential number of clauses. We present a new, small encoding for HCP based on the Chinese remainder theorem. We demonstrate the effectiveness of the encoding on challenging HCP instances.

1 Introduction

Satisfiability (SAT) solvers have become very powerful tools to solve many hard combinatorial problems in a broad range of applications. However, the quality of the encoding can have a significant impact on the effectiveness of a SAT solver, in particular for problems with complicated constraints.

One problem class for which the encoding plays a crucial role in solver performance is the Hamiltonian Cycle Problem (HCP) [14], an NP-complete problem that has been studied from theoretical and practical viewpoints [2,3,6,13]. Given a graph, HCP asks whether there exists a cycle that visits all vertices of the graph exactly once. One graph with and one without a Hamiltonian cycle are shown in Figure 1. On a high level, HCP requires two constraints: a *degree constraint* stating that each vertex contributes exactly two edges to the cycle and an *exactly-one-cycle constraint*. The degree constraint can be compactly encoded with arc consistency [4], a property that is important for efficient solving.

Effectively dealing with the exactly-one-cycle constraint is more challenging. Several encodings have been proposed use $\Theta(|V|^3)$ clauses. Determining the existence of a Hamiltonian cycle is easy for small graphs (< 100 vertices). For larger graphs, $\Theta(|V|^3)$-sized encodings result in a huge formula that are hard to solve [9–11]. The challenge is to come up with a compact encoding that can also be solved efficiently. Our encoding will be quasilinear in the number of edges.

One way to avoid the costliness of the exactly-one-cycle constraint is to use incremental SAT [1,12]. In this setting, the initial formula only consists of the degree constraint. If the SAT solver produces a solution that represents multiple cycles, then a clause is added that blocks the shortest cycle. This is repeated

C.-M. Li and F. Manyà (Eds.): SAT 2021, LNCS 12831, pp. 216–224, 2021.
https://doi.org/10.1007/978-3-030-80223-3_15

until either a Hamiltonian cycle is found or if the formula becomes unsatisfiable, showing that no such cycle exists.

Recently two new HCP encodings have been proposed. Both encodings assign a binary index to each vertex using $k = \lceil \log_2 |V| \rceil$ variables per vertex. The first one is based on linear-feedback shift registers (LFSR) [5,8]. LFSR loops through the numbers $\{1, \ldots, 2^k - 1\}$ by shifting a binary number by one position to the left and puts the parity of some bits in the vacated position. This facilitates a compact SAT encoding. The second encoding uses a binary adder that loops through the numbers $\{0, \ldots, 2^k - 1\}$ in ascending order and returns to 0 after $2^k - 1$ [14]. The binary adder encoding requires auxiliary variables, more clauses, and/or longer clauses compared to LFSR. Yet, the binary adder is more effective as it facilitates quick refutation of some subcycles, e.g., cycles of odd length.

In this paper, we present the Chinese remainder encoding that aims to combine the best of the incremental SAT, binary adder, and LFSR approaches. From the incremental approach, we borrow the observation that only some subcycles need to be blocked. From the binary adder approach we borrow techniques to easily refute some subcycles. Finally, from the LFSR approach we borrow the compact encoding with short clauses without auxiliary variables.

We implemented the binary adder, LSFR, and the Chinese remainder encodings (and corresponding decoding tools), and evaluated their effectiveness on graphs from the Flinders HCP challenge [7]. This is a suite of 1001 graphs with HCP instances of varying difficulty. The experimental results show that the Chinese remainder encoding beats the other two on most large graphs.

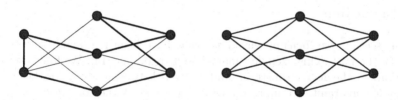

Fig. 1. The left graph has a Hamiltonian cycle (bold), while the right one does not.

2 Preliminaries

Boolean Satisfiability: We consider formulas in *conjunctive normal form* (CNF), defined as follows. A *literal* is either a variable x or the negation $\overline{x}$ of a variable x. For a literal l, $var(l)$ denotes the variable of l. A *clause* is a disjunction of literals and a *formula* is a conjunction of clauses. An *assignment* is a function from a set of variables to the truth values 1 (*true*) and 0 (*false*). A formula is *satisfiable* if there exists an assignment that satisfies it and is *unsatisfiable* otherwise.

A *unit clause* is a clause that contains only one literal. The result of applying the unit-clause rule to a formula F is the formula F without all clauses containing the unit literal and without all occurrences of the negated unit literal. The iterated application of the unit-clause rule to a formula, until no unit clauses are left, is called unit propagation. If unit propagation on a formula F yields the empty clause, we say that it derived a conflict on F.

Linear-Feedback Shift Register: An LFSR [5] is a register that in each step shifts all bits by one position to the left and replaces the vacated position by the result of an XOR operation of some of the bits. Given the right XOR, an LFSR visits all bit-vectors of a given length except the all-zero bit-vector. The shift and the XOR operations can be compactly encoded using clauses.

Example 1. An example 16-bit LFSR fills the vacant bit by $x_{11} \oplus x_{13} \oplus x_{14} \oplus x_{16}$, resulting in $2^{16} - 1 = 65,535$ states. The figure below illustrates this LFSR with state 1001011100101101. The next state is 00101110010110011.

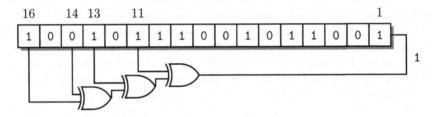

3   Encodings

In this section, we focus on encodings that have been reasonably effective for HCP in the past. This excludes unary-based encodings [14]. We first discuss an encoding for the degree constraint and afterwards two encodings for the exactly-one-cycle constraint. To improve readability, we show the constraints using the logical connectives $\wedge$ (and), $\vee$ (or), $\rightarrow$ (implies), $\leftrightarrow$ (equivalence), and $\not\leftrightarrow$ (xor).

3.1   Degree Constraint

All of the encodings share the same variables and clauses to enforce that exactly two edges from each vertex are in the cycle, thereby ensuring that each vertex is in exactly one cycle. Given an undirected graph $G = (V, E)$, we introduce two variables $e_{i,j}$ and $e_{j,i}$ for each edge $(i, j) \in E$. In the case that G is a directed graph, only $e_{i,j}$ is used for arcs from i to j and only $e_{j,i}$ is used for arcs from j to i. The degree constraint is encoded by enforcing that for each vertex $v \in V$ exactly one of the literals $e_{i,v}$ is true (one incoming edge) and exactly one of the literals $e_{v,j}$ is true (one outgoing edge). Each ExactlyOne constraint is partitioned into an AtLeastOne constraint (i.e., a clause) and an AtMostOne constraint.

HCP is typically only hard for graphs with low degree. For graphs with high degree, we expect dedicated heuristics to outperform SAT solving. The constraint $\mathsf{AtMostOne}(x_1, \ldots, x_n)$ can therefore simply be encoded using the pairwise encoding $(\overline{x}_i \lor \overline{x}_j)$ for $1 \leq i < j \leq n$. However, some graphs in the Flinders HCP challenge set are dense. To avoid a blow-up in size due to the pairwise encoding, we only use the pairwise encoding for AtMostOne constraints of 4 or less inputs. Larger AtMostOne constraints are split recursively as follows:

$$\mathsf{AtMostOne}(x_1, \ldots, x_n) := \mathsf{AtMostOne}(x_1, x_2, x_3, \overline{y}) \land \mathsf{AtMostOne}(y, x_4, \ldots, x_n)$$

3.2   Binary Adder

Given a graph $G = (V, E)$, the binary adder encoding assigns a unique index from the range $\{0, 1, \ldots, |V| - 1\}$ to each vertex in the graph. Each vertex has two neighbors, of which one is the successor $(+1 \pmod{|V|})$, while the other is its predecessor $(-1 \pmod{|V|})$. If edge variable $e_{u,v}$ is true, then the successor property is enforced, i.e., u is assigned i and v is assigned $i + 1 \pmod{|V|}$. The clauses that enforce the successor property also enforce the predecessor property.

We will use parts of the binary encoding in the Chinese remainder encoding. For consistency we therefore use the naming of the bit-vectors. The ith bit of the bit-vector of vertex v is denoted by the Boolean variable v_{2^i} with $i \in \{1, \ldots, k\}$.

Example 2. Consider a graph with 7 vertices, thus $k = \lceil \log_2 7 \rceil = 3$. For vertex v, the variables v_2, v_4, and v_8 denote the least, middle, and most significant bit, respectively. For an edge variable $e_{u,v}$, we add the clauses represented by:

$$e_{u,v} \rightarrow (u_2 \not\leftrightarrow v_2) \qquad \begin{aligned} (e_{u,v} \land \overline{u}_2) &\rightarrow (u_4 \leftrightarrow v_4) \\ (e_{u,v} \land u_2) &\rightarrow (u_4 \not\leftrightarrow v_4) \end{aligned} \qquad \begin{aligned} (e_{u,v} \land \overline{u}_2) &\rightarrow (u_8 \leftrightarrow v_8) \\ (e_{u,v} \land \overline{u}_4) &\rightarrow (u_8 \leftrightarrow v_8) \\ (e_{u,v} \land u_2 \land u_4) &\rightarrow (u_8 \not\leftrightarrow v_8) \end{aligned}$$

No auxiliary variables are introduced in our implementation, resulting in $O(k^2)$ clauses per edge variable. Using auxiliary variables can reduce the number of clauses to $O(k)$ per edge variables, but this is only effective for large k.

It is important to observe that this encoding is able to quickly refute certain subcycles. For example, if an assignment to the edge variables forms a subcycle of odd length, then assigning v_2 (of any vertex v in that cycle) to true or false results in a conflict by unit propagation. Thus with two conflicts the cycle can be refuted. In a similar way, one can additionally refute all cycles of length 2 (mod 4) by the four assignments to the variables v_2 and v_4. This is the key property that will be used in the Chinese remainder encoding.

3.3   Linear-Feedback Shift Register

Haythorpe and Johnson propose to use LFSR to enforce the exactly-one-cycle constraint in HCP [8]. This encoding has several aspects that are similar to the binary adder encoding. It uses bit-vectors of length $k = \lceil \log_2(|V| + 1) \rceil$ for each vertex. One vertex is assigned the bit-vector with all-zeros except for the least significant bit. The bit-vectors of adjacent vertices are forced to be the next and previous state of a k-bit LFSR.

We use the following variable naming: Given a k-bit LFSR, let $n = 2^k - 1$. For each $i \in \{1, \ldots, k\}$, position i in the bit-vector of vertex v is denoted by $v_{n,i}$. We block the all-zero bit-vector, by adding $(\overline{v}_{n,1} \vee \cdots \vee \overline{v}_{n,k})$ for each $v \in V$.

Example 3. Consider a 7-vertex graph, thus $k = \lceil \log_2(7+1) \rceil = 3$. A 3-bit LFSR filling the vacant bit by $x_2 \oplus x_3$ has 7 states. The bit-vector variables of vertex v are $v_{7,1}$, $v_{7,2}$, and $v_{7,3}$. For an edge variable $e_{u,v}$, we add the clauses:

$$e_{u,v} \rightarrow (v_{7,1} \leftrightarrow (u_{7,2} \not\leftrightarrow u_{7,3}))$$
$$e_{u,v} \rightarrow (v_{7,2} \leftrightarrow u_{7,1})$$
$$e_{u,v} \rightarrow (v_{7,3} \leftrightarrow u_{7,2})$$

For most small k, there exists a k-bit LFSR of $2^k - 1$ states that uses just a single XOR of 2 bits. For such an LFSR, the encoding uses $2k - 2$ ternary clauses and 4 clauses of length 4, as in the above example. An encoding based on LFSR is thus compact with short clauses and without auxiliary variables. We will use this property in the Chinese remainder encoding.

In contrast to the binary adder encoding, the LFSR encoding cannot quickly refute some subcycles. If an assignment to the edge variables forms a subcycle, then one needs $2^k - 1$ conflicts (i.e., all states of a k-bit LFSR) to refute it. This helps explain why the LFSR encoding is less effective in practice.

4   Chinese Remainder Encoding

The challenge in coming up with an effective SAT encoding for HCP lies in enabling the solver to quickly refute an assignment for which the edge variables represent a subcycle. The encodings described in the previous section may require many conflict clauses to a refute a subcycle. Our encoding tries to reduce that number, while keeping the encoding compact. We aim to get the best of three worlds (incremental SAT, binary adder, and LFSR).

From the incremental SAT approach, we borrow the partial encoding of the exactly-one-cycle constraint. One vertex is special in the encoding and indicates where the Hamiltonian cycle "starts". This vertex is denoted by s. The encoding picks the first vertex (based on its index) of smallest degree as s, because reasoning from a vertex with a small degree is considered effective to find a Hamiltonian cycle. Recall that the degree constraint ensures that every vertex is in exactly one cycle. We use a parameter m and additionally enforce that any cycle that does not include s must have length 0 (mod m). Moreover, the cycle that includes s must have length $|V|$ (mod m). The expectation is that one can frequently use $m < |V|$, while still managing to find a Hamiltonian cycle with high probability as it will be difficult to satisfy the constraints for multiple cycles if m is large. Using $m < |V|$ reduces the size of the encoding, which improves solver performance.

Next, we combine ideas of the binary adder and the LFSR encodings. Instead of enforcing cycle lengths to be 0 (mod m) or $|V|$ (mod m), we factorize m into $m = m_1 \times m_2 \times \cdots \times m_q$ such that $m_i = p_i{}^{k_i}$ with prime p_i and positive integer k_i. Furthermore the m_i are pairwise coprime, i.e., for each pair m_i and

m_j holds that $p_i \neq p_j$. We enforce that each subcycle has length 0 (mod m_i). By the Chinese remainder theorem, we know that the cycles will be of length 0 (mod m) or $|V|$ (mod m), respectively. In case $k_i > 1$ for some m_i, the Chinese remainder encoding constructs a p_i-ary counter (but with LFSRs for $p_i > 2$). This is shown in Example 2 for $m = 8$, thus $p = 2$ and $k = 3$.

For the prime factors of 2 in m, we use the binary adder encoding, while for the primes of the form $2^k - 1$, such as 3 and 7, we use LFSR. This, of course, excludes several primes. For such a prime p, we use a scheme similar to the binary adder, but having 0 as the successor of $p - 1$. Furthermore, we block all assignments representing indices p to $2^k - 1$ with $k = \lceil \log_2 p \rceil$.

Example 4. For the prime 5, we can encode the cycle $0 \to 1 \to 2 \to 3 \to 4 \to 0$ using three variables for each vertex. For a specific vertex v, they are denoted by $v_{5,1}$, $v_{5,2}$, and $v_{5,3}$. We prevent that variables are assigned to values corresponding to 5, 6, or 7 by adding the binary clauses $(\overline{v}_{5,1} \vee \overline{v}_{5,3}) \wedge (\overline{v}_{5,2} \vee \overline{v}_{5,3})$ for $v \in V$. For an edge variable $e_{u,v}$, we add the ten clauses represented by:

$$e_{u,v} \to (v_{5,1} \leftrightarrow (\overline{u}_{5,1} \wedge \overline{u}_{5,3}))$$
$$e_{u,v} \to (v_{5,2} \leftrightarrow (u_{5,1} \not\leftrightarrow u_{5,2}))$$
$$e_{u,v} \to (v_{5,3} \leftrightarrow (u_{5,1} \wedge u_{5,2}))$$

The main constraint in this encoding enforces that if an edge variable $e_{u,v}$ is true, then v is the successor of u based on the binary adder or LFSR. This is enforced for all edge variables apart from the ones of the form $e_{u,s}$, i.e., the final edge that creates the cycle starting with s. Instead, if an edge variable $e_{u,s}$ is true, then all variables $u_{p_i,j}$ of u must be assigned in such a way that it enforces $|V| - 1$ (mod p_i). Note that for the primes that are encoded using LFSR, the assignment would be the $|V|^{th}$ (mod p_i) state of the LFSR with the bit-vector 1 being the first state.

Finally, we apply the following symmetry-breaking clauses: $(\overline{e}_{s,u} \vee \overline{e}_{v,s})$ for $u > v$ for some total ordering of the vertices. We use the vertex number in the input file. This ensures that every Hamiltonian cycle is represented by a unique assignment to the variables.

5   Results

We implemented an encoding tool, called HCP-encode[1], that takes as input a graph and an integer m. Using the techniques described in the earlier sections, it enforces that all cycles, apart from the one that includes the initial vertex, must have length 0 (mod m). We solved all resulting formulas with the default settings of CADICAL SAT solver, version 1.4. We selected two subsets of the Flinders HCP challenge: 1) graphs that were used in the 2019 XCSP competition; and 2) some larger graphs that resulted in rather high runtimes during our experiments.

Table 1 shows statistics of the graphs in our benchmark suite and the runtimes for the binary adder encoding and the LSFR encoding. The graphs used

---

[1] The encoding and decoding tools together with the graphs are available on GitHub at https://github.com/marijnheule/ChineseRemainderEncoding.

in the 2019 XCSP competition are shown on top, the larger ones below them. The results confirm earlier work that the binary adder encoding is more effective compared to LSFR on these challenge graphs [14]: only once did LSFR outperform the binary adder. However, we observed shorter runtime in our experiments with the binary adder encoding and LSFR compared to recent work [14]. These experiments differ in two ways. First, we use a more recent and possibly a stronger SAT solver for these instances. Second, our implementation does not include preprocessing techniques. It is not clear whether preprocessing helps or hurts performance on these instances. Note that the binary adder and LFSR encodings timed out after an hour for some of the larger graphs.

Table 2 shows the results of our Chinese remainder encoding for various values of the cycle length. We selected cycle lengths that have only small primes in their factorization. The largest cycle length used in the experiments is 420, a number that is divisible by 4, 5, 6, and 7. The table shows the runtime and whether the solution produced by the solver represented a single cycle. The shortest runtime resulting in a single cycle are shown in bold. In general, the larger the cycle, the longer the runtime and the more likely that the result is a single cycle. In particular, for all graphs a cycle length of 0 (mod 2) resulted in multiple cycles, while a cycle length of 0 (mod 420) resulted in a single cycle, i.e., a Hamiltonian cycle. In some cases, a smaller cycle length resulted in a single cycle, while a larger cycle length resulted in multiple cycles (see graphs #237 and #526).

Table 1. Statistics of the selected Flinders HCP challenge graphs and the CADICAL runtime in seconds on the binary adder encoding and the LFSR encoding.

graph #	$|V|$	$|E|$	adder (2^k)	LSFR ($2^k - 1$)
48	338	776	47.22	> 3600
162	909	206571	171.23	180.24
171	996	1495	10.12	20.05
197	1188	1783	10.89	84.75
223	1386	2268	272.46	80.01
237	1476	2215	13.65	22.45
249	1558	2338	19.69	150.70
252	1572	2359	13.71	86.07
254	1582	2374	36.31	127.35
255	1584	2799	48.98	40.60
424	2466	4240	> 3600	> 3600
446	2557	4368	> 3600	> 3600
470	2740	4509	2500.61	> 3600
491	2844	4267	173.46	245.92
506	2964	4447	78.29	244.48
522	3060	4591	84.51	611.46
526	3108	4663	160.73	544.97
529	3132	4699	69.69	275.13

Table 2. Runtime statistics in seconds of the selected Flinders HCP challenge graphs using CaDiCaL and various values for the cycle length. The symbols ✓ and ✗ denote whether the satisfying assignment represents a single or multiple cycles, respectively.

graph #	2	6	12	60	105	420
48	0.10 ✗	6.14 ✗	10.02 ✗	45.20 ✗	84.33 ✓	**73.63** ✓
162	53.62 ✗	34.96 ✓	**32.12** ✓	39.43 ✓	35.75 ✓	40.11 ✓
171	0.01 ✗	2.37 ✗	**2.92** ✓	12.76 ✓	4.89 ✓	5.86 ✓
197	0.02 ✗	0.83 ✗	7.16 ✓	**6.77** ✓	8.87 ✓	14.62 ✓
223	0.02 ✗	1.77 ✗	11.65 ✗	22.14 ✓	**15.93** ✓	70.67 ✓
237	0.04 ✗	2.19 ✗	**7.81** ✓	12.64 ✓	6.90 ✗	16.80 ✓
249	0.19 ✗	**0.81** ✓	4.52 ✓	4.36 ✓	3.01 ✓	7.29 ✓
252	0.02 ✗	1.76 ✗	25.33 ✓	14.62 ✓	**9.66** ✓	32.73 ✓
254	0.33 ✗	2.95 ✓	**0.76** ✓	3.11 ✓	2.42 ✓	4.09 ✓
255	1.27 ✗	2.56 ✗	5.17 ✗	14.31 ✗	8.36 ✗	**9.03** ✓
424	9.81 ✗	665.18 ✗	340.11 ✗	307.71 ✗	494.11 ✓	**488.70** ✓
446	13.24 ✗	334.62 ✗	169.52 ✗	380.47 ✗	**573.38** ✓	722.23 ✓
470	17.08 ✗	166.16 ✗	152.31 ✗	933.36 ✗	501.91 ✗	**840.89** ✓
491	0.06 ✗	22.04 ✗	**7.47** ✓	34.45 ✓	123.36 ✓	135.22 ✓
506	0.11 ✗	31.75 ✗	**19.24** ✓	33.48 ✓	28.73 ✓	63.20 ✓
522	0.63 ✗	5.66 ✗	32.95 ✓	133.40 ✓	**30.40** ✓	67.03 ✓
526	0.05 ✗	24.16 ✗	71.67 ✓	**34.37** ✓	34.69 ✗	158.69 ✓
529	0.40 ✗	17.90 ✗	60.19 ✓	48.09 ✓	**42.33** ✓	365.58 ✓

The Chinese remainder encoding with cycle length 420 outperformed the binary adder encoding for most graphs. Also, none of the experiments with cycle length 420 timed out. Using a smaller cycle length can frequently reduce the runtime, although that increases the probability of multiple cycles. In practice one could run the Chinese remainder encoding for various cycle lengths in parallel.

6 Conclusions

We presented the Chinese remainder encoding for HCP, which combines elements from the incremental SAT, binary adder, and LFSR approaches. Experimental results on graphs from the Flinders HCP challenge show that the Chinese remainder encoding generally outperforms the alternatives when using a cycle length that can be factored into multiple small primes. In the experiments we used a cycle length of $420 = 2^2 \times 3 \times 5 \times 7$. The Chinese remainder encoding is equivalent to the binary adder encoding when the cycle length is the smallest power of 2 that is larger than the number of vertices, so it can be seen as a generalization of the binary adder.

We only experimented with a single SAT call for each encoding. The effectiveness of a small cycle length, in particular $m = 12$, indicates that an incremental SAT approach using that encoding could be effective. Recent work showed that the pure incremental SAT approach is not effective for large graphs [14], but blocking some cycles with our encoding could be helpful. Also, we plan to explore the best combination of cycle lengths in a parallel solving approach.

Acknowledgements. Supported by the NFS under grant CCF-2006363.
We thank Emre Yolcu and Neng-Fa Zhou for comments on an earlier draft.

References

1. Bomanson, J., Gebser, M., Janhunen, T., Kaufmann, B., Schaub, T.: Answer set programming modulo acyclicity. In: Calimeri, F., Ianni, G., Truszczynski, M. (eds.) Logic Programming and Nonmonotonic Reasoning. pp. 143–150. Springer International Publishing (2015)
2. Buratti, M., Del Fra, A.: Cyclic Hamiltonian cycle systems of the complete graph. Discrete Mathematics 279(1), 107–119 (2004), in Honour of Zhu Lie
3. Chiba, N., Nishizeki, T.: The Hamiltonian cycle problem is linear-time solvable for 4-connected planar graphs. Journal of Algorithms **10**(2), 187–211 (1989)
4. Gent, I.P.: Arc consistency in SAT. In: Proceedings of the 15th European Conference on Artificial Intelligence. p. 121–125. ECAI'02, IOS Press, NLD (2002)
5. Golomb, S.W.: Shift Register Sequences. Aegean Park Press (1982)
6. Grebinski, V., Kucherov, G.: Reconstructing a Hamiltonian cycle by querying the graph: Application to DNA physical mapping. Discrete Applied Mathematics 88(1), 147–165 (1998), computational Molecular Biology DAM - CMB Series
7. Haythorpe, M.: FHCP challenge set: The first set of structurally difficult instances of the Hamiltonian cycle problem (2019), https://arxiv.org/abs/1902.10352v1
8. Haythorpe, M., Johnson, A.: Change ringing and Hamiltonian cycles: The search for Erin and Stedman triples. EJGTA **7**, 61–75 (2019)
9. Hertel, Alexander, Hertel, Philipp, Urquhart, Alasdair: Formalizing Dangerous SAT Encodings. In: Marques-Silva, João., Sakallah, Karem A. (eds.) SAT 2007. LNCS, vol. 4501, pp. 159–172. Springer, Heidelberg (2007). https://doi.org/10.1007/978-3-540-72788-0_18
10. Lin, F., Zhao, J.: On tight logic programs and yet another translation from normal logic programs to propositional logic. In: Proceedings of the 18th International Joint Conference on Artificial Intelligence. p. 853–858. IJCAI'03, Morgan Kaufmann Publishers Inc., San Francisco, CA, USA (2003)
11. Prestwich, S.: SAT problems with chains of dependent variables. Discrete Appl. Math. **130**(2), 329–350 (2003)
12. Soh, T., Le Berre, D., Roussel, S., Banbara, M., Tamura, N.: Incremental SAT-based method with native boolean cardinality handling for the Hamiltonian cycle problem. In: Fermé, E., Leite, J. (eds.) Logics in Artificial Intelligence. pp. 684–693. Springer International Publishing (2014)
13. Velev, M.N., Gao, P.: Efficient SAT techniques for absolute encoding of permutation problems: Application to hamiltonian cycles. In: Bulitko, V., Beck, J.C. (eds.) Eighth Symposium on Abstraction, Reformulation, and Approximation, SARA 2009, Lake Arrowhead, California, USA, 8–10 August 2009. AAAI (2009)
14. Zhou, N.F.: In pursuit of an efficient SAT encoding for the Hamiltonian cycle problem. In: Simonis, H. (ed.) Principles and Practice of Constraint Programming, pp. 585–602. Springer International Publishing, Cham (2020)

Efficient SAT-Based Minimal Model Generation Methods for Modal Logic S5

Pei Huang[1,3], Rundong Li[1,3], Minghao Liu[1,3], Feifei Ma[1,2,3(✉)], and Jian Zhang[1,3(✉)]

[1] State Key Laboratory of Computer Science, Institute of Software, Chinese Academy of Sciences, Beijing, China
{huangpei,lird,liumh,maff,zj}@ios.ac.cn
[2] Laboratory of Parallel Software and Computational Science, Institute of Software, Chinese Academy of Sciences, Beijing, China
[3] University of Chinese Academy of Sciences, Beijing, China

Abstract. Modal logic S5 is useful in various applications of artificial intelligence. In recent years, the advance in solving the satisfiability problem of S5 has allowed many large S5 formulas to be solved within a few minutes. In this context, a new challenge arises: how to generate a minimal S5 Kripke model efficiently? The minimal model generation can be useful for tasks such as model checking and debugging of logical specifications. This paper presents several efficient SAT-based methods and provides a symmetry-breaking technique for the minimal model generation problem of S5. Extensive experiments demonstrate that our methods are good at tackling many large instances and achieve state-of-the-art performances. We find that a minimal model of a large S5 formula is usually very small, and we analyze this phenomenon via a graph model. Due to this characteristic, our incremental method performs best in most cases, and we believe that it is more suitable for minimal S5 Kripke model generation.

Keywords: SAT · MaxSAT · Modal logic S5 · Minimal model · Symmetry breaking

1 Introduction

Modal logics provide a theoretical framework for applications in various areas of artificial intelligence. In the past two decades, modal logics have been used in game theory [12], knowledge compilation [5], contingent planning [20] and formal verification [2,18]. Moreover, they also have potential in database theory [10] and distributed computing [13].

S5 is one of the five oldest systems of modal logic. It is suitable for representing and reasoning about the knowledge of a single agent [8,24] and has been used in knowledge compilation [5], contingent planning [20] and epistemic planner [25]. The huge application potential promotes us to improve the practical automated reasoning technique for S5.

© Springer Nature Switzerland AG 2021
C.-M. Li and F. Manyà (Eds.): SAT 2021, LNCS 12831, pp. 225–241, 2021.
https://doi.org/10.1007/978-3-030-80223-3_16

In this paper, we focus on how to efficiently find a minimal S5 Kripke model (MinS5-SAT). In Hardware Verification and Model Checking (e.g. safety property), the model is in fact an explanation of the bug found in the design. A smaller model is easier to understand; it can be more meaningful and helpful to the user for checking or locating the bug precisely. Since the 1990s, a few theoretical works (considering soundness and completeness) about minimal Herbrand model generation were given for modal logic S5 [21,22], but very little work focuses on MinS5-SAT. As for practical algorithms (or solvers), they were designed to decide the satisfiability of modal formulas but rarely considered generating a minimal S5 Kripke model.

The significant improvements of SAT-based S5 solvers in recent years [6,14] pave the way for well handling the MinS5-SAT problem. In 2018, Jean-Marie Lagniez et al. proposed an SAT-based method to solve the MinS5-SAT problem [17], but the translation method can cause the space explosion in many cases which greatly wears out the efficiency of the back-end SAT/MaxSAT solver. For some complex input S5 formulas, it consumes more than 60G of memory.

We provide several practical and efficient SAT-based methods for the MinS5-SAT problem. Compared with the previous works, our methods can make good use of the structural and semantic information to reduce memory usage and eliminate a lot of symmetric (isomorphic) search spaces. A more compact encoding can make the most of the performance of the SAT engine. Experimental results show that our SAT-based methods are efficient in tackling the MinS5-SAT problem, and the method which queries an SAT oracle incrementally is the most efficient one. We noticed that a minimal Kripke model is usually very small. So, we propose a graph model to analyze the reason and find out that "a small model is a high probability event". It also explains why the method based on the incremental framework performs better in both time and memory consumption compared with other methods.

2   Preliminaries

This section briefly reviews the syntax, the semantics and some concepts of modal logic S5.

2.1   Syntax and Semantics

The set of formulas ϕ of S5 is a language $\mathcal{L}$ which extends the propositional language with the modal connectives (or modal operators) $\Box$ and $\Diamond$. The language $\mathcal{L}$ is defined by the grammar:

$$\phi ::= \bot \mid \top \mid p \mid \neg\phi \mid \phi \wedge \phi \mid \phi \vee \phi \mid \Box\phi \mid \Diamond\phi$$

where $p \in \mathbb{P}$ and $\mathbb{P}$ denotes a countably infinite non-empty set of propositional variables. Logical connectives '$\rightarrow$' and '$\leftrightarrow$' are omitted here.

Standard Kripke semantics for modal logic defines a frame, which consists of a non-empty set W of **possible worlds**, and a binary relation R. The relation

R, also known as the **accessibility relation**, is defined between the possible worlds in W. The axioms $\mathcal{K}$, $\mathcal{T}$, $\mathcal{B}$ and 4 restrict that the relation R in S5 is **reflexive, symmetric** and **transitive**. So the possible world semantics for S5 can be simplified as a simple version without accessibility relation [9]. The satisfiability relation $\vDash$ for formulas in $\mathcal{L}$ is recursively defined as follows:

$(W, I, w) \vDash \top$
$(W, I, w) \vDash p$ iff $I(w, p) = 1$
$(W, I, w) \vDash \neg\phi$ iff $(W, I, w) \nvDash \phi$
$(W, I, w) \vDash \phi \wedge \varphi$ iff $(W, I, w) \vDash \phi$ and $(W, I, w) \vDash \varphi$
$(W, I, w) \vDash \phi \vee \varphi$ iff $(W, I, w) \vDash \phi$ or $(W, I, w) \vDash \varphi$
$(W, I, w) \vDash \Box\phi$ iff $\forall w' \in W, (W, I, w') \vDash \phi$
$(W, I, w) \vDash \Diamond\phi$ iff $\exists w' \in W, (W, I, w') \vDash \phi$

2.2 Satisfiability

There are three types of satisfiability problems for S5.

- **[S5-Satisfiability (S5-SAT)]** Determining if there exists a model (W, I, w) that satisfies a given S5 formula θ.
- **[S5-K-Satisfiability (S5-K-SAT)]** Determining if there exists a model (W, I, w) where $|W| = K$ that satisfies a given S5 formula θ.
- **[Minimal S5-Satisfiability (MinS5-SAT)]** Finding a model (W, I, w) that satisfies a given S5 formula θ and it has no model (W', I', w') such that $|W'| < |W|$.

S5-SAT and S5-K-SAT are decision problems and both are NP-complete. MinS5-SAT is NP-hard and can be seen as an optimization problem.

2.3 The Number of Possible Worlds

In 1977, Ladner gave the upper bound of the number of possible worlds to decide the satisfiability of an S5 formula [16]. He proved that if an S5 formula with m modal operators is satisfiable, then there exists an S5-model satisfying the formula with at most $m + 1$ worlds. In 2017, a new upper-bound $dd(\theta) + 1$ was found where $dd(\theta)$ is called diamond degree [6] and it is recursively defined as:

$dd(\theta) = dd'(\mathrm{nnf}(\theta))$
$dd'(\top) = dd'(\neg\top) = dd'(p) = dd'(\neg p) = 0$
$dd'(\phi \wedge \varphi) = dd'(\phi) + dd'(\varphi)$
$dd'(\phi \vee \varphi) = max(dd'(\phi), dd'(\varphi))$
$dd'(\Box\phi) = dd'(\phi)$
$dd'(\Diamond\phi) = 1 + dd'(\phi)$

In 2019, a more compact upper bound, $\chi + 1$ was given by Huang et al. [14]. For most cases, we have:

$$\chi \leq dd(\theta) \leq m \tag{1}$$

The upper-bound $\chi + 1$ is reasoned from the relationship among diamond subformulas via a polynomial-time approximation graph coloring algorithm.

2.4   S5-NF

Every S5 formula can be converted into an equivalent one that is in S5-NF. S5-NF is helpful for improving efficiency and saving memory when solving the S5 satisfiability problems. Identifying structural information and semantic information of an S5-NF formula is relatively easy. The definition of S5-NF is in [14]. We only briefly review it here. S5-NF is a kind of CNF-like first degree normal form but with some textural difference. The basic unit that makes it up is **S5-literal**:

> **Propositional literal:** p
> **B-literal:** $\Box(p \vee q \vee ... \vee r)$
> **D-literal:** $\Diamond(p \wedge q \wedge ... \wedge r)$

where p, q, r are propositional literals.

The disjunction of S5-literals is called **S5-clause** and the conjunction of S5-clauses is called **S5-NF**.

Example 1. An S5 formula θ and its S5-NF ϕ with three S5-clauses.

$$\theta = \Diamond\Box((r \rightarrow p \wedge q) \wedge (\Diamond(\neg r \rightarrow \neg p \wedge q))) \wedge (\neg p \rightarrow \neg\Box(q \wedge r))$$

$$\phi = \underbrace{\Box(p \vee q \vee \neg r)}_{C_1} \wedge \underbrace{\{\Diamond(\neg p \wedge q) \vee \Diamond r\}}_{C_2} \wedge \underbrace{\{p \vee \Diamond(\neg q \wedge \neg r)\}}_{C_3}$$

2.5   Complexity Analysis

The MinS5-SAT is in $\mathcal{P}^{SAT}$ (or $\mathcal{FP}^{SAT}$).

> Assuming that $\mathcal{M}^{S5\text{-}K\text{-}SAT}$ is an oracle Turing machine that has the capability to query an oracle for S5-K-SAT. For a given S5 formula, the upper bound μ of possible worlds can be computed in polynomial time, and it is less than the length (n) of input formula. As the Turing machine $\mathcal{M}^{S5\text{-}K\text{-}SAT}$ can find a minimal model via querying S5-K-SAT at most polynomial (μ) times, MinS5-SAT is in $\mathcal{P}^{S5\text{-}K\text{-}SAT}$. We know that S5-K-SAT is in $\mathcal{NPC}$, so MinS5-SAT $\in \mathcal{P}^{SAT}$.

It reveals that MinS5-SAT can be solved via iteratively calling an SAT engine at most $\mathcal{O}(n)$ times. On the other hand, the MinS5-SAT problem can be reduced to the MaxSAT problem.

In addition to SAT-based approaches, tableau, FOL-based and resolution-based methods can also tackle MinS5-SAT in theory. However, their practical execution efficiency is far less than SAT-based methods.

3   Methodology

In this section, we present the basic SAT-based methods. The encoding process is premised on S5-NF.

3.1   Querying SAT Iteratively

First, we will give the method via querying SAT iteratively. We use propositional variable p_j to denote the truth value of p in the possible world w_j. Then the S5-K-SAT can be encoded as SAT.

Definition 1. *Translation function $tr_{SAT}^-(\phi, K)$ can produce a propositional formula for an input S5-NF ϕ with K possible worlds:*

1. $\top \Rightarrow \top \quad \bot \Rightarrow \bot$
2. *For all propositional literals p in ϕ: $p \Rightarrow p_0$*
3. *For all B-literals in ϕ:*
   $\square(p \vee q \vee \cdots \vee s) \Rightarrow \bigwedge_{j=0}^{K-1}(p_j \vee q_j \vee \cdots \vee s_j)$
4. *For all D-literals in ϕ:*
   $\Diamond(p \wedge q \wedge \cdots \wedge r) \Rightarrow \bigvee_{j=0}^{K-1}(p_j \wedge q_j \wedge \cdots \wedge r_j)$

If $tr_{SAT}^-(\phi, K)$ is satisfiable then we can conclude that the formula ϕ has a model with K possible worlds. So, the MinS5-SAT problem can be seen as an optimization problem:

$$\text{minimize} \quad K \quad \text{s.t.} \quad tr_{SAT}^-(\phi, K) \text{ is satisfiable.} \tag{2}$$

One can iterate the value of K between 0 and upper bound μ in an increasing (or decreasing, binary search, etc.) way to find a minimal K that can satisfy $tr_{SAT}^-(\phi, K)$. The advantage of this method is that it can make full use of the efficiency of the SAT engine.

3.2   Partial MaxSAT Model

If there is a D-literal $\Diamond\psi$ and $(W, I, w) \vDash \psi$, we say that the possible world w is assigned to $\Diamond\psi$ or w realizes $\Diamond\psi$. The key to find a minimal Kripke model for an S5-NF is how to assign the possible worlds to D-literals. For example, suppose that the upper bound for the formula in Example 1 is calculated to be 3 by some method. Then, we can construct a Kripke model M_1 in Fig. 1. The world w_1 is assigned to $\Diamond r$ in C_2 and w_2 is assigned to $\Diamond(\neg q \wedge \neg r)$. Now, if we want to save a possible world, we can try to assign w_0 to $\Diamond(\neg q \wedge \neg r)$ as shown in M_2. In this context, w_2 can be removed from the model because no diamond formula needs it.   Based on this insight, some switch variables can be added for the D-literals. For each possible world w_j, we use a Boolean variable v_j to open or close it. When v_j is falsified, the possible world w_j will be closed. So, we can encode the MinS5-SAT as a partial MaxSAT (PMS) problem [7].

Definition 2. *Translation function $tr_{PMS}^-(\phi, \mu)$ can produce a partial MaxSAT formula for an input S5-NF ϕ with at most μ (upper bound) possible worlds:*

1. $\top \Rightarrow \top \quad \bot \Rightarrow \bot$
2. *For all propositional literals: $p \Rightarrow p_0$*

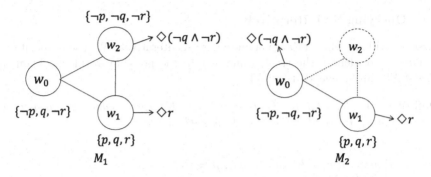

Fig. 1. Two Kripke models of the S5-NF in Example 1.

3. *For all B-literals:*
   $$\Box(p \vee q \vee \cdots \vee s) \Rightarrow \bigwedge_{j=0}^{\mu-1}(p_j \vee q_j \vee \cdots \vee s_j)$$
4. *For all D-literals:*
   $$\Diamond(p \wedge q \wedge \cdots \wedge r) \Rightarrow \bigvee_{j=0}^{\mu-1}(v_j \wedge p_j \wedge q_j \wedge \cdots \wedge r_j)$$
5. *Add a unit clause:* v_0
6. *Add unit soft clauses:* $\bigwedge_{j=1}^{\mu-1}(\neg v_j)$

Except for the clauses generated by rule 6, all other clauses are hard. The possible world w_0 must exist, so we add a hard unit clause v_0. The idea behind this partial MaxSAT formula is to close as many worlds as possible. Since the possible worlds do not need to be really removed, we just apply switch variables to diamond formulas. The number of satisfied switch variables is the size of a minimal model.

Example 2. If the upper bound μ for the S5-NF ϕ in Example 1 is 3, then the $tr_{PMS}^-(\phi, 3)$ is :

$$\bigwedge_{j=0}^{2}(p_j \vee q_j \vee \neg r_j) \wedge \{\bigvee_{j=0}^{2}(v_j \wedge \neg p_j \wedge q_j) \vee \bigvee_{j=0}^{2}(v_j \wedge r_j)\}$$

$$\wedge\{p_0 \vee \bigvee_{j=0}^{2}(v_j \wedge \neg q_j \wedge \neg r_j)\} \wedge v_0 \wedge \underbrace{\neg v_1}_{Soft} \wedge \underbrace{\neg v_2}_{Soft}$$

The advantage of the MaxSAT-based method is that UNSAT core and heuristics for optimization can be well used in finding a minimal model.

4   Improved Methods

Finding a minimal model for an S5-NF can be seen as searching for an optimal assignment of possible worlds for satisfied D-literals. In the basic model, the realization of D-literals will be tested in all possible worlds $\{w_0, w_1, ..., w_{\mu-1}\}$, so there are a lot of symmetric (or isomorphic) situations. Suppose the process of finding kripke model is considered in order, clause by clause. Like Example 1, when we are considering how to realize the D-literals in C_2, and w_2, w_3 have not been considered for other D-literals now, actually, there is no difference trying to realize the D-literals in C_2 via w_2 or w_3.

4.1   SIF Strategy

We design a static symmetry breaking technique called **Smallest Index First** (SIF) strategy. Assuming that $tr_{SAT}^-(\phi, K)$ and $tr_{PMS}^-(\phi, \mu)$ translate the S5-NF ϕ from left to right, the index set of possible worlds $\{0, 1, ..., \mu - 1\}$ (or $\{0, 1, ..., K - 1\}$) can be divided into two parts: $\Omega_1 = \{l \in \mathbb{N} | 0 \leq l \leq L - 1\}$ and $\Omega_2 = \{l \in \mathbb{N} | L \leq l \leq \mu - 1\}$ (or $\{l \in \mathbb{N} | L \leq l \leq K - 1\}$). The index in Ω_1 marks the possible worlds which have been used to test the realization of some D-literals. Ω_2 represents the possible worlds which have not been considered. If the S5-clause currently under consideration has D-literals, we only need to consider one more possible world at most. There is no difference for any one in Ω_2, because we can always find a permutation to rename the worlds in Ω_2. So we can add the w_L with the smallest index to Ω_1.

4.2   Improved S5-K-SAT Model

For S5-K-SAT encoding, initially $L = 1$, $\Omega_1 = \{0\}$, $\Omega_2 = \{1, ..., K-1\}$. Whenever the translation procedure encounters an S5-clause which has D-lierals, update L to $Min(L + 1, K - 1)$.

Definition 3. *Translation function $tr_{SAT}(\phi, K)$ is the improved version of $tr_{SAT}^-(\phi, K)$ with the SIF strategy:*

> *When the procedure is translating S5-clause C_i, update L, iff C_i has D-literals. For all D-literals in C_i:*
> $$\Diamond(p \wedge q \wedge \cdots \wedge r) \Rightarrow \bigvee_{j \in \Omega_1}(p_j \wedge q_j \wedge \cdots \wedge r_j)$$

Example 3. Assume that ϕ is the formula in Example 1 and $K = 3$, then the procedure of $tr_{SAT}(\phi, 3)$ can be like this:

- Step 1. Translating C_1. $L = 1$, $\Omega_1 = \{0\}$, $\Omega_2 = \{1, 2\}$.
  $\Box(p \vee q \vee \neg r) \Rightarrow \bigwedge_{j=0}^{2}(p_j \vee q_j \vee \neg r_j)$
- Step 2. Translating C_2. $L = L + 1$, $\Omega_1 = \{0, 1\}$, $\Omega_2 = \{2\}$.
  $\Diamond(\neg p \wedge q) \vee \Diamond r \Rightarrow \bigvee_{j=0}^{1}(\neg p_j \wedge q_j) \vee \bigvee_{j=0}^{1} r_j$
- Step 3. Translating C_3. $L = L + 1$, $\Omega_1 = \{0, 1, 2\}$, $\Omega_2 = \{\}$.
  $p \vee \Diamond(\neg q \wedge \neg r) \Rightarrow p_0 \vee \bigvee_{j=0}^{2}(\neg q_j \wedge \neg r_j)$

In the second step, we only consider that whether $\Diamond(\neg p \wedge q)$ and $\Diamond r$ can be realized via possible worlds w_0 and w_1. We do not need to consider the possible worlds in Ω_2 for it.

4.3   Improved PMS Model

For PMS encoding, initially $L = 1$, $\Omega_1 = \{0\}$ and $\Omega_2 = \{1, ..., \mu\}$. Whenever the translation procedure encounters an S5-clause which has diamond formula, update L to $Min(L + 1, \mu - 1)$.

Translation function $tr_{PMS}(\phi, \mu)$ is the improved version of $tr_{PMS}^{-}(\phi, \mu)$ with the SIF strategy:

(i) Add : $\bigwedge_{j=0}^{\mu-2}(v_{j+1} \rightarrow v_j)$
   When the procedure is translating S5-clause C_i, update L, iff C_i has D-literals.
(ii) For all D-literals in C_i:
   $\Diamond(p \wedge q \wedge \cdots \wedge r) \Rightarrow \bigvee_{j \in \Omega_1}(v_j \wedge p_j \wedge q_j \wedge \cdots \wedge r_j)$

The effect of (ii) is the same as the previous one. The added clauses (i) restrict that the indexes of the possible worlds in a minimal model are contiguous. This is a specific symmetry breaking for the MaxSAT encoding.

4.4   The Benefit of SIF

If we ignore the box subformulas and propositional literals, a minimal S5 model finding procedure for an S5-NF can be simply abstracted as a tree search process. It tests various assignments for D-literals and finds the one that uses the least number of possible worlds. Similarly, S5-K-SAT are searching for an assignment for these D-literals using just K possible worlds. The basic encoding of D-literals can be seen as testing possible assignments to realize it. In this perspective, the comparison of the basic methods with the improved methods is shown in Fig. 2. In the basic methods, all the possible assignments for D-literals will be tested. In the improved methods, fewer assignments will be tested for the D-literals at a high level of the tree. The D-literals in the first S5-clause only test $\{w_0, w_1\}$, and the D-literals in the second S5-clause only test $\{w_0, w_1, w_2\}$, and so on. So the search tree of the improved methods can be much "thinner" and a lot of symmetric situations are eliminated. When the upper bound μ is big, the search space reduced by the SIF strategy is considerable.

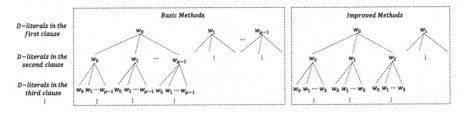

Fig. 2. The search spaces of the basic and improved methods.

5   Comparison

The state-of-the-art MinS5-SAT solver S52SAT 2.0 also uses a SAT based method [17]. The input formula θ will be translated to a MaxSAT formula. The main translation procedure $tr_s(\theta, \mu)$ is recursively defined as:

$$tr_s(\theta, \mu) = tr_s'(\theta, 0, \mu - 1)$$
$$tr_s'(p, i, \mu - 1) = p_i \qquad tr_s'(\neg p, i, \mu - 1) = \neg p_i$$
$$tr_s'((\varphi \wedge \delta), i, \mu - 1) = tr_s'(\varphi, i, \mu - 1) \wedge tr_s'(\delta, i, \mu - 1)$$
$$tr_s'((\varphi \vee \delta), i, \mu - 1) = tr_s'(\varphi, i, \mu - 1) \vee tr_s'(\delta, i, \mu - 1)$$
$$tr_s'(\Box \varphi, i, \mu - 1) = \bigwedge_{j=0}^{\mu-1}(s_j \rightarrow tr_s'(\varphi, j, \mu - 1))$$
$$tr_s'(\Diamond \varphi, i, \mu - 1) = \bigvee_{j=0}^{\mu-1}(s_j \wedge tr_s'(\varphi, j, \mu - 1))$$
$$\text{Add: } \bigwedge_{j=0}^{\mu-2}(s_{j+1} \rightarrow s_j)$$

Variables s_i are added to enable or disable worlds w_i.

In general, the input formula θ can be in a very complex form, which has nested modal operators and arbitrary combinations of logical connectives. This translation method can produce a large SAT formula with redundancies. Besides, there are a lot of symmetric situations in $tr_s(\theta, \mu)$. Compared with it, our translation method has three advantages: First, the input formula θ will be transformed to an equivalent S5-NF and the nested modal operators are eliminated. It makes our methods produce a relatively small formula in the translation phase. And our method will not add variables for box formulas. Second, the structural information of the formula can be used to eliminate a lot of isomorphic models and improve the efficiency in the search phase. Third, the reasoning can be relatively efficient in possible worlds except for w_0. The diamond formulas only have "$\wedge$". When the process tests whether some D-literals can be realized by a certain world, the unit propagation can be activated.

6   Experimental Evaluation

Based on the approaches presented in this article, we implemented the MinS5-SAT solver *S5cheetah 2.0*[1]. The upper bound used in *S5cheetah 2.0* is $\chi + 1$. The *Glucose 4.0* [3] is used as the back-end SAT solver and *RC2* [15] is used as the back-end MaxSAT solver which has the best performance in the MaxSAT competition 2019[2].

First, we clarify some notations in the experimental part:

[**Inc.**] It denotes the method which queries the satisfiability of $tr_{SAT}(\phi, K)$ with increasing values of K from 1 to the upper bound $\chi + 1$.

[**Dec.**] It denotes the method which queries the satisfiability of $tr_{SAT}(\phi, K)$ with decreasing values of K from the upper bound $\chi + 1$ to 1.

[**Bs.**] It denotes the method which queries the satisfiability of $tr_{SAT}(\phi, K)$ using binary search for the optimal K between 1 and the upper bound $\chi + 1$.

---

[1] S5cheetah and benchmarks: http://www.square16.org/tools/s5cheetah/.

[2] https://maxsat-evaluations.github.io/2019/rankings.html.

[PMS.] It denotes our MaxSAT method.

[S52SAT 2.0] It is a state-of-the-art MinS5-SAT solver[3].

[S52SAT 1.0] It is an S5-SAT solver and used as a reference in our experiment. In general, the MinS5-SAT problem is harder than the S5-SAT problem. So, the time and memory consumption of *S52SAT 1.0* can be regarded as the lower bound of the time and memory consumption of *S52SAT 2.0*. Based on the reports in paper [17], *S52SAT 1.0* uses a similar translation method like $tr_s()$ but without selector s_i and consumes less time than *S52SAT 2.0*.

[Lck.] It denotes the S5-SAT solver *LCKS5TabProver* [1]. It is the state-of-the-art tableau method solver for S5 and used as a reference. The advantage of SAT-based methods can be seen from the comparison of LCK with other SAT-based methods.

We cannot directly compare *S5cheetah 2.0* with other MinS5-SAT solvers, but we can infer the strength of our methods from the experimental results. The correctness of *S5cheetah 2.0* is cross-validated by our different methods.

6.1 Benchmarks

The well-established modal logic benchmarks include $QMLTP$[4], $3CNF$ [23], $3CNF_{mu}$ $QS5\_1$, $QS5\_2$, $MQBF_K$ [19], and $LWB_{K,KT,S4}$ [4]. $QMLTP$ is designed for testing automated theorem proving (ATP) systems for first-order modal logics. It contains 177 propositional benchmarks for S5 from different domains (e.g. planning, querying databases, natural language processing, general algebra). All the benchmarks in $QS5\_1$ and $QS5\_2$ are satisfiable and large, they are generated based on hard combinatorial designs about quasigroups. Most benchmarks in $3CNF$ are unsatisfiable, so we generate $3CNF_{mu}$ based on $3CNF$. All the instances in $3CNF_{mu}$, which are generated from small mutations of all the unsatisfiable instances in $3CNF$, are satisfiable. Note that $MQBF_K$ and $LWB_{K,KT,S4}$ are not designed for S5. However, the results on those benchmarks are still valuable. They share the same grammar and S5-SAT entails K, KT and S4-SAT. Furthermore, the size of a minimal S5 Kripke model can be seen as an upper bound for K, KT and S4. All the benchmarks can be downloaded from the link (See footnote 1).

6.2 Environment

The experiments are performed on a server with Intel(R) Xeon (R) CPU (2.40 GHz), Ubuntu 16.04 and 64G RAM. The time bound is set to 300 s for each instance. The experiments were performed on all SATISFIABLE instances.

---

[3] S52SAT 2.0. is not available at moment. So, we compare with S52SAT 1.0 as reference. http://www.cril.univ-artois.fr/%7emontmirail/s52SAT/v2/index.html.

[4] http://www.iltp.de/qmltp/.

6.3   Experimental Results

Table 1 shows the comparison of efficiency on each instance family. For each solver on each instance family, we report the number of instances where the solver uses the least time among all solvers in the table, denoted by "#Win" and the average time ($T_{avg}(ms)$) for tackling each instance family. The unsolved instances are counted with the time bound. The sum of "#Win" of all solvers is not necessarily equal to "#total", since all solvers may fail. "#Mem" records the maximum memory usage.

- **[Lck vs. Other solvers]** Lck failed in tackling many instances compared with SAT-based methods. Even on some small examples, it is much slower than other SAT-based methods.
- **[PMS vs. S52SAT 1.0]** Our PMS method consumes less time and memory than *S52SAT 1.0*. We infer that PMS performs better than *S52SAT 2.0*.
- **[PMS vs. Dec and Bs]** The time consumption of Dec and Bs is close to that of PMS, but PMS consumes more memory than the methods which are based on querying S5-K-SAT iteratively.
- **[Inc vs. Dec, Bs and PMS]** For most instances, the incremental method performs best in terms of memory usage and efficiency. Figure 3 shows the comparison of running time on some hard families (3CNF and QS5). We find that minimal Kripke models are usually small. So, the incremental method has the best performance in solving the MinS5-SAT problem.
- **[SIF vs. No SIF]** SIF is a symmetry-breaking strategy that hardly introduces extra computation cost. It really can help us solve more instances and improve the efficiency of our methods. For $3CNF_{mu}$, it can help Inc solve 5 more instances (943 vs. 938), help Dec solve 67 more instances (401 vs. 334), help Bs solve 53 more instances (401 vs. 334) and help PMS solve 180 more instances (409 vs. 229). For $QS5\_2$, it cannot help Inc solve more instances (154 vs 154) but can help Dec solve 43 more instances (154 vs. 111), help Bs solve 2 more instances (127 vs. 125) and help PMS solve 6 more instances (116 vs 110). For other benchmarks, all the instances can be solved by all methods (with or without SIF) but the methods with SIF consume less time. Figure 4 shows the comparison of running time of the methods with SIF and without SIF on $3CNF_{mu}$ and $QS5\_2$. Sometimes the method using SIF will take a little longer time because of the fluctuation of the CPU and randomized strategy of the SAT solver. SIF has more obvious advantages when the instance is more difficult and the minimum model is larger.

Table 2 shows the average size of minimal models ($MinW$) with the estimated upper bounds ($\chi + 1$) and ($dd(\theta) + 1$). We can see that a minimal model is very small and sometimes the theoretical upper bound is much larger than the size of the number of minimal possible worlds.

7   Why Is a Minimal Model Small?

Although basic modal logics have small model property, the concept is equivalent to the finite model property [11]. Sometimes this theoretical "small" model can

Table 1. The comparison of efficiency on all benchmarks. "-" means no instance can be solved within the time bound.

Ins (#Total)	Inc.			Dec.			Bs.			PMS.			S52SAT1.0		Lck.	
	#Win	T_{avg}	Mem	#Win	T_{avg}	Mem	#Win	T_{avg}	Mem	#Win	T_{avg}	Mem	T_{avg}	Mem	T_{avg}	Mem
QMLTP(41)	41	0.5	0.8M	0	1.3	1.0M	0	0.91	0.9M	0	1.1	20.1M	78.90	25.0M	43910.9	21G
QS5_1(252)	248	1995.6	4.8G	0	29745.3	5.5G	0	6800.64	5.3G	4	5846.4	6.6G	107378.2	64G	-	-
QS5_2(240)	149	129303.9	3.1G	0	189785.7	8.5G	0	164857.9	6.2G	5	181272.8	8.8G	290205.8	64G	-	-
3CNF (55)	54	19476.2	62.8M	0	223919.6	109.7M	0	40669.2	76.1M	0	238946.2	250.1M	126804.3	2.35G	-	-
3CNF_{mu}(945)	939	7776.2	59.9M	0	207520.2	100.7M	0	48329.9	55.5M	0	187422.1	174.0M	290205.9	64G	-	-
LWB_k (42)	42	154.5	46.8M	0	180.6	51.5M	0	166.7	48.8M	0	176.4	59.4M	81326.9	64G	147467.9	64G
LWB_kt (105)	105	7.8	48.1M	0	15.6	55.1M	0	14.2	55.9M	0	18.4	62.8M	30916.2	64G	61103.1	58G
LWB_s4(105)	105	40.4	6.8M	0	47.6	7.1M	0	46.5	7.1M	0	51.8	7.7M	38299.4	24.5G	57393.4	62G
qbfS (177)	177	1.59	3.0M	0	5.78	4.8M	0	3.19	3.0M	0	3.24	12.4M	591.44	84.0M	-	-

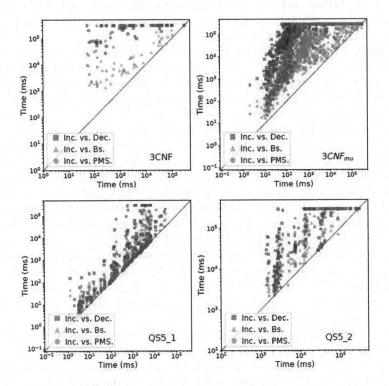

Fig. 3. The comparison of running time on $3CNF$ and $QS5$.(The x-axis corresponds to the time used by incremental method and the y-axis corresponds to the time used by other methods. The axes are in logarithmic scale. The point above the line y=x means that the incremental method consumes less time on this instance.)

be very large. To our best knowledge, there is no literature about the minimal number of possible worlds of modal logics. So, we try to figure out whether a minimal S5 Kripke model is so small frequently.

Suppose the input formula ϕ is an S5-NF, and there are m S5-clauses containing at least one D-literal. Based on the definition of diamond degree, we know that $dd(\phi)=m$. So the satisfiability of ϕ can be decided with at most $m+1$

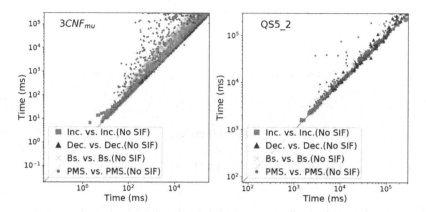

Fig. 4. The comparison of running time on $3CNF_mu$ and $QS5\_2$.(The x-axis corresponds to the time used by methods with SIF and the y-axis corresponds to the time used by methods without SIF. The axes are on a logarithmic scale. The point above the line y=x means the method with SIF consumes less time on this instance.)

Table 2. The minimal number of possible worlds VS. estimated upper bounds.

Ins	MinW	$\chi + 1$	$dd(\theta) + 1$	$m + 1$
$QMLTP$	1.31	1.75	6.87	242.73
$QS5\_1$	1.00	16.05	2826.70	8333.36
$QS5\_2$	1.92	40.93	1329.41	35095.44
$3CNF$	7.03	125.45	152.82	427.85
$3CNF_{mu}$	6.89	233.47	316.50	797.16
LWB_k	1.50	3.47	440.92	1049.48
LWB_kt	1.40	4.00	217.89	1035.52
LWB_s4	1.20	2.57	236.22	1130.41
$qbfS$	2.00	3.00	45.07	1637.87

possible worlds. If ϕ is satisfiable then at least one S5-literal in each S5-clause must be true in its minimal model and we call that S5-literal as the "key S5-literal". Actually, the number of possible worlds is decided by all key D-literals. We can build a graph G for these "key D-literals". The vertices set are key D-literals and the edges are used to denote whether there is a conflict (they cannot be realized by the same world) between two key D-literals. Figure 5 is a schematic. We assume that P_k is the probability of that the key S5-literal is a D-literal in an S5-clause or whether a vertex appears in the graph. We use P_c to denote the probability of the appearance of a conflicting edge between two key D-literals. In this context, if the minimal chromatic number of the graph coloring problem of G is $\chi(G)$, then the minimal size of the model is either $\chi(G)$ or $\chi(G)+1$. According to literature [24], the chromatic number upper bound is

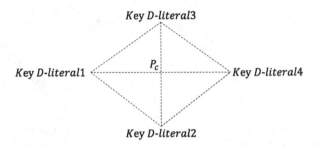

Fig. 5. The conflict graph of four key D-literals.

$\chi(G) \leq \delta = max_{i \in V} min(d_i + 1, i)$, where d_i denotes the degree of vertex i and $d_1 \geq d_2 \geq ... \geq d_{|V|}$. Then the probability that the chromatic number less than some constant H is:

$$P(\delta \leq H) = P(|\{d_i | d_i \geq H\}| \leq H)$$

We simplify the model and use independent random variable $X_{ij}(i, j \in \{1, 2, ..., m\})$ to denote the appearance of edge between two vertexes i and j. $X_{ij} = 1$ means that vertex i appears in graph otherwise, $X_{ij} = 0$.

$$P(d_i \geq H) = P(\sum_{j=1}^{m} X_{ij} \geq H) = P(\frac{\sum_{j=1}^{m} X_{ij} - mp_k^2 p_c}{\sqrt{mp_k^2 p_c(1 - p_k^2 p_c)}} \geq \frac{H - mp_k^2 p_c}{\sqrt{mp_k^2 p_c(1 - p_k^2 p_c)}})$$

Based on central limit theorem, we have:

$$Z = \frac{\sum_{j=1}^{m} X_{ij} - mp_k^2 p_c}{\sqrt{mp_k^2 p_c(1 - p_k^2 p_c)}} \sim N(0, 1)$$

So, $P(d_i \geq H) = \Phi(1 - \frac{H - mp_k^2 p_c}{\sqrt{mp_k^2 p_c(1 - p_k^2 p_c)}})$ where Φ is the cumulative distribution function (CDF) of normal distribution $N(0, 1)$.

We simply use independent random variable Y_i to denote whether $d_i \geq H$ and $P(Y_i = 1) = P(d_i \geq H) = p_d$. Then we have:

$$P(|\{d_i | d_i \geq H\}| \leq H) = P(\sum_{i=1}^{m} Y_i \leq H) = P(\frac{\sum_{i=1}^{m} Y_i - mp_d}{\sqrt{p_d(1 - p_d)}} \leq \frac{H - mp_d}{\sqrt{p_d(1 - p_d)}})$$

Reuse the central limit theorem, we have:

$$P(\delta \leq H) = P(|\{d_i | d_i \geq H\}| \leq H) = \Phi(\frac{H - mp_d}{\sqrt{p_d(1 - p_d)}})$$

If $m = 200$, $P_k = \frac{1}{3}$ (There are 3 types of S5-literals in an S5-clause and they are chosen as key S5-literal with equal probability.) and $P_c = \frac{1}{2}$ (Simply assuming that the existence of an edge follows the uniform distribution.), then $P(\delta \leq \frac{m}{10} =$

Efficient SAT-Based Minimal Model Generation Methods for Modal Logic S5   239

20) $= 99.99\%$. If $m = 300$, $P(\delta \leq \frac{m}{10}) \approx 100\%$. In practice, m is much smaller than $|\phi|$. Besides, the minimal chromatic number can be much smaller than the estimated upper bound δ. The upper bound $\chi+1$ is estimated from conflicting relationship among D-literals, but one cannot know which D-literals are key D-literals and get the accurate conflicting relationships in advance. So the upper bound $\chi+1$ can also be much larger than $\chi(G)+1$. So the minimal number of possible worlds can be many times smaller than estimated upper bound with a high probability. This also shows that there is room for improvement in the upper bound.

Intuitively, P_k is inversely proportional to the average number of S5-literals in each S5-clause. P_c is proportional to the length of the D-literal. In general, the key D-literal is not too long for a satisfiable formula, because its conjunctive structure determines that if it is too long, it will make the assignment of a certain world very demanding, which is easy to make the whole formula to be unsatisfiable. As P_k and P_c get smaller in some larger formulas, δ will be smaller than a smaller constant H with a higher probability. To some extent, this model can help us figure out why a minimal model can be so small and the incremental method is more efficient.

8 Conclusion

In this paper, we propose some efficient SAT-based methods with a symmetry-breaking technique to generate minimal Kripke models for modal logic S5 formulas. Extensive experiments show that our methods achieve state-of-the-art performances and the incremental method is more efficient and consumes less memory compared with other methods. We notice that the minimal S5 Kripke model is usually very small. So, we analyze the reason with a graph model and find that "a small Kripke S5 model is a high probability event". It explains why querying an SAT oracle incrementally performs best in most cases. In the future, we would like to migrate these methods to other modal logics such as S4 and KD45 which are similar to S5.

Acknowledgements. This work has been supported by the National Natural Science Foundation of China (NSFC) under grant No.61972384 and the Key Research Program of Frontier Sciences, Chinese Academy of Sciences under grant number QYZDJ-SSW-JSC036. Feifei Ma is also supported by the Youth Innovation Promotion Association CAS under grant No. Y202034. The authors would like to thank the anonymous reviewers for their comments and suggestions.

References

1. Abate, P., Goré, R., Widmann, F.: Cut-free single-pass tableaux for the logic of common knowledge. In: Workshop on Agents and Deduction at TABLEAUX. vol. 2007. Citeseer (2007)

2. Aguilera, J.P., Fernández-Duque, D.: Verification logic: an arithmetical interpretation for negative introspection. In: Advances in Modal Logic 11, proceedings of the 11th conference on Advances in Modal Logic, held in Budapest, Hungary, August 30 - September 2, 2016. pp. 1–20 (2016)

3. Audemard, G., Simon, L.: Predicting learnt clauses quality in modern SAT solvers. In: IJCAI 2009, Proceedings of the 21st International Joint Conference on Artificial Intelligence, Pasadena, California, USA, 11–17 July 2009, pp. 399–404 (2009)

4. Balsiger, P., Heuerding, A., Schwendimann, S.: A benchmark method for the propositional modal logics k, kt, S4. J. Autom. Reason. **24**(3), 297–317 (2000)

5. Bienvenu, M., Fargier, H., Marquis, P.: Knowledge compilation in the modal logic S5. In: Proceedings of the Twenty-Fourth AAAI Conference on Artificial Intelligence, AAAI 2010, Atlanta, Georgia, USA, July 11–15, 2010 (2010)

6. Caridroit, T., Lagniez, J., Berre, D.L., de Lima, T., Montmirail, V.: A SAT-based approach for solving the modal logic S5-satisfiability problem. In: Proceedings of the Thirty-First AAAI Conference on Artificial Intelligence, 4–9 February 2017, San Francisco, California, USA. pp. 3864–3870 (2017)

7. Chu, Y., Luo, C., Cai, S., You, H.: Empirical investigation of stochastic local search for maximum satisfiability. Frontiers Comput. Sci. **13**(1), 86–98 (2019). https://doi.org/10.1007/s11704-018-7107-z

8. Fagin, R., Halpern, J.Y., Moses, Y., Vardi, M.: Reasoning about knowledge. MIT press, Cambridge (2004)

9. Fitting, M.: A simple propositional S5 tableau system. Ann. Pure Appl. Log. **96**(1–3), 107–115 (1999)

10. Fitting, M.: Modality and databases. In: Dyckhoff, R. (ed.) TABLEAUX 2000. LNCS (LNAI), vol. 1847, pp. 19–39. Springer, Heidelberg (2000). https://doi.org/10.1007/10722086_2

11. Goranko, V., Otto, M.: Model theory of modal logic. In: Handbook of Modal Logic, pp. 249–329 (2007)

12. Grossi, D., Rey, S.: Credulous acceptability, poison games and modal logic. In: Proceedings of the 18th International Conference on Autonomous Agents and MultiAgent Systems, AAMAS 2019, Montreal, QC, Canada, 13–17 May 2019, pp. 1994–1996 (2019)

13. Hella, L., et al.: Weak models of distributed computing, with connections to modal logic. Distrib. Comput. **28**(1), 31–53 (2013). https://doi.org/10.1007/s00446-013-0202-3

14. Huang, P., Liu, M., Wang, P., Zhang, W., Ma, F., Zhang, J.: Solving the satisfiability problem of modal logic S5 guided by graph coloring. In: Proceedings of the Twenty-Eighth International Joint Conference on Artificial Intelligence, IJCAI 2019, Macao, China, 10–16 August 2019. pp. 1093–1100 (2019)

15. Ignatiev, A., Morgado, A., Marques-Silva, J.: RC2: an efficient maxsat solver. J. Satisf. Boolean Model. Comput. **11**(1), 53–64 (2019)

16. Ladner, R.E.: The computational complexity of provability in systems of modal propositional logic. SIAM J. Comput. **6**(3), 467–480 (1977)

17. Lagniez, J.-M., Le Berre, D., de Lima, T., Montmirail, V.: An assumption-based approach for solving the minimal S5-satisfiability problem. In: Galmiche, D., Schulz, S., Sebastiani, R. (eds.) IJCAR 2018. LNCS (LNAI), vol. 10900, pp. 1–18. Springer, Cham (2018). https://doi.org/10.1007/978-3-319-94205-6_1

18. Leuştean, I., Moangă, N., Şerbănuţă, T.F.: Operational semantics and program verification using many-sorted hybrid modal logic. In: Cerrito, S., Popescu, A. (eds.) TABLEAUX 2019. LNCS (LNAI), vol. 11714, pp. 446–476. Springer, Cham (2019). https://doi.org/10.1007/978-3-030-29026-9_25

19. Massacci, F.: Design and results of the tableaux-99 non-classical (Modal) systems comparison. In: Murray, N.V. (ed.) TABLEAUX 1999. LNCS (LNAI), vol. 1617, pp. 14–18. Springer, Heidelberg (1999). https://doi.org/10.1007/3-540-48754-9_2

20. Niveau, A., Zanuttini, B.: Efficient representations for the modal logic S5. In: Proceedings of the Twenty-Fifth International Joint Conference on Artificial Intelligence, IJCAI 2016, New York, 9–15 July 2016. pp. 1223–1229 (2016)

21. Papacchini, F., Schmidt, R.A.: A tableau calculus for minimal modal model generation. Electron. Notes Theor. Comput. Sci. **278**, 159–172 (2011)

22. Papacchini, F., Schmidt, R.A.: Terminating minimal model generation procedures for propositional modal logics. In: Demri, S., Kapur, D., Weidenbach, C. (eds.) IJCAR 2014. LNCS (LNAI), vol. 8562, pp. 381–395. Springer, Cham (2014). https://doi.org/10.1007/978-3-319-08587-6_30

23. Patel-Schneider, P.F., Sebastiani, R.: A new general method to generate random modal formulae for testing decision procedures. J. Artif. Intell. Res. **18**, 351–389 (2003)

24. Soto, M., Rossi, A., Sevaux, M.: Three new upper bounds on the chromatic number. Discret. Appl. Math. **159**(18), 2281–2289 (2011)

25. Wan, H., Yang, R., Fang, L., Liu, Y., Xu, H.: A complete epistemic planner without the epistemic closed world assumption. In: Proceedings of the Twenty-Fourth International Joint Conference on Artificial Intelligence, IJCAI 2015, Buenos Aires, Argentina, 25–31 July 2015. pp. 3257–3263 (2015)

DiMo – Discrete Modelling Using Propositional Logic

Norbert Hundeshagen, Martin Lange[(✉)], and Georg Siebert

Theoretical Computer Science/Formal Methods, University of Kassel,
Kassel, Germany
martin.lange@uni-kassel.de

Abstract. We present a learning tool that addresses competences in using propositional logic for modelling purposes. It provides a language for specifying parametrised propositional formula schemes, a backend tool using an incremental SAT solver to exemplify instances of such a scheme to a user learning how to write correct propositional formulas, and a web-based frontend for easy access.

1 Propositional Logic in Formal Modelling

Propositional Logic (PL) constitutes one of the foundations of computer science as a simple, yet broadly applicable modelling language. It is used in a wide range of areas, from the description of computational process in Boolean circuits on the hardware level to high-level applications in planning [8], computer-aided verification [2], cryptanalysis [10], etc. Typical problems in these areas can be reduced to a few fundamental and tightly linked decision and computation problems on propositional formulas, most of all satisfiability checking (SAT) but also equivalence checking, (counter-)model generation, etc.

Moreover, there is a steady and impressive advancement in SAT solving technology as witnessed regularly for instance by results of the SAT solvers competitions [6]. These industrial-strength tools open up the possibilities for practical solutions in areas whose decision/computation problems can be (efficiently) encoded in propositional logic, provided that users are able to correctly model their problems in SAT. This is one good reason for propositional logic being part of any standard computer science/engineering curriculum. It is in fact recommended to be taught in the the contexts of digital design, mathematical foundations and intelligent systems [7].

The syntactic and semantic simplicity of propositional logic does not necessarily make it an easy topic for students, especially not in times of an apparent decrease in mathematical abilities to grasp and apply abstract concepts, of which propositional logic is one. Students typically have no problem understanding the mechanism of evaluating a propositional formula, including the mechanics of Boolean operators like conjunction, negation etc. They also do not normally struggle with *solving* simple satisfiability tasks like

© Springer Nature Switzerland AG 2021
C.-M. Li and F. Manyà (Eds.): SAT 2021, LNCS 12831, pp. 242–250, 2021.
https://doi.org/10.1007/978-3-030-80223-3_17

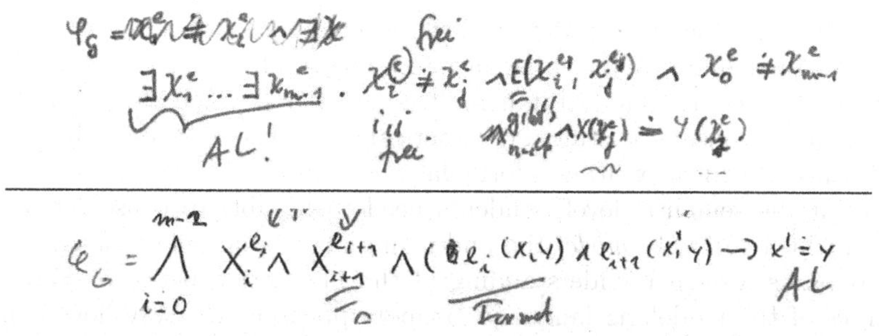

Fig. 1. Typical erroneous use of propositional logic in modelling.

(a) Find a satisfying assignment for $(\neg A \vee B \vee C) \wedge (A \vee \neg B) \wedge (A \vee \neg C)$.

Such tasks, however, merely address the issues arising with the celebrated use of propositional logic in application domains as recalled above, namely *modelling* problems in the language of propositional logic. Such a task would rather be something like

(b) Construct a propositional formula $\Phi(R,n)$ *which is satisfiable iff there is a way for the robot to traverse through room R in order to reach the target area in at most n steps.*

Task (b) addresses an entirely different level of required analytical competences as task (a): he/she needs to transpose the simple planning problem into the language of propositional logic, in other words model it in SAT. By doing so, the student shows the ability to leverage the power of generic black-box solutions (here: SAT solvers) to solve problems from a specific application domain, and this addresses exactly one of the core competences that computer science students should acquire.

Hence, in order to proficiently use propositional logic as a modelling tool, it does not suffice to be able to read and write propositional formulas $\varphi(A_1, \ldots, A_n)$ but instead one needs to deal with formula *schemes* $\varphi_{p_1, \ldots, p_k}(\vec{A})$ in which the propositional variables $\vec{A}$ and also the junctors may depend on external parameters $p_1, \ldots, p_k$ of some domain.

Didactical Considerations. In a programming-language perspective, the key difference between the two tasks stated above can be described as computing the result of a *given* program (a) versus *writing* a program for a given problem (b). To meet task (b) students typically have to master two levels:

(I) On the syntactic level they need to be able to write down well-formed formula schemes. The biggest pitfall is typically the separation of parameter and propositional variables, and to strictly stay within propositional logic over a given set of variables. Figure 1 shows some wild but not atypical attempts at writing a formula φ_G which is satisfiable if the graph G has an Euler tour, using propositional variables X_i^e stating *"the i-th edge on the tour is e."*

Learning can easily be supported on this level by tools which reject malformed input with immediate feedback like error messages (cf. [1]) or syntax highlighting. Note that this is standard in compilers and IDEs, which also explains why students rarely consider writing a (syntactically) correct program to be as problematic and difficult as writing a formula.

(II) On the semantic level, students need to be able to construct formula schemes which correctly *model* the underlying domain-specific problem. It typically requires a deeper understanding of the interaction between syntax and semantics of the modelling language, or more precisely, the way how syntactical change influences semantical change. Modelling in propositional logic can be compared to writing programs in a high-level language like Prolog, both syntactically – see the proposal of the DiMo language below – and semantically through the common use of logical principles.

The issues of understanding and correctly using Prolog and therefore to some extent, the process of modelling in propositional logic, are well explained by the theory of Cognitive Dimension of Notations [4], that is, "Prolog [...] allows many different program structures to be built by combining a very small number of notational elements in different ways", cf. [5]. Hence, there is also a (generic) way to support learning on this level, namely by visualising the *effect* of a program or, in terms of this paper's main focus, a candidate formula (scheme). We take this to mean, for instance, displaying the set of propositional models of the instantiated formula scheme for a suitably large set of parameter values. Provided the student has understood the problem to be modelled, seeing the propositional models for some problem instances is typically sufficient to judge whether the formula "does the right thing or not."

In the following we describe the DiMo language and tool. It supports learning efforts in the area of discrete modelling using propositional logic by implementing the principles described here and thus addresses both the syntactic and semantic level for this task.

2   The DiMo Language and Tool

DiMo Programs. Input to the DiMo Tool is given in a language used to specify parametrised propositional formulas and what to do with them. A DiMo *program* consists of the specification of . . .

- a decision/computation problem. Currently supported are (I) satisfiability checking and (II) model enumeration, as well as generalisations of (III) validity and (IV) equivalence checking of/between propositional formula schemes.
- formal parameters to the formula scheme as well as their (possibly infinite) ranges. Currently, the only supported parameter type is that of integers. Ranges can be any finite or linear subset of $\mathbb{Z}$.

- (optionally) a family of propositions. These are the "main" ones in the sense that others are regarded as auxiliary ones. Those whose values are determined by others can thus be excluded from output and from model comparisons for instance. (Ex.: the auxiliary variables introduced in the well-known Tseitin transformation [11].)
- one or two formula schemes, possibly with abbreviated subformula schemes in order to enhance readability. These are the ones to be checked for satisfiability, equivalence, etc.

A formal specification of the DıMo language can be found in the DıMo manual [9]. It follows standard context-free syntax principles of logics and programming languages and also explains in detail the possibilities to perform arithmetic operations on integer parameters in order to achieve higher expressiveness. Here we present one example of a DıMo program to introduce the main features available in this formal modelling language.

Example 1. Consider the task of writing a formula $\text{ExactlyMofN}(n, m)$ over propositions $A_1, \ldots, A_n$ which is true under some evaluation ϑ iff ϑ maps exactly m of these n propositions to *true*. The DıMo program

```
1   EQUIVALENT    ExactlyMofN_with_aux(n,m)
2   TO            ExactlyMofN_rec(n,m)
3   PROPOSITIONS  A
4   PARAMETERS    n: {1,..}, m: NAT WITH m <= n
5   FORMULAS
6
7     ExactlyMofN_with_aux(n,m) =
8       AtLeastMChosen(n,m) & AtMostMChosen(n,m)
9
10    AtLeastMChosen(n,m) =
11      B(n,m) & BsWellBehaved(n,m) & BsEndOk(m)
12    BsWellBehaved(n,m) =
13      FORALL i : {1,..,n}.
14        FORALL j: {1,..,m}.
15          B(i,j) -> ( (A(i) & B(i-1,j-1)) | B(i-1,j))
16    BsEndOk(m) = FORALL j : {1,..,m}. -B(0,j)
17
18    AtMostMChosen(n,m) = AtLeastNminusMNotChosen(n,n-m)
19    AtLeastNminusMNotChosen(n,m) =
20      N(n,m) & NsWellBehaved(n,m) & NsEndOk(m)
21    NsWellBehaved(n,m) =
22      FORALL i : {1,..,n}.
23        FORALL j: {1,..,m}.
24          N(i,j) -> ( (-A(i) & N(i-1,j-1)) | N(i-1,j))
25    NsEndOk(m) = FORALL j : {1,..,m}. -N(0,j)
26
27    ExactlyMofN_rec(n,m) = Choose(m,0,n)
28    Choose(0,1,n) = FORALL i:{1+1,..,n}. -A(i)
29    Choose(m,1,n) =
```

```
30      FORSOME i:{1+1,..,n-m+1}. A(i) &
31         (FORALL j:{1+1,..,i-1}. -A(j)) & Choose(m-1,i,n)
```

asks for two formalisations of this property to be compared. The first one in lines 7–25 uses auxiliary variables $B(i,j)$ and $N(i,j)$ in order to abbreviate statements like "*exactly j amongst $A_1, \ldots, A_i$ are true*" in order to achieve an encoding of length $\mathcal{O}(n \cdot m)$. The second one in lines 27–31 defines this predicate recursively which basically amounts to enumerating all subsets of $A_1, \ldots, A_n$ having m elements.

Even though both formulas schemes represent correct solutions to the task at hand, they are not semantically equivalent as propositional formulas due to the use of auxiliary variables. They are equivalent in the sense that for each $m, n \in \mathbb{N}$, the Π_2-sentence

$$\left(\forall \vec{A} \, \exists \vec{B} \, \exists \vec{N}. \, \texttt{ExactlyMofN\_with\_aux}(m,n) \rightarrow \texttt{ExactlyMofN\_rec}(m,n)\right) \wedge$$

$$\left(\forall \vec{A} \, \exists \vec{B} \, \exists \vec{N}. \, \texttt{ExactlyMofN\_rec}(m,n) \rightarrow \texttt{ExactlyMofN\_with\_aux}(m,n)\right)$$

is true. For formulas without auxiliary variables, this notion of Π_2-truth boils down to ordinary propositional equivalence. Hence, DiMo's equivalence mode can also be used to test students' solutions against a standard solution.

The Backend. The DiMo tool consists of two parts: front- and backend. The latter runs DiMo programs in the style of a semi-decision procedure. It combines

- an *enumerator* for the parameter spaces,
- an *instantiator* which turns a formula scheme and concrete parameter values into a propositional formula, and
- an *engine* which translates the DiMo problem into a (series of) satisfiability problems of formulas in conjunctive normal form and calls an incremental SAT solver in order to solve the satisfiability, model enumeration or the aforementioned generalisations of validity and equivalence problem for the current instance of the formula schemes. This uses the standard technique of incrementally adding clauses to exclude previously found models.

Remember that DiMo's primary purpose is the training of modelling competences using propositional logic, in particular the design of parametrised formula schemes adhering to some specification. It should be clear that correctness of formula schemes with integer parameters, with addition and multiplication available, is undecidable. However, for learning purposes, the feedback given by analysing each instance of a formula scheme is much more valuable anyway, as it provides the user with an understanding of what the formula scheme written down as a DiMo program expresses.

Example 2. Suppose the header of the DiMo program of Example 1 in lines 1–4 is changed to the following code.

```
 1  MODELS          ExactlyMofN_with_aux(n,m)
 2  PROPOSITIONS    A
 3  PARAMETERS      n: {1,..}, m: NAT WITH m <= n
```

This now asks for all models (restricted to the propositional variables A(i)) of any instantiation of this scheme with $n, m \in \mathbb{N}, n \geq 1, m \leq n$ to be shown. Running DiMo on that program results in the following output.

```
 1  Instance m=0, n=1 .............................
 2    Found model -A(1)
 3  1 model found.
 4  Instance m=0, n=2 .............................
 5    Found model -A(1), -A(2)
 6  1 model found.
 7  Instance m=1, n=1 .............................
 8    Found model A(1)
 9  1 model found.
10  Instance m=0, n=3 .............................
11    Found model -A(1), -A(2), -A(3)
12  1 model found.
13  Instance m=1, n=2 .............................
14    Found model A(1), -A(2)
15    Found model -A(1), A(2)
16  2 models found.
17  Instance m=0, n=4 .............................
18    Found model -A(1), -A(2), -A(3), -A(4)
19  1 model found.
20  Instance m=1, n=3 .............................
21    Found model A(1), -A(2), -A(3)
22    Found model -A(1), A(2), -A(3)
23    Found model -A(1), -A(2), A(3)
24  3 models found.
25  Instance m=2, n=2 .............................
26    Found model A(1), A(2)
27  1 model found.
```

From this one can quickly see that the formula scheme correctly formalises this property. Note that the output has been truncated for obvious reasons; in fact, DiMo reports models for larger parameters with no notable delay: within $10\,\mathrm{s}$, instances up to $m = 5$ and $n = 16$ are handled on a standard MacBook, showing all $4368 = \binom{16}{5}$ models.

The output generated by the backend supports the user to master the semantic level of learning how to correctly use propositional logic in discrete modelling. The syntactic level is mainly addressed by the frontend described below. The DiMo backend is implemented in OCaml for reasons of speed and high-level programming constructs. It is openly available under the BSD-3-license.[1] It connects to an incremental SAT solver through the ocaml-sat-solvers interface

---

[1] https://github.com/muldvarp/DiMo.

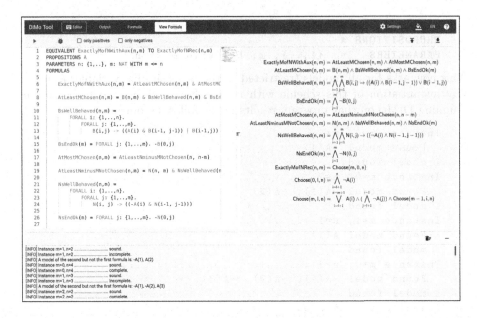

Fig. 2. The frontend with editor (left), formula view (right) and output (below).

which currently supports MINISAT. Extending it to others is merely a matter of implementation, but MINISAT also works very well for these purposes.

The backend can also be run as a stand-alone application reading input from files and producing console output. This is recommended for advanced usage, for instance when long output needs to be generated beyond the limitations of the frontend or the hosting webserver.

The Frontend is a web-based user interface that allows students to write and run DIMO programs in order to learn how to correctly use propositional logic as a modelling tool. It is inspired by modern IDEs with features like syntax and error highlighting, code completion, and basic text editor functions.

This functionality helps to prevent syntax errors at the time of writing formula schemes and thus supports the user in mastering the first, syntactic level in this learning exercise. It is additionally supported and reinforced by the displaying of formula schemes in a mathematical style which students are probably more familiar with from lecture slides. The correspondence between the computer-readable DIMO syntax and the mathematical style is basically one-to-one which makes it easy to learn the former from the latter.

Figure 2 shows a screenshot of the frontend with the DIMO program from Example 1. The main view of the frontend consists of three components:

- The left pane contains the editor in which DIMO programs can be created. Some syntax highlighting can be seen in Fig. 2 for instance the distinction

between DıMo keywords, parameter variables, propositions and Boolean operators. Potential errors would be marked using squiggly red underlining.
- The right pane shows the output of an on-the-fly typesetting of the formula scheme using LaTeX.
- The pane at the bottom contains output taken from a run of the backend on this program.

The frontend is hosted on a server so that users do not need to undergo a potentially laborious setup of a development environment. A (modern) web-browser suffices for access, hence the system is platform independent, easy and uncomplicated to start, and the user can focus on the task of learning how to model problems in propositional logic.

The foundation of the frontend is written in `Typescript`[2] with `Angular` (See footnote 2) as a web application framework. The editing functionality is provided by the `Monaco Editor` (See footnote 2), a web-based port of the Visual Studio Code editor. It offers interfaces for syntax highlighting and visual support for code completion and error highlighting. For this reason, a parser was created with `ANTLR` (See footnote 2) to check the program for syntax errors and extract positional information of the syntax constructs. The information from the parser is then further processed and subsequently inserted in the `Monaco Editor`. With regex operations, the DıMo program is converted into LaTeX source code and displayed using a `Katex` (See footnote 2) environment.

The backend does not include an interface for HTTP requests; it is wrapped by a `Node.js` (See footnote 2) server, written in `Typescript` as well. It uses `Express.js` (See footnote 2) as a web framework. Nearly all functions of the backend can be accessed by HTTP using the server's API. To provide an easy way to set up the DıMo tool a `Docker` (See footnote 2) script is available in the public repository.[3] Alternatively, the latest version is usable on a website hosted at the University of Kassel[4]. The associated wiki provides further support.

3   Conclusion

We have presented a framework for learning how to correctly use propositional logic as a modelling tool. The tool itself makes extensive use of an incremental SAT solver in order to visualise the result of a student's effort to create a parametrised formula according to some requirements. This targets the modelling aspect directly, and this is what also distinguishes DıMo from other logic learning tools like ILTIS [3] for instance which is more general-purpose and rather focuses on tasks like the one named (a) in the introduction.

There is room for further work on the DıMo tool and in particular the DıMo language. Next steps will include the extension by further data types, for instance

[2] https://www.typescriptlang.org, https://angular.io, https://www.docker.com, https://microsoft.github.io/monaco-editor, https://www.antlr.org, https://katex.org, https://nodejs.org, https://expressjs.com.
[3] https://syre.fm.cs.uni-kassel.de/Georg/dimotoolweb.
[4] https://dumbarton.fm.cs.uni-kassel.de.

strings or finite graphs. These will allow DIMO to be used in order to train further modelling tasks, including fundamental problems like 3-colourability or longest common subsequence. There is also need for tool support in learning how to use richer languages in modelling, for instance QBF or first-order logic. Both, and the latter in particular, raise questions though about the right presentation of models for users to see how to correct faulty tries.

References

1. Anderson, J.R., Corbett, A.T., Koedinger, K.R., Pelletier, R.: Cognitive tutors: lessons learned. J. Learn. Sci. **4**(2), 167–207 (1995)
2. Clarke, E.M., Biere, A., Raimi, R., Zhu, Y.: Bounded model checking using satisfiability solving. Formal Methods Syst. Des. **19**(1), 7–34 (2001)
3. Geck, G., Ljulin, A., Peter, S., Schmidt, J., Vehlken, F., Zeume, T.: Introduction to Iltis: an interactive, web-based system for teaching logic. In: Proceedings 23rd Annual ACM Conference on Innovation and Technology in Computer Science Education, ITiCSE 2018, pp. 141–146. ACM (2018)
4. Green, T.R.G.: Cognitive dimensions of notations. In: People and Computers V, pp. 443–460. University Press (1989)
5. Green, T.R.G.: Instructions and descriptions: some cognitive aspects of programming and similar activities. In: Proceedings of Working Conference on Advanced Visual Interfaces, AVI 2000, pp. 21–28. ACM (2000)
6. Järvisalo, M., Berre, D.L., Roussel, O., Simon, L.: The international SAT solver competitions. AI Mag. **33**(1), 89–92 (2012)
7. Joint Task Force on Computing Curricula, ACM and IEEE Computer Society. Computer Science Curricula 2013: Curriculum Guidelines for Undergraduate Degree Programs in Computer Science. ACM (2013)
8. Kautz, H.A., Selman, B.: Planning as satisfiability. In: Proceedings of 10th European Conference on Artificial Intelligence, ECAI 1992, pp. 359–363 (1992)
9. Lange, M.: DiMo - a tool for discrete modelling using propositional logic (version 0.2.2) (2021). https://github.com/muldvarp/DiMo/blob/master/doc/dimo.pdf
10. Massacci, F., Marraro, L.: Logical cryptanalysis as a SAT problem. J. Autom. Reasoning **24**(1/2), 165–203 (2000)
11. Tseytin, G.S.: On the complexity of derivation in propositional calculus. In: Studies in Constructive Mathematics and Mathematical Logic II, volume 8 of Zapiski Nauchnykh Seminarov LOMI, pp. 235–259. Nauka (1968). (In Russian)

SAT-Based Rigorous Explanations
for Decision Lists

Alexey Ignatiev[1][(✉)] and Joao Marques-Silva[2]

[1] Monash University, Melbourne, Australia
alexey.ignatiev@monash.edu
[2] IRIT, CNRS, Toulouse, France
joao.marques-silva@irit.fr

Abstract. Decision lists (DLs) find a wide range of uses for classification problems in Machine Learning (ML), being implemented in a number of ML frameworks. DLs are often perceived as interpretable. However, building on recent results for decision trees (DTs), we argue that interpretability is an elusive goal for some DLs. As a result, for some uses of DLs, it will be important to compute (rigorous) explanations. Unfortunately, and in clear contrast with the case of DTs, this paper shows that computing explanations for DLs is computationally hard. Motivated by this result, the paper proposes propositional encodings for computing abductive explanations (AXps) and contrastive explanations (CXps) of DLs. Furthermore, the paper investigates the practical efficiency of a MARCO-like approach for enumerating explanations. The experimental results demonstrate that, for DLs used in practical settings, the use of SAT oracles offers a very efficient solution, and that complete enumeration of explanations is most often feasible.

1 Introduction

Decision lists (DLs) [64] find a wide range of uses for classification problems in Machine Learning (ML) [1,2,12,15–18,65,71–73], being implemented in a number of ML frameworks (e.g. [10,22]). DLs can be viewed as ordered rules, and so are often perceived as interpretable[1]. This explains in part the recent interest in DLs [1,2,12,65,71–73], most of which is premised on the interpretability of DLs. However, building on recent results for decision trees (DTs) [37], which demonstrate the possible non-interpretability of DTs when representing specific

---

[1] Interpretability is a subjective concept, for which no rigorous accepted definition exists [46]. As clarified later in the paper, for a given pair ML model and instance, we equate interpretability with how succinct is the justification for the model's prediction.

This work was supported by the AI Interdisciplinary Institute ANITI, funded by the French program "Investing for the Future – PIA3" under Grant agreement no. ANR-19-PI3A-0004, and by the H2020-ICT38 project COALA "Cognitive Assisted agile manufacturing for a Labor force supported by trustworthy Artificial intelligence".

C.-M. Li and F. Manyà (Eds.): SAT 2021, LNCS 12831, pp. 251–269, 2021.
https://doi.org/10.1007/978-3-030-80223-3_18

functions, we show that interpretability can also be an elusive goal for some DLs. As a result, and for some concrete applications of DLs, it is important to compute (rigorous) explanations.

Explanations can be broadly categorized into heuristic [47,62,63] and nonheuristic [32,66]. Recent work has provided extensive evidence regarding the lack of quality of heuristic explanation approaches [11,25,34,40,57,68]. Nonheuristic (or rigorous) approaches for computing explanations can be organized into abductive (AXp) [19,32,33,66] and contrastive (CXp) [31,54]. (Abductive explanations are also referred to as PI-explanations [66] (i.e. prime implicant explanations), since these represent subset-minimal sets of feature value pairs that are sufficient for a prediction.) Most work on rigorous explanations either exploits knowledge compilation approaches [3,19,66,67], or approaches based on iterative calls to some oracle for NP (e.g. SAT, SMT, MILP, etc.) [31–33]. As a result, improvements to automated reasoning tools, can have a profound impact on the deployment of rigorous explanation approaches.

Furthermore, recent work proposed polynomial time algorithms for finding explanations of a number of ML models, including DTs [37], naive-Bayes classifiers [49], and also different knowledge representation languages [3]. Unfortunately, and in contrast with these recent tractability results, this paper proves that finding one PI-explanation for a DL is NP-hard.

Motivated by the NP-hardness of finding explanations of DLs, the paper proposes propositional encodings for computing abductive and contrastive explanations of DLs. Furthermore, the paper investigates the practical efficiency of a MARCO-like [43] approach for enumerating explanations. The experimental results demonstrate that, for DLs used in practical settings, the use of SAT oracles offers a very efficient solution, and that complete enumeration of explanations is most often feasible.

The paper is organized as follows. The notation and definitions used throughout the paper are introduced in Sect. 2. Section 3 proves the NP-hardness of finding rigorous explanations for DLs. In addition, this section develops a propositional encoding for finding one AXp or one CXp, and briefly overviews the online enumeration of explanations. Section 4 presents the experimental results. The paper concludes in Sect. 5.

2 Preliminaries

2.1 Propositional Satisfiability

Definitions standard in propositional satisfiability (SAT) and maximum satisfiability (MaxSAT) solving are assumed [8]. In what follows, we will assume formulas to be propositional. A conjunction of literals is referred to as *term* while a disjunction of literals is referred to as *clause*; also note that a literal is either a Boolean variable or its negation. Whenever convenient, terms and clauses are treated as sets of literals. A formula is said to be in *conjunctive* or *disjunctive normal form* (CNF or DNF, respectively) if it is a conjunction of clauses or disjunction of terms, respectively. Set theory notation will be also used with respect to CNF and DNF formulas when necessary.

A *truth assignment* μ is a mapping from the set of variables to $\{0,1\}$. An assignment is said to satisfy a literal l ($\neg l$, resp.) if it maps variable l to 1 (to 0, resp.). A clause is said to be satisfied by assignment μ if μ satisfies at least one of its literals. If for a CNF formula ϕ there exists an assignment μ that satisfies all clauses of ϕ, formula ϕ is referred to as satisfiable and μ is its *satisfying assignment* (or *model*). In addition, we use the notation $\vDash$ to denote *entailment*, i.e. $\phi_1 \vDash \phi_2$ if any model of ϕ_1 is also a model of ϕ_2.

One of the central concepts in rigorous explainable AI (XAI) [32,66] is of prime implicants as defined below.

Definition 1. *A term π is an* implicant *of formula ϕ if $\pi \vDash \phi$. An implicant π of ϕ is called* prime *if none of the proper subsets $\pi' \subsetneq \pi$ is an implicant of ϕ.*

In the context of unsatisfiable formulas, the maximum satisfiability (MaxSAT) problem is to find a truth assignment that maximizes the number of satisfied clauses. A number of variants of MaxSAT exist [8, Chapters 23 and 24]. Hereinafter, we are mostly interested in Partial (Unweighted) MaxSAT, which can be formulated as follows. The formula ϕ is represented as a conjunction of *hard* clauses $\mathcal{H}$, which must be satisfied, and *soft* clauses $\mathcal{S}$, which represent a preference to satisfy those clauses, i.e. $\phi = \mathcal{H} \wedge \mathcal{S}$. Therefore, the Partial MaxSAT problem consists in finding an assignment that satisfies all the hard clauses and maximizes the total number of satisfied soft clauses. In the following, the concepts of minimal unsatisfiable subsets (MUSes) and minimal correction subsets (MCSes) taking into account the hard clauses $\mathcal{H}$ will also be helpful. Concretely, consider unsatisfiable CNF formula $\phi = \mathcal{H} \wedge \mathcal{S}$ with $\mathcal{H}$ and $\mathcal{S}$ defined as the set of hard and soft clauses, respectively.

Definition 2. *A subset of soft clauses $\mathcal{M} \subseteq \mathcal{S}$ is a* Minimal Unsatisfiable Subset *(MUS) iff $\mathcal{H} \cup \mathcal{M}$ is unsatisfiable and $\forall_{\mathcal{M}' \subsetneq \mathcal{M}}, \mathcal{H} \cup \mathcal{M}'$ is satisfiable.*

Definition 3. *A subset of soft clauses $\mathcal{C} \subseteq \mathcal{S}$ is a* Minimal Correction Subset *(MCS) iff $\mathcal{H} \cup \mathcal{F} \setminus \mathcal{C}$ is satisfiable and $\forall_{\mathcal{C}' \subsetneq \mathcal{C}}, \mathcal{H} \cup \mathcal{F} \setminus \mathcal{C}'$ is unsatisfiable.*

MUSes and MCSes of a CNF formula are known to be related through the minimal hitting set (MHS) duality [5,9,45,61], which has been recently exploited in a number of practical settings [21,27,30,36,45] including XAI [31].

2.2 Classification Problems, Decision Lists, and Explanations

This section introduces definitions and notation related with classification problems in ML, but also formal definitions of explanations proposed in recent work [32,66].

Classification Problems. We consider a classification problem, characterized by a set of (categorical) features $\mathcal{F} = \{1, \ldots, m\}$, and by a set of classes $\mathcal{K} = \{c_1, \ldots, c_K\}$. Each feature $j \in \mathcal{F}$ is characterized by a domain D_i. As a result,

$$\tau(\mathbf{x}) = \begin{cases} \oplus & \text{if } [2x_1 - x_2 > 1] \\ \ominus & \text{if } [2x_1 - x_2 \le 1] \end{cases}$$

R_0:	IF x_1 THEN $\oplus$
R_1:	ELSE IF x_2 THEN $\oplus$
R_{DEF}:	ELSE THEN $\ominus$

R_0: IF x_1 THEN $\oplus$
R_1: IF x_2 THEN $\oplus$
R_2: IF $\neg x_1 \wedge \neg x_2$ THEN $\ominus$

(a) Example linear classifier   (b) Example decision list   (c) Example decision set

Fig. 1. Example classifiers

feature space is defined as $\mathbb{F} = D_1 \times D_2 \times \ldots \times D_m$. A specific point in feature space is represented by $\mathbf{v} = (v_1, \ldots, v_m)$. A point $\mathbf{v}$ in feature space denotes an *instance* (or an *example*). Moreover, we use $\mathbf{x} = (x_1, \ldots, x_m)$ to denote an arbitrary point in feature space. In general, when referring to the value of a feature $j \in \mathcal{F}$, we will use a variable x_j, with x_j taking values from D_j. (To keep the notation simple, we opt not to introduce an assignment function, mapping each feature j to some value in D_j.) For simplicity, throughout this paper we will restrict $\mathcal{K}$ to two classes, i.e. $\mathcal{K} = \{\oplus, \ominus\}$. However, most of the ideas described in this document also apply in the more general case of $\mathcal{K}$ with more than two elements; the general case of non-binary classification is also considered in the experimental results presented in Sect. 4. (In settings where $\mathcal{K} = \{\oplus, \ominus\}$, we will also equate $\oplus$ with 1, and $\ominus$ with 0.)

A classifier implements a *total classification function* $\tau : \mathbb{F} \to \mathcal{K}$. In some settings, e.g. when computing explanations, it will be convenient to represent the classification function as a *decision predicate* $\tau_c : \mathbb{F} \to \{0,1\}$, parametrized by some fixed class $c \in \mathcal{K}$, and such that $\forall(\mathbf{x} \in \mathbb{F}).\tau_c(\mathbf{x}) \leftrightarrow (\tau(\mathbf{x}) = c)$.

Example 1. To illustrate the definitions above, we consider a very simple linear classifier, defined as follows. Let $\mathcal{F} = \{1,2\}$, with $D_1 = D_2 = \{0,1,2\}$, and let $\mathcal{K} = \{\ominus, \oplus\}$. As a result, feature space is given by $\mathbb{F} = \{0,1,2\} \times \{0,1,2\}$. Furthermore, the classification function associated with the classifier is shown in Fig. 1a. Concretely, the prediction is $\oplus$ if $2x_1 - x_2 > 1$, and it is $\ominus$ otherwise. □

Decision Lists (DLs) & Decision Sets (DSs). A *rule* is of the form "IF antecedent THEN prediction", where the antecedent is of the form $\bigwedge$feature-literals. The interpretation of a rule is that if the antecedent is consistent (i.e. all the literals are true), then the rule *fires* and the prediction is the one associated with the rule. A decision list (DL) [64] is an *ordered* list of rules, whereas a decision set (DS) [14,39] is an *unordered* list of rules.

Throughout the paper, we will consider ordered sets of rule indices $\mathfrak{R} = \{1, \ldots, R\}$, such that for $i \in \mathfrak{R}$, we will use $\mathfrak{c}$, $\mathfrak{l}$ and $\mathfrak{o}$ to denote, respectively, the class associated with rule i, the set of literals associated with rule i and the order of rule i.

Example 2. Consider another classifier. Let $\mathcal{F} = \{1,2\}$, with $D_1 = D_2 = \{0,1\}$, and so $\mathbb{F} = \{0,1\} \times \{0,1\}$. The decision list for the classifier is shown in Fig. 1b

while an equivalent decision set is shown in Fig. 1c. The classification function
for the DL can be represented as follows:

$$\tau(\mathbf{x}) = \begin{cases} \oplus & \text{if } [(x_1) \vee (\neg x_1 \wedge x_2)] \\ \ominus & \text{if } [(\neg x_1 \wedge \neg x_2)] \end{cases}$$

(Note how the lack of order in DS rules results in a simpler classifier representa-
tion $\tau(\mathbf{x})$ for class $\oplus$, e.g. it can be explicitly represented as $x_1 \vee x_2$ since rules
R_0 and R_1 are unordered in the decision set of Fig. 1c.)   □

Note that following the standard convention, we will *always* assume that DLs
have a *default rule*, with no literals, that *fires* when for all the preceding rules,
the conjunction of literals associated with that rule is inconsistent. An example
default rule for the DL shown in Example 2 is marked as R_{DEF}.

Interpretability and Explanations. Interpretability is generally accepted to
be a subjective concept, without a formal definition [46]. In this paper we measure interpretability in terms of the overall succinctness of the information provided by an ML model to justify a given prediction. We say that a model is *not*
interpretable if for some instance, the justification of a prediction is arbitrarily
larger (on the number of features) than a rigorous explanation (which we define
next). Moreover, and building on earlier work, we equate explanations with the
so-called PI-explanations [3,19,32,66], i.e. subset-minimal sets of feature-value
pairs that are sufficient for the prediction. More formally, given an instance
$\mathbf{v} \in \mathbb{F}$, with prediction $c \in \mathcal{K}$, i.e. $\tau(\mathbf{v}) = c$, a PI-explanation is a minimal subset
$\mathcal{X} \subseteq \mathcal{F}$ such that,

$$\forall(\mathbf{x} \in \mathbb{F}). \bigwedge_{j \in \mathcal{X}} (x_j = v_j) \to (\tau(\mathbf{x}) = c) \tag{1}$$

Another name for a PI-explanation is (a minimal/minimum) *abductive explanation* (AXp) [31,32]. For simplicity, and depending on the context, we will use
PI-explanation and the acronym *AXp* interchangeably.

In a similar vein, we consider *contrastive explanations* (CXps) [31,54]. Contrastive explanation can be defined as a (subset-)minimal set of feature-value
pairs ($\mathcal{Y} \subseteq \mathcal{F}$) that suffice to changing the prediction if they are allowed to take
some arbitrary value from their domain. Formally and as suggested in [31], a
CXp is defined as a minimal subset $\mathcal{Y} \subseteq \mathcal{F}$ such that,

$$\exists(\mathbf{x} \in \mathbb{F}). \bigwedge_{j \notin \mathcal{Y}} (x_j = v_j) \wedge (\tau(\mathbf{x}) \neq c) \tag{2}$$

(It is possible and simple to adapt the definition to target a specific class $c' \neq c$.)
Moreover, building on the seminal work of Reiter [61], recent work demonstrated
a minimal hitting set relationship between AXps and CXps [31], namely each
AXp is a minimal hitting set (MHS) of the set of CXps and vice-versa.

For computing both kinds of explanations (AXps and CXps), we will work
with sets of features, aiming at finding minimal subsets. It will also be helpful to
describe explanations (concretely AXps) as sets of literals. As a result, starting

from an instance $\mathbf{v}$, we create a set of literals $I_{\mathbf{v}} = \{(x_j, v_j) | j \in \mathcal{F}\}$. When clear from the context, we will just use I to denote the literals of an instance.

An AXp $\mathcal{X} \subseteq \mathcal{F}$ can also be viewed as a conjunction ρ of a subset of the literals $I_{\mathbf{v}}$ induced by the instance $\mathbf{v}$ that is *sufficient* for the prediction. Moreover, given a conjunction of literals ρ, we will associate a predicate $\rho : \mathbb{F} \to \{0, 1\}$ (with the symbol duplication deliberately aiming at simplifying the notation) to represent the values taken by the conjunction of literals for each point $\mathbf{x}$ in feature space. As a result, we use $\rho \models \tau_c$ to denote that ρ is sufficient for the prediction, i.e.

$$\forall(\mathbf{x} \in \mathbb{F}).\rho(\mathbf{x}) \to \tau_c(\mathbf{x}) \tag{3}$$

We can also associate a conjunction of literals η with each CXp, such that the literals in η are *not* the literals specified by the CXp, and such that the following condition holds,

$$\exists(\mathbf{x} \in \mathbb{F}).\eta(\mathbf{x}) \wedge \neg\tau_c(\mathbf{x}) \tag{4}$$

It should be noted that since a CXp is a minimal set of features, each η is a maximal set of literals such that there exists at least one point in feature space such that the ML model predicts a class other than c.

Example 3. For the linear classifier of Example 1, let $\mathbf{v} = (2, 0)$, with prediction $\oplus$. In this case, the (only) AXp is $\mathcal{X} = \{1\}$, indicating that, as long as $x_1 = 2$, the value of the prediction is $\oplus$, independently of the value of x_2. Moreover, the AXp can also be represented by $\rho \triangleq (x_1 = 2)$. For this very simple example, $\mathcal{Y} = \{1\}$ is also a CXp. Indeed, if we allow feature 1 to take a value other than 2, then the assignment $\mathbf{v}' = (0, 0)$ will change the prediction. (More complex examples of CXps are studied later in the paper.) □

Example 4. For the decision list of Example 2, let $\mathbf{v} = (0, 1)$, with prediction $\oplus$. In this case, the (only) AXp is $\mathcal{X} = \{2\}$, indicating that, as long as $x_2 = 1$, the value of the prediction is $\oplus$, independently of the value of x_1. Moreover, the AXp can also be represented by $\rho \triangleq (x_2 = 1)$. In this case, a CXp is also $\mathcal{Y} = \{2\}$. For example, the point in feature space $\mathbf{v} = (0, 0)$ will cause the prediction to change to $\ominus$. □

Example 5. To illustrate the hitting set duality relationship between AXps and CXps established in [31], we consider a simple classifier represented as a decision list (DL) of three rules (including the default rule). Let $\mathcal{F} = \{1, 2, 3, 4, 5\}$, $D_i = \{0, 1, 2\}$, with $i = 1, \ldots, 5$, and $\mathcal{K} = \{\ominus, \oplus\}$. Let the decision list be:

R_0:	IF	$x_1 = 1 \wedge x_2 = 1$ THEN $\ominus$
R_1:	ELSE IF	$x_3 \neq 1$ THEN $\oplus$
R_{DEF}:	ELSE	THEN $\ominus$

We consider the instance $\mathbf{v} = (1, 1, 1, 1, 1)$, which results in prediction $\ominus$. It is straightforward to see that, as long as $x_1 = x_2 = 1$, then the prediction is $\ominus$.

Also, it is less trivial (but still observable) that, as long as $x_3 = 1$, the prediction is guaranteed to be $\ominus$ as well. Moreover, it suffices to change the value of feature 3 and the value of *either* feature 1 or feature 2 to change the prediction to $\oplus$, e.g. set $x_3 = x_1 = 0$ or set $x_3 = x_2 = 2$. As a result, we can conclude that the set of AXps is: $\mathbb{X} = \{\{1, 2\}, \{3\}\}$, and the set of CXps is: $\mathbb{Y} = \{\{1, 3\}, \{2, 3\}\}$. Furthermore, from the minimal hitting set duality relationship between AXps and CXP's [31], the sets in $\mathbb{X}$ are MHSes of the sets in $\mathbb{Y}$ and vice-versa. (Clearly, we could follow the definitions and reach the same conclusions.)   □

3 Explaining Decision Lists

It is easy to see that just like DTs [37], DLs can also exhibit redundancy in the literals used, and so the computation of PI-explanations can be instrumental to conveying short explanations to a human decision maker.

Example 6. Consider a possible DL shown below for the function $f(x_1, \ldots, x_4) = (x_1 \wedge x_2) \vee (x_3 \wedge x_4)$. (This DL is constructed by applying a "direct translation" of all the paths of the DT shown in [37, Figure 1b] from left to right into rules followed by appending a default rule predicting class $f = 1$.)

R_0:	IF	$x_1 = 0 \wedge x_3 = 0$	THEN $f = 0$
R_1:	ELSE IF	$x_1 = 0 \wedge x_3 = 1 \wedge x_4 = 0$	THEN $f = 0$
R_2:	ELSE IF	$x_1 = 0 \wedge x_3 = 1 \wedge x_4 = 1$	THEN $f = 1$
R_3:	ELSE IF	$x_1 = 1 \wedge x_2 = 0 \wedge x_3 = 0$	THEN $f = 0$
R_4:	ELSE IF $x_1 = 1 \wedge x_2 = 0 \wedge x_3 = 1 \wedge x_4 = 0$		THEN $f = 0$
R_5:	ELSE IF $x_1 = 1 \wedge x_2 = 0 \wedge x_3 = 1 \wedge x_4 = 1$		THEN $f = 1$
R_6:	ELSE IF	$x_1 = 1 \wedge x_2 = 1$	THEN $f = 1$
R_{DEF}:	ELSE		THEN $f = 1$

Consider a data instance $\mathbf{v} = (1, 0, 1, 1)$ and observe that rule R_5 fires the prediction $f = 1$. Although rule R_5 has four literals, an AXp for instance $\mathbf{v}$ is $(x_3 = 1) \wedge (x_4 = 1)$. Similarly, in practice one may expect examples of DLs s.t. AXps will be significanlty smaller than the rules that fire the corresponding predictions.

This observation is confirmed by the experimental results in Sect. 4, in that explanations can play an important role in understanding the predictions made by DLs.   □

3.1 DL Explainability

Perhaps surprisingly, whereas DTs can be explained in polynomial time, DLs cannot. This section proves a number of theoretical results related to explainability of DLs. Here we will be using the *knowledge compilation* (KC) map [20], which studied a wealth of queries on knowledge representation languages. We consider the concrete setting of classification, i.e. a language L denotes a classifier τ and a target prediction c. Let us briefly define the queries of interest [20]:

1. **Satisfiability (SAT):** *if there exists a polynomial-time algorithm for deciding the satisfiability of $\tau(\mathbf{x}) = c$, i.e. to decide in polynomial time whether there exists $\mathbf{x} \in \mathbb{F}$ such that $\tau(\mathbf{x}) = c$. In the case of DLs, this problem will be referred to as DLSAT.*
2. **Implicant test (IM):** *if there exists a polynomial-time algorithm that decides whether a conjunction of literals ρ is such that $\rho \vDash \tau_c$, i.e. $\forall(\mathbf{x} \in \mathbb{F}).\rho(\mathbf{x}) \rightarrow \tau_c(\mathbf{x})$. In the case of DLs, this problem will be referred to as DLIM.*

Similarly, we can define DNFSAT (which is trivially in P) and DNFIM (which is well-known to be in P only if P = NP [20]).

Proposition 1. *DLSAT is NP-complete.*

Proof. It is easy to see that the DLSAT is in NP. We simply guess an assignment to the features and check whether the prediction is the expected one according to the DL. To prove NP-hardness, the reduction of CNFSAT to DLSAT is organized as follows:

1. Consider a CNF formula ϕ with clauses $c_1, c_2, \ldots, c_m$.
2. Let the variables in ϕ denote the features (w.l.o.g. assume the features to be Boolean).
3. Consider the negation of each clause $\neg c_i$ which represents a conjunction of literals $\bigwedge_{l_j \in c_i} \neg l_j$.
4. For each $\neg c_i$, create a rule π_i with antecedent $\bigwedge_{l_j \in c_i} \neg l_j$ and prediction $\ominus$.
5. Create a default rule with prediction $\oplus$.
6. Hence, formula ϕ is satisfiable if and only if there is an assignment to the features which results in prediction $\oplus$.

The prediction is $\ominus$ if some clause c_i is falsified, i.e. $\neg c_i$ is satisfied (and hence rule π_i fires). Otherwise, if all clauses are satisfied, and so all $\neg c_i$ are falsified, then the prediction is $\oplus$. □

Proposition 2. *No polynomial-time algorithm exists for DLIM unless* P = NP.

Proof. We reduce DNFIM (i.e. IM for DNF) to DLIM, given that IM for DNF is well-known to be solvable in polynomial time only if P = NP [20]. Let ψ denote a DNF, with k terms, i.e. $\psi = t_1 \vee \ldots \vee t_k$, and let p denote a conjunction of literals. IM for DNF is to decide whether p is an implicant of ψ, i.e. $p \vDash \psi$. The reduction of DNFIM to DLIM is organized as follows:

1. For each conjunction of literals t_i in ψ, create a rule with antecedent given by t_i, i.e. $\pi_i = t_i$, and prediction $\ominus$.
2. The $(k+1)^{\text{th}}$ rule is created as follows: the antecendent is p and the prediction is $\oplus$.
3. Finally, we add a default rule with prediction $\ominus$.

As a result, the prediction will be $\oplus$ if and only if $p \wedge \bigwedge_{i \in [k]} (\neg t_i)$ is satisfied, and so $p \nvDash \psi$, in which case p is not an implicant of ψ. □

Given the above results, we can conclude the following.

Proposition 3. *There is no polynomial-time algorithm for finding an AXp of a decision list unless* P = NP.

Proof (sketch). If there was a polynomial-time algorithm for finding an AXp for a DL then we would be able to solve IM for DL in polynomial time. This would in turn imply that IM for DNF is solvable in polynomial time.   □

A Word on Decision Sets. Although decision sets are unordered (in contrast to DLs), this fact does not simplify the computation of PI-explanations. (In what follows, we assume that a DS implements a total classification function, which is not the case in general due to the issue of overlap [35]—otherwise, PI-explanations would be ill-defined.)

Proposition 4 *Finding an AXp for a DS is hard for* D^P.

Proof (sketch). It is known [35] that decision sets can be associated with DNF formulas. It is also known [70] that finding a prime implicant (PI) of a DNF D given a satisfying assignment $\mathbf{v}$ is complete for D^P. Given the aforementioned connection between DSs and DNFs, we show here that the above problem can be reduced to finding a PI-explanation of a DS.

Let the terms in the DNF D become the rules for prediction $\oplus$ in the corresponding DS. Also, let the default rule of the DS predict $\ominus$. Hence, a set of literals ρ (contained in the literals induced by $\mathbf{v}$) is a PI of the DNF D iff ρ is a PI-explanation for the DS prediction $\oplus$ given $\mathbf{v}$.   □

Remark 1. In the case of decision sets, it is also simple to observe that deciding whether a set of literals ρ is an AXp is in D^P. For that, one needs to prove first that the set of literals ρ entails prediction $\oplus$; this problem is clearly in coNP. Additionally, one also needs to prove subset-minimality of ρ, i.e. that removing any single literal from ρ results in a subset of literals that does not entail the prediction $\oplus$. (We can consider $|\rho|$ sets of literals, each of which removes a literal from ρ to get a set of literals ρ_k, and check that there are $|\rho|$ assignments such for each ρ_k we get a different prediction $\ominus$.) The latter problem is in NP. Therefore and given Proposition 4, we can establish D^P-completeness of the decision version of finding a PI-explanation in the case of DSs.

DLs vs. DTs and vs. DSs. The results of this section are somewhat surprising in terms of comparing DTs with DLs and DSs. On the one hand, satisfiability query is trivially in P for DTs and DSs, but it is NP-complete for DLs. On the other hand, AXps can be computed in polynomial time for DTs [37], but a polynomial-time algorithm for computing AXps for DLs and DSs would imply P = NP.

3.2   Explaining Arbitrary DLs with SAT

When explaining decision lists, one can use the work on computing rigorous abductive [32,66] and contrastive explanations [31] for ML models. This section describes a novel propositional encoding for DL classifiers that can be exploited by the generic approach of [31,32].

Let $\mathbf{v}$ denote a point in feature space with prediction $c \in \mathcal{K}$. Moreover, let the rule that fires on $\mathbf{v}$ be $i \in \mathfrak{R}$. Note that for an arbitrary rule $k \in \mathfrak{R}$ to fire, the following constraint must hold true:

$$\bigwedge_{\substack{r_j \in \mathfrak{R} \\ o(j) < o(k)}} \neg(\mathfrak{l}(j)) \wedge \mathfrak{l}(k) \tag{5}$$

Constraint (5) encodes the fact that the literals in all the rules preceding rule k must not fire and the rule k must fire. (Recall that $\mathfrak{l}(i)$ represents the set of literals of rule i). This constraint is straightforward to clausify, i.e. convert to CNF. Moreover, let $\varphi(i)$ denote the set of clauses resulting from clausification of the constraint (5) for rule i to fire.

Given a set of literals ρ, ρ is an implicant of the decision function associated with the DL (i.e. ρ is an AXp) for the instance $\mathbf{v}$ and the corresponding prediction $\mathfrak{c}(i)$ if:

$$\rho \models \bigvee_{\substack{j \in \mathfrak{R} \\ \mathfrak{c}(j) = \mathfrak{c}(i)}} \varphi(j) \tag{6}$$

i.e. for any point $\mathbf{x}$ in feature space, if $\rho(\mathbf{x})$ holds true, then one of the rules predicting the same class $\mathfrak{c}(i)$ as rule i must hold true as well. Constraints (5) and (6) comprise the propositional encoding that can be used in the framework of [32] to compute one AXp for the prediction made by a decision list for a given input instance. Note that computing such an AXp ρ is typically done by reducing the initial set of literals $I_{\mathbf{v}}$, which clearly entails the right-hand side of (6), i.e. $I_{\mathbf{v}} \models \bigvee_{j \in \mathfrak{R}, \mathfrak{c}(j) = \mathfrak{c}(i)} \varphi(j)$. Also note that in practice it is convenient to negate this tautology and instead deal with its negation, which is obviously unsatisfiable. Following [31,32], this enables one to apply the well-developed apparatus for computing one AXp (resp. CXp) as an MUS (resp. MCS) of the negated formula [6,7,26,36,38,42,45,48,50,52,53], but also for enumerating a given number of all AXps (resp. CXps) through MUS (resp. MCS) enumeration [41,43,44,55,60].

Example 7. As mentioned above, when computing an AXp in the form of (6), it is convenient to negate the tautology $I_{\mathbf{v}} \models \bigvee_{j \in \mathfrak{R}, \mathfrak{c}(j) = \mathfrak{c}(i)} \varphi(j)$ and instead work with unsatisfiable formula

$$I_{\mathbf{v}} \wedge \bigwedge_{\substack{j \in \mathfrak{R} \\ \mathfrak{c}(j) = \mathfrak{c}(i)}} \neg \varphi(j)$$

Here, the left part $I_{\mathbf{v}}$ of the conjunction serves as the set $\mathcal{S}$ of unit-size soft clauses, each represented by a literal assigning a value to a feature. This way

AXps and CXps can be found as minimal subsets of $\mathcal{S}$ (i.e. MUSes or MCSes, respectively), subject to the hard clauses $\mathcal{H} \triangleq \bigwedge_{j \in \mathfrak{R}, c(j)=c(i)} \neg \varphi(j)$. Also observe that the negation $\neg \varphi(k)$ (recall that $\varphi(k)$ enforces rule k to fire) constitutes the disjunction

$$\neg \mathfrak{l}(k) \vee \bigvee_{\substack{r_j \in \mathfrak{R} \\ o(j) < o(k)}} \mathfrak{l}(j)$$

which enforces that either rule k does not fire or one of the preceding rules fires. Also, to enforce that the default rule does not fire, we can simply require one of the non-default rules of the DL to fire. Finally, note that the hard clauses $\mathcal{H}$ encode the fact of *misclassification*, which is clearly impossible when the input instance $I_\mathbf{v}$ is given as the soft clauses $\mathcal{S}$, thus making formula $\mathcal{H} \wedge \mathcal{S}$ unsatisfiable.

Now, consider the DL from Example 6 and recall that rule R_5 fires prediction $f = 1$ for the instance $\mathbf{v} = (1, 0, 1, 1)$. As prediction $f = 1$ is represented by rules R_2, R_5, R_6, R_{DEF}, our hard clauses $\mathcal{H}$ must enforce that none of them fires. Given the above, the hard clauses $\mathcal{H}$ are formed by

$$\mathcal{H} = \left\{ \begin{array}{l} \neg\varphi(2) \triangleq \left[\neg\mathfrak{l}(2) \vee \bigvee_{j=0}^{1} \mathfrak{l}(j) \right]; \ \neg\varphi(5) \triangleq \left[\neg\mathfrak{l}(5) \vee \bigvee_{j=0}^{4} \mathfrak{l}(j) \right]; \\ \neg\varphi(6) \triangleq \left[\neg\mathfrak{l}(6) \vee \bigvee_{j=0}^{5} \mathfrak{l}(j) \right]; \ \neg\varphi_{\text{DEF}} \triangleq \qquad\quad \left[\bigvee_{j=0}^{6} \mathfrak{l}(j) \right] \end{array} \right\}$$

Here, CNF encoding of terms $\mathfrak{l}(j)$ is omitted as it is trivial to obtain.   □

As can be observed in Example 7, the propositional encoding described in this section targets simplicity and for this reason it exhibits redundancy, e.g. expressions $\bigvee_{j=0}^{k-1} \mathfrak{l}(j)$ in the representation of $\neg\varphi(k)$ are repeated for every $k' > k$. As shown in Sect. 4, the performance results suggest that the proposed encoding scales well on DLs of realistic size. Nevertheless, a number of improvements can be envisioned, which add more structure to the encoding, but with the cost of using additional auxiliary variables. Our initial experiments suggest no significant gains were obtained with a more complex propositional encoding.

4   Experimental Results

This section aims at assessing the proposed SAT-based approach to computing and enumerating rigorous abductive explanations (AXps) [32,66] as well as contrastive explanations (CXps) [31] for decision list models. First, the approach will be tested from the perspective of raw performance, followed by additional information on the comparative number of AXps and CXps as well as their length.

Experimental Setup. The experiments were performed on a MacBook Pro laptop running macOS Big Sur 11.2.3. Therefore, each individual process was run on a Quad-Core Intel Core i5-8259U 2.30 GHz processor with 16 GByte of memory. The memory limit was set to 4 GByte while the time limit used was set to 1800 1800 s, for each individual process to run.

Prototype Implementation. A prototype implementation[2] of the proposed approach was developed as a Python script instrumenting incremental calls to the Glucose 3 SAT solver [4] using the PySAT toolkit [28]. The implementation targets the computation of one explanation (either an AXp or a CXp) and enumeration of a given number of those, with a possibility to enumerate all.

It is known [31] that a CXp can be computed as an MCS for the encoding formula discussed above and hence CXp enumeration is implemented in the prototype as LBX-based MCS enumeration [53]. Similarly, AXp corresponds to an MUS of the formula and, as a result, AXp enumeration is done using the MARCO-like MUS enumeration approach [41,43,60] due to the hitting set duality between AXps and CXps [31]. Concretely, the MARCO-like explainer is organized as two interconnecting oracles: (i) a SAT oracle checking (un)satisfiability of a selected set of clauses of the formula, and (ii) a minimal hitting set (MHS) oracle, which computes minimal hitting sets of a current collection of MCSes of the formula obtained so far. The MHS oracle was implemented on top of the RC2 MaxSAT solver exploited incrementally [29]. Each iteration of the MARCO-like explainer computes either an AXp or a CXp. The former are reported and blocked (by adding a single clause to the MHS oracle) while the latter are used later as the sets *to hit*. The explainer stops as soon as there are no more minimal hitting set identified by the MHS oracle. As a result, the MARCO-like explainer produces both AXps and CXps upon the end of execution. Note that thanks to the use of MaxSAT-based MHS oracle, AXps computed this way are irredundant, i.e. subset-minimal, and do not have to be reduced further while CXps do need to be reduced by a dedicated reduction procedure (see below). Also note that the MARCO-like approach can also be used in a *dual way*, i.e. targeting CXp enumeration and computing AXps as a by-product. This mode of operation of the explainer has also been implemented in the developed prototype.

It is also important to mention that all the three modes of operation make incremental use of the underlying SAT oracles. As such, the LBX-like CXp enumeration computes an explanation, blocks it by adding a single clause and proceeds to the next CXp. Furthermore, once all explanations for a given data instance are enumerated, all the previously added blocking clauses are *disabled* and the enumeration process starts again for a new data instance. This is done with the use of unique *selector* variables introduced for each data instance. On the contrary, the MARCO-like approaches accumulate and block all explanations on the MHS oracle side. This enables one to keep the same SAT oracle on the checking side of the approach while restarting the MHS oracle from scratch, i.e. with an empty collection of sets to hit, for each new data instance.

Finally, the following heuristics are used. LBX-like computation of a single CXp makes use of the *Clause D* (CLD) heuristic [50]. Computation of a single AXp is done as a simple deletion-based linear search procedure [51], strengthened by exhaustive enumeration of unit-size MCSes used to bootstrap the MHS oracle. Although a more sophisticated algorithm QuickXPlain [38] has been also

---

[2] The prototype is available at https://github.com/alexeyignatiev/xdl-tool.

implemented, it turned out to be outperformed by the aforementioned simpler alternative in this concrete setting.

Benchmarks and Methodology. Experimental evaluation was performed on a subset of datasets selected from a few publicly available sources. In particular, these include datasets from UCI Machine Learning Repository [69] and Penn Machine Learning Benchmarks [58] as well as datasets previously studied in the context of ML explainability [63] and fairness [23,24]. The number of selected datasets is 72. We applied the approach of 5-fold cross validation, i.e. each dataset was randomly split into 5 chunks of instances; each of these chunks served as test data while the remaining 4 chunks were used to train the classifiers. As a result, each dataset (out of 72) resulted in 5 individual pairs of training and test datasets represented by 80% and 20% of data instances. Therefore, the total number of training datasets considered in the evaluation is 360.

Given a training dataset, i.e. represented by 4 chunks of the original data, a decision list model was trained with the use of the well-known heuristic algorithm CN2 [14,15][3], the implementation of which was taken from the well-known Python toolkit Orange[4]. The time spent on training the models was ignored. Next, the prototype explainer was run in one of the three modes described above, to enumerate *all* explanations (either AXps, or CXps) for each of the instances of the original 100% data. Also and as mentioned above, the explainer was given 1800 1800seconds for each of the 360 datasets/models.

Note that the number of rules in the decision list models constructed by CN2 for the target datasets varied from 6 to 2055. Also, the total number of non-class, i.e. solely antecedent, literals used in the models varied from 6 to 6754. Finally, propositional formulas encoding the explanation problems for these models had from 7 to 15340 variables and from 9 to 3932987 clauses. It is important to mention that all data was treated as categorical and hence the propositional formulas given to the encoder incorporated cardinality constraints enforcing that a feature can take exactly one value; in the experiments, these constraints were encoded into CNF using the pairwise encoding [59]. Although left untested, other cardinality encodings would result in smaller formulas—the pairwise encoding was selected intentionally in order to produce larger formulas and so to test scalability of the proposed SAT-based approach.

Raw Performance. Figure 2a depicts a cactus plot showing the raw performance of the explainer working in the three selected modes of operation. (Note that the CPU time axis is scaled logarithmically.) As can be observed, all the algorithms are able to finish successful computation of all the target explanations for all the data instances of each of the 360 benchmark datasets within the given time limit. Surprisingly, the best performing configuration overall turns out to

---

[3] Recent alternative approaches to *sparse* decision lists [1,2,65] have also been considered but were eventually discarded for two reasons: (1) they can only deal with binary data and (2) they produce sparse decision lists containing a couple of rules and a few literals in total—i.e. these methods do not provide models that would be of interest for our work.

[4] https://orangedatamining.com/.

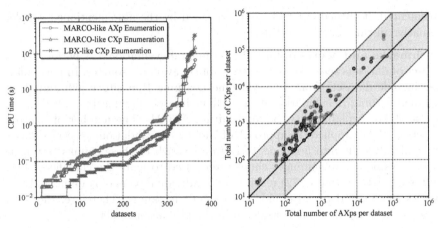

(a) Raw performance comparison   (b) Number of AXps and CXps per dataset

Fig. 2. Performance of the three operation modes and the total number of explanations per dataset they enumerate.

be MARCO-based AXp enumeration. MARCO-based CXp enumeration is a bit slower. Recall that both MARCO-based modes end up enumerating the same sets of explanations including AXps (CXps, resp.) and dual CXps (dual AXps, resp.). Also, recall that the only major difference between the two configurations is the type of the target explanations that are provided by the MHS oracle while the dual explanations have to be reduced by a dedicated reduction procedure. Therefore, the performance difference shown suggests that in practice it may be more beneficial to target AXps and so to reduce dual CXps than doing the opposite (which is not really surprising given that the former correspond to MUS extraction while the latter correspond to MCS extraction). Finally, it should be mentioned that although LBX-like CXp explanation works the most efficiently for most of the benchmarks, in some cases it is outperformed by the competitors, which may be explained by the need to incrementally block a significant number of previously computed solutions (recall that, on the contrary, the MARCO-like configurations restart the MHS oracle from scratch for every new data instance).

AXps vs CXps. As can be seen in Fig. 2b, the total number of AXps per dataset tends to be lower than the total number of CXps. Concretely, the number of AXps per dataset varies from 16 to 72838 while the number of CXps per dataset varies from 23 to 248825. (Observe that the time to compute one explanation is negligible.) These data are in line with the results previously obtained in [31] when explaining a different kind of ML model (namely, XGBoost models [13]) with a different reasoning engine (namely, Z3 SMT solver [56]). Unsurprisingly, the average number of CXps per data instance is also higher than the average number of AXps, as shown in Fig. 3a. In general, the average number of CXps per instance varies from 1 to 20.8 while the average number of AXps goes from 1 to 22.7. However and as one can observe in the scatter plot Fig. 3a,

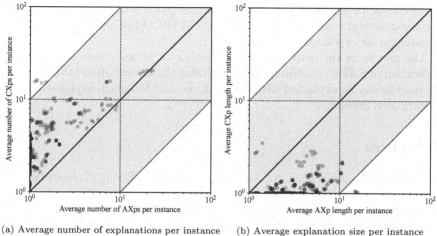

(a) Average number of explanations per instance   (b) Average explanation size per instance

Fig. 3. Average number of AXps and CXps per data instance and their average size.

for the lion's share of data instances there is a single AXp while there are many more CXps. Note that the picture is the opposite for the average explanation length (measured as the number of literals remaining in the explanation). In particular, CXps are shorter than AXps and the average length of a CXp per data instance does not exceed 2.8 while the average length of AXp varies from 1 to 15.8 (which in fact may provide another insight into the underperforming MARCO-like CXp enumeration). Observe that these data also confirms the results previously reported in [31].

Final Remarks. A few conclusions can be made with respect to the experimental results shown above. First, all the explainer configurations scale well and are able to enumerate all explanations for all data instances incrementally, even for DL models with thousands of rules and literals encoded into CNF formulas with millions of clauses. Second, MARCO-like AXp enumeration outperforms both LBX-like and MARCO-like CXp enumeration. Third, the number of CXps per dataset and per instance tends to be higher than the number of AXps. And finally, AXps are on average much larger than CXps.

5   Conclusions

This paper investigates the computation of rigorous (or PI-) explanations for DLs. The paper first argues that, similar to DTs [37], DLs may also not be interpretable. (This observation is also validated by the experimental results.) Furthermore, the paper proves that in contrast to the case of DTs, finding one PI-explanation for DLs (and also for DSs) cannot be in P unless P = NP. As a result, one possible solution for finding AXps and CXps is to encode the problem to propositional logic, and find one or enumerate more than one explanation(s) using SAT oracles. The experimental results demonstrate that SAT-based approaches are effective at finding explanations (both AXps and CXps) of DLs. The experimental results also confirm that a MARCO-like algorithm is effective at enumerating explanations of DLs.

The results in this paper suggest a number of future research topics. The application of SAT to explaining DLs motivates the investigation of which other ML models can be explained with SAT solvers, and for which explanations can be computed efficiently.

References

1. Angelino, E., Larus-Stone, N., Alabi, D., Seltzer, M.I., Rudin, C.: Learning certifiably optimal rule lists. In: KDD, pp. 35–44 (2017)
2. Angelino, E., Larus-Stone, N., Alabi, D., Seltzer, M.I., Rudin, C.: Learning certifiably optimal rule lists for categorical data. J. Mach. Learn. Res. **18**, 234:1–234:78 (2017). http://jmlr.org/papers/v18/17-716.html
3. Audemard, G., Koriche, F., Marquis, P.: On tractable XAI queries based on compiled representations. In: KR, pp. 838–849 (2020)
4. Audemard, G., Lagniez, J., Simon, L.: Improving glucose for incremental SAT solving with assumptions: application to MUS extraction. In: SAT, pp. 309–317 (2013)
5. Bailey, J., Stuckey, P.J.: Discovery of minimal unsatisfiable subsets of constraints using hitting set dualization. In: PADL, pp. 174–186 (2005)
6. Belov, A., Lynce, I., Marques-Silva, J.: Towards efficient MUS extraction. AI Commun. **25**(2), 97–116 (2012)
7. Belov, A., Marques-Silva, J.: Accelerating MUS extraction with recursive model rotation. In: FMCAD, pp. 37–40 (2011)
8. Biere, A., Heule, M., van Maaren, H., Walsh, T. (eds.): Frontiers in Artificial Intelligence and Applications, vol. 336. IOS Press, Amsterdam (2021)
9. Birnbaum, E., Lozinskii, E.L.: Consistent subsets of inconsistent systems: structure and behaviour. J. Exp. Theor. Artif. Intell. **15**(1), 25–46 (2003)
10. Bouckaert, R.R., et al.: WEKA - experiences with a java open-source project. J. Mach. Learn. Res. **11**, 2533–2541 (2010). http://portal.acm.org/citation.cfm?id=1953016
11. Camburu, O., Giunchiglia, E., Foerster, J., Lukasiewicz, T., Blunsom, P.: Can I trust the explainer? verifying post-hoc explanatory methods. CoRR abs/1910.02065 (2019). http://arxiv.org/abs/1910.02065
12. Chen, C., Rudin, C.: An optimization approach to learning falling rule lists. In: AISTATS, pp. 604–612 (2018)
13. Chen, T., Guestrin, C.: XGBoost: a scalable tree boosting system. In: KDD, pp. 785–794 (2016)
14. Clark, P., Boswell, R.: Rule induction with CN2: some recent improvements. In: EWSL, pp. 151–163 (1991)
15. Clark, P., Niblett, T.: The CN2 induction algorithm. Mach. Learn. **3**, 261–283 (1989)
16. Cohen, W.W.: Efficient pruning methods for separate-and-conquer rule learning systems. In: Bajcsy, R. (ed.) Proceedings of the 13th International Joint Conference on Artificial Intelligence, 28 August–3 September 1993, Chambéry, France. pp. 988–994. Morgan Kaufmann (1993)

17. Cohen, W.W.: Fast effective rule induction. In: ICML, pp. 115–123 (1995)
18. Cohen, W.W., Singer, Y.: A simple, fast, and effictive rule learner. In: AAAI, pp. 335–342 (1999)
19. Darwiche, A., Hirth, A.: On the reasons behind decisions. In: ECAI, pp. 712–720 (2020). https://doi.org/10.3233/FAIA200158
20. Darwiche, A., Marquis, P.: A knowledge compilation map. J. Artif. Intell. Res. **17**, 229–264 (2002)
21. Davies, J., Bacchus, F.: Solving MAXSAT by solving a sequence of simpler SAT instances. In: CP, pp. 225–239 (2011)
22. Demsar, J., et al.: Orange: data mining toolbox in python. J. Mach. Learn. Res. **14**(1), 2349–2353 (2013). http://dl.acm.org/citation.cfm?id=2567736, https://orangedatamining.com/
23. Auditing black-box predictive models. https://blog.fastforwardlabs.com/2017/03/09/fairml-auditing-black-box-predictive-models.html (2016)
24. Friedler, S., Scheidegger, C., Venkatasubramanian, S.: On algorithmic fairness, discrimination and disparate impact (2015)
25. Ignatiev, A.: Towards trustable explainable AI. In: IJCAI, pp. 5154–5158 (2020)
26. Ignatiev, A., Janota, M., Marques-Silva, J.: Quantified maximum satisfiability. Constraints An Int. J. **21**(2), 277–302 (2016)
27. Ignatiev, A., Morgado, A., Marques-Silva, J.: Propositional abduction with implicit hitting sets. In: ECAI, pp. 1327–1335 (2016)
28. Ignatiev, A., Morgado, A., Marques-Silva, J.: PySAT: A Python toolkit for prototyping with SAT oracles. In: SAT, pp. 428–437 (2018)
29. Ignatiev, A., Morgado, A., Marques-Silva, J.: RC2: an efficient MaxSAT solver. J. Satisf. Boolean Model. Comput. **11**(1), 53–64 (2019)
30. Ignatiev, A., Morgado, A., Weissenbacher, G., Marques-Silva, J.: Model-based diagnosis with multiple observations. In: IJCAI, pp. 1108–1115 (2019)
31. Ignatiev, A., Narodytska, N., Asher, N., Marques-Silva, J.: From contrastive to abductive explanations and back again. In: AI*IA (2020). preliminary version available from https://arxiv.org/abs/2012.11067
32. Ignatiev, A., Narodytska, N., Marques-Silva, J.: Abduction-based explanations for machine learning models. In: AAAI, pp. 1511–1519 (2019)
33. Ignatiev, A., Narodytska, N., Marques-Silva, J.: On relating explanations and adversarial examples. In: NeurIPS, pp. 15857–15867 (2019)
34. Ignatiev, A., Narodytska, N., Marques-Silva, J.: On validating, repairing and refining heuristic ML explanations. CoRR abs/1907.02509 (2019). http://arxiv.org/abs/1907.02509
35. Ignatiev, A., Pereira, F., Narodytska, N., Marques-Silva, J.: A sat-based approach to learn explainable decision sets. In: IJCAR, pp. 627–645 (2018)
36. Ignatiev, A., Previti, A., Liffiton, M.H., Marques-Silva, J.: Smallest MUS extraction with minimal hitting set dualization. In: CP, pp. 173–182 (2015)
37. Izza, Y., Ignatiev, A., Marques-Silva, J.: On explaining decision trees. CoRR abs/2010.11034 (2020)
38. Junker, U.: QUICKXPLAIN: preferred explanations and relaxations for over-constrained problems. In: AAAI, pp. 167–172 (2004)
39. Lakkaraju, H., Bach, S.H., Leskovec, J.: Interpretable decision sets: a joint framework for description and prediction. In: KDD, pp. 1675–1684 (2016)
40. Lakkaraju, H., Bastani, O.: "How do I fool you?": manipulating user trust via misleading black box explanations. In: AIES, pp. 79–85 (2020)
41. Liffiton, M.H., Malik, A.: Enumerating infeasibility: finding multiple MUSes quickly. In: CPAIOR, pp. 160–175 (2013)

42. Liffiton, M.H., Mneimneh, M.N., Lynce, I., Andraus, Z.S., Marques-Silva, J., Sakallah, K.A.: A branch and bound algorithm for extracting smallest minimal unsatisfiable subformulas. Constraints An Int. J. **14**(4), 415–442 (2009)
43. Liffiton, M.H., Previti, A., Malik, A., Marques-Silva, J.: Fast, flexible MUS enumeration. Constraints An Int. J. **21**(2), 223–250 (2016)
44. Liffiton, M.H., Sakallah, K.A.: On finding all minimally unsatisfiable subformulas. In: SAT, pp. 173–186 (2005)
45. Liffiton, M.H., Sakallah, K.A.: Algorithms for computing minimal unsatisfiable subsets of constraints. J. Autom. Reasoning **40**(1), 1–33 (2008)
46. Lipton, Z.C.: The mythos of model interpretability. Commun. ACM **61**(10), 36–43 (2018)
47. Lundberg, S.M., Lee, S.: A unified approach to interpreting model predictions. In: NeurIPS, pp. 4765–4774 (2017)
48. Lynce, I., Marques-Silva, J.: On computing minimum unsatisfiable cores. In: SAT (2004)
49. Marques-Silva, J., Gerspacher, T., Cooper, M.C., Ignatiev, A., Narodytska, N.: Explaining Naive Bayes and other linear classifiers with polynomial time and delay. In: NeurIPS (2020)
50. Marques-Silva, J., Heras, F., Janota, M., Previti, A., Belov, A.: On computing minimal correction subsets. In: IJCAI, pp. 615–622 (2013)
51. Marques-Silva, J., Lynce, I.: On improving MUS extraction algorithms. In: SAT, pp. 159–173 (2011)
52. Mencia, C., Ignatiev, A., Previti, A., Marques-Silva, J.: MCS extraction with sublinear oracle queries. In: SAT, pp. 342–360 (2016)
53. Mencia, C., Previti, A., Marques-Silva, J.: Literal-based MCS extraction. In: IJCAI, pp. 1973–1979 (2015)
54. Miller, T.: Explanation in artificial intelligence: insights from the social sciences. Artif. Intell. **267**, 1–38 (2019)
55. Morgado, A., Liffiton, M.H., Marques-Silva, J.: MaxSAT-based MCS enumeration. In: HVC, pp. 86–101 (2012)
56. de Moura, L.M., Bjørner, N.: Z3: an efficient SMT solver. In: TACAS, pp. 337–340 (2008)
57. Narodytska, N., Shrotri, A., Meel, K.S., Ignatiev, A., Marques-Silva, J.: Assessing heuristic machine learning explanations with model counting. In: Janota, M., Lynce, I. (eds.) SAT 2019. LNCS, vol. 11628, pp. 267–278. Springer, Cham (2019). https://doi.org/10.1007/978-3-030-24258-9_19
58. Penn Machine Learning Benchmarks. https://github.com/EpistasisLab/penn-ml-benchmarks
59. Prestwich, S.D.: CNF encodings. In: Handbook of Satisfiability: Second Edition, Frontiers in Artificial Intelligence and Applications, vol. 336, pp. 75–100. IOS Press (2021)
60. Previti, A., Marques-Silva, J.: Partial MUS enumeration. In: AAAI (2013)
61. Reiter, R.: A theory of diagnosis from first principles. Artif. Intell. **32**(1), 57–95 (1987)
62. Ribeiro, M.T., Singh, S., Guestrin, C.: "Why should I trust you?": explaining the predictions of any classifier. In: KDD, pp. 1135–1144 (2016)
63. Ribeiro, M.T., Singh, S., Guestrin, C.: Anchors: high-precision model-agnostic explanations. In: AAAI, pp. 1527–1535 (2018)
64. Rivest, R.L.: Learning decision lists. Mach. Learn. **2**(3), 229–246 (1987). https://doi.org/10.1007/BF00058680

65. Rudin, C., Ertekin, S.: Learning customized and optimized lists of rules with mathematical programming. Math. Program. Comput. **10**(4), 659–702 (2018). https://doi.org/10.1007/s12532-018-0143-8
66. Shih, A., Choi, A., Darwiche, A.: A symbolic approach to explaining Bayesian network classifiers. In: IJCAI, pp. 5103–5111 (2018)
67. Shih, A., Choi, A., Darwiche, A.: Compiling Bayesian network classifiers into decision graphs. In: AAAI, pp. 7966–7974 (2019)
68. Slack, D., Hilgard, S., Jia, E., Singh, S., Lakkaraju, H.: Fooling LIME and SHAP: adversarial attacks on post hoc explanation methods. In: AIES, pp. 180–186 (2020)
69. UCI Machine Learning Repository. https://archive.ics.uci.edu/ml
70. Umans, C., Villa, T., Sangiovanni-Vincentelli, A.L.: Complexity of two-level logic minimization. IEEE Trans. Comput. Aided Des. Integr. Circuits Syst. **25**(7), 1230–1246 (2006)
71. Wang, F., Rudin, C.: Falling rule lists. In: AISTATS (2015)
72. Yang, F., Yang, Z., Cohen, W.W.: Differentiable learning of logical rules for knowledge base reasoning. In: NeurIPS, pp. 2319–2328 (2017)
73. Yang, H., Rudin, C., Seltzer, M.I.: Scalable bayesian rule lists. In: ICML, pp. 3921–3930 (2017)

Investigating the Existence of Costas Latin Squares via Satisfiability Testing

Jiwei Jin[1,4], Yiqi Lv[1,3], Cunjing Ge[5], Feifei Ma[1,2,3(✉)], and Jian Zhang[1,3]

[1] State Key Laboratory of Computer Science, Institute of Software,
Chinese Academy of Sciences, Beijing, China
maff@ios.ac.cn
[2] Laboratory of Parallel Software and Computational Science,
Institute of Software, Chinese Academy of Sciences, Beijing, China
[3] University of Chinese Academy of Sciences, Beijing, China
[4] Shandong Jiaotong University, Jinan, China
[5] Johannes Kepler University Linz, Linz, Austria

Abstract. Costas Latin squares are important combinatorial structures in combinatorial design theory. Some Costas Latin squares are found in recent years, but there are still some open problems about the existence of Costas Latin squares with specified properties including idempotency, orthogonality, and certain quasigroup properties. In this paper, we describe an efficient method for solving these problems using state-of-the-art SAT solvers. We present new results of Costas Latin squares with specified properties of even order $n \leq 10$. It is found that within this order range, most Costas Latin squares with such properties don't exist except for a few cases. The non-existence can be certified since SAT solvers can produce a formal proof. Experimental results demonstrate the effectiveness of our method.

1 Introduction

Costas Latin squares (introduced in [4]) are important combinatorial structures which have potential applications in industries [2]. The existence of Costas Latin squares were studied in recent years. J. Dinitz et al. [3] studied Costas Latin squares from a construction as well as a classification point of view, and verified the conjecture that there is no Costas Latin square for any odd order $n>3$. Costas Latin squares which have specified properties are also the interest of mathematicians. These properties include idempotency, orthogonality, and certain quasigroup properties, which are often used as the basis of recursive construction. The existence problems of these Costas Latin squares are still open problems, and are difficult for conventional mathematical methods.

With the rapid advance in SAT solving techniques, some problems, which used to be very difficult for traditional mathematic methods, have been resolved recently by SAT solvers. Marijn Heule et al. solved some long-standing open problem, such as the boolean pythagorean triples problem and Schur Number

C.-M. Li and F. Manyà (Eds.): SAT 2021, LNCS 12831, pp. 270–279, 2021.
https://doi.org/10.1007/978-3-030-80223-3_19

Five problem via parallel SAT solving techniques [5,6]. Curtis Bright et al. developed a SAT+CAS paradigm of coupling SAT solvers with computer algebra systems [1,12], which has tackled various combinatorial problems. SAT solving techniques also play an important role in the study of quasigroups [11]. Pei Huang et al. described a method for solving the large set problem of idempotent quasigroups [8].

In this paper, we focus on open problems about Costas Latin squares with specified properties. We attempt to find instances of Costas Latin squares with those properties, or to decide the non-existence of them if they don't have the specified properties via state-of-the-art SAT solvers.

Searching for Costas Latin squares with specified properties are quite challenging for computers. In this paper we present two effective solving strategies: the transversal matrix and symmetry breaking. The transversal matrix is used to reduce the complexity in modeling, while symmetry breaking is used to prune isomorphic search spaces. Experiments are conducted to test the effectiveness of our strategies. The results show that both strategies are highly efficient.

Since Costas Latin squares of order $n \leq 3$ are trivial or simple, and it is conjectured that there is no Costas Latin square for any odd order $n > 3$ [3], we only focus on Costas Latin squares of order $4, 6, 8, 10$. We derive new results for Costas Latin squares of this order range with aforementioned properties, including some instances of Costas Latin squares with certain properties and the non-existence of most cases. The newly discovered Costas Latin squares have been double checked with another program we developed, and the non-existence results can be validated thanks to the capability of modern SAT solvers.

This paper is organized as follows: In Sect. 2, we introduce some preliminaries about Costas Latin squares; In Sect. 3, 4 we describe how to model these problems in logic language and techniques used for improving the searching efficiency; In Sect. 5 we present the new mathematical results and experimental results with analysis; In the final section, we give conclusions.

2 Preliminaries

A Latin square is a $n \times n$ array filled with n different symbols, each occurring exactly once in each row and exactly once in each column. In this paper we used the integer sequence $1, 2, 3, \cdots, n$ as symbols.

A Costas array of order n is a $n \times n$ array of dots and empty cells such that: (a). There are n dots and $n \times (n-1)$ empty cells, with exactly one dot in each row and column. (b). All the segments between pairs of dots differ in length or in slope.

For notational convenience, Costas arrays are often presented by a certain one-line notation. For a Costas array of order n, we use $\pi(i) = j$ whenever a dot is in cell(i,j). By this notation, a Costas array of order n can be presented as the permutation $(\pi(1), \pi(2), \cdots, \pi(n))$.

A Costas Latin square of order n is a Latin square of order n such that for each symbol $i \in \{1, 2, \cdots, n\}$, a Costas array results if a dot is placed in the cells containing symbol i. We use $CLS(n)$ to denote Costas Latin square of order n. The follows is a $CLS(4)$:

1	2	4	3
2	3	1	4
3	4	2	1
4	1	3	2

The one-line representation of the symbol 1 is $\{1,3,4,2\}$, 2 is $\{2,1,3,4\}$, 3 is $\{4,2,1,3\}$, 4 is $\{3,4,2,1\}$. They are all Costas array, so the Latin square is a Costas Latin square.

For a $CLS(n)$ A, we use $A(i,j)$ to denote the symbol in the i-th row and the j-th column. If A has the property that $A(i,i) = i$ for all $i \in \{1,2,\cdots,n\}$, then it is called an idempotent Costas Latin square.

The orthogonality is an interesting property of Latin squares. For two $CLS(n)$ A and B, if for all $n \times n$ positions, the pair $(A(i,j), B(i,j)), i,j \in \{1,2,\cdots,n\}$ are different, then A and B are called orthogonal. The follows are two orthogonal $CLS(4)$ and the result pairs:

2	3	4	1
4	1	2	3
3	2	1	4
1	4	3	2

4	3	2	1
3	4	1	2
1	2	3	4
2	1	4	3

24	33	42	11
43	14	21	32
31	22	13	44
12	41	34	23

A quasigroup is an algebraic structure such that the multiplication table of a finite quasigroup is a Latin square. Conversely, every Latin square can be taken as the multiplication table of a quasigroup. The existence of quasigroups satisfying the seven short identities has been studied systematically. These identities are:

- 1. $xy \otimes yx = x$: Schröder quasigroup
- 2. $yx \otimes xy = x$: Steins third law
- 3. $(xy \otimes y)y = x$: C_3-quasigroup
- 4. $x \otimes xy = yx$: Steins first law; Stein quasigroup
- 5. $(yx \otimes y)y = x$
- 6. $yx \otimes y = x \otimes yx$: Steins second law
- 7. $xy \otimes y = x \otimes xy$: Schröders first law

If we take a Costas Latin square as a multiplication table of a quasigroup, and it has one of the quasigroup properties mentioned above, then it is called the Costas Latin square with the specified quasigroup property. One task of this paper is to search for Costas Latin square with certain quasigroup property.

3   Modeling

In this section, we will introduce the method to model Costas Latin squares with logic language. We assume that the symbols (numbers) of CLS is an integer sequence $1,2,\cdots,n$, and row index and column index begin with 1. For convenient we use N to denote the set $\{1,2,\cdots,n\}$.

Since in a Latin square A, each number occurs exactly once in each row and exactly once in each column, it is easy to know that:

$$\forall x, y, x_1, x_2, y_1, y_2 \in N :$$
$$x_1 \neq x_2 \mapsto A(x_1, y) \neq A(x_2, y)$$
$$y_1 \neq y_2 \mapsto A(x, y_1) \neq A(x, y_2) \tag{1}$$

For a $CLS(n)$ A, the Costas property requires that for each $i \in N$, all the segments between pairs of i differ in length or in slope. That is for all positions with the same number: a) Each four positions don't form a parallelogram. B) If three or four positions are in a line, the distances between them are different. This can be encoded as:

$$\forall x, y, x', y', u, v, u', v' \in N :$$
$$(A(x, y) = A(x', y') = A(u, v) = A(u', v') \wedge (x - x' = u - u') \wedge (y - y' = v - v'))$$
$$\mapsto x = u \vee x = x' \tag{2}$$

The orthogonality property involves two $CLS(n)$ A, B. This property requires that in all $n \times n$ positions, the pair $(A(i, j), B(i, j)), i, j \in N$ are different. It can be encoded as:

$$\forall x_1, x_2, y_1, y_2 \in N :$$
$$x_1 \neq x_2 \mapsto A(x_1, y_1) \neq A(x_2, y_2) \vee B(x_1, y_1) \neq B(x_2, y_2)$$
$$y_1 \neq y_2 \mapsto A(x_1, y_1) \neq A(x_2, y_2) \vee B(x_1, y_1) \neq B(x_2, y_2) \tag{3}$$

The idempotency property of a $CLS(n)$ A can be encoded simply as:

$$\forall x \in N : A(x, x) = x \tag{4}$$

The quasigroup properties are easy to be encoded, for example, the formula for the first one is: $\forall x, y \in N : A(A(x, y), A(y, x)) = x$. Due to length limitation we omit the logic formulas for them.

4   Improvements in Modeling

Since the basic models in Sect. 3 are hard for SAT solvers, we introduce some search strategies to improve them. The most important strategies are symmetry breaking and the transversal matrix. We say that combinatorial problems have symmetries if they allow isomorphic solutions. Symmetry breaking can reduce the search time spending on revisiting equivalent states of these problems, and is used widely in search algorithms. In this paper we propose a simple but effective symmetry breaking method. For a $CLS(n)$ A, all numbers in it are just symbols, after replacing $1, 2, \cdots, n$ by any its permutation, it is still a Costas Latin square. So the method to break symmetries for Costas Latin squares is just to fix its first column:

$$\forall x \in N : A(x, 1) = x \tag{5}$$

It is easy to see that for *CLS(n)*, the simple symmetry breaking method can reduce the search space by *n!*.

The formula for Costas property and the formula for orthogonality property are difficult to handle. We use a method called transversal finding paradigm to improve the search efficiency. As described by Donald Knuth in [9], transversal-finding paradigm will reduce a factor of more than 1012(!) when searching Eulers conjecture of order 10. In [7,10], the authors show that modeling an orthogonal mate finding problem via transversal-finding paradigm can improve the efficiency of automated reasoning tools. In this paper we will show that the transversal-finding paradigm can also be used for modeling Costas property and improve the solving efficiency.

A transversal in a Latin square is a collection of positions, one from each row and one from each column, so that the elements in these positions are all different. It can be written as a vector, where the i-th element records the row index of the cell that appears in the i-th column. A matrix is called a transversal matrix of Latin square, if it consists of n mutually disjoint transversal vectors. In this paper, we use a variation of transversal matrix. For a Latin square A of order n, we construct a matrix TA for it by this way:

If $A(i,j)=k$, then $TA(k,j)=i$, where $i, j, k \in N$.

We can see that each Latin square has a unique transversal matrix, and each transversal matrix belongs to only one Latin square. Here is an example of a Latin square of order 4 (left) and its transversal matrix (right):

1	2	4	3
2	3	1	4
3	4	2	1
4	1	3	2

1	4	2	3
2	1	3	4
3	2	4	1
4	3	1	2

In transversal matrix, the i-th row represents the row index of i in the original Latin square. Let's see the number 2 of the above example. It is in the 2,1,3,4 row (from left to right) in the original Latin square. In the transversal matrix, this is recorded as the vector of the 2-th row $(2, 1, 3, 4)$.

If a Latin square A doesn't have Costas property, then there is a number i in it and at least two segments between i are same in length and in slope. That is the four points decide a parallelogram. Suppose that the four points are $A(x_1, y_1), A(x_2, y_2), A(x_3, y_3), A(x_4, y_4)$. In order to model Costas property we should consider all the four points in a $n \times n$ matrix. Since in TA, the row information of A are collected in the i-th row, $TA(i, y_1) = x_1, TA(i, y_2) = x_2, TA(i, y_3) = x_3, TA(i, y_4) = x_4$, the formula for Costas property involves only the i-th row of TA, a vector of n.

If a Latin square A doesn't have Costas property, then in some i-th row of its transversal matrix TA, there must be four column x, y, u, v, which make the following hold:

$$TA(i, x) - TA(i, y) = TA(i, u) - TA(i, v) \Leftrightarrow x - y = u - v$$

We use transversal matrix to simplify the formula for Costas property by replacing Formula 2 to the following formula for transversal matrix TA:

$$\forall x, y, z, u, v \in N :$$
$$TA(x, u) - TA(x, y) = TA(x, v) - TA(x, z) \vee u - y = v - z \mapsto y = z \vee u = y \tag{6}$$

Next we will use transversal matrix to reformulate Formula 3 for orthogonality property. From [10], we know that finding a pair of orthogonal Latin squares is equivalent to the transversal-finding phase. The transversal matrix focus on the positions information rather than the elements themselves. For two $CLS(n)$ A, B, their transversal matrix are TA, TB respectively. If we formulate orthogonality property using A, B directly, then we should consider all of the $2 \times n \times n$ positions of A, B. By using transversal matrix TA, TB, we can reduce the formula to involving only $2 \times n$ vectors. For some u and v in TA, TB, obviously for a column x, $A(TA(u, x), x) = u$ and $B(TB(v, x), x) = v$, since $TA(u, x)$ and $TB(v, x)$ are row index of u, v in A, B. If $TA(u, x) = TB(v, x)$, then the positions of u, v in A, B are the same, denoted as p_1, and in this cell, the pair $(A(TA(u, x), x), B(TB(v, x), x))$ is (u, v). Suppose that A and B are orthogonal. If there is another position p_2 for A, B in y-th column, and the pair in it is also (u, v), then p_2 must be same as p_1, and $x = y$ holds. Otherwise A and B can't be orthogonal. So we use the following formula for transversal matrix:

$$\forall x, y, u, v \in N : x \neq y \mapsto TA(u, x) \neq TB(v, x) \vee TA(u, y) \neq TB(v, y) \tag{7}$$

Due to length limitation we don't give more formal definitions of transversal matrix. More formal definitions and details are in [10].

5 New Results and Experimental Evaluation

In this section, we derive new results of our methods on Costas Latin squares of order 4,6,8,10 with aforementioned properties. We find some instances of Costas Latin squares with certain properties and decide the non-existence of most cases. The newly discovered Costas Latin squares have been double checked with another program we developed, and the non-existence results can be validated thanks to the capability of modern SAT solvers. Also we evaluate the efficiency of symmetry breaking and transversal matrix strategies. The experiments are performed on a PC with Intel CPU (1.60 GHz), 4G memory, Ubuntu 18.04. We encode Costas Latin square problems as CNF formulas, and solve them by a SAT solver: Glucose with default setting.

5.1 New Results

Table 1 indicates whether CLS(n) with specified properties exist or not. Here *Ide* means idempotency, *Ort* means orthogonality. s(sat) means that the CLS(n)

Table 1. The overall results of searching for $CLS(n)$

Order n	Ide	Quasigroup							Ort
		.1	.2	.3	.4	.5	.6	.7	
$CLS(4)$	s	s	s	s	s	u	u	s	s
$CLS(6)$	u	u	u	u	u	u	u	u	u
$CLS(8)$	s	u	u	u	u	u	u	u	u
$CLS(10)$	u	u	u	u	u	u	u	u	*

with the certain property exists and u (unsat) means they don't exist. $CLS(10) - Ort$ is very hard and isn't solved within 12 h.

For $CLS(4)$, there is no instance with quasigroup identities 5 and 6, and all other properties hold. For CLS of order 6,8,10, only the instances with idempotency exist for CLS(8). Here are some instances:

CLS(4)-Ide   CLS(4)-Q1   CLS(4)-Q2   CLS(4)-Q3   CLS(4)-Q4   CLS(4)-Q7

1	4	2	3
3	2	4	1
4	1	3	2
2	3	1	4

2	3	1	4
4	1	3	2
3	2	4	1
1	4	2	3

2	4	1	3
3	1	4	2
4	2	3	1
1	3	2	4

1	4	2	3
3	2	4	1
4	1	3	2
2	3	1	4

1	4	2	3
3	2	4	1
4	1	3	2
2	3	1	4

1	4	2	3
3	2	4	1
4	1	3	2
2	3	1	4

CLS(4)-Ort-A   CLS(4)-Ort-B   CLS(8)-Ide

1	3	4	2
2	4	3	1
3	1	2	4
4	2	1	3

3	4	2	1
2	1	3	4
1	2	4	3
4	3	1	2

1	3	5	7	4	2	8	6
4	2	6	8	3	1	5	7
5	7	3	1	6	8	4	2
8	6	2	4	7	5	1	3
6	8	4	2	5	7	3	1
7	5	1	3	8	6	2	4
2	4	8	6	1	3	7	5
3	1	7	5	2	4	6	8

5.2   Experimental Evaluation

In order to evaluate the effectiveness of symmetry breaking and transversal matrix strategies, we compared the running times of algorithms using these strategies against those lack one or two strategies. Since the symmetry breaking strategy is not fit for quasigroup identities and idempotent because it may conflict with these properties, we conducted two groups of experiments. One is for the problems to which this strategy is applicable, as illustrated in Table 2. The other is for problems to which it is not applicable, as shown in Table 3.

Table 2 and Table 3 show the running times (in seconds) of different methods in solving CLS problems. We set the timeout to 3600 s. Each column is the running times of various methods for certain problems. $SB + Tr$ means

Table 2. The run times of different methods in solving CLS-Ord and CLS-Ort

	SB+Tr	SB	Tr	non		SB+Tr	SB	Tr	non
CLS(6)-Ord	0.07	0.08	0.07	0.10	CLS(8)-Ord	1.39	100.04	26.46	2207.91
CLS(6)-Ort	0.28	2.23	TO	TO	CLS(8)-Ort	67.04	1230.96	TO	TO

Table 3. The run times of different methods in solving CLS-Ide and CLS-Qi

	Tr	non		Tr	non		Tr	non
CLS(6)-Ide	0.07	0.10	CLS(8)-Ide	0.97	17.79	CLS(10)-Ide	406.59	TO
CLS(6)-Q1	0.07	0.13	CLS(8)-Q1	1.84	36.58	CLS(10)-Q1	351.70	TO
CLS(6)-Q2	0.08	0.19	CLS(8)-Q2	2.88	97.45	CLS(10)-Q2	889.16	TO
CLS(6)-Q3	0.07	0.10	CLS(8)-Q3	1.00	2.16	CLS(10)-Q3	12.05	38.61
CLS(6)-Q4	0.07	0.09	CLS(8)-Q4	0.98	1.86	CLS(10)-Q4	10.93	36.37
CLS(6)-Q5	0.09	0.12	CLS(8)-Q5	3.73	5.83	CLS(10)-Q5	880.58	84.13
CLS(6)-Q6	0.07	0.10	CLS(8)-Q6	0.94	6.68	CLS(10)-Q6	11.06	TO
CLS(6)-Q7	0.07	0.10	CLS(8)-Q7	1.01	2.21	CLS(10)-Q7	12.09	TO

that the method employs both symmetry breaking and transversal matrix; SB and Tr mean that methods using only symmetry breaking and only transversal matrix respectively. non means that the method uses neither of these two strategies. $CLS(i)$-Ord represents ordinary $CLS(i)$, i.e., $CLS(i)$ without any property. Although the existential problems of $CLS(i)$-Ord have been determined by other work, we still use them to evaluate our strategies. $Q1, \cdots, Q7$ represent the aforementioned seven quasigroup properties.

From Table 2 we can see that symmetry breaking technique is highly efficient. $CLS(6)$-Ort and $CLS(8)$-Ort can only be solved with the symmetry breaking technique. From Table 3 we can see that transversal matrix significantly improves the solving efficiency. For almost all problems, the algorithm with transversal matrix is faster than the one without it.

At last we show the number of variables and the number of clauses (in the best method) of each problem in Table 4.

Table 4. The number of variables and clauses in each case

	Vars	Clauses		Vars	Clauses		Vars	Clauses
CLS(6)-Odr	432	73830	CLS(8)-Odr	1024	628360	CLS(10)-Odr	2000	3245210
CLS(6)-Ide	432	73830	CLS(8)-Ide	1024	628360	CLS(10)-Ide	2000	3245210
CLS(6)-Q1-7	432	75120	CLS(8)-Q1-7	1024	622448	CLS(10)-Q1-7	2000	3255200
CLS(6)-Ort	864	186540	CLS(8)-Ort	2048	1486096	CLS(10)-Ort	4000	7390420

278 J. Jin et al.

6 Conclusion

This paper describes an application of SAT solvers to an important combinatorial structures: Costas Latin Squares. The existence of Costas Latin Squares with specified properties are difficult for mathematical methods. We present two effective solving strategies for these problems: symmetry breaking and transversal matrix. As a result, we find some new instances and prove the non-existence of a number of cases for even order $n \leq 10$. In the future, we will investigate more challenging cases, such as the orthogonal Costas Latin Squares of order 10, as well as Costas Latin Squares of order $n \geq 12$. We believe that finding Costas Latin Squares can be an interesting benchmark for SAT solvers.

Acknowledgments. This work has been supported by the National Natural Science Foundation of China (NSFC) under grant No.61972384, and the Key Research Program of Frontier Sciences, Chinese Academy of Sciences under grant number QYZDJ-SSW-JSC036. Feifei Ma is also supported by the Youth Innovation Promotion Association CAS under grant No. Y202034. We thank professor Lie Zhu at SooChow university for suggesting these open problems and his valuable advice. We also thank the anonymous reviewers for their comments and suggestions.

References

1. Bright, C., Ganesh, V., Heinle, A., Kotsireas, I., Nejati, S., Czarnecki, K.: MATH-CHECK2: A SAT+CAS verifier for combinatorial conjectures. In: Gerdt, V.P., Koepf, W., Seiler, W.M., Vorozhtsov, E.V. (eds.) CASC 2016. LNCS, vol. 9890, pp. 117–133. Springer, Cham (2016). https://doi.org/10.1007/978-3-319-45641-6_9
2. Costas, J.P.: A study of a class of detection waveforms having nearly ideal range-doppler ambiguity properties. Proc. IEEE **72**(8), 996–1009 (1984)
3. Dinitz, J., Ostergard, P., Stinson, D.: Packing costas arrays. J. Comb. Math. Comb. Comput. **80**, 02 (2011)
4. Etzion, T.: Combinatorial designs with costas arrays properties. Discrete Math. **93**(2–3), 143–154 (1991)
5. Heule, M.J.H.: Schur number five. In: McIlraith, S.A., Weinberger, K.Q. (eds.) Proceedings of the Thirty-Second AAAI Conference on Artificial Intelligence, (AAAI-18), the 30th innovative Applications of Artificial Intelligence (IAAI-18), and the 8th AAAI Symposium on Educational Advances in Artificial Intelligence (EAAI-18), New Orleans, Louisiana, USA, 2–7 February 2018, pp. 6598–6606. AAAI Press (2018)
6. Heule, M.J.H., Kullmann, O., Marek, V.W.: Solving and verifying the Boolean Pythagorean triples problem via cube-and-conquer. In: Creignou, N., Le Berre, D. (eds.) SAT 2016. LNCS, vol. 9710, pp. 228–245. Springer, Cham (2016). https://doi.org/10.1007/978-3-319-40970-2_15
7. Huang, P., Liu, M., Ge, C., Ma, F., Zhang, J.: Investigating the existence of orthogonal golf designs via satisfiability testing. In: Davenport, J.H., Wang, D., Kauers, M., Bradford, R.J., (eds.) Proceedings of the 2019 on International Symposium on Symbolic and Algebraic Computation, ISSAC 2019, Beijing, China, 15–18 July 2019, pp. 203–210. ACM (2019)

8. Huang, P., Ma, F., Ge, C., Zhang, J., Zhang, H.: Investigating the existence of large sets of idempotent quasigroups via satisfiability testing. In: Galmiche, D., Schulz, S., Sebastiani, R. (eds.) IJCAR 2018. LNCS (LNAI), vol. 10900, pp. 354–369. Springer, Cham (2018). https://doi.org/10.1007/978-3-319-94205-6_24
9. Knuth, D.E.: The Art of Computer Programming, Volume 4A: Combinatorial Algorithms, Part 2. Pearson Education India, Noida
10. Ma, F., Zhang, J.: Finding orthogonal latin squares using finite model searching tools. Sci. China Inf. Sci. **56**(3), 1–9 (2013)
11. Zhang, H.: Combinatorial designs by SAT solvers. In: Biere, A., Heule, M., van Maaren, H., Walsh, T., (eds.) Handbook of Satisfiability, volume 185 of Frontiers in Artificial Intelligence and Applications, pp. 533–568. IOS Press (2009)
12. Zulkoski, E., Bright, C., Heinle, A., Kotsireas, I.S., Czarnecki, K., Ganesh, V.: Combining SAT solvers with computer algebra systems to verify combinatorial conjectures. J. Autom. Reason. **58**(3), 313–339 (2017)

Assessing Progress in SAT Solvers Through the Lens of Incremental SAT

Stepan Kochemazov[1]([☒]), Alexey Ignatiev[2], and Joao Marques-Silva[3]

[1] ITMO University, St. Petersburg, Russia
`stepan.kochemazov@itmo.ru`
[2] Monash University, Melbourne, Australia
`alexey.ignatiev@monash.edu`
[3] IRIT, CNRS, Toulouse, France
`joao.marques-silva@irit.fr`

Abstract. There is a wide consensus, which is supported by the hard experimental evidence of the SAT competitions, that clear progress in SAT solver performance has been observed in recent years. However, in the vast majority of practical applications of SAT, one is expected to use SAT solvers as oracles deciding a possibly large number of propositional formulas. In practice, this is often achieved through the use of incremental SAT. Given this fundamental use of SAT solvers, this paper investigates whether recent improvements in solver performance have an observable positive impact on the overall problem-solving efficiency in settings where incremental SAT is mandatory or at least expected. Our results, obtained on a number of well-known practically significant applications, suggest that most improvements made to SAT solvers in recent years have no positive impact on the overall performance when solvers are used incrementally.

1 Introduction

Boolean Satisfiability (SAT) solving can only be viewed as one of the most important successes of computer science. SAT was the first decision problem to be proved NP-complete in the early 70s [4]. As a result, and unless P = NP, SAT being NP-complete implies in theory and in practice that the worst-case running time of SAT algorithms grows exponentially with the number of variables. This was indeed the case until the early 90s, with SAT solvers capable at best of deciding formulas with a few hundred variables and a few thousand clauses. However, since the mid 90s, and building on the well-known DPLL algorithm [5,6],

---

[1] It is generally accepted that the term CDCL was coined by L. Ryan [40].

Stepan Kochemazov is supported by the Ministry of Science and Higher Education of Russian Federation, research project no. 075-03-2020-139/2 (goszadanie no. 2019-1339). Joao Marques-Silva is supported by the AI Interdisciplinary Institute ANITI, funded by the French program "Investing for the Future – PIA3" under Grant agreement no. ANR-19-PI3A-0004, and by the H2020-ICT38 project COALA "Cognitive Assisted agile manufacturing for a Labor force supported by trustworthy Artificial intelligence".

C.-M. Li and F. Manyà (Eds.): SAT 2021, LNCS 12831, pp. 280–298, 2021.
https://doi.org/10.1007/978-3-030-80223-3_20

a stream of new algorithmic improvements led to what is now known as CDCL (conflict-driven clause learning) SAT solvers[1]. CDCL SAT solving revolutionized the size and complexity of the formulas that SAT solvers can decide efficiently in practice. Indeed, it is well-known that in many applications, modern CDCL SAT solvers routinely decide formulas with a few million variables and tens of millions clauses. As a direct consequence of these algorithmic improvements, the last two decades have witnessed an ever increasing range of highly significant practical applications [3, Ch. 04]. (The techniques used in SAT solvers have also found widespread use in other automated reasoners, including SMT [3, Ch. 33], ASP [9], CP/LCG [37], ILP and even theorem provers [3].) This success makes SAT one of the few NP-complete problems that has achieved widespread practical deployment. Among the improvements made to DPLL-style SAT solvers, it is generally accepted that clause learning [23,25,26] played a fundamental role, not only because of its remarkable ability to prune the search space for practical formulas, but also because it enables other techniques to become very effective in practice. Other improvements of notice include search restarts [10], branching heuristics [34], watched literals [34], phase saving [39] and literal block distance [2]. (A detailed account can be found in different chapters of the recent SAT handbook [3].) Furthermore, it is generally accepted that the hard experimental evidence offered by the SAT competitions supports the following assertion: *"There has been regular performance improvements in SAT solvers over the years"*.

In terms of practical uses of SAT, incremental SAT is by far the most often used option. The most widely used approach for instrumenting incremental SAT was proposed originally in the MiniSat solver [7], using the so-called activation (or selection variables). Since then, a wealth of practical applications of SAT have resorted to incremental SAT solving (e.g. [3, Ch. 04] and references therein). The importance of incremental SAT is underscored for example by specific optimizations in the engineering of recent SAT solvers [1,11,17]. As yet another example, the PySAT framework for prototyping with SAT solvers makes extensive use of incremental SAT solving [12].

This paper seeks to understand how significant the recent progress made in SAT solvers, as documented by the results from the SAT competitions, is to practical incremental SAT solving. Although there is a well-known incremental track in the SAT competitions, the problem we address is somewhat different. First, our investigation is not limited to the applications considered in the incremental track of the SAT competition; indeed we consider applications of well-known importance, but which are not contemplated in the incremental track. Second, we do not seek to find the best SAT solver, but instead to assess whether specific algorithmic improvements made to SAT solvers contribute visibly to improve solver performance, specifically when the goal is incremental SAT solving[2]. Our results indicate that, contrary to the conclusions obtained from the results of the

---

[2] Similarly, in the area of Satisfiability Modulo Theories (SMT) reasoning [3], it is generally accepted that not all optimizations made to SAT and SMT solvers find widespread use.

SAT competition, most of the improvements made to SAT solvers in recent years do not contribute in a visible way to improving the performance of SAT solving. Furthermore, based on the prominent role of incremental SAT in practical problem solving, one overall recommendation of this work is that the assessment of future SAT solvers should take into account their observed performance improvements with respect to incremental SAT solving.

The paper is organized as follows. Section 2 briefly introduces the notation and definitions used throughout. Section 3 analyzes the results of the SAT competition, aiming to draw the general conclusions that justify our assertion above. Section 4 outlines how a SAT solver was instrumented to enable the proposed study. Section 5 presents the experimental results we have obtained. Section 6 concludes the paper.

2   Preliminaries

Definitions and Notation. The standard definitions used in SAT solving are assumed throughout the paper [3]. A SAT solver decides the decision problem of propositional logic (for formulas represented in conjunctive normal form (CNF)). For satisfiable formulas, a SAT solver returns a model, i.e. an assignment that satisfies the formula. For unsatisfiable formulas, most CDCL SAT solvers will return a non-minimal explanation for unsatisfiability. Most modern CDCL SAT solvers offer an incremental interface, without exception inspired by the incremental interface of MiniSat [7]. Incremental SAT solving finds an ever increasing range of practical applications (a sample of which are documented e.g. [3, Ch. 04]).

Related Work. A number of papers have investigated improvements to the performance of SAT solvers from different perspectives [8,15]. However, none has investigated how improvements made to SAT solvers impact incremental SAT solving. The importance of incremental SAT solving is demonstrated by its ubiquitous use in e.g. the PySAT framework [12]. Before PySAT was developed, incremental SAT was extensively used in a wide range of applications of SAT (a brief account is available from [3, Ch. 04]). The importance of incremental SAT explains a number of recent optimizations made to SAT solvers [1,11,17].

3   Motivation

It is natural to view the winners of recent SAT Competitions as state of the art in CDCL SAT solving. They incorporate the most promising CDCL heuristics aimed at improving solvers' performance over a wide variety of benchmarks originating from different application domains. There are two SAT solvers that played a special role in SAT competitions over the years. They are MiniSat[7] and Glucose [2]. It will not be an exaggeration to say that from 2005 to 2015 the list of competition winners in all categories tended to include at least one version (or sometimes *hack*) of either one or the other.

In 2015 the COMiniSatPS solver [36] combined the Luby series restarts [21] from MiniSat and Glucose-style restarts into a single whole, where the solver switched between two modes, each exploiting one of the restart strategies in conjunction with VSIDS activity values specific to each mode.

In 2016 MapleCOMSPS[20] supplanted Glucose as the source of many of the winners of SAT Competitions 2016 to 2020. The key novel feature of Maple-COMSPS was the use of *learning rate branching* heuristic (LRB) [19] instead of VSIDS joined with Luby restarts in COMiniSatPS. It also replaced the scheme for switching between modes employed by COMiniSatPS by a simple variant where the LRB+Luby restarts mode is used exclusively during the first 2500 s.

In 2017 MapleCOMSPS has been extended with an expensive *inprocessing* [14] technique for improving the quality of learnt clauses, termed *learned clause minimization* [18,22,38], with the resulting solver called MapleLCMDist.

In 2018 the latter was augmented with the *chronological backtracking* [31,35] heuristic aimed at improving the solver behavior in specific cases, in form of MapleLCMDistChronoBT. (The chronological backtracking scheme mimics the organization of backtracking used in the GRASP SAT solver [25].)

The winner of SAT Race 2019 implemented on top of MapleLCMDistChrono-BT the so-called *duplicate learnts heuristic* [16] aimed at detecting and exploiting repeatedly learned clauses, resulting in the MapleLCMDistChronoBT-DL-v3 solver. It also changed the parameters of LBD-based separation between tiers of learnt clauses and used a new scheme for switching between solver modes, which is reminiscent to the one used in MapleCOMSPS but is less frequent.

Finally, Relaxed_LCMDCBDL_newTech [41], that took the 2nd place at SAT Competition 2020, incorporated into MapleLCMDistChronoBT-DL-v3 the stochastic local search (SLS) component, complemented with *rephasing* technique[3], and a novel approach that modifies the activity values of branching heuristic in a CDCL solver based on some of the statistics accumulated by the SLS component. It also modified the scheme for switching between solver modes.

There is a clear agreement that the performance of SAT Competition winners improved significantly over the years[4], thanks to the several major heuristics listed above, among others. In this context, it is very surprising that many applications of SAT solvers still employ the time-tested MiniSat and Glucose first introduced back in 2003 [7] and 2009 [2], respectively. For example, if we look at the participants of the recent MaxSAT Evaluations [28–30], it turns out that the majority of them employ either Glucose (different versions), MiniSat 2.2 or COMiniSatPS as the underlying SAT solver. Of course, there are many possible reasons for this, varying from unwillingness of developers to replace the core components of working tools under pretext that they already work well enough, to the fact that many SAT Competition winners of recent years do not provide incremental interface out of the box. However, whatever the reasons behind this are, it is important to *question* and *evaluate* whether the apparent progress in CDCL SAT solvers indeed translates into the benefits in their practical applications.

---

[3] http://fmv.jku.at/chasing-target-phases/.

[4] http://fmv.jku.at/kissat/.

Of course, it is impossible to cover all possible use cases of SAT solvers in a single study. Therefore, in this paper we concentrate our attention on the ones that can be employed incrementally, in particular, in maximum satisfiability (MaxSAT) solving and minimal unsatisfiable subset (MUS) extraction.

4   Setup and Its Rationale

In order to evaluate whether or not the improvements made to SAT solvers in recent years contribute to their performance in the incremental setting, it is first necessary to choose a solver (or solvers) that could serve as (a) strong representative(s) of the solver "generation". It would be ideal to exploit the winner of the most recent SAT Competition that implements all the recently proposed CDCL heuristics, can be easily modified to enable or disable some of the heuristics whenever needed, and that can be embedded into various tools that could apply it incrementally. Unfortunately, the winner of the SAT Competition 2020, the Kissat solver does not support the incremental mode according to the data available at the moment of writing, and thus is not eligible for the experiments that we need to perform. However, Relaxed_LCMDCBDL_newTech that took the 2nd place in the main track of SAT Competition 2020 satisfies all the aforementioned criteria. Despite not supporting incremental SAT out of the box, it uses the MiniSat codebase and thus can be easily upgraded.

For our experiment we prepared a variant of Relaxed_LCMDCBDL_newTech, which we hereinafter refer to as RLNT[5]. Compared to the original, RLNT supports incremental mode, has several small issues fixed and also allows to separately enable or disable some of its major heuristics. In particular, we are interested in testing the implementations of *stochastic local search* and *rephasing* components (**SLS**) introduced in Relaxed_LCMDCBDL_newTech, the *duplicate learnts* (**DL**) heuristic that appeared in MapleLCMDistChronoBT-DL-v3, the *chronological backtracking* (**CB**) that became a signature of MapleLCMDistChronoBT, the *DISTANCE* (**DIST**) and *learnt clause minimization* heuristics (**LCM**) first introduced in MapleLCMDist. These were modified in order to be enabled or disabled via preprocessor conditional inclusive directives (e.g. `#define SLS` and `#ifdef SLS`). As it happens, these heuristics represent the vital development steps signifying the progress of SAT solvers in the last 4 SAT Competitions and so can serve as *inherent characteristics* of the corresponding generations of SAT solvers.

The listed heuristics employed in RLNT were not specifically adapted to the incremental usage separately. Instead, the variables that govern scheduling of the procedures that switch between solver modes, apply learnt clause minimization, apply rephasing, and so on—these are all reset to initial values with each new call to the SAT solver. The motivation for this adjustment is to alleviate the increase in intervals between, e.g. learnt clause minimization, so that each call of a SAT solver preserves the accumulated knowledge, but still uses all the heuristics as often as it would in the *"standard"* non-incremental mode. In line with this, the call to the

---

[5] https://github.com/veinamond/RLNT.

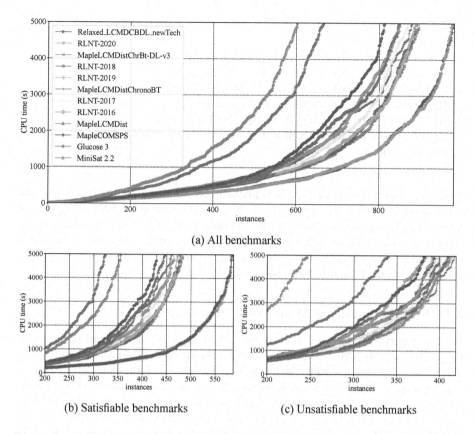

(a) All benchmarks

(b) Satisfiable benchmarks

(c) Unsatisfiable benchmarks

Fig. 1. Evaluation of considered solvers over benchmarks from the main tracks of SAT competitions 2017–2020.

SLS component is scheduled to happen at the start of each SAT solver invocation since this is the way it is used in the original implementation. Due to the fact that it mainly affects rephasing, and also that SLS subsolver calls take negligible amount of time, this implementation should not introduce any adverse effects on the solver's performance. It should be noted that the changes between, say, the SAT competition 2016 winner MapleCOMSPS and Relaxed_LCMDCBDL_newTech certainly cannot be summarized to just the 5 heuristics listed above. There have been also small changes to the handling of conflict clauses with small literal block distance, and to the strategy employed to switch between solver modes that combine branching heuristics with restart strategies (LRB+Luby restarts and VSIDS + glucose restarts). It is natural to assume that these changes are worthwhile, but it should be checked experimentally anyway. Therefore, in the following experiments we opt to use the following SAT solvers:

- MapleCOMSPS – SAT Competition 2016 winner.
- MapleLCMDist – SAT Competition 2017 winner.

- MapleLCMDistChronoBT – SAT Competition 2018 winner.
- MapleLCMDistChronoBT-DL-v3 – SAT Race 2019 winner.
- Relaxed_LCMDCBDL_newTech – SAT Competition 2020 2nd place.
- RLNT-2020 – RLNT with SLS, DL, CB, LCM and DIST enabled.
- RLNT-2019 – RLNT with DL, CB, LCM and DIST enabled.
- RLNT-2018 – RLNT with CB, LCM and DIST enabled.
- RLNT-2017 – RLNT with LCM and DIST enabled.
- RLNT-2016 – RLNT with SLS, CB, DL, LCM and DIST disabled.
- Glucose 3.0.
- MiniSat 2.2.

Thus, our conjecture is that RLNT-2019 should be functionally "equivalent" to the winner of SAT Race 2019, RLNT-2018 to the winner of SAT Competition 2018, etc. (The results of the following section confirm this.) To offset the newer solvers we will use Glucose 3.0 and time-tested MiniSat 2.2, which both are often employed in many practical applications up to these days, although having been released back in 2013 and 2008, respectively.

4.1   SAT Competition Main Track Benchmarks

In this experiment we used the benchmarks from the main tracks of the SAT Competitions 2017–2020; thus, the total number of benchmarks considered is 1550. The experiments were performed on the nodes of the computing cluster [27], equipped with two 18-core Intel Xeon E5-2695 v4 CPUs and 128 GB RAM. All the competitors worked in 36 simultaneous threads with the time limit of 5000 s. As the evaluation criteria, we used the Solution Count Ranking (SCR) and Penalized Average Runtime (PAR-2) following the metrics used in the SAT Competitions.

The results of the evaluation are presented in the form of cactus plots in Fig. 1 and as a more detailed statistics in Table 1. From the presented results, it is easy to conclude that in accordance with the SAT Competition criteria, the RLNT configurations perform as well as (or *better* than) the corresponding SAT Competition winners with negligible deviations. This confirms that the rationale behind the selected baseline solver as well as the implementation choices made is reasonable. Also, one can easily observe the trend according to which the recent competitions favor satisfiable benchmarks over unsatisfiable, thus making the solvers which are stronger on satisfiable benchmarks look better. The particularly distinctive difference between Relaxed_LCMDCBDL_newTech (and RLNT-2020) and the remaining group is thanks to the SLS component that appears to be solely responsible for being able to tackle at least 80 benchmarks. Finally, the performance of Glucose 3 and MiniSat 2.2 when contrasted with that of more modern solvers appears to be an issue. It is especially so if we look at the performance of MiniSat 2.2 on unsatisfiable benchmarks compared to that of the competition.

Table 1. The detailed statistics on the performance of considered solvers over benchmarks from the main tracks of SAT Competitions 2017–2020.

	SCR	SAT	UNSAT	PAR-2
Relaxed_LCMDCBDL_newTech	980	585	395	4199
RLNT-2020	978	586	392	4203
MapleLCMDistChrBt-DL-v3	896	484	412	4772
RLNT-2018	890	479	411	4811
RLNT-2019	889	474	415	4822
MapleLCMDistChronoBT	879	461	418	4933
RLNT-2017	870	470	400	4961
RLNT-2016	849	465	384	5096
MapleLCMDist	849	449	400	5107
MapleCOMSPS	813	430	383	5303
Glucose 3	666	325	341	6238
MiniSat 2.2	603	356	247	6606

Now let us see whether or not the overall picture will change when we move into the incremental context.

4.2   SAT Competition Incremental Track Benchmarks

In this series of experiments we used the benchmarks and applications from the Incremental Track of SAT Competition 2020. The solvers participating in this track have to support the *IPASIR*[6] incremental interface. In the course of the evaluation, the solvers are compiled into an incremental library together with specific IPASIR-based applications that aim to cover various practical domains that may employ incremental solvers. In 2020, the incremental track included the applications for (a) finding backbones of a CNF SAT formula, (b) finding variables essential for the satisfiability of a formula, (c) finding the longest simple path in a graph, (d) a simple MaxSAT solver, (e) Ijtihad QBF solver and (f) the PASAR solver for solving planning instances. For each application, there were 50 instances (which overlapped in the case of finding backbones and the variables essential for satisfiability). Due to high requirements to the execution environment, in particular for it to support C++ 17, we used PCs with 16-core AMD Ryzen 3950x CPUs and 32 GB RAM running Ubuntu 20.04, as the computing platform. The solvers were launched in 16 threads.

The results of this experiment are summarized in Table 2 and cactus plots in Fig. 2. It needs to be noted, that since incremental track is significantly less popular than the main track (at least looking at the number of participants of each), it is less polished and is harder to reproduce. In particular, the outputs and

---

[6] https://github.com/biotomas/ipasir.

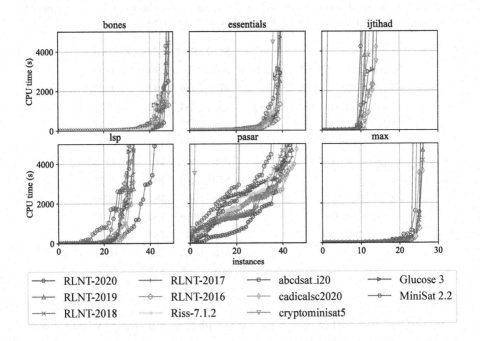

Fig. 2. Evaluation of considered solvers over benchmarks from the incremental track of SAT competitions 2020.

Table 2. The detailed statistics on the performance of considered solvers over benchmarks from the incremental track of SAT Competitions 2020. The best results for each application are marked with bold. Column S refers to the number of solved instances, P2 – to the PAR-2 score.

	bones		essentials		lsp		max		ijtihad		pasar	
	S	P2	S	P2	S	P2	S	P2	S	P2	S	P2
RLNT-2020	49	350	40	2219	**43**	**1987**	26	4869	11	6879	44	2325
RLNT-2019	48	580	40	2170	34	3546	27	4753	12	6845	45	2733
RLNT-2018	49	482	40	2168	34	3577	**27**	**4739**	13	6393	41	3254
RLNT-2017	49	441	40	2174	34	3542	27	4745	12	6845	45	2553
RLNT-2016	**49**	**322**	**40**	**2086**	33	3837	26	4826	14	6369	43	2902
Glucose 3	45	1108	40	2273	32	3845	24	5211	14	6895	42	3387
MiniSat 2.2	48	635	40	2180	34	3811	24	5212	2	9600	22	6380
Riss-7.1.2	45	1108	39	2388	32	3844	25	5013	13	7270	37	3907
abcdsat_i20	48	627	39	2450	32	4205	25	4696	11	7830	36	4295
cadicalsc2020	45	1085	39	2323	34	3381	27	4756	15	6729	**47**	**2400**
cryptoMiniSat5	49	333	37	2737	34	3495	26	4478	**15**	**5966**	3	9496

the success criterion for each application have to be parsed by hand, the number of instances is small, and the majority of instances are too simple. Moreover, there are frequent problems when the built application produces a core-dump and it is unclear whether the application itself is to blame or the solver was not built properly. This is the reason, for example, of the poor performance of the CryptoMiniSat5 solver in the *pasar* application or of MiniSat 2.2 in both *ijtihad* abd *pasar* applications: the majority of launches ended in a core-dump. (It is unclear to us how the organizers treated such situations in their evaluation.) Nevertheless, the results we obtained more-or-less follow the ones available at SAT Competition 2020 web page.[7]

One conclusion to be drawn from the presented data is that the RLNT configurations perform in the incremental setting as well as the participants of the incremental track of SAT Competition 2020, and in several cases outperform them. It means that the RLNT solver and its configurations can be viewed as the state-of-the-art representatives of the modern SAT solvers. Thus, we are justified to use them for the following in-depth evaluation presented below. Another conclusion is that Glucose 3, although it is not a winner in any of the subtracks, is on par with most of the competitors for all the considered benchmarks. Of particular interest is the fact that in contrast to SAT Competition Main Track benchmarks, in the incremental track environment, MiniSat 2.2 is on par with its peers (with the exception of *pasar* and *ijtihad* applications where it has likely suffered from some implementation issue). Finally, one can observe that the incremental track of the SAT Competition 2020 does not provide a solid number of benchmarks that could demonstrate the performance differences (if any) among the competitors of the incremental track, leaving much to be desired. All these points bring us to the need to evaluate the progress in SAT solving in a thorough evaluation from the perspective of two well-known practical use-case scenarios for incremental SAT, which is covered next.

5   Experimental Evidence

This section details the experimental results obtained with the use of the developed configurations of RLNT in the two concrete practical settings of (1) maximum satisfiability (MaxSAT) solving and (2) minimal unsatisfiable subset (MUS) extraction, where incremental calls to a SAT oracle are of crucial importance. Concretely, in all the following experiments we tested the 5 configurations of RLNT (2016–2020) and compared them to the Glucose 3 SAT solver [1], which has been widely used in various incremental settings. Finally, we additionally considered the *"good old"* MiniSat 2.2[8] solver [7] to see how it stands against more advanced SAT solvers.

All the SAT solvers are integrated in the PySAT framework [12] and are used in a *unified* fashion through the same API. The conducted experiments involve testing three practical problem solvers: (1) an award-winning core-guided

---

[7] https://satcompetition.github.io/2020/results.html.
[8] https://github.com/niklasso/minisat.

MaxSAT solver RC2 [13,28–30][9] (namely, competition configurations *RC2-A* and *RC2-B*), (2) a linear search SAT-UNSAT algorithm for MaxSAT [33][10] (in the following referred to as *LSU*), and (3) a simple deletion-based MUS extractor [12,24][11] (referred to as *MUSx*). All the problem solvers used are a part of the PySAT framework.

Note that the rationale behind the choice of the problem solvers is to test the performance of the underlying SAT oracles when dealing with (1) *mostly unsatisfiable* oracle calls, (2) *mostly satisfiable* oracle calls, and (3) *mixed* (satisfiable and unsatisfiable) oracle calls. Hereinafter, given a problem solver $*$, its configuration that exploits the Glucose 3 (resp. MiniSat 2.2) solver is marked as $*_{G3}$ (resp. $*_{M22}$) while the configurations using one of the RLNT solvers are marked by the corresponding year, as $*_{year}$.

Our experimental setup replicates the setup of the annual MaxSAT Evaluations [28–30]. In particular, the experiments were performed on the *StarExec cluster*[12]. Each process was run on an Intel Xeon E5-2609 2.40 GHz processor with 128 GByte of memory, in CentOS 7.7. The memory limit for each individual process was set to 32 GByte. The time limit used was set to 3600 s for each individual process to run.

5.1 RC2 MaxSAT and Mostly Unsatisfiable Calls

The RC2 MaxSAT solver [13] belongs to the large family of core-guided MaxSAT solvers [33] and provides an efficient implementation of the OLL/RC2 algorithm [32]. For this reason, each iteration performed by the solver involves calling a SAT oracle incrementally given an unsatisfiable formula that is slightly modified at each iteration of the algorithm. The solver proceeds until the final iteration, which determines the working formula to be satisfiable. The solver can also be instructed to apply a few additional heuristics [13], some of which may increase the number of satisfiable oracle calls; however, unsatisfiable oracle calls made by RC2 still prevail. Note that the competition configurations RC2-A and RC2-B make use of the Glucose 3 SAT solver. Also note that this part of the experiment tested RC2 on the complete set of benchmarks (both unweighted and weighted) from the MSE'20.

Figure 3 shows two cactus plots depicting the performance of the RC-A and RC2-B solvers on the MSE'20 benchmarks when using either Glucose 3 or one of the variants of RLNT as an underlying SAT oracle. According to Fig. 3a, in total, the best performance of RC2-A is achieved when using RLNT-2016. It solves 792 instances and in average spends 1293.2 s per instance. The default, RC2-A$_{G3}$ is not far away with 790 instances solved and the average time spent being 1290.8 s. The worst performance is demonstrated when RLNT-2020 is in use; here, the average time used per instance is 1549.8 s and the number of

---

[9] https://pysathq.github.io/docs/html/api/examples/rc2.html.
[10] https://pysathq.github.io/docs/html/api/examples/lsu.html.
[11] https://pysathq.github.io/docs/html/api/examples/musx.html.
[12] https://www.starexec.org/.

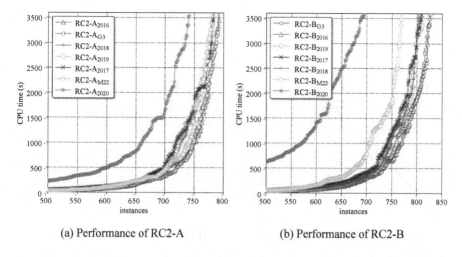

(a) Performance of RC2-A   (b) Performance of RC2-B

Fig. 3. RC2 with various SAT solvers on MSE'20 unweighted and weighted benchmarks.

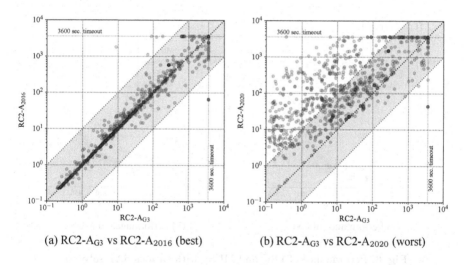

(a) RC2-A$_{G3}$ vs RC2-A$_{2016}$ (best)   (b) RC2-A$_{G3}$ vs RC2-A$_{2020}$ (worst)

Fig. 4. Performance of RC2-A$_{G3}$ compared to RC2-A with *best* and *worst* RLNT.

instances successfully solved is 741. As an additional remark, the MiniSat 2.2 based version is not far behind the top performing competitors – it solves 779 instances and spends 1327.5 s per instance on average. As can be seen in Fig. 3b, similar results are obtained by RC2-B. The worst performance is shown by RC2-B$_{2020}$, which solves 695 benchmarks and spends 1805.8 s per formula on average. The default configuration RC2-B$_{G3}$ outperforms the other competitors with 826 instances solved in 1222.7 s on average while RC2-B$_{2016}$ comes second with 825 instances solved in 1213.3 s on average. RC2-B$_{M22}$ solves 768 instances with the average time of 1385.1 s. The scatter plots shown in Fig. 4 and Fig. 5 detail

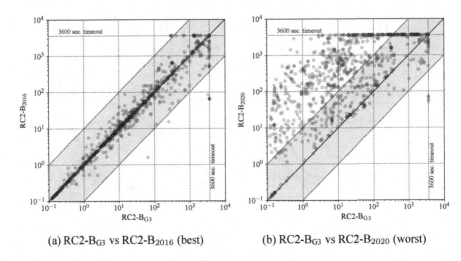

(a) RC2-B$_{G3}$ vs RC2-B$_{2016}$ (best)   (b) RC2-B$_{G3}$ vs RC2-B$_{2020}$ (worst)

Fig. 5. Performance of RC2-B$_{G3}$ compared to RC2-B with *best* and *worst* RLNT.

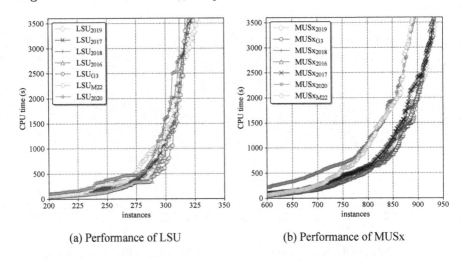

(a) Performance of LSU   (b) Performance of MUSx

Fig. 6. Performance of LSU and MUSx with various SAT solvers.

the performance comparison of the default version of RC2-A$_{G3}$ and RC2-B$_{G3}$ against the best- and worst-performing competitor running RLNT. As can be observed, there is no clear winner in the pair RC2-*$_{G3}$ vs RC2-*$_{2016}$ while for the lion's share of benchmarks the default versions of the solver working on top of Glucose 3 significantly outperform RC2-* with the most advanced RLNT-2020.

5.2   LSU MaxSAT and Mostly Satisfiable Calls

The LSU MaxSAT algorithm performs a linear search strategy iterating over the possible numbers of satisfied soft clauses and decreasing this number as long as

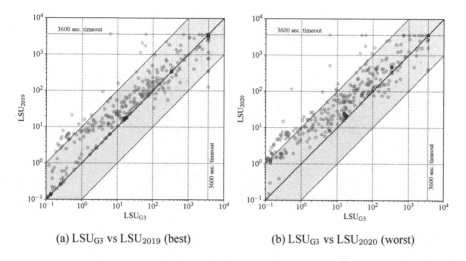

(a) $\mathrm{LSU_{G3}}$ vs $\mathrm{LSU_{2019}}$ (best)   (b) $\mathrm{LSU_{G3}}$ vs $\mathrm{LSU_{2020}}$ (worst)

Fig. 7. Performance of $\mathrm{LSU_{G3}}$ compared to LSU with *best* and *worst* RLNT.

the underlying solver reports the current formula to be satisfiable. As a result, all but one iterations of the algorithm involve satisfiable oracle calls. Similarly to RC2, we used the MSE'20 benchmarks for testing the performance of LSU. One difference, however, is that our implementation of LSU supports only unweighted formulas, i.e. the weighted formulas are discarded.

The performance of LSU is summarized in the cactus plot shown in Fig. 6a. Observe that although the version with Glucose 3 is outperformed by a few other competitors, it is not too far behind. Concretely, it solves 317 benchmarks, each within 1699 s on average. The best performing $\mathrm{LSU_{2019}}$ solves 327 instances, with the average running time of 1714.2 s. The worst configuration is $\mathrm{LSU_{2020}}$, which can cope with 312 formulas in 1771.9 s on average. Finally, observe that $\mathrm{LSU_{M22}}$ also solves 312 instances and the average time spent per formula is 1751.3 s. The scatter plots shown in Fig. 7a and Fig. 7b detail performance comparison of $\mathrm{LSU_{G3}}$ against $\mathrm{LSU_{2019}}$ and $\mathrm{LSU_{2020}}$ (as best- and worst-performing configurations of RLNT). According to these plots, Glucose 3 tends to be significantly faster than both RLNT-2019 and RLNT-2020, although RLNT-2019 manages to solve more instances overall.

5.3   MUS Extraction and Mixed Oracle Calls

The MUS extractor MUSx implements the simple deletion-based algorithm, which is bootstrapped with an unsatisfiable core of a formula and iterates over all clauses of the core trying to incrementally get rid of them one-by-one to get an MUS [12,24]. Therefore and depending on whether the target clause belongs to an MUS, the outcome of the corresponding SAT oracle call may vary. Hence, this part of the experiment aims at representing a practical scenario where the outcomes of incremental SAT solver calls are mixed. As the standard MUS

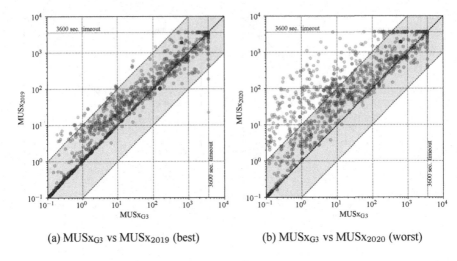

(a) MUSx$_{G3}$ vs MUSx$_{2019}$ (best)   (b) MUSx$_{G3}$ vs MUSx$_{2020}$ (worst)

Fig. 8. Performance of MUSx$_{G3}$ compared to MUSx with *best* and *worst* RLNT.

benchmarks date back to 2011 and most of them are not challenging enough, we opted to generate a large collection of new MUS benchmarks based on the MSE'20 benchmark set. Concretely, we ran RC2 and dumped the working formulas representing the two last unsatisfiable oracle calls. (In practice, these calls are typically the hardest for a SAT solver.) The generation procedure resulted in 1103 formulas in total. Note that in order to make a fair comparison, for each benchmark MUSx was bootstrapped with an initial unsatisfiable core, which was always obtained by Glucose 3. This was done to ensure that the reduction phase computes exactly the same MUS guaranteed by the same initial unsatisfiable core as well as the same order of clauses to traverse.

Figure 6b overviews the performance of MUSx given the competing SAT engines. MUSx$_{2019}$ outperforms the competitors and successfully deals with 934 formulas, within 802.2 sec. on average. MUSx$_{G3}$ comes second with 933 instances solved spending 779.1 s on average. Although the version based on MiniSat 2.2 is slower than all the other configurations for this family of benchmarks (it solves 890 instances with the average time per instance being 926.2 s), once again, the worst RLNT-based configuration uses RLNT-2020. It solves 893 benchmarks spending 983.5 s per benchmark. Scatter plots comparing the performance of MUSx$_{G3}$ against the best- and worst-performing RLNT-based configurations MUSx$_{2019}$ and MUSx$_{2020}$ are shown in Fig. 8a and Fig. 8b, respectively. Observe that MUSx$_{G3}$ is much faster than both competitors, which is especially clear in the case of MUSx$_{2020}$.

5.4 Final Remarks

Observe that none of the tested configurations of RLNT brings any consistent (and significant) performance improvements to the considered problem solvers.

Table 3. PAR-2 measure for each of the tested SAT solvers.

	MiniSat 2.2	Glucose 3	RLNT-2016	RLNT-2017	RLNT-2018	RLNT-2019	RLNT-2020
RC2-A	2536.8	2466.3	**2462.5**	2544.6	2536.7	2543.9	2875.7
RC2-B	2628.1	2287.7	**2281.3**	2406.0	2406.1	2387.5	3272.8
LSU	3391.1	3307.4	3302.7	3306.3	3318.7	**3259.7**	3411.7
MUSx	1621.4	**1333.9**	1345.7	1386.3	1361.8	1353.8	1665.7
Overall	2303.2	2061.9	**2056.3**	2151.8	2153.2	2134.3	2754.0

Motivated by this observation, we decided to measure and report the PAR-2 metric for all the tested SAT solvers per each of the performed experiments as well as across all benchmarks, which is presented in Table 3. As the table suggests, the best overall performance is demonstrated by the solvers with RLNT-2016 "on board" although its advantage over Glucose 3 is negligible. This enables us to conclude that most of the heuristics recently proposed for SAT solvers have no significant (or none at all) positive impact on the performance of practical problem solvers in settings when SAT oracles are to be used incrementally.

6   Conclusions

This paper studies improvements made to SAT solvers in recent years, and analyzes their impact on performance when the SAT solvers are used for solving incremental SAT. Based on Relaxed_LCMDCBDL_newTech a new SAT solver RLNT was developed, to allow the activation/deactivation of specific heuristics and to allow incremental SAT uses. Thus, RLNT is able to be executed under a vast number of possible configurations. The experimental results, on the SAT competition problem instances, demonstrate that RLNT is on par with the best performing SAT solvers. As for the incremental SAT track, the experimental results suggest that recent improvements made to SAT solvers offer no clear gains. Furthermore, the experimental results on two well-known applications of incremental SAT, confirm that most recent improvements have no observable contribution to improving SAT solving performance in incremental settings.

The conclusions drawn from the experimental results can be challenged if other uses of incremental SAT are considered. We feel that MaxSAT and MUS extraction are fairly representative, since a large number of SAT calls is usually required, both with satisfiable and unsatisfiable outcomes. Further validation of our conclusions would require considering additional applications that build on incremental SAT solving. Moreover, the results presented in the paper represent a first step towards a deeper understanding of the interplay between incremental SAT and optimizations used for improving the efficiency of SAT solvers. Additional experiments and analyzes will enable a more comprehensive understanding of this interplay. From a SAT practitioner's perspective, we believe this work demonstrates the need for a discussion within the SAT community on the improvements made to SAT solvers in light of (practical) incremental SAT solving, including more focus on this issue in the annual SAT Competitions. We also believe this work can serve to start such a discussion.

References

1. Audemard, G., Lagniez, J.-M., Simon, L.: Improving glucose for incremental SAT solving with assumptions: application to MUS extraction. In: Järvisalo, M., Van Gelder, A. (eds.) SAT 2013. LNCS, vol. 7962, pp. 309–317. Springer, Heidelberg (2013). https://doi.org/10.1007/978-3-642-39071-5_23
2. Audemard, G., Simon, L.: Predicting learnt clauses quality in modern SAT solvers. In: IJCAI, pp. 399–404 (2009)
3. Biere, A., Heule, M., van Maaren, H., Walsh, T. (eds.): Handbook of Satisfiability, 2nd edn. IOS Press, Amsterdam (2021)
4. Cook, S.A.: The complexity of theorem-proving procedures. In: STOC, pp. 151–158 (1971)
5. Davis, M., Logemann, G., Loveland, D.W.: A machine program for theorem-proving. Commun. ACM 5(7), 394–397 (1962)
6. Davis, M., Putnam, H.: A computing procedure for quantification theory. J. ACM 7(3), 201–215 (1960)
7. Eén, N., Sörensson, N.: An extensible SAT-solver. In: Giunchiglia, E., Tacchella, A. (eds.) SAT 2003. LNCS, vol. 2919, pp. 502–518. Springer, Heidelberg (2004). https://doi.org/10.1007/978-3-540-24605-3_37
8. Fichte, J.K., Hecher, M., Szeider, S.: A time leap challenge for SAT-solving. In: Simonis, H. (ed.) CP 2020. LNCS, vol. 12333, pp. 267–285. Springer, Cham (2020). https://doi.org/10.1007/978-3-030-58475-7_16
9. Gebser, M., Kaminski, R., Kaufmann, B., Schaub, T.: Answer set solving in practice. Synth. Lect. Artif. Intell. Mach. Learn. 6(3), 1–238 (2012). Morgan & Claypool Publishers
10. Gomes, C.P., Selman, B., Kautz, H.A.: Boosting combinatorial search through randomization. In: AAAI, pp. 431–437 (1998)
11. Hickey, R., Bacchus, F.: Speeding up assumption-based SAT. In: Janota, M., Lynce, I. (eds.) SAT 2019. LNCS, vol. 11628, pp. 164–182. Springer, Cham (2019). https://doi.org/10.1007/978-3-030-24258-9_11
12. Ignatiev, A., Morgado, A., Marques-Silva, J.: PySAT: a python toolkit for prototyping with SAT oracles. In: Beyersdorff, O., Wintersteiger, C.M. (eds.) SAT 2018. LNCS, vol. 10929, pp. 428–437. Springer, Cham (2018). https://doi.org/10.1007/978-3-319-94144-8_26
13. Ignatiev, A., Morgado, A., Marques-Silva, J.: RC2: an efficient MaxSAT solver. J. Satisf. Boolean Model. Comput. 11(1), 53–64 (2019)
14. Järvisalo, M., Heule, M.J.H., Biere, A.: Inprocessing rules. In: Gramlich, B., Miller, D., Sattler, U. (eds.) IJCAR 2012. LNCS (LNAI), vol. 7364, pp. 355–370. Springer, Heidelberg (2012). https://doi.org/10.1007/978-3-642-31365-3_28
15. Katebi, H., Sakallah, K.A., Marques-Silva, J.P.: Empirical study of the anatomy of modern sat solvers. In: Sakallah, K.A., Simon, L. (eds.) SAT 2011. LNCS, vol. 6695, pp. 343–356. Springer, Heidelberg (2011). https://doi.org/10.1007/978-3-642-21581-0_27
16. Kochemazov, S., Zaikin, O., Semenov, A.A., Kondratiev, V.: Speeding up CDCL inference with duplicate learnt clauses. In: ECAI, pp. 339–346 (2020)

17. Lagniez, J.-M., Biere, A.: Factoring out assumptions to speed up MUS extraction. In: Järvisalo, M., Van Gelder, A. (eds.) SAT 2013. LNCS, vol. 7962, pp. 276–292. Springer, Heidelberg (2013). https://doi.org/10.1007/978-3-642-39071-5_21
18. Li, C., Xiao, F., Luo, M., Manyà, F., Lü, Z., Li, Y.: Clause vivification by unit propagation in CDCL sat solvers. Artif. Intell. **279**, 103197 (2020)
19. Liang, J.H., Ganesh, V., Poupart, P., Czarnecki, K.: Learning rate based branching heuristic for SAT solvers. In: Creignou, N., Le Berre, D. (eds.) SAT 2016. LNCS, vol. 9710, pp. 123–140. Springer, Cham (2016). https://doi.org/10.1007/978-3-319-40970-2_9
20. Liang, J.H., Oh, C., Ganesh, V., Czarnecki, K., Poupart, P.: MapleCOMSPS, MapleCOMSPS_LRB, MapleCOMSPS_CHB. In: Procceedings of SAT Competition 2016, vol. B-2016-1, pp. 52–53 (2016)
21. Luby, M., Sinclair, A., Zuckerman, D.: Optimal speedup of Las Vegas algorithms. Inf. Process. Lett. **47**(4), 173–180 (1993)
22. Luo, M., Li, C., Xiao, F., Manyà, F., Lü, Z.: An effective learnt clause minimization approach for CDCL SAT solvers. In: IJCAI, pp. 703–711 (2017)
23. Marques-Silva, J.: Search algorithms for satisfiability problems in combinational switching circuits. Ph.D. thesis, University of Michigan (1995)
24. Marques-Silva, J., Lynce, I.: On improving MUS extraction algorithms. In: Sakallah, K.A., Simon, L. (eds.) SAT 2011. LNCS, vol. 6695, pp. 159–173. Springer, Heidelberg (2011). https://doi.org/10.1007/978-3-642-21581-0_14
25. Marques-Silva, J., Sakallah, K.A.: GRASP - a new search algorithm for satisfiability. In: ICCAD, pp. 220–227 (1996)
26. Marques-Silva, J., Sakallah, K.A.: GRASP: a search algorithm for propositional satisfiability. IEEE Trans. Comput. **48**(5), 506–521 (1999). https://doi.org/10.1109/12.769433
27. Irkutsk Supercomputer Center of SB RAS. http://hpc.icc.ru
28. MaxSAT Evaluation 2018. https://maxsat-evaluations.github.io/2018/
29. MaxSAT Evaluation 2019. https://maxsat-evaluations.github.io/2019/
30. MaxSAT Evaluation 2020. https://maxsat-evaluations.github.io/2020/
31. Möhle, S., Biere, A.: Backing backtracking. In: Janota, M., Lynce, I. (eds.) SAT 2019. LNCS, vol. 11628, pp. 250–266. Springer, Cham (2019). https://doi.org/10.1007/978-3-030-24258-9_18
32. Morgado, A., Dodaro, C., Marques-Silva, J.: Core-guided MaxSAT with soft cardinality constraints. In: O'Sullivan, B. (ed.) CP 2014. LNCS, vol. 8656, pp. 564–573. Springer, Cham (2014). https://doi.org/10.1007/978-3-319-10428-7_41
33. Morgado, A., Heras, F., Liffiton, M.H., Planes, J., Marques-Silva, J.: Iterative and core-guided MaxSAT solving: a survey and assessment. Constraints Int. J. **18**(4), 478–534 (2013). https://doi.org/10.1007/s10601-013-9146-2
34. Moskewicz, M.W., Madigan, C.F., Zhao, Y., Zhang, L., Malik, S.: Chaff: engineering an efficient SAT solver. In: DAC, pp. 530–535 (2001)
35. Nadel, A., Ryvchin, V.: Chronological backtracking. In: Beyersdorff, O., Wintersteiger, C.M. (eds.) SAT 2018. LNCS, vol. 10929, pp. 111–121. Springer, Cham (2018). https://doi.org/10.1007/978-3-319-94144-8_7
36. Oh, C.: Between SAT and UNSAT: the fundamental difference in CDCL SAT. In: Heule, M., Weaver, S. (eds.) SAT 2015. LNCS, vol. 9340, pp. 307–323. Springer, Cham (2015). https://doi.org/10.1007/978-3-319-24318-4_23
37. Ohrimenko, O., Stuckey, P.J., Codish, M.: Propagation via lazy clause generation. Constraints Int. J. **14**(3), 357–391 (2009). https://doi.org/10.1007/s10601-008-9064-x

38. Piette, C., Hamadi, Y., Saïs, L.: Vivifying propositional clausal formulae. In: ECAI, pp. 525–529 (2008)
39. Pipatsrisawat, K., Darwiche, A.: A lightweight component caching scheme for satisfiability solvers. In: Marques-Silva, J., Sakallah, K.A. (eds.) SAT 2007. LNCS, vol. 4501, pp. 294–299. Springer, Heidelberg (2007). https://doi.org/10.1007/978-3-540-72788-0_28
40. Ryan, L.: Efficient algorithms for clause-learning SAT solvers. Master's thesis, School of Computing Science, Simon Fraser University (2004)
41. Zhang, X., Cai, S.: Relaxed backtracking with rephasing. In: Proceedings of SAT Competition 2020, vol. B-2020-1, pp. 15–16 (2020)

Projection Heuristics for Binary Branchings Between Sum and Product

Oliver Kullmann[(✉)] and Oleg Zaikin[(✉)]

Swansea University, Swansea, UK
{O.Kullmann,O.S.Zaikin}@Swansea.ac.uk

Abstract. We consider a fundamental problem in the theory of branching heuristics for tree-based solvers, applicable e.g. to SAT, #SAT, CSP, #CSP. Such tree-based solvers are used as the cubing-part in the Cube-and-Conquer paradigm, and are thus of renewed interest for general (#)SAT solving. These solvers build at least implicitly a branching (backtracking) tree, with the goal to minimise tree-size. The heuristics are based on evaluating the progress made in a transition from an instance F to some "simplified" F' by a distance $d(F, F')$ (the bigger the more progress). When a branching $(F'_1, \ldots, F'_k)$ is to be chosen for F, for each possibility we consider its branching tuple t given by $t_i = d(F, F'_i)$, project it to a single number $\pi(t)$, and choose a branching with minimal $\pi(t)$. This paper investigates the choices for $\pi(t)$, in a theoretical framework. The general theory is reviewed, together with the theoretical result on the "canonical projection" $\pi(t) = \tau(t)$. Focusing then on binary branchings ($k = 2$, $t = (a, b)$), we analyse the asymptotics of $\tau(a, b)$, and reflect on the whole possible range of binary projections, arriving at first practical possibilities for dynamic heuristics.

1 Introduction

Historically, look-ahead solvers ([9,16]) were the first successful *complete* SAT solvers. With the rise of CDCL solvers ([17]), they went into oblivion, but the successful Cube-and-Conquer (C&C) framework ([11]) creates some space for them, since the efficient cubing (splitting) depends essentially on a good understanding of the branching process. Look-ahead solvers seem fundamentally tree-based: this restricts their power, but enables perfect parallelisation and a good understanding of the branching process (which needs to be aborted at some point – that's what C&C is doing, passing the task to the conquer-solver).

This paper starts a review of the fundamental theory of branching heuristics for tree-based solvers, looking especially at the question of what makes a "good projection": the heuristical measurement comes up with numbers for each branch, collected into a tuple of positive real numbers, a "branching tuple" t, and the "projection" $\pi(t)$ combines these numbers into a single number, which is to be minimised (maximised) to find the best branching variable. Obviously

O. Kullmann and O. Zaikin—Supported by EPSRC grant EP/S015523/1.

C.-M. Li and F. Manyà (Eds.): SAT 2021, LNCS 12831, pp. 299–314, 2021.
https://doi.org/10.1007/978-3-030-80223-3_21

the projection π is not unique, but what about the induced linear order? In the chapter [16] of the Handbook of Satisfiability on Branching Heuristics, it is outlined that under the assumption, that the branching width k is arbitrarily large, the induced linear ordering is indeed unique, given various natural axiomatic requirements on the consistency of the ordering. We review and extend these basic statements, and provide a proof for the existence and uniqueness of the canonical ordering, in a simplified setting. The canonical ordering is given by the canonical projection, the tau-function $\tau(t)$. Concentrating on binary branching, as in (#)SAT, i.e., $k = 2$, we analyse this fundamental function, and show how to (relatively) efficiently compute $\tau(a, b)$ (with high precision).

When only binary branchings are considered, then the uniqueness-result in fact does not apply (at least not directly). In practice an "approximation" to the tau-function is used, the product (i.e., $(a, b) \mapsto a \cdot b$, which is then to be maximised), improving on the earlier use of the sum. When standardised to form a (generalised) mean, then indeed τ lies in the interval given by the product- and the sum-projections. We consider a range of possible alternative projections in this interval. The final target is an understanding of the many parameters involved, so that they can be chosen offline and/or optimised online to yield efficient SAT solvers, based on proper dynamic heuristics.

Before we come to an outline of this paper, we review some recent literature. The basic method of trees with branching tuples (called "metric trees" in this paper), allowing the branching tuples to contain any positive *real* numbers, is a fundamental tool in the field of exponential upper bounds for algorithms; see [7] for an overview on that field, and see [8] for applications to bounds on circuit size and #SAT. Practical applications include solving vehicle routing problems ([19]), and solving the minimum latency problem ([5]). In [2,4] a similar but restricted branching theory was developed, only considering binary branchings with natural numbers as distances (which in turn allows stronger tools from the theory of recurrences), in the context of branch-and-bound algorithms for MIP.

An outline of the paper is as follows: Sect. 2 reviews the general theory, and provides a proof of the fundamental Lemma 1 on the composition of branching tuples, missing from the literature. The basic Theorem 1 on estimating tree sizes (known since [15]) gets a new proof, and we apply it to control the growth of trees based upon a single branching tuple. Section 3 proves Theorem 2 on the uniqueness of the order of branching tuples, given natural axioms. Corollary 1 gives a formulation suitable for restricted branching width (as used by SAT solvers). Section 4 then studies the binary tau-function, obtaining sharp asymptotic bounds and a method for fast computation. Section 5 finally considers the whole range of possibilities for binary projections, and we conclude in Sect. 6 by a summary and an outlook on future applications.

2   Branching Tuples and Distances

In this section we review the relevant elements of the theory of branching heuristics (for look-ahead solvers), as given in [16]. In Subsect. 2.1 we speak about the background, the (abstract) backtracking tree T of a look-ahead solver, whose size we want to minimise (by polytime means). "Minimising the size" refers to the construction of T, by recursively expanding a node v into its children $w_1, \ldots, w_k$. This is guided by attaching numerical information to each branch, the "distances" $d(v, w_i) > 0$, a positive real number, the greater the more progress was made. A simple example for a distance is measuring the number of variables eliminated in the branch $v \rightsquigarrow w_i$. This numerical information is collected per node in the associated branching tuple $d(v)$. For the actual choice of the branching, in the context of the solving process (note that T is the final result of this process, while d records the progress measurements for the branching chosen by the solver), we assume that a list of branching tuples is given, and a selection is done by minimising the "projected value" of each branching tuple $d(v)$; that there is a canonical choice for a projection is shown in Sect. 3, based on the general theory on tree sizes reviewed in Subsect. 2.2. A fundamental lemma is presented in Lemma 1, connecting the canonical projection of the branching tuples in a tree with the canonical projection of the flattening of the whole tree into a single branching tuple. This lemma is implicit in [16, Lemma 7.5.1], but there is no proof of it in the literature, and the concept of "flattening a tree" is a new device introduced here, simplifying certain aspects of the theory. For the basic Theorem 1 on bounds of tree sizes (which was introduced in [15]), we get in this way a new proof (the proof of [16, Theorem 7.4.8] is based on tree-probability distributions, which are not needed in this paper). This section is concluded by lemmas on expansions of branching tuples into trees, such that a strong handle on the tree sizes and other data are obtained.

2.1 Trees and Distances

The basic object is a *rooted tree* T, which we treat as (special) directed (finite) acyclic graph (dag) with exactly one source. So as a digraph we have the set $V(T)$ of vertices, which we denote here as the set of nodes $\mathrm{nds}(T) := V(T)$. The unique source (the node with no in-neighbours) is denoted by $\mathrm{rt}(T) \in \mathrm{nds}(T)$. The special property of T, which makes it a rooted tree, is that from $\mathrm{rt}(T)$ there is exactly one path to every node of T. As usual we denote by $E(T) \subset \mathrm{nds}(T) \times \mathrm{nds}(T)$ the set of arcs (directed from the root towards the leaves).

Every node $v \in \mathrm{nds}(T)$ has a set $\mathrm{chd}_T(v) \subset \mathrm{nds}(T)$ of children (the out-neighbours of v). The number of children of a node is its degree, denoted by $\deg_T(v) := |\mathrm{chd}(v)| \in \mathbb{N}_0$. The leaves of T are the sinks of T, and the set of leaves is denoted by $\mathrm{lvs}(T) := \{v \in \mathrm{nds}(T) : \mathrm{chd}(v) = \emptyset\} \subseteq \mathrm{nds}(T)$; obviously $v \in \mathrm{lvs}(T) \Leftrightarrow \deg_T(v) = 0$. An inner node of T is a node which is not a leaf, and we use $\mathrm{inds}(T) := \mathrm{nds}(T) \setminus \mathrm{lvs}(T)$ for the set of all inner nodes. To avoid technical difficulties we assume that T has no single-child nodes, that is, for every $v \in \mathrm{inds}(T)$ we have $\deg(v) \geq 2$. The main complexity measure here is $\#\mathrm{nds}(T) := |\mathrm{nds}(T)| \in \mathbb{N}$, the number of nodes of T. Sometimes it is more convenient to consider $\#\mathrm{lvs}(T) := |\mathrm{lvs}(T)| \leq \#\mathrm{nds}(T)$, the number of leaves. By definition holds $\#\mathrm{nds}(T) = \#\mathrm{lvs}(T) + |\mathrm{inds}(T)|$. In a full binary tree (i.e., all inner nodes have degree two) we have $\#\mathrm{nds}(T) = 2 \#\mathrm{lvs}(T) - 1$ and

$|\mathrm{inds}(T)| = \#\mathrm{lvs}(T) - 1$. To be able to speak of the *tuple* of children of an inner node, we make the further assumption that we have *ordered* trees; we could avoid that by using multisets, however using tuples seems more natural in our context. Technically this is handled by considering one infinite linearly ordered set $(\mathcal{U}, \leq)$ (for example $\mathcal{U} = \mathbb{N}$ with the natural order) as the universe of vertices, that is, for every rooted tree T we have $V(T) \subset \mathcal{U}$. When we use now $\mathrm{chd}(v) = \{w_1, \ldots, w_k\}$, then we assume from now one that $w_1 < \cdots < w_k$ (and thus $k = \deg(v)$). As the induced linear order on $\mathrm{lvs}(T)$ we use the lexicographical order as given by the paths from the root to the leaves (that is, the order of the leaves as they show up in the inorder traversal of T); we could use any other linear order on the leaves, but this order lets us avoid certain abstractions here.

The main examples of such trees T are given by the branching trees (back-tracking trees) of look-ahead solvers. At the leaves of T we might have the solved nodes (where either unsatisfiability was determined, or a (partial) satisfying assignment was found), or the nodes as given to a conquer-solver in the C&C setting. For #SAT-solving we naturally have to consider the *whole* tree (as is done in this paper), since we need to count all solutions. For SAT-solving, considering the whole tree means that the basis for the heuristic is the unsatisfiable case (without early abortion by finding a satisfying assignment). This is a natural point of view, since complete SAT-solvers are intrinsically unsatisfiability-driven, while the possible short-cuts for (just) finding a single satisfiable assignment are handled by the choice of the first branch; see [16, Section 7.9] and [9, Subsection 5.3.2] for information on this in the context of look-ahead solvers. We remark that we exclude single-child nodes, since they correspond to an actual reduction performed (no branching occurred), and can be contracted into the parent node.

The basic building block of the branching heuristic, from the theoretical side, is given by a **distance** on T, a map $d : E(T) \to \mathbb{R}_{>0}$ labelling every arc with a positive real number. The intuitive meaning of $d((v, w)) = d(v, w) > 0$ is that it measures the progress made in the transition from v to its child $w \in \mathrm{chd}(v)$. More generally, for any (undirected) graph G and a mapping $d : E(G) \to \mathbb{R}_{>0}$ we obtain a metric, which is a map $d : V(G)^2 \to \mathbb{R}_{\geq 0}$, by defining $d(v, w)$ for arbitrary $v, w \in V(G)$ as the minimum weighted length of a path between v and w. So a distance d on a (rooted, directed) tree T induces a metric, using the underlying (undirected) graph. Thus for $v, w \in \mathrm{nds}(T)$ we have $d(v, w) = d(v, c) + d(c, w)$ for the common ancestor c of v, w in T, and where $d(v, c) = d(c, v)$ resp. $d(c, w)$ is the sum of d-values of arcs on the unique path from c to v resp. w. In this paper we don't travel paths against the direction of the arcs, but the terminology of a "metric tree" for a pair (T, d) is nevertheless a natural choice:

Definition 1. *A **nontrivial rooted tree** T here is a dag $T = (V, E)$ with $V \subset \mathcal{U}$ and $E \subseteq V \times V$ with exactly one source, where the underlying graph is a tree (connected and acyclic), where every inner node has at least two children, and with $\#\mathrm{nds}(T) = |V(T)| \geq 3$. A **distance** on T is a map $d : E(T) \to \mathbb{R}_{>0}$. Pairs (T, d) are called **metric trees**, and the set of all metric trees is $\mathcal{MT}$. For an inner node v with $\mathrm{chd}(v) = \{w_1, \ldots, w_k\}$ the **associated branching tuple***

$d(v) := (d(v, w_1), \ldots, d(v, w_k)) \in \mathbb{R}_{>0}^{\deg(v)}$ *is the tuple of distances from v to its children (using the given linear order on the children).*

As T is the final result of the run of the look-ahead solver, the branching tuple $d(v)$ only records the distances for the (final) choices as made by the algorithm for the branchings. In the process of recursively expanding v, the setting is that the solver actually sees for every possible branching a corresponding branching tuple, and the solver chooses one of them; the distance on T then records this choice, while for the solver a distance $d(F, F')$ between problem instances is needed to construct the branching tuples. The object of study of this paper is not d (which we assume is given), but the choice of "the best" branching tuple. For more information on distances d as used in (look-ahead) SAT solvers see [9, Subsection 5.3.1] and [16, Section 7.7].

So we consider now branching tuples in isolation (later in Subsect. 2.2 we introduce the "canonical projection", which cans the branching tuple into a single number, the smaller the better). Let $\boldsymbol{BT} := \bigcup_{k \geq 2} BT_k$, $\boldsymbol{BT_k} := \mathbb{R}_{>0}^k$ be the set of all branching tuples, i.e., all tuples of positive real numbers of width (length) $k \geq 2$. We use the following natural operations for $t \in BT_k$:

- $|t| := k \in \mathbb{N}_{\geq 2}$ is the length of t;
- $\min(t), \max(t) \in \mathbb{R}_{>0}$ are the minimal resp. maximal values;
- $\Sigma(t) := \sum_{i=1}^{|t|} t_i \in \mathbb{R}_{>0}$ is the sum of all values.

We emphasise that branching tuples contain arbitrary positive *real* numbers, and so the theory is a generalisation of the theory of recurrences, which only consider branching tuples with natural numbers as entries.

From metric trees we extract the set of branching tuples, and for a set of branching tuples we consider the set of all metric trees using only these tuples:

Definition 2. *For* $(T, d) \in \mathcal{MT}$ *let* $\boldsymbol{BT}(\boldsymbol{T}, \boldsymbol{d}) := \{d(v) : v \in \mathrm{inds}(T)\} \subset BT$ *be the (finite) set of branching tuples associated with the inner nodes. And for* $B \subseteq BT$ *let* $\boldsymbol{MT}(\boldsymbol{B}) := \{T \in \mathcal{MT} : BT(T) \subseteq B\}$ *be the (infinite) set of metric trees, where all associated branching tuples are in B.*

A tree with a distance can be flattened to a single branching tuple, forgetting the branching structure:

Definition 3. *For* $T \in \mathcal{MT}$ *let the branching tuple* $\mathbf{fl}(\boldsymbol{T}) \in BT_{\#\mathrm{lvs}(T)}$ *contain for each leaf* $v \in \mathrm{lvs}(T)$ *the sum of distances from* $\mathrm{rt}(T)$ *to* v, *that is, for* $\mathrm{lvs}(T) = \{w_1, \ldots, w_{\#\mathrm{lvs}(T)}\}$ *we set* $\mathrm{fl}(T) := (d(\mathrm{rt}(T), w_1), \ldots, d(\mathrm{rt}(T), w_{\#\mathrm{lvs}(T)}))$.

Example 1. For the metric tree

$$T :=$$

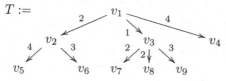

we have

1. $\#\mathrm{nds}(T) = 9$, $\#\mathrm{lvs}(T) = 6$, $|\mathrm{inds}(T)| = 3$.
2. $BT(T) = \{(2, 1, 4), (4, 3), (2, 2, 3)\}$.
3. $\mathrm{fl}(T) = (2 + 4, 2 + 3, \ 1 + 2, 1 + 2, 1 + 3, \ 4) = (6, 5, 3, 3, 4, 4)$.

2.2 The Tau-Function and Bounds on Tree Sizes

Generalising the notion of a root of a "characteristic polynomial" from the theory of recurrences, the "tau-function" is a fundamental tool:

Definition 4. *For $t \in \mathcal{BT}$ we define the characteristic function $\chi_t : \mathbb{R}_{>0} \to \mathbb{R}_{>0}$ by $\chi(t)(x) := \sum_{i=1}^{|t|} x^{-t_i}$. Since $\chi(t)$ is strictly decreasing with $\chi(t)(1) = |t| \geq 2$ and $\lim_{x \to \infty} \chi(t)(x) = 0$, there is exactly one $x_0 \in \mathbb{R}_{>1}$ with $\chi(t)(x_0) = 1$, and we define $\tau(t) := x_0$.*

So $\tau(t) \lesseqgtr x$ for $x > 0$ iff $\chi(t)(x) \gtreqless 1$. The basic intuition behind $\tau : \mathcal{BT} \to \mathbb{R}_{>1}$ can be grasped by considering the "main" solution to a difference equation: One seeks a function $f : \mathbb{N}_0 \to \mathbb{R}_{\geq 0}$ satisfying for some given $a \in \mathbb{N}^k$ a recurrence $\forall n \in \mathbb{N}_0, n \geq a_i : f(n) = \sum_{i=1}^{k} f(n - a_i)$. For example the Fibonacci recurrence $f(n) = f(n-1) + f(n-2)$ is given by $k = 2$ and $a = (1, 2)$. Now $f(n) := \tau(a)^n$ fulfils the recurrence, since $\sum_{i=1}^{k} \tau(a)^{-a_i} = 1$, and multiplying both sides with $\tau(a)^n$ yields $\tau(a)^n = f(n) = \sum_{i=1}^{k} \tau(a)^{n-a_i} = \sum_{i=1}^{k} f(n - a_i)$. Basic properties for $a \in \mathcal{BT}$, $\lambda \in \mathbb{R}_{>0}$ and the restriction $\tau_k := \tau \mid \mathcal{BT}_k$ are (all with easy proofs):

1. τ_k is symmetric (invariant under permutation).
2. τ_k is strictly decreasing in each component.
3. $\tau_k(1, \ldots, 1) = k$.
4. If t is a proper prefix of t' then $\tau(t) < \tau(t')$.
5. $\tau(\lambda \cdot a) = \tau(a)^{1/\lambda}$, $\tau(a)^{\min(a)} \leq |a| \leq \tau(a)^{\max(a)}$.

An important property of all τ_k is that they are strictly convex, that is for all $a, b \in \mathcal{BT}_k$ and $0 < \lambda < 1$ holds $\tau((1 - \lambda)a + \lambda b) < (1 - \lambda)\tau(a) + \lambda \tau(b)$ (this requires more work to check). This implies for example that $\tau(2, 2) < \tau(1, 3)$, using $a := (1, 3)$, $b := (3, 1)$ and $\lambda := 0.5$. Strict convexity is a generalisation of the "penalty" given to "imbalanced" branching tuples, due to the inherent exponential growth: Comparing e.g. (x, x) with $(x - \varepsilon, x + \varepsilon)$, the former is better since the loss in the branch $x - \varepsilon$ is bigger than the win in the branch $x + \varepsilon$, due to the convexity of exponential functions. A simple sufficient criterion for deriving $\tau(a) \leq \tau(b)$ is obtained by using symmetry, monotonicity and the prefix condition; we condense this into the following order relation:

Definition 5. *The order-relation $a \lesssim b$ ("a is trivially smaller than b") holds for $a, b \in \mathcal{BT}$ if the following three conditions are fulfilled: (1) $|a| \leq |b|$; (2) there is a permutation a' of a, such that for all $i \in \{1, \ldots, |a|\}$ holds $a_i \geq b_i$; (3) either $|a| < |b|$ or there is $i \in \{1, \ldots, |a|\}$ with $a_i' > b_i$.*

Some simple properties of the trivially-smaller-relation ("trivially better") are:

1. $\lesssim$ is a strict partial order on $\mathcal{BT}$ (i.e., irreflexive ($a \not\lesssim a$) and transitive ($a \lesssim b \wedge b \lesssim c \Rightarrow a \lesssim c$)), without minimal or maximal elements.
2. If $a \lesssim b$ then $\tau(a) < \tau(b)$.
3. Sufficient criterion for $a \lesssim b$ are:
   (a) $|a| \leq |b| \wedge \min(a) > \max(b) \Rightarrow a \lesssim b$.
   (b) $|a| < |b| \wedge \min(a) \geq \max(b) \Rightarrow a \lesssim b$.

A fundamental lemma is that the tau-value for a flattened metric tree is in the interval given by minimum and maximum tau-values over the inner nodes; for a set of branching tuples B we use $\tau(B) := \{\tau(t) : t \in B\}$ in the usual way:

Lemma 1. *For $T \in \mathcal{MT}$ holds $\min \tau(\mathcal{BT}(T)) \leq \tau(\mathrm{fl}(T)) \leq \max \tau(\mathcal{BT}(T))$.*

Proof. Let $r := \mathrm{rt}(T)$. First consider the special case $|\mathrm{inds}(T)| = 2$. Let $a := d(r)$, and for the other inner node $v \in \mathrm{inds}(T) \setminus \{r\}$ let $b := d(v)$, while $c := \mathrm{fl}(T)$. W.l.o.g. we can assume that v is the first child of r, and thus, using $p := \deg(r)$ and $q := \deg(v)$ we have $c = (a_1 + b_1, \ldots, a_1 + b_q, a_2, \ldots, a_p)$. W.l.o.g. we further assume that $\tau(a) \leq \tau(b)$, and thus $\chi(b)(\tau(a)) \geq 1$ and $\chi(a)(\tau(b)) \leq 1$. So we have to show $\tau(a) \leq \tau(c) \leq \tau(b)$. The first inequality follows by

$$\chi(c)(\tau(a)) = \sum_{i=1}^{q} \tau(a)^{-a_1-b_i} + \sum_{i=2}^{p} \tau(a)^{-a_i} = \tau(a)^{-a_1} \cdot \sum_{i=1}^{q} \tau(a)^{-b_i} + \sum_{i=2}^{p} \tau(a)^{-a_i}$$

$$= \tau(a)^{-a_1} \cdot \chi(b)(\tau(a)) + \sum_{i=2}^{p} \tau(a)^{-a_i} \geq \tau(a)^{-a_1} + \sum_{i=2}^{p} \tau(a)^{-a_i} = 1,$$

and the second inequality follows by

$$\chi(c)(\tau(b)) = \sum_{i=1}^{q} \tau(b)^{-a_1-b_i} + \sum_{i=2}^{p} \tau(b)^{-a_i} = \tau(b)^{-a_1} \cdot \sum_{i=1}^{q} \tau(b)^{-b_i} + \sum_{i=2}^{p} \tau(b)^{-a_i}$$

$$= \tau(b)^{-a_1} + \sum_{i=2}^{p} \tau(b)^{-a_i} = \chi(a)(\tau(b)) \leq 1.$$

Now we prove the statement by induction over $n := |\mathrm{inds}(T)|$. For $n = 1$ we have $\mathrm{fl}(T) = d(r)$ and $\mathcal{BT}(T) = \{d(r)\}$, and thus the assertion trivially holds. It remains the case $n \geq 2$. Consider a node $v \in \mathrm{inds}(T)$ with $\mathrm{chd}(v) \subseteq \mathrm{lvs}(T)$. Let T' be the subtree of T with the leaves of v removed, that is, $V(T') = V(T) \setminus \mathrm{chd}(v)$ and $E(T') = E(T) \setminus \{(v, w) : w \in \mathrm{chd}(T)\}$. So $|\mathrm{inds}(T)| = n - 1$, and we can apply the induction hypothesis to T', that is, we have

$$\min \tau(\mathcal{BT}(T')) \leq \tau(\mathrm{fl}(T')) \leq \max \tau(\mathcal{BT}(T')).$$

We note that $\mathcal{BT}(T) = \mathcal{BT}(T') \cup \{d(v)\}$. Let T'' be the flattening of T' as a tree with one inner node, and so we have $\mathrm{fl}(T'') = \mathrm{fl}(T')$. We assume $\mathrm{rt}(T'') = r$ and $v \in \mathrm{lvs}(T'')$, and thus for the metric tree S obtained by attaching the branching of v in T to T'' we have $\mathrm{fl}(S) = \mathrm{fl}(T)$ and $\mathcal{BT}(S) = \{\mathrm{fl}(T'), d(v)\}$. We can apply the above special case to S and obtain $\min \tau(\mathcal{BT}(S)) \leq \tau(\mathrm{fl}(S)) \leq \max \tau(\mathcal{BT}(S))$. Finally we have $\min \tau(\mathcal{BT}(T)) = \min(\tau(\mathcal{BT}(T')) \cup \{d(v)\}) \leq \min(\{\tau(\mathrm{fl}(T'))\} \cup \{d(v)\}) = \min \tau(\mathcal{BT}(S))$, and similarly holds $\max \tau(\mathcal{BT}(S)) \geq \max(\tau(\mathcal{BT}(T)))$. $\square$

Example 2. For the metric tree

$$T :=$$

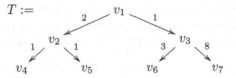

we have

1. $\mathcal{BT}(T) = \{(2,1),(1,1),(3,8)\}$.
2. $\mathrm{fl}(T) = (2+1, 2+1, 1+3, 1+8) = (3,3,4,9)$.
3. $\tau(\mathcal{BT}(T)) = \{1.618\ldots, 2, 1.1461\ldots\}$, $\tau(\mathrm{fl}(T)) = 1.4147\ldots$.

The global meaning of the tau-values of inner nodes over a tree with given distance is that they yield upper (and lower) bounds on the number of leaves, which is expressed by the following theorem (for which we give an alternative, simpler proof here):

Theorem 1 *[16, Theorem 7.4.8]. For $T \in \mathcal{MT}$ holds*

$$(\min \tau(\mathcal{BT}(T)))^{\min \mathrm{fl}(T)} \leq \#\mathrm{lvs}(T) \leq (\max \tau(\mathcal{BT}(T)))^{\max \mathrm{fl}(T)}.$$

Proof. Lemma 1 yields $(\min \tau(\mathcal{BT}(T)))^{\min \mathrm{fl}(T)} \leq \tau(\mathrm{fl}(T))^{\min \mathrm{fl}(T)} \leq |\mathrm{fl}(T)| = \#\mathrm{lvs}(T) \leq \tau(\mathrm{fl}(T))^{\max \mathrm{fl}(T)} \leq (\max \tau(\mathcal{BT}(T)))^{\max \mathrm{fl}(T)}$. $\square$

Theorem 1 gives a global meaning to the target for the branching heuristics to choose branchings with associated branching tuples t minimising $\tau(t)$. Of course, this only makes sense for a "sensible" distance d, with $\max \mathrm{fl}(T)$ being a reasonable parameter of the input. Our main application of Theorem 1 is to show that branching tuples t, t' with $\tau(t) < \tau(t')$ can be expanded so that the tau-relation becomes trivial:

Definition 6. *An **expansion** of $t \in \mathcal{BT}$ is any $\mathrm{fl}(T) \in \mathcal{BT}$ for $T \in \mathcal{MT}(\{t\})$.*

So for any expansion t' of t we have $\tau(t') = \tau(t)$.

Lemma 2. *For $t \in \mathcal{BT}$ and $K \in \mathbb{R}_{\geq \max(t)}$ there exists an expansion t' of t with $\min(t') > K - \max(t)$, $\max(t') \leq K$, and $\tau(t)^{K-\max(t)} < |t'| \leq \tau(t)^K$.*

Proof. Consider any metric tree T with $\mathcal{BT}(T) = \{t\}$, such that $\max \mathrm{fl}(T) \leq K$, while T can not be expanded further (by expanding any leaf) without violating the bound $\max \mathrm{fl}(T) \leq K$; obviously such T exist, since one can start with t itself, and expand leaves as long as one stays below K. Let $t' := \mathrm{fl}(T)$. Then we have $\min(t') > K - \max(t)$, and by Theorem 1 we get $\tau(t)^{K-\max(t)} < |t'| \leq \tau(t)^K$. $\square$

Lemma 3. *For all $a, b \in \mathcal{BT}$ with $\tau(a) < \tau(b)$ there are expansions a' of a and b' of b with $a' \lneq b'$.*

Proof. Let $\alpha := \frac{\ln(\tau(b))}{\ln(\tau(a))}$ (thus $\alpha > 1$). Choose any $K_b \geq \frac{\max(a) + \alpha \cdot \max(b)}{\alpha - 1} > 0$. Thus for $\beta := K_b + \max(a)$ and $\gamma := \alpha \cdot (K_b - \max(b))$ holds $\beta \leq \gamma$, and we can choose (any) K_a with $\beta \leq K_a \leq \gamma$. By Lemma 2 there are expansions a', b' of a, b with

- $\min(a') > K_a - \max(a)$ and $|a'| \leq \tau(a)^{K_a}$;
- $\max(b') \leq K_b$ and $\tau(b)^{K_b - \max(b)} < |b'|$.

From $K_a \geq \beta$ we get $K_a - \max(a) \geq K_b$, and thus $\min(a') > \max(b')$. And from $K_a \leq \gamma$ we get $\tau(a)^{K_a} \leq \tau(b)^{K_b - \max(b)}$, and thus $|a'| < |b'|$. $\square$

3   The Canonical Order of Branching Tuples

As explained in Subsect. 2.2, the canonical projection $\tau(t)$ has a natural *global meaning*, namely it yields an upper bound on the number of leaves in the branching tree. Thus it makes sense to use $\tau(t)$ for projection, and observing its value should be also useful to monitor the state of the search. Here now we give its *local meaning*: the order on branching tuples as stipulated by τ is uniquely given by natural axioms on how we want the projection to behave when comparing different branching tuples. More precisely, recall that a total (or linear) quasi-order on a set X is a binary relation $\leq$ which is reflexive ($x \leq x$), transitive ($x \leq y \wedge y \leq z \Rightarrow x \leq z$) and total ($x \leq y \vee y \leq x$). By defining $t \leq_\tau t' :\Leftrightarrow \tau(t) \leq \tau(t')$ we obtain a total quasi-order on $\mathcal{BT}$ (the smaller the "better"). The task of this section is to give an intrinsic characterisation of this order. This is achieved in Theorem 2, which is equivalent to [16, Theorem 7.5.3], but there is no proof there, while here we give a complete proof. Based on the notion of expansions, we can also provide a natural formulation for the case of restricted width of branching tuples.

What are now the axioms for comparing branching tuples? Consider a total quasi-order $\preceq$ on $\mathcal{BT}$. As usual we define $t \simeq t'$ if $t \preceq t'$ and $t' \preceq t$ ($\simeq$ is an equivalence relation on $\mathcal{BT}$), and $t \prec t'$ if $t \preceq t'$ and $t \not\simeq t'$. We call it a **canonical branching order** if it fulfils the following four properties for all $t, t' \in \mathcal{BT}$:

(S) Symmetry For a permutation t' of t holds $t \simeq t'$.
(E) Expansion If t' is an expansion of t then $t' \simeq t$.
(T) Trivial comparison If $t \leq t'$ then $t \prec t'$.
(D) Density For $t \prec t'$ there is $\varepsilon > 0$ such that $t - \varepsilon \in \mathcal{BT}$ and $t - \varepsilon \prec t'$.

For (D) we used $t - \varepsilon := (t_1 - \varepsilon, \ldots, t_{|t|} - \varepsilon)$.

Theorem 2. *There is exactly one canonical branching order, namely $\leq_\tau$.*

Proof. $\leq_\tau$ is a canonical branching order by Lemma 1 and continuity of τ (for fixed branching-width). Now consider any canonical branching order $\preceq$ and $a, b \in \mathcal{BT}$, where we assume w.l.o.g. $a \preceq b$. In case of $\tau(a) < \tau(b)$ by Lemma 3 there are expansions a', b' with $a' \leq b'$. Thus by (E) and (T) we get $a \simeq a' \prec b' \simeq b$. It remains the case $\tau(a) = \tau(b)$. If $a \simeq b$, then we are done, so assume w.l.o.g. $a \prec b$. By (D), (T) there is $\varepsilon > 0$ with $a \prec a - \varepsilon \prec b$. We have $\tau(a) < \tau(a - \varepsilon)$, and thus $\tau(b) < \tau(a - \varepsilon)$, whence by the first part $b \prec a - \varepsilon$, a contradiction. $\square$

Corollary 1. *For $k \in \mathbb{N}$, $k \geq 2$, the canonical branching order $\leq_\tau$ restricted to $\mathcal{BT}_k$ is uniquely determined by the conditions (S), (T), (D) and*

(E_k) *If for $a, b \in \mathcal{BT}_k$ there are expansions a', b' with $a' \leq b'$, then $a \prec b$.*

Proof. The proof of Theorem 2 works as well. $\square$

4   Analysis and Numerics of Binary Tau

In the remainder of this paper we focus on binary branchings ($k = 2$). In this section we first concentrate $\tau(a, b)$ to its essential core $w\tau(x)$, and show in Lemma 4, that this core is asymptotically very close to a well-known special function, the Lambert-W function. This enables us in Theorem 4 to give good lower and upper bounds for $w\tau(x)$ by elementary functions. Using these bounds as starting points for the Newton-Raphson algorithm, only very few iterations are needed to compute $w\tau(x)$ (and thus $\tau(a, b)$) with full precision (the observed worst-case precision for double is two ulp's, that is, nearly precise in the last machine-digit).

At least for numerical reasons it seems better to consider the logarithm of the tau-function, denoted by $l\tau : \mathcal{BT} \to \mathbb{R}_{>0}$, and defined by $l\tau(t) := \ln(\tau(t))$ (using the natural logarithm). This replaces the computation of arbitrary powers $(x, y) \mapsto x^y$ by the computation of the exponential function $(x, y) \mapsto \exp(x \cdot y)$. It seems indeed best to compute $l\tau(t)$ directly, and then to use $\tau(t) = \exp(l\tau(t))$: $l\tau(t)$ is the unique $x \in \mathbb{R}_{>0}$ such that $\sum_{i=1}^{|t|} \exp(-t_i \cdot x) = 1$. We now have $l\tau(\lambda \cdot t) = \frac{1}{\lambda} \cdot l\tau(t)$ and $l\tau_k(1, \ldots, 1) = \ln(k)$.

We see that $\mathfrak{T}(t) := \frac{\ln(|t|)}{l\tau(t)}$ fulfils $\mathfrak{T}(\lambda \cdot t) = \lambda \cdot \mathfrak{T}(t)$ and $\min(t) \leq \mathfrak{T}(t) \leq \max(t)$. Indeed $\mathfrak{T} : \mathcal{BT} \to \mathbb{R}_{>0}$ has further properties of a (general) "mean", as shown in [16, Section 7.3.3]. We will discuss some further properties of such means in Subsect. 5.1. Here for us only the bounds on $\mathfrak{T}(t)$ from [16, Theorem 7.3.4] are relevant. In general we have $\mathfrak{T}(t) \leq \frac{\Sigma(t)}{|t|}$, that is mean-tau is at most the arithmetic mean. We remark that $\mathfrak{T}(t)$ for fixed $|t|$ is strictly concave.

In the remainder of this paper we concentrate on $l\tau_2 : \mathcal{BT}_2 \to \mathbb{R}_{>0}$, as this is at least currently most important for SAT solving. So $l\tau(a, b)$ is the unique $x > 0$ with $\exp(-a \cdot x) + \exp(-b \cdot y) = 1$. It is an elementary exercise to show that $\mathfrak{T}(a, b) \geq \sqrt{a \cdot b}$ holds, that is, binary mean-tau is at least the geometric mean. Indeed it seems fastest and most accurate to not compute $l\tau(a, b)$ directly, but to eliminate one argument of $l\tau(a, b)$; we use the form which yields a strictly increasing function:

Definition 7. *For $x \in \mathbb{R}_{>0}$:* $\mathbf{w\tau(x)} := l\tau(1, \frac{1}{x}) \in \mathbb{R}_{>0}$.

We have the following easy properties:

1. $w\tau(x) = l\tau(1, \frac{1}{x}) = x \cdot l\tau(1, x)$, $w\tau(x^{-1}) = x^{-1} w\tau(x)$.
2. $w\tau$ is strictly increasing with $\lim_{x \to 0} w\tau(x) = 0$ and $\lim_{x \to +\infty} w\tau(x) = +\infty$.
3. $w\tau(1) = \ln(2)$, $w\tau(2) = 2 \ln(\frac{1+\sqrt{5}}{2})$, $w\tau(\frac{1}{2}) = \ln(\frac{1+\sqrt{5}}{2})$.
4. $l\tau(a, b) = \frac{1}{a} l\tau(1, \frac{b}{a}) = \frac{1}{a} w\tau(\frac{a}{b})$.
5. The characteristic equation for $w\tau(a)$, $a \in \mathbb{R}_{>0}$, and $x \in \mathbb{R}_{>0}$ is

$$\exp(-x) + \exp(-\frac{x}{a}) = 1.$$

The above mentioned bounds, that $\mathfrak{T}(a, b)$ lies between the geometric and the arithmetic mean, yields elementary bounds for $w\tau(x)$:

$$\frac{\ln 4}{1 + x^{-1}} = \ln(4) \frac{x}{x + 1} \leq w\tau(x) \leq \ln(2)\sqrt{x}.$$

We will see that asymptotically $wr(x) \sim \ln(x)$, and thus these bounds are very bad for large x. The best bounds on $wr(x)$ for larger x seem to be obtained by using the principal branch of the Lambert-W function (see [18, Section 4.13]). This is a function $W : \mathbb{R}_{\geq 0} \to \mathbb{R}_{\geq 0}$, defined for $a \in \mathbb{R}_{\geq 0}$ as the unique $x \in \mathbb{R}_{\geq 0}$ with $x \cdot \exp(x) = a$. Thus $W(a) \cdot \exp(W(a)) = a$, $\exp(W(a)) = \frac{a}{W(a)}$, $W(a) = \frac{a}{\exp(W(a))}$, and $\exp(-W(a)) = \frac{W(a)}{a}$ for $a > 0$. Simple values are $W(a) = 0$ iff $a = 0$, $W(e) = 1$, and more generally $W(x \cdot \exp(x)) = x$.

Before we can show the close relation between $wr(x)$ and $W(x)$, we remind at a few elementary properties:

1. For all $x \in \mathbb{R}$: $\exp(x) \geq 1 + x$.
2. Thus for all $x \in \mathbb{R}_{>-1}$: $\exp(-x) \leq \frac{1}{1+x}$.
3. For all $x \in \mathbb{R} \setminus \{0, -1\}$: $\frac{1}{1+x} + \frac{1}{1+\frac{1}{x}} = 1$.

The following relation was pointed out in the discussion [13]:

Lemma 4. *For all $x \in \mathbb{R}_{>0}$ holds $W(x) \leq wr(x) \leq \ln(\exp(W(x)) + 1)$.*

Proof. We show lower and upper bound by substitution into the characteristic equation for wr. First we have $\exp(-W(x)) + \exp(-\frac{1}{x}W(x)) = \frac{W(x)}{x} + \exp(-\frac{1}{x}W(x)) \geq \frac{W(x)}{x} + (1 + -\frac{1}{x}W(x)) = 1$, and thus $W(x) \leq wr(x)$. The upper bound follows similarly:

$$\exp(-\ln(\exp(W(x)) + 1)) + \exp(-\frac{1}{x}\ln(\exp(W(x)) + 1)) =$$

$$\frac{1}{1 + \exp(W(x))} + \exp(-\frac{1}{x}\ln(\exp(W(x)) + 1)) \leq$$

$$\frac{1}{1 + \exp(W(x))} + \frac{1}{1 + \frac{1}{x}\ln(\exp(W(x)) + 1)} \leq$$

$$\frac{1}{1 + \exp(W(x))} + \frac{1}{1 + \frac{1}{x}\ln(\exp(W(x)))} = \frac{1}{1 + \exp(W(x))} + \frac{1}{1 + \frac{1}{x}W(x)} =$$

$$\frac{1}{1 + \exp(W(x))} + \frac{1}{1 + \frac{1}{\exp(W(x))}} = 1.$$

$\square$

So $wr(x)$ is asymptotically equal to $W(x)$. Indeed not just $\lim_{x \to \infty} \frac{wr(x)}{W(x)} = 1$, but also $\lim_{x \to \infty} wr(x) - W(x) = 0$. The best bounds on $W(x)$ seem to be as follows:

Theorem 3 (*[12], Theorems 2.5, 2.7*). *For $x \in \mathbb{R}_{>1}$ holds:*

$$(\ln x - \ln \ln x + 1)\frac{\ln x}{1 + \ln x} \leq W(x).$$

While for $x \in \mathbb{R}_{\geq e}$ holds:

$$W(x) \leq \ln x - \ln \ln x + \frac{e}{e-1}\frac{\ln \ln x}{\ln x}.$$

Thus $\lim_{x\to\infty} \frac{W(x)}{\ln(x)} = 1$, and so also $\lim_{x\to\infty} \frac{w\tau(x)}{\ln(x)} = 1$. We summarise the elementary bounds for $w\tau(x)$:

Theorem 4. *For $x \in \mathbb{R}_{>1}$ holds*

$$\max\left(\frac{\ln 4}{1+x^{-1}}, (\ln x - \ln\ln x + 1)\frac{\ln x}{1+\ln x}\right) \le w\tau(x)$$

$$\le \min\left(\ln(2)\sqrt{x}, \ln\left(\frac{x\cdot(1+\ln x)}{(\ln x - \ln\ln x + 1)\ln x} + 1\right)\right).$$

The first parts of the min- and max are used in the bounds only for very small x (less than 3; but for these x they are crucial), while for large x the second parts are (much) better (indeed very accurate). Using the lower bound of Theorem 4 to compute $w\tau(x)$ via Newton-Raphson iteration (which will converge monotonically from below to $w\tau(x)$, with quadratic convergence), yields very good results: The hardest cases are for say $x \le 1000$, with the maximum observed iterations until fixed-point (typically with one ulp precision, observed never more than two ulp) being six iterations, while the average case for usual SAT-solving seems to be around 3.5 iterations (always for full precision). Not using the bounds obtained by Lambert-W means for x in usual SAT ranges hundreds of iterations, and for very large x thousands of iterations.

We conclude by mentioning that in [14] an algorithm for computing the canonical order of branching tuples is stated, which aims at avoiding to compute the (l)tau-value explicitly, by using the characteristic functions to only perform Newton-Raphson iteration when needed. If this does not start with a good bound, then however this takes, as with the (l)tau-computation, many iterations. And for binary branching tuples, as we have seen above, the number of iterations is now, with the very good bounds, very low anyway, and thus such an approach seems only needed for non-binary branching tuples. For the best branching tuple found, one may want to compute the (l)tau-value anyway, due to its global value, making it possible to monitor the overall progress of the search.

5   On Binary Projections

Practical experience shows that in most cases the maximum-projection (i.e., target is to maximise) $(a,b) \in \mathcal{BT}_2 \mapsto a\cdot b$ is much better than $(a,b) \in \mathcal{BT}_2 \mapsto a + b$. Why is this the case? [16, Section 7.6] offers two explanations: On the one hand, based on Theorem 1 it is argued, that maximising the sum is like maximising a lower bound on the tree-size, while maximising the product is like minimising an upper bound on tree-size, which is intrinsically more meaningful; this argument makes sense, but is purely qualitatively. On the other hand, [16, Lemma 7.6.1] states that the approximation of $\mathfrak{T}(a,b)$ by $\sqrt{a\cdot b}$ is better than the approximation by $\frac{a+b}{2}$, measured in terms of differences; this does not take into account the scale of numbers, and is thus not a very precise argument. We have also the fact that the arithmetic mean is linear (convex and concave), while the geometric mean is concave, which fits better to the expected superlinear growth. In this final section now we want to develop a more precise tool given by the "kernel" of a mean, and we show alternatives to sum, product and tau, by considering the p-mean for $0 \le p \le 1$ as some form of continuum between product and sum. The main argument why Corollary 1 possibly is not the final truth about binary projections is that the trees for concrete instances are not arbitrarily large (which is implicitly assumed in the proof of Corollary 1).

From the outset, one considers total quasi-orders $\prec$ on $\mathcal{BT}_2$ fulfilling (S), (T) and (D). By Corollary 1 we know that $\prec$ is $\le_\tau$ (restricted to binary branchings) iff $\prec$ is compatible with every trivial comparison obtain by expansion, i.e., (E$_2$) holds. We now consider whether there are interesting such orders $\prec$ without (E$_2$). To get a handle on different orderings, we consider maps $m : \mathcal{BT}_2 \to \mathbb{R}_{>0}$, such that $m(a, b)$ is to be *maximised*. In order to be able to compare the numerical values of such projections m, we standardise them to form "means", as we will discuss now (that's why we consider maximisation here instead of minimisation, which was needed for the tau-function).

5.1   On Means in General

The minimum requirements for a mean $m : \mathcal{BT}_2 \to \mathbb{R}_{>0}$ are:

1. $m(a, b) = m(b, a)$ (symmetry).
2. m is strictly increasing in each component.
3. $\min(a, b) \le m(a, b) \le \max(a, b)$ (consistency).

We additionally assume homogeneity here ("scale invariance"), that is, for $\lambda > 0$ holds $m(\lambda \cdot a, \lambda \cdot b) = \lambda \cdot m(a, b)$. As a further requirement, concavity is of importance, assuming that tree-growth is super-linear. We have mentioned three means already:

1. $m_0(a, b) := \sqrt{a \cdot b}$, the geometric mean: this is the default for SAT-solving (note that maximising $m_0(a, b)$ is equivalent to maximising $a \cdot b$).
2. $m_1(a, b) := \frac{a+b}{2}$, the arithmetic mean: this was the older default heuristic, and is typically still used for tie-braking.
3. $\mathfrak{T}(a, b) = \frac{\ln(2)}{\ln \tau(a,b)}$; we have $m_0(a, b) \le \mathfrak{T}(a, b) \le m_1(a, b)$.

A natural generalisation of m_0, m_1, as already considered in [16, Section 7.3.3] for obtaining bounds, are the p-means m_p for $p \in \mathbb{R}$. Since the sum is already bad enough (in most cases), in this initial study we do not go beyond m_1—and indeed m_p is strictly convex iff $p > 1$. We also don't go below the geometric mean, as that seems not fruitful in general (though on selected families of benchmarks this might be different). So we restrict our attention to $0 \le p \le 1$:

1. $m_p(a, b) := (\frac{a^p + b^p}{2})^{1/p}$ for $0 < p \le 1$.
2. $m_1(a, b)$ is the above arithmetic mean.
3. $m_p(a, b) \ge m_{p'}(a, b)$ for $p \ge p'$.
4. $\lim_{p \to 0} m_p(a, b) = m_0(a, b)$.

5.2   Comparing the Various Means by Their Kernels

Due to homogeneity, we can reduce means with two arguments to their "kernels",
which are functions in just one argument:

Definition 8. *For a mean* $m : \mathcal{BT}_2 \to \mathbb{R}_{>0}$ *let the **kernel** $\overline{m} : \mathbb{R}_{\geq 1} \to \mathbb{R}_{\geq 1}$ be
defined as* $\overline{m}(x) := m(1, x)$ *for* $x \geq 1$.

We assume in the following w.l.o.g. $0 < a \leq b$ (using symmetry). Due to homo-
geneity we have $m(a, b) = a \cdot \overline{m}(\frac{b}{a})$. From $m \geq m'$ follows $\overline{m} \geq \overline{m}'$, and thus we
have $\overline{m}_1 \geq \overline{m}_p \geq \overline{m}_0$ as well as $\overline{m}_1 \geq \overline{\mathfrak{T}} \geq \overline{m}_0$. The meaning of the kernel is as
follows:

- We measure the imbalance of $(a, b) \in \mathcal{BT}_2$ by the quotient $x := \frac{b}{a} \geq 1$ (the
  larger x, the greater the imbalance).
- $\frac{\overline{m}(x)}{\overline{m}(1)} = \overline{m}(x)$ is the "reward" given for having $(1, x)$ instead of just $(1, 1)$.
- Due to the standardisation via using means, we can indeed compare the
  kernel-values for different means p, q: if $\overline{p}(x) \geq \overline{q}(x)$, then the mean p gives a
  greater reward to x than the mean q.

The kernels of our means are as follows; we use the symbol $\sim$ here to denote
asymptotic equality (i.e., the quotient approaches 1 as x goes to infinity):

1. $\overline{m}_1(x) = \frac{1}{2} + \frac{x}{2} \sim \frac{x}{2}$.
2. $\overline{m}_p(x) = (\frac{1}{2} + \frac{x^p}{2})^{1/p} \sim \frac{x}{2^{1/p}}$.
3. $\overline{\mathfrak{T}}(x) = \frac{\ln(2)}{\mathrm{wr}(1/x)} = \ln(2)\frac{x}{\mathrm{wr}(x)} \sim \ln(2)\frac{x}{W(x)} \sim \ln(2)\frac{x}{\ln(x)} = \frac{x}{\log_2(x)}$.
4. $\overline{m}_0(x) = \sqrt{x}$.

m_1 gives the greatest reward, m_0 the smallest, while $m_p, \mathfrak{T}$ are incomparable in
general, but there is a clear picture: There is a threshold value $p_0 \approx 0.307$ (the
infimum of $0 \leq p \leq 1$ with $\overline{\mathfrak{T}} \leq \overline{m}_p$), where for $p > p_0$ the mean m_p always gives
a greater reward than $\mathfrak{T}$, while for $p < p_0$ first (i.e., small x) the reward given
by m_p is smaller, and then greater than the reward given by $\mathfrak{T}$ (and the smaller
p, the larger the first realm, being the whole range finally for $p = 0$).

   This paper concentrates on the basic theory, but we can report on the very
first experimental results. As look-ahead solver the simplest SAT-algorithm, the
DLL algorithm ([6]) was used, with a modern implementation and branching
heuristic as given by the `tawSolver` ([1]). The projections $\mathfrak{T}$ and m_p for $0 \leq p \leq 1$
were run on uniform random 3-SAT benchmarks, and compared by average size
of the corresponding backtracking trees. The optimal p obtained was $p \approx 0.26$,
which was still clearly worse here than $\mathfrak{T}$ (by 10%), while slightly better than m_0
(by 1%), and much better than m_1 (by 20%). Clearly the runtime for $\mathfrak{T}$ is higher,
up to a total runtime twice as much compared to m_0, but for a stronger look-
ahead solver (DLL indeed is the "zero-look-ahead look-ahead-solver"), which
spends much more time on each variable, the tau-computation would contribute
far less to the total runtime, while its influence could be much larger. Even for
the `tawSolver`, on selected combinatorial benchmarks the effects (positive and
negative) on tree-sizes can be much higher.

Our first general hypothesis on the (dynamic) choice of a good projection for binary branchings is, phrased in the terminology of means-functions: In general $\mathfrak{T}$ is best, but for large reductions (distances) or for nodes closer towards the leaves the penalty for imbalance can be reduced (there is no "exponential growth" anymore), moving towards m_1, while possibly closer to the root, or when only small reductions are achievable, it is conceivable that an increase in the penalty, moving closer to m_0, might be beneficial (the situation might get "out of control", and thus one needs to be more "cautious").

6   Summary and Outlook

We provided a review of the general theory of branching heuristics for look-ahead-like solvers. Via flattening of metric trees, we gave a new simple proof of the main theorem on bounding tree sizes, and we were able to provide concise proofs showing the uniqueness of the canonical branching order. Turning to binary branchings, the core of the binary tau-function has been condensed into the function $\mathrm{w}\tau(x)$, where strong lower and upper bounds are given, showing $\mathrm{w}\tau(x) \sim \ln(x)$. That "core" (in a variation) yielded the kernel of generalised means, which enabled us to make precise comparisons between alternatives to standard projections for binary branchings. We derived a first general hypothesis on a better *dynamic* numerical control of the branching process.

Perhaps the most important future application of this whole approach is in improving Cube-and-Conquer (see [10] for a high-level overview). In general, having strong methods for splitting is vital here. The Cube-and-Conquer solver needs to use a strong branching scheme in the cubing-phase, creating a tree, where the leaves are the problems given to the conquer-solver. This scheme relies on the analysis of the tree created, with the main target of minimising tree size. More general than a lookahead SAT solver, the leaves here are not those nodes where the residual instances were "solved", but where they are "easy enough" for the conquer-solver. The target is still to minimise tree sizes, and for that the theory outlined in the paper is the very basis. The higher cost of computing $\tau(t)$ should be less relevant in this context.

A further aspect, which should become important in the future, is that for a branching-tuple t by $\tau(t)$ we obtain a *global* evaluation on the goodness of t ("global" in the sense of being comparable in principle over the whole course of computation). Monitoring these values should be valuable to gauge "success" or "failure" of the current strategy, possibly triggering a switch of methods, e.g., cutting off the cube-computation at the current node and switching to the conquer-solver (somewhat similar to random restarts for CDCL solvers).

References

1. Ahmed, T., Kullmann, O., Snevily, H.: On the van der Waerden numbers $\mathrm{w}(2;3,t)$. Disc. Appl. Math. **174**, 27–51 (2014). https://doi.org/10.1016/j.dam.2014.05.007

2. Anderson, D., Bodic, P.L., Morgan, K.: Further results on an abstract model for branching and its application to mixed integer programming. Math. Program. (2020). https://doi.org/10.1007/s10107-020-01556-4
3. Biere, A., Heule, M.J.H., van Maaren, H., Walsh, T. (eds.): Handbook of Satisfiability, volume 185 of Frontiers in Artificial Intelligence and Applications. IOS Press (2009)
4. Bodic, P.L., Nemhauser, G.L.: An abstract model for branching and its application to mixed integer programming. Math. Program. 166(1–2), 369–405 (2017). https://doi.org/10.1007/s10107-016-1101-8
5. Bulhões, T., Sadykov, R., Uchoa, E.: A branch-and-price algorithm for the minimum latency problem. Comput. Oper. Res. 93, 66–78 (2018). https://doi.org/10.1016/j.cor.2018.01.016
6. Davis, M., Logemann, G., Loveland, D.: A machine program for theorem-proving. Commun ACM 5(7), 394–397 (1962). https://doi.org/10.1145/368273.368557
7. Fomin, F.V., Kratsch, D.: Exact Exponential Algorithms. TTCSAES, Springer, Heidelberg (2010). https://doi.org/10.1007/978-3-642-16533-7
8. Golovnev, A., Kulikov, A.S., Smal, A.V., Tamaki, S.: Gate elimination: circuit size lower bounds and #SAT upper bounds. Theor. Comput. Sci. 719, 46–63 (2018). https://doi.org/10.1016/j.tcs.2017.11.008
9. Marijn J. H. Heule and Hans van Maaren. Look-ahead based SAT solvers. In Biere et al. [3], chapter 5, pages 155–184. https://doi.org/10.3233/978-1-58603-929-5-155
10. Heule, M.J.H., Kullmann, O.: The science of brute force. Commun. ACM 60(8), 25–34 (2017). https://doi.org/10.1145/3107239
11. Heule, M.J.H., Kullmann, O., Biere, A.: Cube-and-conquer for satisfiability. In: Handbook of Parallel Constraint Reasoning, pp. 31–59. Springer, Cham (2018). https://doi.org/10.1007/978-3-319-63516-3_2
12. Hoorfar, A., Hassani, M.: Inequalities on the Lambert W function and hyperpower function. J. Inequalities Pure Appl. Math. 9(2), 1–5 (2008). https://www.emis.de/journals/JIPAM/article983.html
13. Pinelis, I.: A certain generalisation of the golden ratio. MathOverflow. https://mathoverflow.net/users/36721/iosifpinelis, https://mathoverflow.net/q/320595
14. Knuth, D.E.: The Art of Computer Programming, Satisfiability (Fascicle 6), vol. 4. Addison-Wesley, Boston (2015). ISBN-13 978–0134397603
15. Kullmann, O.: Obere und untere Schranken für die Komplexität von aussagenlogischen Resolutionsbeweisen und Klassen von SAT-Algorithmen. Master's thesis, Johann Wolfgang Goethe-Universität Frankfurt am Main (1992). (Upper and lower bounds for the complexity of propositional resolution proofs and classes of SAT algorithms (in German); Diplomarbeit am Fachbereich Mathematik)
16. Kullmann, O.: Fundaments of branching heuristics. In: Biere et al. [3], chap. 7, pp. 205–244 (2007). https://doi.org/10.3233/978-1-58603-929-5-205
17. Marques-Silva, J., Lynce, I., Malik, S.: Conflict-driven clause learning SAT solvers. In: Biere et al. [3], chap. 4, pp. 131–153 (1996). https://doi.org/10.3233/978-1-58603-929-5-131
18. Olver, F.W.J., Lozier, D.W., Boisvert, R.F., Clark, C.W. (eds.): NIST Handbook of Mathematical Functions. NIST and Cambridge University Press, Cambridge (2010). ISBN 978-0-521-19225-5
19. Pecin, D., Pessoa, A.A., Poggi, M., Uchoa, E.: Improved branch-cut-and-price for capacitated vehicle routing. Math. Program. Comput. 9(1), 61–100 (2017). https://doi.org/10.1007/s12532-016-0108-8

On Dedicated CDCL Strategies
for PB Solvers

Daniel Le Berre[1] and Romain Wallon[2]([⊠])

[1] Centre de Recherche en Informatique de Lens (CRIL),
Univ. Artois, CNRS, 62300 Lens, France
`leberre@cril.fr`
[2] LIX, Laboratoire d'Informatique de l'X, Ecole Polytechnique,
X-Uber Chair, 91120 Palaiseau, France
`wallon@lix.polytechnique.fr`

Abstract. Current implementations of pseudo-Boolean (PB) solvers working on native PB constraints are based on the CDCL architecture which empowers highly efficient modern SAT solvers. In particular, such PB solvers not only implement a (cutting-planes-based) conflict analysis procedure, but also complementary strategies for components that are crucial for the efficiency of CDCL, namely branching heuristics, learned constraint deletion and restarts. However, these strategies are mostly reused by PB solvers without considering the particular form of the PB constraints they deal with. In this paper, we present and evaluate different ways of adapting CDCL strategies to take the specificities of PB constraints into account while preserving the behavior they have in the clausal setting. We implemented these strategies in two different solvers, namely *Sat4j* (for which we consider three configurations) and *Rounding Sat*. Our experiments show that these dedicated strategies allow to improve, sometimes significantly, the performance of these solvers, both on decision and optimization problems.

Keywords: Pseudo-Boolean solving · Pseudo-Boolean optimization · Branching heuristics · Learned constraint deletion strategies · Restart policies

1 Introduction

The success of so-called *modern* SAT solvers has motivated the generalization of the *conflict-driven clause learning* (CDCL) architecture [13,30,31] to solve *pseudo-Boolean* (PB) problems [35]. The main motivation behind the development of PB solvers is that classical SAT solvers are based on the *resolution* proof system, which is a *weak* proof system: instances that are hard for resolution (for instance those requiring counting capabilities, such as *pigeonhole principle formulae* [20]) are hard for SAT solvers. A stronger alternative is the *cutting planes*

R. Wallon—Most of this paper is based on research conducted by this author while he was working as a PhD student at CRIL (Univ Artois & CNRS).

C.-M. Li and F. Manyà (Eds.): SAT 2021, LNCS 12831, pp. 315–331, 2021.
https://doi.org/10.1007/978-3-030-80223-3_22

proof system [19,21,32], which allows, for instance, to solve pigeonhole principle formulae with a linear number of derivation steps. Generally speaking, this proof system *p-simulates* resolution: any resolution proof can be simulated by a polynomial size cutting planes proof [10]. In theory, PB solvers should thus be able to find shorter unsatisfiability proofs, and thus be more efficient than classical SAT solvers. In practice however, current PB solvers fail to keep the promises of the theory. In particular, most PB solvers [9,12,25,36] implement a subset of the cutting planes proof system known as *generalized resolution* [21]. This subset is convenient as it allows to extend the CDCL algorithm to PB constraints. As soon as a constraint becomes conflicting, the generalized resolution rule is applied between this constraint and the reason for the propagation of one of its literals to derive a new conflicting constraint. This operation is repeated until an assertive constraint is eventually derived. However, solvers implementing this procedure do not exploit the full power of the cutting planes proof system [37], and are still behind resolution-based solvers in PB competitions [34].

Despite the recent improvements brought by *RoundingSat* [16] with the use of the *division* rule during conflict analysis, current implementations of cutting planes still have a critical drawback: they degenerate to resolution when given a CNF as input. Moreover, such implementations are more complex than just replacing resolution during conflict analysis by generalized resolution: finding *which* rules to apply and *when* is not that obvious [17,24]. In particular, PB solvers need to take care about the specific properties of PB constraints and of the cutting planes proof system to fit in the CDCL architecture. Additionally, CDCL comes with many other features, without which the performance of the solver may become very bad (see, e.g., [15]). To the best of our knowledge, little work has been done on extending these components for PB solvers: they are mostly reused from their definition in classical SAT solvers, and adapted just enough to work in the solver, without considering their effective impact in the context of PB solving. In this paper, we focus on such features, namely branching heuristics, learned constraint deletion strategies and restart schemes. We implemented different new strategies for these features, designed to consider the characteristics of PB constraints. Our experiments show that they allow to improve, sometimes significantly, the performance of different PB solvers, both on decision and optimization instances.

2   Preliminaries

We consider a propositional setting defined on a finite set of propositional variables $\mathcal{V}$. A *literal* ℓ is a variable $v \in \mathcal{V}$ or its negation $\bar{v}$. Boolean values are represented by the integers 1 (true) and 0 (false), so that $\bar{v} = 1 - v$.

A *pseudo-Boolean (PB) constraint* is an integral linear equation or inequation over Boolean variables of the form $\sum_{i=1}^{n} \alpha_i \ell_i \vartriangle \delta$, in which the *coefficients* α_i and the *degree* δ are integers, ℓ_i are literals and $\vartriangle \in \{<, \leq, =, \geq, >\}$. Such a constraint can be *normalized* in linear time into a conjunction of constraints of the form $\sum_{i=1}^{n} \alpha_i \ell_i \geq \delta$ in which the coefficients and the degree are all positive integers. In the following, we thus assume that all PB constraints are normalized. A *cardinality constraint* is a PB constraint in which all coefficients are equal to 1 and a *clause* is a cardinality constraint of degree 1. This definition illustrates that PB constraints are a generalization of clauses, and that clausal reasoning is thus a special case of PB reasoning.

PB solvers have thus been designed to extend the CDCL algorithm of classical SAT solvers. In particular, when looking for a solution, PB solvers have to *assign* variables. In the following, we use the notation $\ell(V@D)$ to represent that literal ℓ has been assigned value V at decision level D, and $\ell(?@?)$ to represent that ℓ is unassigned. Assigning variables is achieved either by *making a decision* or by *propagating* a truth value for a variable. In this context, the normalized form of PB constraints is particularly useful for detecting propagations: as for clauses, propagations are triggered after the falsification of some literals in the constraint. However, contrary to clauses, a PB constraint may propagate a literal even if some other literals in this constraint are unassigned or satisfied, as shown in the following example.

Example 1. The PB constraint $5a(0@3) + 5b(?@?) + c(?@?) + d(?@?) + e(0@1) + f(1@2) \geq 6$ propagates the literal b under the current partial assignment. If b is assigned to 0, giving $5a(0@3) + 5b(0@3) + c(?@?) + d(?@?) + e(0@1) + f(1@2) \geq 6$, the constraint becomes conflicting. In both cases, observe that f is satisfied and c and d are unassigned.

After propagations are triggered, it may happen that a constraint becomes conflicting. When this is the case, PB solvers perform a conflict analysis similar to that of SAT solvers, and successively apply the *cancellation* rule between the conflicting constraint and the reason for the propagation of some of its literals, so as to eliminate these literals. However, doing so does not guarantee to preserve the conflict, and several approaches based on the *(partial) weakening* rule have been introduced [11,16,24] to provide such a guarantee, by (locally) assuming that some literals are assigned to 1. Some solvers such as *Sat4j-GeneralizedResolution* [25] apply this rule iteratively until the conflict is guaranteed to be preserved, while others such as *RoundingSat* [16], *Sat4j-RoundingSat* and *Sat4j-PartialRoundingSat* [24] apply it on *all* literals that are not falsified and not divisible by the coefficient of the literals to eliminate, before applying the division rule.

3   Branching Heuristics

An important component in a SAT solver is its *branching heuristic*: to find efficiently a solution or an unsatisfiability proof, the solver has to choose the *right* variables on which to make decisions. Currently, most SAT solvers rely on VSIDS [31] or one of its variants [7], or the more recent LRB [27]. We focus on the former, as it is the one adopted by the native PB solvers we considered.

The most popular variant of VSIDS is *exponential VSIDS* (EVSIDS), introduced in *MiniSat* [13]. In this heuristic, a value g is chosen between 1.01 and 1.2

at the beginning of the execution of the solver. When a variable is encountered during the analysis of the i-th conflict, this variable is *bumped*, i.e., its score is updated by adding g^i to its current score. When it comes to selecting a variable, the solver chooses the variable with the highest score. We remark that, as the original VSIDS, EVSIDS is designed to favor variables appearing in recent conflicts. Moreover, modern implementations of VSIDS not only update the score of variables appearing in the learned clauses, but also that of variables appearing in *all* clauses used to produce them. This approach aims to favor the selection of variables that are *involved* in recent conflicts.

3.1 VSIDS in PB Solvers

Current PB solvers rely thus on the VSIDS heuristic (or one of its variants) to decide which variable should be assigned next. In practice, this heuristic may be used as is by PB solvers, even though doing so does not allow to take into account all the information given by a PB constraint, as observed in [9] (which, however, does not explicitly provide a more suitable heuristic). This is why different variants of this heuristic have been proposed. In [11, Section 4.5], it is proposed to add, for each variable appearing in a *cardinality constraint of the original problem* (i.e., not for *learned* constraints) the degree of this constraint to the *initial* score of the corresponding variables. This approach actually counts the occurrences of the variable in the clauses that are represented by the cardinality constraint.

Example 2 (from [11, Section 4.5]). If the cardinality constraint $a + b + c \geq 2$ is present in the original constraint database, the score of each of its variables is increased by 2. Indeed, this constraint is equivalent to the conjunction of the clauses $a + b \geq 1$, $a + c \geq 1$ and $b + c \geq 1$. If this constraint is learned, the corresponding scores are only increased by 1.

Despite providing a more specific heuristic than the original VSIDS heuristic when considering PB problems, this heuristic is not completely satisfactory, as it does not fit well in modern implementations of VSIDS, and especially of EVSIDS. First, as only the original constraints are considered, the heuristic does not bring any improvement over the classical implementation of the heuristic, which essentially relies on the bumping of variables involved in recent conflicts. Second, the particular form of general PB constraints is not taken into account by this heuristic. The main reason for only considering cardinality constraints in this case is that computing the number of clauses in which a literal of a PB constraint appears is hard in general. Another alternative, implemented in *Pueblo* [36], is estimating the relative importance of a literal in a constraint, by computing the ratio of its coefficient by the degree of the constraint. This value is then added to the VSIDS score of the variable. On the contrary, *Sat4j* [25] and *RoundingSat* [16] both implement a more classical EVSIDS heuristic, by bumping each variable encountered during conflict analysis. However, some implementation details are worth noting for these two solvers. In particular, *Sat4j* bumps these variables *each time they appear in a reason*, while *RoundingSat* bumps them only once (as in *MiniSat* [13]), except if the variable is eliminated during conflict analysis, in which case it is bumped *twice*.

3.2 Towards Better VSIDS for PB Solvers

As mentioned above, current implementations of the VSIDS heuristic in SAT solvers, and in particular the EVSIDS heuristic, are designed to favor the selection of variables that are involved in recent conflicts. When only considering clauses, identifying such literals is straightforward: the literals involved in a conflict are those appearing in the clauses encountered during conflict analysis. However, this is no longer the case when PB constraints are considered. Indeed, given a PB constraint, the literals it contains may not play the same role in the constraint, and thus may not have the same influence in the conflicts in which this constraint is involved. In order to take into account this asymmetry between the literals when computing VSIDS scores, we introduce different ways of bumping the variables appearing in the constraints encountered during conflict analysis. The main reason for the asymmetry of the literals in a PB constraint is the presence of coefficients in the constraint. To take these literals into account, we generalize the heuristics proposed in the PB solvers *pbChaff* [11, Section 4.5], [12] and *Pueblo* [36] by defining the following bumping strategies:

- The *bump-degree* strategy multiplies the increment by the *degree* of the constraint, as a naive generalization of *pbChaff*'s approach, which only considers the degree of the original cardinality constraints.
- The *bump-coefficient* strategy multiplies the increment by the *coefficient* of the literal being bumped, as a tentative measure of the importance of the corresponding variable.
- The *bump-ratio-coefficient-degree* strategy multiplies the increment by the *ratio* of the coefficient of the literal by the degree of the constraint, as proposed in *Pueblo*.
- The *bump-ratio-degree-coefficient* strategy multiplies the increment by the *ratio* of the degree of the constraint by the coefficient of the literal, as a generalization of *pbChaff*'s strategy taking into account the relative importance of the variable in the constraint.

Let us illustrate these different strategies by the following example.

Example 3. When bumping the variable a from the constraint $5a + 5b + c + d + e + f \geq 6$, the increment is multiplied by:

- 6 in the case of *bump-degree*,
- 5 in the case of *bump-coefficient*,
- 5/6 in the case of *bump-ratio-coefficient-degree* (as in *Pueblo*), and
- 6/5 in the case of *bump-ratio-degree-coefficient*

before being added to the variable's score.

Another key observation to take into account to detect literals that are actually *involved* in a conflict is to consider the impact of the current assignment. Indeed, in classical SAT solvers, all variables appearing in the clauses encountered during conflict analysis are always *assigned*, and all but one are actually *falsified*. However, in PB constraints, this is not always the case (see Example 1), and falsified literals may even be *ineffective* [24, Section 3.1].

Definition 1 (Effective Literal). *Given a conflicting (resp. assertive) PB constraint χ, a literal ℓ of χ is said to be* effective *in χ if it is falsified and satisfying it would not preserve the conflict (resp. propagation). We say that ℓ is* ineffective *when it is not effective.*

Remark 1. To identify ineffective literals in a constraint, we use a greedy algorithm that works as follows. The literals of the constraint are successively (and implicitly) weakened away, and only those for which the weakening does not preserve the conflict (resp. propagations) are kept. This operation, yields an (implicit) clause that is both implied by the constraint and conflicting (resp. assertive). Its literals are those considered as effective. Note that this approach is similar to that used by *SATIRE* [38] or *Sat4j-Resolution* [25] to derive clauses during conflict analysis.

Even though they may be encountered during conflict analysis, ineffective literals do not play any role in the conflict, and neither do the corresponding variables. We thus introduce three other bumping strategies taking into account the current assignment:

- The *bump-assigned* strategy bumps only assigned variables appearing in the constraints encountered during conflict analysis.
- The *bump-falsified* strategy bumps only variables whose literals appear as falsified in the constraints encountered during conflict analysis.
- The *bump-effective* strategy bumps only variables whose literals are effective in the constraints encountered during conflict analysis.

Example 4. When bumping the variables of the constraint $5a(0@3) + 5b(1@3) + c(?@?) + d(?@?) + e(0@1) + f(1@2) \geq 6$,

- the strategy *bump-assigned* bumps the variables a, b, e and f,
- the strategy *bump-falsified* bumps the variables a and e, and
- the strategy *bump-effective* bumps only the variable a.

4   Learned Constraint Deletion

PB solvers, similarly to SAT solvers, need to regularly *delete* learned constraints during their execution. Indeed, storing these constraints may not only increase the memory required by the solver, but may also slow down unit propagation. In this context, the key element is to detect *which* constraints to remove. In PB solvers, this feature is mostly inherited directly from SAT solvers. For instance,

Pueblo [36] uses *MiniSat*'s learned constraint deletion, based on the activity of learned constraints (the less active constraints are removed first), *Sat4j* [25] uses also an activity-based strategy but more aggressively as in *Glucose* [2], while *RoundingSat* [16] considers a custom hybrid approach, based on both the *LBD* and the activity measures (the latter is used as a tie-break rule when the former gives identical measures). In other PB solvers, such as *pbChaff* [12] and *Galena* [9], the learned constraint deletion in use (if any) is not documented. In [9], a perspective is however mentioned to weaken learned constraints instead of removing them. However, note that while measures such as those based on the activity may be reused as they are by PB solvers (they do not take into account the representation nor the semantics of the constraints they evaluate), for other evaluation schemes, paying attention to the particular form of PB constraints may be more relevant to properly evaluate the quality of the constraints. This section focuses on two main approaches towards this direction.

4.1 Size-Based Measures

In classical SAT solvers, size-based measures delete the largest clauses in the database, i.e., those containing many literals. The intuition behind this evaluation scheme is that large clauses are weak, especially from a propagation viewpoint: a propagation can only be triggered after many literals have become falsified. When considering PB constraints, this is not the case anymore. Indeed, recall that PB constraints may propagate literals while some other literals remain unassigned, and that the number of literals in a PB constraint does not necessarily reflect its strength.

Another reason that motivated the use of size-based measures in SAT solving is that large clauses are expensive to handle, which is also true for PB constraints. In particular, in such constraints, the size also takes into account the size of the coefficients, which is not negligible: as coefficients may become very large during conflict analysis, arbitrary precision encoding is required to represent these coefficients. As we already discussed, this representation slows down arithmetic operations, and thus the conflict analysis performed by the solver. Different approaches have been studied to limit the growth of the coefficient, such as those based on the division [16] or the weakening [24] rules. However, these approaches lead to the inference of weaker constraints. By using a quality measure that takes into account the size of the coefficients, we can favor the learning of constraints with "small" coefficients. Towards this direction, we introduce quality measures based on the degree of the learned constraints, as described below:

- The *degree* quality measure evaluates the quality of a learned constraint by the *value* of its degree.
- The *degree-bits* quality measure evaluates the quality of a learned constraint by the *minimum number of bits* required to represents its degree

In both cases, the smaller the degree, the better the constraint. Indeed, it is well-known that the degree of a PB constraint can be used as an upper bound of the coefficients of the constraints (because of the *saturation* rule), so that considering only the degree is enough for the purpose of this measure.

Example 5. The degree-based quality measures for the constraint $5a + 5b + c + d + e + f \geq 6$ are:

- 6 in the case of *degree*, and
- 3 in the case of *degree-bits* (as the binary representation of 6, i.e., 110, needs 3 bits).

4.2 LBD-Based Measures

Another alternative to measure the quality of learned clauses in SAT solvers is the so-called *LBD* [2].

Definition 2 (LBD). *Consider a clause γ and the current assignment of its literals. Let π be a partition of these literals, such that literals are partitioned w.r.t. their decision levels. The LBD of γ is the number of classes in π.*

The *LBD* of a clause is first computed when this clause is learned, and is then updated each time the clause is used as a reason. In this context, the notion of *LBD* relies on the fact that all literals in a conflicting clause are falsified, and when the clause is used as a reason, only one literal is not falsified (the propagated literal), but its decision level is also that of another (falsified) literal, which has triggered the propagation. When PB constraints are considered, this is not the case anymore. As such, *LBD* is not well-defined for such constraints. To consider it as a quality measure for learned PB constraints, we thus need to take into account the literals that are unassigned in these constraints. To do so, we introduce five different definitions of this measure. First, we consider a sort of default definition of *LBD* for PB constraints, which only takes into account assigned literals. This definition of *LBD* was used for instance in the first version of *RoundingSat* [16].

Definition 3 (LBD_a). *Consider a PB constraint χ and the current assignment of its assigned literals. Let π be a partition of these literals, such that literals are partitioned w.r.t. their decision levels. The LBD_a of χ is the number of classes in π ("a" stands for "assigned").*

Unassigned literals may be considered as if they were assigned to a "dummy" decision level. This decision level may be the same for all literals, or not.

Definition 4 (LBD_s). *Consider a PB constraint χ and the current assignment of its assigned literals. Let π be a partition of these literals, such that literals are partitioned w.r.t. their decision levels. Let n be the number of classes in π. The LBD_s of χ is n if all literals in χ are assigned, and $n+1$ otherwise ("s" stands for "same").*

Definition 5 (LBD_d). *Consider a PB constraint χ and the current assignment of its assigned literals. Let π be a partition of these literals, such that literals are partitioned w.r.t. their decision levels. Let n be the number of classes in π. The LBD_d of χ is $n + u$, where u is the number of unassigned literals in χ ("d" stands for "different").*

Another possible extension of LBD is to only consider falsified literals, as in the current version of *RoundingSat*:

Definition 6 (LBD_f). *Consider a PB constraint χ and the current assignment of its falsified literals. Let π be a partition of these literals, such that literals are partitioned w.r.t. their decision levels. The LBD_f of χ is the number of classes in π ("f" stands for "falsified").*

The definition above is based on the observation that, when a clause is learned, all literals in this clause are falsified. However, it may happen that falsified literals in a PB constraint are actually *ineffective* (while this is never the case in a clause). As these literals are not involved in the conflict, we should not consider them either. We thus define another extension of LBD that only considers effective literals:

Definition 7 (LBD_e). *Consider a PB constraint χ and the current assignment of its effective literals. Let π be a partition of these literals, such that literals are partitioned w.r.t. their decision levels. The LBD_e of χ is the number of classes in π ("e" stands for "effective").*

Example 6. The LBD-based quality measures for the constraint χ given by $5a(0@3) + 5b(1@3) + c(?@?) + d(?@?) + e(0@1) + f(1@2) \geq 6$ are:

- $LBD_a(\chi) = |\{\{a, b\}, \{e\}, \{f\}\}| = 3$
- $LBD_s(\chi) = |\{\{a, b\}, \{c, d\}, \{e\}, \{f\}\}| = 4$
- $LBD_d(\chi) = |\{\{a, b\}, \{c\}, \{d\}, \{e\}, \{f\}\}| = 5$
- $LBD_f(\chi) = |\{\{a\}, \{e\}\}| = 2$
- $LBD_e(\chi) = |\{\{a\}\}| = 1$

We remark that the definitions of LBD introduced in this section are *extensions* of the original definition of LBD (as given by Definition 2), in the sense that they all coincide when learning clauses.

4.3 Deleting PB Constraints

Taking advantage of the measures described above, we define the following deletion strategies, which are applied each time the learned clause database is reduced:

- *delete-degree*, which deletes the constraints with the highest degree,
- *delete-degree-bits*, which deletes the constraints with the largest degree,
- *delete-lbd-a*, which deletes the constraints with the highest LBD_a,
- *delete-lbd-s*, which deletes the constraints with the highest LBD_s,
- *delete-lbd-d*, which deletes the constraints with the highest LBD_d,
- *delete-lbd-f*, which deletes the constraints with the highest LBD_f, and
- *delete-lbd-e*, which deletes the constraints with the highest LBD_e.

5   Restarts

Restarts are a very powerful feature of CDCL SAT solvers [18]. Even though this feature is not completely understood, it seems required to exploit more power of the resolution proof system [1,14,33]. Restarting is mainly forgetting all decisions made by the solver, and go back to the root decision level. The main advantage of doing so is that wrong decisions made at the very beginning of the search can be cancelled to avoid being stuck in a subpart of the search space. To this end, many restart schemes have been proposed [8], either static such as those based on the Luby series [22,28] or dynamic, as in *PicoSAT* [5] or *Glucose* [3]. In this section, we focus on the latter, considering restart strategies based on the quality of learned constraints. Such restarts are not exploited in current PB solvers. In solvers such as *pbChaff* [12] or *Galena* [9], it is not clear whether restarts are implemented or not, as they do not mention this feature. As *Pueblo* [36] is heavily based on *MiniSat* [13], it is most likely to inherit its restart policy, even though no mention of this feature is made in [36] either. Regarding more recent solver, *Sat4j* [25] implements *PicoSAT*'s static and aggressive restart scheme [6] and *RoundingSat* [16] uses a Luby-based restart policy [22,28]. Note that a common point to these two strategies is that they do not take into account the constraints that are being considered, as they are both static policies. They may thus be reused without any modification since they are independent from the type of the constraints being considered. In this section, we propose instead to follow *Glucose*'s restart policy [3]. In this solver, the decision of whether a restart should be performed depends on the quality of the constraints that are currently being learned: when this quality decreases, the solver is most likely exploring the wrong search space. As of *Glucose*, the quality of learned clauses is measured with their *LBD* (see Definition 2). To measure the decrease in the quality of learned clauses, the average *LBD* is computed over the most recent clauses (in practice, the last 100 clauses). Whenever this average is greater than 70% of the average *LBD* computed over all learned clauses, a restart should be performed. *Glucose* also implements a wide variety of tricks to improve its restart policy (such as restart blocking) that are beyond the scope of this paper.

We thus define 7 restarts strategies, that exploit the quality measures defined in Sect. 4, namely *restart-degree*, *restart-degree-bits*, *restart-lbd-a*, *restart-lbd-s*, *restart-lbd-d*, *restart-lbd-f* and *restart-lbd-e*.

6   Experimental Results

This section presents an empirical evaluation of the different strategies presented in this paper implemented in two PB solvers, namely *Sat4j* [25] and *RoundingSat* [16]. All experiments have been executed on a cluster of computers equipped with quadcore bi-processors Intel XEON X5550 (2.66 GHz, 8 MB cache). The time limit was set to 1200 s and the memory limit to 32 GB. For space reasons, this section does not report the results of all individual strategies presented in this paper, but focuses on the performance of those providing

the best improvements to the considered solvers. The interested reader may still
have a look to the publicly available detailed results of our experiments [26].

6.1 Solver Configurations

Let us first describe our implementation of the different strategies in *Sat4j*
[25], which are available in its repository[1]. For this solver, we considered three
main configurations, namely *Sat4j-GeneralizedResolution*, *Sat4j-RoundingSat*
and *Sat4j-PartialRoundingSat* [24]. For these three configurations, the default
strategies are given below:

- the branching heuristic bumps all variables appearing in each constraint
  encountered during conflict analysis each time they are encountered,
- learned constraints are stored in a *mono-tiered* database, and are regularly
  deleted using *MiniSat*'s learned constraint deletion strategy [13], based on
  the *activity* of learned constraints (i.e., the constraints to remove are those
  that are less involved in recent conflicts), and
- the restart policy is that of *PicoSAT* [6].

Based on our experiments, the best combination of strategies for *Sat4j-
GeneralizedResolution* is *bump-effective*, *delete-lbd-s* and *restart-degree*, while the
best combination for both *Sat4j-RoundingSat* and *Sat4j-PartialRoundingSat* is
bump-assigned, *delete-degree-bits* and the static restart policy of *PicoSAT* [6].

For *RoundingSat* [16], our implementation is available in a dedicated repository[2]. We refactored this solver starting from commit a17b7d0e (denoted master
in the following) to support the use of the different strategies presented in this
paper. The default configuration of this solver corresponds to the refactored
version of *RoundingSat* set up with the default strategies originally used by this
solver, i.e.:

- the branching heuristic bumps all variables appearing in each constraint
  encountered during conflict analysis once, and twice when eliminated,
- learned constraints are stored in a *mono-tiered* database, and are regularly
  deleted using the LBD_f of the constraints and their activity as a tie-break,
  and
- the restart policy uses the Luby series (with factor 100) [22].

The best combination of strategies for this solver, according to our experiments, is *bump-assigned* (with a bumping on the variables each time they are
encountered), *delete-lbd-e* and *restart-lbd-e*.

6.2 Decision Problems

We first consider the performance of the different solvers on decision problems.
To this end, we ran the different solvers on the whole set of decision benchmarks containing "small" integers used in the PB competitions since the first
edition [29], for a total of 5582 instances. Figure 1 gives the results of the different
solvers on these inputs, with their default and best configurations.

---
[1] https://gitlab.ow2.org/sat4j/sat4j/tree/cdcl-strategies
[2] https://gitlab.com/pb-cdcl-strategies/roundingsat/-/tree/cdcl-strategies

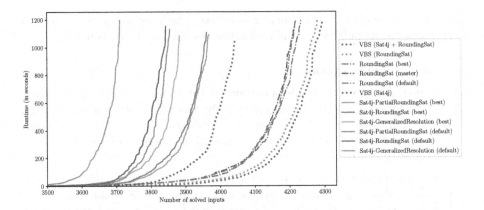

Fig. 1. Cactus plots of different configurations of *Sat4j* and *RoundingSat* on decision problems. For more readability, the first (easy) 3500 instances are cut out.

The cactus plot shows that the different configurations of *Sat4j* are significantly improved by the use of our dedicated strategies. Quite interestingly, we can also observe that *Sat4j-GeneralizedResolution* with the best combination of the strategies beats both implementations of *RoundingSat* in *Sat4j* with their default strategies. In the case of *RoundingSat*, we can also note a small improvement over its default configuration, but this improvement is not as significant as in *Sat4j*. Let us remark that combining the best strategies is not enough to get the best of all the strategies we investigated. In particular, for each feature we considered, the *Virtual Best Solver* (*VBS*) of the different strategies, i.e., the one obtained by selecting the best performing strategies on each individual input, has far better performance than each individual strategy, and this applies to all configurations of *Sat4j* and *RoundingSat* This suggests that no strategy is better than the other on all benchmarks, and that they are actually complementary.

6.3   Optimization Problems

Let us now consider the performance of the different solvers on optimization problems, by using as input the whole set of optimization benchmarks containing "small" integers used in the PB competitions since the first edition [29], for a total of 4374 instances. Considering the huge amount of computation time needed to perform our exhaustive experiments on decision problems (more than 8 years of CPU time), we focused for these experiments on the **best** configurations of the different solvers we identified on decision problems (which still took about 9 months of CPU computation time). Figure 2 shows the results we obtained for these configurations.

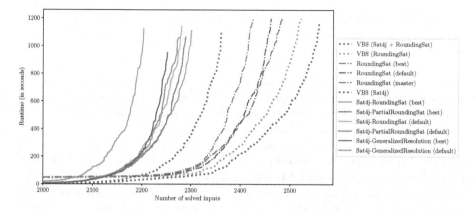

Fig. 2. Cactus plots of different configurations of *Sat4j* and *RoundingSat* on optimization problems. For more readability, the first (easy) 2000 instances are cut out.

Similarly to decision problems, we can observe on the cactus plots that all solvers are improved by the dedicated strategies on optimization problems, with a particularly significant improvement to *Sat4j-GeneralizedResolution*.

6.4   Discussion

Let us now make a more detailed analysis of our experimental results.

Not so surprisingly, the strategy that has the most important impact, especially in *Sat4j*, is the bumping strategy, i.e., the branching heuristic. On the one hand, our experiments showed that the strategies *bump-degree* and *bump-ratio-degree-coefficient* have really poor performance in all considered solvers (including *RoundingSat*). As described in [11, Section 4.5], these strategies are designed to estimate the number of clauses that are represented by the PB constraint whose literals are being bumped. However, when a conflict occurs, not all these clauses are actually involved in the conflict, and thus some variables get "more bumped" than they should be.

On the other hand, assignment-based bumping strategies are, among all individual strategies, those having the biggest impact on the performance of *Sat4j*. For instance, we observed that *Sat4j-GeneralizedResolution* solves the (optimization) instances of the `factor` family much faster thanks to the *bump-effective* strategy (changing the learned constraint deletion or restart strategies makes almost no difference on this family). We made further investigations to understand why there was such an improvement, and it appears that the production of *irrelevant literals* (i.e., literals that occur in a PB constraint, but never affect its truth value, whatever their assignment) penalize the solver on this particular family. It is known that such literals may impact the size of the proof built by PB solvers [23]. Our experiments here also show that they may *pollute* the solver's heuristic, as *bump-effective* never bumps irrelevant literals (they are always ineffective). This also proposes another way to deal with such literals.

The big impact of the bumping strategies in *Sat4j* may also explain why the gain in *RoundingSat* is not so significant. Indeed, the aggressive weakening performed by *RoundingSat* tends, in a sense, to already identify the literals that are already involved in the conflict. This is particularly visible if we look at the behavior the different bumping strategies in *RoundingSat*: there is almost no difference between them. This suggests that the gain in this solver comes mostly from the learned constraint deletion strategy or the restart policy, which improve the default strategies without being significantly better.

In particular, we observed that, in *Sat4j*, performing no deletion at all is actually better than the (default) activity-based deletion strategy. This may be explained by the fact that PB solvers are often slower in practice than SAT solvers, especially because the operations they need to perform, such as detecting propagations and applying the cancellation rule, are more complex than their counterpart in SAT solvers. This means that the number of conflicts per second in a PB solver is lower than that in a SAT solver, and so is the number of learned constraints. As a consequence, PB solvers do not need to clean their learned constraint database as regularly as a SAT solver.

Regarding the restart policies, there is no big difference between the strategies, except for `degree-bits`, which does not have good performance compared to the others, and especially to `degree`. This may be explained by the fact that degrees with the same number of bits may take very different values. These are taken into account by the latter while the former does not distinguish them. Nevertheless, there is clearly room for improvement as the VBS performs much better than the individual strategies.

It is also important to note that the different strategies we considered in this paper are often tightly linked in the solver, and may thus interact with each other. This is particularly true for the learned constraint deletion and restart policies, since they use the same quality measures. While using them independently does not necessarily have a big impact on the solver (this is particularly true for the learned constraint deletion strategy), combining them often allows to get better performance. For instance, in *RoundingSat*, while the best (individual) strategies are *PicoSAT*'s restart policy and the deletion based on the LBD_s, the best gain is actually obtained by using the LBD_e quality measure both for learned constraint deletion and restarts.

Another consequence of the tight link between the different strategies and the solver itself is that implementation details may have unintended side effects on the performance of the solver. For instance, to implement the new strategies in *RoundingSat*, we had to adapt the code and change some data structures in the branching heuristic (by replacing an *ordered set* with an *(unordered) hash map*), resulting in the same literals being bumped, but *in a different order*. As the insertion/update order of the variables is used as a tie-break by EVSIDS, the order in which the literals are selected varies between the `master` and `default` configuration of the solver, which increases the difficulty to interpret the results of *RoundingSat*, especially on optimization problems.

To conclude this analysis, let us summarize the main outcomes of our experiments. The biggest impact on the solver is obtained by carefully adapting the bumping strategy: while considering coefficients in this case worsens all tested solvers, considering the current partial assignment may drastically improve them. Regarding constraint deletion, using the activity based measure (which is the default in *Sat4j*, and only a tie-break in *RoundingSat*) has really poor performance. The other strategies have a lesser impact on the solver, and seem more closely dependent on the proof system of the solver to bring improvement. However, if one needs to set up strategies that work well for all different proof systems, it would be `bump-assigned` for the bumping strategies, `delete-lbd-s` for the deletion strategy and either `degree`-based or *PicoSAT*'s restart policy (depending of whether big degrees are expected to be produced or not, respectively).

7 Conclusion

In this paper, we introduced different branching heuristics, learned constraint deletion and restart strategies dedicated to native PB solving. These strategies are generalizations of those classically implemented in SAT solvers, and are designed to take into account the properties of PB constraints to better fit in the CDCL architecture. Our experiments revealed that one of the key aspects of PB constraints to take into account is the current assignment of their literals. This is particularly true for the EVSIDS-based heuristics, but also for the learned constraint deletion strategies and the restart policies through the use of new *LBD*-based measures. When combined, these strategies allow to improve the PB solvers *RoundingSat* and *Sat4j*, with a particularly significant improvement for the latter, both on decision and optimization problems.

Nevertheless, none of these strategies performs better than the others on all benchmarks: their VBS clearly beats each individual strategy, even when considering their combination. Yet, the strategies introduced in this paper show that better adapting SAT strategies may improve the performance of PB solvers. A perspective for future research is to find better ways to adapt such strategies, and to define new strategies that are *specifically* designed for PB solving or PB optimization (rather than *adapting* existing strategies). Another avenue to explore is to find how to properly combine these strategies to get their best, while taking into account the interactions between these different strategies. In particular, it is not clear that combining all single best strategies provides the best combination. A possible approach to identify such a combination is to use dynamic algorithm configuration to select the most appropriate strategies according to the state of the solver [4].

Acknowledgement. The authors are grateful to the anonymous reviewers for their numerous comments, that greatly helped to improve the paper. Part of this work was supported by the French Ministry for Higher Education and Research and the Hauts-de-France Regional Council through the "Contrat de Plan État Région (CPER) DATA". This publication was supported by the Chair "Integrated Urban Mobility", backed by L'X – École Polytechnique and La Fondation de l'École Polytechnique and sponsored by Uber. The Partners of the Chair shall not under any circumstances accept any liability for the content of this publication, for which the author shall be solely liable.

References

1. Atserias, A., Fichte, J.K., Thurley, M.: Clause-learning algorithms with many restarts and bounded-width resolution. JAIR **40**, 353–373 (2011)
2. Audemard, G., Simon, L.: Predicting learnt clauses quality in modern SAT solvers. In: Proceedings of IJCAI 2009, pp. 399–404 (2009)
3. Audemard, G., Simon, L.: Refining restarts strategies for SAT and UNSAT. In: Milano, M. (ed.) Proceedings of CP 2012, pp. 118–126 (2012)
4. Biedenkapp, A., Bozkurt, H.F., Eimer, T., Hutter, F., Lindauer, M.: Dynamic algorithm configuration: foundation of a new meta-algorithmic framework. In: Proceedings of ECAI 2020 (2020)
5. Biere, A.: Adaptive restart strategies for conflict driven SAT solvers. In: Proceedings of SAT 2008, pp. 28–33 (2008)
6. Biere, A.: PicoSAT essentials. JSAT **4**(2–4), 75–97 (2008)
7. Biere, A., Fröhlich, A.: Evaluating CDCL variable scoring schemes. In: Proceedings of SAT 2015, pp. 405–422 (2015)
8. Biere, A., Fröhlich, A.: Evaluating CDCL Restart Schemes. In: Proceedings of Pragmatics of SAT 2015 and 2018. EPiC Series in Computing, vol. 59, pp. 1–17 (2019)
9. Chai, D., Kuehlmann, A.: A fast pseudo-Boolean constraint solver. IEEE Trans. CAD Integrated Circuits Syst., 305–317 (2005)
10. Cook, W., Coullard, C.R., Turán, G.: On the complexity of cutting-plane proofs. Discrete Appl. Math., 25–38 (1987)
11. Dixon, H.: Automating pseudo-boolean inference within a DPLL framework. Ph.D. thesis, University of Oregon (2004)
12. Dixon, H.E., Ginsberg, M.L.: Inference methods for a pseudo-boolean satisfiability solver. In: Proceedings of AAAI 2002, pp. 635–640 (2002)
13. Eén, N., Sörensson, N.: An Extensible SAT-solver. In: Proceedings of SAT 2004, pp. 502–518 (2004)
14. Elffers, J., Giráldez-Crú, J., Nordström, J., Vinyals, M.: Using Combinatorial Benchmarks to Probe the Reasoning Power of Pseudo-Boolean Solvers. In: Proceedings of SAT 2018, pp. 75–93 (2018)
15. Elffers, J., Giráldez-Cru, J., Gocht, S., Nordström, J., Simon, L.: Seeking practical CDCL insights from theoretical SAT benchmarks. In: Proceedings of IJCAI 2018, pp. 1300–1308 (2018)
16. Elffers, J., Nordström, J.: Divide and conquer: towards faster pseudo-boolean solving. In: Proceedings of IJCAI 2018, pp. 1291–1299 (2018)
17. Gocht, S., Nordström, J., Yehudayoff, A.: On Division Versus Saturation in Pseudo-Boolean Solving. In: Proceedings of IJCAI'2019. pp. 1711–1718 (2019)
18. Gomes, C.P., Selman, B., Kautz, H.: Boosting combinatorial search through randomization. In: Proceedings of AAAI 1998, pp. 431–437 (1998)
19. Gomory, R.E.: Outline of an algorithm for integer solutions to linear programs. Bulletin of the American Mathematical Society, pp. 275–278 (1958)
20. Haken, A.: The intractability of resolution. Theoretical Computer Science, pp. 297–308 (1985)
21. Hooker, J.N.: Generalized resolution and cutting planes. Annals of Operations Research, pp. 217–239 (1988)
22. Huang, J.: The Effect of Restarts on the Efficiency of Clause Learning. In: Proceedings of IJCAI 2007, pp. 2318–2323 (2007)

23. Le Berre, D., Marquis, P., Mengel, S., Wallon, R.: On irrelevant literals in pseudo-boolean constraint learning. In: Proceedings of IJCAI 2020, pp. 1148–1154 (2020)
24. Le Berre, D., Marquis, P., Wallon, R.: On Weakening strategies for PB solvers. In: Proceedings of SAT 2020, pp. 322–331 (2020)
25. Le Berre, D., Parrain, A.: The SAT4J library, Release 2.2, System Description. JSAT, pp. 59–64 (2010)
26. Le Berre, D., Wallon, R.: On Dedicated CDCL Strategies for PB Solvers Companion Artifact, May 2021. https://doi.org/10.5281/zenodo.4751685
27. Liang, J.H., Ganesh, V., Poupart, P., Czarnecki, K.: Learning rate based branching heuristic for SAT solvers. In: Proceedings of SAT 2016, pp. 123–140 (2016)
28. Luby, M., Sinclair, A., Zuckerman, D.: Optimal speedup of Las Vegas algorithms. In: Information Processing Letters, pp. 173–180 (1993)
29. Manquinho, V., Roussel, O.: The First Evaluation of Pseudo-Boolean Solvers (PB'05). JSAT, pp. 103–143 (2006)
30. Marques-Silva, J., Sakallah, K.A.: GRASP: a search algorithm for propositional satisfiability. IEEE Trans. Comput., 220–227 (1999)
31. Moskewicz, M.W., Madigan, C.F., Zhao, Y., Zhang, L., Malik, S.: Chaff: engineering an efficient SAT solver. In: Proceedings of DAC 2001, pp. 530–535 (2001)
32. Nordström, J.: On the interplay between proof complexity and SAT solving. ACM SIGLOG News, pp. 19–44 (2015)
33. Pipatsrisawat, K., Darwiche, A.: On the power of clause-learning SAT solvers as resolution engines. Artif. Intell. **175**(2), 512–525 (2011)
34. Roussel, O.: Pseudo-Boolean Competition 2016 (2016). http://www.cril.fr/PB16/. Accessed 20 May 2020
35. Roussel, O., Manquinho, V.M.: Pseudo-Boolean and Cardinality Constraints. In: Biere, A., Heule, M., van Maaren, H., Walsh, T. (eds.) Handbook of Satisfiability, Frontiers in Artificial Intelligence and Applications, vol. 185, pp. 695–733. IOS Press (2009)
36. Sheini, H.M., Sakallah, K.A.: Pueblo: a hybrid pseudo-boolean SAT solver. JSAT, pp. 165–189 (2006)
37. Vinyals, M., Elffers, J., Giráldez-Crú, J., Gocht, S., Nordström, J.: In Between resolution and cutting planes: a study of proof systems for pseudo-boolean SAT solving. In: Proceedings of SAT 2018, pp. 292–310 (2018)
38. Whittemore, J., Kim, J., Sakallah, K.A.: SATIRE: a new incremental satisfiability engine. In: Proceedings of DAC 2001, pp. 542–545 (2001)

Efficient Local Search for Pseudo Boolean Optimization

Zhendong Lei[1,2], Shaowei Cai[1,2(✉)], Chuan Luo[3], and Holger Hoos[4]

[1] State Key Laboratory of Computer Science, Institute of Software,
Chinese Academy of Sciences, Beijing, China
{leizd,caisw}@ios.ac.cn
[2] School of Computer Science and Technology,
University of Chinese Academy of Sciences, Beijing, China
[3] Microsoft Research, Beijing, China
chuan.luo@microsoft.com
[4] Leiden University, Leiden, The Netherlands
hh@liacs.nl

Abstract. Pseudo-Boolean Optimization (PBO) can be used to model many combinatorial optimization problems. PBO instances encoded from real-world applications are often large and difficult to solve; in many cases, close-to-optimal solutions are useful and can be found reasonably efficiently, using incomplete algorithms. Interestingly, local search algorithms, which are known to be effective for solving many other combinatorial optimization problems, have been rarely considered in the context of PBO. In this paper, we are introducing a new and surprisingly effective local search algorithm, *LS-PBO*, for PBO. *LS-PBO* adopts a well designed weighting scheme and a new scoring function. We compare *LS-PBO* with previous PBO solvers and with solvers for related problems, including MaxSAT, Extended CNF and Integer Linear Programming (ILP). We report results on three real-world application benchmarks, from the Minimum-Width Confidence Band, Wireless Sensor Network Optimization and Seating Arrangement Problems, as well as on benchmarks from the most recent PB Competition. These results demonstrate that our *LS-PBO* algorithm achieves much better performance than previous state-of-the-art solvers on real-world benchmarks.

Keywords: Local search · Pseudo boolean optimization

1 Introduction

Leveraging sustained and impressive improvements in the state of the art in practically solving SAT and MaxSAT, high-performance solvers for these problems are now increasingly used for solving suitably encoded real-world problems. However, in many cases, these encodings produce very large problem instances, due to the limited expressive power of CNF. This becomes obvious, for example,

© Springer Nature Switzerland AG 2021
C.-M. Li and F. Manyà (Eds.): SAT 2021, LNCS 12831, pp. 332–348, 2021.
https://doi.org/10.1007/978-3-030-80223-3_23

when contrasting SAT and MaxSAT encodings with formulations in the framework of Pseudo-Boolean Optimization (PBO), which can be used to model a large range of real-world problems from operations research, economics, manufacturing, etc. PBO formulations use linear pseudo-Boolean (LPB) constraints of the form $\sum a_i \cdot l_i \geq k$, where $a_i, k \in \mathbb{R}$, l_i is a variable x_i or its negation $\bar{x}_i$, and x_i takes values from $\{0, 1\}$, in combination with an objective function of the form $\min \sum c_i \cdot l_i$; this facilitates substantially more concise formulations than (weighted) CNF clauses.

Algorithms for solving PBO can be categorized into three families. First, Pseudo-Boolean solvers [7,18,22] are usually based on ideas from *conflict-driven clause learning* (CDCL) SAT solvers [24], and they can be easily extended to solve PBO – instead of stopping when a solution to all constraints is found, one can determine the value of the current solution and add a new constraint, such that a new solution must improve on the best solution found so far [1]. The well-known PBO solver OpenWBO [19] and the recent PBS/PBO solvers RoundingSAT [8] and HYBRID [6] are based on this idea. As a classical approach for solving combinatorial optimization problems, Branch and Bound (BnB) has also been applied to PBO [15]. Most work on BnB for PBO focuses on techniques for calculating lower bounds on the value of the cost function. Whenever the lower bound estimate is higher than or equal to the upper bound, the search can be pruned, since no better solution can be found by extending the current partial assignment. Important techniques for determining lower bounds include Maximum Independent Set [5] and Linear Programming Relaxation [17]. Further pruning of the search tree is usually achieved using cutting planes [10]. Finally, PB constraints can be translated into SAT, and surprisingly, this approach can be quite efficient [23]. However, all of these complete methods may fail to find optimal solutions for very large instances.

One of the most widely used approaches for underlying incomplete algorithms for challenging combinatorial optimization problems is local search. Somewhat surprisingly, the literature on local search algorithms for handling Pseudo-Boolean constraints is very sparse. In fact, the only recent work on local search for PBO introduced Extended CNF (ECNF), which can express cardinality constraints (a special case of LPB) directly, along with a local search solver for ECNF formulae [16].

In this work, we propose *LS-PBO*, a novel, highly effective local search algorithm for PBO. In our method, we transform the objective function into so-called *objective constraints*, which are added to the original constraints in the PBO instances. We introduce a constraint weighting scheme for PB constraints and a scoring function to guide the local search. The weights of constraints, including original and newly generated objective constraints, are updated throughout the search. The scoring function exploits the objective constraints and other constraints, and is used to select the variables that are iteratively modified by the local search procedure.

We evaluate our approach on three real-world problems – Minimum-Width Confidence Band, Wireless Sensor Network Optimization, and Seating Arrangement – as well as the benchmark instances from the latest PB competition (2016). We compare *LS-PBO* with previous PBO solvers, as well as with solvers for related problems, including MaxSAT, Extended CNF and Integer Linear Programming (ILP). Our empirical results show that *LS-PBO* achieves substantial improvements in terms solution quality and running time over state-of-the-art solvers for all these problems on our real-world benchmark instances.

The remainder of this paper is structured as follows. Section 2 provides some background knowledge. Section 3 introduces the weighting scheme and the scoring function used in our algorithm. Section 4 presents our new local search algorithm for PBO. The results from our experiments are presented in Sect. 5. In Sect. 6, we provide some general conclusions and an outlook on future work.

2   Preliminaries

A 0-1 ILP constraint is an inequality of the form:

$$\sum a_i \cdot x_i \left\{ \begin{matrix} \leq \\ = \\ \geq \end{matrix} \right\} b, \quad a_i, b \in \mathbb{N}, \quad x_i \in \{0, 1\} \tag{1}$$

Using the relation $\overline{x}_i = 1 - x_i$, the general form of (1) can be converted into an equivalent normalized LPB constraint involving only $\geq$ and positive coefficients:

$$\sum a_i \cdot l_i \geq k, \quad a_i, k \in \mathbb{N}^+, \quad l_i \in \{x_i, \overline{x}_i\} \tag{2}$$

The l_i are typically referred to as literals, and a literal is either a variable x_i or its negation $\overline{x}_i$. Cardinality constraints are special linear pseudo-Boolean (LPB) constraints, where all coefficients a_i are equal to 1:

$$\sum l_i \geq k, \quad k \in \mathbb{N}^+, \quad l_i \in \{x_i, \overline{x}_i\} \tag{3}$$

An instance of the Pseudo-Boolean Optimization (PBO) Problem consists of a set of LPB constraints and an objective function $min : \sum c_i \cdot l_i, c_i \in \mathbb{N}^+$, and the goal is to minimize the value of the objective function while satisfying all pseudo-Boolean constraints.

A complete assignment for PBO instance F is a mapping that assigns 0 or 1 to each variable. An assignment α of F is feasible if, and only if, it satisfies all constraints in F. The value of the objective function of a feasible solution α is denoted as $obj(\alpha)$.

A CNF clause is a disjunction of literals, which can also be expressed as a set of literals $\{l_1, l_2, ..., l_n\}$; it is satisfied under a given assignment if it has at least one literal evaluate to true, and falsified otherwise. Different methods of encoding LPB constraints into CNF have been studied, using BDDs, adders and sorting networks.

In Extended CNF (ECNF) [16], a clause is of the form $(\{l_1, l_2, ..., l_n\}, k)$, where k is the cardinality of the clause, and an ECNF clause with cardinality

k is satisfied if it has at least k literals evaluate to true, and falsified otherwise. ECNF has the same expressive power as cardinality constraints. LPB constraints can be encoded into ECNF via introducing additional variables and constraints. For example, the LPB constraint $2x_1 + x_2 \geq 2$ can be expressed by three ECNF clauses, $(\{y_1, y_2, x_2\}, 2), (\{\neg y_1, x_1\}, 1), (\{\neg y_2, x_1\}, 1)$.

3 Main Ideas

In this section, we present the main ideas leveraged in our new local search algorithm for solving Pseudo-Boolean Optimization problems.

3.1 Constraint Weighting

Weighting techniques are very commonly used in local search algorithms for discrete optimization problems – mostly, to increase the weight of unsatisfied constraints and thereby bias the search process towards satisfying these. Here, we propose a new weighting scheme for PBO. Specifically, in addition to the (hard) LPB constraints, whose weights we denote $w(c)$, we introduce an *objective constraint*:

- Given a PBO instance with an objective function $min : \sum_{i=1}^{n} c_i \cdot l_i$, the objective constraint is defined as $\sum_{i=1}^{n} c_i \cdot l_i < obj^*$, where obj^* is the objective value of the best solution found in the current run of the algorithm; at the beginning of the search, obj^* is initialized to ∞.

We further define:

- the coefficient of constraint $c : \sum_{i=1}^{n} a_i \cdot l_i$ $(\geq \ or \ <)$ k, $coeff(c) := \sum_{i=1}^{n} a_i/n$;
- the average constraint coefficient of the given PBO instance, $avg\_coeff := \sum_{c=1}^{m} w(c) \cdot coeff(c)/m$, where m is the number of contraints.

Our new weighting scheme, Weighting-PBO, works as follows: We assign an integer weight $w(c)$ with each constraint c, including the hard constraints and the objective constraint; at the beginning of the search, these weights are initialized to 1. Whenever the local search process is "stuck" in a local optimum, the weights of constraints are updated as follows:

- For each unsatisfied hard constraint c, $w(c) := w(c) + 1$;
- If the objective constraint oc is unsatisfied and $w(oc) \cdot coeff(oc) - avg\_coeff \leq \zeta$, then $w(oc) := w(oc) + 1$.

By increasing the weights of hard constraints, we help the local search process to find feasible solutions, by focusing on constraints that are often falsified in local optima. The weight updates for the objective constraint help guide the search towards solutions with better objective values.

We note that our primary goal is to find a feasible solution. Only when a feasible solution is found, we consider it meaningful to decrease cost (i.e., the value of the objective function). With this consideration, the weights of the hard constraint should be treated differently from the weight objective constraint. Intuitively, in order to find a feasible solution, the weight of the objective constraint should not be too large compared to the weights of the hard constraints – otherwise, the search is likely to become limited to a small subspace of assignments that satisfy the objective constraint. To prevent this situation, in our weighting scheme, we set an upper limit to the weight of the objective constraint.

3.2   Scoring Function

Local search algorithms typically use a scoring function and heuristics based on it to guide the search process. For SAT and related problems, these scoring functions usually measure the benefits of flipping a Boolean variable. Here, we define three scoring functions based on the constraint weights. Specifically, we define a scoring function for measuring the benefits w.r.t. satisfying hard constraints and a scoring function w.r.t. the objective score. We also consider the sum of these two functions as a combined scoring function.

- If a hard constraint c of the given PBO instance is unsatisfied ($\sum a_i \cdot l_i < k$), it incurs a penalty of $w(c) \cdot (k - \sum a_i \cdot l_i)$.
- The objective constraint oc, no matter weather it is satisfied or not, incurs a penalty of $w(oc) \cdot \sum c_i \cdot l_i$.
- The *hard score* of a variable x, denoted $hscore(x)$, is the decrease of the total penalty of unsatisfied hard constraints caused by flipping x.
- The *objective score* of a variable x, denoted by $oscore(x)$, is the decrease of the penalty of the objective constraint caused by flipping x.
- The *score* of a variable x is defined as $score(x) := hscore(x) + oscore(x)$.

Example 1. Consider a PBO instance $min : 100 \cdot x_1 + 200 \cdot x_2 + 300 \cdot x_3$, s.t. $c : 2 \cdot x_1 + 3 \cdot x_2 + 4 \cdot x_3 \geq 5$, and suppose the current weights of the hard constraint c and the objective constraint oc are 2 and 1, respectively, given the assignment $(x_1, x_2, x_3) = (1, 0, 0)$, then $hscore(x_1) = -2 \times 2, hscore(x_2) = 2 \times 3, hscore(x_3) = 2 \times 3$ and $oscore(x_1) = 1 \times 100, oscore(x_2) = -1 \times 200, oscore(x_3) = -1 \times 300$. Note that, the reason why $hsore(x_3)$ is 2×3 rather than 2×4 is that the maximum penalty it can reduce for this constraint is 2×3.

Note that the *hscore* and *oscore* functions measure the change on the total weight of the hard constraints and the objective constraint, respectively. Thus, the value of these functions are calculated based on the weights of constraints. Therefore, the weighting scheme provide guidance to the search process via the scoring functions.

Algorithm 1: LS-PBO

Input: PBO instance F, cutoff time *cutoff*
Output: A solution α of F and its objective value

1 **begin**
2      $\alpha^* := \emptyset, \quad obj^* := +\infty$;
3      $\alpha :=$ all variables are set to 0;
4   **while** *elapsed time < cutoff* **do**
5   **if** α *is feasible* **and** $obj(\alpha) < obj^*$ **then** $\alpha^* := \alpha$; $obj^* := obj(\alpha)$;
6   **if** $D := \{x | score(x) > 0\} \neq \emptyset$ **then**
7             $x :=$ a variable in D with the highest score;
8   **else**
9   update constraint weights using Weighting-PBO;
10   **if** $\exists$ *unsatisfied hard constraints* **then**
11                 $c :=$ a randomly chosen unsatisfied hard constraint;
12                 $x :=$ the variable with highest score in c;
13   **else**
14                 $x :=$ a randomly chosen variable with $oscore(x) > 0$;
15          $\alpha := \alpha$ with x flipped;
16   **return** (α^*, obj^*)

---

4   A Local Search Algorithm for PBO

In this section, we introduce *LS-PBO*, a new local search algorithm for PBO that is based on the weighting scheme and scoring functions from the previous section.

An outline of *LS-PBO* is presented in Algorithm 1. In the beginning, *LS-PBO* generates a complete assignment α by assigning each variable to 0 (the default value)[1], and the best found solution α^* and its objective value are initialized as $\emptyset$ and $+\infty$, respectively.

The main part of the algorithm consists of a loop (lines 4–15) in which assignment α is iteratively modified, by flipping the truth value assigned to one variable, until a given time limit is reached. During the search, whenever a better feasible solution is found, the best feasible solution α^*, and obj^* are updated accordingly (line 5).

At each iteration, if the set D of the variables with positive score is not empty, *LS-PBO* selects the variable with the highest score in D, breaking ties by preferring the variable that has been flipped least recently.

If set D is empty (line 8), which means that the search process has reached a local optimum, *LS-PBO* uses the weighting scheme to update the weights of the constraints. Then, a random perturbation is applied: If there exit falsified hard

---

[1] This all-0 initial assignment leads to better results than randomized initial assignments on the WSNO problem, where all hard constraints have at least one negative literal, while has little impact on the other two problems.

constraints, one of them is chosen uniformly at random, and the variable with the highest score in is selected from it. If there are no falsified hard constraints, a variable x with $oscore(x) > 0$ is selected uniformly at random and flipped.

When the time limit is reached, *LS-PBO* returns the best solution α^*, and its objective value obj^*. Note that, if the algorithm fails to find any feasible solution during the search, then $\alpha^* = \emptyset$ and $obj^* = +\infty$.

5   Experiments

We evaluate *LS-PBO* on PBO instances from both real-world application problems and the latest PB competition, comparing *LS-PBO* against state-of-the-art solvers for various encodings, including two PBO solvers, two MaxSAT solvers, one ECNF solver and one ILP solver:

- Open-WBO [19] was one of the best-performing Pseudo-Boolean Optimization solvers in the recent PB competition 2016.
- HYBRID [6] is a very recent PBO solver built upon RoundingSAT [8]; it has been shown to perform better than the PB solver RoundingSAT, the SAT solver SAT4J, the PBO solver NAPS (which re-encodes PBO instances into CNF and solves them using a CDCL solver), and the ILP solver SCIP on a broad range of PBO benchmarks [6].
- Loandra [2] is a MaxSAT solver that won two unweighted categories and was ranked 2nd in two weighted categories of the incomplete track of MSE 2019.
- SATLike-c [4] is a MaxSAT solver that won two unweighted categories, and was ranked 2nd in two weighted categories of incomplete track in MSE 2020.
- *LS-ECNF* [16] is an Extended Partial MaxSAT solver known to perform well on problems with cardinality constraints.
- Gurobi [9] is one of the most powerful ILP solvers [11]; here, we use both its complete and heuristic versions.

Our solver *LS-PBO* has been implemented in C++ and compiled using g++ with -O3 option. The parameter ζ is set to 100, following preliminary experiments with $\zeta = 10, 20, 50, 80, 100, 150, 200, 500$, which indicated a single peak in performance at $\zeta = 100$.

The experiments were conducted on a server using 2.00 GHz Intel Xeon Platinum 8153 CPUs, 512 GB RAM, running the Centos 7.7.1908 Linux operating system. We used time limits of 300 and 3600 s. For each instance, we report the value of the objective function of the best feasible solution found by each solver. For each randomized solver, we performed 20 runs per instance with different seeds, and we report the minimum, median and maximum performance values obtained over these 20 runs.

In our experiments, we used three real-world application benchmarks described in the following as well as instances from the most recent PB competition. For some of these benchmarks, the instances are available in different encodings and we can thus compare the solvers directly, running each on its native formulation. For others, we need to encode the PBO instances into weighted CNF (for MaxSAT), Extended CNF and Integer Liner Programming (ILP) for comparison. For the weighted CNF encoding, we use PBLib [21], a C++ tool for efficiently encoding PB constraints into CNF. The ENCF and ILP encodings are straightforward. Our solver and all benchmark instances are available at https://lcs.ios.ac.cn/~caisw/Resource/LS-PBO/.

5.1   Minimum-Width Confidence Band Problem

The Minimum-Width Confidence Band Problem (MWCB) is a central problem arising from the analysis of multivariate data, namely, determining minimum-width multivariate confidence intervals. We consider a set of n data vectors x_i, each of length m, represented by a matrix $X \in \mathbb{R}^{n \times m}$. Let $x_{ij} \in X$ denote the j-th element of x_i; X can, for instance, represent time series data, where x_i is a sequence of values observed at successive points in time. A confidence band is defined as a pair (l, u) of vectors, where $l, u \in \mathbb{R}^m$ and $l_j \leq u_j$ for all j. The size of the confidence band $CB = (l, u)$ is $SIZE(CB) = \sum_1^m (u_j - l_j)$. The concept of *error* of a confidence band captures the relationship between a confidence band and a dataset. In the following, $I[C]$ denotes an indicator function with value 1 if condition C is satisfied, and 0 otherwise.

Definition 1. *Given a data vector x_i and a confidence band $CB = (l, u)$, the error of x_i w.r.t. CB is defined as the number of points in x_i that lie outside of CB, i.e., $ERROR(x_i, CB) = \sum_{j=1}^m I[x_{ij} < l_j \vee u_j < x_{ij}]$.*

In the MWCB problem, the goal is to find a confidence band CB of minimal size that satisfies the following constraints:

$$\sum_{i=1}^n I[ERROR(x_i, CB) > s] \leq k$$
$$\forall j \in [1, m] \quad \sum_{i=1}^n I[x_{ij} < l_j \vee x_{ij} > u_j] \leq t,$$

The MWCB problem was proposed in [3], where encodings of MWCP instances where solved using MaxSAT and ILP solvers. In that work, a PB encoding of the MWCB problem was also described, which we also use here. For our experiments, we obtained benchmark instances based on the MIT-BIH arrhythmia database,[2] which is often used in this field [3,12]. There are $n = 2027$ observations in heartbeat-pvc for $m = 253$ time points. In our experiments, the number of observations ranges from 1000 to 2000, and the number of time points ranges from 200 to 250. As for parameter values, we consider $k \in \{0.05 \cdot n, 0.1 \cdot n\}$, $s = 0.05 \, \text{m}$ and $t = k$, as done in [3].

Empirical Results on MWCB: The results from our experiments on MWCB are shown in Tables 1 and 2. Note that, according to our results, Open-WBO performs worse than HYBRID (they are both PBO solvers), and SATLike-c performs very similarly to Loandra (both are MaxSAT solvers), so we do not report results for them here.

---

[2] http://physionet.org/physiobank/database/mitdb/.

Table 1. Empirical results on MWCB, using a 300 s time limit.

Instance	LS-PBO	LS-ECNF	Loandra	HYBRID	Gurobi	
n m k	min[median,max]	min[median,max]			Comp.	Heur.
1000_200_90	110877[+1137, +2678]	115437[+688, +1797]	145826	168706	178806	178806
1000_250_90	148419[+1728, +3434]	154520[+810, +1773]	212839	229951	225930	225930
1200_200_90	112315[+1755, +39538]	116215[+1299, +40078]	181602	223161	220532	220532
1200_250_90	152635[+1292, +3085]	156652[+2378, +3361]	258986	294630	292139	292139
1400_200_90	112449[+1697, +43271]	116437[+880, +43576]	162754	224998	221419	221419
1400_250_90	152348[+2055, +3372]	157077[+1432, +2976]	224473	286857	290957	290957
1600_200_90	138877[+3330, +17492]	150257[+2862, +11811]	N/A	353560	353637	353637
1600_250_90	190110[+10081, +21720]	200335[+4720, +11411]	N/A	449511	444099	444099
1800_200_90	226605[+5755, +12123]	237681[+5843, +12136]	325357	378119	371792	371792
1800_250_90	286398[+6610, +14552]	296513[+5038, +13063]	N/A	472753	466396	466396
2000_200_90	251293[+4628, +49657]	260974[+6095, +48602]	N/A	393500	386950	386950
2000_250_90	319214[+4682, +8080]	324478[+8252, +14350]	N/A	483632	484738	484738
1000_200_95	117375[+935, +2624]	124137[+693, +1842]	149161	154645	175815	131435
1000_250_95	157216[+1628, +3041]	165082[+1079, +1427]	208022	204125	226035	226035
1200_200_95	118988[+1030, +41269]	126289[+1327, +40220]	171594	189875	222200	153473
1200_250_95	160248[+1535, +2384]	169527[+1326, +2544]	202194	270289	210573	292950
1400_200_95	119772[+459, +42860]	126961[+750, +45110]	169947	208118	223483	223483
1400_250_95	162509[+960, +2317]	170748[+1427, +2105]	199947	276115	291315	291315
1600_200_95	185417[+7263, +20133]	196546[+3490, +8452]	276634	336499	349746	349746
1600_250_95	239321[+3937, +16837]	254685[+2948, +8332]	388998	442173	446997	446997
1800_200_95	253976[+3498, +7565]	260176[+2906, +5323]	329055	368134	371603	371603
1800_250_95	318906[+2578, +8154]	325120[+2296, +6345]	420992	460488	465933	465933
2000_200_95	277757[+3111, +49303]	278487[+2383, +52978]	N/A	375494	387405	387405
2000_250_95	343670[+5656, +11008]	349308[+3499, +6921]	N/A	491377	484636	484636

For the 300 s time limit, Gurobi performs worst. Loandra may fail to find feasible solutions in some cases, but it performs better than HYBRID for most instances. *LS-PBO* and *LS-ECNF* perform much better than all other solvers. Now we turn our focus to the comparison between *LS-PBO* and *LS-ECNF*. *LS-PBO* consistently outperforms *LS-ECNF* on all MWCB instances. More encouragingly, for each MWCB instance, even the worst solution of *LS-PBO* is better than that found by other solvers.

For the 3600 s time limit, Gurobi shows much improved performance, and in fact performs better than Loandra and HYBRID, but still much worse than *LS-PBO*. The increase in running time does not have much impact on the performance of *LS-PBO*, which clearly remains the best of the solvers we considered for solving these MWCB instances.

5.2 Wireless Sensor Network Optimization Problem

Nowadays, in Internet of Things (IoT) applications, Wireless Sensor Networks (WSN) [13,14] provide an effective and flexible mechanism for accessing information in many real-world applications. We consider the following problem. Given

Table 2. Empirical results on MWCB, using a 3600 s time limit.

Instance	LS-PBO	LS-ECNF	Loandra	HYBRID	Gurobi	
n m k	min[median,max]	min[median,max]			Comp.	Heur.
1000_200_90	110450[+743, +3075]	114602[+899, +1376]	143854	148403	127146	119670
1000_250_90	148181[+1797, +2999]	153101[+732, +1521]	212839	200498	159888	160566
1200_200_90	111060[+2340, +40120]	115803[+703, +38819]	174318	182787	122907	123099
1200_250_90	150212[+2793, +4201]	156568[+843, +1631]	220894	258209	162783	169289
1400_200_90	110792[+2081, +43621]	115383[+794, +42816]	151074	198229	121170	120765
1400_250_90	150981[+1615, +3698]	155964[+896, +2235]	201628	245942	165157	173345
1600_200_90	137763[+4193, +19123]	148050[+2659, +10149]	N/A	294479	353637	207782
1600_250_90	183797[+10768, +25258]	197618[+2333, +7077]	N/A	375047	252988	267170
1800_200_90	221717[+2755, +7563]	228785[+8389, +12156]	309036	343437	275615	310234
1800_250_90	280700[+2553, +7322]	291657[+4226, +7370]	381621	461042	382024	466396
2000_200_90	247557[+3616, +40465]	258033[+2933, +40994]	N/A	372058	330113	386950
2000_250_90	310250[+3577, +9109]	321742[+2311, +5741]	N/A	454465	484738	484738
1000_200_90	117375[+847, +2960]	124055[+501, +1924]	127499	137079	127501	131240
1000_250_90	156625[+1428, +2395]	164512[+975, +1950]	177597	186906	167825	167765
1200_200_90	118045[+1611, +40975]	125787[+748, +40675]	136513	153666	126149	132959
1200_250_90	159310[+1812, +3316]	168346[+1365, +2898]	185112	227155	167596	181787
1400_200_90	119092[+675, +43534]	126229[+912, +45015]	142457	159342	124943	132487
1400_250_90	161814[+852, +2416]	170012[+1093, +2678]	199947	253924	175104	172885
1600_200_90	185822[+5659, +10050]	196658[+1421, +8340]	272554	263979	230254	250291
1600_250_90	239049[+3677, +10498]	251506[+3238, +10852]	361586	366987	446997	298824
1800_200_90	251744[+5171, +7848]	257759[+2635, +7740]	321124	317803	287682	275934
1800_250_90	314968[+3855, +8023]	323095[+2704, +8370]	395373	410809	343816	465933
2000_200_90	274498[+2734, +48493]	278461[+2230, +53004]	N/A	339323	292612	296753
2000_250_90	342836[+4865, +8795]	349537[+1455, +6692]	N/A	446888	360203	484636

n sensor nodes, let r_i denote the range of the i-th sensor node. The greater this range, the shorter is the lifetime L_i of a given sensor node. There are m points of interest that should be covered by at least k sensors each. Let d_{ij} denote the physical distance between the i-th sensor node and the j-th point. Let w_{it} be a Boolean variable that models whether the i-th sensor node is awake at the t-th time interval. If T denotes the sleep/wake-up scheduling length of the WSN, the goal in the Wireless Sensor Network Optimization Problem (WNSO) is to maximize T while fulfilling a set of constraints (outlined later in this section).

In previous work [13,14], WSNO has been encoded into a set of decision problems for fixed scheduling lengths T, which were then solved using a SAT or SMT solver. This process starts with T set to 1; then, whenever an instance has been found satisfiable, T is increased by one. Upon encountering the first unsatisfiable instance in this process, $T - 1$ is returned as the optimal solution of the given WSNO instance.

In practice, this approach has been found to be limited to about 10 sensors, which is far below the instance sizes encountered in real-world applications. Here, we propose an encoding as an optimization problem, which is solved using a single run of a suitable solver. To our best knowledge, we are the first to consider this kind of encoding for WSNO. In our experiments, the number of sensors n ranges from 100 to 500, the number of points m ranges from 40 to 200, and the coverage k ranges from 4 to 6.

To obtain a PBO instance, we introduce additional variables $T_t, t \in [1, ub]$ such that $T_t = 1$ means that the scheduling length of the current solution is at least t, and ub is an upper bound on the value of T; we use $ub = \sum L_i / k$.

- Objective function: The goal is to maximize the scheduling length, i.e.

$$min : \sum_{t=1}^{t=ub} \overline{T}_t \tag{4}$$

- Correctness of variables T_i: If $T_t = 1$, then $T_{t-1} = 1$:

$$\forall t \in [2, ub] \qquad \overline{T}_t + T_{t-1} \geq 1 \tag{5}$$

- Coverage constraint: If $T_t = 1$ then, at the t-th time interval, every point must be covered by at least k nodes:

$$\forall j \in [1, m], t \in [1, ub], S_j = \{i | d_{ij} \leq r_i\} \quad \sum_{i \in S_j} w_{i,t} + k \cdot \overline{T}_t \geq k \tag{6}$$

- Lifetime constraint: For each sensor node, the number of time intervals at which the node is awake must not exceed the node's lifetime:

$$\forall i \in [1, n] \qquad \sum_{t=1}^{t=ub} \overline{w}_{i,t} \geq ub - L_i \tag{7}$$

- Evasive constraint: Each sensor node must not stay active for more than E consecutive time intervals:

$$\forall i \in [1, n], t \in [1, ub - E] \quad \sum_{t'=t}^{t'=t+E} \overline{w}_{i,t'} \geq 1 \tag{8}$$

- Moving target constraint: Some critical points may be required not be covered by the same sensor for more than M consecutive time intervals, where $M < E$:

$$\forall j \in CR, i \in S_j, t \in [1, ub - M], CR \supset [1, m] \quad \sum_{t'=t}^{t'=t+M} \overline{w}_{i,t'} \geq 1 \tag{9}$$

Empirical Results on WSNO: The results of our experiments on WSNO are shown in Tables 3 and 4. Note that, as Open-WBO was found to perform worse than HYBRID, and Loandra worse than SATlike-c in this experiment, we do not show results for these solvers.

Table 3. Empirical results on WSNO, using a 300 s time limit.

Instance	LS-PBO	LS-ECNF	SATLike-c	HYBRID	Gurobi	
n m k	min[median,max]	min[median,max]	min[median,max]		Comp.	Heur.
100_40_4	210[+0, +4]	210[+2, +6]	741[+15, +44]	210	210	210
150_60_4	602[+0, +0]	605[N/A, N/A]	1063[+71, +93]	602	1180	1180
200_80_4	715[+0, +10]	726[N/A, N/A]	N/A[N/A, N/A]	1767	1911	1911
250_100_4	1305[+0, +433]	2200[N/A, N/A]	N/A[N/A, N/A]	2123	2200	2200
300_120_4	1257[+32, +1315]	2572[N/A, N/A]	N/A[N/A, N/A]	2510	2572	2572
350_140_4	1737[+206, +1426]	3163[N/A, N/A]	N/A[N/A, N/A]	3137	3163	3163
400_160_4	2240[+644, +1296]	N/A[N/A, N/A]	N/A[N/A, N/A]	3509	N/A	N/A
450_180_4	1869[+931, +2172]	N/A[N/A, N/A]	N/A[N/A, N/A]	4026	N/A	N/A
500_200_4	3727[+886, +886]	N/A[N/A, N/A]	N/A[N/A, N/A]	4613	N/A	N/A
100_40_6	140[+0, +4]	140[+4, +9]	363[+39, +119]	140	140	140
150_60_6	402[+0, +1]	787[+0, N/A]	727[+30, +53]	402	709	709
200_80_6	477[+0, +8]	504[N/A, N/A]	N/A[N/A, N/A]	911	1274	1274
250_100_6	870[+0, +89]	1467[+0, +0]	N/A[N/A, N/A]	1299	1467	1467
300_120_6	839[+0, +876]	1715[+0, +0]	N/A[N/A, N/A]	1580	1715	1715
350_140_6	1158[+114, +951]	2109[+0, +0]	N/A[N/A, N/A]	2075	2109	2109
400_160_6	1493[+0, +864]	2357[+0, +0]	N/A[N/A, N/A]	2340	2357	2357
450_180_6	1246[+543, +1448]	2694[+0, N/A]	N/A[N/A, N/A]	2670	N/A	N/A
500_200_6	1784[+1291, +1291]	3075[N/A, N/A]	N/A[N/A, N/A]	3075	N/A	N/A

Table 4. Empirical results on WSNO, using a 3600 s time limit. Cases in which a solver was able to prove the optimality of the solution to a given instance are marked "*".

Instance	LS-PBO	LS-ECNF	SATLike-c	HYBRID	Gurobi	
n m k	min[median,max]	min[median,max]	min[median,max]		Comp.	Heur.
100_40_4	210[+0, +3]	210[+0, +1]	214[+51, +78]	210*	210*	210*
150_60_4	602[+0, +2]	602[+23, +578]	802[+67, +127]	602*	602*	602*
200_80_4	715[+0, +6]	720[+9, +126]	1806[+53, +74]	715*	715*	715*
250_100_4	1305[+0, +0]	1307[+893, N/A]	2110[+53, +82]	1305	2200	2200
300_120_4	1257[+0, +48]	1383[N/A, N/A]	N/A[N/A, N/A]	1608	2572	2572
350_140_4	1737[+0, +85]	3163[+0, N/A]	N/A[N/A, N/A]	2635	3163	3163
400_160_4	2240[+0, +10]	N/A[N/A, N/A]	N/A[N/A, N/A]	2915	N/A	N/A
450_180_4	1869[+0, +381]	N/A[N/A, N/A]	N/A[N/A, N/A]	3697	N/A	N/A
500_200_4	2577[+14, +2036]	4613[N/A, N/A]	N/A[N/A, N/A]	4277	N/A	N/A
100_40_6	140[+0, +0]	140[+1, +3]	141[+1, +5]	140*	140*	140*
150_60_6	402[+0, +0]	426[+361, +361]	403[+68, +94]	402*	402*	402*
200_80_6	477[+0, +2]	489[+25, +785]	1150[+51, +85]	477*	1274	1274
250_100_6	870[+0, +6]	1467[+0, +0]	1349[+90, +116]	870*	1109	870
300_120_6	839[+0, +37]	1715[+0, +0]	N/A[N/A, N/A]	839	1715	1715
350_140_6	1158[+0, +34]	2109[+0, +0]	N/A[N/A, N/A]	1158	2109	2109
400_160_6	1493[+0, +22]	2357[+0, +0]	N/A[N/A, N/A]	1493	2357	2357
450_180_6	1246[+0, +269]	2694[+0, N/A]	N/A[N/A, N/A]	2130	N/A	N/A
500_200_6	1718[+0, +79]	3075[+0, +0]	N/A[N/A, N/A]	2559	N/A	N/A

For the 300 s time limit, LS-ECNF and SATLike-c turned out to be unable to find any feasible solutions in most cases, resulting in the worst performance. HYBRID was is able to find feasible solutions for all instances and performs better than Gurobi, but the gap between HYBRID and our solver LS-PBO is very large. For many instances, even the worst solutions found by LS-PBO is better than those obtained from HYBRID. For the 3600 s time limit, LS-ECNF and SATLike-c still performs worse than other solvers. For small instances, *LS-PBO* can find the same optimal solutions as HYBRID and Gurobi in most cases. Nevertheless, for the larger instances, *LS-PBO* usually produces better solutions than HYBRID and Gurobi. Furthermore, we can also see that the performance obtained in independent runs of *LS-PBO* does not vary much. Overall, on this WSNO benchmark, *LS-PBO* represents a substantial improvement over all other methods we considered.

5.3 Seating Arrangements Problem

The Seating Arrangements Problem (SAP) arises frequently in real-world situations, such as weddings and annual meetings of companies: Given n guests, m tables and s labels, where each guest can have multiple labels, let x_{ij} denote whether guest i is seated at table j, and y_{jk} whether there is a guest with label k seated at j. The objective is then assign guests to tables such that the number of different labels found at each table is minimized, i.e., to the largest possible extent to have at each table guests with the same labels, subject to some additional constraints (specified below). We note that this can be regarded as a special kind of clustering problem. A PBO formulation is as follows:

- Objective function: The goal is to minimize the number of labels at each table:

$$min : \sum_{j=1}^{m} \sum_{k=1}^{s} y_{jk} \tag{10}$$

- The number of the labels of each table must not exceed a given number C:

$$\forall j \in [1, m] \qquad \sum_{k=1}^{s} \overline{y}_{jk} \geq s - C \tag{11}$$

- Each guest i can only be seated at exactly one table:

$$\forall i \in [1, n] \qquad \sum_{j=1}^{m} x_{ij} \geq 1, \ \sum_{j=1}^{m} \overline{x}_{ij} \geq m - 1 \tag{12}$$

- Each table has at most U guests:

$$\forall j \in [1, m] \qquad \sum_{i=1}^{n} \overline{x}_{ij} \geq n - U \tag{13}$$

- Each table has at least L guests:

$$\forall j \in [1, m] \qquad \sum_{i=1}^{n} x_{ij} \geq L \tag{14}$$

- Guests which have conflicts with each other cannot be seated at the same table, i.e., for every pair of guests i and i' that have such a conflict:

$$\forall j \in [1, m] \qquad \overline{x}_{ij} + \overline{x}_{i'j} \geq 1 \tag{15}$$

- Table j will contain all the labels of S_i, where S_i denotes the set of all labels of guest i, if i is allocated to table j:

$$\forall i \in [1, n], j \in [1, m], k \in S_i \quad \overline{x}_{ij} + y_{jk} \geq 1 \tag{16}$$

SAP was originally proposed in the MaxSAT Evaluation 2017 [20]. Compared to the original formulation, we introduce an additional constraint (see constraint (11)), since in real-world applications, it seems important that guests seated at any given table should not have too many different labels.

Empirical Results for SAP: The results from our experiments on SAP are shown in Table 5. As Loandra and Open-WBO failed to find any feasible solution for any of the instances, we do not report their experiment results.

We found that all CNF- and PB-based solvers were unable to find feasible solutions for any of the instances, even when using a time limit of 3600 s. For a 300 s time limit, Gurobi was only able to find 2 feasible solutions, and this number increased to 3 for a 3600 s time limit. While both LS-PBO and LS-ECNF can solve all these instances quickly, LS-PBO shows much better performance: For each instance, the worst solution found by LS-PBO turned out to be superior to the best solution produced by LS-ECNF.

5.4 Results on Pseudo-Boolean Competition Benchmark

Finally, we evaluated our solver against state-of-the-art competitors on the OPT-SMALL-INT benchmark from the most recent Pseudo-Boolean Competition in 2016, which has also been used in recent literature to evaluate PBO solvers [6]. For this PB16 benchmark, we report the average score of each solver, which is computed by the sum of the ratios between the best solution found by a given solver and the best solution found by all solvers. This comparison methodology has also been used in recent MaxSAT Evaluations (2017–2020). We did not include MaxSAT solvers in our experiments, since several of the instances from PB16 are too large to admit practical encodings into MaxSAT.

The results from our experiments on PB16 are shown in Table 6. For this benchmark, LS-PBO cannot compete with HYBRID yet, but it tends to perform better than Gurobi. We note that the gap between LS-PBO and HYBRID is not very big, and we are convinced that it can be reduced or eliminated in future work on LS-PBO.

Table 5. Empirical results on SAP, with 300 s and 3600 s time limits.

Instance	LS-PBO	LS-ECNF	SATLike-c	HYBRID	Gurobi	
n	min[median,max]	min[median,max]	min[median,max]		comp	heur
TimeLimit = 300 s						
100	**582**[+4, +9]	606[+14, +30]	N/A[N/A, N/A]	N/A	688	759
110	**623**[+8, +12]	668[+14, N/A]	N/A[N/A, N/A]	N/A	841	841
120	**680**[+10, +13]	698[+8, +12]	N/A[N/A, N/A]	N/A	N/A	N/A
130	**745**[+5, +9]	761[+10, +14]	N/A[N/A, N/A]	N/A	N/A	N/A
140	**762**[+8, +13]	791[+8, +15]	N/A[N/A, N/A]	N/A	N/A	N/A
150	**829**[+5, +10]	845[+10, +16]	N/A[N/A, N/A]	N/A	N/A	N/A
160	**873**[+6, +13]	882[+18, +25]	N/A[N/A, N/A]	N/A	N/A	N/A
170	**907**[+7, +14]	932[+8, +16]	N/A[N/A, N/A]	N/A	N/A	N/A
180	**975**[+10, +14]	994[+20, +28]	N/A[N/A, N/A]	N/A	N/A	N/A
190	**1005**[+10, +17]	1028[+14, +20]	N/A[N/A, N/A]	N/A	N/A	N/A
200	**1066**[+16, +21]	1096[+17, +26]	N/A[N/A, N/A]	N/A	N/A	N/A
210	**1110**[+11, +16]	1145[+10, +15]	N/A[N/A, N/A]	N/A	N/A	N/A
220	**1157**[+17, +26]	1195[+6, +14]	N/A[N/A, N/A]	N/A	N/A	N/A
230	**1202**[+11, +17]	1232[+11, +20]	N/A[N/A, N/A]	N/A	N/A	N/A
240	**1236**[+8, +14]	1262[+20, +28]	N/A[N/A, N/A]	N/A	N/A	N/A
250	**1289**[+12, +24]	1328[+11, +18]	N/A[N/A, N/A]	N/A	N/A	N/A
260	**1333**[+14, +22]	1358[+15, +24]	N/A[N/A, N/A]	N/A	N/A	N/A
270	**1396**[+19, +30]	1432[+19, +30]	N/A[N/A, N/A]	N/A	N/A	N/A
280	**1422**[+13, +21]	1458[+19, +29]	N/A[N/A, N/A]	N/A	N/A	N/A
290	**1473**[+12, +21]	1512[+16, +29]	N/A[N/A, N/A]	N/A	N/A	N/A
300	**1538**[+23, +31]	1582[+18, +31]	N/A[N/A, N/A]	N/A	N/A	N/A
TimeLimit = 3600 s						
100	**580**[+3, +5]	606[+17, +36]	N/A[N/A, N/A]	N/A	622	759
110	**620**[+6, +9]	666[+14, N/A]	N/A[N/A, N/A]	N/A	660	841
120	**679**[+6, +10]	700[+6, +10]	N/A[N/A, N/A]	N/A	N/A	N/A
130	**738**[+7, +10]	761[+9, +15]	N/A[N/A, N/A]	N/A	N/A	N/A
140	**757**[+7, +10]	790[+8, +16]	N/A[N/A, N/A]	N/A	N/A	N/A
150	**822**[+5, +9]	845[+11, +18]	N/A[N/A, N/A]	N/A	N/A	972
160	**869**[+4, +8]	895[+6, +12]	N/A[N/A, N/A]	N/A	N/A	N/A
170	**897**[+9, +13]	928[+12, +20]	N/A[N/A, N/A]	N/A	N/A	N/A
180	**971**[+7, +10]	990[+25, +32]	N/A[N/A, N/A]	N/A	N/A	N/A
190	**996**[+11, +17]	1028[+14, +23]	N/A[N/A, N/A]	N/A	N/A	N/A
200	**1071**[+3, +8]	1096[+17, +26]	N/A[N/A, N/A]	N/A	N/A	N/A
210	**1094**[+15, +25]	1146[+9, +14]	N/A[N/A, N/A]	N/A	N/A	N/A
220	**1152**[+10, +18]	1195[+7, +12]	N/A[N/A, N/A]	N/A	N/A	N/A
230	**1195**[+9, +13]	1225[+15, +26]	N/A[N/A, N/A]	N/A	N/A	N/A
240	**1219**[+15, +20]	1270[+12, +20]	N/A[N/A, N/A]	N/A	N/A	N/A
250	**1274**[+12, +22]	1330[+9, +19]	N/A[N/A, N/A]	N/A	N/A	N/A
260	**1318**[+12, +18]	1358[+13, +24]	N/A[N/A, N/A]	N/A	N/A	N/A
270	**1392**[+11, +16]	1443[+8, +16]	N/A[N/A, N/A]	N/A	N/A	N/A
280	**1407**[+15, +21]	1455[+22, +33]	N/A[N/A, N/A]	N/A	N/A	N/A
290	**1448**[+20, +28]	1513[+17, +29]	N/A[N/A, N/A]	N/A	N/A	N/A
300	**1538**[+8, +18]	1582[+18, +26]	N/A[N/A, N/A]	N/A	N/A	N/A

Table 6. Empirical results on benchmarks from the 2016 PB Competition

Benchmark	#inst.	Timelimit	LS-OPB Score (avg)	HYBRID Score(avg)	Gurobi (comp) Score (avg)	Gurobi(heur) Score (avg)
PB16	1600	300 s	0.6683	0.8018	0.6762	0.6562
PB16	1600	3600 s	0.7283	0.8130	0.6990	0.6859

6 Conclusions and Future Work

We have introduced a new and highly effective local search algorithm for PBO, LS-PBO. Experiments on benchmarks from three real-world application problems, as well as on a suite of benchmark instances from the most recent PB competition demonstrate clearly that LS-PBO performs far better than a broad set of other state-of-the-art solvers not only for PBO, but also for MaxSAT, ECNF and ILP. This establishes our new algorithm as the method of choice for solving many real-world problems that can be easily and naturally formalised in the framework of PBO. In future work, we intend to develop even more efficient local search solvers for PBO and demonstrate their ability to effectively solve additional real-world combinatorial problems.

Acknowledgement. This work was supported by the Beijing Academy of Artificial Intelligence (BAAI), and the Youth Innovation Promotion Association, Chinese Academy of Sciences (No. 2017150), and partly sponsored by China Construction Bank University (Project No. 2020103).

References

1. Barth, P.: A Davis-Putnam enumeration algorithm for linear pseudo-Boolean optimization. In: Technical Report MPI-I-95-2-003. Max Plank Institute for Computer Science (1995)
2. Berg, J., Demirović, E., Stuckey, P.J.: Core-boosted linear search for incomplete MaxSAT. In: Rousseau, L.-M., Stergiou, K. (eds.) CPAIOR 2019. LNCS, vol. 11494, pp. 39–56. Springer, Cham (2019). https://doi.org/10.1007/978-3-030-19212-9_3
3. Berg, J., Oikarinen, E., Järvisalo, M., Puolamäki, K.: Minimum-width confidence bands via constraint optimization. In: Beck, J.C. (ed.) CP 2017. LNCS, vol. 10416, pp. 443–459. Springer, Cham (2017). https://doi.org/10.1007/978-3-319-66158-2_29
4. Cai, S., Lei, Z.: Old techniques in new ways: clause weighting, unit propagation and hybridization for maximum satisfiability. Artif. Intell. **287**, 103354 (2020)
5. Coudert, O., Madre, J.C.: New ideas for solving covering problems. In: Preas, B. (ed.) Proceedings of the 32st Conference on Design Automation, 1995, pp. 641–646. ACM Press (1995)
6. Devriendt, J., Gocht, S., Demirović, E., Stuckey, P., Nordström, J.: Cutting to the core of pseudo-Boolean optimization: combining core-guided search with cutting planes reasoning. In: AAAI 2021, Accepted (2021). http://www.csc.kth.se/~jakobn/research/CuttingToTheCore_AAAI.pdf

7. Elffers, J., Giráldez-Cru, J., Nordström, J., Vinyals, M.: Using combinatorial benchmarks to probe the reasoning power of pseudo-boolean solvers. In: Beyersdorff, O., Wintersteiger, C.M. (eds.) SAT 2018. LNCS, vol. 10929, pp. 75–93. Springer, Cham (2018). https://doi.org/10.1007/978-3-319-94144-8_5

8. Elffers, J., Nordström, J.: Divide and conquer: towards faster pseudo-Boolean solving. In: Lang, J. (ed.) Proceedings of IJCAI 2018, pp. 1291–1299 (2018)

9. Gurobi Optimization, L.: Gurobi optimizer reference manual (2019). http://www.gurobi.com

10. Hooker, J.N.: Logic-based methods for optimization. In: Borning, A. (ed.) PPCP 1994. LNCS, vol. 874, pp. 336–349. Springer, Heidelberg (1994). https://doi.org/10.1007/3-540-58601-6_111

11. Hvattum, L.M., Løkketangen, A., Glover, F.W.: Comparisons of commercial MIP solvers and an adaptive memory (tabu search) procedure for a class of 0–1 integer programming problems. Algorithmic Oper. Res. 7(1), 13–20 (2012)

12. Jussi, K., Kai, P., Aristides, G.: Confidence bands for time series data. In: Data Mining and Knowledge Discovery, pp. 1530–1553 (2014). https://doi.org/10.1007/s10618-014-0371-0

13. Kovasznai, G., Erdelyi, B., Biro, C.: 2018 IEEE International Conference on Future IoT Technologies (Future IoT) - Investigations of Graph Properties in Terms of Wireless Sen, pp. 1–8 (2018)

14. Kovásznai, G., Gajdár, K., Kovács, L.: Portfolio SAT and SMT solving of cardinality constraints in sensor network optimization. In: 21st SYNASC 2019, pp. 85–91. IEEE (2019)

15. Lawler, E.L., Wood, D.E.: Branch-and-bound methods: a survey. Oper. Res. 14(4), 699–719 (1966)

16. Lei, Z., Cai, S., Luo, C.: Extended conjunctive normal form and an efficient algorithm for cardinality constraints. Proc. IJCAI 2020, 1141–1147 (2020)

17. Liao, S.Y., Devadas, S.: Solving covering problems using lpr-based lower bounds. In: Yoffa, E.J., Micheli, G.D., Rabaey, J.M. (eds.) Proceedings of the 34st Conference on Design Automation, Anaheim, 1997, pp. 117–120. ACM Press (1997)

18. Manquinho, V.M., Roussel, O.: The first evaluation of pseudo-Boolean solvers (pb'05). J. Satisf. Boolean Model. Comput. 2(1–4), 103–143 (2006)

19. Martins, R., Manquinho, V., Lynce, I.: Open-WBO: a modular MaxSAT solver. In: Sinz, C., Egly, U. (eds.) SAT 2014. LNCS, vol. 8561, pp. 438–445. Springer, Cham (2014). https://doi.org/10.1007/978-3-319-09284-3_33

20. Martins, R., Sherry, J.: Lisbon wedding: seating arrangements using maxsat. In: MaxSAT Evaluation 2017: Solver and Benchmark Descriptions, pp. 25–26 (2017). http://hdl.handle.net/10138/228949

21. Philipp, T., Steinke, P.: PBLib – a library for encoding pseudo-boolean constraints into CNF. In: Heule, M., Weaver, S. (eds.) SAT 2015. LNCS, vol. 9340, pp. 9–16. Springer, Cham (2015). https://doi.org/10.1007/978-3-319-24318-4_2

22. Prestwich, S.: Randomised backtracking for linear pseudo-Boolean constraint problems. Proc. CPAIOR 2002, 7–20 (2002)

23. Sakai, M., Nabeshima, H.: Construction of an ROBDD for a pb-constraint in band form and related techniques for pb-solvers. IEICE Trans. Inf. Syst. 98-D(6), 1121–1127 (2015)

24. Silva, J.P.M., Sakallah, K.A.: GRASP - a new search algorithm for satisfiability. In: Rutenbar, R.A., Otten, R.H.J.M. (eds.) Proceedings of ICCAD 1996, pp. 220–227. IEEE Computer Society ACM (1996)

Scheduling Reach Mahjong Tournaments Using Pseudoboolean Constraints

Martin Mariusz Lester$^{(\boxtimes)}$ (ID)

University of Reading, Reading, UK
m.lester@reading.ac.uk

Abstract. Reach mahjong is a gambling game for 4 players, most popular in Japan, but played internationally, including in amateur tournaments across Europe. We report on our experience of generating tournament schedules for tournaments hosted in the United Kingdom using pseudoboolean solvers. The problem is essentially an extension of the well-studied Social Golfer Problem (SGP) in operations research. However, in our setting, there are further constraints, such as the positions of players within a group, and the structure of the tournament graph, which are ignored in the usual formulation of the SGP. We tackle the problem primarily using the SAT/pseudoboolean solver clasp, but sometimes augmented with an existing local search-based solver for the SGP.

Keywords: Social Golfer Problem · Mahjong · Tournament scheduling · Pseudoboolean constraints

Reach mahjong (or *riichi* mahjong) is a gambling game for 4 players. A game (or *hanchan*) is played over several rounds. In each round, players seated at a table sequentially draw and discard tiles in an attempt to form a winning hand of 14 tiles. At the end of the round, the losing players pay a number of points to the winner, according to the value of his hand. The player with the most points at the end of the game is the winner.

Reach mahjong is most popular in Japan, although it is played throughout the world. In Europe, a few hundred amateur players compete in tournaments arranged throughout the year and around the continent. Tournaments are typically organised locally, but run following rules published by the European Mahjong Association (EMA) [1], which has approved and ranked tournaments since 2008. This raises the question of how best to schedule games in a tournament.

We report on our experience of using the pseudoboolean (PB) solver *clasp* [8] to generate tournament schedules (such as Table 1) for tournaments run in the United Kingdom since 2013. This includes generating a schedule for 128 players over 10 sessions for the 2016 European Riichi Mahjong Championship (ERMC), which satisfied a complex combination of constraints. Our software CoMaToSe (Constraint Mahjong Tournament Scheduler) and benchmarks are online [13].

In Sect. 1 we describe some details of the tournament scheduling problem and the constraints that they lead to. Then, in Sect. 2, we describe how we encode those

C.-M. Li and F. Manyà (Eds.): SAT 2021, LNCS 12831, pp. 349–358, 2021.
https://doi.org/10.1007/978-3-030-80223-3_24

constraints. The scheduling problem is essentially an extension of the Social Golfer Problem (SGP), which is amenable to solution using SAT solvers [9,12], but we found that for larger tournaments, and with our extended set of constraints, a PB formulation was more tractable. To our knowledge, there is no previous published work considering mahjong tournament scheduling; our encoding of the constraints extending the SGP is original. We evaluate our approach in Sect. 3. Finally, in Sect. 4 we discuss related work on the SGP, and more generally on tournament scheduling for games with more than 2 players, before concluding.

1   Problem Description

Size, length and format. A number of practical constraints and conventions have arisen over time that essentially fix the format of a tournament. Tournaments typically take place at the weekend, so usually last 1–2 days. Players may travel to a tournament and expect to play throughout; tournament rules specify that all players should play the same number of games and, after adding up each player's score in every game, the player with the highest score should be the winner. Games are played to a time limit in a session of 90 min. Allowing time for breaks and so on, it is usual to have 3–5 sessions in a day, for a total of 4–10 sessions in a tournament. A 2-day tournament might typically attract around 48 players. Every 3 years, a European Championship (ERMC) is held, which lasts longer and attracts more players. The main phase of the 2016 championship in the UK had 128 players over 10 sessions; the 2019 championship in the Netherlands had 140 players over 12 sessions. A tournament venue usually has enough tables and equipment to allow all participants to play simultaneously, although this may be variable in quality.

Wind Allocation. During each round, each player is allocated a different compass point (East, South, West or North) as his *wind*. The East player is the *dealer*. When he wins, he gets 50% more points and stays as dealer for the next round. If he does not win, the wind allocations rotate. He becomes North for the next round, the South player becomes East, and so on. In a full game, each player gets to be East twice; being North initially (and hence East last) may be an advantage because it confers some control over when the game ends. However, if a game is curtailed because of a tournament time limit, being North or West initially puts one at a disadvantage, as one often misses a second turn as dealer.

Table 1. A tournament schedule for 24 players and 5 sessions (SGP 6-4-5) with $d = 10$.

Table	1				2				3				4				5				6			
Session	E	S	W	N	E	S	W	N	E	S	W	N	E	S	W	N	E	S	W	N	E	S	W	N
1	1	3	2	4	7	8	5	6	11	12	10	9	14	13	15	16	17	20	18	19	24	22	23	21
2	9	23	7	17	3	19	10	15	16	6	24	2	8	18	21	12	22	5	1	14	20	11	4	13
3	11	18	14	24	21	1	13	17	20	7	3	22	10	4	6	23	2	15	9	8	12	16	19	5
4	15	21	6	20	4	22	16	9	19	23	8	14	2	17	11	5	3	24	12	13	18	10	1	7
5	13	8	22	10	23	2	20	12	5	15	4	18	19	9	24	1	7	16	21	11	6	14	17	3

The core problem is thus how best to schedule 4–12 sessions of a 4-player game for 16–140 players. Initial wind allocations for a table can be included in the schedule, or they can be drawn at random by the players before the game. Players might feel aggrieved if they have a disadvantageous wind allocation, even if it was produced at random. Balanced allocation of winds in the schedule avoids this and reduces setup time at the start of the game.

1.1   Constraints

The following have been suggested as desirable properties in a schedule:

Socialisation: Players want to play as many different opponents as possible.
Wind balance: In order to share the potential penalty of not getting a second turn as dealer across all players, each player should be allocated each starting wind position roughly an equal number of times. Obviously, this is not possible when the number of sessions is not a multiple of 4 and even then, it may not always be possible.
Table movement: To reduce the chances of cheating, and to share the inconvenience of playing on a table with low-quality equipment, a player should not play on the same table twice.

Of these, most players consider socialisation most important. With just this requirement, tournament scheduling is an instance of the well-studied SGP. With the relatively low ratio of players to sessions in many tournaments, satisfying just this requirement leaves relatively little scope for changing who plays who in each round. However, in larger tournaments, we may also wish to consider what properties are desirable in the tournament graph of "who plays who". Intuitively, we can view a tournament as a process by which points flow along edges from losing players to winning players. We then expect that the final scores of players are indicative of a linear ordering of their skill, but this depends on there being adequate potential for points to flow between any two players. This leads to the following desirable properties of the tournament graph:

Graph connectedness: The tournament graph should be connected.
Graph diameter: The diameter of the tournament graph (greatest distance between any pair of players) of the tournament should be as low as possible. In our setting, this usually means 2. This is a stronger version of the requirement that the graph be connected, with the same motivation. If two players cannot face each other directly, points can still flow between them via other players, but we would like the route to be as short as possible.
Multiple short paths: If two players in the tournament graph are not adjacent, there should be multiple paths between them, ideally of length 2. This increases the potential for indirect flow of points between them.

For a tournament graph with diameter 2, we will refer to the minimum number of paths of length 2 between any two non-adjacent players in the tournament graph as d. Necessarily, $d \geq 1$. For the schedule in Table 1, we used graph constraints to enforce $d = 10$; prior to this, the schedule had $d = 9$.

2 Problem Encoding

As the most important constraint is socialisation, we start with a PB encoding for the SGP, then add our other constraints in a monolithic formulation. By convention, we refer to an SGP instance as g-p-w with:

- g — the number of *groups* playing simultaneously
- p — the number of *players* in a group (always 4 for mahjong)
- w — the number of sessions (*weeks* in the SGP)

We chose our solver by evaluating participants in the SAT and PB [4] competitions of 2012, which were the most recent competitions at the time. Of these, we found that *clasp* [8] was most effective, particularly when run with the *crafty* preset for combinatorially hard problems.

Initially, we had focused on the use of SAT, as Triska had developed an effective SAT encoding of the SGP [18]. However, his socialisation constraint is $\mathcal{O}(g^4p^2w^2)$. For large numbers of players, we found that just generating the constraints was too slow, so starting with the 2016 European Championship (SGP 32-4-10), we adopted a PB formulation.

We had assumed that, while a PB might not find an optimal solution, if it ceased to make progress, it would at least have found a locally optimal solution. However, a tournament organiser told us he had been able to improve wind balance in a generated schedule by shuffling wind allocations of two tables. We found that, using an encoding that considered only wind balance, we could fine-tune the schedule generated from the monolithic encoding and automate this.

Although the SAT/PB method for solving SGP instances is competitive, the best automated method currently known is Triska's heuristic-guided local search algorithm [17]; an implementation by Rezaei is available online [15]. Therefore, for tournament schedules that correspond to hard instances of the SGP, we can import a solution to the SGP instance and just tune the wind balance. While fixing group allocations in this way may remove the best solutions from the space considered by the solver, in practice it allows us to find better solutions than using a constraint solver in isolation. In all cases we considered, we were able to find an optimal wind allocation this way.

2.1 Monolithic Constraint Encoding

We now present our monolithic PB constraint encoding of the problem. We set $n = g.p$ as the number of players. The constraints range over the following Boolean variables, where $h, i, j \in [1, n]$ with $j > i$, $h \neq i$ and $h \neq j$, $k \in [1, g]$, $l \in [1, w]$ and $s \in [1, p]$:

- $P_{i,k,l}$ — true just if i plays in group k in session l
- $S_{i,k,l,s}$ — true just if i plays in group k in session l in seat position s
- $M_{i,j,l}$ — true if i and j meet in session l
- $C_{i,j}$ — true only if i and j meet (compete) in any session
- $D_{i,j,h}$ — true only if i and j both meet h (compete *indirectly*)

We encode East as position 1, South as 2 and so on. Constraint sets are as follows; quantification $(\forall, \sum)$ of indices is always implicitly over the ranges above.

Each group must have exactly p players:

$$\forall k, l. \sum_i P_{i,k,l} = p \tag{1}$$

Each player must play in exactly one group in each session:

$$\forall i, l. \sum_k P_{i,k,l} = 1 \tag{2}$$

Optionally, to break symmetries, order players sequentially in the first session:

$$\forall i. P_{i,\lceil i/g \rceil, 1} = 1 \tag{3}$$

If i and j play in the same group in the same session, then they must meet in that session:

$$\forall i, j, k, l. -P_{i,k,l} + -P_{j,k,l} + M_{i,j,l} \geq -1 \tag{4}$$

and they must meet at most once over all sessions:

$$\forall i, j. \sum_l -M_{i,j,l} \geq -1 \tag{5}$$

i and j competed only if they played in the same group in any session:

$$\forall i, j. -C_{i,j} + \sum_{k,l} P_{i,k,l} P_{j,k,l} \geq 0 \tag{6}$$

i and j competed indirectly via h only if they both competed with h:

$$\forall i, j, h. C_{\min(i,h),\max(i,h)} + C_{\min(h,j),\max(h,j)} + -2D_{i,j,h} \geq 0 \tag{7}$$

i and j must compete directly, or compete indirectly d times (d configurable):

$$\forall i, j. d \cdot C_{i,j} + \sum_h D_{i,j,h} \geq d \tag{8}$$

Each player must play in each group at most once over all sessions:

$$\forall i, k. \sum_l -P_{i,k,l} \geq -1 \tag{9}$$

If i sits in a position in a group, he must play in that group:

$$\forall i, k, l, s. -S_{i,k,l,s} + P_{i,k,l} \geq 0 \tag{10}$$

If i plays in a group, he must sit in one of its positions:

$$\forall i, k, l. -P_{i,k,l} + \sum_s S_{i,k,l,s} \geq 0 \tag{11}$$

Exactly one player must sit in every seat:

$$\forall k, l, s. \sum_i S_{i,k,l,s} = 1 \tag{12}$$

Each player must play in each position (roughly) the same number of times:

$$\forall i, s. \sum_{k,l} S_{i,k,l,s} \geq \lfloor w/p \rfloor \quad \forall i, s. \sum_{k,l} -S_{i,k,l,s} \geq -\lceil w/p \rceil \quad (13)$$

Constraints 1–5 follow Walser [20]; the rest are original. The constraint sets are largely orthogonal: any of 4–5 (socialisation), 6–8 (enforcing d), 9 (table movement) and 10–13 (wind balance) can be removed independently. Note constraints 6 are non-linear. Concerning size: 4–5 is $\mathcal{O}(g^2 p^2 w)$ ($\mathcal{O}(g^2 w)$ smaller than Triska's SAT encoding); 6–8 is $\mathcal{O}(g^3 p^3)$; 10–13 is $\mathcal{O}(g^2 p^2 w)$.

In practice, it may not always be possible to satisfy all constraints simultaneously, whether because there is no solution, or because the solver cannot find one. In these cases, constraint sets 5, 8, 9 or 13 can be made soft, turning the problem into a Weighted Boolean Optimisation (WBO) instance.

Apart from the obvious symmetry breaking of fully specifying session 1, most existing symmetry breaking techniques for the SGP violate the extra constraints in our problem. For example, putting players 1–4 on tables 1–4 in later rounds, or requiring that the tables are ordered by lowest numbered player on the table, violates table movement. Formulations of the pure SGP that encode a table as an ordered list usually benefit from breaking symmetry in the ordering of players. In the PB formulation, native cardinality constraints make it easy to encode a table as an unordered set, so there is no symmetry to break. Of course, when one adds wind allocation, ordering of players at a table is no longer a symmetry.

2.2   Wind Balancing Constraint Encoding

Our constraint encoding for fine-tuning wind allocations uses variables $W_{i,l,s}$, which are true just if player i is in position s in session l. The constraints depend on a fixed allocation of players to groups, which we refer to using values of P variables from the monolithic encoding; tuning can only change a player's seat at a table. Our encoding is as follows. Each player must have a seat:

$$\forall i, l. \sum_s W_{i,l,s} = 1 \quad (14)$$

Exactly one player in a group can take each seat:

$$\forall k, l, s. \sum_{\{i | P_{i,k,l}\}} W_{i,l,s} = 1 \quad (15)$$

Each player must play in each position (roughly) the same number of times:

$$\forall i, s. \sum_l W_{i,l,s} \geq \lfloor w/p \rfloor \quad \forall i, s. \sum_l -W_{i,l,s} \geq -\lceil w/p \rceil \quad (16)$$

3   Evaluation

We have used our encoding to generate schedules for the 2016 ERMC and several smaller tournaments in the UK. Timings were generated on a machine running

Debian Linux 10 with a 3.4 GHz Intel Core i5-7500 CPU and 64 GB of RAM. We used *clasp* 3.3.4 with *crafty* preset and Rezaei's local search SGP solver [15].

For the 2016 ERMC (32-4-10), we used our monolithic encoding, incrementally turning on constraints to obtain the best schedule possible. Enforcing just socialisation took 18 s. We turned on table movement and wind balance, tightening the wind constraints (13) to give each player 2 turns in each seat plus 1 turn as East or South and 1 turn as West or North; solving this took 2 m 10 s. The schedule's tournament graph already had diameter 2, but $d = 1$. Adding the constraint $d = 2$, it took 14 m to solve. Changing to $d = 3$, *clasp* found no solution in 1 h. So finally, keeping the hard constraint $d = 2$ and adding a soft constraint $d = 3$, with a timeout of 1 h, we generated a schedule violating only 122 of $\binom{128}{2} = 8128$ soft constraints. Overall, the instance had 1.3M variables and 3.9M constraints. Appendix A shows benchmarks for similar instances.

For comparison, solving the SGP instance with local search and balancing the winds using our constraint formulation yielded a solution in less than 1s. The tournament graph had diameter 2, but with $d = 1$, and there is no easy way to tune the graph while maintaining socialisation.

For the smaller tournaments, the tournament graph was necessarily low diameter, so we did not enforce it with constraints. 1-day tournaments usually had 5 sessions and ranged from 24 to 52 players (6-4-5 to 13-4-5). 2-day tournaments usually had 8 sessions and ranged from 32 to 68 players (8-4-8 to 17-4-8). We benchmarked our monolithic encoding on these intervals, setting a solver time limit of 10m and making wind balance a soft constraint. For instances in the 1-day interval, it took less than 0.5 s to solve constraints for a schedule with maximal socialisation, table movement and wind balance, except for 6-4-5, which took 3.6 s. For the 2-day interval (see Table 2), the 8-4-8 instance is significant as it is the original formulation of the SGP, and remains out of reach for SAT- and PB-based methods, including ours, so we imported a solution to balance. For 9-4-8 and 10-4-8, *clasp* solved the constraints only with wind balance turned off. For the rest of the interval, *clasp* found solutions with 2–21 wind constraint violations. In all cases, whether using schedules generated by our monolithic encoding, or importing schedules generated by local search, we were able to tune wind balance perfectly, satisfying all constraints, usually in under 2 s.

Table 2. Benchmarks applying monolithic encoding to 2-day tournaments (*g*-4-8).

Groups	8	9	10	11	12	13	14	15	16	17
Variables	14k	18k	22k	27k	32k	37k	44k	50k	57k	64k
Constraints	43k	60k	81k	105k	134k	168k	207k	252k	304k	361k
Socialisation only time (s)	–	53	0.52	0.46	0.56	0.77	0.94	1.2	1.5	1.7
Constraints violated after 10 m	–	–	–	2	3	3	3	13	11	21
Total wind constraints	–	–	–	176	192	208	224	240	256	272
Wind balance tuning time (s)	0.045	1.2	0.094	0.15	0.17	0.030	1.5	0.13	15	9.5

Table 3. Comparison of NLC WBO solvers. Constraints violated after 10 m (g-4-8).

Groups	8	9	10	11	12	13	14	15	16	17
clasp	-	-	-	2	3	3	3	13	11	21
SAT4J	-	-	-	36	9	8	10	16	20	28
NaPS	-	-	-	-	38	30	46	67	49	73
ToySat	-	-	-	-	-	-	-	-	-	-
SAT4J-cutting	-	-	-	-	-	-	-	-	65	69
SAT4J-rounding	-	-	-	-	-	-	-	100	-	86
SAT4J-partial	-	-	-	-	-	-	-	-	-	76

To confirm that *clasp* was still an appropriate choice of solver, we compared up-to-date versions of entrants in the relevant track (WBO SOFT-SMALLINT-NLC) of the most recent PB Competition (2016), as well as experimental versions of *SAT4J* using the cutting planes and rounding SAT techniques. Table 3 shows the comparison. Although the standard *SAT4J* solver is competitive, *clasp* is still best. Some new PB solvers have participated in the more active MaxSAT Evaluation competition, but none supports WBO with non-linear clauses.

Summary: For large instances, where the tournament graph structure was of concern, our monolithic constraint encoding allowed the graph to be optimised at the same time as allocating wind positions. For hard SGP instances, we necessarily had to import an SGP solution, but our wind encoding successfully tuned this. In other cases, there was little difference between the quality of schedules generated: using our monolithic encoding, then tuning wind allocations if necessary; and using a local search SGP solver, followed by tuning wind allocation. However, the latter was considerably faster.

4 Related Work and Conclusions

The SGP was posted on the Usenet group sci.op-research in 1998. The original SGP, to find the highest w for which 8-4-w is solvable, is problem 10 in CSPLib [10]. Optimal solutions of the SGP are entry A107431 in OEIS [2]. Walser suggested a PB encoding [20]. Later, Gent and Lynce proposed a SAT encoding [9]. Much work on solving SGP instances focuses on breaking symmetries [3,6,7,11]. Triska studied the problem extensively [16–18].

Recently, Lardeux and others revisited the SAT encoding, exploring efficient, correct translation of set constraints [12]; they seem unaware of PB problems/solvers. Liu and others investigated solving SGP instances in parallel [14].

We found no previous research specifically on scheduling a mahjong tournament. Bridge and whist are 4-player games, but played by 2 co-operating pairs, not 4 competing individuals. Individual bridge tournaments [19] were played in the past, but are currently not popular. Whist games are shorter than mahjong games, and partnership is still significant, which leads to different goals [5].

We have shown how to generate good tournament schedules for reach mahjong tournaments run according to the conventions of the European Mahjong Association. Since 2013, our approach has been used to generate schedules for several tournaments hosted in the UK, including the 2016 ERMC. Our experience reaffirms the message that SAT/PB solvers are an effective and convenient but imperfect tool for solving complex problems that arise in real life. We think it is likely that a custom local search algorithm that considered all our constraints simultaneously would outperform our approach. However, this would have been far less convenient than applying an existing solver.

A   Benchmarks for Large Instances

Table 4. Benchmarks applying monolithic encoding to large tournaments (g-4-10).

Groups	28	29	30	31	32	33	34	35	36
Soc. + wind time (s)	2.7	3.1	4.2	3.3	131	5.3	102	76	241
Soc. + wind + $d = 2$ time (s)	46	46	38	100	847	664	1189	-	-
With $d = 3$ soft: Variables	0.9M	1.0M	1.1M	1.2M	1.3M	1.4M	1.5M	1.7M	1.8M
Constraints	2.6M	2.9M	3.2M	3.5M	3.8M	4.2M	4.6M	5.0M	5.5M
Constraints violated after 1h	0	62	61	1	122	196	-	327	-

References

1. European Mahjong Association. http://mahjong-europe.org/
2. The on-line encyclopedia of integer sequences. https://oeis.org/A000108, sequence A000108
3. Azevedo, F.: An attempt to dynamically break symmetries in the social golfers problem. In: Azevedo, F., Barahona, P., Fages, F., Rossi, F. (eds.) CSCLP 2006. LNCS (LNAI), vol. 4651, pp. 33–47. Springer, Heidelberg (2007). https://doi.org/10.1007/978-3-540-73817-6_2
4. Balint, A., Belov, A., Järvisalo, M., Sinz, C.: Overview and analysis of the SAT challenge 2012 solver competition. Artif. Intell. **223**, 120–155 (2015). https://doi.org/10.1016/j.artint.2015.01.002
5. Berman, D.R., McLaurin, S.C., Smith, D.D.: Ranking whist players. Discret. Math. **283**(1–3), 15–28 (2004). https://doi.org/10.1016/j.disc.2004.01.005
6. Cotta, C., Dotú, I., Fernández, A.J., Van Hentenryck, P.: Scheduling social golfers with memetic evolutionary programming. In: Almeida, F., et al. (eds.) HM 2006. LNCS, vol. 4030, pp. 150–161. Springer, Heidelberg (2006). https://doi.org/10.1007/11890584_12
7. Dotú, I., Van Hentenryck, P.: Scheduling social golfers locally. In: Barták, R., Milano, M. (eds.) CPAIOR 2005. LNCS, vol. 3524, pp. 155–167. Springer, Heidelberg (2005). https://doi.org/10.1007/11493853_13
8. Gebser, M., Kaufmann, B., Neumann, A., Schaub, T.: *clasp*: a conflict-driven answer set solver. In: Baral, C., Brewka, G., Schlipf, J. (eds.) LPNMR 2007. LNCS (LNAI), vol. 4483, pp. 260–265. Springer, Heidelberg (2007). https://doi.org/10.1007/978-3-540-72200-7_23
9. Gent, I.P., Lynce, I.: A SAT encoding for the social golfer problem. In: In IJCAI2005 Workshop on Modelling and Solving Problems with Constraints (2005). https://www.inesc-id.pt/ficheiros/publicacoes/2516.pdf
10. Harvey, W.: CSPLib problem 010: Social golfers problem. http://www.csplib.org/Problems/prob010

11. Harvey, W., Winterer, T.: Solving the MOLR and social golfers problems. In: van Beek, P. (ed.) CP 2005. LNCS, vol. 3709, pp. 286–300. Springer, Heidelberg (2005). https://doi.org/10.1007/11564751_23
12. Lardeux, F., Monfroy, E., Crawford, B., Soto, R.: Set constraint model and automated encoding into SAT: application to the social golfer problem. Ann. Oper. Res. 235(1), 423–452 (2015). https://doi.org/10.1007/s10479-015-1914-5
13. Lester, M.M.: CoMaToSe: Constraint Mahjong Tournament Scheduler (May 2021). https://doi.org/10.5281/zenodo.4764650
14. Liu, K., Löffler, S., Hofstedt, P.: Social golfer problem revisited. In: van den Herik, J., Rocha, A.P., Steels, L. (eds.) ICAART 2019. LNCS (LNAI), vol. 11978, pp. 72–99. Springer, Cham (2019). https://doi.org/10.1007/978-3-030-37494-5_5
15. Rezaei, A.: Golfer: A toolkit for solving social golfer problem (2015). https://github.com/arezae4/golfer
16. Triska, M.: Solution methods for the social golfer problem (2008). https://www.metalevel.at/mst.pdf, Master's thesis
17. Triska, M., Musliu, N.: An effective greedy heuristic for the social golfer problem. Ann. Oper. Res. 194(1), 413–425 (2012). https://doi.org/10.1007/s10479-011-0866-7
18. Triska, M., Musliu, N.: An improved SAT formulation for the social golfer problem. Ann. Oper. Res. 194(1), 427–438 (2012). https://doi.org/10.1007/s10479-010-0702-5
19. English Bridge Union: Individual competitions. https://www.ebu.co.uk/documents/cmh/Individuals.pdf
20. Walser, J.P.: AMPL model of 'maximum socializing on the golf course' (1998). https://www.csplib.org/Problems/prob010/models/AMPLmodel.txt.html

On the Hierarchical Community
Structure of Practical Boolean Formulas

Chunxiao Li[1(✉)], Jonathan Chung[1(✉)], Soham Mukherjee[1,2(✉)],
Marc Vinyals[3(✉)], Noah Fleming[4(✉)], Antonina Kolokolova[5(✉)], Alice Mu[1(✉)],
and Vijay Ganesh[1(✉)]

[1] University of Waterloo, Waterloo, Canada
{jonathan.chung1,soham.mukherjee,xiao.mu,vganesh}@uwaterloo.ca
[2] Perimeter Institute for Theoretical Physics, Waterloo, Canada
[3] Technion, Haifa, Israel
marcviny@cs.technion.ac.il
[4] University of Toronto, Toronto, Canada
noahfleming@cs.toronto.edu
[5] Memorial University of Newfoundland, St. John's, Canada

Abstract. Modern CDCL SAT solvers easily solve industrial instances
containing tens of millions of variables and clauses, despite the theoretical intractability of the SAT problem. This gap between practice
and theory is a central problem in solver research. It is believed that
SAT solvers exploit structure inherent in industrial instances, and hence
there have been numerous attempts over the last 25 years at characterizing this structure via parameters. These can be classified as *rigorous*, i.e., they serve as a basis for complexity-theoretic upper bounds
(e.g., backdoors), or *correlative*, i.e., they correlate well with solver run
time and are observed in industrial instances (e.g., community structure). Unfortunately, no parameter proposed to date has been shown to
be both strongly correlative and rigorous over a large fraction of industrial instances.

Given the sheer difficulty of the problem, we aim for an intermediate goal of proposing a set of parameters that is strongly correlative
and has good theoretical properties. Specifically, we propose parameters
based on a graph partitioning called Hierarchical Community Structure
(HCS), which captures the recursive community structure of a graph
of a Boolean formula. We show that HCS parameters are strongly correlative with solver run time using an Empirical Hardness Model, and
further build a classifier based on HCS parameters that distinguishes
between easy industrial and hard random/crafted instances with very
high accuracy. We further strengthen our hypotheses via scaling studies.
On the theoretical side, we show that counterexamples which plagued flat
community structure do not apply to HCS, and that there is a subset of
HCS parameters such that restricting them limits the size of embeddable
expanders.

J. Li and J. Chung—Joint first author

J. Li—Work done in part while the authors were at the 2021 Satisfiability: Theory,
Practice, and Beyond program at the Simons Institute, Berkeley, CA, USA.

C.-M. Li and F. Manyà (Eds.): SAT 2021, LNCS 12831, pp. 359–376, 2021.
https://doi.org/10.1007/978-3-030-80223-3_25

1   Introduction

Over the last two decades, Conflict-Driven Clause-Learning (CDCL) SAT solvers have had a dramatic impact on many sub-fields of software engineering [10], formal methods [12], security [16,45], and AI [8], thanks to their ability to solve large real-world instances with tens of millions of variables and clauses [38], notwithstanding the fact that the Boolean satisfiability (SAT) problem is known to be NP-complete and is believed to be intractable [15]. A plausible explanation of this apparent contradiction would be that NP-completeness of the SAT problem is established in a worst-case setting, while the dramatic efficiency of modern SAT solvers is witnessed over "practical" instances. However, despite over two decades of effort, we still do not have an appropriate mathematical characterization of practical instances (or a suitable subset thereof) and attendant complexity-theoretic upper and lower bounds. This gap between theory and practice is rightly considered one of the central problems in solver research by theorists and practitioners alike.

The fundamental premise in this line of work is that SAT solvers are able to find short proofs (if such proofs exist) in polynomial time (i.e., they are efficient) for industrial instances and that they are able to do so because they somehow exploit the underlying properties (a.k.a. structure) of such industrial Boolean formulas[1], and, further, that hard randomly-generated or crafted instances are difficult because they do not possess such structure. Consequently, considerable work has been done in characterizing the structure of industrial instances via parameters. The parameters discussed in literature so far can be broadly classified into two categories: correlative and rigorous[2]. The term *correlative* refers to parameters that take a specific range of values in industrial instances (as opposed to random/crafted) and further have been shown to correlate well with solver run time. This suggests that the structure captured by such parameters might explain why solvers are efficient. An example of such a parameter is modularity (more generally community structure [4]). By contrast, the term *rigorous* refers to parameters that characterize classes of formulas that are fixed-parameter tractable (FPT), such as backdoors [44,48], backbones [29], treewidth, and branchwidth [1,37], among many others [37], or have been used to prove complexity-theoretic bounds over randomly-generated classes of formulas such as clause-variable ratio (a.k.a., density) [14,39].

The eventual goal in this context is to discover a parameter or set of parameters that is both strongly correlative and rigorous, such that it can then be used to establish parameterized complexity-theoretic bounds on an appropriate mathematical abstraction of CDCL SAT solvers, thus finally settling this decades-long open question. Unfortunately, the problem with all the previously proposed rigorous parameters is that either "good" ranges of values for these parameters are not witnessed in industrial instances (e.g., such instances can

---

[1] The term industrial is loosely defined to encompass instances obtained from hardware and software testing, analysis, and verification applications.

[2] Using terminology by Stefan Szeider [43].

have both large and small backdoors) or they do not correlate well with solver run time (e.g., many industrial instances have large treewidth and yet are easy to solve, and treewidth alone does not correlate well with solving time [28]).

Consequently, many attempts have been made at discovering correlative parameters that could form the basis of rigorous analysis [4,21]. Unfortunately, all such correlative parameters either seem to be difficult to work with theoretically (e.g., fractal dimension [2]) or have obvious counterexamples, i.e., it is easy to show the existence of formulas that simultaneously have "good" parameter values and are provably hard-to-solve. For example, it was shown that industrial instances have high modularity, i.e., supposedly good community structure [4], and that there is good-to-strong correlation between modularity and solver run time [32]. However, Mull et al. [30] later exhibited a family of formulas that have high modularity and require exponential-sized proofs to refute. Finally, this line of research suffers from important methodological issues, that is, experimental methods and evidence provided for correlative parameters tend not to be consistent across different papers in the literature.

Hierarchical Community Structure of Boolean Formulas: Given the sheer difficulty of the problem, we aim for an intermediate goal of proposing a set of parameters that is strongly correlative and has good theoretical properties. Specifically, we propose a set of parameters based on a graph-theoretic structure called Hierarchical Community Structure (HCS), inspired by a commonly-studied concept in the context of hierarchical networks [13,35], which satisfies all the empirical tests hinted above and has better theoretical properties than previously proposed correlative parameters. The intuition behind HCS is that it neatly captures the structure present in human-developed systems which tend to be modular and hierarchical [41], and we expect this structure to be inherited by Boolean formulas modelling these systems.

Contributions[3]:

1. **Empirical Result 1 (HCS and Industrial Instances):** We show that a set of parameters based on the HCS of the variable-incidence graph (VIG) of Boolean formulas are effective in distinguishing industrial instances from random/crafted ones. Moreover, we build a classifier that robustly classifies SAT instances into the categories they belong to (verification, random, etc.). The classification accuracy is approximately 99% and we perform a variety of tests to ensure there is no overfitting (See Sect. 5.1).
2. **Empirical Result 2 (Correlation between HCS and Solver Run Time):** We build an empirical hardness model based on our HCS parameters to predict the solver run time for a given problem instance. Our model, based on regression, performs well, achieving an R^2 score of 0.83, much stronger than previous such results (See Sect. 5.2)

---

[3] Instance generator and data can be found at https://satsolvercomplexity.github.io/hcs. Also, for the full-length paper and appendices (with proofs of theorems in Sect. 6), please refer to the arXiv version of the paper [26].

3. **Empirical Result 3 (Scaling Experiments of HCS Instances):** We empirically show, via scaling experiments, that HCS parameters such as community degree and leaf-community size positively correlate with solving time. We empirically demonstrate that formulas whose HCS decompositions fall in a good range of parameter values are easier to solve than instances with a bad range of HCS parameter values (See Sect. 5.4).

4. **Theoretical Results:** We theoretically justify our choice of HCS by showing that it behaves better than other parameters. More concretely, we show the advantages of hierarchical over flat community structure by identifying HCS parameters which let us avoid hard formulas that can be used as counterexamples to community structure [30], and by showing graphs where HCS can find the proper communities where flat modularity cannot. We also show that there is a subset of HCS parameters (leaf-community size, community degree, and fraction of inter-community edges) such that restricting them limits the size of embeddable expanders (See Sect. 6).

5. **Instance Generator:** Finally, we provide an HCS-based instance generator which takes input values of our proposed parameters and outputs a formula that satisfies those values. This generator can be used to generate "easy" and "hard" formulas with different hierarchical structures (See Sect. 5.4).

Research Methodology: We also codify a set of empirical tests which we believe parameters must pass in order to be considered for further theoretical analysis. While other researchers have considered one or more of these tests, we bring them together into a coherent and sound research methodology that can be used for future research in formula parameterization (See Sect. 3). We believe that the combination of these tests provides a strong basis for a correlative parameter to be considered worthy of further analysis.

2   Preliminaries

Variable Incidence Graph (VIG): Researchers have proposed a variety of graphs to study graph-theoretic properties of Boolean formulas. In this work we focus on the Variable Incidence Graph (VIG), primarily due to the relative ease of computing community structure over VIGs compared to other graph representations. The VIG for a formula F over variables $x_1, \ldots, x_n$ has n vertices, one for each variable. There is an edge between vertices x_i and x_j if both x_i and x_j occur in some clause C_k in F. One drawback of VIGs is that a clause of width w corresponds to a clique of size w in the VIG. Therefore, large width clauses (of size n^ε) can significantly distort the structure of a VIG, and formulas with such large width clauses should have their width reduced (via standard techniques) before using a VIG.

Community Structure and Modularity: Intuitively, a set of variables (vertices in the VIG) of a formula forms a community if these variables are more densely connected to each other than to variables outside of the set. An (optimal) community structure of a graph is a partition $P = \{V_1, \ldots, V_k\}$ of its vertices into communities that optimizes some measure capturing this intuition, for instance modularity [31], which is the one we use in this paper. Let $G = (V, E)$ be a graph with adjacency matrix A and for each vertex $v \in V$ denote by $d(v)$ its degree. Let $\delta_P \colon V \times V \to \{0, 1\}$ be the community indicator function of a partition, i.e. $\delta_P(u, v) = 1$ iff vertices u and v belong to the same community in P. The *modularity* of the partition P is

$$Q(P) := \frac{1}{2|E|} \sum_{u,v \in V} \left[A_{u,v} - \frac{d(u)d(v)}{2|E|} \right] \delta_P(u, v) \qquad (1)$$

Note that $Q(P)$ ranges from -0.5 to 1, with values close to 1 indicating good community structure. We define the modularity $Q(G)$ of a graph G as the maximum modularity over all possible partitions, with corresponding partition $\mathcal{P}(G)$. Other measures may produce radically different partitions.

Expansion of a Graph: Expansion is a measure of graph connectivity [23]. Out of several equivalent such measures, the most convenient to relate to HCS is *edge expansion*: given a subset of vertices $S \subseteq V$, its edge expansion is $h(S) = |E(S, V \backslash S)|/|S|$, and the edge expansion of a graph is $h(G) = \min_{1 \leq |S| \leq n/2} h(S)$. A graph family G_n is an expander if $h(G_n)$ is bounded away from zero. Resolution lower bounds (of both random and crafted formulas) often rely on strong expansion properties of the graph [5].

3   Research Methodology

As stated above, the eventual goal of the research presented here is to discover a structure and an associated parameterization that is highly correlative with solver run time, is witnessed in industrial instances, and is rigorous, i.e., forms the basis for an upper bound on the parameterized complexity [37] of the CDCL algorithm. Considerable work has already been done in attempting to identify exactly such a set of parameters [32]. However, we observed that there is a wide diversity of research methodologies adopted by researchers in the past. We bring together the best lessons learned into what we believe to be a sound, coherent, and comprehensive research methodology explained below. We argue that every set of parameters must meet the following empirical requirements in order to be considered correlative:

1. **Structure of Industrial vs. Random/Crafted Instances:** A requisite for a structure to be considered correlative is that industrial instances must fall within a certain range of values for the associated parameters, while random and crafted instances must have a different range. An example of such a structure is the community structure of the VIG of Boolean formulas, as parameterized by modularity. Multiple experiments have shown that industrial instances have high modularity (close to 1), while random instances tend to have low modularity (close to 0) [32]. This could be demonstrated via a correlation experiment or by building a classifier that takes parameter values as input features.

2. **Correlation between Structure and Solver Run Time:** Another requirement is correlation between parameters of a structure and solver run time. Once again, community structure (and the associated modularity parameter) forms a good example of a structure that passes this essential test. For example, it has been shown that the modularity of the community structure of industrial instances (resp. random instances) correlates well with low (resp. high) solver run time [32]. One may use either correlation methods or suitable machine learning predictors (e.g., random forest) as evidence here.
3. **Scaling Studies:** To further strengthen the experimental evidence, we require that the chosen structure and its associated parameters must pass an appropriately designed scaling study. The idea here is to vary one parameter value while keeping as much of the rest of the formula structure constant as possible, and see its effect on solver run time. An example of such a study is the work of Zulkoski et al. [47], who showed that increasing the mergeability metric has a significant effect on solver run time.

Limitations of Empirical Conclusions: As the reader is well aware, any attempt at empirically discovering a suitable structure (and associated parameterization) of Boolean formulas and experimentally explaining the power of solvers is fraught with peril, since all such experiments involve pragmatic design decisions (e.g., which solver was used, choice of benchmarks, etc.) and hence may lead to contingent or non-generalizable conclusions. For example, one can never quite eliminate a parameter from further theoretical analysis based on empirical tests alone, for the parameter may fail an empirical test on account of benchmarks considered or other contingencies. Another well-understood issue with conclusions based on empirical analysis alone is that they by themselves cannot imply provable statements about asymptotic behavior of algorithms. However, one can use empirical analysis to check or expose gaps between the behavior of an algorithm and the tightness of asymptotic statements (e.g., the gap between efficient typical-case behavior vs. loose worst-case statements). Having said all this, we believe that the above methodology is a bare minimum that a set of parameters must pass before being considered worthy of further theoretical analysis. In Sect. 5, we go into further detail about how we protect against certain contingent experimental conclusions.

Limits of Theoretical Analysis: Another important aspect to bear in mind is that it is unlikely any small set of parameters can cleanly separate all easy instances from hard ones. At best, our expectation is that we can characterize a large subset of easy real-world instances via the parameters presented here, and thus take a step towards settling the central question of solver research.

4   Hierarchical Community Structure

Given that many human-developed systems are modular and hierarchical [41], it is natural to hypothesize that these properties are transferred over to Boolean formulas that capture the behaviour of such systems. We additionally hypothesize that purely randomly-generated or crafted formulas do not have

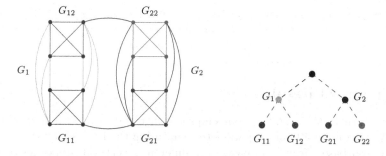

Fig. 1. A hierarchical decomposition (right) constructed by recursively maximizing the modularity of the graph (left).

these properties of hierarchy and modularity, and that this difference partly explains why solvers are efficient for the former and not for the latter class of instances. We formalize this intuition via a graph-theoretic concept called Hierarchical Community Structure (HCS), where communities can be recursively decomposed into smaller sub-communities. Although the notion of HCS has been widely studied [13,35], it has not been considered in the context of Boolean formulas before.

Hierarchical Community Structure Definition: A *hierarchical decomposition* of a graph G is a recursive partitioning of G into subgraphs, represented as a tree T. Each node v in the tree T is labelled with a subgraph of G, with the root labelled with G itself. The children of a node corresponding to a (sub)graph H are labelled with a partitioning of H into subgraphs $\{H_1, \ldots, H_k\}$; see Fig. 1. There are many ways to build such hierarchical decompositions. The method that we choose constructs the tree by recursively maximizing the modularity, as in the hierarchical multiresolution method [22]. We call this the HCS decomposition of a graph G: for a node v in the tree T corresponding to a subgraph H of G, we construct $|\mathcal{P}(H)|$ children, one for each of the subgraphs induced by the modularity-maximizing partition $\mathcal{P}(H)$, unless $|\mathcal{P}(H)| = 1$, in which case v becomes a *leaf* of the tree. In the case of HCS decompositions, we refer to the subgraphs labelling the nodes in the tree as *communities* of G.

We are interested in comparing the hierarchical community structures of Boolean formulas in conjunctive normal form, represented by their VIGs. For this comparison, we use the following parameters:

- The *community degree* of a community in a HCS decomposition is the number of children of its corresponding node.
- A *leaf-community* is one with degree 0.
- The *size* of a community is its number of vertices.
- The *depth* or *level* of a community is its distance from the root.
- The *inter-community edges* of a partition $\mathcal{P}(H)$ are $E_{IC}(H) = \bigcup_{H_i, H_j \in \mathcal{P}(H)} E(H_i, H_j)$, the edges between all pairs of subgraphs, and their endpoints $V_{IC}(H) = \bigcup E_{IC}$ are the *inter-community vertices*. Note that $2|E_{IC}(H)|/|H|$ is an upper bound for the edge expansion of H.

Note that these parameters are not independent. For example, changes in the number of inter-community vertices or inter-community edges will affect modularity. Since our hierarchical decomposition is constructed using modularity, this could affect the entire decomposition and hence the other parameters.

5   Empirical Results

We now turn to the results of our empirical investigations with HCS parameters. We computed 49 unique parameters capturing the HCS structure, together with several base parameters measuring different structural properties of input VIGs[4]. To compute the hierarchical community structure, we used the Louvain method [7] to detect communities and recursively call the Louvain method to produce a hierarchical decomposition. The Louvain method is considered to be more efficient and produces higher-modularity partitions than other known algorithms.

Experimental Design. In our experiments we used a set of 10 869 instances from five classes, which we believe is sufficiently large and diverse to draw sound empirical conclusions (See Appendix [26]). We did not explicitly balance the ratio of satisfiable instances in our benchmark selection because we expect our methods to be sufficiently robust as long as the benchmark contains a sufficient number of SAT and UNSAT instances.

In order to get interesting instances for modern solvers, we considered formulas which were previously used in the SAT competition from 2016 to 2018 [38]. Specifically, we took instances from five major tracks of the competition: agile, verification, crypto, crafted, and random. We also generated additional instances for some classes: for verification, we scaled the number of unrolls when encoding finite state machines for bounded model checking; for crypto, we encoded SHA-1 and SHA-256 preimage problems; for crafted, we generated combinatorial problems using `cnfgen` [25]; and for random, we generated k-CNFs at the corresponding threshold CVRs for $k \in \{3,5\}$, again using `cnfgen`. A summary of the instances is presented in the Appendix.

We preprocessed all formulas using the MiniSAT preprocessor [17], and used MapleSAT [27] as our CDCL solver of choice since it is a leading and representative solver. The core of the preprocessing was a combination of variable elimination with subsumption and self-subsuming resolution [17]. For computing satisfiability and running time, we used SHARCNET's Intel E5-2683 v4 (Broadwell) 2.1 GHz processors [40], limiting the computation time to 5000 s[5]. For parameter computation we did not limit the type of processor because structural parameter values are independent of processing power.

5.1   HCS-based Category Classification of Boolean Formulas

The question whether our set of HCS parameters is able to capture the underlying structure that differentiates industrial instances from the rest naturally

---

[4] For a complete list, see: https://satsolvercomplexity.github.io/hcs/data.
[5] This value is the time limit used by the SAT competition.

Table 1. Results for classification and regression experiments with HCS parameters. For regression we report R^2 values, whereas for classification we report the mean of the balanced accuracy score over 5 cross-validation datasets.

	Category	Runtime
Score	0.996 ± 0.001	0.825 ± 0.016
Top 5 features	rootMergeability	rootInterEdges
	maxInterEdges/CommunitySize	lvl2Mergeability
	cvr	cvr
	leafCommunitySize	leafCommunitySize
	lvl2InterEdges/lvl2InterVars	lvl3Modularity

lends itself to a classification problem. Therefore, we built a multi-class Random Forest classifier to classify a given SAT instance into one of the five categories: verification, agile, random, crafted, or crypto. Random Forests [9] can learn complex, highly non-linear relationships while having simple structure, and hence are easier to interpret than other models (e.g., deep neural networks).

We used an off-the-shelf implementation of a Random Forest classifier implemented as sklearn.ensemble.RandomForestClassifier in scikit-learn [33]. Using the default set of parameters in scikit-learn version 0.24, we trained our classifier using 800 randomly sampled instances of each category on a set of 49 features to predict the class of the problem instance. We found that our classifier performs extremely well, giving an average accuracy score of 0.99 over 5 cross-validation datasets. Further, the accuracy did not depend on our choice of classifier. In particular, we found similar accuracy scores when we used C-Support Vector classification [34] instead of Random Forests.

We also determined the five most important features used by our classifier. Since several features in our feature set are highly correlated, we first performed a hierarchical clustering on the feature set based on Spearman rank-order correlations. From the 22 clusters that were generated, we arbitrarily chose a single feature from each cluster as a representative member of the cluster f[6]. Using these 22 representative features, we then computed their importance using permutation importance [9]. In Table 1 we list the top five representative features from each cluster, not necessarily in order of importance.

5.2   HCS-based Empirical Hardness Model

We used our HCS parameters to build an empirical hardness model (EHM) to predict the run time of MapleSAT on a given instance. Since the solving time is a continuous variable, we considered a regression model built using Random Forests, namely sklearn.ensemble.RandomForestRegressor from scikit-learn [33]. Before training our regression model, we removed instances which timed-out at 5000 s and those instances that were solved almost immediately (in

---

[6] See https://satsolvercomplexity.github.io/hcs/data for details on clusters.

zero seconds) to avoid issues with artificial cut-off boundaries. We then trained our Random Forest model using the default set of parameters in scikit-learn version 0.24 to predict the logarithm of the solving time using the remaining 1880 instances, equally distributed between different categories.

We observed that our regression model performs quite well, with an R^2 score [42] of 0.83, which implies that in the training set, almost 83% of the variability of the dependent variable (i.e., in our case, the logarithm of the solving time) is accounted for, and the remaining 17% is still unaccounted for by our choice of parameters. Similar to category classification, we also looked for the top five predictive features used by our Random Forest regression model using the exact same process. We list the representative features in Table 1.

Additionally, we trained our EHM on each category of instances separately. We found that the performance of our EHM varies with instance category. Concretely, agile outperformed all other categories with an average R^2 value of 0.94, followed by random, crafted and verification instances with scores of $0.81, 0.85$ and 0.74 respectively. The worst performance was shown by the instances in crypto, with a score of 0.48.

5.3   HCS Parameter Value Ranges for Industrial/Random Instances

In the previous section, we reported on the top five parameters most predictive of the solver runtime in the context of our Random Forest regression model. These parameters can be divided into five distinct classes of parameters: mergeability-based, modularity-based, inter-community edge based, CVR, and leaf-community size. The parameters CVR, mergeability and modularity have been studied by previous work. CVR [11] is perhaps the most studied parameter among the three. Zulkoski et al. [47] showed that mergeability, along with combinations of other parameters, correlates well with solver run time; Ansotegui et al. [4] showed that industrial instances have good modularity compared to random instances; and Newsham et al. [32] showed that modularity has good-to-strong correlation with solver run time. We examined the remaining parameters, i.e. inter-community edge based parameters (`rootInterEdges`) and leaf-community size to gain a better understanding of the impact of these parameters on the problem structure and solver runtime, respectively. In this subsection, we look at how HCS parameters scale as the size of industrial instances increases. And in Sect. 5.4, we introduce a HCS instance generator, which we use to perform a set of controlled experiments. We then discuss how the hardness of the instances changes when certain HCS parameters are increased/decreased.

Observations. We observe that hierarchical decomposition generally produces leaf communities of maximal size comparable to the largest clause width, except for very unbalanced formulas (easy for other reasons). The community degree is highest at root level of every instance, and seems to be bounded by $O(\log n)$. This fits within the range of parameters considered in Sect. 6.

In Fig. 2, we show how the inter-community edge based parameter `rootInterEdges` scales with the number of variables in a formula, for verification and random instances. We note that for random instances, `rootInterEdges`

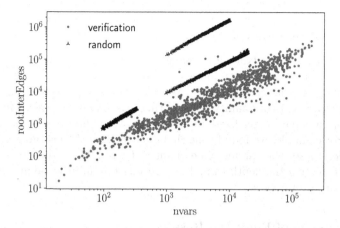

Fig. 2. Dependence of the number of inter-community edges at the root level (rootInterEdges) vs. the number of variables in a formula, for verification and random instances in our dataset. The two distinct lines (starting from the bottom) for random instances correspond to 3-CNFs and 5-CNFs, respectively.

grows linearly with the instance size, whereas in verification instances it grows sublinearly. This supports our intuition that graphs of hard (random) instances are expanders, whereas graphs of industrial instances are not.

5.4 Scaling Experiments with HCS Parameters

Instance Generator. To isolate the effects of HCS parameters on solver runtime, we built an HCS instance generator to construct SAT instances with varying leaf-community size and other HCS parameters. On a high level, the instance generator constructs instances bottom-up, starting with random disjoint formulas of predefined CVR as leaf communities, then combining them recursively by introducing bridge clauses with variables in at least two sub-communities to form super-communities at that level, which in turn are combined at the following level. We point out that in our generator, modularity is specified implicitly through the above parameters, and we do not control for mergeability at all. We refer the reader to the works by Zulkoski et al. [47] and Giráldez-Cru [20] for literature on the empirical behaviours of mergeability and power law, respectively.

It is important to note that our HCS instance generator is not intended to be perfectly representative of real-world instances. In fact, there are multiple properties of our generated instances which are not reflective of industrial instances. For example, our generator assumes that all leaf-communities have the same size and depth, which is demonstrably untrue of industrial instances. In some cases, the communities produced by our generator might not be the same as the communities which would be detected using the Louvain method to perform a hierarchical community decomposition. For example, it might be possible to further decompose the generated "leaf-communities" into smaller communities.

Thus, our generator is only intended to demonstrate the effect of varying HCS parameters on solver runtime.

Observations. We constructed formulas with varying CVR, power law parameter, hierarchical degree, depth, inter-community edge density, inter-community variable density, and clause width. We found evidence which suggests that increasing any of leaf-community size, depth, or community degree, while keeping every other HCS parameter fixed, increases the overall hardness of the generated formula. For example, we found that changing the size of leaf-communities from 15 variables to 20, the solving time changed from 4.96 s to upwards of 5000 s. Similarly, changing the depth from 4 to 5 resulted in an increase in solving time from 0.03 s to over 5000 s.

5.5 Discussion of Empirical Results

The goal of our experimental work was to first ascertain whether HCS parameters can distinguish between industrial and random/crafted instances, and whether these parameters show any correlation with CDCL solver runtime. The robustness of our classifier indicates that HCS parameters are indeed representative of the underlying structure of Boolean formulas from different categories. Further, our empirical hardness model confirms that the correlation of HCS parameters with solver run time is strong—much stronger than previously proposed parameters. We also find that our HCS parameters are more effective in capturing the hardness or easiness of formulas from industrial/agile/random/crafted, but not crypto. The crypto class is an outlier. It is not clear from our experiments (nor any previous ones) as to why crypto instances are hard for CDCL solvers.

We also identified the top five (representative) parameters in terms of their importance in predicting the category (classification) or runtime of an instance (regression). The accuracy for classification and regression with only the top features dropped to 0.94 and 0.77, respectively, suggesting that only a few parameters are likely to play a role in closing the question on why solvers are efficient for industrial instances. Note that a classification accuracy of 0.99 is likely to suggest that our model is over-fitting. Fortunately, in our case our models are trained over a large set of instances obtained via very different methods (e.g., random over various widths, different kinds of crafted, verification instances from different domains), and therefore, there is sufficient entropy in our data set so that overfitting is unlikely to be a concern for the robustness of our model.

In our investigation of parameters based on inter-community edges and leaf-community size, we found that industrial instances typically have small average leaf-community size, high modularity, and relatively few inter-community edges, while random/crafted have larger average leaf-community size, low modularity, and a very high number of inter-community edges. This suggests that leaf-community size and the fraction of inter-community edges, as well as community degree, are important HCS parameters to consider further.

6   Theoretical Results

In this section, we show that hierarchical decomposition avoids some of the pitfalls of flat community structure, a promising correlative parameter for explaining easiness of the industrial instances [32]. Community structure was theoretically shown to be insufficient by Mull et al. [30], where they showed that formulas with good community structure can have random formulas embedded in them either in a community or over the inter-community edges. To avoid embedding a random formula in a community, its size has to be small (relative to the entire graph), and avoiding expanders over inter-community edges requires that there not be too many communities. A way to be able to restrict both is to consider a hierarchical decomposition, limiting both the number of sub-communities (community degree) in each level of the decomposition, as well as the leaf community size thus avoiding the most important issues that flat community structure suffers from.

Based on our experimental work, we narrow down the most predictive HCS parameters to be leaf-community size, community degree, and the number inter-community edges in each decomposition. These parameters also play a role in our theoretical results below. For a formula to have "good" HCS, we restrict the parameter ranges as follows: the graph must exhibit $O(\log n)$ leaf-community size and community degree, and have a small number of inter-community edges in each decomposition of a community. These assumptions are supported by our experimental results (See Appendix [26]). We show that these restrictions are necessary in Appendix, where we also present a significantly simplified proof of the result of Mull et al. [30].

Bounding the Size of Expanders in Good HCS Graphs. Ideally, we would like to be able to prove an upper bound on proof size or search time which depends on the HCS parameters of a formula. Unfortunately, our current state of understanding does not allow for that. A step towards such a result would be to show that formulas with good HCS (and associated parameter value ranges) are not susceptible to typical methods of proving resolution lower bounds. Currently, all resolution bounds exploit *expansion* properties – typically *boundary expansion* – of the CNF formula (or more precisely its bipartite constraint-variable incidence graph (CVIG)). Therefore our goal is to show that formulas with good HCS parameters have poor expansion properties, and also do not have large expanding subgraphs embedded within them. Note that the VIG is related to the CVIG by taking the square of its adjacency matrix, from where it follows that, for formulas with low width, if the VIG is not edge-expanding then the CVIG is not vertex-expanding. Furthermore, again for formulas with low width, vertex expansion is closely related to boundary expansion. Hence we only need to focus on VIG edge expansion. With this in mind, we state several positive and negative results.

First, we observe (see Appendix) that if the number of inter-community edges at the top level of the decomposition grows sub-linearly with n and at least two sub-communities contain a constant fraction of vertices, then this graph family is not an expander. Unfortunately, we can also show (see Appendix) that graphs with good HCS can simultaneously have sub-graphs that are large expanders, with the worst case being very sparse expanders, capable of "hiding" in the hierarchical decomposition by contributing relatively few edges to any cut. To avoid that, we require an explicit bound on the number of inter-community edges, in addition to small community degree and small leaf-community size. This lets us prove the following statement.

Theorem 1. *Let $G = \{G_n\}$ be a family of graphs. Let $f(n) \in \omega(poly(\log n))$, $f(n) \in O(n)$. Assume that G has HCS with the number of inter-community edges $o(f(n))$ for every community C of size at least $\Omega(f(n))$ and depth is bounded by $O(\log n)$. Then G does not contain an expander of size $f(n)$ as a subgraph.*

Note that our experiments show that the leaf size and depth in industrial instances are relatively small and the number of inter-community edges grows slowly. From this and the theorem above, we can show that graphs with *very* good HCS properties do not contain linear-sized expanders.

Lower Bounds Against HCS: We are also able to show several of strong lower bounds on formulas with good HCS (see Appendix). For a number of combinations of parameters, we show that restricting ourselves to "good" ranges of these parameters does not rule out formulas which require superpolynomial size resolution refutations. Our most striking counterexample essentially shows that if the degree of the VIG is more than a small constant, then it is possible to embed formulas of superpolynomial resolution complexity. In contrast with the previous results on the size of embeddable expanders in instances with good HCS, this result shows how to embed a sparse expander of superlogarithmic size.

Hierarchical vs. Flat Modularity: It is well-known that modularity suffers from a *resolution limit* and cannot detect communities smaller than a certain threshold [18], and that HCS can avoid this problem in some instances [7]. In Appendix we provide an asymptotic, rigorous statement of this observation.

Theorem 2. *There exists a graph G whose natural communities are of size $\log(n)$ and correspond to the (leaf) HCS communities, while the partition maximizing modularity consists of communities of size $\Theta\left(\sqrt{n/\log^3 n}\right)$.*

7   Related Work

Community Structure: Using modularity to measure community structure allows one to distinguish industrial instances from randomly-generated ones [4]. Unfortunately, it has been shown that expanders can be embedded within formulas with high modularity [30], i.e., there exist formulas that have good community structure and yet are hard for solvers.

Heterogeneity: Unlike uniformly-random formulas, the variable degrees in industrial formulas follow a powerlaw distribution [3]. However, degree heterogeneity alone fails to explain the hardness of SAT instances. Some heterogeneous random k-SAT instances were shown to have superpolynomial resolution size [6], making them intractable for current solvers.

SATzilla: SATzilla uses 138 disparate parameters [46], some of which are probes aimed at capturing a SAT solver's state at runtime, to predict solver running time. Unfortunately, there is little or no evidence that most of these parameters are amenable to theoretical analysis.

Clause-Variable Ratio (CVR): Cheeseman et al. [11] observed the satisfiability threshold behavior for random k-SAT formulas, where they show formulas are harder when their CVR are closer to the satisfiability threshold. Outside of extreme cases, CVR alone seems to be insufficient to explain hardness (or easiness) of instances, as it is possible to generate both easy and hard formulas with the same CVR [19]. Satisfiability thresholds are poorly defined for industrial instances, and Coarfa et al. [14] demonstrated the existence of instances for which the satisfiability threshold is not equal to the hardness threshold.

Treewidth: Although there are polynomial-time non-CDCL algorithms for SAT instances with bounded treewidth [1], treewidth by itself does not appear to be a predictive parameter of CDCL solver runtime. For example, Mateescu [28] showed that some easy instances have large treewidth, and later it was shown that treewidth alone does not seem to correlate well with solving time [47].

Backdoors: In theory, the existence of small backdoors [36,44] should allow CDCL solvers to solve instances quickly, but empirically backdoors have been shown not to strongly correlate with CDCL solver run time [24].

8   Conclusions and Future Work

In this paper, we propose HCS as a correlative set of parameters for explaining the power of CDCL SAT solvers over industrial instances, which also has good theoretical properties. Empirically, HCS parameters are much more predictive than previously proposed correlative parameters in terms of classifying instances into random/crafted vs. industrial, and in terms of predicting solver run time. Among the top five most predictive parameters, three are HCS parameters, namely leaf-community size, modularity and fraction of inter-community edges. The remaining two are cvr and mergeability. We further identify the following core HCS parameters that are the most predictive among all HCS parameters, namely, leaf-community size, modularity, and fraction of inter-community edges. Indeed, these same parameters also play a role in our subsequent theoretical analysis, where we show that counterexamples to flat community structure do not apply to HCS, and that restricting certain HCS parameters limits the size of embeddable expanders. In the final analysis, we believe that HCS, along with other parameters such as mergeability or heterogeneity, will play a role in finally settling the question of why solvers are efficient over industrial instances.

References

1. Alekhnovich, M., Razborov, A.: Satisfiability. Branch-width and Tseitin tautologies. Comput. Complex. **20**(4), 649–678 (2011). https://doi.org/10.1007/s00037-011-0033-1
2. Ansótegui, C., Bonet, M.L., Giráldez-Cru, J., Levy, J.: The fractal dimension of SAT formulas. In: Proceedings of the 7th International Joint Conference on Automated Reasoning - IJCAR 2014, pp. 107–121 (2014). https://doi.org/10.1007/978-3-319-08587-6_8
3. Ansótegui, C., Bonet, M.L., Levy, J.: Towards industrial-like random SAT instances. In: IJCAI 2009, Proceedings of the 21st International Joint Conference on Artificial Intelligence, pp. 387–392 (2009)
4. Ansótegui, C., Giráldez-Cru, J., Levy, J.: The community structure of SAT formulas. In: Proceedings of the 15th International Conference on Theory and Applications of Satisfiability Testing - SAT 2012, pp. 410–423 (2012). https://doi.org/10.1007/978-3-642-31612-8_31
5. Ben-Sasson, E., Wigderson, A.: Short proofs are narrow—resolution made simple. J. ACM (JACM) **48**(2), 149–169 (2001)
6. Bläsius, T., Friedrich, T., Göbel, A., Levy, J., Rothenberger, R.: The impact of heterogeneity and geometry on the proof complexity of random satisfiability. In: Proceedings of the 2021 ACM-SIAM Symposium on Discrete Algorithms, SODA 2021, pp. 42–53 (2021). https://doi.org/10.1137/1.9781611976465.4
7. Blondel, V., Guillaume, J.L., Lambiotte, R., Lefebvre, E.: Fast unfolding of communities in large networks. J. Stat. Mech. Theory Exp. **2008**, P10008 (2008). https://doi.org/10.1088/1742-5468/2008/10/P10008
8. Blum, A.L., Furst, M.L.: Fast planning through planning graph analysis. Artif. Intell. **90**(1–2), 281–300 (1997)
9. Breiman, L.: Random forests. Mach. Learn. **45**(1), 5–32 (2001). https://doi.org/10.1023/A:1010933404324
10. Cadar, C., Ganesh, V., Pawlowski, P.M., Dill, D.L., Engler, D.R.: EXE: automatically generating inputs of death. ACM Trans. Inf. Syst. Secur. (TISSEC) **12**(2), 1–38 (2008)
11. Cheeseman, P., Kanefsky, B., Taylor, W.M.: Where the really hard problems are. In: Proceedings of the 12th International Joint Conference on Artificial Intelligence IJCAI 1991, pp. 331–337. (1991)
12. Clarke Jr, E.M., Grumberg, O., Kroening, D., Peled, D., Veith, H.: Model Checking. MIT Press (2018)
13. Clauset, A., Moore, C., Newman, M.E.J.: Hierarchical structure and the prediction of missing links in networks. Nature **453**(7191), 98–101 (2008). https://doi.org/10.1038/nature06830
14. Coarfa, C., Demopoulos, D.D., San Miguel Aguirre, A., Subramanian, D., Vardi, M.Y.: Random 3-SAT: the plot thickens. Constraints **8**(3), 243–261 (2003). https://doi.org/10.1023/A:1025671026963
15. Cook, S.A.: The complexity of theorem-proving procedures. In: Proceedings of the 3rd Annual ACM Symposium on Theory of Computing, pp. 151–158 (1971). https://doi.org/10.1145/800157.805047
16. Dolby, J., Vaziri, M., Tip, F.: Finding bugs efficiently with a SAT solver. In: Proceedings of the 6th Joint Meeting of the European Software Engineering Conference and the ACM SIGSOFT International Symposium on Foundations of Software Engineering, pp. 195–204 (2007). https://doi.org/10.1145/1287624.1287653

17. Eén, N., Biere, A.: Effective preprocessing in SAT through variable and clause elimination. In: Bacchus, F., Walsh, T. (eds.) SAT 2005. LNCS, vol. 3569, pp. 61–75. Springer, Heidelberg (2005). https://doi.org/10.1007/11499107_5
18. Fortunato, S., Barthélemy, M.: Resolution limit in community detection. Proc. Natl. Acad. Sci. 104(1), 36–41 (2007). https://doi.org/10.1073/pnas.0605965104
19. Friedrich, T., Krohmer, A., Rothenberger, R., Sutton, A.M.: Phase transitions for scale-free SAT formulas. In: Proceedings of the Thirty-First AAAI Conference on Artificial Intelligence, AAAI 2017, pp. 3893–3899. AAAI Press (2017)
20. Giráldez-Cru, J.: Beyond the structure of SAT formulas. Ph.D. thesis, Universitat Autònoma de Barcelona (2016)
21. Giráldez-Cru, J., Levy, J.: A modularity-based random SAT instances generator. In: Proceedings of the Twenty-Fourth International Joint Conference on Artificial Intelligence, IJCAI 2015, pp. 1952–1958 (2015). http://ijcai.org/Abstract/15/277
22. Granell, C., Gomez, S., Arenas, A.: Hierarchical multiresolution method to overcome the resolution limit in complex networks. Int. J. Bifurcat. Chaos 22(07), 1250171 (2012)
23. Hoory, S., Linial, N., Wigderson, A.: Expander graphs and their applications. Bull. Am. Math. Soc. 43(4), 439–561 (2006)
24. Kilby, P., Slaney, J., Thiebaux, S., Walsh, T.: Backbones and backdoors in satisfiability. Proc. Natl. Conf. Artif. Intell. 3, 1368–1373 (2005)
25. Lauria, M., Elffers, J., Nordström, J., Vinyals, M.: CNFgen: a generator of crafted benchmarks. In: Proceedings of the 20th International Conference on Theory and Applications of Satisfiability Testing (SAT 2017), pp. 464–473 (2017). https://doi.org/10.1007/978-3-319-94144-8_18
26. Li, C., et al.: On the hierarchical community structure of practical sat formulas. arXiv preprint arXiv:2103.14992 (2021)
27. Liang, J.H., Ganesh, V., Poupart, P., Czarnecki, K.: Learning rate based branching heuristic for SAT solvers. In: Proceedings of the 19th International Conference on Theory and Applications of Satisfiability Testing - SAT 2016, pp. 123–140 (2016). https://doi.org/10.1007/978-3-319-40970-2_9
28. Mateescu, R.: Treewidth in industrial SAT benchmarks. Tech. Rep. MSR-TR-2011-22, Microsoft (2011). https://www.microsoft.com/en-us/research/publication/treewidth-in-industrial-sat-benchmarks/
29. Monasson, R., Zecchina, R., Kirkpatrick, S., Selman, B., Troyansky, L.: Determining computational complexity from characteristic 'phase transitions'. Nature 400(6740), 133–137 (1999)
30. Mull, N., Fremont, D.J., Seshia, S.A.: On the hardness of SAT with community structure. In: Proceedings of the 19th International Conference on Theory and Applications of Satisfiability Testing (SAT), pp. 141–159 (2016). https://doi.org/10.1007/978-3-319-40970-2_10
31. Newman, M.E.J., Girvan, M.: Finding and evaluating community structure in networks. Phys. Rev. E 69(2), 026113 (2004). https://doi.org/10.1103/physreve.69.026113
32. Newsham, Z., Ganesh, V., Fischmeister, S., Audemard, G., Simon, L.: Impact of community structure on SAT solver performance. In: Theory and Applications of Satisfiability Testing - SAT 2014-17th International Conference, Held as Part of the Vienna Summer of Logic, VSL 2014, Vienna, Austria, 14–17 July, 2014. Proceedings, pp. 252–268 (2014). https://doi.org/10.1007/978-3-319-09284-3_20
33. Pedregosa, F., et al.: Scikit-learn: machine learning in python. J. Mach. Learn. Res. 12, 2825–2830 (2011)

34. Platt, J.C.: Probabilistic outputs for support vector machines and comparisons to regularized likelihood methods. In: Advances in Large Margin Classifiers, pp. 61–74. MIT Press (1999)
35. Ravasz, E., Somera, A.L., Mongru, D.A., Oltvai, Z.N., Barabási, A.L.: Hierarchical organization of modularity in metabolic networks. Science 297(5586), 1551–1555 (2002)
36. Samer, M., Szeider, S.: Backdoor trees. In: Automated Reasoning, vol. 1, pp. 363–368. Springer (2008)
37. Samer, M., Szeider, S.: Fixed-parameter tractability. In: Biere, A., Heule, M., van Maaren, H., Walsh, T. (eds.) Handbook of Satisfiability, Frontiers in Artificial Intelligence and Applications, 2nd edn., vol. 336. IOS Press (2021)
38. SAT: The International SAT Competition. http://www.satcompetition.org. Accessed 06 Mar 2021
39. Selman, B., Mitchell, D.G., Levesque, H.J.: Generating hard satisfiability problems. Artif. Intell. 81(1–2), 17–29 (1996)
40. SHARCNET: SHARCNET: Graham Cluster. https://www.sharcnet.ca/my/systems/show/114. Accessed 06 Mar 2021
41. Simon, H.A.: The architecture of complexity. Proc. Am. Philos. Soc. 106(6), 467–482 (1962). http://www.jstor.org/stable/985254
42. Steel, R.G.D., Torrie, J.H.: Principles and Procedures of Statistics. McGraw-Hill (1960)
43. Szeider, S.: Algorithmic utilization of structure in SAT instances. Theoretical Foundations of SAT/SMT Solving Workshop at the Simons Institute for the Theory of Computing (2021)
44. Williams, R., Gomes, C.P., Selman, B.: Backdoors to typical case complexity. In: IJCAI-2003, Proceedings of the Eighteenth International Joint Conference on Artificial Intelligence, pp. 1173–1178 (2003). http://ijcai.org/Proceedings/03/Papers/168.pdf
45. Xie, Y., Aiken, A.: Saturn: a SAT-based tool for bug detection. In: Proceedings of the 17th International Conference on Computer Aided Verification, CAV 2005, pp. 139–143 (2005). https://doi.org/10.1007/11513988_13
46. Xu, L., Hutter, F., Hoos, H., Leyton-Brown, K.: Features for SAT (2012). http://www.cs.ubc.ca/labs/beta/Projects/SATzilla/. Accessed Feb 2021
47. Zulkoski, E., Martins, R., Wintersteiger, C.M., Liang, J.H., Czarnecki, K., Ganesh, V.: The effect of structural measures and merges on SAT solver performance. In: Proceedings of the 24th International Conference on Principles and Practice of Constraint Programming, pp. 436–452 (2018). https://doi.org/10.1007/978-3-319-98334-9_29
48. Zulkoski, E., et al.: Learning-sensitive backdoors with restarts. In: Proceedings of the 24th International Conference on Principles and Practice of Constraint Programming, pp. 453–469 (2018). https://doi.org/10.1007/978-3-319-98334-9_30

Smt-Switch: A Solver-Agnostic C++ API for SMT Solving

Makai Mann[1]([⊠]) [iD], Amalee Wilson[1] [iD], Yoni Zohar[1] [iD], Lindsey Stuntz[1],
Ahmed Irfan[1] [iD], Kristopher Brown[1] [iD], Caleb Donovick[1] [iD], Allison Guman[3],
Cesare Tinelli[2] [iD], and Clark Barrett[1] [iD]

[1] Stanford University, Stanford, USA
{makaim,amalee,yoniz,lstuntz,irfan,donovick}@cs.stanford.edu,
ksb@stanford.edu
[2] The University of Iowa, Iowa City, USA
cesare-tinelli@uiowa.edu
[3] Columbia University, New York City, USA
ag3910@columbia.edu

Abstract. This paper presents Smt-Switch, an open-source, solver-agnostic API for SMT solving. Smt-Switch provides simple, uniform, and high-performance access to SMT solving for applications in areas such as automated reasoning, planning, and formal verification. It defines an abstract interface, which can be implemented by different SMT solvers. The interface allows the user to create, traverse, and manipulate terms, as well as dynamically dispatch queries to various underlying SMT solvers.

1 Introduction

Smt-Switch is an open-source, solver-agnostic C++ API for interacting with SMT-LIB-compliant SMT solvers. While SMT-LIB [1] provides a standard textual interface for SMT solving, there are limitations to that interface. In particular, applications that need to manipulate solver formulas or respond to solver output are easier and more efficient with an integrated API. Common approaches for addressing these limitations include committing to a specific solver (and its API) or using a custom internal expression representation, which is then translated to SMT-LIB and sent to a solver. In contrast, Smt-Switch provides a generic in-memory API, but without a custom representation, instead providing a lightweight wrapper around the underlying solver expressions. Smt-Switch already has support for many prominent SMT solvers and a variety of theories, and it provides an extensible abstract interface which makes it easy to add new solvers and theories. Smt-Switch is open-source and uses the permissive BSD license. It is available at https://github.com/makaimann/smt-switch.

The remainder of the paper is organized as follows. We start by describing the architecture of the tool in Sect. 2. Section 3 illustrates how to use the API with a simple example. We cover related work in Sect. 4 and give an experimental evaluation in Sect. 5. Finally, Sect. 6 concludes.

© Springer Nature Switzerland AG 2021
C.-M. Li and F. Manyà (Eds.): SAT 2021, LNCS 12831, pp. 377–386, 2021.
https://doi.org/10.1007/978-3-030-80223-3_26

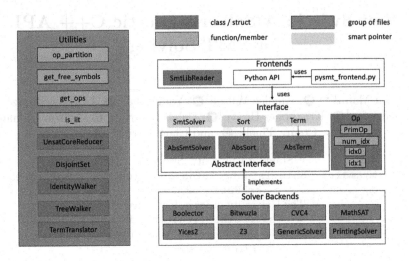

Fig. 1. Architecture diagram

2 Design

Figure 1 depicts an overview of the `Smt-Switch` architecture. After some general comments, we explain the various components in the figure. Throughout this paper, we refer to the external code of some SMT solver used by `Smt-Switch` as an *underlying* solver, and we use *backend* to refer to the `Smt-Switch` wrapper for an underlying solver. `Smt-Switch` delegates as much of the functionality to the underlying solvers as possible. This reduces redundancy and results in simpler implementations and lower memory overhead. The API is implemented in C++, and `Smt-Switch` also provides Python bindings using Cython [4].

Building and Linking. `Smt-Switch` uses CMake [13]. The build infrastructure is designed to be modular with respect to backend solvers. This allows the user to build `Smt-Switch` once and then link solver backends to their project as needed. The build configuration script also has options to enable static and debug builds.

Testing. We use *Google Test* [10] and *Pytest* [14] for the C++ test infrastructure and the Python test infrastructure, respectively. Tests are parameterized by solver so that each test can easily be run over all solvers.

Custom Exceptions. `Smt-Switch` defines its own set of exceptions inherited from `std::exception`. Each of them has a `std::string` message. The defined exceptions are: i) `SmtException` – the generic base class exception, ii) `NotImplementedException`, iii) `IncorrectUsageException`, and iv) `InternalSolverException`.

License. The `Smt-Switch` code is distributed under the BSD 3-clause license and provides setup scripts for building underlying solvers with similarly liberal open-source licenses. For solvers with more restrictive licenses, users are responsible for obtaining the underlying solver libraries themselves.

2.1   Interface

Smt-Switch provides abstract classes that define an interface for interacting with an underlying SMT solver. The interface corresponds closely to SMT-LIB version 2.6 [1], making it straightforward to connect solvers that are SMT-LIB compliant. At the Smt-Switch API level, the user interacts with smart pointers to the abstract classes. The virtual method functionality of C++ allows the interface to be agnostic to the underlying solver. The three primary abstract classes are: i) AbsSort; iii) AbsTerm; and iii) AbsSmtSolver. The Op class is not abstract and does not need to be implemented by the backend. However, the backend must interpret an Op when building terms.

AbsSort. The AbsSort abstract class represents logical sorts in Smt-Switch. A Sort is a pointer to an AbsSort. An enum called SortKind is used to represent built-in SMT-LIB sorts. In some cases, additional parameters are needed to create a sort. For example, bitvector sorts all have SortKind BV, and to create a bitvector sort, an additional parameter for bit-width is needed. Smt-Switch currently supports the following sorts, as they are defined in the SMT-LIB standard: i) Booleans, ii) integers, iii) reals, iv) fixed-width bitvectors, v) uninterpreted functions, vi) arrays, vii) uninterpreted sorts, and viii) algebraic datatypes. Each backend is responsible for creating an AbsSort object, given a SortKind (and its parameters if any). The backend must also be able to provide the SortKind and parameter information from a given sort.

Op. Op is a struct that represents logical function operators in Smt-Switch. As with sorts, there is an enum (called PrimOp) that contains built-in SMT-LIB functions from various theories. An Op stores a PrimOp and up to two integer indices. Unindexed operators are defined only by their PrimOp. Indexed operators use one or two indices. For example, integer addition is represented as PrimOp::Plus without any indices, while bitvector extraction uses PrimOp::Extract together with two indices specifying the most and least significant bits of the extracted slice. Smt-Switch uses a simple naming scheme for PrimOp's based on the corresponding SMT-LIB names.

AbsTerm. The AbsTerm abstract class represents logical terms, and a Term is a pointer to an AbsTerm. A Term can be a symbol (uninterpreted constant or function), a parameter (variable to be bound by a quantifier), a value (term corresponding to a model value such as 0 or 1), or an operator applied to one or more terms. Parameters are bound using the Forall or Exists operators. Terms can be queried to obtain their Sort, Op, and children (if a Term is not a function application, its Op is null). Note that, unlike the current SMT-LIB standard, we consider uninterpreted functions themselves to be terms. To create an uninterpreted function application, the Apply Op is used, where the first argument is the function to be applied and the rest of the arguments are

`Terms` representing the arguments to the function. This simplifies the interface and also makes it possible to support higher-order constructs if an underlying solver supports it. It also facilitates an invariant maintained by `Smt-Switch`: any `Term` with a non-null operator is equal to the result of querying its `Op` and children and then creating a new `Term` with the obtained `Op` and children.

AbsSmtSolver. The `AbsSmtSolver` class provides the main interface that a user interacts with. It has methods for declaring `Sorts`, building `Terms`, asserting formulas, and checking for satisfiability. The method names mirror the commands of SMT-LIB, replacing "-" with "_." One exception is `assert`, which is `assert_formula` in `Smt-Switch` to avoid clashing with the C assertion macro. `SmtSolver` is a pointer to an `AbsSmtSolver`.

Solver Factories. A solver factory defines a single static method: `create`. Each backend solver implementation defines a corresponding factory in a dedicated header file. The `create` function produces an `SmtSolver` for its corresponding backend. It takes a single Boolean parameter called `logging`, which specifies whether to add a layer to keep track of the structure of terms being created. This is useful if the underlying solver does not preserve term structure (e.g., if it performs on-the-fly rewriting of created terms) and the user needs the invariant that if you create a term with a given `Op` and children and then query the `Op` and children of the new term, you get back the `Op` and children you started with (note that this is the inverse of the invariant mentioned in the AbsTerm section above). `Smt-Switch` currently has backends for `Boolector` [18], `Bitwuzla` [17], `CVC4` [3], `MathSAT` [5], `Yices2` [6], and `Z3` [16]. It also provides two more special implementations of `AbsSmtSolver`: i) `PrintingSolver` – a wrapper around a backend that logs all API calls and dumps them as an SMT-LIB script to an output stream – especially useful for debugging as it provides a way to reproduce a behavior seen in `Smt-Switch` using just the underlying solver with an SMT-LIB file; and ii) `GenericSolver` – communicates interactively with an arbitrary SMT-LIB-compliant solver binary through pipes.

2.2 Additional Features

Analysis. `Smt-Switch` provides utility functions for i) gathering all subterms matching some given criteria in a term; ii) reducing an unsatisfiable core; iii) returning a flat list of all the arguments of a commutative and associative operator (e.g., Boolean `and` or `or`); iv) manipulating disjoint sets (union-find data structures) of `Smt-Switch Terms`; and v) traversing and rewriting `Smt-Switch Terms` – by inheriting from the `IdentityWalker` or `TreeWalker` classes. In the former, each sub-term is visited once, regardless of how many times it occurs in the formula. In the latter, every occurrence of every sub-term is visited.

Term Translation. The `TermTranslator` class can be used to copy terms from one backend solver to another. The only requirement for this to work is that the source solver must implement the term traversal interface methods. This functionality makes it easy to communicate information among several solvers.

Portfolio Solving. Smt-Switch provides infrastructure for using a portfolio of backend solvers to solve a single problem in parallel (i.e., the first to finish reports the answer).

Additional Frontends. In addition to its C++ library, Smt-Switch provides a Flex [20] and Bison [8] parser for the SMT-LIB language, and a Python module for translating between PySMT [9] terms and Smt-Switch terms.

3   Example

In this section, we demonstrate the Smt-Switch API with a simple example. Figure 2 (left) uses Smt-Switch with the CVC4 backend to solve simple queries over bitvectors and uninterpreted functions. It starts by including C++ and Smt-Switch headers and invoking the relevant using declarations. The main function then begins by creating a backend SmtSolver using CVC4 without logging. Note that changing the backend solver can easily be done by only changing this line and the factory being included. The logic is set to quantifier-free formulas over bitvectors and uninterpreted functions (QF_UFBV), and solver options are used to enable incremental solving, models, and the production of "unsat assumptions" (an SMT-LIB variant of unsatisfiable core functionality, in which the core is taken from a specified set of assumptions). This is followed by creating two sorts: a bitvector sort of width 32, and a function sort with that sort as both domain and codomain. The next three lines create two bitvector symbolic constants and an uninterpreted function. Next, the terms x0 and y0 are created, corresponding to the least significant half of the bitvectors x and y, respectively, by applying the bitvector extract operator with upper index 15 and lower index 0.

We then assert that applying the function to x and y results in different values and push a new context, in which we assert that the bottom halves of x and y are equal. This is followed by a successful satisfiability check, after which we print the value assigned to x and pop to the top level context. The query is satisfiable because x and y can have different most significant bits, and thus the function applications could return different values.

We then create a term that represents the bit-wise and of x and y and three Boolean terms built in various ways from x and y. The final satisfiability check is done with these terms as assumptions and is unsatisfiable, because the assumptions entail that x equals y, contradicting the top-level assertion that f applied to x is different from f applied to y. Finally, we extract a subset of the assumptions that (together with existing assertions) is sufficient for unsatisfiability. The output of the program is shown at the top right-hand side of the figure. Looking at the output, we can see that only the last two assumptions are needed for unsatisfiability.

The remainder of the right-hand side of Fig. 2 shows the corresponding SMT-LIB commands for the C++ code. An artifact containing the example in both

```
#include <iostream>                          Output:
#include "smt-switch/cvc4_factory.h"         -------
#include "smt-switch/smt.h"                  sat
using namespace smt;                         (_ bv0 32)
using namespace std;                         unsat
int main()                                   (bvuge (bvand x y) y)
{                                            (bvuge (bvand x y) x)
  SmtSolver s =
    CVC4SolverFactory::create(false);        SMT-LIB:
                                             --------
  s->set_logic("QF_UFBV");                   (set-logic QF_UFBV)
  s->set_opt("incremental", "true");         (set-option :incremental true)
  s->set_opt("produce-models", "true");      (set-option :produce-models true)
  s->set_opt("produce-unsat-assumptions",    (set-option :produce-unsat-assumptions
    "true");                                     true)
  Sort bvs = s->make_sort(BV, 32);           (define-sort bvs () (_ BitVec 32))
  Sort funs =
    s->make_sort(FUNCTION, {bvs, bvs});

  Term x = s->make_symbol("x", bvs);         (declare-const x bvs)
  Term y = s->make_symbol("y", bvs);         (declare-const y bvs)
  Term f = s->make_symbol("f", funs);        (declare-fun f (bvs) bvs)

  Op ext = Op(Extract, 15, 0);               (define-fun x0 () (_ BitVec 16)
  Term x0 = s->make_term(ext, x);              ((_ extract 15 0) x))
  Term y0 = s->make_term(ext, y);            (define-fun y0 () (_ BitVec 16)
                                               ((_ extract 15 0) y))
  Term fx = s->make_term(Apply, f, x);
  Term fy = s->make_term(Apply, f, y);
  s->assert_formula(                         (assert (distinct (f x) (f y)))
    s->make_term(Distinct, fx, fy));

  s->push(1);                                (push 1)
  s->assert_formula(                         (assert (= x0 y0))
    s->make_term(Equal, x0, y0));
  cout << s->check_sat() << endl;            (check-sat)

  cout << s->get_value(x) << endl;           (get-value (x))
  s->pop(1);                                 (pop 1)

  Term xy = s->make_term(BVAnd, x, y);       (define-fun xy () bvs (bvand x y))
  Term a1 = s->make_term(BVUge, x0, y0);     (define-fun a1 () Bool (bvuge x0 y0))
  Term a2 = s->make_term(BVUge, xy, x);      (define-fun a2 () Bool (bvuge xy x))
  Term a3 = s->make_term(BVUge, xy, y);      (define-fun a3 () Bool (bvuge xy y))
  cout <<
    s->check_sat_assuming({a1, a2, a3})      (check-sat-assuming (a1 a2 a3))
    << endl;
  UnorderedTermSet ua;
  s->get_unsat_assumptions(ua);              (get-unsat-assumptions)
  for (Term t : ua) { cout << t << endl; }
}
```

Fig. 2. Left: C++ API Example. Right: the output from running the program, as well as the SMT-LIB script that corresponds to the C++ example.

C++ and Python (as well as scripts for reproducing the results in Sect. 5) is available at https://doi.org/10.6084/m9.figshare.14566449.v1.

4   Related Work

The most closely related tools are smt-kit [11] and *metaSMT* [19], other C++ APIs for SMT solving. Both utilize templates to be solver agnostic and have term representations that are separate from the underlying solver, as opposed to Smt-Switch which provides an abstract interface and only a light wrapper around the term representations of the underlying solvers. This design choice reduces overhead and keeps maintenance simple. *metaSMT* makes clever use of C++ template meta-programming to help reduce its overhead. Furthermore, it provides several features including bit-blasting and infrastructure for portfolio solving. However, *metaSMT* only supports bitvectors, arrays, and uninterpreted functions. Adding new theories to either smt-kit or *metaSMT* would likely be a bigger undertaking than in the comparatively simple Smt-Switch. Neither smt-kit nor *metaSMT* appear to be under active development since 2014 and 2016, respectively.

Two other related tools are PySMT [9] and sbv [7]. PySMT is a solver-agnostic SMT solving API for Python. PySMT has its own term representation and translates formulas to the underlying solvers dynamically once they are asserted. It also uses a class hierarchy to support different solvers. sbv is a solver-agnostic SMT-based verification tool for Haskell. It provides its own datatypes for representing various SMT queries and communicates with solvers through SMT-LIB with pipes. A similar related tool in the context of SAT-solving is PySAT [12], which provides a solver-agnostic Python interface to SAT-solvers.

5   Evaluation

We evaluate Smt-Switch by comparing several state-of-the-art SMT solvers with Smt-Switch (using backends for those same solvers). We use default options for the (underlying) solvers in both cases.[1] We compare on SMT-LIB [2] divisions with bitvectors and arrays, because all solvers support these theories (we use the SMT-LIB frontend for Smt-Switch). We ran on all combinations of incremental vs. non-incremental, and quantified vs. quantifier-free for those theories.[2] We sampled benchmarks from other divisions and obtained comparable results. All experiments were run on a 3.5 GHz Intel Xeon E5-2637 v4 CPU with a timeout of 20 min and a memory limit of 8 Gb.

Our results are shown for non-incremental and incremental benchmarks in Figs. 3 and 4, respectively. The total number of benchmarks in the division is shown next to the logic in the top row. The tables display the number solved

---

[1] GitHub Commit or Version
  Smt-Switch: 17c57ac0f0574cf76125ead56a598fce15c56004
  Boolector: 95859db82fe5b08d063a16d6a7ffe4a941cb0f7d
  CVC4:   3dda54ba7e6952060766775c56969ab920430a8a
  MathSAT: 5.6.4 (697e45d7ef56)
  Yices2:   98fa2d882d83d32a07d3b8b2c562819e0e0babd0
  Z3:   6cc52e04c3ea7e2534644a285d231bdaaafd8714

[2] Note that ABV – incremental, quantified arrays and bitvectors does not have any benchmarks in SMT-LIB.

solver	QF_BV (41713)	QF_ABV (15084)	BV (5846)	ABV (169)
btor	41313 (6.1s)	15045 (1.2s)	5544 (3.8s)	-
ss-btor	41298 (6.0s) -1.8%	15045 (1.2s) 3.5%	5543 (3.7s) -4.0%	-
bitwuzla	41366 (5.8s)	15046 (1.0s)	5557 (4.5s)	-
ss-bitwuzla	41357 (6.2s) 5.8%	15046 (1.0s) 2.2%	5559 (4.5s) 0.6%	-
cvc4	38424 (14.2s)	14480 (8.5s)	5465 (1.1s)	17 (0.1s)
ss-cvc4	38425 (15.2s) 6.9%	14618 (4.4s) -48.1%	5472 (1.0s) -13.6%	17 (0.1s) 6.2%
msat	39609 (17.3s)	14940 (2.7s)	-	-
ss-msat	39598 (18.5s) 6.7%	14937 (2.9s) 6.1%	-	-
yices2	40707 (5.8s)	15015 (2.1s)	-	-
ss-yices2	40695 (6.1s) 4.7%	15007 (2.2s) 9.1%	-	-
z3	40261 (15.6s)	14916 (3.0s)	5522 (1.5s)	44 (2.4s)
ss-z3	40092 (15.9s) 1.7%	14915 (2.8s) -5.3%	5523 (1.8s) 22.5%	44 (1.5s) -40.3%

Fig. 3. Results on non-incremental SMT-LIB benchmarks.

and average runtime on commonly solved instances. The number solved for incremental benchmarks is the sum of all completed satisfiability checking calls. An incremental benchmark is counted as commonly solved for the average runtime calculation if both solvers completed all queries. The Smt-Switch rows also show the percent increase in runtime when using Smt-Switch.

The data are a rough approximation of the overhead incurred when using Smt-Switch. It is rough because our experiment measures parsing time as well as expression construction and solving time. CVC4, for example, uses an ANTLR-based parser, which is a bit slower than other parsers. There is also some noise due to differences in how a solver's API performs relative to its standalone binary. For example, one outlier in the incremental MathSAT QF_BV results skews the overhead significantly for that dataset, though this is due to some difference in the search rather than parsing or expression-building overhead. When Smt-Switch solves fewer benchmarks, it is often due to benchmarks that were already close to the timeout with the standalone solver. Overhead is most pronounced on large files, where both parsing and expression-building are exercised more often. Still, the data over many benchmarks and solvers does suggest that the overhead of using Smt-Switch is low, generally less than 10% (and some of this is due to parsing differences). Given the flexibility provided by Smt-Switch, this level of overhead should be acceptable for many applications.

solver	QF_BV (2589)	QF_ABV (1272)	BV (18)
btor	52375 (6.5s)	3243 (21.5s)	-
ss-btor	52395 (6.9s) 5.8%	3247 (21.1s) -1.8%	-
bitwuzla	52366 (7.1s)	3247 (22.4s)	12445 (1.6s)
ss-bitwuzla	52366 (7.3s) 2.8%	3246 (22.9s) 2.2%	12445 (0.8s) -49.8%
cvc4	51262 (17.5s)	2504 (22.1s)	36097 (54.4s)
ss-cvc4	51252 (15.4s) -12.2%	2740 (2.3s) -89.6%	35852 (26.0s) -52.3%
msat	52333 (8.4s)	3121 (5.7s)	-
ss-msat	52255 (10.0s) 19.4%	3119 (6.3s) 10.5%	-
yices2	52538 (6.2s)	3242 (6.3s)	-
ss-yices2	52490 (6.7s) 7.0%	3243 (6.7s) 6.0%	-
z3	52347 (18.1s)	2911 (31.3s)	37433 (33.6s)
ss-z3	52238 (18.2s) 0.6%	2871 (30.0s) -4.2%	37231 (25.0s) -25.6%

Fig. 4. Results on incremental SMT-LIB benchmarks.

6 Conclusion

We presented Smt-Switch, a solver-agnostic C++ API for SMT solving. This system is open-source, supports a variety of solvers and theories, and has already been used in several projects [15,21]. Future work includes i) further reducing the overhead with additional performance tuning; ii) support for more theories (e.g., the floating point and string theories); and iii) providing additional utility functions and classes.

References

1. Barrett, C., Fontaine, P., Tinelli, C.: The SMT-LIB Standard: Version 2.6. Technical Report, Department of Computer Science, The University of Iowa (2017). www.SMT-LIB.org
2. Barrett, C., Fontaine, P., Tinelli, C.: The Satisfiability Modulo Theories Library (SMT-LIB) (2021). www.SMT-LIB.org
3. Barrett, C., et al.: CVC4. In: Gopalakrishnan, G., Qadeer, S. (eds.) CAV 2011. LNCS, vol. 6806, pp. 171–177. Springer, Heidelberg (2011). https://doi.org/10.1007/978-3-642-22110-1_14
4. Behnel, S., Bradshaw, R., Citro, C., Dalcin, L., Seljebotn, D.S., Smith, K.: Cython: The best of both worlds. Comput. Sci. Eng. **13**(2), 31–39 (2011)
5. Cimatti, A., Griggio, A., Schaafsma, B.J., Sebastiani, R.: The MathSAT5 SMT solver. In: Piterman, N., Smolka, S.A. (eds.) TACAS 2013. LNCS, vol. 7795, pp. 93–107. Springer, Heidelberg (2013). https://doi.org/10.1007/978-3-642-36742-7_7
6. Dutertre, B.: Yices 2.2. In: Biere, A., Bloem, R. (eds.) CAV 2014. LNCS, vol. 8559, pp. 737–744. Springer, Cham (2014). https://doi.org/10.1007/978-3-319-08867-9_49
7. Erkok, L.: SBV: SMT Based Verification in Haskell (2019). http://leventerkok.github.io/sbv/
8. Free Software Foundation: bison (2021). https://www.gnu.org/software/bison/
9. Gario, M., Micheli, A.: PySMT: a solver-agnostic library for fast prototyping of SMT-based algorithms. In: Proceedings of the 13th International Workshop on Satisfiability Modulo Theories (SMT), pp. 373–384 (2015)
10. Google: GoogleTest. https://github.com/google/googletest
11. Horn, A.: Smt-kit: C++11 library for many sorted logics. http://ahorn.github.io/smt-kit/
12. Ignatiev, A., Morgado, A., Marques-Silva, J.: PySAT: a python toolkit for prototyping with sat oracles. In: Beyersdorff, O., Wintersteiger, C.M. (eds.) SAT 2018. LNCS, vol. 10929, pp. 428–437. Springer, Cham (2018). https://doi.org/10.1007/978-3-319-94144-8_26
13. KitWare: CMake. https://cmake.org
14. Krekel, H., Oliveira, B., Pfannschmidt, R., Bruynooghe, F., Laugher, B., Bruhin, F.: pytest 5.4.2 (2004). https://github.com/pytest-dev/pytest
15. Mann, M., et al.: Pono: a flexible and extensible SMT-based model checker. In: CAV. Lecture Notes in Computer Science, Springer (2021)
16. de Moura, L., Bjørner, N.: Z3: an efficient SMT solver. In: Ramakrishnan, C.R., Rehof, J. (eds.) TACAS 2008. LNCS, vol. 4963, pp. 337–340. Springer, Heidelberg (2008). https://doi.org/10.1007/978-3-540-78800-3_24

17. Niemetz, A., Preiner, M.: Bitwuzla at the SMT-COMP 2020. CoRR abs/2006. 01621 (2020). https://arxiv.org/abs/2006.01621
18. Niemetz, A., Preiner, M., Wolf, C., Biere, A.: BTOR2, BtorMC and Boolector 3.0. In: Chockler, H., Weissenbacher, G. (eds.) CAV 2018. LNCS, vol. 10981, pp. 587–595. Springer, Cham (2018). https://doi.org/10.1007/978-3-319-96145-3_32
19. Riener, H., et al.: metaSMT: focus on your application and not on solver integration. Int. J. Softw. Tools Technol. Transf. **19**(5), 605–621 (2017)
20. Vern Paxson: flex (2021). https://github.com/westes/flex
21. Zohar, Y., Irfan, A., Mann, M., Nötzli, A., Reynolds, A., Barrett, C.: lazybv2int at the SMT Competition 2020. https://github.com/yoni206/lazybv2int (2020)

The MERGESAT Solver

Norbert Manthey[✉]

TU Dresden, Dresden, Germany
nmanthey@conp-solutions.com

Abstract. Successful SAT solvers in recent competitions are typically based on the winner of the previous competition. Due to this procedure, for multiple years relevant features like incremental solving have not been supported by winning solvers anymore. Furthermore, bug fixes in one solver do not evolve into predecessors. This work presents MergeSat, a SAT solver that is also based on leading solvers of the past years. However, MergeSat can replace MiniSat or Glucose, as relevant features have been added back. Also, new techniques from other solvers of the community have been adapted, and implementation issues have been identified and fixed. These issues did not surface in an original solver or its successor during competitions. Finally, we provide a mechanism to easily incorporate changes of other solver, as well as a development and test environment to identify potential issues when merging techniques early. With this setup, MergeSat is a good starting point for future research development and integration into other solvers.

1 Introduction

An emerging pattern in top SAT solvers of recent SAT competitions is the following: a winning or top solver of the current year is typically based on a top performing solver of the previous year. Unfortunately, most solvers do not share the same code base continuously, nor are maintained by the same research team. Consequently, fixes and patches to a solver of last year are lost, as they do not make it into next years variant of that solver. Furthermore, abandoned features like incremental solving are hard to bring back, and hence, novel development cannot make it into tools that are based on SAT solvers easily.

On the other hand, the modification between solver versions is rather small, and can be identified by comparing the formatted code for the given solver versions. Many tools that deal with other logics, e.g. CBMC [16], MONOSAT [9], still use older SAT solvers, such as MINISAT [17] or GLUCOSE [2] and their interface. These facts and the potential to positively influence a broad range of tools motivated the development of MERGESAT.

The solver is based on the winning solver of the SAT competition 2018, namely the tool MAPLE_LCM_DIST_CHRONoBT [42]. The major improvements are that the solver is deterministic again, supports incremental SAT solving, implements runtime checkers for satisfiability and DRAT proofs, as well as provides a development environment that checks for these features continuously.

C.-M. Li and F. Manyà (Eds.): SAT 2021, LNCS 12831, pp. 387–398, 2021.
https://doi.org/10.1007/978-3-030-80223-3_27

Furthermore, techniques presented in the 2020 competition have been added. Implementation issues in these extensions have been identified, reported to the original authors, and fixed in the implementation. MERGESAT implements the extensions in a configurable way, and supports automated configuration tools, also when being used as a solver library. On the SAT 2020 benchmark, MERGE-SAT performance outperforms all participating MINISAT based solver engines.

New Contribution and Goal of MergeSat

The goal of MERGESAT is to encapsulate recent developments in SAT research into a tool that can be integrated easily into tools that currently use MINISAT [17] or GLUCOSE [2]. This goal should be achieved with low maintenance effort, also providing an easy starting point for collaboration and future research. For easy integration, a script is provided to identify the diff of two MINISAT based solvers. This diff can then be integrated into MERGESAT. Furthermore, the integrity of the implemented features and the solver itself are tested continuously, to make sure the solver can be used widely. Only a few solvers come with such a development environment.

Beyond MAPLE_LCM_DIST_CHRONOBT, the solver implements more techniques: MINISAT's incremental solving interface has been activated again and the IPASIR interface [4] is supported. Next, MERGESAT can be used as engine in the parallel solver HORDESAT [6]. Furthermore, *conflict refinement* [33] has been extended to be used adaptively. Similarly, *assumption prefetching* (similarly to [24,32] is used in an adaptive way, depending on whether the last solver call ended in ⊤ or ⊥. *Trail saving* [25], polarity rephasing and SLS solving have been adapted from [46], as well as removing good learned (*core*) clauses from [31] have been integrated.

Structure

This paper describes how the solver development is setup, and how the solver has evolved since 2018. Furthermore, the list of relevant fixes to existing solvers, as well as brief experimental results are presented.

2   Recent SAT Competitions

SAT competitions are an annual event, with different tracks, scoring systems and varying settings. Besides the plain satisfiability track, there have been incremental tracks and even minimal unsatisfiability tracks. Various research teams submit SAT solvers to these competitions, as well as solver descriptions. After the event, the solver sources and proceedings are published, e.g. [3–5,7,8,10,22,23]. Recently, top solvers of the main track of the competition do not participate in the incremental track, likely due to missing support for multiple solver calls.

2.1 Benchmark Selection

The annual solver competitions are an independent snapshot of the development of solving technology and implementation details. The used benchmarks are a collection of user submitted formulas of the participants, or selected CNFs from a pool of previously known formula sets. In some years, the benchmarks have been separated into categories, such as *crafted* or *application*. Benchmark selection approaches like [27] or analysis along the ideas of [38] are currently not considered.

Still, the annual competitions help to boost the solver performance, even when running on a different benchmark. General comparisons between solvers are difficult, as solvers might be specialized for applications or benchmark categories. Hence, typically new solvers evolve from the best solvers of the previous year.

2.2 Winning Solvers and Top Solvers

The following Table 1 shows the for MERGESAT relevant top performing solvers of the most recent five SAT competitions, as well as the solver variant of the previous year these solvers are based on.

Table 1. For MERGESAT relevant winners and top solvers of recent SAT competition, sorted by year, and showing the previous solver variant as well as the relevant tool description. The table shows the history of the solver development.

Year	Top solver	Based on
2020	RELAXED_LCMDCBDL_newTech [46]	MapleLCMDiscChronoBT-DL-v3 [44]
2019	MapleLCMDiscChronoBT-DL-v3 [44]	Maple_LCM_Dist_ChronoBT [42]
2018	Maple_LCM_Dist_ChronoBT [42]	Maple LCM Dist [19]
2017	Maple LCM Dist [19]	MapleCOMSPS [29]
2016	MapleCOMSPS [29]	COMiniSatPS [41]

The solvers in the list typically add one or two techniques to the existing solver. The initial solver COMiniSatPS is based on MiniSat [17] and implements ideas of GLUCOSE [1], as well as [41]. To show-case a relevant solver extension, research groups seem to pick the winner or a close top performing solver of the previous year to extend it with their current research idea[1]. This leads to a chain of solvers with varying author teams.

2.3 SAT Solver Evolution

Independently of the history of the top solver of a given year, there are other forks in the *solver evolution tree*. For example, in 2011 partial restarts have been

---

[1] Such a chain might likely be related to publications that aim at improving the current state of the art.

presented to reduce the cost of unit propagation, but this change was not added to MiniSat or Glucose, nor COMiniSatPS. To the best of my knowledge, feature relevance analysis like [30] has not been repeated since 2011, although solvers like CryptoMiniSat [43] or CaDiCaL [14] implement a large amount of techniques in one solver. Hence, for each year of a solver competition, it is hard to tell which solver extension is relevant with respect to performance. For the solvers presented in Sect. 2.2, the current solver evolution only selects the improvements of one solver, and ignores all other proposed modifications. Follow-up improvements of a previous-year solver are not incorporated back into the main solver. As solvers are produced as research prototype, the implementation of the solver meets the requirements for publications and competitions, but might lack best implementation practices, like for example memory usage.

There are a few solvers that are independent from the above evolution tree, for example Lingeling [12], CaDiCaL [13] or KissSat [14] as well as CryptoMiniSat [43]. These systems try to keep up with the broader development of techniques, at the cost of a higher maintenance effort. Most solving techniques have to be re-implemented to fit into the correspondent eco system. Older solvers like Lingeling by Biere et al. do not receive updates with new techniques.

3   Development Model of MergeSat

MergeSat bridges the gap between research prototypes that are based on the previous years top solver, as well as the independent systems that try to maintain more relevant solving techniques. The development of the solver is moved forward by incorporating solver modifications of submissions to the SAT competition, e.g. the IPASIR interface from the incremental competition track. The solver itself is then continuously tested to meet expected standards and not break features.

3.1   Supported Features and Selected Techniques

MergeSat provides the same features well established SAT solvers like MiniSat or Glucose. Besides solving plain and compressed CNF formulas from files in DIMACS format, MergeSat can emit proofs in the commonly used DRUP format [21]. MergeSat also supports incremental SAT solving via MiniSat's interface, and implements the IPASIR [4] interface. The solver was already used as SAT backend in the MaxSAT solver open-wbo [36]. Furthermore, MergeSat implements the required hooks to be used as HordeSat SAT engine [6], which allows to use the solver for multi-core and multi-machine parallel SAT solving.

3.1.1   Additionally Implemented Solving Techniques
The following major techniques are implemented in the solver, and are not present in MiniSat or Glucose.

▷ Simplifying learned clauses with Learnt clause minimization [35], and additionally repeat successful simplifications in reverse order [33].

▷ Chronological backtracking [39], which allows to reduce repetitive unit propagations by maintaining an unordered search stack.

▷ Reduce the simplification time on large formulas by using step limits for simplification and search, similarly to [12].

▷ Faster simplification by using linear resolution for clause simplification, along [18] instead of the quadratic default implementation.

▷ Deleting learned clauses from the most relevant set of learned clauses [31], but skipping every second attempt when not removing more than 5% of the clauses.

▷ Avoiding duplicate clauses, by using a small cache of recent new clauses instead of a full hashmap of all learned clauses as in [44]. MAPLELCMDISCCHRONOBT-DL-V3 keeps all learned clauses in a hash map. To avoid this additional memory, and still be able to get a partial benefit, MERGESAT uses a cache of the most recently added 20 simplified clauses during LCM. Clauses present in this set are used to reject new simplified clauses.

▷ Simplification during search (inprocessing) [11], using self-subsuming resolution and subsumption.

▷ Switching between VSIDS and LRB/Distance decision heuristic frequently, along [44], using a single heap structure to implement the priority queue.

▷ Exploiting hardware features by using prefetching watchlists [26] and supporting use transparent huge pages [20], when being compiled with the provided docker infrastructure.

▷ Partial restarts, that allow to safe effort when restarting the search [45].

▷ Use SLS solving to participate in the solving process and use phase saving rephasing to guide the search [46].

▷ Trail saving, i.e. saving the propagation information during backtracking to re-use it during the next search [25].

3.1.2 Incremental SAT Solving

Most successful solvers of recent competitions do not participate in the incremental track of these competitions – likely because the lack of support for incremental solving in recent successful solvers. MERGESAT supports incremental solving again, and improves it as follows:

▷ Instead of assigning all assumption literals and alternating these assignments with propagation, **assumption prefetching** is used. All assumptions are assigned before propagation is executed [32].

▷ To improve judging the quality of learned clauses, ignore LBD levels of assumption literals, similarly to GLUCOSE [1].

▷ For unsatisfiable formulas, the set of unsatisfiable assumption literals is simplified adaptively [33], by running vivification in reversed order; and disabling this simplification for a call in case the attempt in the previous attempt was not successful.

▷ The SLS engine in initialized **lazily**. Instead of the eager initialization, as done in [46], the SLS engine is called just before data for rephasing is required for rephasing or attempting to solve the formula.

3.1.3   Parameter Configuration

As the default setup might not fit a certain application best, MERGESAT allows to tune the implemented techniques via the tool command line. To adapt the solver better to a given use case, the *PCS configuration file format* is supported. This file format allows to use tools like SMAC3 [37] or PARAMILS [28] to tune the configuration. Furthermore, the configuration debugging tool SPYBUG [34] can be used. As MERGESAT can generate the PCS file itself, future parameters can be integrated into the process easily.

In contrast to other tools, the configuration can also be specified via an environment variable. This setup allows to also tune the SAT engine when it is used as a SAT backend as part of another tool.

3.2   Incorporating Patches

Today, solvers that are submitted to the SAT competition typically do not come with a version controlled source code. Consequently, solver dependencies have to be found manually. The source code difference between solvers have to be detected manually. To reduce the manual effort, the following steps are used:

1. Move the relevant solver versions to separate branches in MERGESAT's repository
2. Format the source code of all solvers with the same coding style
3. Create a patch that corresponds to the difference that was introduced by the new solver
4. Eventually split the difference along features into multiple patches
5. Cherry-pick feature patches and apply them to MERGESAT

The above steps allow to apply a solver diff to MERGESAT, which likely carries changes that are not present in the other solver variants. Splitting patches into chunks allows to reduce conflicts during applying patches, as well as improves the quality of the history of the changes in the solver. Finally, with all solvers being present in the repository, reasoning about their differences can be done by using tools. To simplify the process, a script is provided with MERGESAT to extract the difference between two solvers.

3.3   Provided Implementation Improvements

MERGESAT has been tested with memory sanitizer, undefined behavior sanitizer and the Coverity code analysis tool. This testing revealed non-critical memory issues when initializing data structures for new variables, as well as when parsing compressed formulas. The memory consumption of the solver has also been reduced slightly. Besides picking features from existing solvers, the following issues in feature implementations have been addressed to improve the solver further. The issues have also been reported to the author of the original implementation.

Avoid Clause Header Expansion. The implementation of learnt clause minimization (LCM) [35] introduces an additional bit per stored clause to indicate whether a clause has been used for LCM already. In contrast to recommendations of [26], this additional bit results in an increased clause header size, which leads to slower unit propagation. This issue has been spotted by manually investigating the code. While the authors of the initial implementation in [35] have been notified, the bit is still present in the winning solver of 2019 and its successors[2].

Avoid Resource Leaks. In case a MINISAT based solver is used as a SAT backend in another tool, and MINISAT internal realloc implementation fails, e.g. when hitting a memory limit, the tool might leak memory in case it can recover from the SAT solvers memory failure. MERGESAT carries a fix for this behavior, to avoid this resource leak. This issue has been found by testing MERGESAT as a SAT backend of a MaxSAT solver in a low-memory situation and by using the VALGRIND tool [40].

Avoid Unsoundness Due To Decision Heuristic Switch. The solver MAPLECOMSPS introduced switching decision heuristics from VSIDS for initialization to LRB [29]. As this solver initialized all data structures for all decision heuristics, simply switching from one implementation to another results in sound behavior. However, when re-activating incremental solving together with this heuristic switch implementation, switching heuristics by just using other data structures without synchronizing their state can lead to unsound behavior. Successor solvers frequently switch between the two heuristics, which also carry the risk of unsound behavior. To not result in unsound behavior, MERGESAT moves the full state from one heuristic to another. As a follow up modification, the three decision heaps of predecessors have been merged into a single one. This issue has been found by using MERGESAT as a SAT backend in the MaxSAT solver OPEN-WBO [36]. Without the fix, OPEN-WBO produced incorrect answers for certain input.

Cyclic Search in Chronological Backtracking. During chronological backtracking [39], conflict clauses detected during unit propagation might be spurious, because they would be entailed clauses on a previous level. The original implementation updates the watch list of this conflict, and re-tries propagation. There exist input formulas, that undo this watch list update, and next hit the same spurious conflict again. MERGESAT jumps back higher in case such a cycle is detected, to resolve the situation properly.

Combining Trail Saving with Chronological Backtracking. Trail saving [25] stores the literals and the clauses that imply them for all backtracked assignments. Next, during propagation, this information is used to speedup propagation and conflict detection. However, solver invariants – like always storing the asserting variable on the first position – are neglected. When combining trail saving with chronological backtracking, the invariants can be violated. Hence, MERGESAT checks the invariants, and aborts trail saving in case of violation.

---

[2] See   http://sat-race-2019.ciirc.cvut.cz/solvers/MapleLCMDiscChronoBT-DL-v3.zip.

3.4 Development Environment

To improve confidence into the tool, model validation has been implemented. This technique stores a read-only copy of the parsed formula, and checks whether the given model satisfies this copy of the formula. Similarly, a runtime DRAT proof checker is integrated. This checker allows to verify each modification of the proof during runtime, and interrupt execution as soon as a proof modification is invalid. Both checkers are disabled by default, but can be enabled from the command line.

MERGESAT is developed as an open source tool on github[3], and features can be extended via *pull requests*. Each pull request runs through continuous integration checks. These test make sure that the starexec package can be constructed, the IPASIR integration works, as well as whether CNF files are solved as expected by using the CNFUZZ tool suite [15], as well as the two additional checkers mentioned above.

The continuous integration checks are executed via *TravisCI*[4] and *github workflows*[5].

4 Tool Comparison

To demonstrate the performance of the tool, we use the benchmark of the SAT competition 2020 [5]. A cluster of Intel(R) Xeon(R) CPU E5-2680 CPUs has been user. From the 24 core CPU, every fourth core is used to reduce impact from resource sharing. Run time is limited to 1 h, and the memory consumption is limited to 6 GB.

MERGESAT and state-of-the-art solvers have been compared on this setup. Besides KISSSAT [14], the winning solver of the 2020 competition, the base solver CADICAL [14] for the hack-track of the 2021 competition has been added. As further reference, the best MINISAT based solvers for solving satisfiable and unsatisfiable formulas have been added to the comparison, RELAXED_LCMDCBDL_NEWTECH [44] and MLCDBT-DL-F2TRC [31], respectively.

Table 2 shows the number of solved instances, and the overall PAR2 time. Next, it also reports the number of solved formulas that are known to be satisfiable and unsatisfiable, as well as the time it took to solve these subsets.

In the given set, MERGESAT is the best MINISAT based solver. Furthermore, MERGESAT outperforms CADICAL. The current setup of MERGESAT is stronger on satisfiable formulas. With the support for tool configuration also for libraries, a fitting configuration for other applications can be found as well.

---

[3] https://github.com/conp-solutions/mergesat.

[4] https://travis-ci.org.

[5] https://help.github.com/en/actions.

Table 2. This table compares the performance of recent top performing SAT solvers with MERGESAT. The table shows the solver as well as its variant, either as git commit or competition year. Next, the number of solved formulas and the related PAR2 value is given. Finally, the solved instances and the sum of time it took to solve them is presented for satisfiable and unsatisfiable formulas separately.

Solver	Variant	Solved	PAR2	Solved$_\top$	$\sum_t^\top$	Solved$_\perp$	$\sum_t^\perp$
KISSSAT	59813ad	253	1215310	131	72618	122	84291
CADICAL	f726e9a	237	1362661	127	105244	110	83816
MERGESAT	d208424	248	1278947	142	83582	106	100964
R_LCMDCBDL_NT	SC2020	243	1279091	147	72836	96	75854
MLCDBT-DL-F2TRC	SC2020	206	1566977	102	100468	104	69709

5 Conclusion and Future Work

MERGESAT in its current form is a SAT solver that provides recent SAT technology with the interface of the widely used solvers MINISAT and GLUCOSE. With the workflow to easily integrate solver modifications, the solver allows to easily combine the contributions of several research groups in a single solver. Combined with the offered – and widely used – MiniSat-interface, as well as supporting IPASIR, MERGESAT is an attractive target for both new research as well as tools that utilize SAT backends. Tools that currently use a MINISAT based SAT backend today might consider experimenting and benchmarking with MERGESAT.

Future work includes to support more solver extensions, as well as to exchange the SAT backend in tools that still rely on MINISAT or GLUCOSE to MERGESAT. Additionally, multi-core parallel SAT solving should be implemented within the same MINISAT solver interface, to allow other tools to use an even more powerful solver. Finally, given that MERGESAT implements many recently published techniques for SAT solving, this solver can be used to repeat the relevance analysis of components as done in [30].

Acknowledgement. MERGESAT is combination of the research ideas and implementation of many other research groups. Without this input, the solver would not exist in its form. These research groups own a big part of the success of the solver.

References

1. Audemard, G., Lagniez, J.-M., Simon, L.: Improving glucose for incremental SAT solving with assumptions: application to MUS extraction. In: Järvisalo, M., Van Gelder, A. (eds.) SAT 2013. LNCS, vol. 7962, pp. 309–317. Springer, Heidelberg (2013). https://doi.org/10.1007/978-3-642-39071-5_23
2. Audemard, G., Simon, L.: Predicting learnt clauses quality in modern sat solvers. In: Proceedings of the 21st International Jont Conference on Artifical Intelligence, IJCAI'09, pp. 399–404. Morgan Kaufmann Publishers Inc., San Francisco (2009)

3. Balint, A., Belov, A., Heule, M.J., Järvisalo, M. (eds.): Proceedings of SAT Challenge 2013, Department of Computer Science Series of Publications B, vol. B-2013-1. University of Helsinki, Helsinki, Finland (2013)
4. Balyo, T., Biere, A., Iser, M., Sinz, C.: SAT race 2015. Artif. Intell. **241**, 45–65 (2016)
5. Balyo, T., Froleyks, N., Heule, M., Iser, M., Järvisalo, M., Suda, M. (eds.): Department of Computer Science Report Series B, vol. B-2020-1. University of Helsinki (2020)
6. Balyo, T., Sanders, P., Sinz, C.: HordeSat: a massively parallel portfolio SAT solver. In: Heule, M., Weaver, S. (eds.) SAT 2015. LNCS, vol. 9340, pp. 156–172. Springer, Cham (2015). https://doi.org/10.1007/978-3-319-24318-4_12
7. Balyo, T., Heule, M., Järvisalo, M.: Proceedings of SAT Competition 2017: Solver and Benchmark Descriptions, Series of Publications B, vol. B-2017-1. Department of Computer Science, University of Helsinki, Finland (2017)
8. Balyo, T., Heule, M.: Proceedings of SAT Competition 2016: Solver and Benchmark Descriptions. Department of Computer Science Series of Publications B, University of Helsinki, Finland (2016)
9. Bayless, S., Bayless, N., Hoos, H.H., Hu, A.J.: Sat modulo monotonic theories. In: Proceedings of the Twenty-Ninth AAAI Conference on Artificial Intelligence, AAAI'15, pp. 3702–3709. AAAI Press (2015)
10. Belov, A., Diepold, D., Heule, M.J., Järvisalo, M. (eds.): Proceedings of SAT Competition 2014, Department of Computer Science Series of Publications B, vol. B-2014-2. University of Helsinki, Helsinki, Finland (2014)
11. Biere, A.: PrecoSAT system description (2009). http://fmv.jku.at/precosat/preicosat-sc09.pdf
12. Biere, A.: Lingeling, Plingeling, PicoSAT and PrecoSAT at SAT Race 2010. FMV Report Series Technical Report 10/1, Johannes Kepler University, Linz, Austria (2010)
13. Biere, A.: CaDiCaL, Lingeling, Plingeling, Treengeling, YalSAT entering the SAT competition 2017. In: Balyo, T., Heule, M., Järvisalo, M. (eds.) Proceedings of SAT Competition 2017 - Solver and Benchmark Descriptions. Department of Computer Science Series of Publications B, vol. B-2017-1, pp. 14–15. University of Helsinki (2017)
14. Biere, A., Fazekas, K., Fleury, M., Heisinger, M.: CaDiCaL, kissat, paracooba, plingeling and treengeling entering the SAT competition 2020. In: Balyo, T., Froleyks, N., Heule, M., Iser, M., Järvisalo, M., Suda, M. (eds.) Proc. of SAT Competition 2020 - Solver and Benchmark Descriptions. Department of Computer Science Report Series B, vol. B-2020-1, pp. 51–53. University of Helsinki (2020)
15. Brummayer, R., Biere, A.: Fuzzing and delta-debugging SMT solvers. In: Workshop SMT 2010, pp. 1–5. ACM (2009)
16. Clarke, E., Kroening, D., Lerda, F.: A tool for checking ANSI-C programs. In: Jensen, K., Podelski, A. (eds.) TACAS 2004. LNCS, vol. 2988, pp. 168–176. Springer, Heidelberg (2004). https://doi.org/10.1007/978-3-540-24730-2_15
17. Eén, N., Sörensson, N.: An extensible SAT-solver. In: Giunchiglia, E., Tacchella, A. (eds.) SAT 2003. LNCS, vol. 2919, pp. 502–518. Springer, Heidelberg (2004). https://doi.org/10.1007/978-3-540-24605-3_37
18. Ehlers, T., Nowotka, D.: Tuning parallel sat solvers. In: Berre, D.L., Järvisalo, M. (eds.) Proceedings of Pragmatics of SAT 2015 and 2018. EPiC Series in Computing, vol. 59, pp. 127–143. EasyChair (2019). https://easychair.org/publications/paper/NkG7

19. Xiao, F., Luo, M., Li., C.M., Manya F., Lü, Z.: MapleLRB_LCM, Maple_LCM, Maple_LCM_Dist, MapleLRB_LCMoccRestart and Glucose-3.0+width in SAT Competition (2017)
20. Fichte, J.K., Manthey, N., Stecklina, J., Schidler, A.: Towards faster reasoners by using transparent huge pages (2020). https://arxiv.org/abs/2004.14378
21. Heule Jr, M., Warren, A.H., Wetzler, N.: Trimming while checking clausal proofs. In: FMCAD (2013)
22. Heule, M., Järvisalo, M., Suda, M. (eds.): Proceedings of SAT Competition 2018: Solver and Benchmark Descriptions, Department of Computer Science Series of Publications B, vol. B-2018-1. Department of Computer Science, University of Helsinki, Finland (2018)
23. Heule, M., Järvisalo, M., Suda, M. (eds.): Proceedings of SAT Race 2019: Solver and Benchmark Descriptions, Department of Computer Science Report Series B, vol. B-2019-1. Department of Computer Science, University of Helsinki, Finland (2019)
24. Hickey, R., Bacchus, F.: Speeding up assumption-based SAT. In: Janota, M., Lynce, I. (eds.) SAT 2019. LNCS, vol. 11628, pp. 164–182. Springer, Cham (2019). https://doi.org/10.1007/978-3-030-24258-9_11
25. Hickey, R., Bacchus, F.: Trail saving on backtrack. In: Pulina, L., Seidl, M. (eds.) SAT 2020. LNCS, vol. 12178, pp. 46–61. Springer, Cham (2020). https://doi.org/10.1007/978-3-030-51825-7_4
26. Hölldobler, S., Manthey, N., Saptawijaya, A.: Improving resource-unaware SAT solvers. In: Fermüller, C.G., Voronkov, A. (eds.) LPAR 2010. LNCS, vol. 6397, pp. 519–534. Springer, Heidelberg (2010). https://doi.org/10.1007/978-3-642-16242-8_37
27. Hoos, H.H., Kaufmann, B., Schaub, T., Schneider, M.: Robust benchmark set selection for boolean constraint solvers. In: Nicosia, G., Pardalos, P. (eds.) LION 2013. LNCS, vol. 7997, pp. 138–152. Springer, Heidelberg (2013). https://doi.org/10.1007/978-3-642-44973-4_16
28. Hutter, F., Hoos, H.H., Leyton-Brown, K., Stützle, T.: Paramils: an automatic algorithm configuration framework. J. Artif. Int. Res. 36(1), 267–306 (2009)
29. Liang, J.H., Chanseok Oh, V.G.K.C., Poupart, P.: MapleCOMSPS, MapleCOMSPS_LRB, MapleCOMSPS_CHB. In: Proceedings of SAT Competition 2016 (2016). http://hdl.handle.net/10138/164630
30. Katebi, H., Sakallah, K.A., Marques-Silva, J.P.: Empirical study of the anatomy of modern sat solvers. In: Sakallah, K.A., Simon, L. (eds.) SAT 2011. LNCS, vol. 6695, pp. 343–356. Springer, Heidelberg (2011). https://doi.org/10.1007/978-3-642-21581-0_27
31. Kochemazov, S.: Improving implementation of SAT competitions 2017–2019 winners. In: Pulina, L., Seidl, M. (eds.) SAT 2020. LNCS, vol. 12178, pp. 139–148. Springer, Cham (2020). https://doi.org/10.1007/978-3-030-51825-7_11
32. Kottler, S.: Description of the sapperlot, sartagnan and moussaka solvers for the sat-competition 2011 (2011)
33. Manthey, N.: Refining unsatisfiable cores in incremental SAT solving. Technical report, TU Dresden (2015)
34. Manthey, N., Lindauer, M.: Spybug: Automated bug detection in the configuration space of sat solvers. In: SAT, pp. 554–561 (2016)
35. Luo, M., Li, C.M., Xiao, F., Manya, F., Lü, Z.: An effective learnt clause minimization approach for CDCL SAT solvers. In: Proceedings of the Twenty-Sixth International Joint Conference on Artificial Intelligence, IJCAI-17, pp. 703–711 (2017). https://doi.org/10.24963/ijcai.2017/98

36. Martins, R., Manquinho, V., Lynce, I.: Open-WBO: a modular MaxSAT solver. In: Sinz, C., Egly, U. (eds.) SAT 2014. LNCS, vol. 8561, pp. 438–445. Springer, Cham (2014). https://doi.org/10.1007/978-3-319-09284-3_33

37. ML4AAD Group: SMAC v3 project. https://github.com/automl/SMAC3 (2017), version visited last on August 2017

38. Möhle, S., Manthey, N.: Better evaluations by analyzing benchmark structure, pp. 1–10 (2016). http://www.pragmaticsofsat.org/2016/reg/POS-16_paper_4.pdf

39. Nadel, A., Ryvchin, V.: Chronological backtracking. In: Beyersdorff, O., Wintersteiger, C.M. (eds.) SAT 2018. LNCS, vol. 10929, pp. 111–121. Springer, Cham (2018). https://doi.org/10.1007/978-3-319-94144-8_7

40. Nethercote, N., Seward, J.: Valgrind: A framework for heavyweight dynamic binary instrumentation. SIGPLAN Not. **42**(6), 89–100 (2007). https://doi.org/10.1145/1273442.1250746

41. Oh, C.: Between SAT and UNSAT: the fundamental difference in CDCL SAT. In: Heule, M., Weaver, S. (eds.) SAT 2015. LNCS, vol. 9340, pp. 307–323. Springer, Cham (2015). https://doi.org/10.1007/978-3-319-24318-4_23

42. Ryvchin, V., Nadel, A.: Maple_LCM_Dist_ChronoBT: featuring chronological backtracking. In: Proceedings of SAT Competition 2018 (2018). http://hdl.handle.net/10138/237063

43. Soos, M., Nohl, K., Castelluccia, C.: Extending SAT solvers to cryptographic problems. In: Kullmann, O. (ed.) SAT 2009. LNCS, vol. 5584, pp. 244–257. Springer, Heidelberg (2009). https://doi.org/10.1007/978-3-642-02777-2_24

44. Kochemazov, S., Oleg Zaikin, V.K., Semenov, A.: Maplelcmdistchronobt-dl, duplicate learnts heuristic-aided solvers at the sat race 2019 (2019)

45. van der Tak, P., Ramos, A., Heule, M.: Reusing the assignment trail in cdcl solvers. JSAT **7**(4), 133–138 (2011)

46. Zhang, X., Cai, S.: Relaxed backtracking with rephasing. In: Balyo, T., Froleyks, N., Heule, M., Iser, M., Järvisalo, M., Suda, M. (eds.) Proceedings of SAT Competition 2020 - Solver and Benchmark Descriptions. Department of Computer Science Report Series B, vol. B-2020-1, pp. 15–15. University of Helsinki (2020)

Proof Complexity of Symbolic QBF Reasoning

Stefan Mengel[1,2] and Friedrich Slivovsky[3(✉)]

[1] CNRS, UMR 8188, Centre de Recherche en Informatique de Lens (CRIL),
62300 Lens, France
[2] Univ. Artois, UMR 8188, 62300 Lens, France
[3] TU Wien, Vienna, Austria

Abstract. We introduce and investigate symbolic proof systems for
Quantified Boolean Formulas (QBF) operating on Ordered Binary Decision Diagrams (OBDDs). These systems capture QBF solvers that perform symbolic quantifier elimination, and as such admit short proofs of
formulas of bounded path-width and quantifier complexity. As a consequence, we obtain exponential separations from standard clausal proof
systems, specifically (long-distance) QU-Resolution and IR-Calc.

We further develop a lower bound technique for symbolic QBF proof
systems based on strategy extraction that lifts known lower bounds from
communication complexity. This allows us to derive strong lower bounds
against symbolic QBF proof systems that are independent of the variable ordering of the underlying OBDDs, and that hold even if the proof
system is allowed access to an NP-oracle.

1 Introduction

Unlike in SAT solving, which is dominated by Conflict-Driven Clause Learning
(CDCL), in QBF solving there is no single approach that is clearly dominant
in practice. Instead, modern solvers are based on variety of techniques, such as
(quantified) CDCL [29,32,40], expansion of universal variables [9,10,25], and
abstraction [26,35,38].

In practice, these techniques turn out to be complementary, each having
strengths and weaknesses on different classes of instances [23,30,34]. This com-
plementarity of solvers can be analyzed theoretically by considering proof complexity. Essentially, the different paradigms used in solvers can be formalized as
proof systems for QBF, which then can be analyzed with mathematical methods.
Then, by separating the strength of different proof systems, one can show that
the corresponding solvers are unable to solve problems efficiently that can be
dealt with by other solvers. This motivation has led to a great interest in QBF

S. Mengel—Partially supported by the PING/ACK project of the French National
Agency for Research (ANR-18-CE40-0011).

F. Slivovsky—Supported by the Vienna Science and Technology Fund (WWTF) under
grant ICT19-060.

C.-M. Li and F. Manyà (Eds.): SAT 2021, LNCS 12831, pp. 399–416, 2021.
https://doi.org/10.1007/978-3-030-80223-3_28

proof complexity over the last few years and resulted in a good understanding of common QBF proof systems and how they relate to each other (see [7,8] and the references therein).

In this paper, we focus on a *symbolic* approach to QBF solving that was originally implemented in the QBDD system [31]. Its underlying idea is to use OBDDs to represent constraints inside the solver, instead of clauses as used by most other SAT and QBF solvers. We formalize QBDD as a proof system in which the lines are OBDDs. More specifically, we consider QBF proof systems that are obtained from propositional OBDD-proof systems by adding ∀-reduction (cf. [7]). Propositional proof systems using OBDDs as lines have been studied intensively since the introduction of this model in [1], see e.g. [12]. We thus consider lifting these systems to QBF by adding ∀-reduction as very natural.

Analyzing the strength of OBDD-refutations, we first show that, even for a weak propositional system that allows only conjunction of lines and forgetting of variables, the resulting QBF proof system, which we refer to as OBDD($\land, \exists, \forall$) and which corresponds to traces of QBDD, p-simulates QU-resolution. We also show that OBDD($\land, \exists, \forall$), and in fact also QBDD, can make use of structural properties of QBF in the sense that instances of bounded pathwidth and bounded quantifier alternation can be solved efficiently. We do this by using a recent result on variable elimination for OBDDs from [13] to show that the intermediate OBDDs in QBDD are not too big in this setting. We then observe that other QBF proof systems from the literature have hard instances of bounded pathwidth and bounded quantifier alternation. This shows that OBDD($\land, \exists, \forall$) can efficiently refute QBFs that are out of reach for many other systems. In particular, it is exponentially separated from (long-distance) QU-resolution [3] and the expansion based IR-calc [8]. It follows that, at least in principle, QBDD can solve instances that other, more modern solvers cannot.

The main technical contribution of this work is a lower bound technique for OBDD-refutations. Here, we consider the strongest possible propositional system, which is semantic entailment of OBDDs. We first show that this system admits efficient strategy extraction of decision lists whose terms are OBDDs. Functions that can be succinctly encoded in this way have short protocols in a communication model from [24] for which it is known that lower bounds can be obtained by proving that a function does not have large monochromatic rectangles. To the best of our knowledge, such bounds are only known for fixed variable partitions. To prove lower bounds for OBDD-refutations that are independent of the variable order chosen for the OBDDs, we lift classical bounds on the inner product function to a graph-based generalization which we show has essentially the same properties as the inner product function, but for *all* variable partitions.

2 Preliminaries

2.1 Propositional Logic and Quantified Boolean Formulas

We assume an infinite set of propositional *variables* and consider *propositional formulas* built up from variables and the constants true (1) and false (0) using conjunction ($\wedge$), disjunction ($\vee$), and negation ($\neg$). We write $\mathsf{var}(\varphi)$ for the set of variables occurring in a formula φ. In particular, we are interested in formulas in *conjunctive normal form (CNF)*. A formula is in CNF if it is a conjunction of *clauses*. A clause is a disjunction of *literals*, and a literal is variable x or a negated variable $\neg x$. An *assignment* of a set X of variables is a mapping $\tau : X \to \{0,1\}$ of variables to truth values. We write $[X]$ for the set of assignments of X. Given assignments $\tau : X \to \{0,1\}$ and $\sigma : Y \to \{0,1\}$ such that X and Y are disjoint, we let $\tau \cup \sigma$ denote the assignment of $X \cup Y$ such that $(\tau \cup \sigma)(x) = \tau(x)$ if $x \in X$ and $(\tau \cup \sigma)(x) = \sigma(x)$ if $x \in Y$. Furthermore, we write $\tau|_{X'}$ for the restriction of τ to $X' \subseteq X$. The result of applying an assignment τ to formula φ and propagating constants is denoted $\varphi[\tau]$. If $\varphi[\tau] = 1$ we say that τ *satisfies* φ, and if $\varphi[\tau] = 0$, the assignment τ *falsifies* φ. A *Quantified Boolean Formula (QBF)* is a pair $\Phi = \mathcal{Q}.\varphi$ consisting of a *quantifier prefix* $\mathcal{Q}$ and a propositional formula φ, called the *matrix* of Φ. If the matrix is in CNF, then Φ is in *Prenex Conjunctive Normal Form (PCNF)*. The quantifier prefix is a sequence $\mathcal{Q} = Q_1 x_1 \ldots Q_n x_n$ where the $Q_i \in \{\forall, \exists\}$ are *quantifiers* and the x_i are propositional variables such that $\{x_1, \ldots, x_n\} = \mathsf{var}(\varphi)$. We write $D_\Phi(x_i) = \{x_1, \ldots, x_{i-1}\}$ for the set of variables that come before x_i in the quantifier prefix, and say x_i *left of* x_j and x_j *is right of* x_i if $i < j$. A variable x_i is *existential* if $Q_i = \exists$, and *universal* if $Q_i = \forall$. We write $\mathsf{var}_\exists(\Phi)$ for the set of existential variables, $\mathsf{var}_\forall(\Phi)$ for the set of universal variables, and $\mathsf{var}(\Phi)$ for the set of all variables occurring in Φ. Let Φ be a QBF. A *universal strategy* for Φ is a family $\boldsymbol{f} = \{f_u\}_{u \in \mathsf{var}_\forall(\Phi)}$ of functions $f_u : [\mathsf{var}(\Phi)] \to \{0,1\}$ such that $f_u(\tau) = f_u(\sigma)$ for any assignments τ and σ that agree on $D_\Phi(u)$. If $\boldsymbol{f}$ is a universal strategy and $\tau : \mathsf{var}_\exists(\Phi) \to \{0,1\}$ and assignment of existential variables, we write $\tau \cup \boldsymbol{f}(\tau)$ for the assignment of $\mathsf{var}(\Phi)$ such that $(\tau \cup \boldsymbol{f}(\tau))(x) = \tau(x)$ for existential variables $x \in \mathsf{var}_\exists(\Phi)$ and $(\tau \cup \boldsymbol{f}(\tau))(u) = f_u(\tau \cup \boldsymbol{f}(\tau))$ for universal variables $u \in \mathsf{var}_\forall(\Phi)$. A universal strategy $\boldsymbol{f}$ is a *universal winning strategy* for Φ if $\tau \cup \boldsymbol{f}(\tau)$ falsifies the matrix of Φ for every assignment τ of the existential variables. A QBF is *false* if it has a universal winning strategy, and *true* otherwise.

2.2   Graphs and Pathwidth of Formulas

Let $G = (V, E)$ a graph and for every set $V' \subseteq V$ let $N[V']$ denote the open neighborhood of V, i.e., the set of all vertices in $V \setminus V'$ that have a neighbor in V'. The *expansion* of G is then defined as $\min_{V' \subseteq V, |V'| \le |V|/2} \frac{|N(V')|}{|V'|}$.

A *path decomposition* of a graph $G = (V, E)$ is a pair (P, λ) where $P = p_1, \ldots, p_n$ is a sequence of *nodes* p_i, and $\lambda : \{p_1, \ldots, p_n\} \to 2^V$ maps nodes p_i to subsets $\lambda(p_i) \subseteq V$ of vertices called *bags*, subject to the following constraints:

1. Each vertex appears in some bag, that is, $V \subseteq \bigcup_{i=1}^n \lambda(p_i)$,
2. For each edge $vw \in E$ there is a node p_i such that $\{v, w\} \subseteq \lambda(p_i)$.
3. If $v \in \lambda(p_i)$ and $v \in \lambda(p_j)$ for $1 \le i < j \le n$, then $v \in \bigcap_{k=i}^j \lambda(p_k)$.

The *width* of a path decomposition is $\max_{i=1}^n |\lambda(p_i)| - 1$, and the *pathwidth* of a graph G is the minimum width of any path decomposition of G. The pathwidth of a CNF formula φ is the pathwidth of its *primal graph*, which is the graph with vertex set $\mathsf{var}(\varphi)$ and edge set $\{xy \mid \exists C \in \varphi \text{ s.t. } x, y \in \mathsf{var}(C)\}$, and the pathwidth of a PCNF formula is the pathwidth of its matrix.

2.3 OBDD

We only give a short introduction into ordered binary decision diagrams (short OBDDs), a classical representation of Boolean functions [11]; see [39] for a textbook treatment.

Let X be a set of variables and π an ordering of X. A π-OBDD on variables X is defined to be a directed acyclic graph B with one source s and two sinks labeled 0 and 1, called the 0- and 1-sink respectively. All non-sink nodes are labeled with variables from X such that on every path P in B the variables appear in the order π. Moreover, all non-sink nodes have two outgoing edges, one labeled with 0, the other with 1. The size of B, denoted by $|B|$, is defined as the number of nodes in B. Given an assignment $a \in \{0,1\}$, the OBDD B computes a value $B(a)$ as follows: starting in the root, we construct a path by taking for every node v labeled be a variable x the edge labeled with $a(x)$. We continue until we end up in a sink, and the label of the sink is the value of B on a denoted by $B(a)$. This way B computes a Boolean function and every Boolean function can be computed by an OBDD. The OBDD B is called complete if on every source-sink path P all variables in X appear as node labels. The *width* of a complete OBDD B is defined as the maximal number of nodes that are labeled with the same variable.

Observation 1. *There is a polynomial time algorithm that, given an OBDD B, computes an equivalent complete OBDD B'. Moreover, $|B'| \leq (|X| + 1)|B|$.*

Binary Boolean functions can be efficiently applied to OBDDs as stated in the following result.

Lemma 2. *Let $f : \{0,1\}^2 \to \{0,1\}$ be a binary Boolean function. Then there is an algorithm that, given two π-OBDDs B_1 and B_2, computes in time polynomial in $|B_1| + |B_2|$ a π-OBDD B such that B computes on input $a \in \{0,1\}^X$ the value $B(a) := f(B_1(a), B_2(a))$. In particular, the size of B is polynomial in that of B_1 and B_2.*

OBDDs are well-known to be *canonical* in the sense that, for fixed variable order π, there is a unique representation of any Boolean function f by a π-OBDD.

Lemma 3. *Let f be a Boolean function on variables X and let π be a variable order of X. Then there is a unique π-OBDD of minimal size (up to isomorphism) computing f. Moreover, given a π-OBDD representing f, this unique OBDD can be computed in polynomial time. The same is true for complete OBDDs.*

Throughout this paper, we always assume that OBDDs are minimized with the help of the algorithm of Lemma 3.

2.4   Combinatorial Rectangles

Let X be a set of variables and $\Pi = (X_1, X_2)$ a partition of X. We call Π *balanced* if $\min(|X_1|, |X_2|) \geq \lfloor |X|/2 \rfloor$. More generally, for $0 < b \leq 1/2$ we say that Π is b-balanced if $\min(|X_1|, |X_2|) \geq \lfloor b|X| \rfloor$. A combinatorial rectangle with partition Π is a Boolean function $R(X) = R_1(X_1) \wedge R_2(X_2)$. A dual way of seeing R is defining A to be the models of R_1 and B those of R_2. Then the models of R are exactly $A \times B$ and in a slight abuse of notation we then also write $R = A \times B$. The *size* of R is $|A| \cdot |B|$. A function R is called a balanced rectangle if and only if R is a combinatorial rectangle with a partition Π that is balanced.

Let f be a Boolean function and let R be a combinatorial rectangle. We say that R is monochromatic with respect to f if either all models of R are models of f or no model of R is a model of f. When f is clear from the context, we simply call R a monochromatic rectangle without remarking f explicitly. We also say that f *has* the monochromatic rectangle R. The *color* of a monochromatic rectangle R with respect to f is the value $f(x)$ taken by the function on $x \in R$. We will use the following well-known connection between OBDD and rectangles [28].

Theorem 4. *Let g be a function in variables X computed by a π-OBDD of width w. Let X_1 be a prefix of the variable order π and let $X_2 := X \setminus X_1$. Then $g(X) = \bigvee_{i=1}^{w} R_i(X)$, where every R_i is rectangle with partition (X_1, X_2).*

3   Symbolic QBF Proof Systems

We consider line-based QBF proof systems for PCNF formulas where each line is an OBDD. Each derivation begins with a sequence of OBDDs corresponding to the clauses in the matrix of the PCNF formula. New OBDDs are derived by propositional reasoning or universal reduction (cf. Frege systems with universal reduction [7]). Formally, let $\Phi = Q_1 x_1 \ldots Q_n x_n . C_1 \wedge \ldots \wedge C_m$ be a PCNF formula. An *OBDD derivation* of L_k from Φ is a sequence $L_1, \ldots, L_k$ of OBDDs—all with the same variable order π—such that each L_i represents clause C_i for $1 \leq i \leq m$, or is derived using one of the following rules:

1. **conjunction** ($\wedge$): L_i represents $L_j \wedge L_k$ for $j, k < i$.
2. **projection** ($\exists$): L_i represents $\exists x. L_j$ for some $x \in \mathsf{var}(L_j)$ and $j < i$.
3. **entailment** ($\models$): L_i is entailed by $L_{i_1}, \ldots, L_{i_k}$, for $i_1, \ldots i_k < i$.[1]
4. **universal reduction** ($\forall$): L_i represents $L_j[u/c]$, where $j < i$, u is a universally quantified variable that is rightmost among variables in L_j and $c \in \{0, 1\}$.

Here, $L_j[u/c]$ denotes the OBDD obtained from L by removing each node labeled with variable u and rerouting all incoming edges to its neighbor along the c-labeled edge (effectively substituting c for u). The *size* of an OBDD derivation

---

[1] Note that OBDD derivations using the entailment rule do not lead to proof systems in the sense of Cook and Reckhow [15], since checking entailment is coNP-hard.

is the sum of the sizes of the OBDDs in the derivation, and the *width* of an OBDD derivation is the maximum width of any OBDD in the derivation.

With the exception of entailment, each of these proof rules can be checked in polynomial time by applying an operation or transformation to the OBDDs in the premises, and verifying that the result—which is unique due to canonicity— matches the OBDD in the conclusion. Moreover, the entailment rule does not trivialize OBDD proofs since it only considers *propositional* entailment, and a QBF can be false without its matrix being unsatisfiable. Finally, it is not difficult to see that OBDD derivations are sound.

Proposition 5. *Let* $L_1, \ldots, L_k$ *be an OBDD derivation from* Φ. *If* Φ *is true then* $.L_1 \wedge \ldots \wedge L_k$ *is true.*

An *OBDD-refutation* of Φ is an OBDD derivation of an OBDD representing 0. A π-*OBDD derivation* is an OBDD derivation where all OBDDs use variable order π. We sometimes explicitly mention the derivation rules used in a proof. For instance, an OBDD($\wedge, \exists, \forall$) derivation is OBDD derivation using only conjunction, projection, and universal reduction.

A Proof System for Symbolic Quantifier Elimination

We can use symbolic QBF proof systems to study the QBF solver QBDD proposed by Pan and Vardi [31]. Given a PCNF formula $\Phi = Q_1 x_1 \ldots Q_n x_n.\varphi$, QBDD maintains *buckets* $S_1, \ldots, S_n$ of OBDDs such that x_i is the rightmost variable (with respect to the quantifier prefix) occurring in the OBDDs of S_i. Initially, the S_i are the sets of clauses in φ that have x_i as their rightmost variable, represented as OBDDs. QBDD proceeds by eliminating variables from the inside out, starting with the variable x_n. To eliminate the variable x_i, it computes the conjunction of OBDDs in bucket S_i, then removes x_i from the result by quantifying either existentially or universally, depending on the quantifier Q_i. The resulting OBDD is then added to the correct bucket. The procedure terminates with a constant 1 or constant 0 OBDD, depending on whether the QBF Φ is true or false. Since any universal variable is innermost upon elimination, a run of QBDD corresponds to an OBDD($\wedge, \exists, \forall$)-derivation.

Let $\mathsf{tower}(k, 0) := 2^k$ and $\mathsf{tower}(k, q + 1) := \mathsf{tower}(2^k, q)$. In this subsection, we prove the following result:

Proposition 6. QBDD *solves PCNF formulas* Φ *with* q *quantifier blocks and pathwidth* k *in time* $\mathsf{tower}(k, q + 1) \, \mathsf{poly}(|\Phi|)$.

Since, as stated above, the runs of QBDD are proofs in OBDD($\wedge, \exists, \forall$), we directly get the following result on the strength of OBDD($\wedge, \exists, \forall$).

Corollary 7. *Every false PCNF* Φ *with* q *quantifier width and pathwidth* k *has an* OBDD($\wedge, \exists, \forall$)-*refutation of size* $\mathsf{tower}(k, q + 1)\mathsf{poly}(|\Phi|)$.

As the basic tool, we use the following variable elimination result for OBDDs.

Lemma 8 ([13]). *Let B be an OBDD of width w and let X be a subset of the variables in B. Then there is an OBDD B' of width 2^w that encodes $\exists X.B$ with the same variable order as B. Moreover B' can be computed in time $2^w \mathsf{poly}(|B|)$.*

Note that since OBDD can be negated without increase of the representation size, we get that the same result is true for $\forall$-elimination. Iterating this result directly yields the following corollary.

Corollary 9. *Let B be an OBDD of width w and let $\mathcal{Q} = Q_1 X_1 \ldots Q_q X_q$ a quantifier prefix with q blocks. Then the QBF $Q_1 X_1 \ldots Q_q X_q.B$ has an OBDD representation B' of width $\mathsf{tower}(w, q)$. Moreover, B' can be computed in time $\mathsf{tower}(w, q)\mathsf{poly}(|B|)$.*

An analogous construction for the more general representation of structured DNNF [33] is at the heart of the treewidth based QBF-algorithm in [13].

We can now proceed with the proof of Proposition 6.

Proof (of Proposition 6). Let $\Phi = Q_1 X_1 \ldots Q_q X_q.\varphi$, and let (P, λ) be a path decomposition of width k of the primal graph of φ. In [20] it is shown that there is a variable order π depending only on (P, λ) such that there is a complete OBDD B of width 2^k computing φ. Let $P_i := \bigwedge_{j \in [i]} S_i$. Then P_i is the conjunction of some clauses of φ, so (P, λ) yields a path decomposition of P_i of width at most k. It follows that for every $i \in [q]$, there is a complete OBDD representation of P_i with order π and width at most 2^k.

We claim that all OBDDs that are computed by QBDD have width at most $\mathsf{tower}(k, q + 1)$. Note first that all S_i have pathwidth at most k as above, so we can compute all of them by only conjoining OBDDs with order π and of width at most 2^k. Now whenever we eliminate a variable, the result is a a function that we get from P_i by eliminating some variables. But since these variables are only in q quantifier blocks and we eliminate from the inside out, we have by Corollary 9 that the width of the result is at most $\mathsf{tower}(2^k, q) = \mathsf{tower}(k, q + 1)$. Noting that a complete OBDD of width w in n variables has size at most wn and using canonicity and Lemma 2 in all steps completes the proof. □

4   Relation to Other Proof Systems

In this section, we show that $\mathsf{OBDD}(\wedge, \exists, \forall)$ is separated from several clausal QBF proof systems. These results are obtained by identifying classes of QBFs that are hard for these proof systems but having bounded pathwidth and a fixed number of quantifier blocks.

We first consider *Q-Resolution* [27], *QU-Resolution* [21], and *Long-Distance Q-Resolution* [2,19], which can be further generalized and combined into *Long-Distance QU-Resolution* [3].[2] QU-Resolution allows resolution on universal pivots, Long-Distance Q-Resolution can derive tautological clauses in certain cases,

---

[2] This system is typically referred to as LQU^+-*Resolution*.

and Long-Distance QU-Resolution additionally permits the derivation of tauto-logical clauses by resolution on universal pivots.

For all the proof systems above, we define the size of a refutation to be the number of clauses in it. As usual, we say a proof system P p-simulates another proof system P′ if for every proof Π' in P′ there is a proof Π in P such that the length of Π is polynomial in that of Π'.

Proposition 10. OBDD$(\wedge, \exists, \forall)$ p-simulates QU-Resolution.

Proof. We simulate QU-resolution line by line, using the fact that all clauses have small OBDD representations. An application of universal reduction in QU-resolution that removes literal l corresponds to an application of universal reduction in an OBDD derivation that replaces l by 0. Resolution of clauses $C_1 \vee x$ and $\neg x \vee C_2$ can be simulated by first computing an OBDD L' representing $(C_1 \vee x) \wedge (\neg x \vee C_2)$. Each clause C can be represented by an OBDD of size $O(|C|)$, for any variable ordering, so by Lemma 2, the OBDD L' can be computed in time polynomial in the size of the premises. To obtain an OBDD L representing the resolvent $C_1 \vee C_2$, we simply project out the pivot x, that is, $L = \exists x.L'$.

$\square$

Lower bounds against QU-Resolution can be obtained by lifting lower bounds against bounded-depth circuits and decision lists [6,8]. This is because a decision list [36] encoding a universal winning strategy can be efficiently extracted from QU-Resolution refutations [2], and decision lists can be succinctly represented by bounded-depth circuits. For instance, the class QPARITY of formulas with the parity function as a unique universal winning strategy is hard for QU-Resolution [8]. This class was modified so as to also demonstrate hardness for Long-Distance QU-Resolution, resulting in the class of formulas defined below.

$$\text{QUPARITY}_n := \exists x_1 \ldots \exists x_n \forall z_1 \forall z_2 \exists t_2 \ldots \exists t_n.$$

$$\text{xor}_u(x_1, x_2, t_2, z_1, z_2) \wedge \text{xor}_u(x_1, x_2, t_2, \neg z_1, \neg z_2) \wedge$$

$$\bigwedge_{i=3}^{n} (\text{xor}_u(t_{i-1}, x_i, t_i, z_1, z_2) \wedge \text{xor}_u(t_{i-1}, x_i, t_i, \neg z_1, \neg z_2)) \wedge$$

$$(z_1 \vee z_2 \vee t_n) \wedge (\neg z_1 \vee \neg z_2 \vee \neg t_n),$$

where

$$\text{xor}_u(o_1, o_2, o, l_1, l_2) := (l_1 \vee l_2 \vee \neg o_1 \vee o_2 \vee o) \wedge (l_1 \vee l_2 \vee o_1 \vee \neg o_2 \vee o) \wedge$$
$$(l_1 \vee l_2 \vee \neg o_1 \vee \neg o_2 \vee \neg o) \wedge (l_1 \vee l_2 \vee o_1 \vee o_2 \vee \neg o).$$

We restate the following result without a proof.

Theorem 11 ([8]). QUPARITY$_n$ *requires exponential-size refutations in Long-Distance QU-Resolution.*

At the same time, the QUPARITY formulas have a very simple structure that can be exploited by symbolic proof systems.

Lemma 12. *The class* $\{\text{QUPARITY}_n\}_{n \in \mathbb{N}}$ *has bounded pathwidth.*

Proof. Let $n \in \mathbb{N}$ and consider the path $P = p_1, \ldots, p_n$ and node labeling λ such that $\lambda(p_1) = \{x_1, x_2, t_2, z_1, z_2\}$, $\lambda(p_i) = \{t_i, x_{i+1}, t_{i+1}, z_1, z_2\}$ for $2 \le i < n$, as well as $\lambda(p_n) = \{z_1, z_2, t_n\}$. It is straightforward to verify that (P, λ) is a path decomposition of QUPARITY_n, and its width is 4. □

Since QUPARITY_n only has three quantifier blocks, we obtain the following results by Proposition 6 and Theorem 11.

Corollary 13. *The formulas* QPARITY_n *have polynomial-size* $\text{OBDD}(\wedge, \exists, \forall)$ *refutations.*

Theorem 14. *QU-Resolution does not p-simulate* $\text{OBDD}(\wedge, \exists, \forall)$.

Next, we look at the expansion-based proof system *IR-calc* [8]. For classes of formulas with a bounded number of quantifier blocks, lower bounds against IR-calc can be obtained by considering the *strategy size*, which is the minimum range of any universal winning strategy (as a function mapping assignments of existential variables to assignments of universal variables) [4].

Definition 15 (Strategy Size [4]). *The strategy size* $S(\Phi)$ *of a false QBF* Φ *is the minimum cardinality of the range of a universal winning strategy for* Φ.

Theorem 16 ([4]). *A false PCNF formula* Φ *with at most k universal quantifier blocks requires IR-calc proofs of size* $\sqrt[k]{S(\Phi)}$.

We use this correspondence to establish a proof size lower bound for the following class of formulas, which is a variant of the *equality formulas* [5] obtained by splitting the "long" clause $(t_1 \vee \ldots \vee t_n)$ into smaller clauses using auxiliary variables e_i:

$$\text{EQ}'_n := \exists x_1 \ldots \exists x_n \forall u_1 \ldots \forall u_n \exists t_1 \ldots \exists t_n \exists e_1 \ldots \exists e_n.$$

$$\bigwedge_{i=1}^{n} ((x_i \vee u_i \vee \neg t_i) \wedge (\neg x_i \vee \neg u_i \vee \neg t_i)) \wedge$$

$$(t_1 \vee e_1) \wedge \bigwedge_{i=2}^{n-1} (\neg e_{i-1} \vee t_i \vee e_i) \wedge (\neg e_{n-1} \vee t_n)$$

Lemma 17. EQ'_n *is false and the function* $\boldsymbol{f} : \sigma \mapsto \boldsymbol{f}(\sigma)$ *with* $\boldsymbol{f}(\sigma)(u_i) = \sigma(x_i)$ *for* $1 \le i \le n$ *is the unique universal winning strategy.*

Proof. Given any assignment σ of the existential variables x_i, applying the joint assignment $\sigma \cup \boldsymbol{f}(\sigma)$ results in unit clauses $\bigwedge_{i=1}^{n}(\neg t_i)$, and unit propagation derives a contradiction. Thus $\boldsymbol{f}$ is a universal winning strategy and EQ'_n is false. Consider an assignment σ of the x_i together with an assignment τ of the u_i such that $\sigma(x_i) \ne \tau(u_i)$ for some i. It is not difficult to see that the formula obtained by applying $\sigma \cup \tau$ can be satisfied by assigning the t_i and e_i appropriately, so the universal player can only win the evaluation game if they play according to $\boldsymbol{f}$. □

Proposition 18. *Any IR-calc refutation of* EQ'_n *has size* $\Omega(2^n)$.

Proof. By Lemma 17 the function f is the unique universal winning strategy for EQ'_n, and the cardinality of its range is 2^n. Thus $2^n = S(EQ'_n)$ is a proof size lower bound for IR-calc by Theorem 16. $\quad\square$

Lemma 19. *The class* $\{EQ'_n\}_{n\in\mathbb{N}}$ *has bounded pathwidth.*

Proof. For $n \in \mathbb{N}$, we construct a path decomposition (P, λ) of EQ'_n as follows. We let $P = p_1, \ldots, p_n$ and define the labeling λ as $\lambda(p_1) = \{x_1, u_1, t_1, e_1\}$, $\lambda(p_i) = \{e_{i-1}, x_i, u_i, t_i, e_i\}$ for $2 \le i \le n-1$, and $\lambda(p_n) = \{e_{n-1}, x_n, u_n, t_n\}$. $\quad\square$

Corollary 20. *The formulas* EQ'_n *have polynomial-size* $OBDD(\wedge, \exists, \forall)$ *refutations.*

Theorem 21. *IR-calc does not p-simulate* $OBDD(\wedge, \exists, \forall)$.

5   A Lower Bound on OBDD Refutations

In this section, we present a technique for proving lower bounds on the size of OBDD-proofs even with the entailment ($\models$) rule. We first show that such proofs admit efficient extraction of universal winning strategies as *OBDD-decision lists*, a model which can in turn be efficiently transformed into *rectangle decision lists*. We then use a result by Impagliazzo and Williams [24] to show that lower bounds for such decision lists reduce to size bounds of rectangles for Boolean functions.

While the variable order must be the same for all OBDDs appearing in an OBDD-proof, it can be chosen arbitrarily so as to minimize proof size. To derive a lower bound using the method sketched above, we thus have to construct a function that does not have large monochromatic rectangles with respect to *any* balanced partition of its arguments. We obtain such a function as a generalization of the well-known *inner product* function.

5.1   From OBDD Proofs to Rectangle Decision Lists

Definition 22. *Let* $\mathcal{C}$ *be a class of Boolean functions. A* $\mathcal{C}$*-decision list of length* s *is a sequence* $(L_1, c_1), \ldots, (L_s, c_s)$ *where the* $c_i \in \{0, 1\}$ *are truth values and the* $L_i \in \mathcal{C}$ *are circuits, and* L_s *computes the constant function* 1. *Let* V *be the set of variables occurring in the circuits* L_i. *The decision list computes a function* $f : \{0, 1\}^V \to \{0, 1\}$ *as follows. Given an assignment* $\tau : V \to \{0, 1\}$, *let* $i = \min\{1 \le j \le s \mid L_j(\tau) = 1\}$. *The we have* $f(\tau) = c_i$.

A (w, π)-*OBDD-decision list* is a $\mathcal{C}$-decision list where $\mathcal{C}$ is the class of Boolean functions computed by π-OBDDs of maximum width w. Similarly, for a partition (X, Y) of a set V of variables, an (X, Y)-*rectangle decision list* is a $\mathcal{C}$-decision list where $\mathcal{C}$ is the class of rectangles with respect to (X, Y).

The next result states that OBDD-decision lists can be efficiently extracted from OBDD-proofs. Due to space constraints, we omit the proof.

Theorem 23 (Strategy Extraction [2,7]). *There is a linear-time algorithm that takes a π-OBDD-refutation of a PCNF formula Φ and outputs a family of (w, π)-OBDD-decision lists computing a universal winning strategy for Φ, where w is the width of the refutation.*

Lemma 24. *If there is a (w, π)-OBDD-decision list of length s computing a function $f : \{0,1\}^V \to \{0,1\}$, and (X, Y) is a bipartition of V such that X is the set of variables appearing in a prefix of π, then there is an (X, Y)-rectangle decision list of length $w(s - 1) + 1$ computing f.*

Proof. Let $(L_1, c_1), \ldots, (L_s, c_s)$ be a (w, π)-OBDD-decision list computing function $f : \{0,1\}^V \to \{0,1\}$, and let (X, Y) be a bipartition of V such X corresponds to the variables in a prefix of π. By Theorem 4, each OBDD L_i for $1 \leq i < s$ is equivalent to a disjunction $\bigvee_{j=1}^{w} R_{ij}(V)$ of rectangles with respect to (X, Y). We construct an (X, Y)-rectangle decision list by replacing each pair (L_i, c_i) for $1 \leq i < s$ by the sequence $(R_{i1}, c_i), \ldots, (R_{iw}, c_i)$. We can simply append (L_s, c_s) to this sequence since the constant L_s trivially is a rectangle. The resulting (X, Y)-rectangle decision list computes f and has length $w(s - 1) + 1$. □

5.2 From Rectangle Decision Lists to Communication Complexity

We next use a result of Impagliazzo and Williams [24] to prove lower bounds for rectangle decision lists. The following definition has been slightly simplified for our setting.

Definition 25. *Let f be a Boolean function on variables V and let $\Pi = (X, Y)$ be a partition of V. An AND-protocol for f with partition Π is the following: two players are given an assignment to X and Y, respectively, and want to compute f on the joint assignment. To this end, they play in several rounds. In each round, they deterministically compute one bit each and send it to a third party. The third party computes the conjunction of the two bits and sends it to the players. If the conjunction evaluates to 1, then the protocol ends and the players have to output the value of f on the given input.*

The length of the AND-protocol is the maximal number of rounds the players have to play to compute f taken over all possible inputs for f.

AND-protocols are interesting for us because of the following simple connection already observed without proof by Chattopadhyay et al. [14].

Proposition 26. *Let f be a function in variables V and let Π be a partition of V. If f is computed by a rectangle decision list of length s in which all rectangles have the partition Π, then there is an AND-protocol for φ with partition Π of length at most s.*

Proof. The players simply evaluate the rectangle decision list: for every line (R_i, c_i) where $R_i = R_{i,1}(X_1) \wedge R_{i,2}(X_2)$, the players evaluate $R_{i,1}$ and $R_{i,2}$ on their part of the input individually. Then the third party gives them the conjunction, so the value of the rectangle on the input. If it is 1, then the players know that f evaluates to c_i on their input.   □

Lower bounds on the length of AND-protocols can be shown thanks to the following result from [24].

Theorem 27. *Let f be a function in variables V and let Π be a balanced partition of V. If f has an AND-protocol with partition Π of length s, then there is a monochromatic rectangle with respect to f with partition Π of size at least $\frac{1}{4es}2^{|V|}$.*

5.3   A Function with only Small Monochromatic Rectangles

With Theorem 27, showing lower bounds for rectangle decision lists, and thus for OBDD-refutations, boils down to showing that functions do not have larger monochromatic rectangles. Such function are known in the literature, see e.g. [28], but all results that we are aware of are for a fixed partition of the variables. However, since we want to show lower bounds independent of the choice of the variable order used in the OBDD-refutation, we need functions that have no big monochromatic rectangles for *any* balanced partition of their variables. We will construct such functions in this section.

The following result will be a building block in our construction.

Proposition 28. *Let $F := \bigoplus_{i \in [n]} g_i(x_i, y_i)$ where every function g_i is either $g_i = x_i \wedge y_i$, $g_i = \neg x_i \wedge y_i$, $g_i = x_i \wedge \neg y_i$, or $g_i = x_i \vee y_i$. Then every monochromatic rectangle of F has size at most 2^n.*

To show Proposition 28, we will use the following well known result from communication complexity: Let $\mathsf{IP}(x_1, \ldots, x_n, y_1, \ldots, y_n)$ be the inner product function defined as $\mathsf{IP}(x_1, \ldots, x_n, y_1, \ldots, y_n) := \bigoplus_{i \in [n]} x_i \cdot y_i$ where $\cdot$ denotes the multiplication over $\{0, 1\}$ or equivalently conjunction. The following is well known, see e.g. [28].

Lemma 29. *All monochromatic rectangles of $\mathsf{IP}(x_1, \ldots, x_n, y_1, \ldots, y_n)$ have size at most 2^n.*

It is easy to see that the function F from Proposition 28 is a generalization of the inner product function. We will see that one can easily lift the bound on monochromatic rectangles.

Proof (of Proposition 28). First observe that $x_i \vee y_i = 1 \oplus (\neg x_i \wedge \neg y_i)$, so substituting every occurrence of $x_i \vee y_i$ by $\neg x_i \wedge \neg y_i$ will only change the color but not the size of any monochromatic rectangle. So in the remainder, we assume that there is no $g_i = x_i \vee y_i$ in F.

In a next step, we substitute all occurrences of negated variables by the respective variables without the negation. Call the resulting formula F'. This substitution is clearly a bijection σ between assignments that maintains the value, i.e., $F(X, Y) = F'(\sigma(X, Y))$. Since σ acts on the variables independently, we have that for every monochromatic rectangle $A \times B$ of F, the set $\sigma(A \times B)$ is a monochromatic rectangle as well and $A \times B$ and $\sigma(A \times B)$ have the same size. Now observing that F' is in fact the inner product function completes the proof using Lemma 29. □

We now introduce a generalization of IP with respect to an underlying graph structure. So let X be a set of Boolean variables and let G be a graph with vertex set X and edge set E. Then we define

$$\mathsf{IP}_G(X) = \bigoplus_{xy \in E} x \cdot y.$$

Note that with this definition $\mathsf{IP} = \mathsf{IP}_{M_n}$ where M_n is a matching with n edges. For the statement of the following lemma, recall that a matching is *induced* if it can be obtained as the subgraph induced by the endpoints of its edges.

Lemma 30. *Let $G = (X, E)$ be a graph with n variables. Let $\{e_1, \ldots, e_m\}$ be an induced matching of G and let (X_1, X_2) be a partition of X such that for every e_i one of the end points is in X_1 and one is in X_2. Then every monochromatic rectangle for IP_G respecting the partition (X_1, X_2) has size at most 2^{n-m}.*

Proof. Let X' be the variables that are no end point in any of the e_i. Fix an assignment $a : X' \to \{0, 1\}$. Let $e_i = x_i y_i$ and assume that $x_i \in X_1$ while $y_i \in X_2$. Let $\mathsf{IP}_{G,a}$ be the function in $X'' := \{x_i, y_i \mid i \in [m]\}$ that we get from IP_G by plugging a into the variables X'. Let g_i be the function that, given an assignment a_i to x_i and y_i, counts the number of edges e modulo 2 that are incident to at least one of x_i and y_i and such that $a_i \cup a$ assigns 1 to both end points of e. Clearly, $\mathsf{IP}_{G,a} = \bigoplus_{i \in [m]} g_i(x_i, y_i) \oplus c_a$ where $c_a \in \{0, 1\}$ is a constant depending only on a. We will show that, up to the constant c_a which does not change the size of monochromatic rectangles, the function $\mathsf{IP}_{G,a}$ has the form required by Proposition 28.

To this end, let us analyze g_i. Let $N'(x_i)$ be the neighbors of x_i different from y_i and let $N'(y_i)$ be the neighbors of y_i different from x_i. Let $p_a(x_i)$ be the parity of variables in $N'(x_i)$ that are assigned 1 by a and let $p_a(y_i)$ be defined analogously for y_i. Then $g_i = (p_a(x_i) \wedge x_i) \oplus (p_a(y_i) \wedge y_i) \oplus (x_i \wedge y_i)$. We analyze the different cases:

- If $p_a(x_i) = 0$ and $p_a(y_i) = 0$, then $g_i(x_i, y_i) = x_i \wedge y_i$.
- If $p_a(x_i) = 1$ and $p_a(y_i) = 0$, then $g_i(x_i, y_i) = x_i \oplus (x_i \wedge y_i)$. If $x_i = 0$, then this term is 0, so in all models we must have $x_i = 1$. But $g_i(1, y_i) = 1 \oplus y_i = \neg y_i$, so $g_i(x_i, y_i) = x_i \wedge \neg y_i$.
- If $p_a(x_i) = 0$ and $p_a(y_i) = 1$, then $g_i(x_i, y_i) = \neg x_i \wedge y_i$ is obtained by a symmetric argument.
- Finally, if $p_a(x_i) = 1$ and $p_a(y_i) = 1$ then $g_i(x_i, y_i) = x_i \oplus y_i \oplus (x_i \wedge y_i)$. Clearly, if $x_i = y_i = 0$, then g_i evaluates to 0. Moreover, all other assignments evaluate to 1. So $g_i(x_i, y_i) = x_i \vee y_i$.

Thus, in any case, g_i is of the form required by Proposition 28. It follows that every monochromatic rectangle of $\mathsf{IP}_{G,a}$ has size at most 2^m.

Now consider a monochromatic rectangle R in IP. Then, for every assignment $a : X' \to \{0,1\}$, restricting the variables X' according to a must give a monochromatic rectangle R_a as well. It follows that

$$|R| = \sum_{a:X' \to \{0,1\}} |R_a|.$$

But as we have seen, $|R_a| \leq 2^m$. Moreover, there are $2^{|X'|} = 2^{n-2m}$ assignments to X' and thus $|R| \leq 2^{n-2m}2^m = 2^{n-m}$ as claimed. $\square$

Theorem 31. *Let $G = (X,E)$ be a graph with expansion d, degree Δ and n vertices. Let (X_1, X_2) be a b-balanced partition of X. Then all monochromatic (X_1, X_2)-rectangles have size at most $2^{n\left(1 - \frac{nbd^2}{\Delta^2}\right)}$.*

Proof. We show that there is an induced matching of size $\frac{nbd^2}{\Delta^2}$ as in Lemma 30. Then the result follows directly.

Assume w.l.o.g. that $|X_1| \leq |X_2|$. Then, by the expansion property of G, there are at least $d|X_1|$ neighbors of X_1 in X_2. Call these neighbors X_2'. Note that X_2' has at least $d\min(\frac{|X|}{2}, |X_2'|) \geq d^2|X_1|$ neighbors in X_1 where the latter inequality is true because $d \leq 1$. Denote the set of vertices in X_1 that have a neighbor in X_2' by X_1'. Then $|X_1'| \geq d^2|X_1|$.

We now construct a matching between X_1' and X_2'. To this end, first delete all vertices not in $X_1' \cup X_2'$ from G. We then choose a matching iteratively as follows: pick a vertex $x_i \in X_1$ that has not been eliminated and that still has a neighbor y_i in X_2. We add x_iy_i to the matching and delete x_i and y_i and all their neighbors from G. If there are now any vertices in X_i that have no neighbors outside of X_i anymore, we delete those as well. We continue until G is empty.

We now analyze how many rounds we can make at least. First note that we delete at most $2\Delta - 2$ neighbors of x_i and y_i. Moreover, each of them can result in at most $\Delta - 1$ vertices that have no neighbor on the other side of the partition anymore. So overall we delete at most $2\Delta + (2\Delta-2)(\Delta-1) = 2\Delta^2 - 2\Delta + 2 \leq 2\Delta^2$ vertices. Since we start with at least $2d^2|X_1| \geq 2nbd^2$ vertices, we can make $\frac{2nbd^2}{2\Delta^2}$ iterations before running out of vertices. $\square$

5.4   Putting It All Together

In this section, we will finally show the promised lower bound for OBDD-refutations by putting together the results of the last sections.

Theorem 32. *There is an infinite sequence (Φ_n) of false PCNF formulas such that $|\Phi_n| = O(n)$ and every OBDD-refutation of Φ_n has size $2^{\Omega(n)}$.*

Proof. Choose a family of graphs of degree at most Δ and expansion d for some constants Δ and d. Such families are well known to exist, see e.g. [22]. Out of this family, choose a sequence (G_n) such that G_n has n vertices X_n. Now let $\varphi_n' = \neg IP_{G_n}$. Clearly, φ_n' can be computed by a Boolean circuit C_n of size $O(n)$.

We apply Tseitin-transformation on that circuit to get a CNF formula φ_n that has as satisfying assignments exactly the values of all gates in C_n under an assignment to inputs. Note that φ_n has variables for all non-inputs of C_n and thus in particular also for the output; let z be the variable corresponding to the output of C_n and let Y denote the remaining variables of φ_n introduced in the Tseitin-transformation. Then $\mathsf{var}(\varphi_n) = X_n \cup Y \cup \{z\}$. Moreover, φ_n has size $O(n)$. Now define

$$\Phi_n = \exists X_n \forall z \exists Y \varphi_n.$$

Then the only universal winning strategy f_z is to return for every assignment a to X_n the negation of the value that C_n evaluates to under a. But then, using Theorem 23 and Lemma 24, from every refutation of size s and width w of Φ_n, we get a rectangle decision list of length $s' = w(s-1)+1$ for $\neg C_n = \mathsf{IP}_{G_n}$. Using Proposition 26 and Theorem 27, we get that IP_{G_n} has a monochromatic rectangle of size $\frac{1}{4es'}2^{|X_n|} = \frac{1}{4es'}2^n$. But all monochromatic rectangles in IP_{G_n} have size at most $2^{n\left(1 - \frac{nbd^2}{\Delta^2}\right)}$ by Theorem 31. Since d, b and Δ are positive constants, it follows that $s' = 2^{\Omega(n)}$. But then at least one of s and w are in $2^{\Omega(n)}$, which gives the desired size bound.   □

6   Conclusion

We have introduced OBDD-refutations that model symbolic OBDD-based reasoning for QBF. We have shown that these systems, already in the form that was used (implicitly) in a symbolic QBF solver [31], are surprisingly strong as they allow solving instances that are hard for the proof systems underlying state-of-the-art QBF solvers. In view of this, it may be worthwhile to revisit these techniques in practice. There has been considerable progress in the computation of tree decompositions over the last few years (see e.g. [17]) that could benefit a symbolic approach. Moreover, it could be interesting to use progress in knowledge compilation on generalizations of OBDDs that have similar properties but can be exponentially more succinct [16]. While we consider it unlikely that such an approach would strictly beat current solvers, it might be sufficiently complementary to substantially improve the performance of a portfolio, much like the recently developed ADD-based symbolic model counter ADDMC has been shown to be highly complementary to DPLL-based state-of-the-art solvers [18].

   We have also demonstrated limitations of OBDD-refutations by proving exponential lower bounds. Our results require that all OBDDs appearing in a proof have the same variable order, but practical OBDD libraries such as CUDD [37] allow for dynamic variable reordering. While it is not clear how to use this to give more efficient refutations in an implementation of a QBF solver, it would be interesting to see if we can still show lower bounds in this generalized setting. For refutations with variable reordering, the strategy extraction step and the transformation to rectangle decision lists go through unchanged, but there seems to be no equivalent of Theorem 27 for rectangle decision lists with varying partitions. It would be interesting to develop new techniques to show lower bounds in this setting.

References

1. Atserias, A., Kolaitis, P.G., Vardi, M.Y.: Constraint propagation as a proof system. In: Wallace, M. (ed.) CP 2004. LNCS, vol. 3258, pp. 77–91. Springer, Heidelberg (2004). https://doi.org/10.1007/978-3-540-30201-8_9
2. Balabanov, V., Jiang, J.-H.R.: Unified QBF certification and its applications. Formal Methods Syst. Des. **41**(1), 45–65 (2012)
3. Balabanov, V., Widl, M., Jiang, J.-H.R.: QBF resolution systems and their proof complexities. In: Sinz, C., Egly, U. (eds.) SAT 2014. LNCS, vol. 8561, pp. 154–169. Springer, Cham (2014). https://doi.org/10.1007/978-3-319-09284-3_12
4. Beyersdorff, O., Blinkhorn, J.: Lower bound techniques for QBF expansion. Theory Comput. Syst. **64**(3), 400–421 (2020)
5. Beyersdorff, O., Blinkhorn, J., Hinde, L.: Size, cost, and capacity: A semantic technique for hard random QBFs. Log. Methods Comput. Sci. **15**(1) (2019)
6. Beyersdorff, O., Blinkhorn, J., Mahajan, M.: Hardness characterisations and size-width lower bounds for QBF resolution. In: Hermanns, H., Zhang, L., Kobayashi, N., Miller, D. (eds.) LICS 2020: 35th Annual ACM/IEEE Symposium on Logic in Computer Science, Saarbrücken, Germany, 8–11 July 2020, pp. 209–223. ACM (2020)
7. Beyersdorff, O., Bonacina, I., Chew, L., Pich, J.: Frege systems for quantified boolean logic. J. ACM **67**(2), 9:1–9:36 (2020)
8. Beyersdorff, O., Chew, L., Janota, M.: New resolution-based QBF calculi and their proof complexity. ACM Trans. Comput. Theory **11**(4), 26:1–26:42 (2019)
9. Biere, A.: Resolve and expand. In: SAT 2004 - The Seventh International Conference on Theory and Applications of Satisfiability Testing, Vancouver, BC, Canada, 10–13 May 2004, Online Proceedings (2004)
10. Bloem, R., Braud-Santoni, N., Hadzic, V., Egly, U., Lonsing, F., Seidl, M.: Expansion-based QBF solving without recursion. In: Bjørner, N., Gurfinkel, A. (eds.) 2018 Formal Methods in Computer Aided Design, FMCAD 2018, Austin, TX, USA, 30 October–2 November 2018, pp. 1–10. IEEE (2018)
11. Bryant, R.E.: Graph-based algorithms for boolean function manipulation. IEEE Trans. Comput. **35**(8), 677–691 (1986)
12. Buss, S., Itsykson, D., Knop, A., Sokolov, D.: Reordering rule makes OBDD proof systems stronger. In: Servedio, R.A. (ed.) 33rd Computational Complexity Conference, CCC 2018, San Diego, CA, USA, 22–24 June 2018, vol. 102 of LIPIcs, pp. 16:1–16:24. Schloss Dagstuhl - Leibniz-Zentrum für Informatik (2018)
13. Capelli, F., Mengel, S.: Tractable QBF by knowledge compilation. In: Niedermeier, R., Paul, C. (eds.) 36th International Symposium on Theoretical Aspects of Computer Science, STACS 2019, 13–16 March 2019, vol. 126 of LIPIcs, pp. 18:1–18:16. Schloss Dagstuhl - Leibniz-Zentrum für Informatik (2019)
14. Chattopadhyay, A., Mahajan, M., Mande, N.S., Saurabh, N.: Lower bounds for linear decision lists. Chic. J. Theor. Comput. Sci. **2020** (2020)
15. Cook, S.A., Reckhow, R.A.: The relative efficiency of propositional proof systems. J. Symb. Log. **44**(1), 36–50 (1979)
16. Darwiche, A.: SDD: a new canonical representation of propositional knowledge bases. In: Walsh, T. (ed.) IJCAI 2011, Proceedings of the 22nd International Joint Conference on Artificial Intelligence, Barcelona, Catalonia, Spain, 16–22 July 2011, pp. 819–826. IJCAI/AAAI (2011)

17. Dell, H., Komusiewicz, C., Talmon, N., Weller, M.: The PACE 2017 parameterized algorithms and computational experiments challenge: the second iteration. In: Lokshtanov, D., Nishimura, N. (eds.) 12th International Symposium on Parameterized and Exact Computation, IPEC 2017, Vienna, Austria, 6–8 September 2017, vol. 89 of LIPIcs, pp. 30:1–30:12. Schloss Dagstuhl - Leibniz-Zentrum für Informatik (2017)
18. Dudek, J.M., Phan, V., Vardi, M.Y.: ADDMC: weighted model counting with algebraic decision diagrams. In: The Thirty-Fourth AAAI Conference on Artificial Intelligence, AAAI 2020, The Thirty-Second Innovative Applications of Artificial Intelligence Conference, IAAI 2020, The Tenth AAAI Symposium on Educational Advances in Artificial Intelligence, EAAI 2020, New York, NY, USA, 7–12 February 2020, pp. 1468–1476. AAAI Press (2020)
19. Egly, U., Lonsing, F., Widl, M.: Long-distance resolution: proof generation and strategy extraction in search-based QBF solving. In: McMillan, K., Middeldorp, A., Voronkov, A. (eds.) LPAR 2013. LNCS, vol. 8312, pp. 291–308. Springer, Heidelberg (2013). https://doi.org/10.1007/978-3-642-45221-5_21
20. Ferrara, A., Pan, G., Vardi, M.Y.: Treewidth in verification: local vs. global. In: Sutcliffe, G., Voronkov, A. (eds.) LPAR 2005. LNCS (LNAI), vol. 3835, pp. 489–503. Springer, Heidelberg (2005). https://doi.org/10.1007/11591191_34
21. van Gelder, A.: Contributions to the theory of practical quantified boolean formula solving. In: Milano, M. (ed.) CP 2012. LNCS, pp. 647–663. Springer, Heidelberg (2012). https://doi.org/10.1007/978-3-642-33558-7_47
22. Hoory, S., Linial, N., Wigderson, A.: Expander graphs and their applications. Bull. Am. Math. Soc. 43(4), 439–561 (2006)
23. Hoos, H.H., Peitl, T., Slivovsky, F., Szeider, S.: Portfolio-based algorithm selection for circuit QBFs. In: Hooker, J. (ed.) CP 2018. LNCS, vol. 11008, pp. 195–209. Springer, Cham (2018). https://doi.org/10.1007/978-3-319-98334-9_13
24. Impagliazzo, R., Williams, R.: Communication complexity with synchronized clocks. In: Proceedings of the 25th Annual IEEE Conference on Computational Complexity, CCC 2010, Cambridge, Massachusetts, USA, 9–12 June 2010, pp. 259–269. IEEE Computer Society (2010)
25. Janota, M., Klieber, W., Marques-Silva, J., Clarke, E.M.: Solving QBF with counterexample guided refinement. Artif. Intell. 234, 1–25 (2016)
26. Janota, M., Marques-Silva, J.: Solving QBF by clause selection. In: Yang, Q., Wooldridge, M.J. (eds.) Proceedings of the Twenty-Fourth International Joint Conference on Artificial Intelligence, IJCAI 2015, Buenos Aires, Argentina, 25–31 July 2015, pp. 325–331. AAAI Press (2015)
27. Kleine Büning, H., Karpinski, M., Flögel, A.: Resolution for quantified boolean formulas. Inf. Comput. 117(1), 12–18 (1995)
28. Eyal, K., Noam, N.: Communication Complexity. Cambridge University Press, Cambridge (1997)
29. Lonsing, F., Biere, A.: Depqbf: a dependency-aware QBF solver. J. Satisf. Boolean Model. Comput. 7(2–3), 71–76 (2010)
30. Lonsing, F., Egly, U.: Evaluating QBF solvers: quantifier alternations matter. In: Hooker, J. (ed.) CP 2018. LNCS, vol. 11008, pp. 276–294. Springer, Cham (2018). https://doi.org/10.1007/978-3-319-98334-9_19
31. Pan, G., Vardi, M.Y.: Symbolic decision procedures for QBF. In: Wallace, M. (ed.) CP 2004. LNCS, vol. 3258, pp. 453–467. Springer, Heidelberg (2004). https://doi.org/10.1007/978-3-540-30201-8_34
32. Peitl, T., Slivovsky, F., Szeider, S.: Dependency learning for QBF. J. Artif. Intell. Res. 65, 180–208 (2019)

33. Pipatsrisawat, K., Darwiche, A.: New compilation languages based on structured decomposability. In: Fox, D., Gomes, C.P. (eds.) Proceedings of the Twenty-Third AAAI Conference on Artificial Intelligence, AAAI 2008, Chicago, Illinois, USA, 13–17 July 2008, pp. 517–522. AAAI Press (2008)
34. Pulina, L., Tacchella, A.: A self-adaptive multi-engine solver for quantified boolean formulas. Constraints An. Int. J. **14**(1), 80–116 (2009)
35. Rabe, M.N., Tentrup, L.: CAQE: a certifying QBF solver. In: Kaivola, R., Wahl, T. (eds.) Formal Methods in Computer-Aided Design, FMCAD 2015, Austin, Texas, USA, 27–30 September 2015, pp. 136–143. IEEE (2015)
36. Ronald, L.: Rivest. Learning decision lists. Mach. Learn. **2**(3), 229–246 (1987)
37. Somenzi, F.: CUDD: CU decision diagram package-release 2.4. 0. University of Colorado at Boulder (2009)
38. Tentrup, L.: Non-prenex QBF solving using abstraction. In: Creignou, N., Le Berre, D. (eds.) SAT 2016. LNCS, vol. 9710, pp. 393–401. Springer, Cham (2016). https://doi.org/10.1007/978-3-319-40970-2_24
39. Wegener, I.: Branching Programs and Binary Decision Diagrams. SIAM (2000)
40. Zhang, L., Malik, S.: Conflict driven learning in a quantified boolean satisfiability solver. In: Pileggi, L.T., Kuehlmann, A. (eds.) Proceedings of the 2002 IEEE/ACM International Conference on Computer-aided Design, ICCAD 2002, San Jose, California, USA, 10–14 November 2002, pp. 442–449. ACM/IEEE Computer Society (2002)

XOR Local Search for Boolean Brent Equations

Wojciech Nawrocki[1]($\boxtimes$)(iD), Zhenjun Liu[1], Andreas Fröhlich[2](iD), Marijn J.H. Heule[1](iD), and Armin Biere[2](iD)

[1] Carnegie Mellon University, Pittsburgh, USA
wnawrock@andrew.cmu.edu, zhenjunl@andrew.cmu.edu, mheule@andrew.cmu.edu
[2] Johannes Kepler University, Linz, Austria
andreas.froehlich@jku.at, biere@jku.at

Abstract. Combining clausal and XOR reasoning has been studied for almost two decades, in particular in the context of CDCL and look-ahead, but not in classical local search. To stimulate research in this direction, we propose to standardize a hybrid format, called XNF, which allows both clauses and XORs. We implemented a tool to extract XOR constraints from a CNF, simplify them, and produce an XNF formula. The usefulness of XNF formulas is demonstrated by focusing on the impact of combined clausal and XOR reasoning on local search. Native support for XOR facilitates satisfying any falsified long XOR using a single flip, similarly to satisfying a falsified clause. When combined with XOR-based heuristics, local search performance is significantly improved on matrix multiplication challenges which are hard for CDCL.

1 Introduction

Two of the most successful approaches to SAT solving are Conflict-Driven Clause Learning (CDCL) and Stochastic Local Search (SLS). Modern CDCL solvers are very sophisticated and able to efficiently solve a broad range of problems. In contrast, the idea of SLS is simple yet works well on certain formulas. Also look-ahead solvers have been quite successful in the past, but suffer from having few applications that are not already successfully covered by CDCL.

These solving paradigms usually operate on conjunctive normal form (CNF) and thus expect their input to be a set of clauses. While in principle all problems can be translated into pure CNF, additionally allowing the use of XOR constraints can provide a more natural representation, which in turn can possibly lead to more efficient solving approaches. Examples include problems from cryptography, with corresponding formulas often originally denoted in algebraic normal form, but also all formulas that simply contain parity constraints [4,5,18,31]. Similarly, XOR constraints are important for approximate model counting [13]. As a result, the combination of clausal and XOR reasoning has been considered an interesting topic and has been studied [37] as well as applied in several algorithms—usually in the context of CDCL and look-ahead solvers [14,20], with

C.-M. Li and F. Manyà (Eds.): SAT 2021, LNCS 12831, pp. 417–435, 2021.
https://doi.org/10.1007/978-3-030-80223-3_29

CryptoMiniSAT probably being the most prominent example [38]. Nevertheless, most state-of-the-art solvers still do not support XOR reasoning.

Research on XOR constraints in the context of SLS is sparse and, aside from loosely related work on gates [6,33], satisfiability modulo theories [17], and continuous local search [29,30], there have been few successful attempts on improving SLS solvers by incorporating support for non-CNF representations. In particular, up-to-date there is no SLS algorithm that combines clausal and XOR reasoning during the search process by supporting native XOR constraints.

Moreover, SLS solvers have different strengths than other types of solvers. For instance, they are considered to work well on random $k-$SAT and satisfiable, hard combinatorial problems. On some crafted combinatorial problems such as VanDerWaeden_pd_3k and battleship, the SLS solver Swcca outperforms the CDCL solver Glucose in both success rate and average time [12]. Another well-known example is the boolean Pythagorean Triples problem [23]: the satisfiable $[1, 7824]$ instance can be solved using DDFW local search [24] in one CPU minute, while complete methods can take years.

A recent problem of interest on which SLS performed particularly well is related to matrix multiplication [21] expressed as a SAT problem using Boolean Brent equations [22]. The corresponding matrix multiplication (challenge 1) benchmarks[1], MM-Challenge-1, turn out to be hard for CDCL solvers, but could be solved by the SLS solver YalSAT. This is particularly surprising since the benchmark formulas contain a large number of XOR constraints which, encoded into CNF, should (and actually do) hinder the performance of SLS solvers.

Why do we consider CNF-encoded XOR constraints to be problematic for SLS solvers? To avoid combinatorial explosion in the number of clauses, the Tseitin transformation has to be used, particularly for long XOR constraints. While shortening the formula, this encoding introduces a large number of auxiliary variables which, roughly speaking, obscure the XOR constraint from the solver's view and drastically affect the neighbourhood of assignments visited during the local search. We will give a detailed explanation in Sect. 2. This observation, together with the already good performance of SLS on MM-Challenge-1, provides even more reason to assume that it might be possible to further push the state-of-the-art by incorporating native XOR support into SLS.

Our Contribution. The core observation on which we base our work is that XOR constraints fit quite naturally into SLS algorithms. Every time a literal is flipped, the truth values of all XOR constraints containing the literal get flipped as well, and the core solver loop can be adapted to do this. To support this, we extended our input format from CNF to XNF, allowing XORs to exist as another type of constraint alongside the usual disjunctive clauses. We also developed a tool cnf2xnf, which extracts XOR constraints from a formula given in CNF and saves the result in XNF format, as well as a related tool extor which reconstructs solutions for the original CNF from solutions for the XNF. Both algorithms are described in Sect. 3. Our main contribution is xnfSAT, an SLS solver based on the state-of-the-art YalSAT [8] solver—we outline its implemen-

---

[1] https://github.com/marijnheule/matrix-challenges.

tation in Sect. 4. We then present experimental results in Sect. 5 and show that xnfSAT achieves significant performance improvements on all benchmarks within MM-Challenge-1, thus confirming the usefulness of our combined representation and pushing the state-of-the-art on these challenging instances.

2   XOR Constraints

An SLS solver starts with a complete assignment of truth values to variables. While the formula is not satisfied, it loops flipping literals chosen according to some probability distribution. The choice of this distribution forms the heart of an SLS solver [2].

To see why CNF-encoded XOR constraints can negatively impact the performance of SLS solvers, let us first summarize briefly a simplified version of the SLS algorithm as used in YalSAT [8].

Algorithm 1 outlines the high-level structure of YalSAT, omitting certain details such as restarts and corresponding strategy changes. The basic loop originates from WalkSAT [34]. The solver first builds up internal data structures, preprocesses the formula via unit propagation, and sets an initial truth-value assignment. It then loops until a solution is found. On each iteration, it picks a falsified clause and flips the truth value of a literal in it. Details of this process will be outlined in Sect. 4—for now, a bird's eye view suffices.

Algorithm 1. Outline of a typical WalkSAT-based solver

1: **for** clause in input file **do**
2:     parse and store clause to data structure
3: **end for**
4: preprocess formula
5: $\alpha \leftarrow$ complete initial assignment of truth values
6: **while** there exists a clause falsified by α **do**
7:     $C \leftarrow pickUnsatClause()$
8:     $x \leftarrow pickVar(C)$
9:     $\alpha \leftarrow \alpha$ with x flipped
10:     update solver state
11: **end while**

CNF Encodings

Let us now look at how this algorithm interacts with the CNF encoding of XOR constraints. The direct encoding of an XOR constraint on k variables uses 2^{k-1} clauses of length k, where each clause consists of variables $x_1, \ldots, x_k$ with an even number of them negated:

$$\texttt{XOR\_d}(x_1, x_2, \ldots, x_k) = \bigwedge_{\text{even } \#\neg} (\pm x_1 \vee \pm x_2 \vee \cdots \vee \pm x_k)$$

To avoid an exponential growth in the number of clauses, it is common to use the Tseitin transformation [40] instead, which recursively translates arbitrary formulas into CNF by introducing fresh auxiliary variables for its sub-formulas:

$$f(g(x_1, \ldots, x_k)) = f(y) \wedge (y \leftrightarrow g(x_1, \ldots, x_k))$$

The resulting formula is equisatisfiable to the original one. Due to its recursive nature and the associative property of certain binary operations, the final CNF representation can differ in the number of variables and clauses depending on the structure of the original formula.

We consider two different parameters that describe this structure in the case of pure XOR constraints and, thus, influence the final CNF representation: the *cutting number* and the *mode*.

The cutting number, roughly speaking, defines the size of the individual slices that are cut out of an XOR constraint and then encoded in a direct fashion [4]. The smaller the slices (with a minimum of size $n = 3$), the shorter and fewer the resulting clauses, since each slice will be encoded into 2^{n-1} clauses of length n. However, with larger n, fewer slices are required and, thus, fewer auxiliary variables need to be introduced.

It is not clear whether there is a universally optimal setting for the cutting number. Soos and Meel [37] argue that a cutting number of 4 experimentally turned out to be optimal for their use case in approximate model counting. In contrast, for some problems in cryptography, it is suggested that a cutting number of 6 would be the optimal setting for the respective applications [5,10]. In Sect. 5, we analyze results for xnfSAT on CNF benchmarks constructed using several cutting numbers.

The second parameter, which we call the mode of translation, influences the fashion in which the XOR constraint is recursively traversed. For the mode, we distinguish between *linear* and *pooled* encodings. While the linear mode might be considered the standard approach and has been used before [5], we are not aware of any previous work using the pooled mode—however, a similar approach for at-most-one constraints has been contributed to Knuth's book "The Art of Computer Programming, Volume 4, Fascicle 6: Satisfiability" [27] (p. 134, Ex. 12) by the fourth author.

From an implementational point of view, the difference between the two modes basically boils down to whether a stack or a queue is used when removing a chunk of variables from the XOR constraint and adding fresh auxiliary variables during translation. In particular, a stack will lead to a linear translation, whereas a queue will produce a pooled one. We can assume $k > n$, with k being the length of the XOR constraint and n denoting the cutting number. If this were not the case, we could simply use the direct encoding. Let XOR_1_n and XOR_p_n denote the linear and the pooled encoding, respectively, with cutting number n:

$$\text{XOR\_1\_n}(x_1, \ldots, x_k) = \text{XOR\_d}(x_1, \ldots, x_{n-1}, \overline{y}) \wedge \text{XOR\_1\_n}(y, x_n, \ldots, x_k)$$
$$\text{XOR\_p\_n}(x_1, \ldots, x_k) = \text{XOR\_d}(x_1, \ldots, x_{n-1}, \overline{y}) \wedge \text{XOR\_p\_n}(x_n, \ldots, x_k, y)$$

Note that XOR chunks (with length $n - 1$) are always sliced from the left. The new auxiliary variable in linear mode or pooled mode is then added to the left or the right of the remaining XOR constraint, respectively. For the sliced chunks, the position of $\overline{y}$ does not matter since the direct encoding is not affected by variable order. To illustrate the practical difference of the two modes, let us take a closer look at a short example for an XOR constraint of length 6 (for simplicity, using a fixed cutting number of 3).

Example 1.

$\text{XOR\_1\_3}(x_1, x_2, x_3, x_4, x_5, x_6)$
$= \text{XOR\_d}(x_1, x_2, \overline{y_1}) \wedge \text{XOR\_1\_3}(y_1, x_3, x_4, x_5, x_6)$
$= \text{XOR\_d}(x_1, x_2, \overline{y_1}) \wedge \text{XOR\_d}(y_1, x_3, \overline{y_2}) \wedge \text{XOR\_1\_3}(y_2, x_4, x_5, x_6)$
$= \text{XOR\_d}(x_1, x_2, \overline{y_1}) \wedge \text{XOR\_d}(y_1, x_3, \overline{y_2}) \wedge \text{XOR\_d}(y_2, x_4, \overline{y_3}) \wedge \text{XOR\_1\_3}(y_3, x_5, x_6)$
$= \text{XOR\_d}(x_1, x_2, \overline{y_1}) \wedge \text{XOR\_d}(y_1, x_3, \overline{y_2}) \wedge \text{XOR\_d}(y_2, x_4, \overline{y_3}) \wedge \text{XOR\_d}(y_3, x_5, x_6)$

$\text{XOR\_p\_3}(x_1, x_2, x_3, x_4, x_5, x_6)$
$= \text{XOR\_d}(x_1, x_2, \overline{y_1}) \wedge \text{XOR\_p\_3}(x_3, x_4, x_5, x_6, y_1)$
$= \text{XOR\_d}(x_1, x_2, \overline{y_1}) \wedge \text{XOR\_d}(x_3, x_4, \overline{y_2}) \wedge \text{XOR\_p\_3}(x_5, x_6, y_1, y_2)$
$= \text{XOR\_d}(x_1, x_2, \overline{y_1}) \wedge \text{XOR\_d}(x_3, x_4, \overline{y_2}) \wedge \text{XOR\_d}(x_5, x_6, \overline{y_3}) \wedge \text{XOR\_p\_3}(y_1, y_2, y_3)$
$= \text{XOR\_d}(x_1, x_2, \overline{y_1}) \wedge \text{XOR\_d}(x_3, x_4, \overline{y_2}) \wedge \text{XOR\_d}(x_5, x_6, \overline{y_3}) \wedge \text{XOR\_d}(y_1, y_2, y_3)$

While the structure of the resulting CNF formula (for different modes) as well as the number of variables and clauses (for different cutting numbers) will vary, all combinations are effective in reducing the number of clauses at the expense of adding linearly more variables—a relatively small price to pay. Nevertheless, this translation can greatly hinder the performance of local search solvers.

To see this, consider $\text{XOR\_1\_n}(x_1, \ldots, x_k)$. For original variables $x_1, \ldots, x_k$, the encoding introduces auxiliary variables $y_1, \ldots, y_r$ (with $r \in \Theta(k)$) and $r - 1$ XOR constraints of length $n < k$. For simplicity, let us again assume $n = 3$:

$\text{XOR\_1\_3}(x_1, .., x_k) = \text{XOR\_d}(x_1, x_2, \overline{y_1}) \wedge \text{XOR\_d}(y_1, x_3, \overline{y_2}) \wedge \cdots \wedge \text{XOR\_d}(y_r, x_{k-1}, x_k)$

Observe that for each assignment of $x_1, \ldots, x_k$ satisfying $\text{XOR\_d}(x_1, \ldots, x_k)$, there exists a unique assignment of $y_1, \ldots, y_r$ that satisfies $\text{XOR\_1\_3}(x_1, \ldots, x_k)$. This is because, given an assignment of $x_1, \ldots, x_k$ satisfying $\text{XOR\_d}(x_1, \ldots, x_k)$, there is only one assignment of y_1 satisfying $\text{XOR\_d}(x_1, x_2, \overline{y_1})$, which subsequently forces the assignment of y_2 in order to satisfy $\text{XOR}(y_1, x_3, \overline{y_2})$, and so on. The same kind of argument holds for the general encodings XOR_1_n and XOR_p_n.

We say that an assignment satisfies the CNF-encoded XOR constraint (by XOR_1_n or XOR_p_n) *on a high level* if an odd number of $x_1, \ldots, x_k$ are set to true (i.e., if the original XOR constraint would be satisfied). However, even when the constraint is satisfied on a high level, it is possible that the auxiliary variables do not have the correct unique values. In this way, an XOR constraint can be satisfied on a high level but falsified in the (low-level) Tseitin CNF encoding.

For the SLS solver to move from a falsifying assignment of $x_1, \ldots, x_k$ to a satisfying assignment of $x_1, \ldots, x_k$, it additionally needs to flip the correct auxiliary variables to match the corresponding assignment of $y_1, \ldots, y_r$. However, there is only one assignment of $y_1, \ldots, y_r$ satisfying the Tseitin-encoded CNF representation of $(x_1 \oplus \cdots \oplus x_k)$ out of 2^r many. While this might not be a big issue for CDCL solvers (since corresponding values could be propagated), this is particularly difficult for the probabilistic approach taken by SLS solvers.

Hence, after the XOR constraint becomes satisfied on a high level, the probability of an SLS solver flipping the correct auxiliary variables and satisfying the low-level Tseitin-encoded clauses is small. Worse still, it may end up flipping one of the original variables x_i and invalidating the XOR constraint.

Another issue with the Tseitin encoding of XOR constraints that particularly affects SLS solvers is the change in neighbourhood of assignments within the search space. If we look at an XOR constraint $(x_1 \oplus \cdots \oplus x_k)$ that just got falsified under a certain assignment by flipping x_1, we could easily fix this by flipping an arbitrary variable in this constraint using a single step, including x_k. This does not hold for the Tseitin-encoded CNF version of the XOR constraint anymore. Once again, consider XOR_1_3: If the CNF version of the constraint is falsified due to x_1, this can only be fixed by x_2 or y_1. In order to flip x_k, we first would have to take r intermediate steps by flipping all $y_1, \ldots, y_r$. This can be particularly problematic with probabilistic algorithms, considering that the correct variable has to be chosen in each step, decreasing the overall probability for x_k being reached exponentially. Similar arguments have been made in the context of configuration checking [32] and might have contributed to the success of CCA-based solvers, such as CCAnr [11].

It is possible to trade off some auxiliary variables for an increased clause count by increasing the cutting number. However, as the number of clauses grows exponentially, this explodes quickly. Using pooled mode, the exponential decrease in probability can be avoided since the resulting structure will roughly be tree-like, i.e., $O(\log(r))$ steps are sufficient for possibly reaching any other variable from the original XOR constraint. Nevertheless, the overall probability distribution is still skewed heavily towards "close" variables and the high-level vs low-level satisfiability issue is not resolved either. Thus, we can only expect small improvements compared to the linear version.

XNF Format

Overall, the currently widely-used Tseitin encoding of XOR constraints is ineffective in SLS solvers. Thus, our goal is to avoid this conversion by including XOR constraints natively as part of the input format. This would enable an SLS solver to handle XOR constraints more effectively, and we hope to standardize this format to facilitate research on SAT solvers with XOR reasoning.

We use the following extension of the existing CNF format that is compatible with XOR constraints. For simplicity, we will call this format XNF. This format is in the spirit of the DIMACS format, which makes it natural to standardize. An XOR constraint is denoted as a sequence of literals preceded by the symbol x; OR constraints are denoted the same as in the original CNF format. The header is changed slightly to "p xnf #variables #constraints". For example, the formula $(x_1 \vee x_2 \vee \overline{x_3}) \wedge (\overline{x_1} \oplus x_2)$ is denoted by the following XNF input:

```
p xnf 3 2
1 2 -3 0
x -1 2 0
```

While we came up with this format independently, we later stumbled upon a blog post[2] that briefly mentions CryptoMiniSAT's [38] support of a very similar input format[3]. Support for inputs in XNF also was recently added to the CDCL solver Satch[4], which is CNF-based and uses the pooled encoding presented in Sect. 2 to encode XOR constraints into CNF. This extension to Satch turned out very useful for testing the tools discussed in the next section.

3 Extracting XORs

Existing propositional problems do have XOR constraints but are usually only available in CNF. Therefore, we have implemented a stand-alone extraction tool cnf2xnf which allows to extract an XNF file from a given CNF in DIMACS format. We implemented this tool to make sure that our approach for hybrid local search also works, in a practical sense, with benchmarks given in CNF. The more general goal of this tool is to promote the XNF format and thus further encourage research into hybrid XNF solving.

The SAT solver CryptoMiniSAT [38] contains an internal procedure for extracting XORs [37] in order to take advantage of sophisticated XOR reasoning [35] for applications in approximate model counting [13]. The aim of that extractor is to recover XORs after encoding them into CNF and running CNF-based inprocessing. It takes shortened clauses into account—a common side-effect of CNF-level preprocessing. In earlier work by the fourth author [19], XORs were found by sorting the CNF, which fails to extract XORs with shortened clauses. Our new extractor cnf2xnf[5] shares the same problem for preprocessed formulas, but otherwise follows the same principles as used by Soos and Meel [37], apart from not using Bloom filters. In addition to extracting directly encoded XORs, our tool also finds XORs encoded in a Tseitin encoding of And-Inverter-Graphs (AIGs) [28]. Our algorithm is simpler and has successfully been used for gate-extraction to improve bounded variable elimination [15] and to implement Gaussian-elimination in some of the last author's SAT solvers [7,9].

Our extraction algorithm works as follows. We go over all clauses (including binary clauses) and as soon as we find a clause of length k with at most one positive literal, called "base clause", we check whether we can find all 2^{k-1}

---

[2] https://www.msoos.org/xor-clauses/.
[3] We are not aware of any formal publication about this format.
[4] https://github.com/arminbiere/satch.
[5] https://github.com/arminbiere/cnf2xnf.

target clauses obtained from the base clause by negating an even number of literals. As in subsumption algorithms [15], we only traverse the occurrence list of a single literal in a target clause with the smallest number of occurrences. If all clauses are found, they are marked as garbage and the corresponding XOR constraint is added. Extracting ternary XORs from AIGs starts with a ternary base clause which, together with two binary clauses, encodes an AND gate. For each of the two inputs of that outer AND gate, we then try to find another three clauses encoding an inner AND gate, which share the same inputs but negated. The implied XOR constraint is extracted. If the variables encoding the output of the two inner AND gates occur exclusively in these nine clauses, the clauses are then marked as garbage.

After extracting all XOR constraints, we eliminate variables which only occur in XOR constraints through substitution, simulating Gaussian elimination. The resulting XNF is written to the output file. Optionally, the user can request to produce an "extension stack", listing all the eliminated XOR constraints as well as those sets of nine clauses for XORs extracted from AIGs. This extension stack can be used to map a satisfying assignment of the XNF back to the original CNF. This is implemented in another tool called `extor`[6]. It takes a satisfying assignment of the XNF in the output format of the SAT competition together with the extension stack as inputs and produces a satisfying assignment for the original CNF—again in the SAT competition output format. The algorithm is exactly the same as for reconstructing solutions for CNF preprocessing [16,25, 26], except for the semantics of XOR constraints: for those, the value of the first literal of a processed constraint on the stack is flipped if it has an even number of true literals. For regular clauses, the value is only flipped if all literals are false.

As mentioned above, XNF parsing was also added to the new SAT solver Satch, which was then used to test the `cnf2xnf` extractor as well as solution reconstruction with `extor`. For 235 benchmarks of the main track of the SAT competition 2020, we were able to find and extract XORs successfully. From those, a subset of 118 allowed to eliminate variables by Gaussian elimination. This reduced the number of variables substantially—often to less than 50%. However, note that extracting binary XORs partially simulates equivalent literal substitution. Thus, it is difficult to give a precise account of the effectiveness of this flow as a preprocessing technique, which is available in other SAT solvers anyhow and not the target of this paper. Without any bounds, running XOR extraction until completion was able to extract all XORs of 224 benchmarks within one second and all XORs of 333 benchmarks within 10 s. For only 30 benchmarks, it took more than 100 s.

While these experiments are successful in showing that XNF extraction is feasible on standard competition instances, running Satch on the extracted XNF benchmarks had almost identical performance to running it on the original CNF versions. Furthermore, none of the satisfiable benchmarks was solved through local search, neither before nor after XNF extraction—however, the focus of

---

[6] also available at https://github.com/arminbiere/cnf2xnf.

this paper is to improve local search on specific benchmarks where local search already has an advantage. We consider it a challenge and future work to improve XOR-based reasoning on competition benchmarks.

4 Implementation

To support the XNF format which natively encodes XOR constraints, we modified YalSAT [8], a state-of-the-art SLS solver. We call our modified solver xnfSAT.[7]

Recall the structure of the YalSAT algorithm as outlined in Algorithm 1. Most of the modifications are natural analogies to XOR constraints. The bulk of our modifications concerns the internal data structures and the implementation of *pickVar* (line 8). To perform preprocessing efficiently, we adapted this step to carry out unit propagation on XOR constraints. We did not significantly change *pickUnsatClause* (line 7), as the existing code was sufficient to handle the newly added XOR constraints. For formulas that are encoded in pure CNF, our modification does not change the behavior of YalSAT.

For preprocessing, we carry out two rounds of unit propagation on clauses as YalSAT does, including also unitary XOR constraints. After unit propagation terminates, we want to utilize the partial assignment forced by unit propagation on XOR constraints. To deduce contradiction is easy, by examining whether there is a falsified XOR constraint. However, to remove satisfied literals, an XOR constraint should have its parity flipped: initially, an XOR constraint is satisfied iff an *odd* number of its literals are set to true; if one of its literals is forced to true by unit propagation, then the XOR constraint is true iff an *even* number of its remaining literals are set to true. As a result, we need an array to keep track of the parity of each XOR constraint.

Define **parity** of an XOR to be 0 if the constraint is satisfied when an odd number of its literals are set to true, and define **parity** to be 1 otherwise. This definition has the convenient property that it is precisely the "base truth value" of the XOR, so that the actual truth value of the constraint in a local search step can be calculated by comparing its current value to its **parity**. Using this definition, we only need to store the variables (but not whether they are negated) appearing in each XOR constraint and initialize its **parity** to the number of negations modulo 2.

Next to basically being a WalkSAT-based algorithm, YalSAT, more specifically, is also a probSAT-based algorithm. In probSAT [3], the probability that a variable x is picked is proportional to $c_b^{-break(x)}$, where c_b is a constant, called the *break coefficient*, and $break(x)$ denotes the number of clauses that would be falsified when x was flipped. A key extension of YalSAT compared to probSAT is that it uses a weighted version of break instead. In YalSAT [8], the probability of choosing a variable x is proportional to $c_b^{-break_w(x)}$, with $break_w(x) = \sum_{C \in B(x)} w(C)$, where $B(x)$ is the set of clauses that would be falsified by flipping x, and $w(C)$ is

---

[7] https://github.com/Vtec234/xnfsat.

the weight of a particular clause C. In its current implementation within YalSAT, $w(C)$ is not specific to each single clause though, but defined as a function of its length—we will get back to that later.

For xnfSAT, we first extend the definition of $break$ and $break_w$ by also taking into account the XORs that would be falsified. This is straightforward from a theoretic perspective, but requires to address the concrete implementation as part of an efficient SLS solver architecture. In the original YalSAT [8], calculating $break_w$ values using critical literals is crucial to its performance. A literal in a clause C is *critical* if flipping it falsifies C. Say a clause is k-satisfied if k literals in this clause are set to true. Then a clause contains a critical literal iff it is 1-satisfied. Since $break(x)$ is equal to the number of clauses in which x is critical, $break(x)$ can be cached and updated efficiently by tracking the number of true literals in each clause. Whenever a literal is flipped, this can be efficiently updated while looping through each clause where the corresponding variable occurs [1]. This is also where weighting is addressed when implementing $break_w$ in YalSAT [8]—instead of just increasing or decreasing the cached value by 1, it can be increased or decreased by $w(C)$, respectively. To generalize this idea to XORs, note that each time a literal in an XOR constraint is flipped, the truth value of the XOR constraint changes. Thus, in a satisfied XOR constraint, every literal is critical. When an XOR constraint C becomes satisfied or unsatisfied, increase or decrease $break_w(x)$ by $w(C)$, respectively, for all its literals x.

In YalSAT [8], the weight $w(C)$ is a function of the length of the clause C. However, this is not necessarily a good heuristic to measure the importance of an XOR compared to a clause, especially when XOR constraints are significantly longer. For example, in MM-Challenge-1, all XORs are more than six times longer than all the clauses. To simplify the algorithm and not to overtune on specific parameters, we assign a fixed weight w_X to all XOR constraints. Similarly, we will write w_k for $w(C)$ when C is a clause of length k.

Finally, a good choice for c_b is very important and has been extensively studied in the context of distribution-based SLS solvers [1–3]—however, mainly on random k−SAT problems. With hard combinatorial formulas usually not having uniform clause lengths, the original YalSAT [8] automatically configures c_b as a function of the maximum length of all clauses. This is no longer suitable when XOR constraints are added: For one thing, it is not clear whether the length of native XORs should be considered in the same way as the one of clauses. For another, when translated into CNF, the length of the resulting clauses depends on the encoding. To facilitate a thorough evaluation, we thus decided to re-expose c_b as a parameter in xnfSAT.

Now there is one remaining issue with YalSAT, which initially was very helpful to show the general usefulness of SLS on the MM-Challenge-1 benchmarks [21], but would prevent a clear analysis of the contribution of native XORs to the algorithm. In its original version [8], YalSAT changes *strategy* after each restart interval[8]. This can help find good settings for a broad range of instances and thus is supposed to increase overall robustness. On the negative side, it obfuscates

---

[8] A detailed explanation of strategies in YalSAT is out of the scope of this paper.

what exactly contributes to a successful run by possibly causing hard to predict, unknown interactions. In preliminary experiments, we still had strategies switched on. Implementing XOR support in xnfSAT with strategies significantly improved performance (cf. Fig. 1), but we soon realized that it is hard to tell if this effect was really just because of the XORs and not due to some hidden interaction with a complex strategy—this could then prevent the same approach to work with other solvers. We thus decided to disable all strategies and to instead figure out which were the individual components that contributed to the good performance on MM-Challenge-1. As a side effect, the resulting version of xnfSAT became much faster. However, note that our goal was not to overtune to a specific benchmark class nor should this be considered our contribution—instead, the aim was to simplify the algorithm. As our results in Table 1 show, adding native XOR support on top of this much simpler, strategy-free version, still significantly improves performance and we can now conjecture that this is indeed due to our hybrid implementation. The changes we made by switching off strategies:

- Caching is always on, i.e. after a restart the algorithm will pick a previous local minimum. (Had a small effect.)
- c_b is now fixed and never modified during run. (Had a medium effect.)
- Weights w_k for different clause lengths are now exposed as a parameter and never modified during run. (Had a large effect.)
- The initial assignment is now always $0 \ldots 0$. (Had the largest effect.)

5 Experiments

We benchmark xnfSAT on MM-Challenge-1. These instances are hard for CDCL, and best known performance on them has been achieved by SLS [21]. We compare several encodings:

- original, handcrafted XNF (before conversion to CNF)
- CNF with linear XOR_1_n constraints and cutting number $n \in [3,8]$
- CNF with pooled XOR_p_n constraints and cutting number $n \in [3,8]$
- reconstructed XNF as extracted from CNF by cnf2xnf[9]

Running on different CNF variants allows us to observe the impact of the choice of XOR encoding on performance. Running on both handcrafted and extracted XNF allows us to verify that the cnf2xnf outputs perform adequately compared to hand-written formulas. Note that the runtime of cnf2xnf on these instances is negligible, around 0.3 s per formula. All benchmark formulas involve a significant amount (more than 700) of XORs or their clausal encodings.

Parameter choices are crucial to the performance of SLS solvers. We optimize parameter classes outlined in Sect. 4: the break coefficient c_b, the weight w_X assigned to XOR constraints, and the weights w_k assigned to clauses of length k.

---

[9] The CNF encoding was generated by using XOR_p_4 on the handcrafted XNF.

In preliminary experiments with the strategy-based version described in Sect. 4, we first searched for optimal values of c_b and w_X on the 4-cut pooled CNF (recall that it was conjectured optimal [37]) and on the original XNF. On both formulas, we sampled c_b in the range $[1.5, 5.5]$. On XNF, we also sampled w_X in $[2, 8]$. These ranges were observed to contain most acceptable values. On CNF, the break constant was sampled with a step size of 0.25—on XNF, a step size of 1.0 was used for both parameters due to the higher computational resource requirements of the two-dimensional (c_b, w_X) grid. We found that the average best-performing c_b value for all instances is around 2.5. Interestingly, this does not change with the addition of XOR constraints. The best-performing w_X is around 5.0. The strategy-based versions will not be discussed in detail, but the runtime CDF of the best configuration (with $c_b = 2.5, w_X = 5.0$) on CNF and XNF is plotted in Fig. 1 for comparison.

For our full experiments, we then switched off strategies and fixed $c_b = 2.5$ as well as $w_X = 5.0$, next sampling w_k for $k \in [2, 8]$ (there are no clauses of other lengths) on every variant of the instances. The sampled ranges varied as we analyzed preliminary experiments but tended to be within $[2, 5]$. This roughly corresponds to the range that was previously used by the strategies in the original YalSAT. However, these values are now fixed and do not change after each restart, making the solver much simpler. Having sampled a broad range of values for w_k, we decided to go for $w_2 = w_3 = 2$, $w_4 = w_5 = 4.5$, and $w_6 = w_7 = w_8 = 5.0$ for all encodings, aside from the 3-cut one, where we chose $w_3 = 4.5$ for reasons that we will explain later. While this setting was not necessarily optimal for each instance, the overall results were solid[10]—recall that our goal was not to perfectly tune every single formula, but to show that the underlying algorithm profits from adding native XOR support. Note that we invested significant computational resources into optimizing CNF weights in order to ensure that our results persist even against well-tuned CNF encodings.

We ran all benchmarks on the Lonestar 5 cluster of Texas at Texas Advanced Computing Center, which has Xeon E5-2690 processors with 24 hardware threads per node. Each variant of each instance was attempted $8 \times 24 = 192$ times (for 192 *runs*) with a timeout of 1000 s. Performance is measured by three metrics: the percentage of instances solved within our timeout, the average number of variable megaflips (flips$\times 10^6$) before reaching the solution, and the average time to solution (in seconds). In Table 1, these are abbreviated by frac, Mflips and time, respectively. In addition, to gain more insights into how the specific encoding of XOR constraints impacts performance, we measured the percentage of flips spent on auxiliary variables (aux) for the CNF instances.

Results

Figure 1 shows the overall results of our experiments, plotting a runtime CDF of what we consider to be the most interesting configurations. For each encoding, we show the configuration (i.e., choice of parameters) that performed best regarding

---

[10] In the final version, we will replace this note by a link to the full experimental data.

the overall number of solved instances with that encoding. In general, hardness of the individual instances did not differ a lot among the various encodings and parameter configurations, i.e., easy instances or hard instances for one setting were also easy or hard, respectively, for all other settings.

We can see that the XNF-based solver outperforms all CNF versions by a huge margin for both the handcrafted encoding as well as the reconstructed XNF. In particular, it takes only 200 s for the XNF version to solve approximately the same number of instances as the best CNF configuration.

Furthermore, both XNF versions perform roughly equally—this confirms that cnf2xnf was successful in extracting the XORs and shows that the resulting structure is not negatively affected in any way.

Next, we can take a closer look at the different CNF encodings. One trend seems to be that performance on MM-Challenge-1 increases with larger cutting numbers, reaching peak at 6. In particular, the 4-cut encoding that we initially conjectured to be optimal turned out to perform worse than higher cutting numbers, with just the 3-cut encoding being worse. Note that the 4-cut encoding was used for initially creating the publicly available CNF representation of the MM-Challenge-1 benchmark set and for first solving it using YalSAT [21]. This points towards another central benefit of our native XOR representation, which we have not explicitly discussed so far: while the optimal cutting number turned out to be 6, we do not need to care about finding that out since XNF still outperforms it.

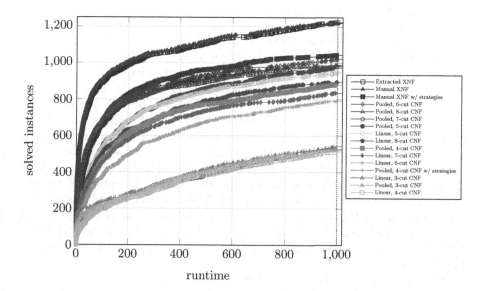

Fig. 1. Runtime CDF of xnfSAT performance on various encodings and solver versions.

Regarding CNF encodings, there is some mild evidence that the proposed pooled mode is generally better than the linear mode. While this is not true for the 3-cut encoding, we think that this might be a special case that could also be influenced by other factors. Notably, the original XNFs only contain clauses of length 2 and 3. After encoding the instances into CNF, new clauses of length n will be introduced for the n-cut encoding. As a result, the 3-cut encoding is the only one having to use the same weight for original 3-clauses as well as for clauses representing CNF-encoded XORs. Yet again, this points to another benefit of using native XORs: for formulas other than in MM-Challenge-1, it may well be the case that clauses in the original XNF have lengths above 3. Thus, even for n-cut encodings with $n > 3$, there is no guarantee that the clauses representing CNF-encoded XORs can be weighted differently from the original clauses.

Looking at Table 1, we can see a detailed analysis of the best-performing linear CNF, pooled CNF, and the XNF version. We chose to display the extracted XNF version because in problems without handcrafted XNF, this could still be obtained using cnf2xnf. The XNF version outperforms both CNF encodings across all benchmarks.

6 Conclusion

Combining clausal and XOR reasoning has frequently been looked at in the past. However, rarely so in the context of SLS solvers. With many possible applications, particularly in the domain of cryptography [4,5,18,31] or for approximate model counting [37], progress in this area is certainly of interest.

We argued why CNF encodings of XOR constraints can hinder the performance of SLS solvers and, next to presenting the pooled CNF encoding, advocate for a hybrid representation that allows clauses as well as native XOR constraints. We thus proposed to standardize a format that we call XNF, being a natural extension of the CNF DIMACS format, in order to further support research in that direction. To enable broader use, we also developed the tools cnf2xnf and extor to find and extract XOR constraints in CNF formulas, convert them into XNF, and to allow reconstructing the solution for the original formula afterwards. We then proceeded by presenting our main contribution, a hybrid SLS solver called xnfSAT. Our detailed experimental evaluation on the matrix multiplication challenge benchmarks [21] showed that xnfSAT solves XNF representations way faster than the corresponding CNF representations, thereby confirming the benefit of supporting native XOR constraints and pushing the state-of-the-art on these instances. As further side results, we presented several other evaluations, providing insights into possible effects that various different CNF encodings as well as parameter settings might have on the performance of SLS solvers.

We hope that our contributions further spark community interest in hybrid SAT solving for clauses and XORs, and expect our results to generalize to other instances with XOR constraints. There are certainly many possible directions of relevance, some of those related to the present work:

While xnfSAT implements support for various clause selection heuristics [1], we sticked to the default setting, using *unfair breadth first search* during our

Table 1. Performance of xnfSAT on benchmarked instances at the optimal settings: CNF ($c_b = 2.5, w_2 = w_3 = 2, w_6 = 5$) and XNF ($c_b = 2.5, w_2 = w_3 = 2, w_X = 5$).

MM-23-*	frac	aux	Mflips	time	frac	aux	Mflips	time	frac	Mflips	time
4-4-4-4-1	76.6	7.8	280.8	67.4	99.5	19.8	31.3	8.2	100.0	0.4	0.1
2-2-2-2-A	94.3	4.1	602.6	154.6	100.0	12.0	245.3	72.7	100.0	55.9	15.6
2-2-2-2-D	79.2	3.2	1171.8	299.6	99.0	10.0	345.7	105.7	100.0	77.1	22.0
2-2-2-3-4	85.4	3.8	967.1	234.6	99.5	11.1	430.0	122.3	100.0	269.0	73.1
2-2-2-2-C	60.4	3.4	1174.1	297.6	85.4	9.7	652.9	192.8	98.4	332.6	90.9
2-2-2-4-B	12.5	4.5	2020.1	487.9	30.7	11.2	1748.8	515.0	42.7	1648.9	432.6
2-2-2-2-B	2.1	4.8	2703.6	676.0	12.5	13.3	1756.5	529.5	41.1	1574.6	429.7
2-2-2-2-M	0.5	3.1	1182.2	316.3	0	–	–	–	29.2	1516.4	450.3
2-2-2-2-3	1.6	3.8	1543.5	385.6	5.7	11.3	2118.0	612.8	23.4	1439.7	392.3
2-2-2-4-A	0	–	–	–	0	–	–	–	2.1	2943.1	835.0
Formula	Linear, 6-cut CNF				Pooled, 6-cut CNF				Extracted XNF		

evaluation. Note that all those clause selection heuristics were originally developed for pure CNF-based solvers. Nevertheless, preliminary experiments showed that changing the clause selection heuristic can affect the performance of our solver. For future work, it might be interesting to look in more detail at new heuristics which allow treating clauses and XORs in a different manner.

We also noted that using a starting assignment of $0\dots0$ was important and performed much better than random initialization for the benchmarks we considered. However, this does not necessarily mean that $0\dots0$ is already optimal. Besides, other problem classes could benefit from different initial assignments. Thus, another interesting direction of research could go into the direction of combining the approach used by NLocalSAT [41] with xnfSAT or with hybrid representations in general.

As we saw in Sect. 5, the CNF encoding using a cutting number of 3 performed worse compared to the other CNF representations. One reason might be due to the fact that the formulas originally already contain clauses of length 3, but also the XOR constraints are mapped to clauses of this length. While it is likely that the two kinds of clauses should be treated differently, both are assigned the same weight w_3. To address this, individual clause weighting heuristics as part of other solvers [2,39] could be of use. Beyond that, more sophisticated approaches [36] could potentially also be adapted to find individual weights.

Finally, it would also be interesting to look at whether pure CNF-based CDCL solvers can profit from different encodings of XOR constraints, e.g., using the pooled mode in contrast to a standard linear encoding.

Acknowledgements. The authors acknowledge the Texas Advanced Computing Center (TACC) at The University of Texas at Austin for providing HPC resources that have contributed to the research results reported within this paper. The work is also supported by the National Science Foundation (NSF) under grant CCF-2010951, Austrian Science Fund (FWF), NFN S11408-N23 (RiSE), and the LIT AI Lab funded by the State of Upper Austria.

References

1. Balint, A., Biere, A., Fröhlich, A., Schöning, U.: Improving implementation of SLS Solvers for SAT and new Heuristics for k-SAT with long clauses. In: Sinz, C., Egly, U. (eds.) SAT 2014. LNCS, vol. 8561, pp. 302–316. Springer, Cham (2014). https://doi.org/10.1007/978-3-319-09284-3_23

2. Balint, A., Fröhlich, A.: Improving stochastic local search for SAT with a new probability distribution. In: Strichman, O., Szeider, S. (eds.) SAT 2010. LNCS, vol. 6175, pp. 10–15. Springer, Heidelberg (2010). https://doi.org/10.1007/978-3-642-14186-7_3

3. Balint, A., Schöning, U.: Choosing probability distributions for stochastic local search and the role of make versus break. In: Cimatti, A., Sebastiani, R. (eds.) SAT 2012. LNCS, vol. 7317, pp. 16–29. Springer, Heidelberg (2012). https://doi.org/10.1007/978-3-642-31612-8_3

4. Bard, G.V.: Introduction: How to Use this Book, pp. 1–6. Springer, US, Boston, MA (2009). https://doi.org/10.1007/978-0-387-88757-9_1

5. Bard, G.V., Courtois, N.T., Jefferson., C.: Efficient methods for conversion and solution of sparse systems of low-degree multivariate polynomials over GF(2) via SAT-solvers. Cryptology ePrint Archive, Report 2007/024 (2007), https://eprint.iacr.org/2007/024

6. Belov, A., Järvisalo, M., Stachniak, Z.: Depth-driven circuit-level stochastic local search for SAT, pp. 504–509 (2011)

7. Biere, A.: Lingeling and friends entering the SAT challenge 2012. In: Balint, A., Belov, A., Diepold, D., Gerber, S., Järvisalo, M., Sinz, C. (eds.) Proceedings of SAT Challenge 2012: Solver and Benchmark Descriptions. Department of Computer Science Series of Publications B, vol. B-2012-2, pp. 33–34. University of Helsinki (2012)

8. Biere, A.: CaDiCaL, Lingeling, Plingeling, Treengeling, YalSAT entering the SAT competition 2017. In: Balyo, T., Heule, M., Järvisalo, M. (eds.) Proceedings of SAT Competition 2017 - Solver and Benchmark Descriptions. Department of Computer Science Series of Publications B, vol. B-2017-1, pp. 14–15. University of Helsinki (2017)

9. Biere, A.: CaDiCaL at the SAT Race 2019. In: Heule, M., Järvisalo, M., Suda, M. (eds.) Proceedings of SAT Race 2019 - Solver and Benchmark Descriptions. Department of Computer Science Series of Publications B, vol. B-2019-1, pp. 8–9. University of Helsinki (2019)

10. Bulygin, S., Buchmann, J.: Algebraic cryptanalysis of the round-reduced and side channel analysis of the Full PRINTCipher-48. In: Lin, D., Tsudik, G., Wang, X. (eds.) CANS 2011. LNCS, vol. 7092, pp. 54–75. Springer, Heidelberg (2011). https://doi.org/10.1007/978-3-642-25513-7_6

11. Cai, S., Luo, C., Su, K.: CCAnr: a configuration checking based local search solver for non-random satisfiability. In: Heule, M., Weaver, S. (eds.) SAT 2015. LNCS, vol. 9340, pp. 1–8. Springer, Cham (2015). https://doi.org/10.1007/978-3-319-24318-4_1

12. Cai, S., Su, K.: Local search for Boolean satisfiability with configuration checking and subscore. Artif. Intell. **204**, 75–98 (2013)

13. Chakraborty, S., Meel, K.S., Vardi, M.Y.: A scalable approximate model counter. In: Schulte, C. (ed.) CP 2013. LNCS, vol. 8124, pp. 200–216. Springer, Heidelberg (2013). https://doi.org/10.1007/978-3-642-40627-0_18

14. Chen, J.: Building a Hybrid SAT solver via conflict-driven, look-ahead and XOR reasoning techniques. In: Kullmann, O. (ed.) SAT 2009. LNCS, vol. 5584, pp. 298–311. Springer, Heidelberg (2009). https://doi.org/10.1007/978-3-642-02777-2_29

15. Eén, N., Biere, A.: Effective Preprocessing in SAT Through Variable and Clause Elimination. In: Bacchus, F., Walsh, T. (eds.) SAT 2005. LNCS, vol. 3569, pp. 61–75. Springer, Heidelberg (2005). https://doi.org/10.1007/11499107_5

16. Fazekas, K., Biere, A., Scholl, C.: Incremental inprocessing in SAT solving. In: Janota, M., Lynce, I. (eds.) SAT 2019. LNCS, vol. 11628, pp. 136–154. Springer, Cham (2019). https://doi.org/10.1007/978-3-030-24258-9_9

17. Fröhlich, A., Biere, A., Wintersteiger, C.M., Hamadi, Y.: Stochastic local search for satisfiability modulo theories. In: Proceedings of AAAI. AAAI, January 2015. https://www.microsoft.com/en-us/research/publication/stochastic-local-search-for-satisfiability-modulo-theories/

18. Gwynne, M., Kullmann, O.: On SAT representations of XOR constraints. In: Dediu, A.-H., Martín-Vide, C., Sierra-Rodríguez, J.-L., Truthe, B. (eds.) LATA 2014. LNCS, vol. 8370, pp. 409–420. Springer, Cham (2014). https://doi.org/10.1007/978-3-319-04921-2_33

19. Heule, M.J.H.: SmArT solving: tools and techniques for satisfiability solvers. Ph.D. thesis, Delft University of Technology, Netherlands (2008). http://resolver.tudelft. nl/uuid:d41522e3-690a-4eb7-a352-652d39d7ac81
20. Heule, M., van Maaren, H.: Aligning CNF- and equivalence-reasoning. In: Hoos, H.H., Mitchell, D.G. (eds.) SAT 2004. LNCS, vol. 3542, pp. 145–156. Springer, Heidelberg (2005). https://doi.org/10.1007/11527695_12
21. Heule, M.J.H., Kauers, M., Seidl, M.: Local search for fast matrix multiplication. CoRR abs/1903.11391 (2019). http://arxiv.org/abs/1903.11391
22. Heule, M.J.H., Kauers, M., Seidl, M.: New ways to multiply 3 × 3-matrices. J. Symb. Comput. **104**, 899–916 (2021). https://doi.org/10.1016/j.jsc.2020.10.003
23. Heule, M.J.H., Kullmann, O., Marek, V.W.: Solving and verifying the Boolean Pythagorean triples problem via cube-and-conquer. CoRR abs/1605.00723 (2016). http://arxiv.org/abs/1605.00723
24. Ishtaiwi, A., Thornton, J., Sattar, A., Pham, D.N.: Neighbourhood clause weight redistribution in local search for SAT. In: van Beek, P. (ed.) CP 2005. LNCS, vol. 3709, pp. 772–776. Springer, Heidelberg (2005). https://doi.org/10.1007/11564751_62
25. Järvisalo, M., Biere, A.: Reconstructing solutions after blocked clause elimination. In: Strichman, O., Szeider, S. (eds.) SAT 2010. LNCS, vol. 6175, pp. 340–345. Springer, Heidelberg (2010). https://doi.org/10.1007/978-3-642-14186-7_30
26. Järvisalo, M., Heule, M.J.H., Biere, A.: Inprocessing rules. In: Gramlich, B., Miller, D., Sattler, U. (eds.) IJCAR 2012. LNCS (LNAI), vol. 7364, pp. 355–370. Springer, Heidelberg (2012). https://doi.org/10.1007/978-3-642-31365-3_28
27. Knuth, D.E.: The Art of Computer Programming, vol. 4, Fascicle 6: Satisfiability. Addison-Wesley Professional, 1st edn. (2015)
28. Kuehlmann, A., Paruthi, V., Krohm, F., Ganai, M.K.: Robust Boolean reasoning for equivalence checking and functional property verification. IEEE Trans. Comput.-Aided Des. Integr. Circ. Syst. **21**(12), 1377–1394 (2002)
29. Kyrillidis, A., Shrivastava, A., Vardi, M.Y., Zhang, Z.: FourierSAT: a Fourier expansion-based algebraic framework for solving hybrid Boolean constraints (2020)
30. Kyrillidis, A., Vardi, M.Y., Zhang, Z.: On continuous local BDD-based search for hybrid SAT solving (2020)
31. Leventi-Peetz, A., Zendel, O., Lennartz, W., Weber, K.: CryptoMiniSat switches-optimization for solving cryptographic instances. In: Berre, D.L., Järvisalo, M. (eds.) Proceedings of Pragmatics of SAT 2015 and 2018. EPiC Series in Computing, vol. 59, pp. 79–93. EasyChair (2019). https://easychair.org/publications/paper/5g6S
32. Luo, C., Cai, S., Wu, W., Su, K.: Double configuration checking in stochastic local search for satisfiability, pp. 2703–2709 (2014)
33. Pham, D.N., Thornton, J., Sattar, A.: Building structure into local search for SAT. In: Veloso, M.M. (ed.) IJCAI 2007, Proceedings of the 20th International Joint Conference on Artificial Intelligence, 6–12 January 2007, Hyderabad, India, pp. 2359–2364 (2007). http://ijcai.org/Proceedings/07/Papers/380.pdf
34. Selman, B., Kautz, H., Cohen, B.: Local search strategies for satisfiability testing. Cliques, Coloring, and Satisfiability DIMACS Series in Discrete Mathematics and Theoretical Computer Science, pp. 521–531 (1996). https://doi.org/10.1090/dimacs/026/25
35. Soos, M., Gocht, S., Meel, K.S.: Tinted, Detached, and Lazy CNF-XOR Solving and Its Applications to Counting and Sampling. In: Lahiri, S.K., Wang, C. (eds.) CAV 2020. LNCS, vol. 12224, pp. 463–484. Springer, Cham (2020). https://doi.org/10.1007/978-3-030-53288-8_22

36. Soos, M., Kulkarni, R., Meel, K.S.: CrystalBall: gazing in the Black box of SAT solving. In: Janota, M., Lynce, I. (eds.) SAT 2019. LNCS, vol. 11628, pp. 371–387. Springer, Cham (2019). https://doi.org/10.1007/978-3-030-24258-9_26
37. Soos, M., Meel, K.S.: BIRD: engineering an efficient CNF-XOR SAT solver and its applications to approximate model counting. In: AAAI, pp. 1592–1599. AAAI Press (2019). http://dblp.uni-trier.de/db/conf/aaai/aaai2019.html#SoosM19
38. Soos, M., Nohl, K., Castelluccia, C.: Extending SAT solvers to cryptographic problems. In: Kullmann, O. (ed.) SAT 2009. LNCS, vol. 5584, pp. 244–257. Springer, Heidelberg (2009). https://doi.org/10.1007/978-3-642-02777-2_24
39. Thornton, J., Pham, D.N., Bain, S., Jr, V.F.: Additive versus multiplicative clause weighting for SAT. In: McGuinness, D.L., Ferguson, G. (eds.) Proceedings of the Nineteenth National Conference on Artificial Intelligence, Sixteenth Conference on Innovative Applications of Artificial Intelligence, 25–29 July 2004, San Jose, California, USA, pp. 191–196. AAAI Press/The MIT Press (2004). http://www.aaai.org/Library/AAAI/2004/aaai04-031.php
40. Tseitin, G.S.: On the complexity of derivation in propositional calculus. Automation of Reasoning, pp. 466–483 (1983)
41. Zhang, W., Sun, Z., Zhu, Q., Li, G., Cai, S., Xiong, Y., Zhang, L.: NLocalSAT: boosting local search with solution prediction. In: Proceedings of the Twenty-Ninth International Joint Conference on Artificial Intelligence, July 2020

A Fast Algorithm for SAT in Terms of Formula Length

Junqiang Peng and Mingyu Xiao$^{(\boxtimes)}$ (iD)

School of Computer Science and Engineering, University of Electronic Science and Technology of China, Chengdu, China

Abstract. In this paper, we prove that the general CNF satisfiability problem can be solved in $O^*(1.0646^L)$ time, where L is the length of the input CNF-formula (*i.e.*, the total number of literals in the formula), which improves the current bound $O^*(1.0652^L)$ given by Chen and Liu 12 years ago. Our algorithm is a standard branch-and-search algorithm analyzed by using the measure-and-conquer method. We avoid the bottleneck in Chen and Liu's algorithm by simplifying the branching operation for 4-degree variables and carefully analyzing the branching operation for 5-degree variables. To simplify case-analyses, we also introduce a general framework for analysis, which may be able to be used in other problems.

Keywords: Parameterized algorithms · Satisfiability · Measure-and-conquer

1 Introduction

Propositional Satisfiability is the problem of determining, for a formula of the propositional calculus, if there is an assignment of truth values to its variables for which that formula evaluates to true. By SAT, we mean the problem of propositional satisfiability for formulas in conjunctive normal form (CNF) [5]. The SAT problem is the first problem proved to be NP-complete [4] and it plays an important role in computational complexity and artificial intelligence [1]. There are numerous investigations on this problem in different fields, such as approximation algorithms, randomized algorithms, heuristic algorithms, and exact and parameterized algorithms. In this paper, we study parameterized algorithms for SAT parameterized by the input length.

To measure the running time bound for the SAT problem, there are three frequently used parameters: the number of variables n, the number of clauses m, and the input length L. The input length L is defined as the sum of the number of literals in each clause. The number of variables n should be the most basic parameter. The simple brute force algorithm to try all 2^n possible assignments of the n variables will get the running time bound of $O^*(2^n)$.[1] After decades of

---

[1] The O^* notation supervises all polynomial factors, i.e., $f(n) = O^*(g(n))$ means $f(n) = O(g(n)n^{O(1)})$.

© Springer Nature Switzerland AG 2021
C.-M. Li and F. Manyà (Eds.): SAT 2021, LNCS 12831, pp. 436–452, 2021.
https://doi.org/10.1007/978-3-030-80223-3_30

Table 1. Previous and our upper bound for SAT

Running time bounds	References
$O^*(1.0927^L)$	Van Gelder 1988 [16]
$O^*(1.0801^L)$	Kullmann and Luckhardt 1997 [12]
$O^*(1.0758^L)$	Hirsch 1998 [9]
$O^*(1.074^L)$	Hirsch 2000 [10]
$O^*(1.0663^L)$	Wahlström 2005 [17]
$O^*(1.0652^L)$	Chen and Liu 2009 [2]
$O^*(1.0646^L)$	**This paper 2021**

hard work, no one can break this trivial bound. The Strong Exponential Time Hypothesis conjectures that the SAT problem cannot be solved in time $O^*(c^n)$ for some constant $c < 2$ [11]. For a restricted version, the k-SAT problem (the length of each clause in the formula is bounded by a constant k), better results have been developed. For example, 3-SAT can be solved in $O^*(1.3279^n)$ time [13], 4-SAT can be solved in $O^*(1.4986^n)$ time [13], and k-SAT can be solved in $O^*(c(k)^n)$ time for some value $c(k)$ depending on k [13]. When it comes to the parameter m, Monien et al. first gave an algorithm with time complexity $O^*(1.260^m)$ in 1981 [14]. Later, the bound was improved to $O^*(1.239^m)$ by Hirsch in 1998 [9], and then improved to $O^*(1.234^m)$ by Yamamoto in 2005 [19]. Now the best result is $O^*(1.2226^m)$ obtained by Chu, Xiao, and Zhang [3].

The input length L is another important and frequently studied parameter. It is probably the most precise parameter to describe the input CNF-Formula. From the first algorithm with running time bound $O^*(1.0927^L)$ by Van Gelder in 1988 [16], the result was improved several times. In 1997, the bound was improved to $O^*(1.0801)$ by Kullmann and Luckhardt [12]. In 1998, the bound was improved to $O^*(1.0758^L)$ by Hirsch [9], and improved again by Hirsch to $O^*(1.074^L)$ in 2000 [10]. Then Wahlström gave an $O^*(1.0663^L)$-time algorithm in 2005 [17]. In 2009, Chen and Liu [2] used the measure-and-conquer method to analyze the running time bound and further improved the result to $O^*(1.0652^L)$. We list the major progress and our result in Table 1.

Our algorithm, as well as most algorithms for the SAT problem, is based on the branch-and-search process. The idea of branch-and-search is simple and practical: for a given CNF-formula $\mathcal{F}$, we iteratively branch on a variable or literal x into two branches by assigning value 1 or 0 to it. Let $\mathcal{F}_{x=1}$ and $\mathcal{F}_{\overline{x}=1}$ be the resulted CNF-formula by assigning value 1 and 0 to x, respectively. It holds that $\mathcal{F}$ is satisfiable if and only if at least one of $\mathcal{F}_{x=1}$ and $\mathcal{F}_{\overline{x}=1}$ is satisfiable. To get a running time bound, we need to analyze how much the parameter L can decrease in each branch. To break some bottlenecks in direct analysis, some references [2,17] analyzed the algorithm based on some other measures and gave the relation between the new measure and L. The current best result [2] was obtained by using the measure-and-conquer method, which is also to use a new measure. This is the first time to bring the measure-and-conquer method to this research line. In this paper, we further improve the running time bound by still using the measure-and-conquer method. Similar to many measure-and-conquer algorithms, our algorithm and the algorithm in [2] deal with variables from high degree to low degree. The algorithm in [2] carefully analyzed branching operations for variables of degree 4. Our algorithm will simplify the branching operation for 4-degree variables and carefully analyze the branching operation for 5-degree variables. Finally, we can improve the bound to $O^*(1.0646^L)$.

Due to the limited space, the proofs of some lemmas marked with (*) are omitted, which can be found in the full version of this paper [15].

2   Preliminaries

Let $V = \{x_1, x_2, ..., x_n\}$ denote a set of n boolean *variables*. Each variable x_i ($i \in \{1, 2, ..., n\}$) has two corresponding *literals*: positive literal x_i and negative literal $\overline{x_i}$ (we use $\overline{x}$ to denote the negation of a literal x, and $\overline{\overline{x}} = x$). A *clause* on V consists of some literals on V. Note that we allow a clause to be empty. A clause $\{z_1, z_2, \ldots, z_q\}$ is also simply written as $z_1 z_2 \ldots z_q$. Thus, we use zC to denote the clause containing literal z and all literals in clause C. We also use $C_1 C_2$ to denote the clause containing all literals in clauses C_1 and C_2. We use $\overline{C}$ to denote a clause that contains the negation of every literal in clause C. That is, if $C = z_1 z_2 ... z_q$, then $\overline{C} = \overline{z_1} \overline{z_2} ... \overline{z_q}$. A *CNF-formula* on V is the conjunction of a set of clauses $\mathcal{F} = \{C_1, C_2, ..., C_m\}$. When we say a variable x is contained in a clause (or a formula), it means that the clause (at least one clause of the formula) contains a literal x or its negative $\overline{x}$.

An assignment for V is a map $A : V \rightarrow \{0, 1\}$. A clause C_j is *satisfied* by an assignment if and only if there exists at least one literal in C_j such that the assignment makes its value 1. A CNF-formula is *satisfied* by an assignment A if and only if each clause in it is satisfied by A. We say a CNF-formula is *satisfiable* if it can be satisfied by at least one assignment. We may assign value 0 or 1 to a literal, which is indeed to assign a value to its variable to make the corresponding literal 0 or 1.

A literal z is called an (i, j)-*literal* (resp., an (i^+, j)-*literal* or (i^-, j)-*literal*) in a formula $\mathcal{F}$ if z appears i (resp. at least i or at most i) times and $\overline{z}$ appears j times in the formula $\mathcal{F}$. Similarly, we can define (i, j^+)-literal, (i, j^-)-literal, (i^+, j^+)-literal, (i^-, j^-)-literal, and so on. Note that literal z is an (i, j)-literal if and only if literal $\overline{z}$ is a (j, i)-literal. A variable x is an (i, j)-*variable* if the positive literal x is an (i, j)-literal. For a variable or a literal x in formula $\mathcal{F}$, the *degree* of it, denoted by $deg(x)$, is the number of x appearing in $\mathcal{F}$ plus the number of $\overline{x}$ appearing in $\mathcal{F}$, i.e., $deg(x) = i + j$ for an (i, j)-variable or (i, j)-literal x. A d-*variable* (resp., d^+-*variable* or d^--*variable*) is a variable with the degree exactly d (resp., at least d or at most d). The degree of a formula $\mathcal{F}$ is the maximum degree of all variables in $\mathcal{F}$. For a clause or a formula C, the set of variables whose literal appears in C is denoted by $var(C)$.

The *length* of a clause C, denoted by $|C|$, is the number of literals in C. A clause is a k-*clause* or k^+-*clause* if the length of it is k or at least k. We use

$L(\mathcal{F})$ to indicate the length of a formula $\mathcal{F}$. It is the sum of the lengths of all clauses in $\mathcal{F}$, which is also the sum of the degrees of all variables in $\mathcal{F}$. A formula $\mathcal{F}$ is called k-*CNF formula* if each clause in $\mathcal{F}$ has a length of at most k.

In a formula $\mathcal{F}$, a literal x is called a *neighbor* of a literal z if there is a clause containing both z and x. The set of neighbors of a literal z in a formula $\mathcal{F}$ is denoted by $N(z, \mathcal{F})$. We also use $N^{(k)}(x, \mathcal{F})$ (resp., $N^{(k+)}(z, \mathcal{F})$) to denote the neighbors of z in k-clauses (resp., k^+-clauses) in $\mathcal{F}$, i.e., for any $z' \in N^{(k)}(z, \mathcal{F})$ (resp., $z' \in N^{(k+)}(z, \mathcal{F})$), there exists a k-clause (resp., k^+-clause) containing both z and z'.

3   Branch-and-Search and Measure-and-Conquer

Our algorithm is a standard branch-and-search algorithm, which first applies some reduction rules to reduce the instance as much as possible and then searches for a solution by branching. The branching operations may exponentially increase the running time. We will use a measure to evaluate the size of the search tree generated in the algorithm. For the SAT problem, the number of variables or clauses of the formula is a commonly used measure. More fundamentals of branching heuristics about the SAT problem can be found in [1].

We use $T(\mu)$ to denote the maximum size or number of leaves of the search tree generated by the algorithm for any instance with the measure being at most μ. For a branching operation that branches on the current instance into l branches with the measure decreasing by at least a_i in the i-th branch, we get a a recurrence relation

$$T(\mu) \leq T(\mu - a_1) + T(\mu - a_2) + \cdots + T(\mu - a_l).$$

The recurrence relation can also be simply represented by a *branching vector* $[a_1, a_2, \ldots, a_l]$. The largest root of the function $f(x) = 1 - \sum_{i=1}^{l} x^{-a_i}$ is called the *branching factor* of the recurrence. If the maximum branching factor for all branching operations in the algorithm is at most γ, then $T(\mu) = O(\gamma^\mu)$. If on each node of the search tree, the algorithm runs in polynomial time, then the total running time of the algorithm is $O^*(\gamma^\mu)$. For two branching vectors $\mathbf{a} = [a_1, a_2, \ldots, a_l]$ and $\mathbf{b} = [b_1, b_2, \ldots, b_l]$, if $a_i \geq b_i$ holds for all $i = 1, 2 \ldots, l$, then the branching factor of $\mathbf{a}$ is not greater than that of $\mathbf{b}$. For this case, we say $\mathbf{b}$ *dominates* $\mathbf{a}$. This property will be used in many places to simplify some arguments in the paper. More details about analyzing recurrences can be found in the monograph [8].

The measure-and-conquer method [7] is a powerful tool to analyze branch-and-search algorithms. The main idea of the method is to adopt a new measure in the analysis of the algorithm. For example, instead of using the number of variables as the measure, it may set weights to different variables and use the sum of all variable weights as the measure. This method may be able to catch more structural properties and then get further improvements. Nowadays, the fastest exact algorithms for many NP-hard problems were designed by using this method. In this paper, we will also use the measure-and-conquer method.

We introduce a weight to each variable in the formula according to the degree of the variable, $w \colon \mathbb{Z}^+ \to \mathbb{R}^+$, where $\mathbb{Z}^+$ and $\mathbb{R}^+$ denote the sets of nonnegative integers and nonnegative reals, respectively. Let w_i denote the weight of a variable with degree i. A variable with lower degree will not receive a higher weight. i.e., $w_i \geq w_{i-1}$. In our algorithm, the measure of a formula $\mathcal{F}$ is defined as

$$\mu(\mathcal{F}) = \sum_x w_{deg(x)}. \tag{1}$$

In other words, $\mu(\mathcal{F})$ is the sum of the weight of all variables in $\mathcal{F}$. Let n_i denote the number of i-variables in $\mathcal{F}$. Then we also have that $\mu(\mathcal{F}) = \sum_i w_i n_i$.

One important step is to set the value of weight w_i. Different values of w_i will generate different branching vectors and factors. We need to find a good setting of w_i so that the worst branching factor is as small as possible. We will get the value of w_i by solving a quasiconvex program after listing all our branching vectors. However, we pre-specify some requirements of the weights to simplify arguments. Some similar assumptions were used in previous measure-and-conquer algorithms. We set the weight such that

$$\begin{aligned} & w_1 = w_2 = 0, \\ & 0 < w_3 < 2, w_4 = 2w_3, \text{ and} \\ & w_i = i \text{ for } i \geq 5. \end{aligned} \tag{2}$$

We use δ_i to denote the difference between w_i and w_{i-1} for $i > 0$, i.e., $\delta_i = w_i - w_{i-1}$. By (2), we have

$$w_3 = \delta_3 = \delta_4. \tag{3}$$

We also assume that

$$\begin{aligned} & \delta_i \leq \delta_{i-1} \text{ for } i \geq 3, \text{ and} \\ & w_3 \geq \delta_5. \end{aligned} \tag{4}$$

Under these assumptions, it holds that $w_i \leq i$ for each i. Thus, we have

$$\mu(\mathcal{F}) \leq L(\mathcal{F}). \tag{5}$$

This tells us that if we can get a running time bound of $O^*(c^{\mu(\mathcal{F})})$ for a real number c, then we also get a running time bound of $O^*(c^{L(\mathcal{F})})$ for this problem. To obtain a running time bound in terms of the formula length $L(\mathcal{F})$, we consider the measure $\mu(\mathcal{F})$ and show how much the measure $\mu(\mathcal{F})$ decreases in the branching operations of our algorithm and find the worst branching factor among all branching vectors.

4 The Algorithm

We will first introduce our algorithm and then analyze its running time bound by using the measure-and-conquer method. Our algorithm consists of reduction operations and branching operations. When no reduction operations can be applied anymore, the algorithm will search for a solution by branching. We first introduce our reduction rules.

4.1   Reduction Rules

We have ten reduction rules. They are well-known and frequently used in the literature (see [2,17] for examples). So we may omit the proofs of the correctness of some rules. We introduce the reduction rules in the order as stated and a reduction rule will be applied in our algorithm only when all previous reduction rules can not be applied on the instance.

R-Rule 1 (Elimination of duplicated literals).   *If a clause C contains duplicated literals z, remove all but one z in C.*

R-Rule 2 (Elimination of subsumptions).   *If there are two clauses C and D such that $C \subseteq D$, remove clause D.*

R-Rule 3 (Elimination of tautology).   *If a clause C contains two opposite literals z and $\bar{z}$, remove clause C.*

R-Rule 4 (Elimination of 1-clauses and pure literals).   *If there is a 1-clause $\{x\}$ or a $(1^+, 0)$-literal x, assign $x = 1$.*

Davis-Putnam Resolution, proposed in [6], is a classic and frequently used technology for SAT. Let $\mathcal{F}$ be a CNF-formula and x be a variable in $\mathcal{F}$. Assume that clauses containing literal x are $xC_1, xC_2, ..., xC_a$ and clauses containing literal $\bar{x}$ are $\bar{x}D_1, \bar{x}D_2, ..., \bar{x}D_b$. A *Davis-Putnam resolution* on x is to construct a new CNF-formula $DP_x(\mathcal{F})$ by the following method: initially $DP_x(\mathcal{F}) = \mathcal{F}$; add new clauses C_iD_j for each $1 \leq i \leq a$ and $1 \leq j \leq b$; and remove $xC_1, xC_2, ..., xC_a, \bar{x}D_1, \bar{x}D_2, ..., \bar{x}D_b$ from the formula. It is known that

Proposition 1 ([6]). *A CNF-formula $\mathcal{F}$ is satisfiable if and only if $DP_x(\mathcal{F})$ is satisfiable.*

In the resolution operation, each new clause C_iD_j is called a *resolvent*. A resolvent is *trivial* if it contains both a literal and the negation of it. Since trivial resolvents will always be satisfied, we can simply delete trivial resolvents from the instance directly. So when we do resolutions, we assume that all trivial resolvents will be deleted.

R-Rule 5 (Trivial resolution).   *If there is a variable x with at most one non-trivial resolvent, then apply resolution on x.*

R-Rule 6 ([2]). *If there are a 2-clause z_1z_2 and a clause C containing both z_1 and $\overline{z_2}$, then remove $\overline{z_2}$ from C.*

R-Rule 7. *If there are two clauses $z_1z_2C_1$ and $z_1\overline{z_2}C_2$, where literal $\overline{z_2}$ appears in no other clauses, then remove z_1 from clause $z_1z_2C_1$.*

Lemma 1. *(*) Let $\mathcal{F}$ be a CNF-formula and $\mathcal{F}'$ be the resulting formula after applying R-Rule 7 on $\mathcal{F}$. Then $\mathcal{F}$ is satisfiable if and only if $\mathcal{F}'$ is satisfiable.*

R-Rule 8 ([2]). *If there is a 2-clause z_1z_2 and a clause $\overline{z_1z_2}C$ such that literal $\overline{z_1}$ appears in no other clauses, remove the clause z_1z_2 from $\mathcal{F}$.*

R-Rule 9 ([2]). *If there is a 2-clause $z_1 z_2$ such that either literal z_1 appears only in this clause or there is another 2-clause $\overline{z_1}\overline{z_2}$, then replace z_1 with $\overline{z_2}$ in $\mathcal{F}$ and then apply R-Rule 3 as often as possible.*

R-Rule 10 ([2]). *If there are two clauses CD_1 and CD_2 such that $|D_1|, |D_2| \geq 1$ and $|C| \geq 2$, then remove CD_1 and CD_2 from $\mathcal{F}$, and add three new clauses xC, $\overline{x}D_1$, and $\overline{x}D_2$, where x is a new 3-variable.*

This is like the Davis-Putnam resolution in reverse and thus it is correct.

Definition 1 (Reduced formulas). *A CNF-formula $\mathcal{F}$ is called reduced, if none of the above reduction rules can be applied on it.*

Our algorithm will first iteratively apply above reduction rules in the order to get a reduced formula. We will use $R(\mathcal{F})$ to denote the resulting reduced formula obtained from $\mathcal{F}$. Next, we show some properties of reduced formulas.

Lemma 2. *(*) In a reduced CNF-formula $\mathcal{F}$, all variables are 3^+-variables.*

Lemma 3. *(*) In a reduced CNF-formula $\mathcal{F}$, if there is a 2-clause xy, then no other clause in $\mathcal{F}$ contains xy, $\overline{x}y$, or $x\overline{y}$.*

Lemma 4. *(*) In a reduced CNF-formula $\mathcal{F}$, if there is a clause xyC, then*

(i) no other clause contains xy;
(ii) no other clause contains $\overline{x}y$ or $\overline{x}\overline{y}$ if x is a 3-variable.

Lemma 5. *(*) In a reduced CNF-formula $\mathcal{F}$, if there is $(1,i)$-literal x and xC is the only clause containing x, then*

(i) $|C| \geq 2$;
(ii) all variables in C are different from all variables in $N^{(2)}(\overline{x}, F)$, that is, if $y \in N^{(2)}(\overline{x}, F)$, then $y, \overline{y} \notin C$.

4.2   Branching Rules and the Algorithm

After getting a reduced formula, we will search for a solution by branching. In a branching operation, we will generate two smaller CNF-formulas such that the original formula is satisfiable if and only if at least one of the two new formulas is satisfiable. The two smaller formulas are generated by specifying the value of a set of literals in the original formula.

The simplest branching rule is that we pick up a variable or literal x from $\mathcal{F}$ and branch into two branches $\mathcal{F}_{x=1}$ and $\mathcal{F}_{x=0}$, where $\mathcal{F}_{x=1}$ and $\mathcal{F}_{x=0}$ are the formulas after assigning $x = 1$ and $x = 0$ in $\mathcal{F}$, respectively. When the picked literal x is a $(1, 1^+)$-literal, we will apply a stronger branching. Assume that xC is the only clause containing x. Then we branch into two branches $\mathcal{F}_{x=1\ \&\ C=0}$ and $\mathcal{F}_{x=0}$, where $\mathcal{F}_{x=1\ \&\ C=0}$ is the resulting formula after assigning 1 to x and 0 to all literals in C in $\mathcal{F}$. The correctness of this branching operation is also easy to observe. Only when all literals in C are assigned 0, we need to assign 1 to x.

Algorithm 1: SAT($\mathcal{F}$)

Input: a CNF-formula $\mathcal{F}$

Output: 1 or 0 to indicate the satisfiability of $\mathcal{F}$

Step 1. If $\mathcal{F} = \emptyset$, return 1. If $\mathcal{F}$ contains an empty clause, return 0.

Step 2. If $\mathcal{F}$ is not a reduced CNF-formula, iteratively apply the reduction rules to reduce it.

Step 3. If there is a d-variable x with $d \geq 6$, return SAT($\mathcal{F}_{x=1}$)$\vee$SAT($\mathcal{F}_{x=0}$).

Step 4. If there is a $(1,4)$-literal x (assume xC is the only clause containing x), return SAT($\mathcal{F}_{x=1 \,\&\, C=0}$)$\vee$SAT($\mathcal{F}_{x=0}$).

Step 5. If there is a 5-variable x contained in a 2-clause, return SAT($\mathcal{F}_{x=1}$)$\vee$SAT($\mathcal{F}_{x=0}$).

Step 6. If there is a 5-variable x contained in a 4^+-clause, return SAT($\mathcal{F}_{x=1}$)$\vee$SAT($\mathcal{F}_{x=0}$).

Step 7. If there is a clause containing both a 5-variable x and a 4^--variable, return SAT($\mathcal{F}_{x=1}$)$\vee$SAT($\mathcal{F}_{x=0}$).

Step 8. If there are still some 5-variables, then $\mathcal{F} = \mathcal{F}^* \wedge \mathcal{F}'$, where $\mathcal{F}^*$ is a 3-CNF with $var(\mathcal{F}^*)$ be the set of 5-variables in $\mathcal{F}$ and $var(\mathcal{F}^*) \cap var(\mathcal{F}') = \emptyset$. We return SAT($\mathcal{F}^*$) $\wedge$ SAT($\mathcal{F}'$) and solve $\mathcal{F}^*$ by using the 3-SAT algorithm by Liu [13].

Step 9. If there is a $(1,3)$-literal x (assume xC is the only clause containing x), return SAT($\mathcal{F}_{x=1 \,\&\, C=0}$)$\vee$SAT($\mathcal{F}_{x=0}$).

Step 10. If there is a $(2,2)$-literal x, return SAT($\mathcal{F}_{x=1}$)$\vee$SAT($\mathcal{F}_{x=0}$).

Step 11. Apply the algorithm by Wahlström [18] to solve the instance.

The main steps of our algorithm for the SAT problem are given in Algorithm 1. The algorithm will execute one step only when all previous steps can not be applied. In Step 2, the algorithm first reduces the formula by applying the reduction rules. Step 3 will branch on a variable of degree ≥ 6 if it exists. Steps 4–8 deal with 5-variables. Note that if Steps 1–7 do not apply, then $\mathcal{F}$ can be written as $\mathcal{F} = \mathcal{F}^* \wedge \mathcal{F}'$, where $\mathcal{F}^*$ is a 3-CNF with $var(\mathcal{F}^*)$ be the set of 5-variables in $\mathcal{F}$ and $var(\mathcal{F}^*) \cap var(\mathcal{F}') = \emptyset$. So we can do Step 8. Steps 9–10 deal with 4-variables. When the algorithm comes to the last step, all variables must have a degree of 3 and the algorithm deals with this special case.

We compare our algorithm with the previous algorithm by Chen and Liu [2]. We can see that they used a simple and uniform branching rule to deal with variables of degree at least 5 and used careful and complicated branching rules for 4-variables. Their bottlenecks contain one case of branching on $(2,3)$-variables (or $(3,2)$-variables) and one case of dealing with 4-variables. To get further improvements, we carefully design and analyze the branching rules for 5-variables to avoid one previous bottleneck, and also refine the branching rules for 4-variables.

5   Framework of the Analysis

We use the measure-and-conquer method to analyze the running time bound of our algorithm, and adopt $\mu(\mathcal{F})$ defined in (1) as the measure to construct recurrence relations for our branching operations. Before analyzing each detailed step of the algorithm, we first introduce the general framework of our analysis.

In each sub-branch of a branching operation, we assign value 1 or 0 to some literals and remove some clauses and literals. If we assign value 1 to a literal x in the formula $\mathcal{F}$, then we will remove all clauses containing x and all $\bar{x}$ literals from the clauses containing $\bar{x}$. The assignment and removing together are called an *assignment operation*. We may assign values to more than one literal and we do assignment operations for each literal. Let S be a subset of literals. We use $\mathcal{F}_{S=1}$ to denote the resulting formula after assigning 1 to each literal in S and doing assignment operations. Note that $\mathcal{F}_{S=1}$ may not be a reduced formula and we will apply our reduction rules to reduce it. We use $\mathcal{F}'_{S=1}$ to denote the reduced formula obtained from $\mathcal{F}_{S=1}$, i.e., $\mathcal{F}'_{S=1} = R(\mathcal{F}_{S=1})$. We analyze how much we can reduce the measure in each branch by establishing some lower bounds for

$$\Delta_S = \mu(\mathcal{F}) - \mu(\mathcal{F}'_{S=1}).$$

We also define

$$\xi_S^{(1)} = \mu(\mathcal{F}) - \mu(\mathcal{F}_{S=1});$$

$$\xi_S^{(2)} = \mu(\mathcal{F}_{S=1}) - \mu(\mathcal{F}'_{S=1}).$$

Thus, $\Delta_S = \xi_S^{(1)} + \xi_S^{(2)}$.

In a branching operation, we will branch into two sub branches. Assume that the set of literals in S_1 are assigned the value in the first sub branch and the set of literals in S_2 are assigned the value in the second sub branch. If we can show

$$\min(\Delta_{S_1}, \Delta_{S_2}) \geq a \quad \text{and} \quad \Delta_{S_1} + \Delta_{S_2} \geq b,$$

then we can always get a branching vector covered by one of

$$[a, b-a] \quad and \quad [b-a, a].$$

This technique will be frequently used in our analysis.

5.1   Some Lower Bounds

Next, we show some detailed lower bounds for Δ_S (as well as for $\Delta_{S_1} + \Delta_{S_2}$). We first consider $\xi_S^{(1)}$ and $\xi_S^{(2)}$.

According to the assignment operation, we know that all variables of the literals in S will be deleted in $\mathcal{F}_{S=1}$. So we have a trivial bound

$$\xi_S^{(1)} \geq \sum_{v \in S} w_{deg(v)}. \tag{6}$$

To get better bounds, we first define some notations. For a literal x in a reduced formula $\mathcal{F}$, we define:

- $n_i(x)$: the number of i-variables whose literals appear in $N(x, \mathcal{F})$;

- $n'_i(x)$: the number of i-variables whose literals appear in $N^{(2)}(x,\mathcal{F})$;
- $n''_i(x)$: the number of i-variables whose literals appear in $N^{(3+)}(x,\mathcal{F})$.

Note that by the definition, we always have that $n_i(x) = n'_i(x) + n''_i(x)$.

Next, we give some lower bounds on $\xi_S^{(1)}$, $\xi_S^{(2)}$, and $\Delta_{S_1} + \Delta_{S_2}$, which will be used to prove our main results.

Lemma 6. *(*) Assume that $\mathcal{F}$ is a reduced CNF-formula. Let $S = \{x\}$, where x is a literal in $\mathcal{F}$. It holds that*

$$\xi_S^{(1)} \geq w_{deg(x)} + \sum_{i\geq 3} n_i(x)\delta_i. \tag{7}$$

Lemma 7. *(*) Assume that $\mathcal{F}$ is a reduced CNF-formula of degree d. Let $S = \{x\}$, where x is a $(j, d-j)$-literal in $\mathcal{F}$. It holds that*

$$\xi_S^{(1)} \geq w_d + j\delta_d. \tag{8}$$

Lemma 8. *(*) Assume that $\mathcal{F}$ is a reduced CNF-formula of degree d. Let $S = \{x\}$, where x is a literal in $\mathcal{F}$. It holds that*

$$\xi_S^{(2)} \geq n'_3(\overline{x})w_3 + \sum_{4\leq i\leq d} n'_i(\overline{x})w_{i-1}. \tag{9}$$

Lemma 9. *(*) Assume that $\mathcal{F}$ is a reduced CNF-formula of degree d. Let $S_1 = \{x\}$ and $S_2 = \{\overline{x}\}$, where the corresponding variable of x is a d-variable in $\mathcal{F}$. It holds that*

$$\Delta_{S_1}+\Delta_{S_2} \geq 2w_d+2d\delta_d+(n'_3(x)+n'_3(\overline{x}))(2w_3-2\delta_d)+ \sum_{4\leq i\leq d} (n'_i(x) + n'_i(\overline{x}))(w_i - 2\delta_d). \tag{10}$$

Lemma 10. *(*) Assume that $\mathcal{F}$ is a reduced CNF-formula of degree d. Let x be a $(1, d-1)$-literal and xC be the only clause containing x in $\mathcal{F}$. Let $S = \{x\}\cup\overline{C}$. It holds that*

$$\Delta_S \geq w_d + 2w_3 + \sum_{3\leq i\leq d} n'_i(\overline{x})w_i. \tag{11}$$

Lemma 11. *(*) Assume that $\mathcal{F}$ is a reduced CNF-formula of degree d. Let x be a $(1, d-1)$-literal and xC be the only clause containing x in $\mathcal{F}$. Let $S_1 = \{x\}\cup\overline{C}$ and $S_2 = \{\overline{x}\}$. It holds that*

$$\Delta_{S_1} + \Delta_{S_2} \geq 2w_d + 2w_3 + 2(d-1)\delta_d. \tag{12}$$

Lemma 12. *(*) Assume that $\mathcal{F}$ is a reduced CNF-formula of $d = 5$. Let $S_1 = \{x\}$ and $S_2 = \{\overline{x}\}$, where the corresponding variable of x is a 5-variable in $\mathcal{F}$. If all clauses containing x or $\overline{x}$ are 3^+-clauses, it holds that*

$$\Delta_{S_1} + \Delta_{S_2} \geq 2w_5 + (\sum_{3\leq i\leq 5} (n_i(x) + n_i(\overline{x})))\delta_5 + (\sum_{3\leq i\leq 4} (n_i(x) + n_i(\overline{x})))(w_3 - \delta_5). \tag{13}$$

6   Step Analysis

Equipped with the above lower bounds, we are ready to analyze the branching vector of each step in the algorithm.

6.1   Step 2

In this step, we do not branch and only apply reduction rules to reduce the formula. However, it is still important to show that the measure will never increase when applying reduction rules, and reduction operations use only polynomial time.

Lemma 13. *(*) For any CNF-formula $\mathcal{F}$, it holds that*

$$\mu(R(\mathcal{F})) \leq \mu(\mathcal{F}).$$

Lemma 14. *(*) For any CNF-formula $\mathcal{F}$, we can apply the reduction rules in polynomial time to transfer it to $R(\mathcal{F})$.*

6.2   Step 3

In this step, we branch on a variable x of degree at least 6. The two sub-branches are: $S_1 = \{x\}$; $S_2 = \{\overline{x}\}$. We have the following result:

Lemma 15. *The branching vector generated by Step 3 is covered*

$$[w_6 + \delta_6, w_6 + 11\delta_6] \text{ or } [w_6 + 11\delta_6, w_6 + \delta_6]. \tag{14}$$

Proof. Since R-Rule 4 is not applicable, both x and $\overline{x}$ are $(1^+, 1^+)$-literals. By the condition of this case, we have $d \geq 6$ and $\delta_d = \delta_6$ by (2).

By Lemma 7, we can get that $\Delta_{S_1} \geq \xi_{S_1}^{(1)} \geq w_d + j\delta_d \geq w_6 + \delta_6$ since x is a $(j, d-j)$-literal with $j \geq 1$. Also, we can get $\Delta_{S_2} \geq w_6 + \delta_6$ by the same method.

By Lemma 9, we have that $\Delta_{S_1} + \Delta_{S_2} \geq 2w_d + 2d\delta_d + (n_3'(x) + n_3'(\overline{x}))(2w_3 - 2\delta_d) + \sum_{4 \leq i \leq d} (n_i'(x) + n_i'(\overline{x}))(w_i - 2\delta_d) \geq 2w_6 + 12\delta_d$ since $w_3 > \delta_d$ and $w_i > 2\delta_d$ for $4 \leq i \leq d$.

With $\min(\Delta_{S_1}, \Delta_{S_2}) \geq w_6 + \delta_6$ and $\Delta_{S_1} + \Delta_{S_2} \geq 2w_6 + 12\delta_6$, we can know that the branching vector of this case is covered by $[w_6 + \delta_6, w_6 + 11\delta_6]$ or $[w_6 + 11\delta_6, w_6 + \delta_6]$. □

6.3   Step 4

In this step, the algorithm will consider a $(1, 4)$-literal x. Assume that xC is the only clause containing x. The two sub-branches are: $S_1 = \{x\} \cup \overline{C}$; $S_2 = \{\overline{x}\}$. We have the following result:

Lemma 16. *The branching vector generated by step 4 is covered by*

$$[w_5 + 2w_3, w_5 + 8\delta_5] \text{ or } [w_5 + 8\delta_5, w_5 + 2w_3]. \tag{15}$$

Proof. By Lemma 10, we get that $\Delta_{S_1} \geq w_d + 2w_3 + \sum_{3 \leq i \leq d} n_i'(\overline{x})w_i \geq w_5 + 2w_3$.
By Lemma 7, we have that $\Delta_{S_2} \geq \xi_{S_2}^{(1)} \geq w_d + j\delta_d = w_5 + 4\delta_5$ since $\overline{x}$ is a $(4,1)$-literal.

By Lemma 11, we can get that $\Delta_{S_1} + \Delta_{S_2} \geq 2w_d + 2w_3 + 2(d-1)\delta_d = 2w_5 + 2w_3 + 8\delta_5$.

Since $w_3 < 2$ and $w_5 = 5$ by (2), we have $2w_5 > 5w_3$, i.e., $2w_5 - 4w_3 > w_3$. Since $w_4 = 2w_3$ by (4), we have $2w_5 - 2w_4 > w_3 \Rightarrow 2\delta_5 > w_3$. So $\min(\Delta_{S_1}, \Delta_{S_2}) \geq w_5 + 2w_3$. Since $\Delta_{S_1} + \Delta_{S_2} \geq 2w_5 + 2w_3 + 8\delta_5$, we know that the branching vector of this case is covered by $[w_5 + 2w_3, w_5 + 8\delta_5]$ or $[w_5 + 8\delta_5, w_5 + 2w_3]$. □

6.4   Step 5

In this step, we branch on a 5-variable x such that either x or $\overline{x}$ is in a 2-clause. The two sub-branches are: $S_1 = \{x\}$; $S_2 = \{\overline{x}\}$. We have the following result:

Lemma 17. *The branching vector generated by step 5 is covered by one of*

$$[w_5 + 2\delta_5, w_5 + 4w_3 + 4\delta_5], \ [w_5 + 4w_3 + 4\delta_5, w_5 + 2\delta_5],$$
$$[w_5 + 3\delta_5, w_5 + 2w_3 + 5\delta_5], \ and \ [w_5 + 2w_3 + 5\delta_5, w_5 + 3\delta_5].$$

Proof. We will consider two subcases:

Case 1. There are at least two 2-clause containing literal x or $\overline{x}$. Now it holds that $\sum_{3 \leq i \leq d} n_i'(x) + n_i'(\overline{x}) \geq 2$. By Lemma 7, we get that $\Delta_{S_1} \geq \xi_{S_1}^{(1)} \geq w_d + j\delta_d \geq w_5 + 2\delta_5$ since x is a $(2,3)$-literal or $(3,2)$-literal. In a similar way, we can get that $\Delta_{S_2} \geq w_5 + 2\delta_5$.

By Lemma 9, we have $\Delta_{S_1} + \Delta_{S_2} \geq 2w_d + 2d\delta_d + (n_3'(x) + n_3'(\overline{x}))(2w_3 - 2\delta_d) + \sum_{4 \leq i \leq d}(n_i'(x) + n_i'(\overline{x}))(w_i - 2\delta_d) \geq 2w_5 + 10\delta_5 + \sum_{3 \leq i \leq 5}(n_i'(x) + n_i'(\overline{x}))(2w_3 - 2\delta_5) \geq 2w_5 + 10\delta_5 + 2(w_3 - 2\delta_5) \geq 2w_5 + 4w_3 + 6\delta_5$ since $w_4, w_5 \geq 2w_3$ and $\sum_{3 \leq i \leq 5} n_i'(x) + n_i'(\overline{x}) \geq 2$.

By $\min(\Delta_{S_1}, \Delta_{S_2}) \geq w_5 + 2\delta_5$ and $\Delta_{S_1} + \Delta_{S_2} \geq 2w_5 + 4w_3 + 6\delta_5$, we know that the branching vector of this case is covered by $[w_5 + 2\delta_5, w_5 + 4w_3 + 4\delta_5]$ or $[w_5 + 4w_3 + 4\delta_5, w_5 + 2\delta_5]$.

Case 2. There is only one 2-clause containing literal x or $\overline{x}$. Note that $\sum_{3 \leq i \leq d} n_i'(x) + n_i'(\overline{x}) = 1$. For literal x, it is contained in at least two clauses and at most one of them is 2-clause. So $\sum_{3 \leq i \leq d} n_i(x) \geq 3$ holds.

By Lemma 6, we get that $\Delta_{S_1} \geq \xi_{S_1}^{(1)} \geq w_5 + \sum_{3 \leq i \leq d} n_i(x)\delta_i \geq w_5 + (\sum_{3 \leq i \leq d} n_i(x))\delta_5 \geq w_5 + 3\delta_5$. Similarly, we also can get that $\Delta_{S_2} \geq w_5 + 3\delta_5$. By Lemma 9, we get that $\Delta_{S_1} + \Delta_{S_2} \geq 2w_d + 2d\delta_d + (n_3'(x) + n_3'(\overline{x}))(2w_3 - 2\delta_d) + \sum_{4 \leq i \leq d}(n_i'(x) + n_i'(\overline{x}))(w_i - 2\delta_d) \geq 2w_5 + 10\delta_5 + \sum_{3 \leq i \leq 5}(n_i'(x) + n_i'(\overline{x}))(2w_3 - 2\delta_5) \geq 2w_5 + 10\delta_5 + (2w_3 - 2\delta_5) \geq 2w_5 + 2w_3 + 8\delta_5$ since $w_4, w_5 \geq 2w_3$ and $\sum_{3 \leq i \leq d} n_i'(x) + n_i'(\overline{x}) = 1$.

Since $\min(\Delta_{S_1}, \Delta_{S_2}) \geq w_5 + 3\delta_5$ and $\Delta_{S_1} + \Delta_{S_2} \geq 2w_5 + 2w_3 + 8\delta_5$, we know that the branching vector of this subcase is covered by $[w_5 + 3\delta_5, w_5 + 2w_3 + 5\delta_5]$ or $[w_5 + 2w_3 + 5\delta_5, w_5 + 3\delta_5]$.

These two cases complete the proof. □

6.5 Step 6

In this step, all clauses containing a 5-variable are 3^+-clauses now. We branch on a 5-variable x contained in a 4^+-clause. The two sub-branches are: $S_1 = \{x\}$; $S_2 = \{\overline{x}\}$. We have the following result:

Lemma 18. *The branching vector generated by step 6 is covered by*

$$[w_5 + 4\delta_5, w_5 + 7\delta_5] \ or \ [w_5 + 7\delta_5, w_5 + 4\delta_5]. \tag{16}$$

Proof. Literal x is contained in at least two 3^+-clauses. So $\sum_{3 \leq i \leq d} n_i(x) \geq 4$ holds. By Lemma 6, we get that $\Delta_{S_1} \geq \xi_{S_1}^{(1)} \geq w_5 + (\sum_{3 \leq i \leq d} n_i(x))\delta_d \geq w_5 + 4\delta_5$. Similarly, we get that $\Delta_{S_2} \geq w_5 + 4\delta_5$.

Let m_4 be the number of 4^+-clauses containing x. We have that $\sum_{3 \leq i \leq 5} n_i(x) + n_i'(x) \geq 2(5 - m_4) + 3m_4 \geq 10 + m_4 \geq 11$ since $m_4 \geq 1$. By Lemma 12, We get that $\Delta_{S_1} + \Delta_{S_2} \geq 2w_5 + (\sum_{3 \leq i \leq 5} (n_i(x) + n_i(\overline{x})))\delta_5 + (\sum_{3 \leq i \leq 4} (n_i(x) + n_i(\overline{x})))(w_3 - \delta_5) \geq 2w_5 + 11\delta_5$ since $w_3 \geq \delta_5$.

Since $\min(\Delta_{S_1}, \Delta_{S_2}) \geq w_5 + 4\delta_5$ and $\Delta_{S_1} + \Delta_{S_2} \geq 2w_5 + 11\delta_5$, we know that the branching vector of this case is covered by $[w_5 + 4\delta_5, w_5 + 7\delta_5]$ or $[w_5 + 7\delta_5, w_5 + 4\delta_5]$. $\qquad\square$

6.6 Step 7

In Step 7, all clauses containing a 5-variable are 3-clauses. We branch on a 5-variable x whose literal and a literal of a 4^--variable are in the same clause. The two sub-branches are: $S_1 = \{x\}$; $S_2 = \{\overline{x}\}$. We have that

Lemma 19. *The branching vector generated by step 7 is covered by*

$$[w_5 + 4\delta_5, w_5 + w_3 + 5\delta_5] \ or \ [w_5 + w_3 + 5\delta_5, w_5 + 4\delta_5]. \tag{17}$$

Proof. There is at least one 4^--variable whose literal is in $N(x, \mathcal{F}) \cup N(\overline{x}, \mathcal{F})$. So it holds that $\sum_{3 \leq i \leq 4} (n_i(x) + n_i(\overline{x})) \geq 1$.

For literal x, it is contained in at least two 3-clauses, which means that $\sum_{3 \leq i \leq d} n_i(x) \geq 4$ holds. By Lemma 6, we get that $\Delta_{S_1} \geq \xi_{S_1}^{(1)} \geq w_5 + \sum_{3 \leq i \leq 5} n_i(x)\delta_i \geq w_5 + (\sum_{3 \leq i \leq d} n_i(x))\delta_5 = w_5 + 4\delta_5$. Similarly, we can get that $\Delta_{S_2} \geq w_5 + 4\delta_5$.

By Lemma 12, we get that $\Delta_{S_1} + \Delta_{S_2} \geq 2w_5 + (\sum_{3 \leq i \leq 5} (n_i(x) + n_i(\overline{x})))\delta_5 + (\sum_{3 \leq i \leq 4} (n_i(x) + n_i(\overline{x})))(w_3 - \delta_5) \geq 2w_5 + w_3 + 9\delta_5$ since $\sum_{3 \leq i \leq 4} n_i(x) + n_i(\overline{x}) \geq 1$.

Since $\min(\Delta_{S_1}, \Delta_{S_2}) \geq w_5 + 4\delta_5$ and $\Delta_{S_1} + \Delta_{S_2} \geq 2w_5 + 2w_3 + 8\delta_5$, we know that the branching vector is covered by $[w_5 + 4\delta_5, w_5 + w_3 + 5\delta_5]$ or $[w_5 + w_3 + 5\delta_5, w_5 + 4\delta_5]$. $\qquad\square$

6.7   Step 8

In Step 8, the literals of all 5-variables form a 3-SAT instance $\mathcal{F}^*$. We apply the $O^*(1.3279^n)$-time algorithm in [13] for 3-SAT to solve our problem, where n is the number of variables in the instance. Since $w_5 = 5$, we have that $n = \mu(\mathcal{F}^*)/w_5 = \mu(\mathcal{F}^*)/5$. So the running time for this part will be

$$O^*(1.3279^{\mu(\mathcal{F}^*)/w_5}) = O^*(1.0584^{\mu(\mathcal{F}^*)}).$$

6.8   Step 9

In this step, we branch on a $(1,3)$-literal x. The two sub-branches are: $S_1 = \{x\}$; $S_2 = \{\overline{x}\}$. We have the following result:

Lemma 20. *(*) The branching vector generated by step 9 is covered by*

$$[w_4 + 2w_3, w_4 + 6\delta_4] \ or \ [w_4 + 6\delta_4, w_4 + 2w_3]. \tag{18}$$

6.9   Step 10

In this step, we branch on a $(2,2)$-literal x. The two sub-branches are: $S_1 = \{x\}$; $S_2 = \{\overline{x}\}$. We have the following result:

Lemma 21. *The branching vector generated by step 10 is covered by*

$$[w_4 + 2\delta_4, w_4 + 6\delta_4] \ or \ [w_4 + 6\delta_4, w_4 + 2\delta_4]. \tag{19}$$

Proof. By Lemma 7, we get that $\Delta_{S_1} \geq \xi_{S_1}^{(1)} \geq w_d + j\delta_d = w_4 + 2\delta_4$ since x is a $(2,2)$-literal. Similarity, we can get that $\Delta_{S_2} \geq w_4 + 2\delta_4$.

By Lemma 9, we have $\Delta_{S_1} + \Delta_{S_2} \geq 2w_d + 2d\delta_d + (n_3'(x) + n_3'(\overline{x}))(2w_3 - 2\delta_d) + \sum_{4 \leq i < d} (n_i'(x) + n_i'(\overline{x}))(w_i - 2\delta_d) = 2w_4 + 8\delta_4 + (n_3'(x) + n_3'(\overline{x}))(2w_3 - 2\delta_4) + (n_4'(x) + n_4'(\overline{x}))(w_4 - 2\delta_4) = 2w_4 + 8\delta_4$.

Since $\min(\Delta_{S_1}, \Delta_{S_2}) \geq w_4 + 2\delta_4$ and $\Delta_{S_1} + \Delta_{S_2} \geq 2w_4 + 8\delta_4$, we know that the branching vector is covered by $[w_4 + 2\delta_4, w_4 + 6\delta_4]$ or $[w_4 + 6\delta_4, w_4 + 2\delta_4]$. □

6.10   Step 11

All variables are 3-variables now. We apply the $O^*(1.1279^n)$-time algorithm by Wahlström [18] to solve this special case, where n is the number of variables. For this case, we have that $n = \mu(\mathcal{F})/w_3$. So the running time of this part is

$$O^*((1.1279^{1/w_3})^{\mu(\mathcal{F})}).$$

7   The Final Result

Each one of the branching vectors above will generate a constraint in our quasi-convex program to solve the best value for w_3 and w_4. Let α_i denote the branching factor for branching vector (i) where $14 \leq i \leq 21$. We want to find the minimum value α such that $\alpha \leq \alpha_i$ and $\alpha \leq 1.1279^{1/w_3}$ (generated by Step 11) under the assumptions (2) and (4). By solving this quasiconvex program, we get that $\alpha = 1.0646$ by letting $w_3 = 1.9234132344759123$ and $w_4 = 3.8468264689518246$. Note that $\alpha = 1.0646$ is greater than 1.0584 the branching factor generated in Step 8. So 1.0646 is the worst branching factor in the whole algorithm. By (5), we get the following result.

Theorem 1. *Algorithm 1 solves the SAT problem in $O^*(1.0646^L)$ time.*

Table 2. The weight setting

$w_1 = w_2 = 0$	
$w_3 = 1.9234132344759123$	$\delta_3 = 1.9234132344759123$
$w_4 = 3.8468264689518246$	$\delta_4 = 1.9234132344759123$
$w_5 = 5$	$\delta_5 = 1.1531735310481754$
$w_i = i(i \geq 6)$	$\delta_i = 1(i \geq 6)$

Table 3. The branching vector and factor for each step

Steps	Branching vectors	Branching factors
Step 3	$[w_6 + \delta_6, w_6 + 11\delta_6]$	1.0636
Step 4	$[w_5 + 2w_3, w_5 + 8\delta_5]$	1.0632
Step 5	$[w_5 + 3\delta_5, w_5 + 2w_3 + 5\delta_5]$	1.0618
	$[w_5 + 2\delta_5, w_5 + 4w_3 + 4\delta_5]$	1.0636
Step 6	$[w_5 + 4\delta_5, w_5 + 7\delta_5]$	1.0636
Step 7	$[w_5 + 4\delta_5, w_5 + 5\delta_5 + w_3]$	1.0646
Step 8	$O^*((1.3279^{1/w_5})^\mu)$	1.0584
Step 9	$[w_4 + 2w_3, w_4 + 6\delta_4]$	1.0646
Step 10	$[w_4 + 2\delta_4, w_4 + 6\delta_4]$	1.0646
Step 11	$O^*((1.1279^{1/w_3})^\mu)$	1.0646

We also show the whole weight setting in Table 2 and the branching vector of each step under the setting in Table 3. From Table 3, we can see that we have four bottlenecks: Steps 7, 9, 10, and 11. In fact, Steps 9, 10, and 11 have the same branching vector $[4w_3, 8w_3]$ under the assumption that $w_4 = 2w_3$ (for Step 11, the worst branching vector in [18] is $[4, 8]$). The branching factor for these three steps will decrease if the value of w_3 increases. On the other hand, the branching factor for Step 7 will decrease if the value of w_3 decreases. We set the best value of w_3 to balance them. If we can either improve Step 7 or improve Steps 9, 10, and 11 together, then we may get a further improvement. However, the improvement is very limited and several other bottlenecks will appear.

8   Concluding Remarks

In this paper, we show that the SAT problem can be solved in $O^*(1.0646^L)$ time, improving the previous bound in terms of the input length obtained more than 10 years ago. Nowadays, improvement becomes harder and harder. However, SAT is one of the most important problems in exact and parameterized algorithms, and the state-of-the-art algorithms are frequently mentioned in the literature. Furthermore, in order to give a neat and clear analysis, we introduce a general analysis framework, which can even be used to simplify the analysis for other similar algorithms based on the measure-and-conquer method.

Acknowledgements. The work is supported by the National Natural Science Foundation of China, under grant 61972070.

References

1. Biere, A., Heule, M., van Maaren, H., Walsh, T. (eds.): Handbook of Satisfiability, Frontiers in Artificial Intelligence and Applications, vol. 185. IOS Press (2009)
2. Chen, J., Liu, Y.: An improved SAT algorithm in terms of formula length. In: Dehne, F., Gavrilova, M., Sack, J.-R., Tóth, C.D. (eds.) WADS 2009. LNCS, vol. 5664, pp. 144–155. Springer, Heidelberg (2009). https://doi.org/10.1007/978-3-642-03367-4_13
3. Chu, H., Xiao, M., Zhang, Z.: An improved upper bound for SAT. Proc. AAAI Conf. Artif. Intell. **35**(5), 3707–3714 (2021). https://ojs.aaai.org/index.php/AAAI/article/view/16487
4. Cook, S.A.: The complexity of theorem-proving procedures. In: Harrison, M.A., Banerji, R.B., Ullman, J.D. (eds.) Proceedings of the 3rd Annual ACM Symposium on Theory of Computing, Shaker Heights, Ohio, USA, 3–5 May 1971, pp. 151–158. ACM (1971). https://doi.org/10.1145/800157.805047
5. Cook, S.A., Mitchell, D.G.: Finding hard instances of the satisfiability problem: a survey. In: Du, D., Gu, J., Pardalos, P.M. (eds.) Satisfiability Problem: Theory and Applications, Proceedings of a DIMACS Workshop, Piscataway, New Jersey, USA, 11–13 March 1996. DIMACS Series in Discrete Mathematics and Theoretical Computer Science, vol. 35, pp. 1–17. DIMACS/AMS (1996). https://doi.org/10.1090/dimacs/035/01
6. Davis, M., Putnam, H.: A computing procedure for quantification theory. J. ACM **7**(3), 201–215 (1960). https://doi.org/10.1145/321033.321034
7. Fomin, F.V., Grandoni, F., Kratsch, D.: A measure & conquer approach for the analysis of exact algorithms. J. ACM **56**(5), 25:1–25:32 (2009). https://doi.org/10.1145/1552285.1552286

8. Fomin, F.V., Kratsch, D.: Exact Exponential Algorithms. TTCSAES. Springer, Heidelberg (2010). https://doi.org/10.1007/978-3-642-16533-7
9. Hirsch, E.A.: Two new upper bounds for SAT. In: Karloff, H.J. (ed.) Proceedings of the Ninth Annual ACM-SIAM Symposium on Discrete Algorithms, San Francisco, California, USA, 25–27 January 1998, pp. 521–530. ACM/SIAM (1998). http://dl.acm.org/citation.cfm?id=314613.314838
10. Hirsch, E.A.: New worst-case upper bounds for SAT. J. Autom. Reason. **24**(4), 397–420 (2000). https://doi.org/10.1023/A:1006340920104
11. Impagliazzo, R., Paturi, R.: On the complexity of k-sat. J. Comput. Syst. Sci. **62**(2), 367–375 (2001). https://doi.org/10.1006/jcss.2000.1727
12. Kullmann, O., Luckhardt, H.: Deciding propositional tautologies: Algorithms and their complexity. preprint 82 (1997)
13. Liu, S.: Chain, generalization of covering code, and deterministic algorithm for k-sat. In: Chatzigiannakis, I., Kaklamanis, C., Marx, D., Sannella, D. (eds.) 45th International Colloquium on Automata, Languages, and Programming, ICALP 2018, Prague, Czech Republic, 9–13 July 2018. LIPIcs, vol. 107, pp. 88:1–88:13. Schloss Dagstuhl - Leibniz-Zentrum für Informatik (2018). https://doi.org/10.4230/LIPIcs.ICALP.2018.88
14. Monien, B., Speckenmeyer, E., Vornberger, O.: Upper bounds for covering problems. Methods Oper. Res. **43**, 419–431 (1981)
15. Peng, J., Xiao, M.: A fast algorithm for SAT in terms of formula length (2021). https://arxiv.org/abs/2105.06131
16. Van Gelder, A.: A satisfiability tester for non-clausal propositional calculus. Inf. Comput. **79**(1), 1–21 (1988). https://doi.org/10.1016/0890-5401(88)90014-4
17. Wahlström, M.: An algorithm for the SAT problem for formulae of linear length. In: Brodal, G.S., Leonardi, S. (eds.) ESA 2005. LNCS, vol. 3669, pp. 107–118. Springer, Heidelberg (2005). https://doi.org/10.1007/11561071_12
18. Wahlström, M.: Faster exact solving of SAT formulae with a low number of occurrences per variable. In: Bacchus, F., Walsh, T. (eds.) SAT 2005. LNCS, vol. 3569, pp. 309–323. Springer, Heidelberg (2005). https://doi.org/10.1007/11499107_23
19. Yamamoto, M.: An improved $\tilde{\mathcal{O}}(1.234^m)$-time deterministic algorithm for SAT. In: Deng, X., Du, D.-Z. (eds.) ISAAC 2005. LNCS, vol. 3827, pp. 644–653. Springer, Heidelberg (2005). https://doi.org/10.1007/11602613_65

MedleySolver: Online SMT Algorithm Selection

Nikhil Pimpalkhare[1], Federico Mora[1(✉)], Elizabeth Polgreen[1,2], and Sanjit A. Seshia[1]

[1] University of California, Berkeley, USA
`fmora@cs.berkeley.edu`
[2] University of Edinburgh, Edinburgh, Scotland

Abstract. Satisfiability modulo theories (SMT) solvers implement a wide range of optimizations that are often tailored to a particular class of problems, and that differ significantly between solvers. As a result, one solver may solve a query quickly while another might be flummoxed completely. Predicting the performance of a given solver is difficult for users of SMT-driven applications, particularly when the problems they have to solve do not fall neatly into a well-understood category. In this paper, we propose an *online* algorithm selection framework for SMT called MedleySolver that predicts the relative performances of a set of SMT solvers on a given query, distributes time amongst the solvers, and deploys the solvers in sequence until a solution is obtained. We evaluate MedleySolver against the best available alternative, an *offline* learning technique, in terms of pure performance and practical usability for a typical SMT user. We find that with no prior training, MedleySolver solves 93.9% of the queries solved by the virtual best solver selector achieving 59.8% of the par-2 score of the most successful individual solver, which solves 87.3%. For comparison, the best available alternative takes longer to train than MedleySolver takes to solve our entire set of 2000 queries.

1 Introduction and Motivation

State-of-the-art Satisfiability Modulo Theory (SMT) solvers employ highly optimized and unique techniques to efficiently solve queries. One example of differentiation between solvers is in quantifier reasoning, where the number of different algorithms implemented is reflected in the wide spectrum of literature on the subject, e.g. [7,16,23,27,34]. In the same vein, solvers use very different techniques for different theories; for example, there are various techniques that can be used for bit-precise reasoning, e.g. [6,9,10,14,15,17,20,22,30,31].

SMT solvers are becoming more widely used across various applications including verification, automated software testing, and policy verification, e.g. [4,8,24], making them particularly useful to industry practitioners and non-SMT researchers. Given the performance differential between solvers, a key question for such practitioners wishing to apply SMT solving to a problem in a specific

© Springer Nature Switzerland AG 2021
C.-M. Li and F. Manyà (Eds.): SAT 2021, LNCS 12831, pp. 453–470, 2021.
https://doi.org/10.1007/978-3-030-80223-3_31

domain is "which solver should I use?" In this work, we endeavor to provide a simple answer to this question: "Let MedleySolver choose for you!"

MedleySolver frames the problem of choosing an SMT-solver as a modified Multi-Armed Bandit (MAB) problem, a classic reinforcement learning formulation in which an agent must repeatedly pick from several different choices with unknown reward distributions, minimizing overall regret. This agent must trade-off between exploitation (choosing a solver that is already believed to be fast) and exploration (testing out other solvers). For a given SMT query, MedleySolver selects a sequence of solvers to run, running the solver it believes is most likely to solve the query first and the solver that is least likely last. MedleySolver also predicts the time it should spend running each solver before it should give up and move onto the next solver in the sequence.

We apply classic algorithm selection techniques from the domain of Multi-Armed Bandit problems to the order selection problem. In this paper, we highlight Thompson Sampling and k-Nearest-Neighbor (k-NN) classification. We select these two as high-performing instances of a non-contextual and a contextual algorithm respectively but perform a more extensive comparison with a variety of other Multi-Armed Bandit algorithms for completeness. These algorithms traditionally predict one optimal action, but we use them to *rank* SMT solvers on a given query based on the behavior observed on previous queries and, in the case of the contextual bandit algorithms, a feature vector. This ranking allows the algorithm to explore and exploit in a single round.

Non-contextual multi-armed bandit algorithms have been directly applied to selecting search heuristics and variable orderings for constraint satisfaction problems [39,43], and to implementing co-operative sharing of clauses in parallel SAT solving [25]. Our use of a contextual multi-armed bandit framework to select a sequence of SMT solvers for a given SMT query is novel.

We pair these order selection algorithms with two runtime prediction algorithms. The first runtime prediction algorithm estimates the time each solver should be run by modeling its performance as exponential distributions with a parameter that is updated dynamically. The second fits a linear model using stochastic gradient descent (SGD). Runtime estimation helps reduce the cost of exploratory solver choices that do not produce rewards by stopping solvers when we are confident they will not finish before the overall timeout.

Our work is inspired by recent work showing machine learning techniques can be used to solve SMT queries faster. For example, FastSMT [5] is a tool that uses machine learning to find an optimal sequence of tactics, or query transformations, for SMT solvers to use on queries from a given domain. One issue with such approaches is that the complexity of the learning methods leads to training times grossly larger than the time spent solving. In this paper, we achieve comparable performance boosts with no pre-training or additional burden on the SMT end-user. To meet this goal, we approached the problem of algorithm selection for SMT solvers in a dynamic, or "online," manner. This ensures the cost of our training remains small, proportional, and justified by how SMT practitioners use SMT solvers. For example, techniques such as counterexample-guided inductive synthesis (CEGIS) [38] produce long sequences of similar SMT queries that are not easy to obtain prior to solving for offline training.

Contributions. The key contributions of this work are:

1. An adaptation of standard regression techniques to predicting when a given solver will timeout on a query, and a novel approach for the same time allocation problem that models runtime as exponential distributions and estimates timeouts dynamically and with context.
2. A framing of the SMT solver selection problem as a Multi-Armed Bandit (MAB) problem combined with a timeout prediction scheme. Specifically, we extend the MAB problem to selecting sequences of solvers per query instead of a single solver and use the timeout prediction scheme to allocate time to each solver in the sequence. This interaction lets us use lightweight techniques for both problems that do not require pre-training while retaining comparable performance to pre-trained techniques.
3. An empirical evaluation on a set of 2000 benchmarks representing a typical user's workload. Our approach solves 1813 queries on this set; 128 more than the next best solver in $3/5th$ of the time, with no pre-training.

2   Related Work

MedleySolver is most related to algorithm selection techniques for SAT and SMT. Our motivation, however, is similar to portfolio-based approaches.

Algorithm/Solver Selection. Early approaches to learning-based algorithm selection in solvers included picking between different encodings of SMT to SAT in the UCLID solver [11,36] and selecting input parameters for SAT solvers [19]. **SatZilla** [44] used empirical-hardness models to map queries to SAT solvers. Models are learned offline, then combined with a fixed order of "pre-solvers"— solvers that are called before featurization with a short timeout—when online. MedleySolver differs from SATZilla in that it targets SMT, learns solver orders, distributes time among solvers, and does not require training. **ArgoSmArT** *k*-**NN** [32] applies a pre-trained *k*-Nearest-Neighbor algorithm to portfolio SAT solving. Given a query, they deploy the most successful solver on the *k* nearest neighbors. Although one algorithm we apply is *k*-NN, we use it to select sequences of solvers and apply it in combination with the time-prediction algorithm. **MachSMT** [35] is a pre-trained tool like SatZilla but for SMT. Like SatZilla, MachSMT pre-trains to learn an empirical hardness model, then used to predict solving time for a given query. This is related to our timeout estimation, however, our version requires no pre-training. We achieve similar performance to MachSMT without pre-training by decoupling solver choice from time allocation and allowing for mistakes by selecting a sequence of solvers to run, instead of a single solver. **Where4** [18] is a portfolio-based SMT solver that uses regression models to select which solver to run. It extracts features from WhyML programs rather than SMT queries and does not allocate time between solvers. **CPHydra** [33] does allocate time between solvers but does so by solving an NP-Hard problem (knapsack). CPHydra also ignores solver order, requires offline training, and is aimed at CSP, which is related to, but different from, SMT. **FastSMT** [5] is a pre-trained learning tool for speeding up the Z3 SMT solver that works by selecting algorithmic "tactics" or strategies inside the solver itself. FastSMT is interesting because it produces an interpretable strategy that can often be significantly faster than Z3 out-of-the-box. MedleySolver differs from FastSMT in that it learns to combine solvers, rather than to combine the tactics of a single solver. FastSMT also requires significant training time.

Parallel Portfolio Solvers. Parallel portfolio solvers execute sets of solving processes in parallel for each query. Our approach is complementary in that we focus on speeding up sequential computation: different configurations of Medley-Solver could be run in parallel with a portfolio approach. Nevertheless, portfolio approaches share a similar goal, so we highlight related works in this space. **PAR4** [40] is a basic portfolio parallel SMT solver that won several tracks in the SMT-competition in 2019. Wintersteiger et al. [42] implement **Parallel Z3**, a portfolio solver for SMT with the additional feature that learned clauses are shared between processes. Menouer and Baarir [28] combine search space-splitting with portfolio solving by using EXP3 to dynamically allocate cores to each search space splitting solver from a set. Our approach differs in that we focus on SMT, not SAT; we allocate time, not cores; and we use bandit algorithms (like EXP3) to pick the order of solvers, not the number of cores.

3   Problem Statement and Approach Overview

SMT users rarely aim to solve a single query in isolation and usually care about resource consumption. For example, verification engines generate many verification queries for one verification problem and aim to solve these queries in the least amount of time. As such, we define the *practical* SMT problem as that of taking a set of SMT queries $Q = \{q_1, ..., q_m\}$, a set of SMT algorithms (usually solvers) S, and producing a set of answers $A = \{a_1, ..., a_m\}$, where each a_i corresponds to the matching q_i, while using the least computational resources.

Our approach to the practical SMT problem, MedleySolver, is a program that takes Q, S, and a timeout T per query, and aims to maximize the number of instances solved while minimizing the cumulative time spent. We decompose our approach into two parts. For each query $q \in Q$, we predict 1. which solvers are most likely to solve a given query and return a list of solvers ordered by chance of success; and 2. the time each solver is likely to take to solve a given query and distribute the timeout T to the solvers in the sequence accordingly.

Given a query q_i, MedleySolver generates a sequence of solvers σ, and a sequence of time-allocations $t_1, ..., t_n$, so that the solver in σ_1 is run for t_1 seconds and so on. If a solver in the sequence successfully solves the query, we do not run the rest of the solver sequence on that query and instead move onto the next query. For the remainder of the paper, we use σ to denote a sequence of solvers and σ_i to denote the ith solver in the sequence σ. We process each query $q_1, ..., q_m$ in order and our solver selection algorithms learn as we go, so the solver selection for q_m uses information from queries $q_1, ..., q_{m-1}$. In practice,

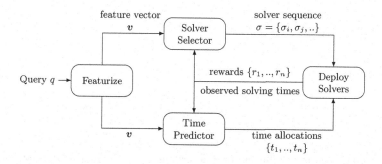

Fig. 1. Overview of one iteration of our approach.

this historical information can be reset whenever and in our experimental results, we reset it when confronting a new set of queries (for instance, a new category of the SMT competition). An overview of our approach is shown in Fig. 1. We describe the three main components of Fig. 1: the solver selector, the timeout predictor, and the featurization of queries, in detail in the next two sections.

4 Dynamic Solver Selection

In the **multi-armed bandit (MAB)** problem [13] an agent sequentially selects between choices with unknown associated reward distributions, aiming to maximize the reward achieved over time. The agent must trade off exploration (trying new actions and learning about them) and exploitation (deploying actions we know have the potential for high reward).

We frame the solver selection problem as a MAB problem. The agent is selecting the solver to use and the payout is based on successfully solving queries. We assume that running a solver for a randomly selected SMT query is equivalent to sampling from some unknown distribution that we seek to approximate. Contextual MABs extend the problem by giving agents access to a feature vector before each round. This allows us to add information about the characteristics of the SMT query we are trying to solve in each round, as described in Sect. 4.2.

We modify the MAB problem in one key way: we select a sequence of solvers to run (with corresponding time allocations that we consider later), instead of selecting a single solver. This contribution allows solver selection to perform exploration on each query until it observes a reward, has tried all solvers, or reaches the time-out per query. We also use a time-prediction algorithm, described in Sect. 5 which predicts the time it is worth running a solver on a given query, allowing us to perform "partial exploration" instead of committing to running a single solver until time-out or termination. Both of these extensions to the MAB algorithms allow the solver selection to correct incorrect solver choices, reducing the cost of exploration vs exploitation. In the following subsections, we adapt one non-contextual algorithm and one contextual algorithm (i.e., algorithms that use the feature vector) from the literature to our domain. We choose the algorithms based on their popularity in the classic literature for

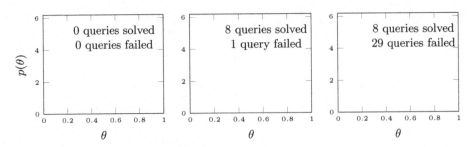

Fig. 2. Updating the distribution of θ according to Bayes' rule. A distribution for a solver that has failed on more queries than it has solved will have a $\theta < 0.5$.

MAB, and the compatibility of the assumptions the algorithm makes with our domain (for instance, we omit algorithms such as LinUCB [26], which assumes that the reward is linearly correlated with the feature vector). In Sect. 6 we evaluate our choices against other MAB algorithms for completeness.

Rewards. We use a binary reward structure where a solver receives a reward of 1 if it is observed solving a query and 0 if it is observed failing to solve a query, which decouples solving time from rewards. We also explored an exponential reward structure where a solver receives a reward of $(1 - t/T)^4$ if it solves a query in time t, but found the binary reward more effective which we believe is due to its ability to differentiate more clearly between benchmarks that are slow to solve and benchmarks that are not solved.

4.1   Thompson Sampling

Thompson Sampling [1,2] uses Bayes' rule to choose an action, or arm in the MAB problem, that maximizes the expected reward. Each round of the MAB in this context is picking a random query from the set of queries and trying to solve it with a specific solver σ_i. To adapt non-contextual Thompson Sampling to our SMT solver selection problem, we model the outcome of an experiment with a Bernoulli distribution where the solver solves the query with a probability θ_i and fails to solve it within the time-out with a probability $1 - \theta_i$. In Thompson Sampling, the agent does not know the value of each θ_i but begins with some prior belief over each one. These priors are beta-distributed: the prior for θ_i is

$$p(\theta_i) = \frac{\Gamma(\alpha_i + \beta_i)}{\Gamma(\alpha_i)\Gamma(\beta_i)}\theta_i^{\alpha_i - 1}(1 - \theta_i)^{\beta_i - 1}.$$

We initially take this distribution to be uniform i.e., $\alpha_i = \beta_i = 1$. That is, we assume a prior that, for a random query, each solver has a 50% chance of solving the query and a 50% chance of failing to solve the query within the timeout.

To select a solver to deploy, Thompson Sampling takes a sample from each distribution $p(\theta_i)$ corresponding to a solver. Note that, because Thompson Sampling takes a sample from the distributions $p(\theta_1)...p(\theta_n)$, it is more likely to pick solvers that we are uncertain about instead of simply returning the solvers

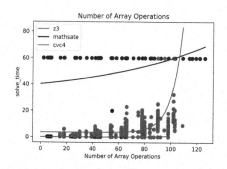
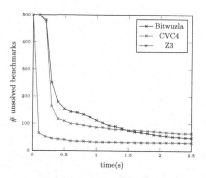

(a) Solver performance on Uclid5 queries as the number of array operations increases.

(b) Three solver's runtime over a sample of bit-vector queries.

Fig. 3. Empirical intuition for features and time predictors.

in order of the $p(\theta)$ with the highest mean, allowing exploration. Conventional Thompson Sampling returns the solver with the highest valued sample. Our algorithm returns a sequence of solvers in descending order of these sampled values i.e., the solver with the θ closest to 1 is first.

After deploying the solvers and observing the results, the distributions over $\theta_1, .., \theta_n$ are updated according to Bayes's rule. Each time a solver σ_i is run, a reward r_i is observed. The posterior distribution for the beta distribution [12] is obtained by adding the reward r_i to α_i and $1 - r_i$ to β_i, as illustrated in Fig. 2.

Thompson Sampling assumes events are independent, i.e., the probability of a solver being able to solve a query is independent of all queries the solver has seen before. This could be true if our time-out prediction algorithm is perfect so that if a solver can solve a query within the timeout T, the solver will also always be able to solve that query within the time t allocated to the solver.

4.2 Features for Contextual Approaches

Contextual approaches depend on the assumption that queries with similar characteristics will cause SMT solvers to perform similarly. We capture the characteristics of each SMT query q_i in a feature vector $v_i \in V$. We use these feature vectors both in contextual bandit algorithms (described next) and in our contextual time-prediction (described in Sect. 5).

We identify a list of 24 features that are quick to extract and that we believe correlate with solving time for specific solvers. These features include context-free qualities like counts for specific operators (e.g. array store operators), the maximum value of literals, the sum of literal values, and so on. The features also include context-sensitive qualities like quantifier nesting and alternations, as well as the size of a given queries' abstract-syntax-tree as a minimal graph (we refer to this representation as a term graph). All feature extraction procedures run in $\mathcal{O}(n)$ where n is the size of the term graph. The term graph construction is efficient and the term graph itself is often exponentially smaller than the input query. Therefore, the cost of extracting features is relatively small.

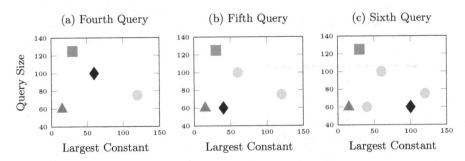

Fig. 4. Example k-NN run with $k = 1$, solvers A, B, C, and 2 features. A, B, and C are represented by a square, a triangle, and a circle, respectively; the new query is represented by a diamond. A and B fail on the new query in (a); solver B fails on the new query in (b); and solver C succeeds on both.

As a heuristic, we try to build features that can differentiate solver performance on their own. For example, Fig. 3a shows the performance of three different SMT solvers as the number of array operations in the term graph increases accompanied by an exponential regression fit. For this example, intuitively, we would want to favor the use of Z3 as the number of array operations increases. While we did not do any empirical feature selection, we did use our prior knowledge of SMT solvers to decide which feature extractors to build, and we evaluate the impact of our decisions in Sect. 6.3.

4.3 k-Nearest-Neighbor

The k-Nearest-Neighbor algorithm(k-NN) is a simple contextual approach. Viewed from the perspective of a MAB problem, given solvers $s_1, ..., s_n$, k-NN classifies SMT queries into n classes: queries where solver s_1 is the best choice, queries where solver s_2 is the best choice, and so on. We extend the standard k-NN algorithm to return a sequence of solvers.

Given a query, q, the basic k-NN algorithm looks at the k nearest queries to q, tallies the number solved by each solver, and orders the solvers by their tallies. We calculate the distance between two queries—how "near" two queries are—by computing the Euclidean distance between their feature vectors. The idea behind this algorithm is that if a solver succeeded on many queries similar to q, then it is likely to succeed on q. If any solvers in the solver set are not included in the neighbors, we randomly shuffle these solvers and append them to the end of the sequence—we make an exception for the $k = 1$ case: when $k = 1$ we return the solver that solved the nearest neighbor, followed by the solver that solved the next nearest neighbor and so on, without replacement.

Once an order is selected, we run the solvers in sequence. If a solver s in this sequence succeeds, we add the feature vector of that query to our data-set of previously solved queries along with the label s. See Fig. 4 for three steps of a hypothetical 1-nearest neighbor example.

5   Runtime Prediction

The second component of our approach comprises time predictors, which we use to split the per-query timeout T into sub-timeouts per solver $t_1 \ldots t_n$. We train a time-predictor for each solver. Our goal is to find a time t_i such that we can stop running the ith solver in the sequence and be highly confident it was unlikely to solve the current query after this point. Formally, we are trying to find the minimum t_i such that $P(t_i < u_i < T) \leq \delta$, where u_i is the true runtime of σ_i on q_i and δ is the accepted error probability. We consider this event the only relevant error scenario because it implies if we had allocated more time to solver σ_i we could have solved the current query.

To calculate each t_i, we model each solver's runtime as an exponential distribution, justified by our experimental observations illustrated in Fig. 3b: solvers usually succeed early or not at all. We employ Maximum Likelihood Estimation (MLE) [29] to fit an exponential distribution to the runtime samples which we have gathered up to that point. In MLE, we find $\min_\lambda P(u_1 \ldots u_m | \lambda)$, where $u_1 \ldots u_m$ are the observed runtime samples we have seen, which we assume are drawn from $Exponential(\lambda)$. We use the exponential's probability distribution function as a measure of likeliness, so this problem is equal to $\min_\lambda n \ln \lambda - \lambda(\sum_i u_i)$, leading to the following minimizer:

$$\lambda^* = \frac{n}{\sum_i u_i}$$

Applying the cumulative distribution function and using the memoryless property of the exponential distribution, we can calculate t_i as follows:

$$t_i = \frac{-\ln(\delta + e^{-\lambda^* T})}{\lambda^*}$$

We split T into sub-timeouts greedily; we use the above process to allocate time for solvers starting from the beginning of our ordering and stop once we reach the overall timeout, allocating zero time to the remaining solvers in the order. If we reach the end of the ordering and still have time remaining, we give the remaining timeout to the last solver.

k-NN Runtime Prediction. We present a contextual runtime prediction system based on the k-NN algorithm. Instead of using every past sample point to estimate λ^*, we limit our estimation scheme to the k nearest data-points. As with the k-NN based solver selection, the distance between two queries is the Euclidean distance between their feature vectors. The rest of the estimation scheme remains identical to the non-contextual scheme.

Linear Regression Runtime Prediction. Finally, we present a contextual runtime prediction system that finds a linear relationship between our feature vector and the associated runtime. To do so, it minimizes the L2-regularized squared loss of the linear model using stochastic gradient descent, solving:

$$\min_{w,b} \sum_i (w^T x_i + b - u_i) + \alpha||w||_2,$$

where w is the learned weight of our features, b is a learned coefficient, x_i is the feature vector of the ith query, u_i is the true runtime of the ith query, and α is a regularization constant.

6   Empirical Evaluation

We implemented a prototype of MedleySolver in Python.[1] The input is a directory of queries, and the output is the result, solver used, and time elapsed per query. In this section, we evaluate this prototype and aim to answer the following research questions: 1. How does MedleySolver compare to individual solvers on the practical SMT problem? 2. How does MedleySolver compare to the best available alternatives on the practical SMT problem? 3. How do the individual components of MedleySolver affect the overall performance?

Subjects and Methods. We equip MedleySolver with six SMT solvers (CVC4 v1.8 [6], MathSAT v5.6.3 [9], Z3 v4.8.7 [14], Boolector v2.4.1 [31], Bitwuzla v.0.9999 [30] and Yices v2.6.2 [15]) and run on four benchmark sets, each with 500 queries. Some SMT solvers do not support all needed syntax. For example, the BV set includes quantifiers that Boolector cannot handle. We expect MedleySolver to learn to avoid solvers that fail on specific kinds of queries.

The benchmark queries simulate a typical user's workload in that they are similar in nature, i.e. use related logical theories and come from similar applications, but are diverse enough to expose issues a normal user will encounter, i.e. deviations in SMT-LIB conformance. We selected a random sample of 500 queries from an existing benchmark set, Sage2, derived from a test generation tool; 500 queries from 140 Uclid5 [37] verification tasks; and 500 queries each from the BV and QF_ABV theory SMT-COMP tracks, respectively.

We ran every individual solver with a timeout of 60 s for every query on a Dell PowerEdge C6220 server blade equipped with two Intel Xeon 10-core Ivy Bridge processors running Scientific Linux 7 at 2.5 GHz with 64 GB of 1866 Mhz DDR3 memory. We saved these results and used them to simulate runs of MedleySolver. This helped ensure results are deterministic, reproducible, and lowered our carbon emissions. The overhead of running MedleySolver on all 2000 queries varies between learning algorithms and features used but is always less than two minutes for the full set of queries, and is therefore negligible.

6.1   RQ1: Comparison with Individual Solvers

To evaluate the utility of MedleySolver for a typical user, we ran k-NN and Thompson with the three timeout predictors on every set individually and then

---

[1] Code and data: https://github.com/uclid-org/medley-solver/tree/SAT2021.

Table 1. Par-2 score (lower is better) and the number of queries solved for each solver across benchmarks. MedleySolver configurations are selectors (e.g. 10-NN) over time predictors (e.g. Linear time prediction). Learning algorithms use binary reward and every query is given a 60 s timeout. 'Split' refers to the sum over all individual benchmark sets where the learning algorithms are restarted between sets, while 'Combined' refers to the aggregated set with no resets. Individual sets contain 500 queries; 'Combined' and 'Split' contain 2000.

| Solver | Benchmark set | | | | | |
	BV	QFABV	Sage2	Uclid5	Split	Combined
10-NN	**2081.8**	1208.2	14855.4	5386.9	**23532.3**	29111.2
Expo	484	492	396	457	1829	1799
10-NN	2857.7	1039.7	17558.2	5386.9	26842.5	**25133.8**
10-Nearest-Expo	477	493	367	457	1794	1813
10-NN	4229.1	**824.4**	**13789.0**	8136.4	26978.9	87898.4
Linear	468	496	409	452	1825	1308
Thompson	2986.4	1308.5	15323.1	5540.9	25158.9	51757.3
Expo	480	491	401	456	1828	1676
Thompson	2840.8	1105.1	17949.7	5536.0	27431.6	27555.9
10-Nearest-Expo	479	493	365	456	1793	1816
Thompson	4291.1	1474.1	15661.3	**4344.6**	25771.1	45267.7
Linear	466	489	392	473	1820	1658
Boolector	60000.0	1408.7	31502.3	60000.0	152911.1	
	0	491	265	0	756	
Bitwuzla	3872.3	**822.9**	22316.4	60000.0	87011.7	
	471	496	349	0	1316	
CVC4	3332.1	5874.1	49161.5	7395.5	65763.3	
	477	459	117	459	1512	
MathSat	11455.0	1724.0	34159.4	50783.3	98121.7	
	406	488	232	77	1203	
Yices	7244.3	922.1	**13544.4**	60000.0	81710.9	
	442	494	411	0	1347	
Z3	**2888.6**	1202.0	35279.2	**2637.2**	**42007.1**	
	477	492	232	484	1685	
Virtual best	964.6	530.8	9006.2	2192.1	12786.5	
	493	497	453	476	1931	

over the combined set. The combined set represents a realistic combination of queries a typical user might want to solve.

Table 1 reports the results of our experiment in terms of Par-2 score,[2] where "virtual best" is calculated by using the best-performing individual solver for each query. On individual sets where one solver dominates, like Z3 on Uclid5, MedleySolver approaches the best solver but does not reach it. Conversely, on sets where no one solver is close to the virtual best, like BV, we find the MedleySolver can exploit this performance differentiation and approach the virtual best solver.

---

[2] Sum of all runtimes for solved instances + 2*timeout for unsolved instances [41].

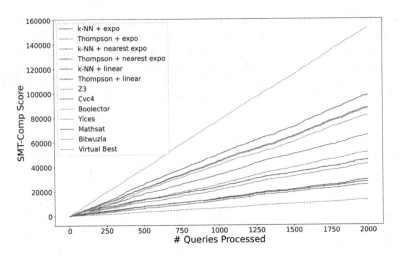

Fig. 5. Par-2 score over queries solved in the combined set.

The combined set, which is less uniform than BV but less dominated than Uclid5, demonstrates the power of MedleySolver: with no training, MedleySolver solves 94.5% of the queries solved by the virtual best using only 72.3% of the time taken by the most successful individual solver, Z3, which solves 87.3%. Figure 5 shows the performance of every solver over the number of queries processed, and visually depicts the proximity of MedleySolver to the virtual best. Together, Table 1 and Fig. 5 answer RQ3: MedleySolver outperforms every individual solver on the practical SMT problem.

The Thompson MAB selector generally does better when summing up individual sets than when running on the combined set, while the k-NN selector is the opposite. This suggests contextual approaches can effectively carry over lessons between sets, and non-contextual approaches benefit from being used in the context of a benchmark.

6.2   RQ2: Comparison with State-of-the-Art

We now compare MedleySolver to alternative portfolio approaches, including those based on pre-trained machine learning techniques. Parallel portfolio solvers like PAR4 [40] run multiple solvers in parallel and stop all solvers when the first one solves the query. We can calculate the hypothetical performance of such a solver by multiplying the virtual best solver time by the number of solvers we run. This would give a Par-2 score of 65481, in comparison to 10-NN's better score of 32632 over the combined benchmark set.

MachSMT [35] uses a neural network to select which solver to run on a given query. Table 2 shows the performance of MachSMT and MedleySolver on the same benchmarks as in Table 1 but with 2/5 of the queries set aside for MachSMT to train on per set. Although MachSMT slightly outperforms MedleySolver on

Table 2. Par-2 score (lower is better) and training time for MedleySolver, MachSMT, and the Virtual Best of all individual solvers. Individual benchmarks consist of 200 training queries and 300 test queries; 'Combined' consists of 800 training queries and 1200 test queries. Only MachSMT uses the training queries.

Solver	Benchmark Set				
	BV	QFABV	Sage2	Uclid5	Combined
MedleySolver	1638.7	310.5	9245.3	4248.0	18565.5
	N/A	N/A	N/A	N/A	N/A
MachSMT	1458.3	919.2	8516.1	2430.9	12539.1
	33895.5 s	4498.9 s	55115.5 s	276419.8 s	300072.8 s
Virtual best	801.7	184.3	5204.2	1464.7	6746.0
	N/A	N/A	N/A	N/A	N/A

the test sets, the training time required by MachSMT is orders of magnitude larger than the time required to solve, particularly because, to have training data on which to train, MachSMT must run all the solvers on all the queries in the training set which takes a considerable amount of time. So, on the practical SMT problem, MedleySolver achieves similar results with significantly less resource consumption and we argue the cost of training is not worth it if online learning can achieve competitive performance. Preiner et al. do make a trained model available that could eliminate training time for a user. However, this pre-trained model is trained on specific versions of a specific set of SMT solvers running on a specific system. In practice and in our example, the user's specifics do not match and local training is required.

FastSMT [5] is an offline approach that synthesizes strategies for the Z3 SMT solver. FastSMT requires significant training time and needs to be trained per benchmark set. We can run the pre-trained FastSMT model on the Sage2 benchmark set, where it solves 358 queries in 12766s (par-2 score of 29806). This is a substantial performance gain over Z3, but all MedleySolver configurations still outperform this without any pre-training. FastSMT improves on Z3 but it is limited to one single solver and, unlike MedleySolver, is not able to take advantage of the range of different SMT solvers implementing different heuristics.

6.3   RQ3: Impact of Individual Components

In this section, we evaluate the performance of the individual pieces of MedleySolver. Specifically, we aim to answer the following questions. 1. How do our learning algorithms compare to other well-known MAB algorithms? 2. How well do our order selectors perform? 3. What is the impact of selecting an order instead of a single solver on performance? 4. Which query features are most responsible for MedleySolver's performance?

Performance of Other Multi-Armed Bandit Algorithms. We have highlighted the results from Thompson Sampling and k-NN but we also adapted and evaluated the following Multi-Armed Bandit algorithms: the classic non-contextual epsilon-greedy bandit algorithm [21]; LinUCB [26], an upper-confidence bound algorithm that assumes a linear relationship between the rewards and the feature vector; Exp3 [3]: an adversarial bandit algorithm; and an adaptation of a neural network classification based bandit [45]. All of these bandits performed comparably or better than the best individual solver, but no non-contextual algorithm performed as well as Thompson Sampling, and no contextual algorithm performed as well as k-NN.

Order Selection Accuracy. To better understand MedleySolver's performance, we measure how frequently it selects the best solver as the first solver to try. Over our five case-study benchmarks, the best performing selector is k-Nearest-Neighbor with $k = 10$ (10-NN), which correctly picks the best solver 74.3% of the time. The highest success rate is on the BV benchmark, where 10-NN is 92.0% accurate. The lowest success rate is on the QF_ABV benchmark, where 10-NN is 52.0% accurate. This difference demonstrates MedleySolver's accuracy is proportional to the cost of mistakes: solvers are much better overall on the QF_ABV category so MedleySolver can frequently pick a sub-optimal solver that will still terminate quickly; on the other hand, in BV, picking the wrong solver will often lead to a timeout.

Timeout Prediction Impact. To better understand MedleySolver's performance, we measure the impact of selecting an order of solvers instead of a single solver. To do this we run MedleySolver without timeout prediction, giving the entire time per query to the first solver in the sequence. We find, all else equal, on the combined set, selecting a single solver produces a par-2 score 350% worse than our best MedleySolver configuration. This difference is due to the direct cost of mispredictions and because, without the time prediction, MedleySolver is unable to learn from mistakes on a given query.

Feature Evaluation. In this section, we aim to interpret what our results tell us about SMT solvers and optimize performance through feature analysis. To better understand the SMT solvers we use, we measure how well each feature correlates with solver performance differentiation. Specifically, for every feature f, for every pair of solvers $(s_i, s_j) \in S \times S$, we measure the Pearson correlation coefficient between f and $\text{time}(s_i) - \text{time}(s_j)$. Using this technique we found, on the BV benchmark set, the most distinguishing features were the number of universal quantifiers for Bitwuzla and MathSat5; the number of free variables for Yices and Boolector; the number of bound variables for Boolector and Bitwuzla; and the size of the term graph for Bitwuzla and Z3.

To optimize performance, we search for the subset of features that induce the best performance from MedleySolver. Specifically, we use backward step-wise feature selection (BSFS) to iteratively remove features from our feature vector whose removal does not negatively affect performance. Using this technique we found that, all else equal, using only three features on the BV benchmark (number of quantifiers, number of variables, and term graph size) improves the par-2 score of the best configuration of MedleySolver by 30%. We observe a similar reduction in feature vector size across benchmarks and an average par-2 performance improvement of 11%. Interestingly, BSFS often removes the feature with the smallest correlation score, as described above.

6.4   Threats to Validity

We evaluated MedleySolver on a set of benchmarks and a combination of solvers we believe represent a real user's SMT workload, but we understand these results may not generalize. To mitigate this possibility, we evaluated the SMT-Competition data curated by the MachSMT authors. On the QF_UFBV benchmark, the best individual solver was Bitwuzla with a score of 2614.6 while MedleySolver scored 2600.5; on the QF_LIA benchmark, the best individual solver was Yices with a score of 45871.2 while MedleySolver scored of 25737.2; on the QF_BVFPLRA benchmark, the best individual solver was MathSAT5 with a score of 3015.2 while MedleySolver scored 567.7; and on the NRA benchmark, the best individual solver was Z3 with a score of 1455.6 while MedleySolver scored 1068.6. In all cases, MedleySolver outperformed every individual solver while using no pre-training–often by margins greater than those observed in our case study–suggesting our results do generalize.

The queries MedleySolver has seen in the past affect the prediction Medley-Solver makes for the current query, and thus the order MedleySolver receives the queries could affect the overall performance on the full dataset. MAB algorithms such as Thompson Sampling use random sampling and choice of random seed could also affect the results. To gain confidence in our claims, we repeated our experiments with 20 different random seeds and found the standard deviation in MedleySolver's overall par-2 score to be approximately 1% of its average score. The margins between MedleySolver and any individual solver are significantly larger than 1% and so MedleySolver is consistently comfortably better than any individual solver in our evaluation regardless of deviation.

7   Conclusions and Future Work

We presented MedleySolver, an online learning algorithm for SMT that uses a novel application of multi-armed bandits to predict the best order in which to deploy a sequence of SMT solvers, in combination with a novel time-prediction algorithm, allowing the solver selection to recover from mistakes. Our approach solves more queries in less time per query than any individual solver on a set of benchmarks taken from the SMT-competition and verification tasks. Unlike offline techniques, MedleySolver requires no pre-training.

In the future, we intend to explore white-box techniques for solver termination prediction. We hypothesize that monitoring a solver's execution can help identify when the solver is unlikely to terminate. We are also interested in exploring online feature selection techniques.

Acknowledgments. This work was supported in part by NSF grants CNS-1739816 and CCF-1837132, by the DARPA LOGiCS project under contract FA8750-20-C-0156, by the iCyPhy center, and by gifts from Intel, Amazon, and Microsoft.

References

1. Agrawal, S., Goyal, N.: Analysis of Thompson sampling for the multi-armed bandit problem. In: COLT. JMLR Proceedings, vol. 23, pp. 39.1–39.26. JMLR.org (2012)
2. Agrawal, S., Goyal, N.: Thompson sampling for contextual bandits with linear payoffs. In: ICML (3). JMLR Workshop and Conference Proceedings, vol. 28, pp. 127–135. JMLR.org (2013)
3. Auer, P., Cesa-Bianchi, N., Freund, Y., Schapire, R.E.: The nonstochastic multi-armed bandit problem. SIAM J. Comput. **32**(1), 48–77 (2002)
4. Backes, J., et al.: Semantic-based automated reasoning for AWS access policies using SMT. In: FMCAD, pp. 1–9. IEEE (2018)
5. Balunovic, M., Bielik, P., Vechev, M.T.: Learning to solve SMT formulas. In: NeurIPS, pp. 10338–10349 (2018)
6. Barrett, C., et al.: CVC4. In: Gopalakrishnan, G., Qadeer, S. (eds.) CAV 2011. LNCS, vol. 6806, pp. 171–177. Springer, Heidelberg (2011). https://doi.org/10.1007/978-3-642-22110-1_14
7. Barth, M., Dietsch, D., Fichtner, L., Heizmann, M.: Ultimate eliminator: a quantifier upgrade for smt solvers at smt-comp **2019** (2019)
8. Bjørner, N.: SMT solvers for testing, program analysis and verification at microsoft. In: SYNASC, p. 15. IEEE Computer Society (2009)
9. Bruttomesso, R., Cimatti, A., Franzén, A., Griggio, A., Sebastiani, R.: The MATH-SAT 4 SMT Solver. In: Gupta, A., Malik, S. (eds.) CAV 2008. LNCS, vol. 5123, pp. 299–303. Springer, Heidelberg (2008). https://doi.org/10.1007/978-3-540-70545-1_28
10. Bryant, R.E., Kroening, D., Ouaknine, J., Seshia, S.A., Strichman, O., Brady, B.: Deciding bit-vector arithmetic with abstraction. In: Grumberg, O., Huth, M. (eds.) TACAS 2007. LNCS, vol. 4424, pp. 358–372. Springer, Heidelberg (2007). https://doi.org/10.1007/978-3-540-71209-1_28
11. Bryant, R.E., Lahiri, S.K., Seshia, S.A.: Modeling and verifying systems using a logic of counter arithmetic with lambda expressions and uninterpreted functions. In: Brinksma, E., Larsen, K.G. (eds.) CAV 2002. LNCS, vol. 2404, pp. 78–92. Springer, Heidelberg (2002). https://doi.org/10.1007/3-540-45657-0_7
12. Castillo, E.F., Hadi, A.S., Solares, C.: Learning and updating of uncertainty in dirichlet models. Mach. Learn. **26**(1), 43–63 (1997)
13. Cesa-Bianchi, N., Lugosi, G.: Prediction, Learning, and Games. Cambridge University Press, Cambridge (2006)
14. de Moura, L., Bjørner, N.: Z3: an efficient SMT solver. In: Ramakrishnan, C.R., Rehof, J. (eds.) TACAS 2008. LNCS, vol. 4963, pp. 337–340. Springer, Heidelberg (2008). https://doi.org/10.1007/978-3-540-78800-3_24
15. Dutertre, B.: Yices 2.2. In: Biere, A., Bloem, R. (eds.) CAV 2014. LNCS, vol. 8559, pp. 737–744. Springer, Cham (2014). https://doi.org/10.1007/978-3-319-08867-9_49
16. Ge, Y., de Moura, L.: Complete instantiation for quantified formulas in satisfiabiliby modulo theories. In: Bouajjani, A., Maler, O. (eds.) CAV 2009. LNCS, vol. 5643, pp. 306–320. Springer, Heidelberg (2009). https://doi.org/10.1007/978-3-642-02658-4_25

17. Hansen, T.: A constraint solver and its application to machine code test generation. Ph.D. thesis, University of Melbourne, Australia (2012). http://hdl.handle.net/11343/37952
18. Healy, A., Monahan, R., Power, J.F.: Predicting SMT solver performance for software verification. In: F-IDE@FM. EPTCS, vol. 240, pp. 20–37 (2016)
19. Hutter, F., Babic, D., Hoos, H.H., Hu, A.J.: Boosting verification by automatic tuning of decision procedures. In: 7th International Conference on Formal Methods in Computer-Aided Design (FMCAD), pp. 27–34 (2007)
20. Jha, S., Limaye, R., Seshia, S.A.: Beaver: engineering an efficient SMT solver for bit-vector arithmetic. In: Bouajjani, A., Maler, O. (eds.) CAV 2009. LNCS, vol. 5643, pp. 668–674. Springer, Heidelberg (2009). https://doi.org/10.1007/978-3-642-02658-4_53
21. Johnson, J.D., Li, J., Chen, Z.: Reinforcement Learning: An Introduction: Sutton, R.S., Barto, A.G. MIT press, Cambridge, MA 1998, 322, ISBN 0-262-19398-1. Neurocomputing **35**(1-4), 205–206 (2000)
22. Jonáš, M., Strejček, J.: Solving quantified bit-vector formulas using binary decision diagrams. In: Creignou, N., Le Berre, D. (eds.) SAT 2016. LNCS, vol. 9710, pp. 267–283. Springer, Cham (2016). https://doi.org/10.1007/978-3-319-40970-2_17
23. Kovács, L., Robillard, S., Voronkov, A.: Coming to terms with quantified reasoning. In: Proceedings of the 44th ACM SIGPLAN Symposium on Principles of Programming Languages, pp. 260–270 (2017)
24. Kroening, D., Strichman, O.: Decision Procedures - An Algorithmic Point of View. Texts in Theoretical Computer Science. An EATCS Series, Springer, Heidelberg (2016). https://doi.org/10.1007/978-3-540-74105-3
25. Lazaar, N., Hamadi, Y., Jabbour, S., Sebag, M.: BESS: Bandit Ensemble for parallel SAT Solving. Research Report RR-8070 (2012). https://hal.inria.fr/hal-00733282
26. Li, L., Chu, W., Langford, J., Schapire, R.E.: A contextual-bandit approach to personalized news article recommendation. In: Proceedings of the 19th international conference on World Wide Web, pp. 661–670. ACM (2010)
27. Löding, C., Madhusudan, P., Peña, L.: Foundations for natural proofs and quantifier instantiation. In: Proceedings of the ACM on Programming Languages, vol. 2, no. POPL, pp. 1–30 (2017)
28. Menouer, T., Baarir, S.: Parallel learning portfolio-based solvers. Procedia Comput. Sci. **108**, 335–344 (2017)
29. Myung, I.J.: Tutorial on maximum likelihood estimation. J. Math. Psychol. **47**(1), 90–100 (2003). https://doi.org/10.1016/S0022-2496(02)00028-7
30. Niemetz, A., Preiner, M.: Bitwuzla at the SMT-COMP 2020 (2020). CoRR abs/2006.01621, https://arxiv.org/abs/2006.01621
31. Niemetz, A., Preiner, M., Biere, A.: Boolector 2.0. J. Satisf. Boolean Model. Comput. **9**(1), 53–58 (2014). https://doi.org/10.3233/sat190101
32. Nikolic, M., Maric, F., Janicic, P.: Simple algorithm portfolio for SAT. Artif. Intell. Rev. **40**(4), 457–465 (2013)
33. O'Mahony, E., Hebrard, E., Holland, A., Nugent, C., O'Sullivan, B.: Using case-based reasoning in an algorithm portfolio for constraint solving. In: Irish Conference on Artificial Intelligence and Cognitive Science, pp. 210–216 (2008)
34. Reynolds, A., Deters, M., Kuncak, V., Tinelli, C., Barrett, C.: Counterexample-guided quantifier instantiation for synthesis in SMT. In: Kroening, D., Păsăreanu, C.S. (eds.) CAV 2015. LNCS, vol. 9207, pp. 198–216. Springer, Cham (2015). https://doi.org/10.1007/978-3-319-21668-3_12

35. Scott, J., Niemetz, A., Preiner, M., Nejati, S., Ganesh, V.: Machsmt: a machine learning-based algorithm selector for SMT solvers. In: Groote, J.F., Larsen, K.G. (eds.) Tools and Algorithms for the Construction and Analysis of Systems - 27th International Conference, TACAS 2021, Held as Part of the European Joint Conferences on Theory and Practice of Software, ETAPS 2021, Luxembourg City, Luxembourg, 27 March–1 April 2021, Proceedings, Part II. Lecture Notes in Computer Science, vol. 12652, pp. 303–325. Springer, Heidelberg (2021). https://doi.org/10.1007/978-3-030-72013-1_16

36. Seshia, S.A.: Adaptive Eager Boolean Encoding for Arithmetic Reasoning in Verification. Ph.D. thesis, Carnegie Mellon University (2005)

37. Seshia, S.A., Subramanyan, P.: UCLID5: integrating modeling, verification, synthesis and learning. In: MEMOCODE, pp. 1–10. IEEE (2018)

38. Solar-Lezama, A., Tancau, L., Bodík, R., Seshia, S.A., Saraswat, V.A.: Combinatorial sketching for finite programs. In: ASPLOS, pp. 404–415. ACM (2006)

39. Wattez, H., Koriche, F., Lecoutre, C., Paparrizou, A., Tabary, S.: Learning variable ordering heuristics with multi-armed bandits and restarts. In: ECAI. Frontiers in Artificial Intelligence and Applications, vol. 325, pp. 371–378. IOS Press (2020)

40. Weber, T.: Par4 system description. https://smt-comp.github.io/2019/system-descriptions/Par4.pdf

41. Weber, T., Conchon, S., Déharbe, D., Heizmann, M., Niemetz, A., Reger, G.: The SMT competition 2015–2018. J. Satisf. Boolean Model. Comput. **11**(1), 221–259 (2019)

42. Wintersteiger, C.M., Hamadi, Y., de Moura, L.: A concurrent portfolio approach to SMT solving. In: Bouajjani, A., Maler, O. (eds.) CAV 2009. LNCS, vol. 5643, pp. 715–720. Springer, Heidelberg (2009). https://doi.org/10.1007/978-3-642-02658-4_60

43. Xia, W., Yap, R.H.C.: Learning robust search strategies using a bandit-based approach. In: AAAI, pp. 6657–6665. AAAI Press (2018)

44. Xu, L., Hutter, F., Hoos, H.H., Leyton-Brown, K.: Satzilla: portfolio-based algorithm selection for SAT. J. Artif. Intell. Res. **32**, 565–606 (2008)

45. Zhou, D., Li, L., Gu, Q.: Neural contextual bandits with upper confidence bound-based exploration (2019). CoRR abs/1911.04462

Leveraging GPUs for Effective Clause Sharing in Parallel SAT Solving

Nicolas Prevot[1], Mate Soos[2], and Kuldeep S. Meel[2(✉)]

[1] London, United Kingdom
[2] School of Computing, National University of Singapore, Singapore, Singapore
meel@comp.nus.edu.sg

Abstract. The past two decades have witnessed an unprecedented improvement in runtime performance of SAT solvers owing to clever software engineering and creative design of data structures. Yet, most entries in the annual SAT competition retain the core architecture of MiniSat, which was designed from the perspective of single core CPU architectures. Since 2005, however, there has been a significant shift to heterogeneous architectures owing to the impending end of Dennard scaling.

The primary contribution of this work is a novel multi-threaded CDCL-based framework, called GPUShareSat, designed to take advantage of CPU+GPU architectures. The core underlying principle of our approach is to divide the tasks among the CPU and the GPU so as to attempt to achieve the best of both worlds. We observe that bit-vector based operations can allow a GPU to efficiently determine the usefulness of a learnt clause to different threads and accordingly notify the thread of the presence of relevant clauses. This approach of checking all clauses against all assignments from different threads allows the GPU to exploit its potential for massive parallelism through clever group-testing strategy and bitwise operations.

Our detailed empirical analysis shows practical efficiency of our approach: in particular, GPUShareSat augmented with the state-of-the-art single-threaded solver Relaxed_LCMDCBDL_newTech solved 19 more instances than the winner of the 2020 SAT competition's parallel track, P-MCOMSPS-STR.

1   Introduction

Given a Boolean formula φ over the set of variables v, the problem of Boolean Satisfiability (SAT) is to determine whether there exists an assignment $\mathcal{A}$ such that φ evaluates to True under $\mathcal{A}$. SAT is a fundamental problem in computer science with applications in various domains ranging from computational biology, automated theorem proving, spectrum allocations, and the like. The past

---

The accompany open source library is available at https://github.com/nicolasprevot/GpuShareSat.

N. Prevot—Independent Researcher.

© Springer Nature Switzerland AG 2021
C.-M. Li and F. Manyà (Eds.): SAT 2021, LNCS 12831, pp. 471–487, 2021.
https://doi.org/10.1007/978-3-030-80223-3_32

25 years have witnessed the development of efficient SAT solvers allowing modern solvers to handle problems involving millions of variables. Such an unprecedented improvement in the runtime performance of SAT solvers is often dubbed as the *SAT revolution*. Quoting Knuth, "The story of satisfiability is the tale of a triumph of software engineering, blended with rich doses of beautiful mathematics" [16].

From the perspective of software engineering and the creative design of data structures, Een and Sorrenson's MiniSat [13], first introduced in 2005, taking concepts from both Chaff [17] and GRASP, has remained a cornerstone for the design of modern SAT solvers. Even fifteen years later, most of the entries in the annual SAT competition continue to retain the architecture proposed by MiniSat. It is worth noting that the design of data structures of MiniSat was primarily targeted for single-core CPUs. Since 2006, however, the end of Dennard scaling [10] has prompted the leading hardware designers to explore multi-core and heterogeneous architectures. The SAT community acknowledged the importance of multi-core architectures since the early days, and there has been a consistent interest in the design of parallel SAT solvers.

Returning to the hardware landscape, among a wide array of hardware architectures proposed over the years, one of the dominant architectures is CPU+GPU, wherein the CPU consist of a small number of *fat* cores while GPUs consist of a large number of *thin* cores, and the general computational paradigm is to perform complex computational tasks on CPUs while employing GPUs to perform embarrassingly parallel computational tasks, often involving matrix-based arithmetic operations. The crucial importance of CPU+GPU to unprecedented advances in machine learning [9] serves as a strong motivator for the design of frameworks in other domains to take advantage of heterogeneous architectures. While there have been recent efforts in the context of SAT to take advantage of GPUs as well as the CPUs, such efforts have not materialized in achieving runtime performance improvements. To summarize, a major challenge in the community is the *design of an efficient framework for heterogeneous architectures*.

The primary contribution of this work is a novel CDCL-based framework called GPUShareSat, designed to take advantage of CPU+GPU heterogeneous architectures. Our aim is to divide the tasks in CDCL to CPU and GPU so as to achieve the best of both worlds. To this end, we focus on the major Achilles heel of parallel SAT solvers: identifying which clauses to import from other threads. We observe that efficient bit-vector-based operations can allow a GPU to efficiently determine the usefulness of a learnt clause to different threads and accordingly notify the thread of the presence of these relevant clauses. The identification of relevance of a clause for a thread is based on the assumption of the locality of assignments. Furthermore, based on the observation that a clause is often not useful to most threads, we design a group testing-based strategy to perform efficient checks of usefulness.

To demonstrate the practical efficiency of our framework, we augment two state of the art SAT solvers, one multi-threaded, glucose-syrup [3], and one single-threaded, Relaxed_LCMDCBDL_newTech [1], with GPUShareSat and perform detailed analysis on benchmarks from the 2020 SAT competition on a high-performance single-GPU multi-core CPU computing cluster. Our empirical analysis demonstrates that glucose-syrup, when augmented with GPUShareSat, solves 11 more instances than glucose-syrup alone. Similarly, Relaxed_LCMDCBDL_newTech, augmented with GPUShareSat, solves 19 instances more than P-MCOMSPS-STR, the winner of the parallel track of the 2020 SAT competition.

To encourage adoption, we sought to perform minimal changes to the MiniSat-based architecture of glucose-syrup and Relaxed_LCMDCBDL_newTech. To this end, we achieved adding GPUShareSat to the respective solvers by keeping largely intact the source code running CDCL on CPU threads, modifying only the code responsible for sharing clauses.

2   Definitions

We will use lowercase to represent variables and boldface to represent (possibly, multi-dimensional) sets/vectors. For a vector x, we use x_i to represent the i-th coordinate of x. Let $v = \{v_1, v_2, \ldots v_n\}$ be the set of Boolean variables. A literal ℓ is a variable v or its negation $\neg v$. A clause C of size s is a disjunction of s literals, i.e., $C = (\ell_1 \vee \ell_2 \ldots \ell_k)$. A formula φ in Conjunctive Normal Form (CNF) is represented as conjunction of finitely many clauses.

We define a truth value as a member of the set $\{T, F, U\}$ where T stands for True, F for False, and U for unassigned. The negation of a truth value w is denoted as $\neg w$, with $\neg T = F$, $\neg F = T$, $\neg U = U$. An assignment $\mathcal{A}$ is a function that maps a variable to a truth value. Given an assignment $\mathcal{A}$ and a literal ℓ, $\mathcal{A}(l) = \mathcal{A}(v)$ if $l = v$ and $\mathcal{A}(l) = \neg \mathcal{A}(v)$ if $l = \neg v$. An assignment $\mathcal{A}$ is complete when each variable is mapped to either T or F. We say that $\mathcal{A}$ satisfies φ if $\mathcal{A}$ is complete and φ evaluates to T under $\mathcal{A}$.

In rest of the text, we assume the reader is familiar with the standard terminology such as *conflict, propagation* related to Conflict Driven Clause Learning (CDCL) paradigm; the interested reader is referred to [19] for details.

Bitwise Representation of Assignments. A vector x of truth values of size k can be represented using two size k bit-vectors (Se, Tr) wherein x_i is represented by (Se[i], Tr[i]). Se[i] is set if $x_i \neq U$. Tr[i] is set if $x_i = T$, not set if $x_i = F$, and may be set or not if $x_i = U$

We now define three functions, isFalse, isUndef, and isTrue, which are employed in our algorithmic descriptions. For a given vector x, isFalse(x) returns a bit-vector of size k whose i-th bit is set to 1 if $x_i = F$. Observe that isFalse(x) can be obtained from bitwise operations over Se and Tr, i.e., isFalse(x) = Se& $\sim$ Tr wherein & represents the bitwise AND, which operates over k bits, and $\sim$ represents the bitwise negation. Similarly, isUndef(x) returns a bit-vector such that isUndef(x)= $\sim$ Se. Finally, isTrue(x) is a size k bit-vector which can be computed as Se&Tr.

3   Related Work

Our work touches on two separate topics within the area of SAT solving: (1) multi-threaded SAT solving and (2) using GPGPUs for improving the speed of SAT solving.

Multithreaded SAT Solving. There are two main categories of parallel SAT solving strategies: one called divide-and-conquer [28] that divides the problem into always non-overlapping, and hopefully equal parts, and one called portfolio [14] that does not attempt to divide the problem, and instead relies on the cooperation of the different solver threads to attack the problem from different angles thanks to their differing configurations. This latter is the approach we take in this paper.

The original divide-and-conquer method by Zhang et al. [28] relied on so-called guiding paths to cut the problem into smaller chunks. A more modern and performant version of this approach by van der Tak et al. is called concurrent cube-and-conquer [27] that uses a lookahead solver to cut the problem into many smaller chunks that are expected to be of equivalent complexity.

ManySAT [14] pioneered the so-called portfolio approach that uses a CDCL system configured differently for each thread, each sharing some information with the other. The different configurations used by the threads are such as using different restart strategies [5,25] or different variable polarity policies [24]. The different threads in ManySAT share certain clauses with each other using lockless queues: if the CDCL algorithm's learnt clause is less than eight long, the clause is shared with other threads. Modern portfolio method SAT solvers use a number of heuristics to decide which clauses to share. In glucose-syrup [3] and Plingeling [6], clauses are shared only if their size and LBD (Literal Block Distance) is smaller than a constant. Finally, Vallade et al. [26] improved on these results by using a metric based on both community structure [7] and LBDs in their winning parallel SAT solver of the 2020 SAT competition, P-MCOMSPS-STR.

GPU Aided SAT Solving. The state-of-the-art SAT solving approach of CDCL SAT solvers does not translate well from the CPU to the GPGPU domain. One difficulty is that although the GPU can run many times more threads at once than the CPU, the memory and cache available per thread is much smaller on the GPU, and a group of threads not following the same decision path (i.e., diverging threads) cause all other threads in the same so-called 'warp' to stall. Running CDCL using the well-known watched literal scheme requires both a large amount of memory and a highly non-uniform decision path for each thread. This would make running the CDCL procedure separately in each GPU thread too slow.

Various approaches have been proposed to take advantage of GPUs to speed up SAT solving but have not yet seen widespread adoption. In [23], the GPU is used to perform unit propagation. In [21,22], the GPU is used for pre-processing the formula with techniques such as Bounded Variable Elimination and subsumption [12]. In [18], the GPU is used to perform survey propagation [8]. Finally, in [4] the authors use the GPU to execute a version of the Tabu Search algorithm [20] while the CPU is executing a multi-threaded CDCL algorithm.

4 GPUShareSat: GPU-Based Parallel SAT Solving

We now present the primary technical contribution of this paper, GPUShareSat, a GPU-based framework for parallel SAT solving. GPUShareSat bears similarity to the traditional parallel SAT solvers in its reliance on several CPU threads, wherein each thread runs its own CDCL algorithm. GPUShareSat differs crucially from its contemporaries in its usage of a dedicated CPU thread, henceforth referred to as MasterThread, to which all CPU threads export and import learnt clauses. MasterThread, in turn, relies on the adjoining GPU to inform the threads on the clauses that they should import. We present the high-level overview of GPUShareSat in Fig. 1.

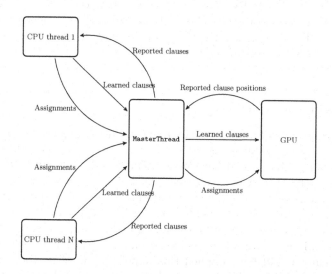

Fig. 1. Interactions between CPU threads and with the GPU

In our design of GPUShareSat, we sought to minimize modification to the overall CDCL architecture so as to ease adoption to other solvers. To this end, we only modified the subroutine for importing clauses in the context of CPU clauses wherein instead of only importing clauses at toplevel (i.e. decision level 0), we enable the solver to import clauses at the highest decision level possible while keeping the watched literal scheme consistent. Another significant modification lies in the export of the current assignment trails to MasterThread since the MasterThread decides on exporting clauses to CPU threads based on their recent

Algorithm 1. CPUSolver

```
 1: while noOtherThreadHasFoundAnAnswer() do
 2:     importFromGPU()
 3:     if propagate() == conflict then
 4:         c ← ConflictAnalysis()
 5:         if level == 0 then
 6:             return UNSAT
 7:         SendtoGPU(c)
 8:         addClauseToDatabase(c)
 9:         backtrack
10:     else
11:         if allVariablesAreSet() then
12:             return SAT
13:         sendCurrentAssignToGpu()
14:         decide()
```

assignments. We present the simplified pseudocode for the CPU thread's solver in Algorithm 1 in Appendix. The pseudocode follow the standard CPU solver along with three additions: (1) The CPU thread seeks to eagerly import the clauses from GPU (line 2), (2) the CPU thread sends the learnt clause to GPU (line 7), (3) the CPU thread send the current assignment to the GPU thread (line 13).

4.1 Usefulness of Clauses

From the perspective of a CPU thread, a natural desiderata would be to import clauses that will be useful in its search in the future. To this end, we hypothesize that clauses that would have been useful recently are likely to be useful in the future since the search space of CDCL tends to be local. To this end, MasterThread needs to decide how to determine whether a clause cl would be useful to a given thread, say Thread. Consider an assignment of a thread where unit propagation completed without conflict, and a clause cl which this thread does not have. If all literals of this clause are false except for one which is undef, then this clause would have implied this undef literal. So it would have been used in unit propagation. If all literals of this clause are false, then this clause would have been in conflict, so it would have been useful as well.

We formalize the above observation via the notion of *triggering*: let $\mathcal{A}$ be a partial assignment. We say that cl would trigger $\mathcal{A}$ if cl would result in unit propagation with respect to $\mathcal{A}$ or trigger a conflict with respect to $\mathcal{A}$. We capture the notion of trigger, formally, in the following definition:

Definition 1. *A clause* cl *of size s triggers on an assignment* $\mathcal{A}$ *if both of the following conditions hold true:*

1. *For each literal ℓ in* cl, $\mathcal{A}(\ell) \neq T$
2. *For at least s - 1 literals $\ell \in$* cl, $\mathcal{A}(\ell) = F$

Therefore, we view that a clause cl would have been useful to Thread, if it would have triggered on a recent assignment trail of Thread. Informally, the presence of such a clause cl would have influenced the recent state of the solver in Thread. It is worth remarking that Audemard and Simon had also put forth a similar thesis in the context of glucose solver [2] in that they measured a clause usefulness by how often it is used in unit propagation or conflict analysis. At this point, a natural question is to determine the partial assignments for which we should determine if a given clause would trigger them or not. While on one end of the spectrum, we could perform such a check for every partial assignment but this would overwhelm MasterThread. Therefore, a given thread Thread only sends partial assignment where unit propagation completed without conflict.

4.2 Assignment Trigger Check

We now discuss how to perform an efficient check whether a clause triggers on the assignments sent from different CPU threads. To this end, we focus on the efficient bitwise operations for checking whether a clause triggers on the assignments, which were first proposed in [15]. We consider that we are given the k assignments $\mathcal{A}$; we use $\mathcal{A}_i$ for $1 \leq i \leq k$ to represent the i-th assignment. Recall, for every variable v, we represent $\mathcal{A}(v)$ with two bit-vectors of size k. Their i-th bit will represent $\mathcal{A}_i(v)$. For a literal $\ell = \neg v$, $\mathcal{A}(\ell)$ is computed as the negation of $\mathcal{A}(v)$. These representations allows us to check if a clause cl of size s triggers over k assignments at once using bitwise operations. We present the pseudocode of assignmentTrigger in Algorithm 2. assignmentTrigger returns a bit-vector res of size k, where res[i] is set to 1 if the clause cl triggers on the assignment $\mathcal{A}_i$. In this algorithm, & represent the bitwise AND. | represents the bitwise OR. They operate over k bits at once and are executed in only one clock cycle on the GPU provided that $k \leq 32$.

Algorithm 2. assignmentTrigger($\mathcal{A}$, cl)

1: allFalse ← [1, ··· 1]   ▷ bit-vector of size k with each bit initialized to 1
2: oneUndef ← [0, ··· , 0]   ▷ bit-vector of size k with each bit initialized to 0
3: for $\ell \in$ cl do
4:    oneUndef ← (allFalse&isUndef($\mathcal{A}(\ell)$)) | (oneUndef&isFalse($\mathcal{A}(\ell)$))
5:    allFalse ← allFalse&isFalse($\mathcal{A}(\ell)$)
6: res ← oneUndef | allFalse
7: **return** res

All the clauses can be tested in parallel from each other, so assignmentTrigger is massively parallelisable, it fits well with the GPU.

4.3 Pooling-Based Efficient Trigger Check

While the standard GPU-based implementations allow us to perform check for k up to 32 assignments in parallel, the latency of each check is not sufficient to handle the rate of assignments sent by CPU threads. Observe that a CPU thread sends an assignment for every decision that did not result in conflict upon unit propagation. In this context, one wonders whether we need to perform a check for every assignment. To this end, we relied on two preliminary analyses:

Locality. We performed a preliminary evaluation on 100 instances randomly chosen from the SAT 2020 competition, and for each variable, we compute the set of all the values taken between 32 conflicts. Our preliminary evaluation results are presented in Table 1

Table 1. Behavior of successive assignments

Set of values	{T}	{F}	{T, F}	{U}	{T, U}	{F, U}	{T, F, U}
Fraction of variables	0.063	0.182	0.000	0.588	0.031	0.085	0.048

The first row of Table 1 lists the set of values while the second row indicates the fraction of variables with the corresponding set of values. For example, the entry, $\{T, U\}$ indicates that 3.1% of the variables were assigned the values T and U at least once, but not F, between the 32 conflicts. The entry $\{U\}$ tells us that 58.8% of variables only took the value U between the 32 conflicts. Therefore, we observe that the successive assignments coming from the same CPU thread share a significant similarity.

Sparsity. The second key observation, based on preliminary evaluation, is that, on average, less than 1% assignments are triggered by a given clause.

The observations of *locality* and *sparsity* lead us to draw parallels to a fundamental problem in information theory: group testing, pioneered by Dorfman [11]. In the context of the second world war, the task under consideration was to determine the relatively small fraction of sick soldiers in a large army by performing as few tests as possible. Dorfman suggested a simple but effective idea: pool the blood samples of soldiers into groups and perform individualized testing only for the groups that test positive.

We seek to design a similar strategy in the context of determining assignments triggers by a clause. To this end, we aim to capture the concept of *pooling* by defining the notion of an *pooled assignment*.

Definition 2. *Given the assignments* $(\mathcal{A}_i)_{1 \leq i \leq k}$ *, the pooled assignment* $P : V \mapsto 2^{\{T,F,U\}}$ *is defined by* $P(v) = \bigcup_{1 \leq i \leq k} \{\mathcal{A}_i(v)\}$. *Similarly, for a literal* ℓ, *we define* $P(\ell)$ *as* $\bigcup_{1 \leq i \leq k} \{\mathcal{A}_i(\ell)\}$

Definition 3. *For* $p \subseteq \{T, F, U\}$, *we denote* $\neg p = \{\neg x \mid x \in p\}$

Proposition 1. *Given the assignments* $(\mathcal{A}_i)_{1 \leq i \leq k}$, P *their pooled assignments and a literal* $\ell = \neg v$, $P(\ell) = \neg P(v)$

Proof. $P(\ell) = P(\neg v) = \bigcup_{1 \leq i \leq k} \{\mathcal{A}_i(\neg v)\} = \bigcup_{1 \leq i \leq k} \{\neg \mathcal{A}_i(v)\} = \neg \bigcup_{1 \leq i \leq k} \{\mathcal{A}_i(v)\} = \neg P(v)$

Example 1. Given the assignments $(v_1 \mapsto T, v_2 \mapsto F, v_3 \mapsto U)$ and $(v_1 \mapsto T, v_2 \mapsto U, v_3 \mapsto T)$, their pooled assignment is $(v_1 \mapsto \{T\}, v_2 \mapsto \{F, U\}, v_3 \mapsto \{U, T\})$

Remark 1. The value of a pooled assignment for a variable is a set of truth value p. It can be represented using three Boolean variables (t, f, u), where t (resp. f, u) indicates if $T \in p$ (resp. $F \in p$, $U \in p$).

Remark 2. Given a vector of m pool assignments P and a variable v, we can represent the vector values for v as $(\mathsf{canBeTrue}(P(v)), \mathsf{canBeFalse}(P(v)), \mathsf{canBeUndef}(P(v)))$. $(\mathsf{canBeTrue}(P(v)), \mathsf{canBeFalse}(P(v)))$ and $\mathsf{canBeUndef}(P(v)))$ are bit-vectors of size m. For a literal $\ell = \neg v$, we have $\mathsf{canBeTrue}(P(\ell)) = \mathsf{canBeFalse}(P(v)), \mathsf{canBeFalse}(P(\ell)) = \mathsf{canBeTrue}(P(v)), \mathsf{canBeUndef}(P(\ell)) = \mathsf{canBeUndef}(P(v))$

Akin to group testing, we seek to first determine whether a clause cl *triggers* a polled assignment. To this end, we extend the definition of trigger.

Definition 4. *A clause* cl *of size s triggers on an pooled assignment P if both of the following conditions hold true:*

1. *For each literal ℓ in* cl, $P(\ell) \cap \{U, F\} \neq \emptyset$
2. *For at least s - 1 literals $\ell \in$* cl, $F \in P(\ell)$

Next we make a simple but crucial observation:

Theorem 1. *Given the assignments* $(\mathcal{A}_i)_{1 \leq i \leq k}$ *and their associated pooled assignment P, if there exists an assignment $\mathcal{A}_i$ such that a clause* cl *triggers on $\mathcal{A}_i$, then* cl *triggers on P.*

Proof. Let $(\mathcal{A}_i)_{1 \leq i \leq k}$ be assignments, P their associated pooled assignment, $1 \leq i \leq k$, and cl a clause of size s which triggers $(\mathcal{A}_i)$.

From condition 1 of Definition 1, for each literal ℓ in cl, $\mathcal{A}_i(\ell) \neq T$, so $\mathcal{A}_i(\ell) \in \{F, U\}$. In addition, $\mathcal{A}_i(\ell) \in P(l)$. So condition 1. of Definition 4 $P(\ell) \cap \{U, F\} \neq \emptyset$ is met. From condition 2 of Definition 1, there are at least s - 1 literals in cl with $\mathcal{A}_i(\ell) = F$. For all of these, since $\mathcal{A}_i(\ell) \in P(l)$, condition 2. of Definition 4: $F \in P(\ell)$ is met.

By contraposition of this theorem: if a clause does not trigger on a pooled assignment, it does not trigger on all the individual assignments.

Example 2. Given the assignments $(v_1 \mapsto F, v_2 \mapsto T)$ and $(v_1 \mapsto T, v_2 \mapsto F)$, The clause $v_1 \vee v_2$ does not trigger on either of them. It does trigger on their associated pooled assignment $(v_1 \mapsto \{T, F\}, v_2 \mapsto \{T, F\})$ though. This example shows that a clause may trigger on a pooled assignment without triggering on any individual assignment.

We now discuss how the notion of pooling can be efficiently employed to determining assignments triggered by a clause. We previously proposed an algorithm that tested which clause triggered over k assignments (with $k \leq 32$). We propose a new algorithm that returns whether a clause triggers over up to $k \times m$ assignments, where in practice, we choose $m = 32$.

To this end, we employ a two-step process: we first check which pooled assignment a clause triggers. For each pooled assignment it triggers, we employ assignmentTrigger to locate the corresponding assignments, if any. The successive assignments from a CPU solver thread are pooled together by the `MasterThread` into m pools (in practice, we choose $m = 32$). If the number of CPU threads is lower than m, then we can also create several pools for each CPU solver thread.

The assignments are: $(\mathcal{A}_{ij})_{1 \leq i \leq m, 1 \leq j \leq k}$ where i represents the groups and j the assignment within the pool. While it is possible in practice not to have the same number of assignments within a pool, we will assume that they all have k assignments for simplicity. Note that each assignment maps a variable to a truth value. For each $1 \leq i \leq m$, P_i will be the pooled assignment associated with the assignments $(\mathcal{A}_{ij})_{1 \leq j \leq k}$, that is for every variable v, $P_i(v) = \bigcup_{1 \leq j \leq k}\{\mathcal{A}_{ij}(v)\}$.

Algorithm 3. poolTrigger($\mathcal{A} = (\mathcal{A}_{ij})_{1 \leq i \leq m, 1 \leq j \leq k}$, $\boldsymbol{P} = (P_i)_{1 \leq i \leq m}$, cl)

1: allFalse $\leftarrow [1, \cdots 1]$ ▷ bit-vector of size m with each bit initialized to 1
2: oneUndef $\leftarrow [0, \cdots, 0]$ ▷ bit-vector of size m with each bit initialized to 0
3: **for** $\ell \in$ cl **do**
4:     oneUndef $\leftarrow$ (allFalse&canBeUndef($\boldsymbol{P}(\ell)$)) | (oneUndef&canBeFalse($\boldsymbol{P}(\ell)$))
5:     allFalse $\leftarrow$ allFalse&canBeFalse($\boldsymbol{P}(\ell)$)

6: agTrigger $\leftarrow$ oneUndef | allFalse
7: **for** bit position i set in agTrigger **do**
8:     assigTrigger $\leftarrow$ assignmentTrigger(($\mathcal{A}_{ij})_{1 \leq j \leq k}$, cl)
9:     **if** assigTrigger $\neq 0$ **then**
10:         report(i, assigTrigger)

We present the pseudocode of the pooling-based trigger check procedure, called poolTrigger, in Algorithm 3. We now discuss the pseudocode of poolTrigger in detail. The algorithm first performs the check to determine the pooled assignments $\{P_i\}$ such that the clause cl triggers P_i. The check is similar to that of assignmentTrigger, wherein we substitute the usage of bit-vector(isSet, isUndef) with bit-vectors (canBeTrue, canBeFalse, canBeUndef) to account for the need for 3 bits to represent a pooled assignment. Observe that the bit-vectors (canBeTrue, canBeFalse, canBeUndef) represent the set of m pooled assignments, and therefore, are of the size $n \times m$. The bit-vector agTrigger stores which of the pooled assignments are triggered by cl. Observe that even though a pooled assignment P_i may be triggered by cl, it does not necessarily imply that there exists an assignment $\mathcal{A}_{i,j}$ in the assignments associated with P_i such that cl triggers $\mathcal{A}_{i,j}$. Therefore, for each of the pooled assignments triggered by cl, we employ assignmentTrigger to determine whether there exists an assignment triggered by cl and whenever such an assignment exists, the corresponding thread is notified of the clause cl, which is encapsulated in the subroutine report.

4.4 GPU Implementation

The representation on the GPU of the assignments is as follows: for each solver thread, we have an array of size n (number of variables), whose elements are the two bit-vectors of size k (Se, Tr) which represent the values of this variable for the assignments of this solver. In addition, there is another array of size n representing the pooled assignments. Its elements are the three bit-vectors (canBeTrue, canBeFalse, canBeUndef).

During a GPU run, we start by updating the assignments on the GPU with the new values of the assignments sent by the CPU threads. Only the modifications with the previous assignments are sent. The pooled assignments are updated at the same time as the assignments. A precise description of the algorithm to update the assignments and pooled assignments is not in scope for this paper.

Then, the GPU finds which clauses trigger on which assignments, using the Algorithm 3. Finally, the clauses that did trigger are reported to the CPU threads, which can then import them. We then start the next GPU run.

Similar to CPU solvers, MasterThread needs to regularly delete clauses to avoid running out of memory and becoming too slow. So, MasterThread performs memory management via activity-based clause deletion. We bump the activity of a clause whenever the clause triggers an assignment. Thus, similar to CPU solvers, we try to keep good clauses and delete bad ones on the GPU.

Assignment of GPU Clauses to GPU Threads. In our implementation, during a GPU run, each clause is looked at by only one GPU thread. In the CUDA computation model, GPU threads are grouped into warps of fixed size, which, in practice, is 32. Therefore, in our case, the 32 threads in a warp will look at 32 different clauses and find which ones trigger by also reading assignments and pooled assignments. Once they are done with these, they will look at the next set of 32 clauses and so on. The GPU is most efficient if all the threads in a warp execute the same instructions at the same time. If divergence happens and only some threads take an execution path, then the others will have to wait. Some instructions have to be executed at the beginning of execution over a clause and at the end. So, it is better if all threads in a warp execute these instructions at the same time. We also chose to have all the threads in a warp look at clauses of the same size. This avoids the case where a single thread looks at a very long clause and blocks the entire warp from moving to the next set of clauses. To achieve this, we chose to group all the clauses on the GPU by their size. Each warp will only look at clauses of a given size.

Using Memory Coalescing in CUDA. Reading the GPU memory is most efficient if the reads are coalesced, which happens, for example, if successive threads in a warp read successive 4-byte words in memory. We chose to coalesce reading the clauses by reordering how we represent them in memory to how they are accessed. Firstly, all the threads in a warp will read the first literal of their clauses. Then, they will read their second literal, and so on. So, we chose to order clauses in memory following this pattern. The first 32 4-bytes words will represent the first 32 literals of the clauses of a warp. The next 32 4-bytes words will represent the next 32 literals of the clauses of a warp, and so on.

Thanks to this coalescing, reading the clauses can be performed efficiently. Whenever a literal from a clause is read, we need to read the value of that literal for the pooled assignments or assignments. That variable might be anywhere in memory, so the access pattern for reading the assignments is not as efficient. However, they might be cached, especially if there are fewer variables.

Whenever a GPU thread finds a clause that triggers, it needs to report the clause to the CPU. We chose to only report an identifier of the clause (its size and position within that size), as well as the assignment it triggers on. By keeping a copy of all the clauses on the CPU, we can reconstruct the full clause just from this clause identifier. The clause reported is added to a queue. We use an atomic operation to increment the position in the queue by one and write to that position. This avoids having two threads writing to the same position in the queue at the same time.

Avoiding Clause Duplication on the CPU. We aim to avoid a CPU thread having the same clause multiple times in its database, as it slows down the thread due to unit propagation overhead and uses up memory. If a CPU thread has a clause cl in its database, then cl will not trigger on assignments sent by this thread to `MasterThread`, so cl will not be reported again. However, after a thread sends an assignment to `MasterThread`, the thread does not wait to receive clauses before sending more assignments. Therefore, it is possible for a thread to send two assignments to `MasterThread` and for a clause cl to trigger on both the assignments. Therefore, in order to avoid reporting cl multiple times to the same thread, `MasterThread` keeps for every thread a set of GPU clause identifiers that have been reported recently.

5   Evaluation

We developed a prototype implementation of GPUShareSat in the form of a library, and we augmented two state-of-the-art award-winning SAT solvers with GPUShareSat[1]. The objective of our empirical evaluation was two-fold: runtime performance comparison of solvers augmented with GPUShareSat vis-a-vis state of the art parallel solvers, and an in-depth investigation of the inner working of GPUShareSat. In particular, we sought to answer the following questions:

---

[1] The accompanying artefact consisting of detailed statistics is available at https://doi.org/10.5281/zenodo.4764813.

RQ 1. How does the runtime performance of solvers augmented with GPUShareSat compare to that of the winners of parallel track in recent SAT competitions?

RQ 2. How effective is the pooling-based strategy?

RQ 3. What are the characteristics of the workload on the GPU?

Experimental Setup. Our empirical evaluation seeks to follow the recently released SAT practitioner manifesto. We use the standard 5000 s wall-clock time-out on the benchmarks from SAT competition 2020. All experiments were conducted on a high-performance computer cluster, each node consisting of nodes with 2×E5-2690v3 CPUs containing 2×12 real cores, 96 GB of RAM, and an NVidia K40 GPU.

To answer **RQ 1**, we integrated GPUShareSat with Relaxed_LCMDCBDL_newTech, which scored 2nd place at the 2020 SAT Competition's main (i.e. single-core) track, and called the resulting implementation Relaxed-Gpu. In Relaxed-Gpu, we removed the duplicate learnt clause detection (`is_duplicate`) and associated data structures, as they could use up to 50 GB of memory for a single thread. We used the same parameters and search strategy for all CPU threads to isolate the performance improvement to our system. The diversity of search came only from the fact that clause exchange is non-deterministic due to scheduling differences. If we were to use differing parameters for the threads, as solvers taking the portfolio approach usually do, we would expect performance to improve.

We perform a runtime performance comparison of Relaxed-Gpu vis-a-vis P-MCOMSPS-STR, the winner of the SAT competition 2020 parallel track. We analyzed the performance of P-MCOMSPS-STR for 12 and 24 threads, and surprisingly, the implementation of P-MCOMSPS-STR with 12 threads outperformed P-MCOMSPS-STR with 24 threads by 14 more problems solved and 10% better PAR-2 score and therefore, we perform a comparison of Relaxed-Gpu for 12 threads.

Furthermore, for **RQ 2** and **RQ 3**, we augmented GPUShareSat with glucose-syrup given the ease of collection of detailed statistics from glucose-syrup. We refer to the augmented version by glucose-syrup-gpu. Since the objective of **RQ 3** is to understand the workload with as many CPU threads as possible, we run the experiments with 24 threads. We report the average of all the statistics over all the benchmark instances.

Summary of the Results

We observe that Relaxed-Gpu significantly outperforms P-MCOMSPS-STR, the winning parallel SAT solver of the 2020 SAT competition, both in terms of the number of solved instances and PAR-2 score. In particular, while P-MCOMSPS-STR could only solve 276 instances with a PAR-2 score of 3493, Relaxed-Gpu could solve 296 instances with a PAR-2 score of 3164. In the context of **RQ 2**, we observe that usage of pooling allows us to skip invoking of assignmentTrigger for over 99.8% of the assignments. Finally, GPUShareSat managed to keep up with as many as 24 CPU threads both in clauses checked per second and in the number of clauses kept in memory, enabling GPUShareSat to efficiently and effectively inform the CPU threads of the clauses they should import. Observe that the GPU employed in our experiments, the NVidia K40, would be classified as a relatively slow GPU from the perspective of GPUs typically employed by the deep learning community. A more modern GPU such as an NVidia RTX 3080 has $\approx$ 10x the performance relative to the K40.

Overall, our results demonstrate that GPUShareSat can be used either as a drop-in tool to improve already parallel SAT solvers, or to make single-threaded SAT solvers into powerful, multi-threaded SAT solvers that can outperform state of the art parallel SAT solvers.

RQ 1: Relaxed-Gpu **vis-a-vis P-MCOMSPS-STR.** Figure 2 presents the run-time performance comparison of Relaxed-Gpu vis-a-vis P-MCOMSPS-STR in form of a cactus plot. A point (x, y) represents the corresponding solver solved x instances in less than y seconds. The figure clearly shows the performance improvement achieved by Relaxed-Gpu in comparison to P-MCOMSPS-STR. In particular, Relaxed-Gpu solved 296 instances with a PAR-2 score of 3164, while P-MCOMSPS-STR could only solve 276 instances with a PAR-2 score of 3493. In particular, P-MCOMSPS-STR solved 143 SAT and 133 UNSAT instances while Relaxed-Gpu solved 175 SAT and 121 UNSAT instances. Note that Relaxed_LCMDCBDL_newTech was significantly stronger on SAT than UNSAT instances in the SAT Competition of 2020; hence the slanted distribution towards SAT in the case of Relaxed-Gpu is expected.

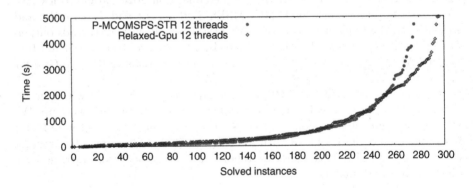

Fig. 2. Relaxed-Gpu vis-a-vis P-MCOMSPS-STR.

RQ 2: Impact of Pooling-Based Trigger Check. The primary rationale behind the usage of pooling-based trigger check was the potential benefits due to avoidance of the redundant invocation for assignmentTrigger for a large number of assignments when their associated pooled assignment does not trigger the clause of interest. To this end, we computed *no-triggers*, defined as the fraction of tuples (P, cl) such that the clause cl did not trigger the pooled assignment P over the set of all possible tuples. Our evaluation indicated *no-triggers*, averaged over the entire set of instances, is 0.9984, which represents a significant reduction in the number of invocations of assignmentTrigger. The primary reason behind a surprisingly high value of *no-triggers* is that the average learnt clause size for glucose-syrup was 54.43 literals/learnt clauses. For such large learnt clauses, there is a high likelihood of a learnt clause containing two unassigned literals with respect to a given pooled assignment.

RQ 3: Characteristics of the Workload of GPU. Since our analysis of the characteristics appeals to the performance improvement due to GPUShareSat in the context of glucose-syrup, we first present the corresponding cactus plot in Fig. 3. It is worth remarking that while glucose-syrup solved 252 instances with a PAR-2 score of 4208, glucose-syrup-gpu solved 263 instances with a PAR-2 score of 3853.

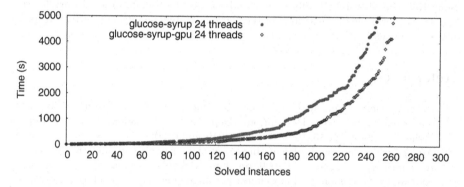

Fig. 3. Glucose-syrup vis-a-vis glucose-syrup-gpu. glucose-syrup solved 124 SAT and 127 UNSAT instances. Glucose-syrup-gpu solved 132 SAT and 131 UNSAT instances.

We now delve deeper into analyzing the characteristics of the workload of the GPU. The average number of clauses imported per thread was 0.120 per conflict or 0.210 per assignment sent to the GPU. In the case of glucose-syrup, the corresponding number was 1.27 clauses per conflict, which is 10.6 times higher. Therefore, glucose-syrup-gpu is able to import fewer but useful clauses.

The number of clauses checked by the GPU in glucose-syrup-gpu was 160.3 million clauses/s on average. Clause checks were performed over a number of assignments at once, and the number of clause tests on individual assignments was 18.66 billion per second on average. Note that most of these clause tests did not require a call to assignmentTrigger thanks to the pool checks. To put this number into perspective, glucose-syrup propagated 0.850 million literals/thread/s and checked for propagation 16.69 million clauses/thread/s. Therefore, from the perspective of checking clauses, a single 12 core E5-2690v3 CPU performed on a much lower scale than a single NVidia K40 GPU.

When it comes to learnt clauses kept in memory, we see a similar pattern. glucose-syrup-gpu kept an average of 1.50 million learnt clauses in the GPU during solving, while a single thread of glucose-syrup kept 77,436, amounting to 1.85 million learnt clauses for 24 threads.

6   Conclusion

We design an efficient framework, called GPUShareSat, to take advantage of heterogeneous architectures. We identified that GPUs can efficiently determine the clauses that a CPU thread should import from other threads. We observed that GPUShareSat integrated with Relaxed_LCMDCBDL_newTech significantly outperforms the parallel track's winning solver from the 2020 SAT competition. We have released GPUShareSat as an open source library and we hope our results will encourage the community to integrate GPUShareSat into existing solvers.

Acknowledgments. This work was supported in part by National Research Foundation Singapore under its NRF Fellowship Programme [NRF-NRFFAI1-2019-0004] and Sung Kah Kay Assistant Professorship Endowment. The computational work for this article was performed on resources of the National Supercomputing Centre, Singapore https://www.nscc.sg.

References

1. Relaxed backtracking with rephasing. In Proceedings of SAT Competition 2020: Solver and Benchmark Descriptions, Department of Computer Science Report Series B 2020–1, pp. 15–16. University of Helsinki (2020)
2. Audemard, G., Simon, L.: Predicting learnt clauses quality in modern SAT solvers. In: Boutilier, C. (ed.) IJCAI 2009, pp. 399–404 (2009)
3. Audemard, G., Simon, L.: Lazy clause exchange policy for parallel SAT solvers. In: Sinz, C., Egly, U. (eds.) SAT 2014. LNCS, vol. 8561, pp. 197–205. Springer, Cham (2014). https://doi.org/10.1007/978-3-319-09284-3_15
4. Beckers, S., De Samblanx, G., De Smedt, F., Goedeme, T., Struyf, L., Vennekens, J.: Parallel hybrid SAT solving using OpenCL. In: Benelux Conference on Artificial Intelligence. Springer (2012)
5. Biere, A.: Adaptive restart strategies for conflict driven SAT solvers. In: Kleine Büning, H., Zhao, X. (eds.) SAT 2008. LNCS, vol. 4996, pp. 28–33. Springer, Heidelberg (2008). https://doi.org/10.1007/978-3-540-79719-7_4
6. Biere, A.: Lingeling, plingeling and treengeling entering the SAT competition 2013. In: Proceedings of SAT Competition 2013, vol. B-2013-1 of Department of Computer Science Series, pp. 51–52. University of Helsinki (2013)
7. Blondel, V.D., Guillaume, J.L., Lambiotte, R., Lefebvre, E.: Fast unfolding of communities in large networks. J. Stat. Mech. Theor. Exp. **2008**(10), P10008 (2008)
8. Braunstein, A., Mézard, M., Zecchina, R.: Survey propagation: an algorithm for satisfiability. Random Struct. Algorithms **27**(2), 201–226 (2005)
9. Coates, A., Huval, B., Wang, T., Wu, D.J., Catanzaro, B., Andrew, Y.N.: Deep learning with COTS HPC systems. In: Proceedings of the 30th International Conference on Machine Learning, ICML 2013, Atlanta, GA, USA, 16–21 June 2013, volume 28 of JMLR Workshop and Conference Proceedings, pp. 1337–1345. JMLR.org (2013)

10. Dennard, R.H., Gaensslen, F.H., Yu, H., Rideout, V.L., Bassous, E., LeBlanc, A.R.: Design of ion-implanted MOSFET's with very small physical dimensions. IEEE J. Solid-State Circuits **9**(5), 256–268 (1974)
11. Dorfman, R.: The detection of defective members of large populations. Ann. Math. Stat. **14**(4), 436–440 (1943)
12. Eén, N., Biere, A.: Effective preprocessing in SAT through variable and clause elimination. In: Bacchus, F., Walsh, T. (eds.) SAT 2005. LNCS, vol. 3569, pp. 61–75. Springer, Heidelberg (2005). https://doi.org/10.1007/11499107_5
13. Eén, N., Sörensson, N.: An extensible SAT-solver. In: Giunchiglia, E., Tacchella, A. (eds.) SAT 2003. LNCS, vol. 2919, pp. 502–518. Springer, Heidelberg (2004). https://doi.org/10.1007/978-3-540-24605-3_37
14. Hamadi, Y., Jabbour, S., Sais, L.: Manysat: a parallel SAT solver. J. Satisf. Boolean Model. Comput. **6**(4), 245–262 (2009)
15. Heule, M., van Maaren, H.: Parallel SAT solving using bit-level operations. J. Satisf. Boolean Model. Comput. **4**(2–4), 99–116 (2008)
16. Knuth, D.E.: The Art of Computer Programming, vol. 4, Fascicle 6: Satisfiability, 1st edn. Addison-Wesley Professional, Boston (2015)
17. Malik, S., Zhao, Y., Madigan, C.F., Zhang, L., Moskewicz, M.W.: Chaff: engineering an efficient SAT solver. In: Design Automation Conference, pp. 530–535 (2001)
18. Manolios, P., Zhang, Y.: Implementing survey propagation on graphics processing units. In: Biere, A., Gomes, C.P. (eds.) SAT 2006. LNCS, vol. 4121, pp. 311–324. Springer, Heidelberg (2006). https://doi.org/10.1007/11814948_30
19. Marques-Silva, J., Lynce, I., Malik, S.: Conflict-driven clause learning sat solvers. In: Handbook of Satisfiability, pp. 131–153. IOS Press (2009)
20. Mazure, B., Sais, L., Grégoire, É.: Boosting complete techniques thanks to local search methods. Ann. Math. Artif. Intell. **22**(3–4), 319–331 (1998)
21. Osama, M., Wijs, A.: Parallel SAT simplification on GPU architectures. In: Vojnar, T., Zhang, L. (eds.) TACAS 2019, Part I. LNCS, vol. 11427, pp. 21–40. Springer, Cham (2019). https://doi.org/10.1007/978-3-030-17462-0_2
22. Osama, M., Wijs, A., Biere, A.: Sat solving with GPU accelerated inprocessing. In: Proceedings of TACAS (2021)
23. Dal Palù, A., Dovier, A., Formisano, A., Pontelli, E.: Cud@sat: SAT solving on GPUs. J. Exp. Theor. Artif. Intell. **27**(3), 293–316 (2015)
24. Pipatsrisawat, K., Darwiche, A.: A lightweight component caching scheme for satisfiability solvers. In: Marques-Silva, J., Sakallah, K.A. (eds.) SAT 2007. LNCS, vol. 4501, pp. 294–299. Springer, Heidelberg (2007). https://doi.org/10.1007/978-3-540-72788-0_28
25. Ryvchin, V., Strichman, O.: Local restarts. In: Kleine Büning, H., Zhao, X. (eds.) SAT 2008. LNCS, vol. 4996, pp. 271–276. Springer, Heidelberg (2008). https://doi.org/10.1007/978-3-540-79719-7_25
26. Vallade, V., Le Frioux, L., Baarir, S., Sopena, J., Ganesh, V., Kordon, F.: Community and LBD-based clause sharing policy for parallel SAT solving. In: Pulina, L., Seidl, M. (eds.) SAT 2020. LNCS, vol. 12178, pp. 11–27. Springer, Cham (2020). https://doi.org/10.1007/978-3-030-51825-7_2
27. van der Tak, P., Heule, M., Biere, A.: Concurrent cube-and-conquer. CoRR, abs/1402.4465 (2014)
28. Zhang, H., Bonacina, M.P., Hsiang, J.: PSATO: a distributed propositional prover and its application to quasigroup problems. J. Symb. Comput. **21**(4), 543–560 (1996)

A Proof Builder for Max-SAT

Matthieu Py[(⊠)], Mohamed Sami Cherif, and Djamal Habet

Aix-Marseille Univ, Université de Toulon, CNRS, LIS, Marseille, France
{matthieu.py,mohamed-sami.cherif,djamal.habet}@univ-amu.fr

Abstract. Complete Max-SAT solvers are able to return the optimal value of an input instance but they do not provide any certificate of its validity. In this paper, we introduce for the first time a Max-SAT proof builder, called MS-Builder, which generates Max-SAT proofs under the particular form of a sequence of Max-SAT equivalence-preserving transformations. To generate a Max-SAT proof, MS-Builder iteratively calls a SAT oracle to get a SAT refutation which is handled and adapted into a sound refutation for Max-SAT. We also propose an extendable tool, called MS-Checker, able to verify the validity of any proof using Max-SAT inference rules.

Keywords: Max-SAT · Proof · Max-SAT resolution

1 Introduction

Given a Boolean formula in Conjunctive Normal Form (CNF), the Maximum Satisfiability (Max-SAT) problem consists in determining the maximum number of clauses that it is possible to satisfy by an assignment of the variables. Max-SAT is an optimization extension of the Satisfiability (SAT) problem and a natural way to model many real world and crafted problems [12,15,32] making it a well studied problem in theory as well as in practice. Different complete solving paradigms for Max-SAT have seen the day in recent years including Branch and Bound algorithms [1,18,23], SAT-based algorithms [2,26,27] and reduction to other problems (such as ILP [13], Max-ASP [3] and WCSP [14]).

Recent years have also witnessed a particular interest in proof systems for Max-SAT [9–11,19–21,28]. In particular, Max-SAT resolution [10,11,19] was one of the first known complete systems for Max-SAT and was later extensively used in the context of Max-SAT solving [1,23,27]. However, generating proofs establishing the optimum cost of Max-SAT formulas remains an unexplored topic in practice. Indeed, current Max-SAT solvers are not able to output certificates as it is the case for SAT solvers. This is in part due to the variety of paradigms and techniques for Max-SAT solving which make it difficult to devise a generalized approach to compute certificates.

In this paper, we devise an independent proof builder for Max-SAT, called MS-Builder, which builds proofs for Max-SAT by iteratively calling a SAT oracle to get a resolution refutation. The builder relies on recent work [28] to adapt the

© Springer Nature Switzerland AG 2021
C.-M. Li and F. Manyà (Eds.): SAT 2021, LNCS 12831, pp. 488–498, 2021.
https://doi.org/10.1007/978-3-030-80223-3_33

SAT refutation into a Max-SAT refutation which is then applied to the current formula. Moreover, we introduce an extendable Max-SAT proof checker, called MS-Checker, to verify the validity of any proof using Max-SAT inference rules. Both tools are experimentally evaluated on the unweighted partial benchmark of the 2020 Max-SAT Evaluation [4].

This paper is organized as follows. Section 2 includes some necessary definitions and notations. Section 3 recalls related work on the adaptation of SAT refutations to Max-SAT refutations. MS-Builder and MS-Checker are respectively presented in Sects. 4 and 5 and their experimental evaluation is detailed in Sect. 6. Finally, we conclude and discuss future work in Sect. 7.

2   Preliminaries

2.1   Definitions and Notations

Let X be a set of propositional variables. A literal l is a variable $x \in X$ or its negation $\overline{x}$. A clause c is a disjunction of literals $(l_1 \vee l_2 \vee \cdots \vee l_k)$. A formula ϕ in Conjunctive Normal Form (CNF) is a conjunction of clauses $\phi = c_1 \wedge c_2 \wedge \cdots \wedge c_m$. An assignment $I : X \longrightarrow \{true, false\}$ maps each variable to a boolean value and can be represented as a set of literals. A literal l is satisfied (resp. falsified) by I if $l \in I$ (resp. $\overline{l} \in I$). A clause c is satisfied by I if at least one of its literals is satisfied by I, otherwise it is falsified by I. The empty clause $\square$ contains zero literals and is always falsified. A clause c opposes a clause c' if c contains a literal whose negation is in c', i.e. $\exists l \in c$, $\overline{l} \in c'$. For a given CNF formula, solving the Satisfiability (SAT) problem consists in determining whether there exists an assignment I (called model) that satisfies it. The cost of an assignment I is the number of clauses falsified by I. For a given CNF formula ϕ, solving the (plain) Max-SAT problem consists in determining the maximum number of satisfied clauses in ϕ.

2.2   Resolution Refutations in SAT

To certify that a CNF formula is satisfiable, it is sufficient to exhibit a model of the formula. On the other hand, to prove that a CNF formula is unsatisfiable, we need to refute the existence of a model. A well-known SAT refutation system is based on an inference rule for SAT called resolution [29]. The resolution rule, defined below, deduces a clause called resolvent which can be added to the formula from two opposed clauses.

Definition 1 (Resolution [29]). *Given two clauses* $c_1 = (x \vee A)$ *and* $c_2 = (\overline{x} \vee B)$, *the resolution rule is defined as follows:*

$$\frac{c_1 = (x \vee A) \quad c_2 = (\overline{x} \vee B)}{c_3 = (A \vee B)}$$

A resolution refutation is a sequence of resolutions leading to an empty clause. Many restricted classes of resolution refutations have been studied in the literature namely linear resolution [24], unit resolution [16], input resolution [16], regular resolution [31], read-once resolution [17] and tree (or tree-like) resolution refutations [5] among others. In particular, a resolution refutation is tree-like if every intermediate clause, i.e. resolvent, is used at most once in the proof. Similarly, a resolution refutation is read-once if each clause is used at most once in the proof. Clearly, read-once resolution refutations are also tree-like since they form a restricted class of tree resolution refutations. It was shown in [17] that there exists unsatisfiable CNF formulas which cannot be refuted using read-once resolution. Finally, a resolution is regular if each branch (path from a clause of the initial formula to the empty clause) contains at most one resolution per variable.

Example 1. We consider the CNF formula $\phi = (\overline{x_1} \vee x_3) \wedge (x_1) \wedge (\overline{x_1} \vee x_2) \wedge (\overline{x_2} \vee \overline{x_3})$. The resolution refutation of ϕ, represented in Fig. 1, is tree-like (and) regular, but not read-once because of clause (x_1).

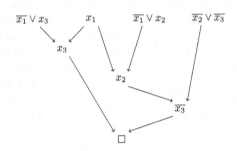

Fig. 1. Resolution refutation

2.3   Proofs for Max-SAT

In the last fifteen years, the study of inference rules for Max-SAT has led to major results in Max-SAT theory and solving. In particular, one of the first proof systems for Max-SAT is based on an inference rule called Max-SAT resolution, which is an extension of the resolution rule. Max-SAT resolution was shown sound and complete for Max-SAT, i.e. it is sufficient to prove the optimum cost of a given CNF formula.

Definition 2 (Max-SAT resolution [10,11,19]). *Given two clauses $c_1 = x \vee a_1 \vee \cdots \vee a_s$ and $c_2 = \overline{x} \vee b_1 \vee \cdots \vee b_t$ with $A = a_1 \vee \cdots \vee a_s$ and $B = b_1 \vee \cdots \vee b_t$, the Max-SAT resolution rule is defined as follows:*

$$\frac{c_1 = x \vee A \qquad\qquad c_2 = \overline{x} \vee B}{\begin{array}{c} c_3 = A \vee B \\ cc_1 = x \vee A \vee \overline{b_1} \\ \cdots \\ cc_t = x \vee A \vee b_1 \vee \cdots \vee b_{t-1} \vee \overline{b_t} \\ cc_{t+1} = \overline{x} \vee B \vee \overline{a_1} \\ \cdots \\ cc_{t+s} = \overline{x} \vee B \vee a_1 \vee \cdots \vee a_{s-1} \vee \overline{a_s} \end{array}}$$

where c_3 is the resolvent clause and $cc_1, \ldots, cc_{t+s}$ are compensation clauses.

In recent work, Max-SAT resolution was augmented with other rules such as the split rule [21,28] defined below or the extension rule [20]. It was shown that the addition of such rules to Max-SAT resolution can improve its efficiency in generating shorter proofs [20,21] or allow, given a resolution refutation for SAT, to generate a Max-SAT resolution refutation [28].

Definition 3 (Split rule). *Given a clause $c_1 = (A)$ where A is a disjunction of literals and x a variable, the split rule is defined as follows:*

$$\frac{c_1 = (A)}{c_2 = (x \vee A) \qquad c_3 = (\overline{x} \vee A)}$$

Remark 1. Unlike the resolution rule, the Max-SAT resolution rule and the split rule replace the premise(s) by the conclusion(s).

To be more exhaustive, we must also mention that other Max-SAT proof systems exist like the Clause Tableau Calculus [22]. If these proofs systems have been extensively studied in theory, generating proofs remains an unexplored topic in practice. Hence, this work aims to contribute to this topic by proposing tools to build and check Max-SAT proofs.

3 Related Work

In this section, we briefly recall recent results established in [28] on the adaptation of resolution refutations to Max-SAT refutations. One of the main results deals with tree resolution refutations showing that a linear adaptation to a Max-SAT refutation is possible in this case. Indeed, if the resolution refutation is tree-like, it is possible to transform it into a smaller refutation which is tree-like regular by iteratively eliminating irregularities (sequences of successive resolutions whose first and last are on the same variable) [30]. To adapt tree regular refutations, Max-SAT resolution is augmented with the split rule to fix the non-read-once clauses, i.e. clauses which are used more than once in the proof. The split rule is applied on a non-read-once clause to augment it with the variable resolved on in the junction point of all the branches starting from it. Thus, the obtained clauses can replace the non-read-once clause as a premise without affecting the validity of the proof. The same treatment is applied until all non-read-once clauses are fixed. Finally, when the proof becomes read-once, it is sufficient to replace each resolution step by a Max-SAT resolution to get a valid Max-SAT refutation [17]. An adaptation of tree regular resolution refutation is showcased in Example 2.

Example 2. We consider the tree regular resolution refutation in Example 1, represented in Fig. 1. We observe that the clause (x_1) is used two times as a premise of a resolution step. The junction point of the left and right branches eliminates variable x_3. Thus, we apply the split rule on clause (x_1) to get $(x_1 \vee x_3)$ and $(x_1 \vee \overline{x_3})$ and we replace (x_1) by $(x_1 \vee x_3)$ and $(x_1 \vee \overline{x_3})$ respectively on the left and right branches. Finally, we replace all resolutions by Max-SAT resolutions to obtain the complete Max-SAT refutation represented in Fig. 2.

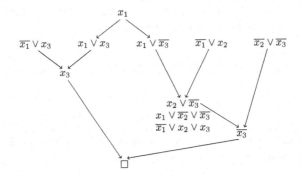

Fig. 2. Adaptation of a tree-like regular resolution refutation

In the generic case where the resolution refutation is not tree-like, it is also possible to adapt it into a Max-SAT refutation but with an exponential cost. To adapt the refutation, the entire proof leading to each non-read-once intermediate clause is duplicated, thus generating as many copies of the clauses as needed to render the proof tree-like. Then, the tree refutation is adapted into a Max-SAT refutation as explained above.

4   MS-Builder

In this section, we describe a Max-SAT proof builder, called MS-Builder based on the adaptation of resolution refutations for Max-SAT recalled in Sect. 3. The idea is to iteratively call a SAT oracle in order to get a resolution refutation for the current formula, adapt it into a Max-SAT refutation and apply it to the formula. The proof builder repeats this step until the SAT oracle returns a model for the final formula.

For practical reasons, we add an additional treatment to the Max-SAT proof builder. If the resolution refutation is not read-once, we first try to fix the effect of unit propagation in the non-read-once part of the proof. To do that, we discard the non-read-once unit clauses and we re-inject them at the end of the resolution refutation. Indeed, some resolution refutations are non-read-once simply because of the effects of unit propagation. It is the case of the resolution refutation proposed in Example 1, which is in fact read-once after fixing the unit propagation as showcased in the following example.

Example 3. We consider the tree regular resolution refutation in Example 1 (represented in Fig. 1). We fix the unit propagation by discarding (x_1) and re-injecting it at the end of the resolution refutation to get the read-once resolution refutation represented in Fig. 3.

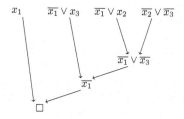

Fig. 3. Fixing unit propagation to get a read-once resolution refutation

The adaptation of any resolution refutation into a Max-SAT refutation is integrated into MS-Builder which can be seen as a core-based Max-SAT proof builder whose correctness is guaranteed by the correctness of the adaptation proposed in [28].

Example 4. Let $\phi = (\overline{x_1} \vee x_3) \wedge (x_1) \wedge (\overline{x_1} \vee x_2) \wedge (\overline{x_2} \vee \overline{x_3})$. The SAT oracle returns the resolution refutation in Fig. 1 which is adapted into the read-once one in Fig. 3 and to a Max-SAT one (by replacing resolutions by Max-SAT resolutions) and then applied to the formula. Now we have $\phi = \square \wedge (x_1 \vee \overline{x_2} \vee \overline{x_3}) \wedge (\overline{x_1} \vee x_2 \vee x_3)$ and the SAT oracle returns that the current formula (without considering the empty clause) is satisfied by the assignment $I(x_1) = I(x_2) = I(x_3) = 0$. MS-Builder thus receives the formula described in Fig. 4 and returns the proof described in Fig. 5.

5   MS-Checker

In this section, we present our extendable Max-SAT checker, called MS-Checker, which requires two input files: a formula and a proof. The formula has to be given in the standard WCNF format, either in the old or new format [4]. The proof file must start with a sequence of Max-SAT transformation lines. A Max-SAT transformation line must start with 't' and must include the name of the inference rule (`msres` for Max-SAT resolution and `split` for the split rule) and its premise(s) (between '<>'). For the split rule, the variable to split on is specified as a parameter after its name. Then, the proof file must contain a line (starting with 'o') with the announced optimum cost of the formula. Finally, it must contain a line (starting with 'v') with a truth assignment satisfying the final formula (without the empty clauses).

c Formula of Example 1
1 -1 3 0
1 1 0
1 -1 2 0
1 -2 -3 0

Fig. 4. Formula file format

t msres < 1 -1 -2 | 1 -2 -3 >
t msres < 1 -1 3 | 1 -1 -3 >
t msres < 1 1 | 1 -1 >
o 1
v 000

Fig. 5. Proof file format

After reading the formula, MS-Checker verifies that the proposed inference rules are correct and that the premises are still in the formula then applies the transformation. Finally, it checks if the truth assignment satisfies the final formula without considering the empty clauses.

6   Experiments

We have implemented MS-Builder and MS-Checker in C++[1]. Resolution Refutations are computed using Booleforce [6] and Tracecheck [7,8]. We consider the benchmark of the unweighted partiel track of the 2020 Max-SAT Evaluation [4]. The experiments are performed on Dell PowerEdge M620 servers with Intel XeonSilver E5-2609 processors (clocked at 2.5–2.6 GHz) under Ubuntu 18.04. Each solving process is allocated a slot of 1 h and at most 16 GB of memory per instance.

MS-Builder has succeeded to construct full proofs for 163 instance while MS-checker has succeeded to check 575 complete or partial proofs over 576 in total. The running time for building and checking instances are plotted respectively in Figs. 6 and 7. Proof checking is obviously much easier than proof building except on rare formulas with an important number of clauses (in the input file or after applying some transformations) which can make difficult the linear operation of extracting a premise to the formula used in MS-Checker.

---

[1] The source code is available on https://pageperso.lis-lab.fr/matthieu.py/en/software.html.

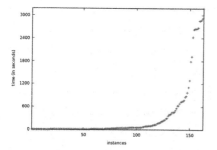

Fig. 6. Running time (in seconds) for building complete proofs

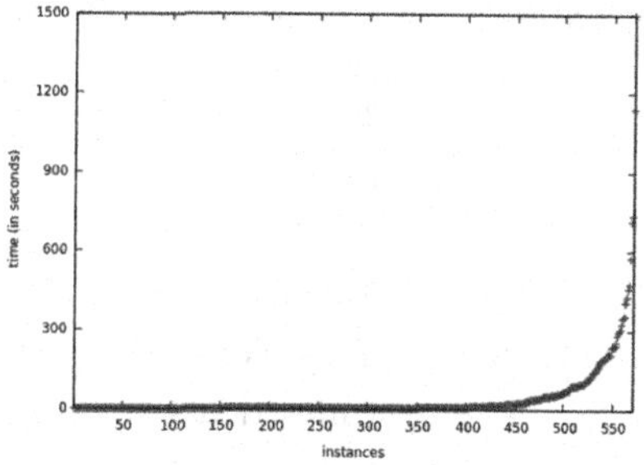

Fig. 7. Running time (in seconds) for checking proof

MS-Builder has also succeed to build at least half of the proofs (with respect to the number of empty clauses) of 302 instances over 463 instances for which the optimum cost is known. This is illustrated in Fig. 8 which reports the percentage of empty clauses built per solved instance. The sizes of the computed proofs vary from few bytes to 1 Gb as illustrated in Fig. 9. Notice how empty (incomplete) proofs are computed for some very hard instances for which the timeout is not sufficient to even compute the first Max-SAT refutation. On the other hand, there are some instances, usually with an optimum cost of 1, which have very small proofs.

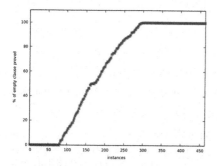

Fig. 8. Percentage of proved □ per instance

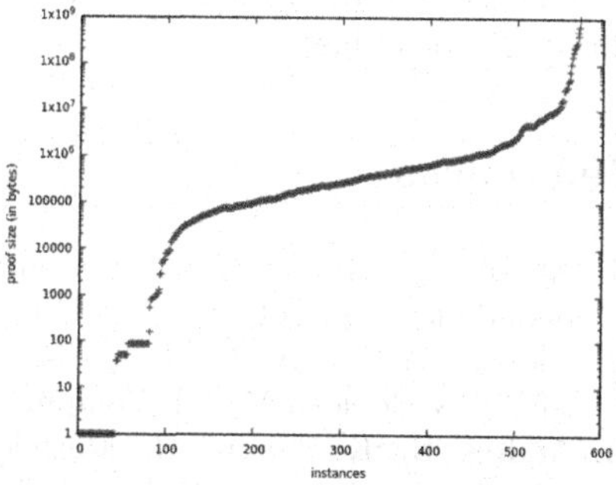

Fig. 9. Size of proof per instance (in logarithmic scale)

Finally, we can observe in Table 1 that read-once resolution refutations and resolution refutations which are read-once after fixing unit propagation appear very often. However, there are many instances such that the last resolution refutation met are the largest and the hardest (i.e. unrestricted) and that is why the last resolution refutations are often the most difficult to adapt and the timeout often stops on these resolution refutations.

Table 1. Encountered types of resolution refutations in the whole benchmark

Type of resolution refutation	Number	Percentage
Read-once	169,239	83.7%
Read-once after UP-fixing	24,556	12.1%
Tree-like regular	2,879	1.4%
Tree-like	1,795	0.9%
Unrestricted	3,799	1.9 %

7   Conclusion

In this paper, we proposed two tools, MS-Builder and MS-Checker, to respectively generate and check Max-SAT proofs. MS-Builder builds proofs by iteratively calling a SAT oracle and adapting the obtained SAT refutations into Max-SAT refutations. MS-Builder has succeeded in building a substantial amount of proofs for unweighted partial instances of the 2020 Max-SAT Evaluation. However, unrestricted resolution refutations are usually hard to adapt due to the exponential overhead caused by duplicating parts of the proofs.

As future work, it would be interesting to include more advanced techniques such as core reduction or minimization [2,25] in order to improve the efficiency of these tools. Furthermore, It would be relevant to study the possibility of extending the UP-fixing mechanism to non-unit clauses. Finally, we are also working on extending our tools to build and check proofs for weighted partial Max-SAT formulas.

References

1. Abramé, A., Habet, D.: Ahmaxsat: description and evaluation of a branch and bound max-SAT solver. J. Satisfiability Boolean Model. Comput. **9**, 89–128 (2015)
2. Alexey Ignatiev, A.M., Marques-Silva, J.: RC2: an efficient maxsat solver. J. Satisfiability Boolean Model. Comput. **11**(1), 53–64 (2019)
3. Andres, B., Kaufmann, B., Matheis, O., Schaub, T.: Unsatisfiability-based optimization in clasp. In: Technical Communications of The Twenty-eighth International Conference on Logic Programming (ICLP 2012) 17 (01 2012)
4. Bacchus, F., Järvisalo, M., Martins, R.: MaxSAT Evaluation (2020). https://maxsat-evaluations.github.io/2020/
5. Ben-sasson, E., Impagliazzo, R., Wigderson, A.: Near optimal separation of tree-like and general resolution. Combinatorica **24**, 585–603 (2004)
6. Biere, A.: Booleforce. http://fmv.jku.at/booleforce/
7. Biere, A.: TraceCheck. http://fmv.jku.at/tracecheck/
8. Biere, A.: PicoSAT essentials. J. Satisfiability Boolean Model. Comput. **4**(2–4), 75–97 (2008)
9. Bonet, M.L., Levy, J.: Equivalence between systems stronger than resolution. In: Pulina, L., Seidl, M. (eds.) SAT 2020. LNCS, vol. 12178, pp. 166–181. Springer, Cham (2020). https://doi.org/10.1007/978-3-030-51825-7_13

10. Bonet, M.L., Levy, J., Manyà, F.: A complete calculus for max-SAT. In: Biere, A., Gomes, C.P. (eds.) SAT 2006. LNCS, vol. 4121, pp. 240–251. Springer, Heidelberg (2006). https://doi.org/10.1007/11814948_24
11. Bonet, M.L., Levy, J., Manyàb, F.: Resolution for Max-SAT. Artif. Intell. **171**, 606–618 (2007)
12. D'Almeida, D., Grégoire, É.: Model-based diagnosis with default information implemented through MAX-SAT technology. In: IEEE 13th International Conference on Information Reuse & Integration, pp. 33–36. IEEE (2012)
13. Davies, J., Bacchus, F.: Solving MAXSAT by solving a sequence of simpler SAT instances. In: Lee, J. (ed.) CP 2011. LNCS, vol. 6876, pp. 225–239. Springer, Heidelberg (2011). https://doi.org/10.1007/978-3-642-23786-7_19
14. de Givry, S., Larrosa, J., Meseguer, P., Schiex, T.: Solving max-sat as weighted csp. Principles Pract. Constraint Program. - CP **2003**, 363–376 (2003)
15. Guerra, J., Lynce, I.: Reasoning over biological networks using maximum satisfiability. In: Milano, M. (ed.) CP 2012. LNCS, pp. 941–956. Springer, Heidelberg (2012). https://doi.org/10.1007/978-3-642-33558-7_67
16. Hertel, A., Urquhart, A.: Algorithms and complexity results for input and unit resolution. J. Satisfiability Boolean Model. Comput. **6**, 141–164 (2009)
17. Iwama, K., Miyano, E.: Intractability of read-once resolution. In: Proceedings of Structure in Complexity Theory. Tenth Annual IEEE Conference (1995)
18. Küegel, A.: Improved exact solver for the weighted max-sat problem. In: POS-10. Pragmatics of SAT. EPiC Series in Computing, vol. 8, pp. 15–27. EasyChair (2012)
19. Larrosa, J., Heras, F.: Resolution in Max-SAT and its relation to local consistency in weighted CSPs. In: IJCAI International Joint Conference on Artificial Intelligence - IJCAI 2005, pp. 193–198 (01 2005)
20. Larrosa, J., Rollon, E.: Augmenting the power of (Partial) MaxSat resolution with extension. In: Proceedings of the AAAI Conference on Artificial Intelligence (2020)
21. Larrosa, J., Rollon, E.: Towards a better understanding of (Partial Weighted) MaxSAT proof systems. In: Pulina, L., Seidl, M. (eds.) SAT 2020. LNCS, vol. 12178, pp. 218–232. Springer, Cham (2020). https://doi.org/10.1007/978-3-030-51825-7_16
22. Li, C.M., Manyà, F., Soler, J.R.: A Clause Tableau Calculus for MaxSAT. In: Proceedings of the Twenty-Fifth International Joint Conference on Artificial Intelligence, IJCAI 2016, pp. 766–772 (2016)
23. Li, C.M., Manyà, F., Planes, J.: New inference rules for Max-SAT. J. Artif. Intell. Res. (JAIR) **30**, 321–359 (2007)
24. Loveland, D.W.: A linear format for resolution. In: Laudet, M., Lacombe, D., Nolin, L., Schützenberger, M. (eds.) Symposium on Automatic Demonstration. LNM, vol. 125, pp. 147–162. Springer, Heidelberg (1970). https://doi.org/10.1007/BFb0060630
25. Marques-Silva, J.: Minimal unsatisfiability: Models, algorithms and applications (invited paper). In: 2010 40th IEEE International Symposium on Multiple-Valued Logic, pp. 9–14 (2010)
26. Martins, R., Manquinho, V.M., Lynce, I.: Open-WBO: a modular MaxSAT solver. In: Theory and Applications of Satisfiability Testing - SAT 2014-17th International Conference. Lecture Notes in Computer Science, vol. 8561, pp. 438–445 (2014)
27. Narodytska, N., Bacchus, F.: Maximum satisfiability using core-guided MaxSAT resolution. In: Proceedings of the Twenty-Eighth AAAI Conference on Artificial Intelligence, pp. 2717–2723 (2014)

28. Py, M., Cherif, M.S., Habet, D.: Towards bridging the gap between sat and max-sat refutations. In: 2020 IEEE 32nd International Conference on Tools with Artificial Intelligence (ICTAI), pp. 137–144 (2020)
29. Robinson, J.A.: A machine-oriented logic based on the resolution principle. J. Assoc. Comput. Mach. **12**, 23–41 (1965)
30. Urquhart, A.: The complexity of propositional proofs. Bull. Symbolic Logic **1**, 425–467 (1995)
31. Urquhart, A.: A near-optimal separation of regular and general resolution. SIAM J. Comput. **40**, 107–121 (2011)
32. Xu, H., Rutenbar, R.A., Sakallah, K.A.: Sub-SAT: a formulation for relaxed Boolean satisfiability with applications in routing. IEEE Trans. Comput. Aided Des. Integr. Circuits Syst. **22**, 814–820 (2003)

Certified DQBF Solving by Definition Extraction

Franz-Xaver Reichl, Friedrich Slivovsky[✉], and Stefan Szeider

TU Wien, Vienna, Austria
{freichl,fs,sz}@ac.tuwien.ac.at

Abstract. We propose a new decision procedure for dependency quantified Boolean formulas (DQBFs) that uses interpolation-based definition extraction to compute Skolem functions in a counter-example guided inductive synthesis (CEGIS) loop. In each iteration, a family of candidate Skolem functions is tested for correctness using a SAT solver, which either determines that a model has been found, or returns an assignment of the universal variables as a counterexample. Fixing a counterexample generally involves changing candidates of multiple existential variables with incomparable dependency sets. Our procedure introduces auxiliary variables—which we call *arbiter variables*—that each represent the value of an existential variable for a particular assignment of its dependency set. Possible repairs are expressed as clauses on these variables, and a SAT solver is invoked to find an assignment that deals with all previously seen counterexamples. Arbiter variables define the values of Skolem functions for assignments where they were previously undefined, and may lead to the detection of further Skolem functions by definition extraction.

A key feature of the proposed procedure is that it is certifying by design: for true DQBF, models can be returned at minimal overhead. Towards certification of false formulas, we prove that clauses can be derived in an expansion-based proof system for DQBF.

In an experimental evaluation on standard benchmark sets, a prototype implementation was able to match (and in some cases, surpass) the performance of state-of-the-art-solvers. Moreover, models could be extracted and validated for all true instances that were solved.

1 Introduction

Sustained progress in propositional satisfiability (SAT) solving [23] has resulted in a growing number of applications in the area of electronic design automation [49], such as model checking [7], synthesis [43], and symbolic execution [5]. Efficient SAT solvers were essential for recent progress in constrained sampling and counting [31], two problems with many applications in artificial intelligence. In these cases, SAT solvers are used to deal with problems from complexity classes beyond NP and propositional encodings that grow super-polynomially in the size of the original instances. As a consequence, these problems are not directly encoded in propositional logic but have to be reduced to a sequence of SAT instances.

© Springer Nature Switzerland AG 2021
C.-M. Li and F. Manyà (Eds.): SAT 2021, LNCS 12831, pp. 499–517, 2021.
https://doi.org/10.1007/978-3-030-80223-3_34

The success of SAT solving on the one hand, and the inability of propositional logic to succinctly encode problems of interest on the other hand, have prompted the development of decision procedures for more succinct generalizations of propositional logic such as Quantified Boolean Formulas (QBFs). Evaluating QBFs is PSPACE-complete [45] and thus believed to be much harder than SAT, but in practice the benefits of a smaller encoding may outweigh the disadvantage of slower decision procedures [13]. A QBF is true if it has a *model*, which is a family of Boolean functions (often called *Skolem functions*) that satisfy the matrix of the input formula for each assignment of universal variables. The arguments of each Skolem function are implicitly determined by the nesting of existential and universal quantifiers. Dependency QBF (DQBF) explicitly state a *dependency set* for each existential variable, which is a subset of universal variables allowed as arguments of the corresponding Skolem function [3,4]. As such, they can succinctly encode the existence of Boolean functions subject to a set of constraints [34], and problems like equivalence checking of partial circuit designs [19] and bounded synthesis [13] can be naturally expressed in this way.

Several decision procedures for DQBF have been developed in recent years (see Sect. 5). Conceptually, these solvers either reduce to SAT or QBF by instantiating [16] or eliminating universal variables [18,20,39,50], or lift Conflict-Driven Clause Learning (CDCL) to non-linear quantifier prefixes by imposing additional constraints [15,47].[1] We believe these methods should be complemented with algorithms that directly reason at the level of Skolem functions [35]. A strong argument in favor of such an approach is the fact that DQBF instances often have a large fraction of unique Skolem functions that can be obtained by definition extraction, but the current solving paradigms have no direct way of exploiting this [40].

In this paper, we develop new decision procedures for DQBF designed around computing Skolem functions by definition extraction. We first describe a simple algorithm that proceeds in two phases. In the first phase, it introduces clauses to make sure each existential variable is defined in terms of its dependency set and auxiliary *arbiter variables*. In the second phase, it searches for an assignment of the arbiter variables under which the definitions are a model. Runs of this algorithm can degenerate into an exhaustive instantiation of dependency sets for easy cases, so we propose an improved version in the Counter-Example Guided Inductive Synthesis (CEGIS) paradigm [28,42,43].

We implemented the CEGIS algorithm in a system named PEDANT. In an experimental evaluation, PEDANT performs very well compared to a selection of state-of-the-art solvers—notably, it achieves good performance without the aid of the powerful preprocessor HQSPRE [51]. One of the benefits of its function-centric design is that PEDANT internally computes a family of Skolem functions, and can output models of true instances at a negligible overhead. Using a simple workflow, we are able to validate models for all true instances solved by PEDANT. Towards validation of false instances, we prove that clauses introduced by PEDANT can be derived in the ∀Exp+Res proof system [6,27].

---

[1] An approach that does not fit this simplified classification is the First-Order solver IPROVER [29].

The remainder of the paper is structured as follows. After covering basic concepts in Sect. 2, we present the new decision algorithms for DQBF and prove their correctness in Sect. 3. We describe the implementation and experimental results in Sect. 4. We discuss related work in Sect. 5, before concluding with an outlook on future work in Sect. 6.

2 Preliminaries

Propositional Logic. A *literal* is either a variable or the negation of a variable. A *clause* is the disjunction of literals. A *term* is a conjunction of literals. A formula is in *Conjunctive Normal Form* (CNF) if it is a conjunction of clauses. Whenever convenient, we identify a CNF with a set of clauses and clauses, respectively terms, with sets of literals. We denote the set of variables occurring in a formula φ by $var(\varphi)$. We denote the truth value *true* by TRUE and *false* by FALSE. An *assignment* of a set V of variables is a function mapping V to $\{$TRUE, FALSE$\}$. We denote the set of all assignments for V by $[V]$. Moreover, we associate an assignment σ with the term $\{x \mid x \in \mathbf{dom}(\sigma), \sigma(x) = $ TRUE$\} \cup \{\neg x \mid x \in \mathbf{dom}(\sigma), \sigma(x) = $ FALSE$\}$. Whenever convenient, we treat assignments as terms. Let $\sigma \in [V]$ and let $W \subseteq V$, then we denote the *restriction of σ to W* by $\sigma|_W$. For a formula φ and an assignment σ we denote the *evaluation of φ by σ* with $\varphi[\sigma]$. A formula φ is *satisfied* by an assignment σ if $\varphi[\sigma] = $ TRUE and it is *falsified* by σ otherwise. A formula φ is *satisfiable* if there is an assignment σ that satisfies φ and it is *unsatisfiable* otherwise. Let φ and ψ be two formulae, φ *entails* ψ, denoted by $\varphi \vDash \psi$, if every assignment satisfying φ also satisfies ψ. A *definition* for a variable x by a set of variables X in a formula φ is a formula ψ with $var(\psi) \subseteq X$ such that for every satisfying assignment σ of φ the equality $\sigma(x) = \psi[\sigma]$ holds [40].

Dependency Quantified Boolean Formulas. We only consider *Dependency Quantified Boolean formulas* (DQBF) in *Prenex Conjunctive Normal Form* (PCNF). A DQBF in PCNF is denoted by $\Phi = \mathcal{Q}.\varphi$, where *(a)* the *quantifier prefix* $\mathcal{Q}$ is given by $\mathcal{Q} = \forall u_1 \ldots \forall u_n \exists e_1(D_1) \ldots \exists e_m(D_m)$. Here $u_1, \ldots, u_n$ and $e_1, \ldots, e_m$ shall be pairwise different variables. We denote the set $\{u_1, \ldots, u_n\}$ by U_Φ and the set $\{e_1, \ldots, e_m\}$ by E_Φ. Additionally, $D_1, \ldots, D_m$ shall be subsets of U_Φ. *(b)* the *matrix* φ shall be a CNF with $var(\varphi) \subseteq U_\Phi \cup E_\Phi$. For $1 \leq i \leq m$ we call the set D_i the *dependencies* of e_i. We refer to the variables in U_Φ as *universal variables* and to the variables in E_Φ as *existential variables*. For an existential variable e we denote its dependencies by $D_\Phi(e)$. If the underlying DQBF is clear from the context we omit the subscript.

Let Φ be a DQBF and F be a set of functions $\{f_{e_1}, \ldots, f_{e_m}\}$ such that for $1 \leq i \leq m$, $f_{e_i} : [D_i] \to \{$TRUE, FALSE$\}$. For an assignment σ to the universal variables we denote the existential assignment $\{f_{e_1}(\sigma|_{D_1}), \ldots, f_{e_m}(\sigma|_{D_m})\}$ by $F(\sigma)$. F is a *model* (or a *winning $\exists$-strategy*) for Φ if for each assignment σ to the universal variables, the assignment $\sigma \cup F(\sigma)$ satisfies the matrix φ. A DQBF is true if it has a model and false otherwise.

$\forall Exp+Res$. The $DQBF$-$\forall Exp+Res$ [6] calculus is a proof system for DQBF, which is based on the $\forall Exp+Res$ calculus for QBF. It instantiates the matrix of a DQBF with a universal assignment and uses propositional resolution on the instantiated clauses. This proof system is sound and refutationally complete [6]. Since we are interested in DQBF, we refer to DQBF-$\forall Exp+Res$ simply as $\forall Exp+Res$.

3   Solving DQBF by Definition Extraction

In this section, we describe two decision procedures for DQBF that leverage definition extraction. We start with an algorithm (Algorithm 1) that is fairly simple but introduces some important concepts. Because this algorithm leads to the equivalent of exhaustive expansion of universal variables on trivial examples, we then introduce a more sophisticated algorithm based on CEGIS (Algorithm 2). We also sketch correctness proofs for both algorithms.

Throughout this section, we consider a fixed DQBF $\Phi := \mathcal{Q}. \varphi$ with quantifier prefix $\mathcal{Q} := \forall u_1 \dots \forall u_n \exists e_1(D_1) \dots \exists e_m(D_m)$.

3.1   A Two-Phase Algorithm

The algorithm proceeds in two phases. In the first phase (GENERATEDEFINI-TIONS), it finds definitions ψ_{Def} for all existential variables. It maintains a set A of auxiliary *arbiter variables* whose semantics are encoded in a set φ_A of *arbiter clauses*, both of which are empty initially. If a variable e_i is defined in terms of its dependency set, the definition is computed using a SAT solver (line 15) capable of generating interpolants [40]. Otherwise, the SAT solver returns an assignment ξ of the dependency set D_i and the arbiter variables A for which the variable is not defined. In particular, e_i is not defined under the restriction $\sigma = \xi|_{D_i}$ to its dependency set. The algorithm then introduces an arbiter variable e_i^σ that determines the value of the Skolem function for e_i under σ. In subsequent iterations, we include these arbiter variables in the set of variables that can be used in a definition of e_i. The newly introduced clauses ensure that e_i and e_i^σ take the same value under the assignment σ (line 13), so that e_i is defined by e_i^σ and D_i. Since the number of assignments σ of the dependency set is bounded, we will eventually find a definition of e_i in terms of its dependency set D_i and the arbiter variables A.

In the second phase (FINDARBITERASSIGNMENT), a SAT solver (line 21) is used to find an assignment of the arbiter variables under which the definitions obtained in the first phase are a model. Starting with an initial assignment τ, we use a SAT solver to check whether the formula $\psi_{Def} \wedge \neg \varphi$ consisting of the definitions from the first phase and the negated matrix of the input DQBF is unsatisfiable under τ (line 23). If that is the case, Algorithm 1 returns TRUE. Otherwise, the SAT solver returns an assignment σ as a counterexample. Since the existential variables are defined in $\varphi \wedge \varphi_A$ by the universal and arbiter variables, the formula $\varphi \wedge \varphi_A$ must be unsatisfiable under the assignment $\tau \wedge \sigma|_U$ consisting of the arbiter assignment and counterexample restricted to universal variables. A *core* ρ of failed assumptions $\tau \wedge \sigma_U$ such that $\rho \models \neg(\varphi \wedge \varphi_A)$ is extracted using another SAT call. The assignment $\rho|_A$ represents a concise reason for the failure of the arbiter assignment τ, and its negation $\neg\rho|_A$ is added as a new clause to the SAT solver used to generate arbiter assignments, which is subsequently invoked to find a new arbiter assignment.

This process continues until a model is found or the SAT solver cannot find a new arbiter assignment, in which case the algorithm returns FALSE.

Algorithm 1. Solving DQBF by Definition Extraction

1: **procedure** SOLVEBYDEFINITIONEXTRACTION(Φ)
2: $\quad$ $(\varphi_A, A, \psi_{Def}) \leftarrow$ GENERATEDEFINITIONS(Φ)
3: $\quad$ **return** FINDARBITERASSIGNMENT($\Phi, \varphi_A, A, \psi_{Def}$)

4: **procedure** GENERATEDEFINITIONS(Φ)
5: $\quad$ ▷ $\Phi = \forall u_1 \dots \forall u_n \exists e_1(D_1) \dots \exists e_m(D_m).\varphi$
6: $\quad$ $A \leftarrow \emptyset, \psi_{Def} \leftarrow \emptyset, \varphi_A \leftarrow \emptyset$
7: $\quad$ ▷ A: arbiter variables, ψ_{Def}: definitions, φ_A: arbiter clauses
8: $\quad$ **for** $i = 1, \dots, m$ **do**
9: $\quad\quad$ $isDefined, \xi \leftarrow$ ISDEFINED($e_i, A \cup D_i, \varphi \wedge \varphi_A$)
10: $\quad\quad$ **while** not $isDefined$ **do**
11: $\quad\quad\quad$ $\sigma \leftarrow \xi|_{D_i}$ $\quad\quad\quad\quad\quad$ ▷ e_i is not defined under $\xi \in [D_i \cup A]$
12: $\quad\quad\quad$ $A \leftarrow A \cup \{e_i^\sigma\}$
13: $\quad\quad\quad$ $\varphi_A \leftarrow \varphi_A \wedge (e_i^\sigma \vee \neg\sigma \vee \neg e_i) \wedge (\neg e_i^\sigma \vee \neg\sigma \vee e_i)$
14: $\quad\quad\quad$ $isDefined, \xi \leftarrow$ ISDEFINED($e_i, A \cup D_i, \varphi \wedge \varphi_A$)
15: $\quad\quad$ $\psi_{Def}^i \leftarrow$ GETDEFINITION($e_i, A \cup D_i, \varphi \wedge \varphi_A$)
16: $\quad\quad$ $\psi_{Def} \leftarrow \psi_{Def} \wedge (e_i \leftrightarrow \psi_{Def}^i)$
17: $\quad$ **return** $(\varphi_A, A, \psi_{Def})$

18: **procedure** FINDARBITERASSIGNMENT($\Phi, \varphi_A, A, \psi_{Def}$)
19: $\quad$ $\tau \leftarrow \bigwedge_{a \in A} a$ $\quad\quad\quad\quad$ ▷ initial assignment to the arbiter variables
20: $\quad$ $validitySolver \leftarrow$ SATSOLVER($\psi_{Def} \wedge \neg\varphi$)
21: $\quad$ $arbiterSolver \leftarrow$ SATSOLVER($\emptyset$)
22: $\quad$ **loop**
23: $\quad\quad$ **if** $validitySolver$.SOLVE(τ) **then**
24: $\quad\quad\quad$ $\sigma \leftarrow validitySolver$.GETMODEL()
25: $\quad\quad\quad$ $\rho \leftarrow$ GETCORE($\varphi \wedge \varphi_A, \tau \wedge \sigma|_U$)
26: $\quad\quad\quad$ $arbiterSolver$.ADDCLAUSE($\neg\rho|_A$)
27: $\quad\quad\quad$ **if** $arbiterSolver$.SOLVE() **then**
28: $\quad\quad\quad\quad$ $\tau \leftarrow arbiterSolver$.GETMODEL()
29: $\quad\quad\quad$ **else**
30: $\quad\quad\quad\quad$ **return** FALSE
31: $\quad\quad$ **else**
32: $\quad\quad\quad$ **return** TRUE

We now argue that Algorithm 1 is a decision procedure for DQBF. Due to space constraints, some proofs are omitted. In the following, A shall denote a set of arbiter variables and φ_A shall denote the associated set of arbiter clauses.

A DQBF has a model if, and only if, there is a propositional formula for each existential variable that defines its Skolem functions using only variables from the dependency set. This can be slightly generalized by allowing the definition to contain existential variables whose dependency sets are a subset.

Lemma 1. *Let Φ be a DQBF and $<_E$ a linear ordering of its existential variables. Then Φ is true if, and only if, for each $e \in E$ there is a formula ψ_e with $var(\psi_e) \subseteq D(e) \cup \{x \in E \mid D(x) \subseteq D(e), x <_E e\}$ such that $\neg\varphi \wedge \bigwedge_{e \in E}(e \leftrightarrow \psi_e)$ is unsatisfiable.*

Theorem 1. *If Algorithm 1 returns* TRUE *for the DQBF Φ then Φ is true.*

Proof. Let $\Phi' := \mathcal{Q}\exists A(\emptyset).\varphi$, and let $<_E$ be any ordering of existential variables in Φ' in which the variables in A come before the remaining variables. If Algorithm 1 returns TRUE, we know that there is an arbiter assignment τ such that $\neg\varphi \wedge \psi_{Def} \wedge \tau$ is unsatisfiable. For each arbiter variable e^σ, we obtain a definition ψ_e^σ as $\psi_e^\sigma := \tau(e^\sigma)$. We can now replace the arbiter assignment τ with these definitions and apply Lemma 1 to conclude that Φ' is true. But if Φ' is true, then necessarily also Φ is true.   □

To show that the algorithm returns FALSE only if the input DQBF is false, one can prove that clauses on arbiter variables introduced by FINDARBITERASSIGN-MENT can be derived (as clauses on annotated literals) in ∀Exp+Res.

Proposition 1. *For each clause C added to the arbiter solver by Algorithm 1 (line 26), a clause $C' \subseteq C$ can be derived from Φ in ∀Exp+Res.*

Theorem 2. *If Algorithm 1 returns* FALSE *for the DQBF Φ then Φ is false.*

Proof. If the algorithm returns FALSE then the set $\mathcal{C}$ of clauses in the arbiter solver is unsatisfiable. By Proposition 1 for each $C \in \mathcal{C}$ we can derive a clause $C' \subseteq C$ subsuming C in ∀Exp+Res, so there is a ∀Exp+Res refutation of Φ. As ∀Exp+Res is sound [6], this shows that Φ is false.   □

Finally, Algorithm 1 terminates since at most one arbiter variable is introduced for each existential variable and assignment of its dependency set in the first phase, and there is a limited number of clauses on arbiter variables that can be introduced in the second phase. In combination with Theorem 1 and Theorem 2, we obtain the following result.

Corollary 1. *Algorithm 1 is a decision procedure for DQBF.*

3.2   Combining Definition Extraction with CEGIS

Discounting SAT calls, the running time of Algorithm 1 is essentially determined by the number of assignments of a dependency set for which the corresponding existential variable is not defined: it introduces an arbiter variable for each such assignment in the first phase, and the number of iterations in the second phase is bounded by the number of arbiter assignments. As a result, even a single existential variable that is unconstrained and has a large dependency set causes the algorithm to get stuck enumerating universal assignments.

A key insight underlying the success of counter-example guided solvers for QBF [25,26,46] is that it is typically overkill to perform complete expansion of universal variables. Instead, they incrementally refine Skolem functions by taking into account universal assignments that pose a problem for the current solution candidate.[2]

Following this idea, we now present an improved algorithm (Algorithm 2) in the style of Counter-Example Guided Inductive Synthesis (CEGIS) [28]. It integrates the two phases of Algorithm 1 into a single loop. In each iteration, it first tries to find definitions for existential variables in terms of their dependency sets and the arbiter variables (FINDDEFINITIONS). The algorithm then proceeds to a validity check of the definitions under the current arbiter assignment (CHECKARBITERASSIGNMENT). A key difference to Algorithm 1 is that we may not have a definition for each variable at this point. In this case, we can simply leave the existential variable unconstrained in the SAT call except for arbiter clauses φ_A (and *forcing clauses* φ_F, which we discuss later). In the implementation, we limit the SAT solver's freedom to generate counterexamples by substituting a default value or a heuristically obtained "guess" for the Skolem function. Here, any function on variables from the dependency set can be used without affecting correctness, one only has to make sure that counterexamples are not repeated to guarantee termination.

If a counterexample σ is found, procedure CHECKARBITERASSIGNMENT returns it to the main loop. Otherwise, (line 25), we have to check whether the SAT call in line 20 returned UNSAT because a model has been found, or whether there is an inconsistency in the formula $\varphi_A \wedge \varphi_F$ comprised of arbiter and forcing clauses under the current arbiter assignment τ. The procedure CHECKCONSISTENCY either finds that the model is consistent, in which case Algorithm 2 returns TRUE, or else computes an assignment σ of the universal variables as a counterexample. If CHECKARBITERASSIGNMENT returns FALSE, the main loop resumes in line 14 with a call to ANALYZECONFLICT.

To see what this procedure does, let us first consider the simple case in which the counterexample σ only contains an assignment of universal variables that was returned by the consistency check. Then, the existential assignment $\rho_\exists = \emptyset$ is empty, the for-loop is skipped and no new arbiter variables are introduced (line 55), and the procedure only tries to further simplify the failed arbiter assignment ρ_A in line 58, before adding its negation to the arbiter solver.

Now assume $\rho_\exists$ is nonempty but the case distinction in the body of the for-loop between lines 43 and 54 always leads to line 51. Then *notforced* = $\rho_\exists$ and the procedure NEWARBITERS creates new arbiter variables A' and clauses φ'_A for each existential variable $e \in \mathbf{dom}(\rho_\exists)$ and the universal counterexample $\sigma_\forall$

---

[2] In these QBF solvers, Skolem functions are typically only indirectly represented by trees of formulas (*abstractions*) that encode viable assignments.

(restricted to the dependency set $D(e)$ in each case). Since these arbiter variables determine the assignment of the existential variables in $\mathbf{dom}(\rho_\exists)$ under $\sigma_\forall$, we can replace $\rho_\exists$ with the assignment $\rho'_A := \{e^\xi \in A' \,|\, e \in \rho_\exists\} \cup \{\neg e^\xi \in A' \,|\, \neg e \in \rho_\exists\}$ (line 57) and conclude that $\varphi \wedge \varphi_A \wedge \varphi_F$ is unsatisfiable under the assignment $\rho_A \cup \rho'_A \cup \sigma_\forall$, which only assigns arbiter variables and universal variables. A clause forbidding the arbiter assignment $\rho_A \cup \rho'_A$ can now be added as before.

Finally, let us turn to the general case, which includes entailment checks for each existential literal $\ell \in \rho_\exists$ in the minimized counterexample. These checks are added to reduce the number of new arbiter variables created. If the literal ℓ is entailed by the assignment $\sigma_\forall \wedge \tau$, we add further literals from τ to the failed arbiter assignment ρ_A (if necessary) to ensure that ℓ is entailed by $\sigma_\forall \wedge \rho_A$. No arbiter variable has to be introduced for $var(\ell)$ in this case. Otherwise, if $\neg\ell$ is entailed by $\sigma_\forall \wedge \tau$, then the counterexample is spurious since $e = var(\ell)$ must be assigned the opposite way under $\sigma_\forall \wedge \tau$ by any Skolem function. To enforce this in the next iteration, the algorithm adds a *forcing clause* C encoding the implication $\sigma_\forall \wedge \tau \to \neg\ell$ (which can be further strengthened by restricting $\sigma_\forall$ to the dependency set of e) to φ_F. It also sets a flag *oppositeForced*, which causes ANALYZECONFLICT to exit with TRUE instead of adding new arbiter variables.

If ANALYZECONFLICT returns TRUE, Algorithm 2 proceeds to the next iteration of its main loop with the same arbiter assignment τ but additional forcing clauses. Otherwise, ANALYZECONFLICT returns FALSE after adding a clause to the SAT solver *arbiterSolver*, and FINDNEWARBITERASSIGNMENT is called to determine a new arbiter assignment τ that satisfies all previously added clauses. Algorithm 2 terminates either when it discovers a model or when it cannot find a new arbiter assignment.

We now sketch a proof that shows that Algorithm 2 is a decision procedure for DQBF. As in Sect. 3.1, A denotes a set of arbiter variables and φ_A denotes the associated set of arbiter clauses.

Definition 1 (Forcing Clause). *Let ℓ be an existential literal, ψ a formula with $var(\psi) \subseteq U \cup E \cup A$ and let σ be a (partial) assignment for $U \cup A$. We say that ℓ is forced by σ in ψ if $\psi \wedge \sigma \wedge \neg\ell$ is unsatisfiable. If ℓ is forced by σ then $\neg\sigma|_{D(var(\ell))\cup A} \vee l$ is a forcing clause.*

In particular, if a literal ℓ is forced by an assignment σ in a formula φ then $\varphi \wedge \sigma \vDash \ell$ holds. Forcing clauses can be added to a DQBF without changing its models. In particular, the resulting DQBF has the same truth value.

Lemma 2. *Let $C_1, \ldots, C_k$ be clauses such that for each index i, the clause C_i is a forcing clause in $\varphi \wedge \varphi_A \wedge \bigwedge_{1 \le j < i} C_j$. Then the DQBF $Q\exists A(\emptyset).\varphi \wedge \varphi_A \wedge \bigwedge_{1 \le i \le k} C_i$ is true if and only if Φ is true.*

Theorem 3. *If Algorithm 2 returns TRUE for a DQBF Φ then Φ is true.*

Proof. We assume that the algorithm returns TRUE and show that the DQBF Φ is true. We know that we have a set A of arbiter variables, a set φ_A of arbiter clauses, a set φ_F of forcing clauses and a set $E' \subseteq E$ such that each $e \in E'$ has

---

Algorithm 2. Solving DQBF by Definition Extraction (CEGIS Version)

1: **procedure** SOLVEBYDEFINITIONEXTRACTIONCEGIS(Φ)
2:     ▷ $\Phi = \forall u_1 \ldots \forall u_n \exists e_1(D_1) \ldots \exists e_m(D_m).\varphi$
3:     ▷ A: arbiter variables, ψ_{Def}: definitions, φ_A: arbiter clauses
4:     $A \leftarrow \emptyset$, $\psi_{Def} \leftarrow \emptyset$, $\varphi_A \leftarrow \emptyset$
5:     $\varphi_F \leftarrow \emptyset$ ▷ forcing clauses
6:     $\tau \leftarrow \emptyset$ ▷ arbiter assignment
7:     $arbiterSolver \leftarrow$ SATSOLVER($\emptyset$)
8:     **loop**
9:         $\psi_{Def} \leftarrow$ FINDDEFINITIONS($\{e \in E \mid e$ undefined$\}, \varphi \wedge \varphi_A \wedge \varphi_F$)
10:         $modelValid, \sigma \leftarrow$ CHECKARBITERASSIGNMENT(τ)
11:         **if** $modelValid$ **then**
12:             **return** TRUE
13:         ▷ σ is a counterexample
14:         **if** ANALYZECONFLICT(σ) **then**
15:             ▷ forcing clauses have been added to φ_F
16:             **continue**
17:         **if not** FINDNEWARBITERASSIGNMENT() **then**
18:             **return** FALSE

19: **procedure** CHECKARBITERASSIGNMENT(τ)
20:     $checker \leftarrow$ SATSOLVER($\neg\varphi \wedge \psi_{Def} \wedge \varphi_F \wedge \varphi_A$)
21:     **if** $checker$.SOLVE(τ) **then**
22:         $\sigma \leftarrow checker$.VALUES($E \cup U$)
23:         **return** FALSE, σ
24:     **else**
25:         $isConsistent, \sigma \leftarrow$ CHECKCONSISTENCY($\varphi_A \wedge \varphi_F, \tau$)
26:         **if** $isConsistent$ **then**
27:             **return** TRUE, $\emptyset$
28:         **else**
29:             ▷ $\sigma \in [U]$ is such that $\varphi_A \wedge \varphi_F \wedge \tau \wedge \sigma$ is unsatisfiable
30:             **return** FALSE, σ

31: **procedure** FINDNEWARBITERASSIGNMENT()
32:     **if** $arbiterSolver$.SOLVE() **then**
33:         $\tau \leftarrow arbiterSolver$.GETMODEL()$|_A$
34:         **return** TRUE
35:     **return** FALSE

---

a definition ψ_e in $\varphi \wedge \varphi_A \wedge \varphi_F$ by $D(e) \cup A$. Let $\psi_{Def} := \bigwedge_{e \in E'}(e \leftrightarrow \psi_e)$ and $\Phi' := Q\exists A(\emptyset).\varphi \wedge \varphi_A \wedge \varphi_F$. By Lemma 2, we know that Φ is true if and only if Φ' is true. As the algorithm returns TRUE, we know that $\neg\varphi \wedge \varphi_A \wedge \varphi_F \wedge \psi_{Def}$ is unsatisfiable. Using a mild generalization of Lemma 1, this implies that Φ' is true. Thus, Φ is true as well. □

As in the case of Algorithm 1, the correctness of FALSE answers for Algorithm 2 follows from a correspondence with ∀Exp+Res derivations.

```
36: procedure ANALYZECONFLICT(σ)
37:     σ∀ ← σ|U                                    ▷ σ∀ assigns all universal variables
38:     ρ ← GETCORE(φ ∧ φA ∧ φF, σ ∧ τ)
39:     ρ∃ ← ρ|E, ρA ← ρ|A
40:     notForced ← ∅                               ▷ collect literals ℓ ∈ ρ∃ that are not implied
41:     oppositeForced ← FALSE
42:     ψ ← φ ∧ φA ∧ φF
43:     for ℓ ∈ ρ∃ do
44:         if ψ ∧ σ∀ ∧ τ ⊨ ℓ then
45:             ρ ← GETCORE(ψ, σ∀ ∧ τ ∧ ¬ℓ)
46:             ρA ← ρA ∪ ρ|A         ▷ add reason for ℓ to failed arbiter assignment ρA
47:         else if ψ ∧ σ∀ ∧ τ ⊨ ¬ℓ then
48:             φF ← φF ∧ GETFORCINGCLAUSE(ψ, σ∀ ∧ τ, ¬ℓ)
49:             oppositeForced ← TRUE
50:         else
51:             notForced ← notForced ∪ {ℓ}
52:     if oppositeForced then
53:         return TRUE
54:     ▷ no literal was forced to the opposite polarity
55:     φ'A, A' ← NEWARBITERS(notForced, σ∀)
56:     φA ← φA ∧ φ'A
57:     ρA ← ρA ∧ SETASSIGNMENT(A', ρ∃)
58:     ρA ← GETCORE(ψ, ρA ∧ σ∀)|A
59:     arbiterSolver.ADDCLAUSE(¬ρA)
60:     return FALSE
```

Proposition 2. *For each clause C added to the arbiter solver by Algorithm 2 (line 59), a clause $C' \subseteq C$ can be derived from Φ in $\forall Exp+Res$.*

Theorem 4. *If Algorithm 2 returns FALSE for a DQBF Φ then Φ is false.*

Each iteration of Algorithm 2 introduces new forcing clauses or forbids another arbiter assignment. Because there is a bound on the number of arbiter variables that can be introduced, the number of such clauses can be bounded as well, and the algorithm eventually terminates. Together with Theorem 3 and Theorem 4, this gives rise to the following corollary.

Corollary 2. *Algorithm 2 is a decision procedure for DQBF.*

4   Experiments

We implemented Algorithm 2 as described in the previous section in a prototype named PEDANT.[3] For definition extraction, it uses a subroutine from UNIQUE [40] that in turn relies on an interpolating version of MINISAT [12] bundled with the EXTAVY model checker [22,48]. Further, CADICAL is used as a

---

[3] Available at https://github.com/perebor/pedant-solver.

SAT solver [8] (we also tested with CRYPTOMINISAT [44] and GLUCOSE [2] but saw no significant differences in overall performance). PEDANT can read DQBF in the standard DQDIMACS format and output models in the DIMACS format.

The implementation incorporates a few techniques not explicitly mentioned in the above pseudocode. We identify *unate* existential literals (a generalization of pure literals) [1], which can be used in any model of a DQBF. Moreover, we set a (configurable) default value for existential variables that applies when there is no forcing clause propagating a different value. This is to limit the freedom of the SAT solver used in the validity check in coming up with counterexamples. Moreover, when checking for definability of an existential variable, we use *extended dependencies* that include existential variables with dependency sets that are contained in the dependencies of the variable that is checked.

For all experiments described below we use a cluster with Intel Xeon E5649 processors at 2.53 GHz running 64-bit Linux.

4.1 Performance on Standard Benchmark Sets

We compare PEDANT with other DQBF solvers on standard benchmark sets in terms of instances solved within the timeout and their PAR2 score.[4] Specifically, we choose the solvers DCAQE [47], IDQ [16], HQS [20], and the recently introduced DQBDD [39]. Both HQS and DQBDD internally use HQSPRE [51] as a preprocessor. For DCAQE and IDQ, we call HQSPRE with a time limit of 300 seconds (the time for preprocessing is included in the total running time). By default, PEDANT is run without preprocessing.

The results are based on a single run with a time and memory limit of 1800 seconds and 8 GB, respectively, which are enforced using RUNSOLVER [36].[5] We report results for two benchmark sets. The first—which we refer to as the "Compound" set—has been used in recent papers on HQS [18]. It is comprised of instances encoding partial equivalence checking (PEC) [14,16,19,37] and controller synthesis [10], as well as succinct DQBF representations of propositional satisfiability [4]. Results are summarized in Table 1. PEDANT solved the most instances overall and for 4 out of 5 families (the "Balabanov" family being the exception), with DQBDD coming in a close second. The performance of PEDANT on the PEC instances in the "Finkbeiner" family is particularly encouraging.

Next, we consider the instances from the DQBF track of QBFEVAL'20 [33]. Results are shown in Table 2. Here, PEDANT falls behind the other solvers, with the exception of IDQ. In particular, significantly fewer instances from the "Kullmann" and "Tentrup" families are solved.

For the autarky finding benchmarks in the "Kullmann" family [30], we noticed that most dependencies can be removed by preprocessing with the reflexive resolution-path dependency scheme [41,52]. The resulting instances are much

---

[4] The Penalized Average Runtime (PAR) is the average runtime, with the time for each unsolved instance calculated as a constant multiple of the timeout.

[5] Due to the heavy-tailed runtime distribution of DQBF solvers, run-to-run variance rarely affects the number of solved instances. However, PAR2 scores should be taken with a grain of salt and only used to compare orders of magnitude.

Table 1. Results for the "Compound" benchmark set.

Family(Total)	DCAQE	DQBDD	HQS	IDQ	PEDANT
	Sol/PAR2	Sol/PAR2	Sol/PAR2	Sol/PAR2	Sol/PAR2
Balabanov(34)	**21**/$1.5 \cdot 10^3$	$13/2.3 \cdot 10^3$	$19/1.8 \cdot 10^3$	**21**/$1.5 \cdot 10^3$	$13/2.3 \cdot 10^3$
Biere(1200)	**1200**/$1.6 \cdot 10^{-1}$	$1197/9.0 \cdot 10^0$	**1200**/$6.4 \cdot 10^{-2}$	$1184/6.6 \cdot 10^1$	**1200**/$1.0 \cdot 10^{-1}$
Bloem(461)	$85/2.9 \cdot 10^3$	$82/3.0 \cdot 10^3$	$82/3.0 \cdot 10^3$	$50/3.2 \cdot 10^3$	**98**/$2.9 \cdot 10^3$
Finkbeiner(2000)	$32/3.5 \cdot 10^3$	$1999/1.1 \cdot 10^1$	$1799/3.9 \cdot 10^2$	$6/3.6 \cdot 10^3$	**2000**/$1.7 \cdot 10^0$
Scholl(1116)	$568/1.8 \cdot 10^3$	$793/1.1 \cdot 10^3$	$676/1.4 \cdot 10^3$	$345/2.5 \cdot 10^3$	**854**/$8.7 \cdot 10^2$
All(4811)	$1906/2.2 \cdot 10^3$	$4084/5.5 \cdot 10^2$	$3776/7.9 \cdot 10^2$	$1606/2.4 \cdot 10^3$	**4165**/$4.9 \cdot 10^2$

easier to solve for PEDANT, and models can still be validated against the original DQBFs. In general, we found that preprocessing with HQSPRE can have both positive and negative effects on PEDANT. The rightmost columns of Table 2 show results when preprocessing is enabled.[6] Overall, performance is clearly improved, but fewer instances from the "Bloem" and "Scholl" families are solved. In prior work, it was observed that preprocessing can destroy definitions [40], and this appears to be the case here as well.

For the instances from the "Tentrup" family, we discovered that the performance of PEDANT is sensitive to which counterexamples are generated by CADICAL. With the right sequence of counterexamples, false instances can be refuted quickly, while otherwise the solver is busy introducing arbiter variables for minor variations of previously encountered cases. Curiously, this also appears to be the case for true instances. We believe that the algorithm can be made more robust against such "adversarial" sequences of counterexamples by achieving better generalization (see Sect. 6).

Table 2. Results for the QBFEVAL'20 DQBF benchmark set.

Family(Total)	DCAQE	DQBDD	HQS	IDQ	PEDANT	PEDANTHQ
	Sol/PAR2	Sol/PAR2	Sol/PAR2	Sol/PAR2	Sol/PAR2	Sol/PAR2
Balabanov(34)	**21**/$1.5 \cdot 10^3$	$13/2.3 \cdot 10^3$	$19/1.8 \cdot 10^3$	**21**/$1.5 \cdot 10^3$	$14/2.3 \cdot 10^3$	$13/2.4 \cdot 10^3$
Bloem(90)	$31/2.4 \cdot 10^3$	$32/2.3 \cdot 10^3$	$33/2.3 \cdot 10^3$	$14/3.1 \cdot 10^3$	**37**/$2.2 \cdot 10^3$	$25/2.7 \cdot 10^3$
Kullmann(50)	$35/1.1 \cdot 10^3$	**50**/$1.5 \cdot 10^1$	$41/6.9 \cdot 10^2$	**50**/$3.4 \cdot 10^0$	$34/1.3 \cdot 10^3$	$40/7.3 \cdot 10^2$
Scholl(90)	$52/1.5 \cdot 10^3$	$78/4.9 \cdot 10^2$	$77/5.3 \cdot 10^2$	$15/3.0 \cdot 10^3$	**82**/$3.3 \cdot 10^2$	$65/1.2 \cdot 10^3$
Tentrup(90)	$77/5.5 \cdot 10^2$	**84**/$2.8 \cdot 10^2$	$78/5.1 \cdot 10^2$	$17/2.9 \cdot 10^3$	$15/3.0 \cdot 10^3$	**84**/$2.9 \cdot 10^2$
All(354)	$216/1.4 \cdot 10^3$	**257**/$1.0 \cdot 10^3$	$248/1.1 \cdot 10^3$	$117/2.4 \cdot 10^3$	$182/1.8 \cdot 10^3$	$227/1.4 \cdot 10^3$

---

[6] With options `--resolution 1 --univ_exp 0 --substitute 0`.

4.2 Distribution of Defined Existential Variables

The main design goal for PEDANT was to create a solver that benefits from unique Skolem functions given by propositional definitions. We thus expect PEDANT to do well on instances where a large proportion of existential variables is defined. Figure 1 shows the distribution of defined existential variables (i.e., unique Skolem functions) as computed by UNIQUE [40]. These definitions are also found by PEDANT without the introduction of arbiter variables. Comparing Table 1 and Table 2 with Fig. 1, we see that PEDANT performed better for instance families with a larger fraction of defined variables. This makes sense: the fewer variables are undefined, the fewer arbiter variables need to be introduced.

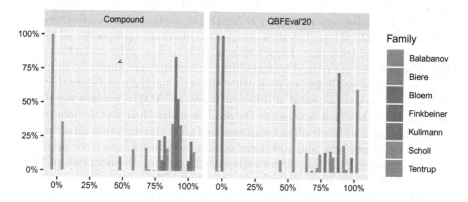

Fig. 1. Distribution of defined variables by benchmark set and family. For a given percentage x_0 on the x-axis, the y-axis shows the fraction of instances from each benchmark family for which x_0 percent of existential variables are defined. For example, the instances in the "Balabanov" family have no defined variables, while the fraction of defined variables for instances in the "Finkbeiner" family ranges from 75% to 100%.

4.3 Solution Validation

When running PEDANT without preprocessing (the default), we had it trace and output models in DIMACS format. We implemented a simple workflow for validating these models in Python 3 using the PySAT library [24]. First, a simple syntactic check is performed to make sure the encoding of each Skolem function only mentions variables in the dependency set of the corresponding variable. Then, a SAT solver is used to verify that substituting the model ψ for existential variables in the matrix φ of the input DQBF is valid, by testing for each clause $C \in \varphi$ whether $\psi \land \neg C$ is unsatisfiable (cf. Lemma 1). In this manner, we are able to validate models for all 648 true DQBFs in the two benchmark sets that were solved by PEDANT without preprocessing. The maximum validation time was 237 s, with a mean of 4.3 s and a median of 0.5 s.

The current validation process is intended as a proof of concept. Since models constructed by PEDANT are circuits, we plan to support the AIGER format [9] in the near future, and provide a workflow along the lines of QBFCERT [32].

5 Related Work

The DQDPLL algorithm lifts the CDCL algorithm to DQBF [15]. While CDCL solvers are free to assign variables in any order, in DQBF a variable may be assigned only after the variables in its dependency set have been assigned. Moreover, its assignment must not differ between branches in the search tree that agree on the assignment of the dependency set. In DQDPLL, this is enforced by temporary *Skolem clauses* that fix the truth value of a variable for a given assignment of its dependencies. The solver DCAQE lifts clausal abstraction from QBF to DQBF [47]. QBF solvers based on abstraction maintain a propositional formula for each quantifier level that characterizes eligible moves in the evaluation game. These *abstractions* are refined by forbidding moves that are known to result in a loss. Abstractions are linked to each other through auxiliary variables that indicate which clauses are satisfied at different levels. DCAQE organizes variables in a dependency lattice that determines the order in which their abstractions may be solved. This can lead to variables being assigned after variables that do not appear in their dependency sets, and additional consistency checks have to be applied to ensure that Skolem functions do not exploit such spurious dependencies. DCAQE uses *fork resolution* as its underlying proof system [34].

Expansion of universal variables can be successively applied to transform a DQBF into a propositional formula that can be passed to a SAT solver [11]. In practice, the space requirements of fully expanding a DQBF are prohibitive. This can be addressed by only expanding some universal variables, as well as considering only a subset of the clauses generated by expansion. Even though such approaches degenerate into full expansion in the worst case, they can be quite effective. The solver IDQ [16] successively expands a DQBF in a counterexample-guided abstraction refinement (CEGAR) loop. Initially, universal variables in each clause are expanded separately. Satisfiability of the resulting propositional formula is checked by a SAT solver. If it is unsatisfiable, so is the original DQBF. Otherwise, IDQ checks whether any pair of literals with consistent annotations are assigned different truth values in the satisfying assignment. If there are no such literals, a model of the DQBF has been found. Otherwise, clauses containing the corresponding clashing literals are further expanded. The system is inspired by the *Inst-Gen* calculus, the proof system underpinning the First-Order solver IPROVER [29]. Originally designed for the effectively propositional fragment of first-order logic (EPR), IPROVER also accepts DQBF as input.

The solver HQS seeks to keep the memory requirements of expansion in check by operating on And-Inverter Graph (AIG) representations of input formulas [20]. It uses expansion alongside several other techniques to transform a DQBF into an equivalent QBF and leverage advances in QBF solving [18,50]. HQS is paired with a powerful preprocessor named HQSPRE that provides an arsenal of additional simplification techniques [51], including an incomplete but efficient method for refuting DQBF by reduction to a QBF encoding [14]. HQSPRE is also used in the recently developed solver DQBDD [39], which is similar to HQS but relies on Binary Decision Diagrams (BDDs) instead of AIGs to represent formulas and perform quantifier elimination.

Evaluating DQBF is NEXPTIME complete [3] in general, but some tractable subclasses have been identified in recent work [17,38].

6 Conclusion

We presented a decision algorithm for DQBF that relies on definition extraction to compute Skolem functions inside a CEGIS loop, and evaluated it in terms of the prototype implementation PEDANT. While the initial results are very promising, we see significant room for improvement and various directions to pursue in future research. Generally, the approach works well when Skolem functions can be computed by definition extraction for a large fraction of existential variables without introducing too many arbiter variables. During testing, we encountered multiple instances for which conflict analysis was occupied dealing with minor variations of a small number of counterexamples. We believe that this is partly due to arbiter variables being introduced for *complete* assignments of dependency sets. Even if the assignment of some universal variables in the dependency set is irrelevant for a given counterexample, the newly introduced arbiter variables only deal with the counterexample as represented by the complete assignment, and each counterexample obtained by varying the assignment of irrelevant universal variables requires a new set of arbiter variables. To avoid this, we plan to experiment with a variant of the algorithm that introduces arbiter variables for *partial* assignments [16,29].

A different approach to generalizing from counterexamples—one that does not require changes in the underlying proof system—is the use of machine learning. By predicting the pattern common to a sequence of counterexamples, it is possible to deal with it wholesale and avoid an exhaustive enumeration [25]. Moreover, recent work on Boolean Synthesis demonstrates the viability of learning Skolem functions by sampling satisfying assignments [21].

Finally, we plan to explore further applications of interpolation-based definition extraction within our algorithm. Currently, its use is limited to existential variables that are defined by their dependency sets in the input DQBF, or are undefined only in a small number of cases. In addition to that, one could search for "partial" definitions under assignments of the dependency set characterized by formulas, or introduce definitions that are valid under assumptions [35].

Acknowledgements. Supported by the Vienna Science and Technology Fund (WWTF) under the grants ICT19-060 and ICT19-065, and the Austrian Science Fund (FWF) under grant W1255.

514   F.-X. Reichl et al.

References

1. Akshay, S., Chakraborty, S., Goel, S., Kulal, S., Shah, S.: What's hard about boolean functional synthesis? In: Chockler, H., Weissenbacher, G. (eds.) CAV 2018. LNCS, vol. 10981, pp. 251–269. Springer, Cham (2018). https://doi.org/10.1007/978-3-319-96145-3_14
2. Audemard, G., Simon, L.: Predicting learnt clauses quality in modern SAT solvers. In: Boutilier, C. (ed.) IJCAI 2009, Proceedings of the 21st International Joint Conference on Artificial Intelligence, pp. 399–404 (2009)
3. Azhar, S., Peterson, G., Reif, J.: Lower bounds for multiplayer non-cooperative games of incomplete information. J. Comput. Math. Appl. **41**, 957–992 (2001)
4. Balabanov, V., Chiang, H.K., Jiang, J.R.: Henkin quantifiers and boolean formulae: a certification perspective of DQBF. Theor. Comput. Sci. **523**, 86–100 (2014)
5. Baldoni, R., Coppa, E., D'Elia, D.C., Demetrescu, C., Finocchi, I.: A survey of symbolic execution techniques. ACM Comput. Surv. **51**(3), 50:1–50:39 (2018)
6. Beyersdorff, O., Blinkhorn, J., Chew, L., Schmidt, R.A., Suda, M.: Reinterpreting dependency schemes: soundness meets incompleteness in DQBF. J. Autom. Reason. **63**(3), 597–623 (2019)
7. Biere, A., Cimatti, A., Clarke, E., Zhu, Y.: Symbolic model checking without BDDs. In: Cleaveland, W.R. (ed.) TACAS 1999. LNCS, vol. 1579, pp. 193–207. Springer, Heidelberg (1999). https://doi.org/10.1007/3-540-49059-0_14
8. Biere, A., Fazekas, K., Fleury, M., Heisinger, M.: CaDiCaL, Kissat, Paracooba, Plingeling and Treengeling entering the SAT Competition 2020. In: Balyo, T., Froleyks, N., Heule, M., Iser, M., Järvisalo, M., Suda, M. (eds.) Proceedings of SAT Competition 2020 - Solver and Benchmark Descriptions. Department of Computer Science Report Series B, vol. B-2020-1, pp. 51–53. University of Helsinki (2020)
9. Biere, A., Heljanko, K., Wieringa, S.: AIGER 1.9 and beyond. Tech. Rep. 11/2, Institute for Formal Models and Verification, Johannes Kepler University, Altenbergerstr. 69, 4040 Linz, Austria (2011)
10. Bloem, R., Könighofer, R., Seidl, M.: SAT-based synthesis methods for safety specs. In: McMillan, K.L., Rival, X. (eds.) VMCAI 2014. LNCS, vol. 8318, pp. 1–20. Springer, Heidelberg (2014). https://doi.org/10.1007/978-3-642-54013-4_1
11. Bubeck, U., Büning, H.K.: Dependency quantified horn formulas: models and complexity. In: Biere, A., Gomes, C.P. (eds.) SAT 2006. LNCS, vol. 4121, pp. 198–211. Springer, Heidelberg (2006). https://doi.org/10.1007/11814948_21
12. Eén, N., Sörensson, N.: An extensible SAT-solver. In: Giunchiglia, E., Tacchella, A. (eds.) SAT 2003. LNCS, vol. 2919, pp. 502–518. Springer, Heidelberg (2004). https://doi.org/10.1007/978-3-540-24605-3_37
13. Faymonville, P., Finkbeiner, B., Rabe, M.N., Tentrup, L.: Encodings of bounded synthesis. In: Legay, A., Margaria, T. (eds.) TACAS 2017. LNCS, vol. 10205, pp. 354–370. Springer, Heidelberg (2017). https://doi.org/10.1007/978-3-662-54577-5_20
14. Finkbeiner, B., Tentrup, L.: Fast DQBF refutation. In: Sinz, C., Egly, U. (eds.) SAT 2014. LNCS, vol. 8561, pp. 243–251. Springer, Cham (2014). https://doi.org/10.1007/978-3-319-09284-3_19
15. Fröhlich, A., Kovásznai, G., Biere, A.: A DPLL algorithm for solving DQBF (2012). http://fmv.jku.at/papers/FroehlichKovasznaiBiere-POS12.pdf, presented at Workshop on Pragmatics of SAT (POS)

16. Fröhlich, A., Kovásznai, G., Biere, A., Veith, H.: idq: instantiation-based DQBF solving. In: Berre, D.L. (ed.) POS-14. Fifth Pragmatics of SAT workshop, a workshop of the SAT 2014 conference, part of FLoC 2014 during the Vienna Summer of Logic, Vienna, Austria, 13 July 2014. EPiC Series in Computing, vol. 27, pp. 103–116. EasyChair (2014)

17. Ganian, R., Peitl, T., Slivovsky, F., Szeider, S.: Fixed-parameter tractability of dependency QBF with structural parameters. In: Calvanese, D., Erdem, E., Thielscher, M. (eds.) Proceedings of the 17th International Conference on Principles of Knowledge Representation and Reasoning, KR 2020, pp. 392–402 (2020)

18. Ge-Ernst, A., Scholl, C., Wimmer, R.: Localizing quantifiers for DQBF. In: Barrett, C.W., Yang, J. (eds.) Formal Methods in Computer Aided Design, FMCAD 2019, pp. 184–192. IEEE (2019)

19. Gitina, K., Reimer, S., Sauer, M., Wimmer, R., Scholl, C., Becker, B.: Equivalence checking of partial designs using dependency quantified boolean formulae. In: IEEE 31st International Conference on Computer Design, ICCD 2013, pp. 396–403. IEEE Computer Society (2013)

20. Gitina, K., Wimmer, R., Reimer, S., Sauer, M., Scholl, C., Becker, B.: Solving DQBF through quantifier elimination. In: Nebel, W., Atienza, D. (eds.) Proceedings of the 2015 Design, Automation & Test in Europe Conference & Exhibition, DATE 2015, pp. 1617–1622. ACM (2015)

21. Golia, P., Roy, S., Meel, K.S.: Manthan: a data-driven approach for boolean function synthesis. In: Lahiri, S.K., Wang, C. (eds.) CAV 2020. LNCS, vol. 12225, pp. 611–633. Springer, Cham (2020). https://doi.org/10.1007/978-3-030-53291-8_31

22. Gurfinkel, A., Vizel, Y.: Druping for interpolates. In: FMCAD 2014, pp. 99–106. IEEE (2014)

23. Heule, M.J.H., Järvisalo, M., Suda, M.: SAT competition 2018. J. Satisf. Boolean Model. Comput. **11**(1), 133–154 (2019)

24. Ignatiev, A., Morgado, A., Marques-Silva, J.: PySAT: a python toolkit for prototyping with SAT oracles. In: SAT, pp. 428–437 (2018)

25. Janota, M.: Towards generalization in QBF solving via machine learning. In: McIlraith, S.A., Weinberger, K.Q. (eds.) Proceedings of the Thirty-Second AAAI Conference on Artificial Intelligence, (AAAI-18), pp. 6607–6614. AAAI Press (2018)

26. Janota, M., Klieber, W., Marques-Silva, J., Clarke, E.M.: Solving QBF with counterexample guided refinement. Artif. Intell. **234**, 1–25 (2016)

27. Janota, M., Marques-Silva, J.: On propositional QBF expansions and Q-resolution. In: Järvisalo, M., Van Gelder, A. (eds.) SAT 2013. LNCS, vol. 7962, pp. 67–82. Springer, Heidelberg (2013). https://doi.org/10.1007/978-3-642-39071-5_7

28. Jha, S., Seshia, S.A.: A theory of formal synthesis via inductive learning. Acta Informatica **54**(7), 693–726 (2017)

29. Korovin, K.: iProver – an instantiation-based theorem prover for first-order logic (system description). In: Armando, A., Baumgartner, P., Dowek, G. (eds.) IJCAR 2008. LNCS (LNAI), vol. 5195, pp. 292–298. Springer, Heidelberg (2008). https://doi.org/10.1007/978-3-540-71070-7_24

30. Kullmann, O., Shukla, A.: Autarkies for DQCNF. In: Barrett, C.W., Yang, J. (eds.) 2019 Formal Methods in Computer Aided Design, FMCAD 2019, pp. 179–183. IEEE (2019)

31. Meel, K.S., et al.: Constrained sampling and counting: Universal hashing meets SAT solving. In: Darwiche, A. (ed.) Beyond NP, Papers from the 2016 AAAI Workshop. AAAI Workshops, vol. WS-16-05. AAAI Press (2016)

32. Niemetz, A., Preiner, M., Lonsing, F., Seidl, M., Biere, A.: Resolution-based certificate extraction for QBF. In: Cimatti, A., Sebastiani, R. (eds.) SAT 2012. LNCS, vol. 7317, pp. 430–435. Springer, Heidelberg (2012). https://doi.org/10.1007/978-3-642-31612-8_33

33. Pulina, L., Seidl, M.: The 2016 and 2017 QBF solvers evaluations (qbfeval'16 and qbfeval'17). Artif. Intell. **274**, 224–248 (2019)

34. Rabe, M.N.: A resolution-style proof system for DQBF. In: Gaspers, S., Walsh, T. (eds.) SAT 2017. LNCS, vol. 10491, pp. 314–325. Springer, Cham (2017). https://doi.org/10.1007/978-3-319-66263-3_20

35. Rabe, M.N., Seshia, S.A.: Incremental determinization. In: Creignou, N., Le Berre, D. (eds.) SAT 2016. LNCS, vol. 9710, pp. 375–392. Springer, Cham (2016). https://doi.org/10.1007/978-3-319-40970-2_23

36. Roussel, O.: Controlling a solver execution with the runsolver tool. J. Satisf. Boolean Model. Comput. **7**(4), 139–144 (2011)

37. Scholl, C., Becker, B.: Checking equivalence for partial implementations. In: Proceedings of the 38th Design Automation Conference, DAC 2001, pp. 238–243. ACM (2001)

38. Scholl, C., Jiang, J.R., Wimmer, R., Ge-Ernst, A.: A PSPACE subclass of dependency quantified boolean formulas and its effective solving. In: The Thirty-Third AAAI Conference on Artificial Intelligence, AAAI 2019, pp. 1584–1591. AAAI Press (2019)

39. Síč, J.: Satisfiability of DQBF using binary decision diagrams. Master's thesis, Masaryk University, Brno, Czech Republic (2020)

40. Slivovsky, F.: Interpolation-based semantic gate extraction and its applications to QBF preprocessing. In: Lahiri, S.K., Wang, C. (eds.) CAV 2020. LNCS, vol. 12224, pp. 508–528. Springer, Cham (2020). https://doi.org/10.1007/978-3-030-53288-8_24

41. Slivovsky, F., Szeider, S.: Soundness of Q-resolution with dependency schemes. Theor. Comput. Sci. **612**, 83–101 (2016)

42. Solar-Lezama, A., Jones, C.G., Bodík, R.: Sketching concurrent data structures. In: Gupta, R., Amarasinghe, S.P. (eds.) Proceedings of the ACM SIGPLAN 2008 Conference on Programming Language Design and Implementation, pp. 136–148. ACM (2008)

43. Solar-Lezama, A., Tancau, L., Bodík, R., Seshia, S.A., Saraswat, V.A.: Combinatorial sketching for finite programs. In: Shen, J.P., Martonosi, M. (eds.) Proceedings of the 12th International Conference on Architectural Support for Programming Languages and Operating Systems, ASPLOS 2006, pp. 404–415. ACM (2006)

44. Soos, M., Nohl, K., Castelluccia, C.: Extending SAT solvers to cryptographic problems. In: Kullmann, O. (ed.) SAT 2009. LNCS, vol. 5584, pp. 244–257. Springer, Heidelberg (2009). https://doi.org/10.1007/978-3-642-02777-2_24

45. Stockmeyer, L.J., Meyer, A.R.: Word problems requiring exponential time: Preliminary report. In: Aho, A.V., et al. (eds.) Proceedings of the 5th Annual ACM Symposium on Theory of Computing, Austin, Texas, USA, 30 April–2 May 1973, pp. 1–9. ACM (1973)

46. Tentrup, L.: CAQE and quabs: Abstraction based QBF solvers. J. Satisf. Boolean Model. Comput. **11**(1), 155–210 (2019)

47. Tentrup, L., Rabe, M.N.: Clausal abstraction for DQBF. In: Janota, M., Lynce, I. (eds.) SAT 2019. LNCS, vol. 11628, pp. 388–405. Springer, Cham (2019). https://doi.org/10.1007/978-3-030-24258-9_27

48. Vizel, Y., Gurfinkel, A., Malik, S.: Fast interpolating BMC. In: Kroening, D., Păsăreanu, C.S. (eds.) CAV 2015. LNCS, vol. 9206, pp. 641–657. Springer, Cham (2015). https://doi.org/10.1007/978-3-319-21690-4_43
49. Vizel, Y., Weissenbacher, G., Malik, S.: Boolean satisfiability solvers and their applications in model checking. Proc. IEEE **103**(11), 2021–2035 (2015)
50. Wimmer, R., Karrenbauer, A., Becker, R., Scholl, C., Becker, B.: From DQBF to QBF by dependency elimination. In: Gaspers, S., Walsh, T. (eds.) SAT 2017. LNCS, vol. 10491, pp. 326–343. Springer, Cham (2017). https://doi.org/10.1007/978-3-319-66263-3_21
51. Wimmer, R., Scholl, C., Becker, B.: The (D)QBF preprocessor hqspre - underlying theory and its implementation. J. Satisf. Boolean Model. Comput. **11**(1), 3–52 (2019)
52. Wimmer, R., Scholl, C., Wimmer, K., Becker, B.: Dependency schemes for DQBF. In: Creignou, N., Le Berre, D. (eds.) SAT 2016. LNCS, vol. 9710, pp. 473–489. Springer, Cham (2016). https://doi.org/10.1007/978-3-319-40970-2_29

Scalable SAT Solving in the Cloud

Dominik Schreiber$^{(\boxtimes)}$ (ID) and Peter Sanders (ID)

Karlsruhe Institute of Technology, Karlsruhe, Germany
{dominik.schreiber,sanders}@kit.edu

Abstract. Previous efforts on making Satisfiability (SAT) solving fit for high performance computing (HPC) have led to super-linear speedups on particular formulae, but for most inputs cannot make efficient use of a large number of processors. Moreover, long latencies (minutes to days) of job scheduling make large-scale SAT solving on demand impractical for most applications. We address both issues with *Mallob*, a framework for job scheduling in the context of SAT solving which exploits *malleability*, i.e., the ability to add or remove processing power from a job during its computation. Mallob includes a massively parallel, distributed, and malleable SAT solving engine based on HordeSat with a more succinct and communication-efficient approach to clause sharing and numerous further improvements over its precursor. Experiments with up to 2560 cores show that Mallob outperforms an improved version of HordeSat and scales significantly better. Moreover, Mallob can solve many formulae in parallel while dynamically adapting the assigned resources, and jobs arriving in the system are usually initiated within a fraction of a second.

Keywords: Parallel SAT solving · Distributed computing · Malleable load balancing

1 Introduction

Today's applications of SAT solving are manifold and include areas such as cryptography [26], formal software verification [23], and automated planning [30]. Application-specific SAT encoders generate formulae which represent the problem at hand stated in propositional logic. Oftentimes, multiple formulae which represent different aspects or horizons of the problem are generated [23, 30]. The individual formulae range from trivial to extremely difficult, and their difficulty is usually not known beforehand. Up to a certain degree, today's high performance computing (HPC) can facilitate the resolution of difficult problems. In particular, we notice increased interest in performing SAT solving in on-demand HPC environments that are often referred to as *cloud* [15,29]. This is also reflected in the International SAT Competition 2020 featuring a cloud track for the first time [11]. However, prior achievements of super-linear speedups for particular application instances [4] must be set in relation with the total work which must be invested in every single formula to achieve such peak speedups. Furthermore, in most HPC systems, long latencies of job scheduling (ranging

© Springer Nature Switzerland AG 2021
C.-M. Li and F. Manyà (Eds.): SAT 2021, LNCS 12831, pp. 518–534, 2021.
https://doi.org/10.1007/978-3-030-80223-3_35

from minutes to days) hinder the quick resolution of a stream of jobs even if most of the jobs are trivial. To address these issues, we believe that a SAT solver tasked with a formula of unknown difficulty should be allotted a flexible amount of computational resources based on the overall system load and further task-dependent parameters. In the context of scheduling and load balancing, this feature is called *malleability*: The ability of an algorithm to deal with a varying number of processing elements during its execution [10]. Malleable algorithms open up opportunities for highly dynamic load balancing techniques: The number of associated processing elements for each job can be adjusted continuously to warrant optimal and fair usage of available system resources [19].

In this work, we present a new framework for the scalable resolution of SAT jobs on demand. Our system named *Mallob* consists of two major contributions. First, we propose a decentralized approach to malleable job scheduling and load balancing in the context of SAT solving. Secondly, we present a distributed and malleable SAT solving engine based on the popular large-scale solver Horde-Sat [4]: Most notably, we introduce a succinct and communication-efficient clause exchange mechanism, adapt HordeSat's solver backend to handle malleability, and integrate a number of performance improvements. Experiments with up to 128 compute nodes (2560 cores) show that Mallob as a standalone SAT solver clearly outperforms an updated and improved version of HordeSat and scales significantly better. Moreover, Mallob can solve many formulae in parallel with minimal overhead and combines parallel job processing with a flexible degree of parallel SAT solving to make best use of the available resources. In most cases, it only takes a split second until an arriving job is initiated.

After describing important preliminaries and related work in Sect. 2, we present the malleable environment which hosts our solver engine in Sect. 3. Thereupon, in Sect. 4 we present the solver engine itself. We present the evaluation of our system in Sect. 5 and conclude our work in Sect. 6.

2 Related Work

Given a propositional formula F, the *SAT problem* is to find an assignment to all variables in F such that F is satisfied, or to report that no such assignment exists. For the sequential resolution of SAT problems, the most commonly used algorithm is *CDCL* [25], which is essentially a highly engineered heuristic depth-first search over the space of partial variable assignments. CDCL features advanced techniques such as non-chronological backtracking and restart mechanisms. Furthermore, when a logical conflict is encountered, the solver *learns* a clause which represents this conflict. The knowledge gained from this learning mechanism can help to speed up the subsequent search. Another branch of notable sequential SAT solving approaches is the family of *local search solvers* which perform stochastic local search over the space of variable assignments [18].

Parallel SAT solvers commonly use sequential SAT solvers as building blocks. One strategy which is often called the *portfolio approach* is to execute several solvers in parallel on the same formula [1,14]. Diversification strategies for an effective portfolio range from supplying different random seeds to the same solver over reconfiguring the solver's parameters to employing wholly different SAT solvers. As an alternative to portfolio approaches, *search space partitioning approaches* subdivide the original formula into several sub-formulae and solve these in parallel [2,31]. An extreme case of this strategy is applied in parallel *Cube&Conquer* approaches where a large number of subproblems is generated and then distributed among all workers [15,17]. Regardless of the means of parallelization, an important feature of parallel solvers is to exchange learnt clauses among all workers and, notably, to find a good tradeoff between the sharing of useful information and the avoidance of unnecessary overhead [9].

The International SAT Competition 2020 [11] established a distinction between modestly parallel SAT solving and high-performance SAT solving by featuring both a parallel track and a cloud track. In the parallel track, a single 32-core node was employed for up to 5000 s per instance while the cloud track was evaluated on 100 8-core nodes for up to 1000 s per instance. These different modes of operation require different solver architectures: For modest parallelism in shared memory, high concurrency and memory consumption can become a considerable issue [20]. On a larger scale, concurrency can be less of an issue while good diversification and communication efficiency becomes critical. HordeSat [4] is a popular solver designed for massive parallelism which served as a baseline in the mentioned cloud track. It features a modular solver interface which allows to plug in and dynamically diversify different core solvers. Clause exchange is performed periodically via all-to-all collective operations. The HordeSat paradigm found adoption in a generic interface for parallel SAT solving [24].

Previously, a distributed system for SAT solving in the cloud was presented in [28,29]. It features a centralized scheduler which precomputes a schedule based on run time predictions and which employs sequential solvers without any communication among them: The authors noted that *"such solutions [for exchange of knowledge] are not necessarily suitable for distributed clouds in which the communication time could be important"* [29]. In contrast, we demonstrate that clause exchange is highly effective and introduce decentralized dynamic load balancing without any run time predictions. Another work related to ours is the distributed Cube&Conquer solver Paracooba [15] which can also resolve multiple jobs in parallel and also performs a kind of malleable load balancing. While Paracooba is designed for Cube&Conquer, we propose a malleable portfolio approach. In the cloud track of the SAT Competition 2020 [11], our system outperformed Paracooba and scored a clear first place.

3   Malleable Environment

We now outline the platform *Mallob* for the scheduling and load balancing of malleable jobs. Mallob is an acronym for **M**alleable **Lo**ad **B**alancer as well as **M**ulti-tasking **A**gile **Log**ic **B**lackbox. As a comprehensive presentation of Mallob in its entirety is too broad in scope for this publication, we present the design

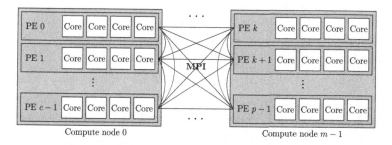

Fig. 1. System architecture used by Mallob

decisions and the features of Mallob that are necessary to understand our SAT
solving system and will describe the internal workings and theoretical properties
of our scheduling and load balancing in a future publication.

We consider a homogeneous[1] distributed computing environment with m
compute nodes (see Fig. 1). For the sake of generality, we do not assume any
kind of shared (RAM or disk) memory between the nodes. As such, the only way
for the nodes to exchange information is to send messages over some broadband
interface. This is enabled by the Message Passing Interface (MPI) [13].

Each compute node contains several *cores*. We partition the cores on a node
into c *groups* of t cores each running one *thread*.[2] Each group is implemented as
a *process* and is also called *PE* (for *processing element*) in the following. Overall,
our system contains a total of $p := c \cdot m$ PEs and $c \cdot m \cdot t$ parallel threads.

A number of *jobs* $1, \ldots, n$ arrive in the system at arbitrary times. A job
is a particular problem statement, in our case given by a propositional logic
formula in *Conjunctive Normal Form* (CNF). Every job j has a constant *priority*
$\pi_j \in (0, 1)$ and a *demand of resources* $d_j \in \mathbb{N}$ which may vary over time. In the
most simple setting, $d_j = p$ at all times. More generally, a job can express with
d_j how many PEs it is able to employ in its current stage of computation. We
expect the number of active jobs to be smaller than the number of workers,
which allows us to restrict each PE to compute on at most one job at a time.

If a job j enters the system, a *request message* $r_0(j)$ performs a random walk
through a sparse regular graph over all PEs until an idle PE $p_0(j)$, named the *root*
of j, adopts the job. This root remains unchanged throughout the job's lifetime
and represents j in collective load balancing computations. Such a balancing
computation is triggered at most once within a certain period e (e.g., $e = 0.1\,s$)
by (a) the arrival of a new job, (b) the completion of a job, and/or (c) the
change of a job's demand. All such events are then broadcast globally with a
single lightweight collective operation. The result of each balancing is a map

---

[1] While we intend to generalize our system to heterogeneous environments in the
future, this undertaking is out of scope for this publication.

[2] The cores may be distributed over several CPU chips (or sockets). Moreover, each
core may be able to run several hardware threads. Our system can handle both
additional levels of hierarchy by appropriately defining c and t.

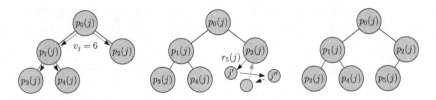

Fig. 2. Illustration of T_j growing from volume 5 to 6. Each circle is a PE.

$j \mapsto v_j$ which assigns to each job j a certain integer, the *volume* $v_j \geq 0$. v_j is proportional to $d_j p_j / \sum_{j'} d_{j'} p_{j'}$ and determines the number of PEs which participate in the resolution of j until the next update of v_j.

The *job tree* T_j of job j is a binary tree of PEs that is rooted at $p_0(j)$. Its purpose is to enforce the volume assigned to j and to enable efficient job-internal communication. Each node $p_x(j)$ in T_j has a unique index $x \geq 0$. Node $p_x(j)$ may have child nodes $p_{2x+1}(j)$ (left child) and $p_{2x+2}(j)$ (right child). T_j is supposed to consist of exactly v_j nodes $p_0(j), \ldots, p_{v_j-1}(j)$ and adjusts accordingly whenever v_j updates: Beginning from $p_0(j)$ which computes a new value of v_j, a message containing v_j is sent through T_j as shown in Fig. 2. If this update arrives at a node $p_x(j)$ for which $x \geq v_j$, then the node will leave T_j and suspend its computation. Conversely, if $p_x(j)$ does not have a left (right) child node and if $2x + 1 < v_j$ ($2x+2 < v_j$), it will send out a request $r_{2x+1}(j)$ ($r_{2x+2}(j)$) for another idle PE to join T_j. These messages are first routed over any former children of $p_x(j)$ before they begin a random walk. As such, our node allocation strategy prioritizes PEs which may still host suspended job nodes of j. In order to make careful use of main memory, we allow each PE to host a small constant number of job nodes and let it discard the oldest job nodes if this limit is exceeded.

Mallob also features a special mode for the isolated resolution of a single job: After a binary tree broadcast of the job description, the i-th PE assumes the role of $p_i(j)$, and no further load balancing is required. As such, Mallob can be employed as a conventional distributed solver without any noticeable overhead compared to static distributed solver architectures such as HordeSat's.

4   The Mallob SAT Engine

We now present our massively parallel, distributed, and malleable SAT solving engine. We focus on (1) a succinct and communication-efficient clause exchange which supports malleability; (2) a rework of HordeSat's solver backend to support malleability; and (3) practical optimizations and performance improvements.

4.1   Succinct Clause Exchange

HordeSat uses synchronous communication in *rounds* to periodically perform an all-to-all clause exchange. The used collective operation is called an *all-gather*: Each PE i contributes a buffer b_i of fixed size β. The concatenation of all buffers,

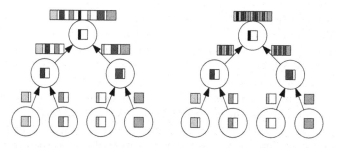

Fig. 3. Exemplary flow of information in the first half of HordeSat's all-gather operation (left) and in our aggregation within a job tree (right). Each circle is a PE; a buffer within a circle represents the PE's locally collected (*exported*) clauses.

$B := b_1 \circ \ldots \circ b_p$, is then broadcast to each PE. This all-gather operation is included by default in all MPI implementations. Each b_i contains a list of learned clauses which were previously *exported* by the solvers of PE i. The clauses are serialized in a compact shape, sorted by their size in increasing order. After the all-gather, each solver *imports* clauses from B into its individual database.

We noticed that the above clause exchange mechanism has various shortcomings. First, whenever a PE does not fill b_i, B contains "holes" which carry no information (see Fig. 3). Secondly, B may contain duplicates: In particular in the beginning of SAT solving when a formula is simplified and basic propagations are done, this may lead to p almost identical buffers b_i. This effect is especially pronounced for unit clauses (see below). Thirdly, B grows proportionally to the number of involved PEs. For sufficiently large HordeSat configurations, this can constitute a bottleneck in terms of communication volume *and* local work.

In our system, we use job tree T_j (as described in Sect. 3) as the communication structure for the clause exchange of each job j. As such, we ensure that the PEs involved in a clause exchange are exactly the PEs that are currently associated with j. As soon as a fixed amount of time s has passed since the last broadcast of shared clauses (e.g., $s = 1\,\text{s}$), each leaf $p_x(j)$ in T_j sends b_x to its parent. When an inner node $p_x(j)$ has received a buffer from each of its children, it exports its own clauses b_x and then performs a two- or three-way merge of the present buffers: All buffers are read simultaneously from left to right and aggregated into a single new buffer b'_x, similar to textbook k-way merge of sorted sequences [27, 5.7.1]. In addition, we use a hash set of seen clauses with hashing that is invariant to the order of literals [4] in order to recognize duplicates.

The size of b'_x is limited and any remaining unread information in the input buffers is discarded. As each b_i is sorted in increasing order by clause length, we aggregate some of the globally shortest clauses while we strictly limit the overall communication volume. Furthermore, we improve the density of useful information in B because each intermediate buffer is compact and contains no duplicate clauses. We limit the size of b'_x as follows: For each aggregation step, i.e., for each further level of T_j that is reached, we discount the maximum buffer size by a factor of α. Specifically, we compute the buffer size limit $l(u) := \lceil u \cdot \alpha^{\log_2(u)} \cdot \beta \rceil$ where u is the number of individual buffers b_i aggregated so far. This limit can be steered by a user parameter $\alpha \in [\frac{1}{2}, 1]$, the *discount factor* at each buffer aggregation. We can see that $l(u)$ converges to β for $\alpha = \frac{1}{2}$ and grows indefinitely for $\alpha > \frac{1}{2}$ with respect to the number u of involved PEs. For $\alpha = 1$, $l(u)$ grows proportionally in u just like HordeSat's shared clause buffer.

HordeSat employs *clause filtering* to detect and discard redundant clauses which have already been imported or exported before. This technique is realized with an approximate membership query (AMQ) data structure. Each PE employs one *node filter* f_n and t *solver filters* (one for each solver thread). At clause export, each clause is registered in its solver filter and then tested against f_n. At clause import, each clause is tested against f_n and then against each solver filter. Unit clauses, however, are always admitted due to their high importance. This is problematic because particular unit clauses can be sent around many times and can waste a considerable amount of space in the buffers.

In our approach we omit f_n because its main use is to filter duplicate clauses which Mallob already detects during the aggregation of buffers. We complemented the solver filters with an additional filtering of unit clauses, using an exact set instead of an AMQ data structure. This way no false positives occur for unit clauses, and each such clause is shared once. We also implemented a probabilistic "restart" mechanism for clause filters: Every X seconds, half of all clauses (chosen randomly) in each clause filter are forgotten and therefore can be shared again. This allows solvers to eventually learn crucial clauses even if they join T_j after these clauses have already been shared for the first time.

4.2 Malleable Solver Backend

In the following we present the most relevant changes we made to HordeSat's solver backend to support malleability.

Malleable Diversification. As in HordeSat, our approach relies on three different sources of diversification: Employing different solver configurations, handing different random seeds to the solvers, and supplying each solver with different default polarities (*phases*) of variables. We diversify a particular solver S with a *diversification index* $x_S \geq 0$ and a *diversification seed* σ_S. We use x_S to determine a particular solver configuration and we use σ_S as a random seed and to select random variable phases. The i-th solver S ($0 \leq i < t$) employed by $p_k(j)$ is assigned $x_S := kt + i$. We obtain σ_S by combining x_S with the solver's thread ID (given by the operating system). As such, each instantiated solver is diversified differently even if a job node is rescheduled and a solver S' is instantiated for which some solver S with $x_S = x_{S'}$ already existed before.

Preemption of Solvers. In our malleable environment, it is essential that a PE's main thread can suspend, resume, and terminate each job node at will. We noticed that we cannot reliably notify a solver thread to stop or suspend its execution because it can get stuck in expensive preprocessing and inprocessing [6] for an extended period. Furthermore, it is impossible to forcefully abort a thread without terminating or, otherwise, potentially corrupting its surrounding process. To still enable seamless preemption and termination, we enabled our solver engine to be launched in a separate process. While this involves some overhead, suspension and termination of a process is supported on the OS level in a safe and elegant manner through signals. For instance, a PE's main thread can terminate a job node by sending "SIGTERM" to the solver process, which then exits immediately regardless of the state of its solver threads.

4.3   Performance Improvements

We now present some further improvements of Mallob over HordeSat.

Solver Portfolio. HordeSat originally featured solver interfaces to Lingeling and Minisat. However, the clause import in HordeSat's Minisat interface treats shared clauses just like original, irredundant clauses and periodically interrupts each solver to add these clauses, what we believe to be detrimental to its performance. Therefore, for this work we focus on Lingeling as an efficient and reliable SAT solver with great diversification options and a dedicated clause import and export mechanism. We updated Lingeling from its 2014 version [5] to its 2018 version [7] with the side effect of rendering all core modules of our system Free Software. Similarly, instead of the 16 diversification options from the former Plingeling [5], we use 13 CDCL diversification options from the newer Plingeling [7]. Every fourteenth solver thread now uses local search solver YalSAT (included in the Lingeling interface), alternatingly with and without preprocessing.

Lock-Free Clause Import. For each solver S within a PE, HordeSat's main thread copies all admitted clauses from clause sharing into a buffer B_S, increasing its size as necessary. The solver thread of S then imports the clauses in B_S one by one. As this implies concurrent access to B_S, a mutually exclusive lock is acquired by the solver thread before reading clauses and by the main thread before writing clauses. If the solver thread cannot acquire this lock, it gives up on importing a clause. We replaced B_S with a lock-free ring buffer[3] R_S and hence achieve a lock-free import of clauses. We also make more careful use of the available memory: The size of R_S is fixed and clauses are eventually discarded if a solver consumes no clauses for some time. We set $|R_S|$ to a low multiple of the maximum number of literals which may be shared in a single round.

Memory Usage. The memory consumption of parallel SAT solvers is a known issue [20]: As each solver commonly maintains its own clause database, memory requirements increase proportionally with the number of spawned solvers. As such, large formulae can cause out-of-memory errors. To counteract this issue, we introduce a simple but effective step of precaution: For a given threshold $\hat{s}$, if a given serialized formula description has size $s > \hat{s}$, then only $t' = \max\{1, \lfloor t \cdot \hat{s}/s \rfloor\}$

---

[3] https://github.com/rmind/ringbuf.

threads will be spawned for each PE. The choice of $\hat{s}$ depends on the amount of available main memory per PE. Based on monitoring the memory usage for different large formulae within a run where 3.2 GB were available per solver, we use $\hat{s} := 10^8$. As t' only depends on s, the t' threads can be started immediately upon the arrival of a formula without the need for any further inspection.

5   Evaluation

We now turn to the evaluation of our work. After explaining our setup, we first evaluate the capabilities of our standalone SAT solver engine, denoted *Mallob-mono*. We then evaluate Mallob with malleable job scheduling.

We implemented Mallob in C++17 and make use of OpenMPI [12]. Our software, all experimental data with supplementary material, and an interactive visualization of experiments can be found at https://github.com/domschrei/mallob.

We experimentally compare Mallob to HordeSat, both with its original portfolio and with the updated portfolio that Mallob uses. As HordeSat does not necessarily represent the state-of-the-art in distributed SAT solving [2], we refer to the SAT Competition 2020 [11] as well as the upcoming SAT Competition 2021 for state-of-the-art comparisons involving Mallob. We fixed a significant performance bug to make HordeSat more competitive: In its original code, Lingeling was not given a callback providing the elapsed time since program start. This caused each solver thread to fall back to frequent expensive system calls.

We ran most experiments on the ForHLR phase II, an HPC cluster with 1152 compute nodes with two 10-core Intel Xeon E5-2660 v3 processors and 64 GB of main memory (RAM) each, connected by an InfiniBand 4X EDR interconnection. In addition, we ran some experiments on SuperMUC-NG, a supercomputer which features 6336 compute nodes with a 24-core Xeon Platinum 8174 processor and 96 GB of DDR4 RAM each and an OmniPath network interconnection. We used the operating system Red Hat Enterprise Linux (RHEL) 7.x on ForHLR II and SUSE Linux Enterprise Server (SLES) 12.x on SuperMUC-NG.

We limited most runs to 300 s per instance. As such, the CPU time per instance at our largest configuration of 2560 cores is at 213 core hours (ch), similar in scale to the 222 ch per instance in the SAT Competition's cloud track. At the next smaller scale of 640 cores, 300 s translate to 53 ch which is similar in scale to the 44 ch per instance in the competition's parallel track.

5.1   Selection of Benchmarks

As the usage of HPC environments is costly in terms of money and energy, we aimed to run experiments responsibly and resource-efficiently while still ensuring statistical relevance and robustness of results. For this means we analyzed the 400 benchmarks of the SAT Competition 2020 with GBD [21] and partitioned them into 80 separate *families* (including families from past competitions). We sorted the instances of each family by the number of contained clauses and then randomly picked one SAT instance from the second (larger) half of each family's sorted instance list. As such, we obtained a selection of 80 instances (35 satisfiable, 35 unsatisfiable, 10 "unknown"). We then compared the official rankings of the SAT Competition 2020 [11] with rankings resulting from our selection of benchmarks. In the cloud track, our selection of benchmarks reproduces the exact same ranking of solvers. In the parallel track, we computed a Kendall rank correlation coefficient [22] of $\tau = 0.82$ over all non-disqualified submissions: 41 pairs of solvers were ranked consistently while four pairs were ranked differently. In particular, the top three solvers were identical. Therefore, we believe that we found a reasonably diverse selection of benchmarks for our means. However, as the reduction of a test set generally increases the risk of overfitting, we treated better performing but more complicated configurations of our system with caution and only adopted them when we found the improvement to be significant.

5.2 Standalone SAT Solving Performance

We now discuss our experiments involving HordeSat and Mallob-mono. We performed our experiments on 128 nodes of ForHLR II with a total of 2560 physical cores. Consistent with the default configuration of HordeSat, we bind each MPI process to four physical cores. Consequently, we execute $20/4 = 5$ MPI processes on each node which results in up to $128 \cdot 5 = 640$ PEs with up to four solvers each. We included HordeSat both with its original solvers ("old") and our updated portfolio ("new"). We included Mallob with different discount factors α in a basic configuration that is as close as possible to HordeSat. HordeSat imposes an upper bound on the LBD or "glue" value [3] of clauses that are exported: Initially, a clause must be unit or have a maximum LBD score of 2 to be shared, and whenever a PE fills its clause buffer by less than 80% this limit is incremented. We also adopted this mechanism in Mallob. We turned off our clause filter half life mechanism (i.e., we set $X = \infty$) for all runs of Mallob-mono.

As Fig. 4 shows, the updated solvers improve HordeSat's performance considerably. Furthermore, the most naïve and untuned configuration of Mallob

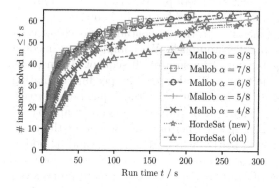

Configuration	#	(+,	-)	PAR-2
HordeSat (old)	51	23	28	252.7
HordeSat	59	28	31	193.7
Mallob $\alpha = 4/8$	59	29	30	196.2
Mallob $\alpha = 5/8$	62	30	32	169.6
Mallob $\alpha = 6/8$	63	30	33	157.4
Mallob $\alpha = 7/8$	63	31	32	**154.0**
Mallob $\alpha = 8/8$	64	31	33	158.2

Fig. 4. Performance of HordeSat and "naïve" Mallob on 128 compute nodes. The table shows solved instances (SAT, UNSAT) and PAR-2 scores [16] (lower is better).

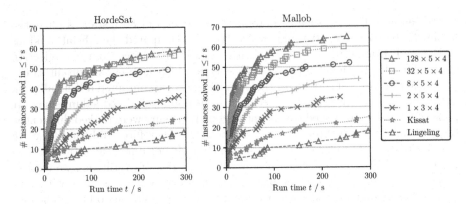

Fig. 5. Scaling behavior of HordeSat (with updated solvers) and Mallob ($\alpha = 7/8$, without any clause length or LBD limits) compared to two sequential solvers.

with $\alpha = 1$ outperforms HordeSat even if both systems make use of the exact same solvers. If $\alpha = 0.5$, only a very small clause buffer of less than 1500 integers is shared each round which proves to be highly detrimental to Mallob's performance and underlines the importance of clause sharing. The best overall performance is achieved with $\alpha = 7/8$ whereas $\alpha = 6/8$ is a close second.

We provide further experimental results for the parametrization of Mallob in the publication's supplementary material (see Sect. 5). Measured on 128 nodes, Mallob achieved best performance without HordeSat's LBD limit mechanism. We also tested a maximum clause length limit of 5 and 10 and found the results to be mostly inconclusive. As such, we continue with a very simple configuration of Mallob without any strict limits on clause lengths or LBD scores.

We now discuss the scalability of our solver. Figure 5 provides an overview on the performance of both HordeSat and Mallob when executed on 12, 40, 160, 640, and 2560 cores. As sequential baselines we included Lingeling (in the 2018 version used by Mallob) as well as Kissat [8], the winner of the SAT Competition 2020's main track. Table 1 shows pairwise speedups. We used a time limit of $\tau_s = 50\,000\,$s for sequential solvers and $\tau_p = 300\,$s for parallel solvers. As in [4] we "generously" attribute a run time of τ_s to the sequential approach for each unsolved instance solved by the parallel approach. We computed the median speedup S_{med} and the total speedup S_{tot} (the sum of all sequential run times divided by the sum of all parallel run times). We also provide speedups emulating "weak scaling", i.e., only considering instances for which the sequential approach took at least as many seconds as the number of cores in the parallel approach.

While both parallel solvers show improved performance whenever the number of cores is quadrupled, HordeSat clearly lacks scalability beyond 32 nodes. As such, Mallob on only 32 nodes outperforms HordeSat on 128 nodes. Furthermore, the 128-node configuration of Mallob achieves a much more pronounced speedup over its 32-node configuration, although we do notice some degree of

Table 1. Parallel speedups for HordeSat (H) and Mallob (M). In the left half, "#" denotes the number of instances solved by the parallel approach and S_{med} (S_{tot}) denotes the median (total) speedup for these instances compared to Lingeling / Kissat. In the right half, only instances are considered for which the sequential solver took at least (num. cores of parallel solver) seconds to solve. Here, "#" denotes the number of considered instances for each combination.

Config.	#	All instances				Hard instances					
		Lingeling		Kissat		Lingeling			Kissat		
		S_{med}	S_{tot}	S_{med}	S_{tot}	#	S_{med}	S_{tot}	#	S_{med}	S_{tot}
H1×3×4	36	3.84	51.90	2.22	29.55	32	4.39	52.01	31	4.03	32.49
H2×5×4	40	12.00	95.80	5.06	64.44	35	12.27	96.83	33	9.11	69.63
H8×5×4	49	22.83	135.55	9.76	90.08	38	32.00	142.76	32	24.88	105.94
H32×5×4	56	42.12	203.66	15.25	112.14	34	97.61	231.77	19	114.86	208.68
H128×5×4	59	50.35	204.10	17.38	111.46	21	356.33	444.12	10	243.42	375.04
M1×3×4	35	4.83	58.15	3.62	64.66	31	5.37	58.24	30	5.29	66.08
M2×5×4	44	12.98	94.44	10.52	67.71	39	14.37	95.28	37	11.54	69.25
M8×5×4	52	28.38	154.62	12.06	89.61	41	34.29	162.23	34	23.43	106.85
M32×5×4	60	53.75	220.92	23.41	148.57	37	152.19	245.54	23	134.07	262.04
M128×5×4	65	81.60	308.48	25.97	175.58	25	363.32	447.97	12	363.32	483.11

diminishing returns as well. This decline in efficiency motivates the next stage of our evaluations where Mallob resolves multiple jobs in parallel.

5.3 Malleable Job Scheduling

To evaluate Mallob in its scheduling mode, we appoint one PE as a designated "client" which introduces jobs to the system and receives results or timeout notifications. Furthermore, the randomized scheduling and load balancing paradigm of Mallob requires that a small ratio ε of PEs is reserved to remain idle. We cautiously chose $\varepsilon = 0.05$ but expect that lower values of ε can be viable. We limited each PE to keep a maximum of three job nodes (active or inactive).

In a first experiment, we test the basic malleability of our solving engine. We use 64 compute nodes of SuperMUC-NG with a total of 1536 cores and partition each node into six PEs à four cores, resulting in 384 PEs in total. As such, we obtain up to $\lfloor (1 - \varepsilon)(p - 1) \rfloor = \lfloor 0.95 \cdot 383 \rfloor = 363$ parallel active job nodes. We introduce a sequential chain of 80 jobs to the system. Periodically (once every 30 s), a "stranger" job arrives and resides in the system for a limited time (15 s) during which it occupies half of the available PEs. We run this experiment with and without a clause filter half life $X = 90$, chosen by preliminary tests, to evaluate its impact in such a malleable setting. As a comparison, we repeat the experiment on 64 and on 32 compute nodes without any disturbances.

Figure 6 shows that the run with disturbances performed worse than the static (i.e., undisturbed) large run and better than the static small run, which is consistent with the available CPU resources in these runs. The periodic reduction

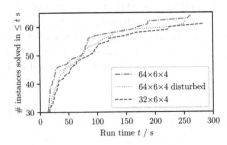

Configuration	#	(+,	-)	PAR-2
32×6×4 $X=\infty$	61	28	33	176.6
64×6×4 $X=90$ dstrb.	61	28	33	174.5
64×6×4 $X=\infty$ dstrb.	62	29	33	166.9
64×6×4 $X=\infty$	64	31	33	153.5

Fig. 6. Performance of Mallob with $X = \infty$ (note the range of the y-axis) with and without periodic disturbances. The table shows solved instances (SAT, UNSAT) and PAR-2 scores [16] (lower is better) and also includes a variant with $X = 90$.

of clause filters was not helpful but rather detrimental to Mallob's performance in this specific setting. Still, for the following experiments we continue with a (potentially suboptimal) value of $X = 90$ because we want to ensure from a design perspective that crucial clauses are eventually shared with the PEs which arrive late to a job. We intend to pursue more reliable and explicit clause re-sharing strategies for malleable SAT solving in the future.

In our next experiment, we let Mallob resolve several jobs at once to evaluate its load balancing. We use 128 compute nodes of ForHLR II and run four PEs à five threads on each compute node (because this fits best the two-socket hardware at hand). As such, we have 512 PEs and up to 485 parallel active job nodes with $\varepsilon = 0.05$. We limit the number of parallel jobs in the system to $J = 4$ (16, 64) which leads to about 121 (30, 7) PEs or 605 (150, 35) threads per job compared to the 640 (160, 40) threads of the closest tested configuration of Mallob-mono.

For 96% of all measurements we counted exactly 485 busy PEs (94.9% system load). The job scheduling times, measured from the introduction of the initial job request $r_0(j)$ to the initiation of the job description transfer to $p_0(j)$, ranged from 0.003 s to 0.781 s (average 0.061 s, median 0.006 s). Our scheduling and load balancing imposes very little overhead: With $J = 4$ (16, 64) we measured an

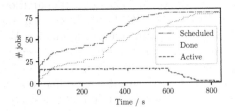

Approach	#	(+,	-)	PAR-2
Mallob $J = 4$	58	26	32	192.7
Mb-mono $m = 32$	**60**	**28**	32	**181.4**
Mallob $J = 16$	**54**	**24**	**30**	**232.7**
Mb-mono $m = 8$	52	23	29	240.1
Mallob $J = 64$	**49**	**21**	**28**	**279.0**
Mb-mono $m = 2$	44	19	25	299.8

Fig. 7. Experiment with a uniform number J of parallel jobs. Left: Number of active jobs and cumulative number of scheduled jobs and done (i.e., finished or cancelled) jobs with $J = 16$ (measured each second). Right: Solved instances and PAR-2 scores (lower is better) of Mallob with $J = 4, 16, 64$ and of comparable Mallob-mono runs.

average of 3.1% (3.0%, 3.0%) of active core time in the PEs' main threads which collectively perform the entire scheduling, load balancing, and communication.

We now compare Mallob with $J = 4$ (16, 64) with Mallob-mono on 640 (160, 40) cores. Figure 7 (right) shows that the run with $J = 4$ performed worse, the run with $J = 16$ performed better and the run with $J = 64$ performed much better than its closest *mono* configuration: When few active jobs are left, additional PEs are available to accelerate the resolution of the remaining jobs. This effect is more pronounced the more jobs are being processed overall.

In a final experiment, we evaluate the performance and resource efficiency of Mallob and its scheduling in a more ambitious setting. We again use 128×4×5 cores of ForHLR II. We immediately introduce all 400 benchmark instances of the SAT Competition 2020 at system start and do not impose any time limit per job. As a comparison, we measured the performance of Mallob-mono on 128 nodes for each instance and computed a *hypothetical optimal sequential scheduler* (HOSS) which knows each job's run time in advance. To minimize average response times, the HOSS schedules the 400 runs of Mallob-mono sorted by their run time in ascending order. We also include two trivial but practical schedulers which process all jobs "embarrassingly parallel" by running 400 instances of Lingeling or Kissat at the same time.

Figure 8 shows that the HOSS outperforms 400 Lingelings, but performs worse than 400 Kissats in terms of median response times. This underlines both the great performance of Kissat and the high resource efficiency of (state-of-the-art) sequential SAT solvers. However, Mallob with malleable scheduling outperforms any of the extremes as it combines parallel job processing with a flexible degree of parallel SAT solving: As more and more jobs finished over time, the average number of cores per job increased steadily from 7.2 to 24. Our system solved 299 instances within 4378 core hours (ch) while the HOSS solves 270 instances with the same resources and takes 7358 ch to solve the same number of instances. To put these measures in perspective [11], Mallob-mono in the SAT Competition 2020 spent 29449 ch for solving 299 instances (7005 ch

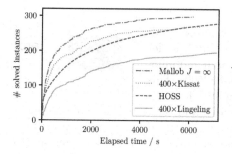

Configuration	R_{all}		R_{slv}	
	avg.	med.	avg.	med.
Mallob $J = \infty$	2422.4	679.8	808.6	260.6
400×Kissat	2998.4	1362.5	975.5	355.5
HOSS	2774.7	2024.5	1396.4	937.3
400×Lingeling	4436.0	7200.0	1559.2	819.9

Fig. 8. Cumulative solved instances by different scheduling approaches on 128 compute nodes within two hours. The table shows average and median response times, calculated for all 400 instances (R_{all}) and for the solved instances per approach (R_{slv}). Each unsolved instance leads to a response time of 7200 s.

for solved instances, 22444 ch for unsolved instances), more instances than any other solver. The winning system of the parallel track solved 284 instances within 6548 ch (1392 ch for solved and 5156 ch for unsolved instances). In both cases we estimate the used hardware to be similar in per-core performance to the hardware we used.

To conclude, Mallob is able to find a flexible trade-off between the resource-efficiency of parallel job processing and the speedups obtained by parallel SAT solving based on the current system load. For real world applications, various mechanisms of Mallob can help to steer this degree of parallelism, such as limiting the maximum number J of concurrent jobs, setting individual job priorities, and limiting a job's maximum volume and its (wallclock or CPU) time budget.

6   Conclusion

In order to improve the scalability and resource efficiency of SAT solving in cloud environments, we introduced the *Mallob* framework for the scalable resolution of SAT jobs on demand. We presented a new approach to malleable job scheduling and a SAT solving engine based on HordeSat which features succinct clause sharing, a reworked solver backend supporting malleability, and various practical improvements. We showed that our standalone SAT solver outperforms an improved version of HordeSat and leads to better speedups. We observed that our job scheduling and load balancing imposes very little overhead and that Mallob's combination of parallel job processing and flexible parallel SAT solving is able to improve resource efficiency and response times in a cloud environment.

While we focused on Mallob's SAT solving capabilities in this work, for future work we intend to evaluate the general scheduling and load balancing properties of Mallob under more realistic job arrival rates and varying job priorities. Secondly, we intend to integrate further solver backends and explore better methods for the re-sharing of crucial clauses in order to improve Mallob's performance. Thirdly, we intend to advance Mallob by adding support for incremental SAT solving and for related applications such as automated planning [30].

Acknowledgments. This project has received funding from the European Research Council (ERC) under the European Union's Horizon 2020 research and innovation programme (grant agreement No. 882500). This work was performed on the supercomputer ForHLR funded by the Ministry of Science, Research and the Arts Baden-Württemberg and by the Federal Ministry of Education and Research. The authors gratefully acknowledge the Gauss Centre for Supercomputing e.V. (www.gauss-centre. eu) for funding this project by providing computing time on the GCS Supercomputer SuperMUC-NG at Leibniz Supercomputing Centre (www.lrz.de). The authors wish to thank Tomáš Balyo and Markus Iser for fruitful discussions, the anonymous reviewers for their helpful feedback and suggestions, and Ekkehard Schreiber and Marvin Williams for kindly proofreading the manuscript.

References

1. Audemard, G., Hoessen, B., Jabbour, S., Piette, C.: Dolius: a distributed parallel SAT solving framework. In: Pragmatics of SAT, pp. 1–11. Citeseer (2014)
2. Audemard, G., Lagniez, J.-M., Szczepanski, N., Tabary, S.: An adaptive parallel SAT solver. In: Rueher, M. (ed.) CP 2016. LNCS, vol. 9892, pp. 30–48. Springer, Cham (2016). https://doi.org/10.1007/978-3-319-44953-1_3
3. Audemard, G., Simon, L.: Predicting learnt clauses quality in modern SAT solvers. In: Twenty-First International Joint Conference on Artificial Intelligence, pp. 399–404 (2009)
4. Balyo, T., Sanders, P., Sinz, C.: HordeSat: a massively parallel portfolio SAT solver. In: Heule, M., Weaver, S. (eds.) SAT 2015. LNCS, vol. 9340, pp. 156–172. Springer, Cham (2015). https://doi.org/10.1007/978-3-319-24318-4_12
5. Biere, A.: Yet another local search solver and Lingeling and friends entering the SAT competition 2014. In: Proceedings of SAT Competition, p. 65 (2014)
6. Biere, A.: Splatz, Lingeling, Plingeling, Treengeling, YalSAT entering the SAT competition 2016. Proceedings of SAT Competition pp. 44–45 (2016)
7. Biere, A.: CaDiCaL, Lingeling, Plingeling, Treengeling and YalSAT entering the SAT competition 2018. In: Proceedings of SAT Competition, pp. 14–15 (2018)
8. Biere, A., Fazekas, K., Fleury, M., Heisinger, M.: CaDiCaL, Kissat, Paracooba, Plingeling and Treengeling entering the SAT competition 2020. In: Proceedings of SAT Competition, p. 50 (2020)
9. Ehlers, T., Nowotka, D., Sieweck, P.: Communication in massively-parallel SAT solving. In: 2014 IEEE 26th International Conference on Tools with Artificial Intelligence, pp. 709–716. IEEE (2014)
10. Feitelson, D.G., Rudolph, L.: Toward convergence in job schedulers for parallel supercomputers. In: Feitelson, D.G., Rudolph, L. (eds.) JSSPP 1996. LNCS, vol. 1162, pp. 1–26. Springer, Heidelberg (1996). https://doi.org/10.1007/BFb0022284
11. Froleyks, N., Heule, M., Iser, M., Järvisalo, M., Suda, M.: SAT Competition 2020. In: Artificial Intelligence (2021, to appear)
12. Graham, R.L., Shipman, G.M., Barrett, B.W., Castain, R.H., Bosilca, G., Lumsdaine, A.: Open MPI: a high-performance, heterogeneous MPI. In: 2006 IEEE International Conference on Cluster Computing, pp. 1–9. IEEE (2006)
13. Gropp, W., Gropp, W.D., Lusk, E., Skjellum, A., Lusk, E.: Using MPI: portable parallel programming with the message-passing interface, vol. 1. MIT Press, Cambridge (1999)
14. Hamadi, Y., Jabbour, S., Sais, L.: ManySAT: a parallel SAT solver. J. Satisf. Boolean Model. Comput. 6(4), 245–262 (2010)
15. Heisinger, M., Fleury, M., Biere, A.: Distributed cube and conquer with paracooba. In: Pulina, L., Seidl, M. (eds.) SAT 2020. LNCS, vol. 12178, pp. 114–122. Springer, Cham (2020). https://doi.org/10.1007/978-3-030-51825-7_9
16. Heule, M., Järvisalo, M., Suda, M.: SAT race 2019 (2019). http://sat-race-2019.ciirc.cvut.cz/downloads/satrace19slides.pdf. Accessed 13 May 2021
17. Heule, M.J.H., Kullmann, O., Wieringa, S., Biere, A.: Cube and conquer: guiding CDCL SAT solvers by Lookaheads. In: Eder, K., Lourenço, J., Shehory, O. (eds.) HVC 2011. LNCS, vol. 7261, pp. 50–65. Springer, Heidelberg (2012). https://doi.org/10.1007/978-3-642-34188-5_8
18. Hoos, H.H., Stützle, T.: Local search algorithms for SAT: an empirical evaluation. J. Autom. Reason. 24(4), 421–481 (2000)

19. Hungershofer, J.: On the combined scheduling of malleable and rigid jobs. In: 16th Symposium on Computer Architecture and High Performance Computing, pp. 206–213. IEEE (2004)
20. Iser, M., Balyo, T., Sinz, C.: Memory efficient parallel SAT solving with inprocessing. In: 2019 IEEE 31st International Conference on Tools with Artificial Intelligence (ICTAI), pp. 64–70. IEEE (2019)
21. Iser, M., Sinz, C.: A problem meta-data library for research in SAT. Proc. Pragmatics SAT **59**, 144–152 (2019)
22. Kendall, M.G.: Rank Correlation Methods. Griffin, London (1948)
23. Kleine Büning, M., Balyo, T., Sinz, C.: Using DimSpec for bounded and unbounded software model checking. In: Ait-Ameur, Y., Qin, S. (eds.) ICFEM 2019. LNCS, vol. 11852, pp. 19–35. Springer, Cham (2019). https://doi.org/10.1007/978-3-030-32409-4_2
24. Le Frioux, L., Baarir, S., Sopena, J., Kordon, F.: PaInleSS: a framework for parallel SAT solving. In: Gaspers, S., Walsh, T. (eds.) SAT 2017. LNCS, vol. 10491, pp. 233–250. Springer, Cham (2017). https://doi.org/10.1007/978-3-319-66263-3_15
25. Marques-Silva, J., Lynce, I., Malik, S.: Conflict-driven clause learning SAT solvers. In: Handbook of Satisfiability, pp. 131–153 (2009). IOS Press
26. Massacci, F., Marraro, L.: Logical cryptanalysis as a SAT problem. J. Autom. Reason. **24**(1), 165–203 (2000)
27. Mehlhorn, K., Sanders, P.: Algorithms and data structures: the basic toolbox. Springer Science & Business Media, Berlin (2008). https://doi.org/10.1007/978-3-540-77978-0
28. Ngoko, Y., Cérin, C., Trystram, D.: Solving SAT in a distributed cloud: a portfolio approach. Int. J. Appl. Math. Comput. Sci. **29**(2), 261–274 (2019)
29. Ngoko, Y., Trystram, D., Cérin, C.: A distributed cloud service for the resolution of SAT. In: 2017 IEEE 7th International Symposium on Cloud and Service Computing (SC2), pp. 1–8. IEEE (2017)
30. Schreiber, D.: Lilotane: a lifted SAT-based approach to hierarchical planning. J. Artif. Intell. Res. **70**, 1117–1181 (2021)
31. Schubert, T., Lewis, M., Becker, B.: PaMiraXT: parallel SAT solving with threads and message passing. J. Satisfiability, Boolean Model. Comput. **6**(4), 203–222 (2010)

DQBDD: An Efficient BDD-Based DQBF Solver

Juraj Síč[1]([✉])[iD] and Jan Strejček[2][iD]

[1] Brno University of Technology, FIT, Brno, Czech Republic
`sicjuraj@fit.vut.cz`
[2] Masaryk University, Brno, Czech Republic
`strejcek@fi.muni.cz`

Abstract. This paper introduces a new DQBF solver called DQBDD, which is based on quantifier localization, quantifier elimination, and translation of formulas to binary decision diagrams (BDDs). In 2020, DQBDD participated for the first time in the *Competitive Evaluation of QBF Solvers (QBFEVAL'20)* and won the *DQBF Solvers Track* by a large margin.

1 Introduction

A *binary decision diagram (BDD)* is a data structure proposed by Bryant [5] to succinctly represent all satisfying assignments of a Boolean formula. Unfortunately, BDDs have limited scalability as there exist formulas such that the corresponding BDDs are exponential in the number of Boolean variables [6]. However, it has been also observed that applying a quantifier to a formula variable often reduces the size of the corresponding BDD [15]. This observation suggests that BDDs could be an appropriate data structure for satisfiability solvers processing formulas with quantifiers. Indeed, recently introduced BDD-based solvers are usually aimed at quantified formulas. For example, eBDD-QBF [21] is a solver for *quantified Boolean formulas (QBFs)* and Q3B [15,16] is an SMT-solver for quantified bit-vector formulas.

This paper introduces another BDD-based solver for quantified formulas, namely the tool called DQBDD deciding satisfiability of *dependency quantified Boolean formulas (DQBFs)*. These formulas are quantified Boolean formulas with existential quantifiers of the form $\exists x(D_x)$, where the value of x can depend only on the values of the universally quantified variables in the *dependency set* D_x. For a precise definition of the syntax and semantics of DQBF, we refer to [11]. While deciding satisfiability of a given Boolean formula is NP-complete, the same problem for QBFs is PSPACE-complete and it is even NEXPTIME-complete for DQBFs [22]. Satisfiability of DQBFs has also some practical applications, in

This work has been supported by the Czech Ministry of Education, Youth and Sports project LL1908 of the ERC.CZ programme, and the FIT BUT internal project FIT-S-20-6427.

particular the *partial equivalence checking (PEC)* [12] which answers the question
of whether a given combinational circuit with unknown parts can be equivalent
to a given specification. Another application is the *controller synthesis problem
(CSP)* [4] which tries to find a controller that keeps a given system in safe states.

The DQBF satisfiability solving is now a hot research topic. The first
algorithm [8], based on DPLL, was introduced in 2012. Since then, several different solving techniques were suggested and implemented in DQBF solvers iDQ [9],
iProver [18], HQS [11,13,34], and dCAQE [33]. Further, there exist DQBF preprocessors HQSpre [35] and Unique [30] which can significantly reduce a given formula
and HQSpre can even directly solve some of them. Research advances in this area
are described in existing overviews [19,28]. Out of the mentioned solvers, the best
performing tool is HQS, which won the *DQBF Solvers Track* of the *Competitive
Evaluation of QBF Solvers (QBFEVAL)* in 2018 and 2019 [23,24].

The following section briefly explains the basic approach of DQBDD to
DQBF solving and compares it to the approach of HQS. Section 3 describes
the implementation, installation, and usage of our tool. The performance of our
tool is then analyzed in Sect. 4.

2   Approach

Let us first assume that we want to build a BDD-based solver for QBFs. The most
straightforward approach is to translate a given formula to the corresponding
BDD in a bottom-up manner, i.e., start with atomic subformulas and build BDDs
for larger subformulas from previously constructed BDDs for smaller subformulas. The whole formula is satisfiable if and only if the resulting BDD represents at
least one satisfying assignment. When processing a quantified subformula $\forall x.\psi$
or $\exists x.\psi$, we handle it as the right side of the corresponding equivalence

$$\forall x.\psi \equiv \psi[1/x] \wedge \psi[0/x] \qquad \text{or} \qquad \exists x.\psi \equiv \psi[1/x] \vee \psi[0/x]$$

where $\psi[v/x]$ for $v \in \{0,1\}$ denotes the formula ψ with all the occurrences of x
replaced by the value v. Given a BDD for ψ, the BDD for $\psi[1/x] \wedge \psi[0/x]$ or
$\psi[1/x] \vee \psi[0/x]$ contains fewer variables than the BDD for ψ (except the case
when the BDD for ψ does not contain x; both BDDs are then identical) and
the number of its nodes is usually also lower. As mentioned before, the main
weakness of BDDs is that they can grow very quickly with an increasing number
of variables and the operations on large BDDs get slower. To reduce the size of
manipulated BDDs, we first push the quantifiers downwards the syntax tree as
far as possible. This process is known as *localization* [11] or *miniscoping* [14].

Now we briefly explain the approach of DQBDD to solving satisfiability of
DQBFs. The full description of the algorithm can be found in the master's thesis
of Juraj Síč [32]. The approach has basically three steps: preprocessing, quantifier
localization, and translation of the input formula to the corresponding BDD.

Formula Preprocessing. The tool gets an input formula in the DQDIMACS
format [9], which implies that the formula is in *prenex conjunctive normal form*

(PCNF). DQBDD then calls HQSpre to reduce the formula. The preprocessed formula is still in prenex normal form, but its matrix (i.e., the part of the formula without the prefix of quantifiers) does not have to be in CNF any more. Alternatively, DQBDD can also read a formula in the prenex cleansed DQCIR format[1] which does not have to be in CNF and HQSpre is thus inapplicable. As the last step of the preprocessing phase, negations are pushed to Boolean variables as the remaining steps of the DQBDD algorithm expect a formula in *negation normal form (NNF)*, where negations appear only in front of variables. Note that NNF has no restrictions on the position of quantifiers, so DQBDD can be easily adjusted to handle DQBFs that are not in prenex normal form.

Quantifier Localization. In this step, DQBDD applies localization rules [11, Theorems 3 and 4] to push the quantifiers downwards as far as possible. Note that the rule (3d) of Theorem 3 [11] is not valid when applied to subformulas [10,32]. However, the rule can be fixed by additional side conditions [10,32].

Translation to a BDD. This step works similarly to the straightforward algorithm for QBFs described at the beginning of this section: the DQBF formula produced by the previous steps is translated to the corresponding reduced ordered BDD in a bottom-up manner. However, handling quantified subformulas is not as simple as for QBF. We use the following quantifier elimination rules.

Universal quantifier elimination. We can apply so-called *universal* or *Shannon expansion* to any subformula $\forall x.\psi$ such that all existential quantifiers $\exists y(D_y)$ in ψ satisfy $x \in D_y$. That is, we replace this subformula with

$$\psi_1[0/x] \wedge \psi_2[1/x]$$

where ψ_1 arises from ψ by removing x from all dependency sets D_y and ψ_2 differs from ψ_1 by replacing each variable y existentially quantified inside this formula by a fresh variable y' with the same dependency set. Hence, any universal quantifier can be eliminated as all potential existential quantifiers $\exists y(D_y)$ in ψ violating $x \in D_y$ can be pushed above the subformula. Note that the elimination can increase the number of variables in the subformula.

Existential quantifier elimination. The situation for subformulas $\exists y(D_y).\psi$ is different. Roughly speaking, such a subformula can be handled as

$$\psi[0/y] \vee \psi[1/y]$$

but only if ψ contains no quantifiers and each variable in ψ is either a free variable, or a variable from D_y, or an existentially quantified variable y' satisfying $D_{y'} \subseteq D_y$ [11, Theorem 5]. To satisfy these requirements, it may be necessary to first eliminate some universal variable in order to remove it from ψ or from some $D_{y'}$. Recall that the elimination of a universal quantifier can again increase the number of existential quantifiers in the formula.

---

[1] This is the prenex cleansed QCIR format [17] extended with quantifiers `depend(v, v1, ..., vn)` representing existential variable `v` with dependencies `v1, ..., vn`.

Now assume that we need to translate a subformula of the form

$$\forall x_1 \forall x_2 \ldots \forall x_n \exists y_1 (D_{y_1}) \exists y_2 (D_{y_2}) \ldots \exists y_m (D_{y_m}).\psi$$

and ψ has already been translated. Note that the order of these quantifiers can be arbitrarily changed without any impact on the formula semantics as long as all variables in each dependency set D_{y_i} are quantified before y_i. We implemented three possible strategies for quantifier elimination called *none*, *simple*, and *all*.

None. Instead of elimination, we push the quantifiers upwards using the reverse version of quantifier localization rules. This strategy is equivalent to an algorithm that skips the quantifier localization and keeps the formula in prenex form.

Simple. We iteratively eliminate all existential quantifiers for which the elimination rule requirements are satisfied and the universal quantifiers that are not in any dependency set D_{y_i} and thus their elimination does not introduce any fresh variable. The remaining quantifiers are pushed up.

All. We iteratively eliminate all quantifiers that can be eliminated. More precisely, we first eliminate all existential quantifiers satisfying the requirements, then we eliminate a selected universal quantifier, and then we repeat the process. If we reach the situation that all universal quantifiers are eliminated and the remaining existential quantifiers cannot be eliminated due to a variable quantified outside the considered subformula, then we push these remaining existential quantifiers up.

If the considered subformula is in fact the whole formula, then we have to apply the *all* strategy as we cannot push any quantifier up in the formula. In this strategy, the universal quantifiers can be eliminated in an arbitrary order. We implemented three heuristics to determine the order, namely *at the beginning*, *current lowest*, and *vars in conjuncts*.

at the beginning. This heuristics determines the elimination order of universal variables $x_1, \ldots, x_n$ at the beginning of the elimination process according to the number of dependency sets each variable appears in (variables with the lowest number are eliminated first). The motivation is to keep the number of variables added by the elimination process low as long as possible.

current lowest. This heuristics is similar to the previous one, but the order is updated according to the current situation every time before the next universal variable is selected for elimination.

vars in conjuncts. This heuristics is motivated directly by the use of BDDs. Elimination of a universal variable x produces the BDD for $\psi_1[0/x] \wedge \psi_2[1/x]$. As we have the BDD for ψ in hand and instantiation of a variable is very cheap, for each universal variable x we compute the set of variables in the BDDs for $\psi_1[0/x]$ and $\psi_2[1/x]$ and select the variable with the smallest set.

An experimental comparison of all combinations of elimination strategies and elimination order heuristics [32] shows significant differences between strategies and only small differences between heuristics. We selected the *simple* strategy with the heuristics *at the beginning* as the default setting. The combination of the *simple* strategy with the heuristics *vars in conjuncts* solved the same number of instances (not the same instances) but it was slightly slower.

Our approach is very close to the current approach of HQS, which also applies preprocessing, quantifier localization, and quantifier elimination using the same elimination strategy *simple* as we use by default. However, there are two important differences. First, HQS uses a succinct representation of Boolean formulas called *and-inverter graphs (AIGs)* [20]. Second, after turning the formula back to prenex normal form, HQS uses *dependency elimination* [34] (which removes universal variables only from some dependency sets) and quantifier elimination to simplify the formula until it gets a QBF, which is then sent to a QBF solver.

3   Implementation and Usage

DQBDD is implemented in C++ under LGPLv3 license. The current stable version is 1.2. For working with BDDs, our tool uses the library CUDD v3.0.0 [31] which also implements Rudell's sifting algorithm [26] for dynamic reordering of BDD variables to keep the size of BDDs small. Further, DQBDD integrates the DQBF preprocessor HQSpre[2] [35] which uses Easylogging++ v9.96.7 library for logging, and SAT solvers PicoSAT [3] and antom [29]. Finally, DQBDD also uses the library cxxopts v2.2.0 for command-line argument parsing.

The sources of DQBDD including all the mentioned libraries can be found at https://github.com/jurajsic/DQBDD. Compilation of the tool requires only a C++ compiler supporting the C++14 standard and CMake v3.5 or higher. DQBDD can be compiled into a dynamically linked executable on Linux and Mac systems while static linking is supported only on Linux systems (and is enabled by default). The executables of DQBDD v1.2 are available in the repository.

The tool is executed from command-line as

```
DQBDD [ARGUMENT...] <input file>
```

where `<input file>` specifies the input formula in DQDIMACS [9] or prenex cleansed DQCIR format. The tool supports the following arguments:

`--preprocess 0/1` turns the preprocessing off/on (not applicable for DQCIR).
`--dyn-reordering 0/1` turns off/on the mentioned sifting algorithm in CUDD.
`--localise 0/1` turns off/on the quantifier localization step. Turning off localization effectively enforces the quantifier elimination strategy *none*.
`--elimination-choice 0/1/2` selects the strategy *none/simple/all* for quantifier elimination. To select *none*, it is more efficient to switch off the quantifier localization step.
`--uvar-choice 0/1/2` selects the heuristics *at the beginning/current lowest/vars in conjuncts* determining the order of universal quantifier elimination.

The default value of all these arguments is 1 except the last argument, where the default value is 0.

---

[2] We use the version distributed with HQS downloaded on March 18, 2021, from http://abs.informatik.uni-freiburg.de/src/projectfiles/21/HQS.zip.

Table 1. For each tool and instance type, the table shows the **total** number of solved instances, the number of solved **sat**isfiable and **unsat**isfiable instances, and the number of instances solved **uniq**uely by the solver. All solved CSP instances are satisfiable.

	PEC				CSP		SAT			
	3277 instances				404 instances		22 instances			
	total	sat	unsat	uniq	total	uniq	total	sat	unsat	uniq
dCAQE	818	132	686	2	**41**	**15**	**7**	3	4	0
DQBDD	**3035**	**364**	**2671**	**384**	26	4	1	0	1	**1**
HQS	2625	246	2379	5	24	0	6	**4**	2	0
iDQ	534	48	486	1	7	0	**7**	**4**	3	0
iProver	677	83	594	0	19	0	**7**	2	**5**	**1**

4   Experimental Comparison

We compared the performance of DQBDD v1.2 against DQBF solvers iDQ v1.0, iProver v3.4[3], dCAQE v4.0.1, and the current version of HQS[4].

For the experiments, we used the DQBF benchmark set considered also in other recent papers on DQBF [10,11]. The set consists of 4316 instances of partial equivalence checking problem (**PEC**) collected from various sources [7,9,12,27], 461 instances of controller synthesis problem (**CSP**) [4], and 34 instances of **SAT** problem encoded as DQBF with an exponentially smaller number of variables [1].

All our experiments were computed on a 24 core machine with 2.10 GHz Intel Xeon CPU. We set the runtime limit to 900 s of CPU time and the memory consumption limit to 4 GB for each tool and input formula. We employed the framework for reliable benchmarking and resource measurement called BenchExec v2.2 [2] to enforce these limits. BenchExec also isolates the measured processes such that they can run in parallel with minimum interference between each other.

First, we run preprocessor HQSpre on all benchmarks and removed the solved instances from our benchmark set. This leaves us with 3277 PEC instances, 404 CSP instances, and 22 SAT instances. Then we run solvers dCAQE, iDQ, and iProver on the remaining instances in the preprocessed form. We run HQS and DQBDD on the remaining instances in their original form as both these tools call HQSpre in their solving routine. All the considered benchmarks with the corresponding BenchExec definitions and obtained results from the solvers can be found at https://github.com/jurajsic/DQBFbenchmarks.

The results are presented in Table 1. DQBDD dominates on PEC instances. This can be also seen in Fig. 1a which shows the cactus plot comparing running times of individual solvers on PEC instances. Only HQS can solve a similar number of PEC instances, but it is significantly slower. The total running time of DQBDD on solved PEC instances is 28 081 s, while for HQS, which solved

---

[3] Called with "--qbf_mode true --inst_out_proof false --res_out_proof false".
[4] Downloaded from http://abs.informatik.uni-freiburg.de/src/projectfiles/21/HQS.zip on March 18, 2021.

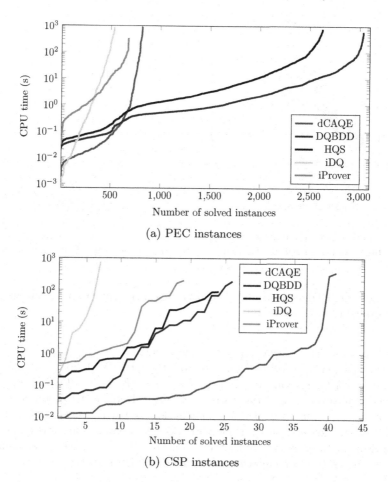

(a) PEC instances

(b) CSP instances

Fig. 1. Cactus plots showing on the x axis the numbers of PEC and CSP instances solved by individual tools for the runtime limit set to values on the y axis.

410 instances less, it is 58 154 s. The scatter plot in Fig. 2a compares running times of DQBDD and HQS on individual PEC instances. Furthermore, there was a discrepancy for 7 PEC instances. All these were determined as satisfiable by dCAQE while at least one other solver determined them as unsatisfiable. We believe that all these instances are unsatisfiable as we were able to find a simple unsatisfiable DQBF that dCAQE solves incorrectly [32, Appendix D].

For CSP instances, dCAQE solved the most instances. The comparison of running times of all tools can be found in Fig. 1b. As dCAQE sometimes returns an incorrect result, we rather focus on the comparison of the two next best solvers, that is DQBDD and HQS. DQBDD needed 190 s to solve the 22 instances solved by both DQBDD and HQS, while HQS needed 238 s. The detailed comparison of running times is shown in Fig. 2b.

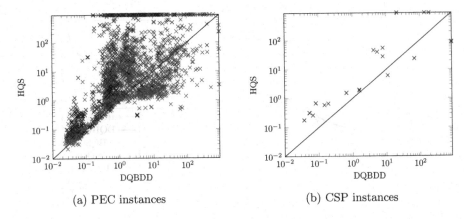

(a) PEC instances   (b) CSP instances

Fig. 2. Scatter plots comparing CPU times of DQBDD and HQS on individual satisfiable (blue) and unsatisfiable (red) instances of PEC and CSP. (Color figure online)

Finally, DQBDD solved only one SAT instance, but other solvers were not able to solve this instance.

QBF. As QBF is a special case of DQBF, DQBDD is also a QBF solver. We tried DQBDD on the QBF benchmarks from the QBFEVAL'20 [25] competition. Out of the 521 QBFs considered in the *Prenex CNF Track*, DQBDD solved 250 instances. However, 214 of them were actually solved by the preprocessor. For the 339 *Prenex non-CNF Track* benchmarks, DQBDD solved 109 instances. As HQSpre works only on CNF benchmarks, no preprocessing was involved. A comparison of these results with the results of QBFEVAL'20 reveals that our solver is currently not competitive with leading QBF solvers.

5   Conclusion

We have presented a new DQBF solver called DQBDD. The tool uses a similar approach based on quantifier localization and elimination as the solver HQS, but DQBDD essentially translates a given formula to the equivalent BDD, which other DQBF solvers do not. Our experimental comparison shows that DQBDD runs significantly faster on instances of the *partial equivalence checking* problem, which is currently the principal application of DQBF solving. The good performance of DQBDD has also been confirmed by winning the *DQBF Solvers Track* of QBFEVAL'20.

References

1. Balabanov, V., Roland Jiang, J.-H.: Reducing satisfiability and reachability to DQBF, 2015. Talk given at International Workshop on Quantified Boolean Formulas - QBF 2015 (2015)
2. Beyer, D., Löwe, S., Wendler, P.: Reliable benchmarking: requirements and solutions. Int. J. Softw. Tools Technol. Transf. **21**(1), 1–29 (2017). https://doi.org/10.1007/s10009-017-0469-y
3. Biere, A.: Picosat essentials. J. Satisfiability, Boolean Model. Comput. (JSAT). **4**, 75–97 (2008)
4. Bloem, R., Könighofer, R., Seidl, M.: SAT-based synthesis methods for safety specs. In: Verification, Model Checking, and Abstract Interpretation, pp. 1–20 (2014)
5. Bryant, R.E.: Graph-based algorithms for Boolean function manipulation. IEEE Trans. Comput. **35**(8), 677–691 (1986)
6. Bryant, R.E.: On the complexity of VLSI implementations and graph representations of Boolean functions with application to integer multiplication. IEEE Trans. Comput. **40**(2), 205–213 (1991)
7. Finkbeiner, B., Tentrup, L.: Fast DQBF refutation. In: Sinz, C., Egly, U. (eds.) SAT 2014. LNCS, vol. 8561, pp. 243–251. Springer, Cham (2014). https://doi.org/10.1007/978-3-319-09284-3_19
8. Fröhlich, A., Kovásznai, G., Biere, A.: A DPLL algorithm for solving DQBF. In: Pragmatics of SAT (PoS 2012, aff. to SAT 2012) (2012)
9. Fröhlich, A., Kovásznai, G., Biere, A., Veith, H.: iDQ: instantiation-based DQBF solving. In: Le Berre, D. (ed.) POS-14. Fifth Pragmatics of SAT Workshop, A Workshop of the SAT 2014 Conference, part of FLoC 2014 during the Vienna Summer of Logic, 13 July, 2014, Vienna, Austria, volume 27 of EPiC Series in Computing, pp. 103–116. EasyChair (2014)
10. Ge-Ernst, A., Scholl, C., Síč, J., Wimmer, R.: Solving dependency quantified Boolean formulas using quantifier localization. Theoretical Computer Science (2021). Submitted. Preprint available as arXiv:1905.04755v2
11. Ge-Ernst, A., Scholl, C., Wimmer, R.: Localizing quantifiers for DQBF. In: Barrett, C.W., Yang, J. (eds.) 2019 Formal Methods in Computer Aided Design, FMCAD 2019, San Jose, CA, USA, 22–25 October, 2019, pp. 184–192. IEEE (2019)
12. Gitina, K., Reimer, S., Sauer, M., Wimmer, R., Scholl, C., Becker, B.: Equivalence checking of partial designs using dependency quantified Boolean formulae. In: 2013 IEEE 31st International Conference on Computer Design, ICCD 2013, Asheville, NC, USA, 6–9 October, 2013, pp. 396–403. IEEE Computer Society (2013)
13. Gitina, K., Wimmer, R., Reimer, S., Sauer, M., Scholl, C., Becker, B.:. Solving DQBF through quantifier elimination. In: Nebel, W., Atienza, D. (eds.) Proceedings of the 2015 Design, Automation and Test in Europe Conference and Exhibition, DATE 2015, Grenoble, France, 9–13 March, 2015, pp. 1617–1622. ACM (2015)
14. Harrison, J.: Handbook of Practical Logic and Automated Reasoning. Cambridge University Press (2009)
15. Jonáš, M., Strejček, J.: Solving quantified bit-vector formulas using binary decision diagrams. In: Creignou, N., Le Berre, D. (eds.) SAT 2016. LNCS, vol. 9710, pp. 267–283. Springer, Cham (2016). https://doi.org/10.1007/978-3-319-40970-2_17
16. Jonáš, M., Strejček, J.: Q3B: an efficient BDD-based SMT solver for quantified bit-vectors. In: Dillig, I., Tasiran, S. (eds.) CAV 2019. LNCS, vol. 11562, pp. 64–73. Springer, Cham (2019). https://doi.org/10.1007/978-3-030-25543-5_4

17. Jordan, C., Klieber, W., Seidl, M.: Non-CNF QBF solving with QCIR. Beyond NP. In: AAAI Workshop (2016)
18. Korovin, K.: iProver – an instantiation-based theorem prover for first-order logic (system description). In: Armando, A., Baumgartner, P., Dowek, G. (eds.) IJCAR 2008. LNCS (LNAI), vol. 5195, pp. 292–298. Springer, Heidelberg (2008). https://doi.org/10.1007/978-3-540-71070-7_24
19. Kovásznai, G.: What is the state-of-the-art in DQBF solving. In: MaCS-16. Joint Conference on Mathematics and Computer Science (2016)
20. Mishchenko, A., Chatterjee, S., Brayton, R.: FRAIGs: a unifying representation for logic synthesis and verification. EECS Dept., UC Berkeley, Technical report (2005)
21. Olivo, O., Emerson, E.A.: A more efficient BDD-based QBF solver. In: Lee, J. (ed.) CP 2011. LNCS, vol. 6876, pp. 675–690. Springer, Heidelberg (2011). https://doi.org/10.1007/978-3-642-23786-7_51
22. Peterson, G., Reif, J., Azhar, S.: Lower bounds for multiplayer noncooperative games of incomplete information. Comput. Math. Appl. 41(7), 957–992 (2001)
23. Pulina, L., Seidl, M.: QBF evaluation 2018 (2018)
24. Pulina, L., Seidl, M., Shukla, A.: QBF evaluation 2019 (2019)
25. Pulina, L., Seidl, M., Shukla, A.: QBF evaluation 2020 (2020)
26. Rudell, R.: Dynamic variable ordering for ordered binary decision diagrams. In: Proceedings of 1993 International Conference on Computer Aided Design (ICCAD), pp. 42–47 (1993)
27. Scholl, C., Becker, B.: Checking equivalence for partial implementations. In: Proceedings of the 38th Design Automation Conference (IEEE Cat. No.01CH37232), pp. 238–243 (2001)
28. Scholl, C., Wimmer, R.: Dependency quantified Boolean formulas: an overview of solution methods and applications. In: Beyersdorff, O., Wintersteiger, C.M. (eds.) SAT 2018. LNCS, vol. 10929, pp. 3–16. Springer, Cham (2018). https://doi.org/10.1007/978-3-319-94144-8_1
29. Schubert, T., Lewis, M., Becker, B.: Antom - solver description (2010)
30. Slivovsky, F.: Interpolation-based semantic gate extraction and its applications to QBF preprocessing. In: Lahiri, S.K., Wang, C. (eds.) CAV 2020. LNCS, vol. 12224, pp. 508–528. Springer, Cham (2020). https://doi.org/10.1007/978-3-030-53288-8_24
31. Somenzi, F.: CUDD: CU decision diagram package release 3.0.0 (2015)
32. Síč, J.: Satisfiability of DQBF using binary decision diagrams. Master's thesis, Masaryk University, Faculty of Informatics (2020)
33. Tentrup, L., Rabe, M.N.: Clausal abstraction for DQBF. In: Janota, M., Lynce, I. (eds.) SAT 2019. LNCS, vol. 11628, pp. 388–405. Springer, Cham (2019). https://doi.org/10.1007/978-3-030-24258-9_27
34. Wimmer, R., Karrenbauer, A., Becker, R., Scholl, C., Becker, B.: From DQBF to QBF by dependency elimination. In: Gaspers, S., Walsh, T. (eds.) SAT 2017. LNCS, vol. 10491, pp. 326–343. Springer, Cham (2017). https://doi.org/10.1007/978-3-319-66263-3_21
35. Wimmer, R., Scholl, C., Becker, B.: The (D)QBF preprocessor HQSpre - underlying theory and its implementation. J. Satisfiability Boolean Model. Comput. 11, 3–52 (2019)

Logical Cryptanalysis with WDSat

Monika Trimoska$^{(\boxtimes)}$, Gilles Dequen, and Sorina Ionica

Laboratoire MIS, Université de Picardie Jules Verne, Amiens, France
{monika.trimoska,gilles.dequen,sorina.ionica}@u-picardie.fr

Abstract. Over the last decade, there have been significant efforts in developing efficient XOR-enabled SAT solvers for cryptographic applications. In [22] we proposed a solver specialised to cryptographic problems, and more precisely to instances arising from the index calculus attack on the discrete logarithm problem for elliptic curve-based cryptosystems. Its most prominent feature is the module that performs an enhanced version of Gaussian Elimination. [22] is concentrated on the theoretical aspects of the new tool, but the running time-per-conflict results suggest that this module uses efficient implementation techniques as well. Thus, the first goal of this paper is to give a comprehensive exposition of the implementation details of WDSat. In addition, we show that the WDSat approach can be extended to other cryptographic applications, mainly all attacks that involve solving dense Boolean polynomial systems. We give complexity analysis for such systems and we compare different state-of-the-art SAT solvers experimentally, concluding that WDSat gives the best results. As a second contribution, we provide an original and economical implementation of a module for handling OR-clauses of any size, as WDSat currently handles OR-clauses comprised of up to four literals. We finally provide experimental results showing that this new approach does not impair the performance of the solver.

1 Introduction

Due to the significant number of improvements in SAT-based parity reasoning over the last decade, SAT solvers are gaining popularity in cryptographic applications. More specifically, they are often used to tackle the solving phase in algebraic cryptanalysis of stream ciphers [11,14,18,19,21], and more recently, of public-key cryptosystems [10,23]. Algebraic cryptanalysis includes all attacks where the underlying problem of a cryptographic system is reduced to the problem of solving a multivariate polynomial system of equations. The resulting system is solved using algebraic techniques, such as Gröbner basis algorithms [9], exhaustive search [5], hybrid methods [2] or algorithms in the XL family [6]. Finding a solution to the polynomial system constitutes a successful attack and results in recovering

We acknowledge financial support from the European Union under the 2014/2020 European Regional Development Fund (FEDER) and from the Agence Nationale de Recherche under project ANR20-ASTR-0011.

C.-M. Li and F. Manyà (Eds.): SAT 2021, LNCS 12831, pp. 545–561, 2021.
https://doi.org/10.1007/978-3-030-80223-3_37

(a part of) the secret key or the plaintext. Boolean polynomial systems may be easily re-written as SAT formulas, which are then solved using a SAT solver. This technique is referred to as logical cryptanalysis [17].

The transformation of a Boolean polynomial system into a CNF formula is done in three steps, each resulting in a propositional formula in different form. First, we obtain an Algebraic Normal Form (ANF) by replacing all multiplications over the binary field by a logical AND and all sums by the XOR operator. The next step is to eliminate all conjunctions through a linearization-like process that consists in replacing all occurrences of $(x_1 \wedge \ldots \wedge x_k)$ by a newly added variable $x_{1,\ldots,k}$ and adding the constraint $x_{1,\ldots,k} \Leftrightarrow (x_1 \wedge \ldots \wedge x_k)$ to the model in its CNF equivalence $(\neg x_{1,\ldots,k} \vee x_1) \wedge \ldots \wedge (\neg x_{1,\ldots,k} \vee x_k) \wedge (\neg x_1 \vee \ldots \vee \neg x_k \vee x_{1,\ldots,k})$. This step results in a so-called CNF-XOR formula which is a conjunction of both OR-clauses and XOR-clauses. Classically, a XOR-clause of size k can be rewritten either as a conjunction of 2^{k-1} k-OR-clauses or as a conjunction of 3-OR-clauses, if the XOR-clause is first cut up into 3-XOR-clauses.

Since the XOR operator is at the core of reasoning models obtained from cryptographic attacks, significant effort has been put into developing XOR-enabled SAT solvers that read formulas in CNF-XOR form and are adapted to reason directly on XOR constraints. In this paper, we give implementation details of one such solver, named WDSAT, proposed in [22]. WDSAT is a built-from-scratch DPLL-based SAT solver that is specifically designed for solving ANF instances derived from cryptographic attacks on public-key cryptosystems. These formulas have few variables, but are highly dense, i.e. they have very long XOR-clauses. The original proposal of WDSAT shows experimental results on formulas derived from an attack on elliptic curve-based cryptosystems. In contrast, in this paper, we experiment with WDSAT and other state-of-the-art SAT solvers using instances derived from the Multivariate Quadratic (MQ) problem, which is the problem of finding all common zeros of a multivariate quadratic system of polynomials. The following toy example shows an MQ system with 4 equations in 3 variables over the binary field.

$$x_1x_2 + x_1x_3 + x_1 + x_2 + x_3 + 1 = 0$$
$$x_1x_2 + x_2x_3 + x_1 + x_3 = 0$$
$$x_1x_2 + x_3 + 1 = 0.$$

In addition, we propose an original technique with reduced amount of memory, which allows to handle large size clauses and thus, solve multivariate polynomial systems of any degree. We report experimental results with WDSAT on multivariate polynomial systems of degree three and four. Solving the multivariate polynomial problem is at the core of algebraic cryptanalysis, as many cryptographic attacks can be reduced to the problem of solving a multivariate polynomial system of equations.

2   Background

WDSAT was proposed at CP 2020 [22] as an XOR-enabled SAT solver dedicated to solving instances derived from a *Weil Descent*. A Weil descent is a technique, commonly used in cryptanalysis, for reducing the problem of finding roots of a polynomial defined over an extension field to the problem of solving a multivariate polynomial system of equations defined over the base field. The WDSAT solver was particularly designed for the Weil descent steps performed in an attack on elliptic curve-based cryptosystems. The solver is built-from-scratch and based on the DPLL algorithm [7]. It is comprised of three reasoning modules that communicate with each other. One is used for reasoning on the CNF part of the formula and the other two are used for XOR reasoning. When an assumption of a truth value is made, the literal is first set in the CNF module. Then, all propagated literals are recovered and are set, together with the initial assumption, in the second module, called XORSET. Finally, all literals propagated by the CNF and XORSET modules are set in the third module, called XORGAUSS. If the XORGAUSS module results in more propagated literals, the process is repeated, until all modules can no longer propagate. Each module is equipped with a corresponding propagation, conflict detection and backtracking technique. The CNF and XORSET modules use classic techniques for unit propagation on OR and XOR-clauses respectively. Handling the XOR-clauses instead of breaking them down into a CNF is beneficial for SAT solving, as it allows us to use powerful techniques inspired from algebraic solving tools, such as the Gaussian Elimination (GE). Performing GE generally results in fewer conflicts, but is computationally expensive. Thus, the purpose of the XORGAUSS module is to perform (GE) on the XOR part of the formula efficiently. In this module, XOR-clauses are represented as Equivalence Classes (EC). A *representative* is chosen for each class and the GE technique consists in assigning a truth value to a variable while applying defined rules that ensure that the so-called unicity-of-representatives property is maintained. This property states that a representative of an EC will never be present in another EC. Thus, the notion of representative of an EC is analogous to the notion of *pivot* in linear algebra.

In addition, starting from the observation that existing SAT-based implementations of the GE are not as efficient as GE in algebraic tools, we proposed in [22] an extended version of the XORGAUSS module (XG-EXT). Indeed, in a Gröbner-basis based approach [13], when a variable $\mathbf{x}_i$ is set to 1, all occurrences of a monomial $\mathbf{x}_i\mathbf{x}_j$ are replaced by $\mathbf{x}_j$ and can be canceled out with other occurrences of $\mathbf{x}_j$. Recall that a monomial $\mathbf{x}_i\mathbf{x}_j$ from the initial Boolean polynomial system becomes $x_i \wedge x_j$ in the equivalent propositional formula and is replaced by a newly added variable $x_{i,j}$. The CNF block that we obtain from this substitution is $(x_i \vee \neg x_{i,j}) \wedge (x_j \vee \neg x_{i,j}) \wedge (\neg x_i \vee \neg x_j \vee x_{i,j})$. When we set x_i to TRUE and apply the unit propagation rules, we are left with the following OR-clauses:

$$(x_j \vee \neg x_{i,j}) \wedge \tag{1}$$
$$(\neg x_j \vee x_{i,j}).$$

In the XOR part of the CNF-XOR formula, x_j and $x_{i,j}$ are two different variables and a possible cancellation of terms can be overseen. To fix this oversight, the following rule is added to WDSAT. When $x_{i,j} \Leftrightarrow (x_i \wedge x_j)$ and we set x_i to TRUE, $x_{i,j}$ is replaced by x_j. To perform the substitution of $x_{i,j}$ by x_j, propagation rules, similar to the ones for truth value assignment, are defined for maintaining the unicity-of-representatives property. This constitutes the XG-EXT module.

Since this oversight is due to the CNF-XOR input form, it is common for all XOR-enabled SAT solvers that perform GE. However, the newest version of CRYPTOMINISAT (5.8.0) implements a technique called BIRD [20] that seems to fix the issue as well. The BIRD technique consists in (i) transforming XOR clauses into CNF, (ii) inprocess over CNF clauses, (iii) recover simplified XOR-clauses and (iv) perform CDCL coupled with GE on the CNF-XOR formula. Since this technique is performed during resolution, the recovery process in the third step should be able to recover the XOR-clause $(x_j \oplus x_{i,j} \oplus \top)$ from the two OR-clauses in Eq. (1). Adding the recovered clause to the XOR system and performing GE should have a similar result as replacing $x_{i,j}$ by x_j.

3 Implementation Details

Input Forms. The WDSAT solver can read formulas in both ANF and CNF-XOR form. Reading a formula in ANF comes with two advantages. The first one is linked to branching rules and the second is that this form allows us to use the extension of the XG module. Since the direct encoding is shorter, in number of clauses, than in CNF-XOR modeling, the use of ANF comes more advantageous within the context of cryptographic problems.

Branching Rules. Reading a formula in ANF, the solver can store the information of which variables comprise the initial system, as opposed to variables that are added to substitute a conjunction. We can thus, distinguish *unary* variables from *substitution* variables. The truth value of a substitution variable is equal to the conjunction of the truth values of the corresponding unary variables. As a result, assigning truth values to all unary variables will necessarily propagate all other variables (see, for instance, Proposition 1 in [23]). In WDSAT, only unary variables are considered in the binary search. Conflict-driven branching heuristics can not be used in WDSAT, as the solver does not perform conflict analysis. In addition, there is a heuristic branching technique specific to SAT instances derived from Boolean polynomial systems developed for WDSAT. This technique, inspired by the Minimal Vertex Cover problem from graph theory, determines the minimal subset of variables that need to be assigned to obtain a formula comprised only of XOR-clauses. This formula is then solved in polynomial time using GE. The technique is currently used only during preprocessing to provide a predetermined branching order that is optimal. Thus, the solver does not use heuristics to decide on the order of branching variables dynamically, but the order can be specified by the user. This feature is to be used if the user has more information on the system or if the preprocessing technique was applied.

3.1   Three Reasoning Modules

In this section, we give a description and implementation details of the three modules that make up the WDSAT solver and we propose a novel CNF module that can handle longer clauses. Each module has its own propagation stack, called the $CNF\_propagation\_stack$, the $XORSET\_propagation\_stack$ and the $XG\_propagation\_stack$, as well as a respective SET_IN function that sets a literal to TRUE in the corresponding module. These stacks are used for communication between the modules. For simplicity, we consider that these stacks and all other data structures relative to the modules are included in a structure F, simply referred to as the propositional formula.

CNF Module. In this module, responsible for unit propagation on OR-clauses, the OR-clauses are treated as lists of implications, following an idea of Heule *et al.* [12] for handling 3-OR-clauses, implemented in the March SAT solver. In addition, the method is extended to handle 4-OR-clauses. Hence, WDSAT is able to solve instances derived from Boolean polynomial systems of degree three at most.

Compressed CNF Reasoning. In this section, we propose an original method for handling OR-clauses, using a compact data structure and simple bitwise operations. Our module serves as an addition to the WDSAT solver, as it allows us to handle OR-clauses of any size. In this module, OR-clauses are stored as bit-vectors comprised of the following three parts: the *value* of the clause is the arithmetic sum of its literals in their *dimacs* representation, the *weight* of the clause is the number of unassigned literals left in the clause and the final part, referred to as the *sat assessment* is composed of only one bit that is set to 1 when the clause is already satisfied by one of its assigned literals, and to 0 otherwise. The *value* and the *weight* bit-vectors have a predetermined static length. The first two lines in Table 1 show an example of the representation of two OR-clauses. As an illustration, the *value* of $\neg x_1 \lor x_4 \lor \neg x_2$ is $(-1) + 4 + (-2) = 1$, and the *weight* equals 3.

Let k be the number of variables in a CNF, and let W be the length of the longest OR-clause. The length of a bit-vector representing a clause in this manner is given by the formula:

$$\lceil \log_2(2Wk) \rceil + \lceil \log_2(W) \rceil + 1. \tag{2}$$

Since the increase is asymptotically logarithmic, a 64-bit integer can easily represent very long clauses. Hence, a formula is an array of integers, denoted *clauses*, where each entry represents a clause. In the remainder of this section, we will use $|W|$ to denote the length (in bits) of the maximal *weight*.

To perform unit propagation, we need to have efficient access to the occurrences of each literal. More specifically, we allocate an array occ_in_clause indexed by signed literals. Each entry in the array holds a list of clauses in which the corresponding literal occurs. When we set a literal l to TRUE, we perform the following operations. As per the first rule of unit propagation, the *sat assessment* is set to 1 in all clauses from the list $occ\_in\_clause[l]$. As per the second unit propagation rule, $-l$ is subtracted from the *value* of all clauses from the list $occ\_in\_clause[-l]$, and the *weight* of these clauses is decremented.

Table 1. Example of two clauses in a CNF with 4 variables and maximum clause length 4.

OR-clause	Bit-vector			Decimal
	Value	Weight	Sat	
$\neg x_1 \lor x_4 \lor \neg x_2$	00001	011	0	22
$x_1 \lor x_3$	00100	010	0	68
Set x_1 to FALSE.				
$\neg x_1 \lor x_4 \lor \neg x_2$	00001	011	1	23
x_3	00011	001	0	50
Propagation: x_3 is set to TRUE.				

With our compact representation, clauses are managed using only bitwise operations. More specifically, we use the following functions, where, as per the C syntax, $\ll$ and $\gg$ denote the left and right bitwise shift, & denotes the bitwise AND , and | denotes the bitwise OR. These functions are used in the SET_IN_CNF function, given in Algorithm 1.

- GET_CLAUSE_VALUE(cl) : $clauses[cl] \gg (|W| + 1)$;
- GET_CLAUSE_WEIGHT(cl) : $(clauses[cl] \gg 1)$ & $(2^{|W|} - 1)$;
- LITERAL_TO_CLAUSE(l) : $(l \ll (|W| + 1))$ | 2;
- IS_CLAUSE_SAT(cl) : $clauses[cl]$ & 1;
- SET_CLAUSE_TO_SAT(cl) : $clauses[cl] \leftarrow clauses[cl]$ | 1;

As we can see in Algorithm 1, a propagation is detected when the *weight* of a clause is equal to 1. In this case, the *value* of the clause is equal to the *dimacs* representation of the only remaining literal that can satisfy the clause, and thus, the literal is directly propagated. A conflict occurs when we try to assign a variable that is already assigned to the opposite truth value. The second part of Table 1 shows an example of the changes that are made in the *clauses* structure from the execution of Algorithm 1.

This economical structure is adapted for the requirements of WDSAT and the classic DPLL algorithm. In this paradigm, it is never required to get all literals from a specific clause, or to check which literals are unassigned, unless there is only one unassigned literal left. Thus, it is not concerning that these operations can not be done efficiently in our CNF module.

XORSET Module. XORSET is a simple module for parity reasoning. In other words, this module performs unit propagation on XOR-clauses. The unit propagation rule can be informally defined as follows. When all except one literal in an XOR-clause are assigned, the remaining literal is given a truth value according to parity reasoning. Recall that an XOR-clause is satisfied if there is an odd number of literals that are set to TRUE.

During the solving process, the solver counts the number of literals in a clause that are set to TRUE, and respectively the ones that are set to FALSE. In order to

Algorithm 1. Function SET_IN_CNF(to_set, F) : Function that sets a list of literals to TRUE.

Input: A list of literals that need to be set to TRUE, the propositional formula F
Output: FALSE if unsatisfiability is detected with unit propagation, TRUE otherwise.

```
1:  CNF_propagation_stack ← to_set.
2:  while CNF_propagation_stack is not empty do
3:      l ← top element from CNF_propagation_stack.
4:      if assignment[l] ≠ TRUE then
5:          if assignment[l] = FALSE then
6:              return FALSE.
7:          end if
8:          assignment[l] ← TRUE.
9:          for each cl in occ_in_clause[l] do
10:             SET_CLAUSE_TO_SAT(cl).
11:         end for
12:         for each cl in occ_in_clause[-l] do
13:             if not IS_CLAUSE_SAT(cl) then
14:                 clauses[cl] ← clauses[cl]- LITERAL_TO_CLAUSE(-l).
15:                 if GET_CLAUSE_WEIGHT(cl) = 1 then
16:                     l_prop ← GET_CLAUSE_VALUE(cl).
17:                     add l_prop to CNF_propagation_stack.
18:                 end if
19:             end if
20:         end for
21:     end if
22: end while
23: return TRUE.
```

do this efficiently, the solver needs to have quick access to the occurrences of each literal. At the implementation level, the structure that keeps this information is an array indexed by both positive and negative literals that contains lists of clauses in which a literal appears. This is a classical technique for implementing basic XOR reasoning in a SAT solver.

XORGAUSS Module. As explained in Sect. 2, in this module, XOR-clauses are represented as equivalence classes. To obtain this representation, the first step is to *normalise* all clauses so that they contain only positive literals and do not contain more than one occurrence of each literal. To eliminate negative literals, normalised clauses may contain a $\top$ constant. All variables in a clause are considered to belong to the same equivalence class (EC), and one literal from the EC is chosen to be the representative. An XOR-clause $(x_1 \oplus x_2 \oplus ... \oplus x_n) \Leftrightarrow \top$ rewrites as $x_1 \Leftrightarrow (x_2 \oplus x_3 \oplus ... \oplus x_n \oplus \top)$. The initialization process of the XG module consists in performing the following steps for each XOR-clause : (i) put the clause in normal form, (ii) transform the clause into an EC and (iii) replace all occurrences of its representative in the system with the right side of the equivalence. Applying this transformation, we obtain a simplified system having the unicity-of-representatives property.

Example 1. Let us consider the following set of three XOR-clauses.

$$x_1 \oplus x_4 \oplus x_5 \oplus x_6$$
$$x_1 \oplus x_2 \oplus \neg x_4$$
$$x_2 \oplus x_3 \oplus \neg x_6$$

The steps of the initialization process of this formula are shown in Table 2. The left column shows the set of equivalence classes that grows with each step. The right column shows the set of remaining XOR-clauses. We consider that all clauses are already put in normal form. This set becomes smaller as each clause is transformed into an equivalence class.

Table 2. Equivalence classes initialization steps.

Set of equivalence classes	Set of XOR-clauses
$\emptyset$	$x_1 \oplus x_4 \oplus x_5 \oplus x_6$
	$x_1 \oplus x_2 \oplus x_4 \oplus \top$
	$x_2 \oplus x_3 \oplus x_6 \oplus \top$
$x_1 \Leftrightarrow x_4 \oplus x_5 \oplus x_6 \oplus \top$	$x_2 \oplus x_5 \oplus x_6$
	$x_2 \oplus x_3 \oplus x_6 \oplus \top$
$x_1 \Leftrightarrow x_4 \oplus x_5 \oplus x_6 \oplus \top$	$x_3 \oplus x_5$
$x_2 \Leftrightarrow x_5 \oplus x_6 \oplus \top$	
$x_1 \Leftrightarrow x_4 \oplus x_5 \oplus x_6 \oplus \top$	$\emptyset$
$x_2 \Leftrightarrow x_5 \oplus x_6 \oplus \top$	
$x_3 \Leftrightarrow x_5 \oplus \top$	

At the implementation level, XOR-clauses are represented as bit-vectors. If a variable is present in the clause, the corresponding bit is set to 1, otherwise it is set to 0. Plus, the first bit in the vector is used for the $\top/\bot$ constant. For a compact representation, bit-vectors are stored in an array of 64-bit integers. For instance, to store a k-bit vector, an array of $\lceil (k+1)/64 \rceil$ integers is allocated. Finally, the clauses represented in this manner are stored in an array indexed by the representatives. This array is the core structure of the XG module and it will be referred to as the EC structure. For an example of the EC structure, see Fig. 1 that illustrates the set of equivalence classes that we obtain through the transformation in Table 2. In this illustration, each line represents one equivalency and is labeled with the representative. The columns are colored in gray if and only if the corresponding variable belongs to the right side of the equivalency. The constant is referenced in the first column.

To explain the implementation choices, in Table 3 we recall the inference rules from [22] for performing GE in the XG module of WDSAT. In this table, R denotes the set of representatives and C denotes the set of clauses. C_x is

Fig. 1. The *EC* structure.

an XOR-clause in C that is represented by an EC with representative x. Finally, $var(C_x)$ denotes the set of literals (plus a $\top/\bot$ constant) in the clause C_x and the notation $C[x_1/\phi]$ is used when the literal x_1 is replaced by ϕ in all clauses, where ϕ may be a clause, a variable or a constant.

Table 3. Inference rules for the substitution of x_1 by a TRUE/FALSE constant.

Premises	Conclusions on C	Updates on R
x_1, C	$C[x_1/\top]$	*N/A*
$x_1 \not\in R$		
x_1, C	$C_{x_2} \leftarrow C_{x_1} \oplus x_2 \oplus \top$	$R \leftarrow R \setminus \{x_1\}$
$x_1 \in R$	$C[x_2/C_{x_2}]$	$R \leftarrow R \cup \{x_2\}$
$x_2 \in var(C_{x_1})$		

This representation of equivalence classes allows for an efficient implementation of the inference rules, where the main operations are XOR-ing bit-vectors and flipping the clause constant. The first rule, for whose application we give pseudo-code in Algorithm 2, corresponds to the case where x_1 is not a representative. In a bit-vector from the *EC* structure, individual bits can be set to 0, set to 1 or their value can be checked. We distinguish variable bits from the constant bit. Other operations that modify the *EC* structure are FLIP_CONSTANT, used simply to inverse the value of the constant bit, and the operator $\oplus$ that denotes the XOR-ing of two bit-vectors. Lines in Algorithm 2 that contain operations that modify the *EC* structure are in bold. For a better understanding of the infer algorithm, we provide an execution example in Fig. 2. In this example, we show the contents of the *EC* structure after the execution of each line in bold. The infer function corresponding to the second inference rule, where x_1 is in the set of representatives, is detailed in Algorithm 3. In this algorithm, a RESET_VECTOR function is used that simply sets all the bits in a given bit-vector to 0. The execution example for this algorithm is given in Fig. 3.

Finally, everything is linked together in the SET_IN function of the XG module, detailed in Algorithm 4. In this algorithm, the GET_PROPOSITIONAL_VARIABLE function extracts the propositional variable from a literal and the GET_TRUTH_VALUE function checks whether l is a positive or a negative literal. For instance, calling GET_PROPOSITIONAL_VARIABLE($\neg x_1$) would return x_1 and GET_TRUTH_VALUE($\neg x_1$) would return FALSE.

Algorithm 2. Function INFER_NON_REPRESENTATIVE(ul, tv, F) : Function that applies the first inference rule to the EC structure.

Input: Propositional variable ul, truth value tv, the propositional formula F
Output: The EC structure and the $XG\_propagation\_stack$ are modified.

1: add ul to R.
2: **if** tv =TRUE **then**
3:     FLIP_CONSTANT($EC[ul]$).
4: **end if**
5: set ul to 1 in $EC[ul]$.
6: **for each** r in R **do**
7:     **if** ul is set to 1 in $EC[r]$ **then**
8:         $EC[r] \leftarrow EC[r] \oplus EC[ul]$.
9:         **if** all variable bits in $EC[r]$ are set to 0 **then**
10:             **if** the constant bit in $EC[r]$ is set to 1 **then**
11:                 add r to $XG\_propagation\_stack$.
12:             **else**
13:                 add $\neg r$ to $XG\_propagation\_stack$.
14:             **end if**
15:         **end if**
16:     **end if**
17: **end for**
18: set ul to 0 in $EC[ul]$.

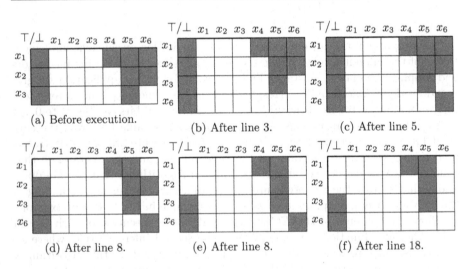

(a) Before execution.   (b) After line 3.   (c) After line 5.

(d) After line 8.   (e) After line 8.   (f) After line 18.

Fig. 2. Setting x_6 to TRUE. Stream of changes on the EC structure after execution of the respective lines of Algorithm 2.

4   Applications in Cryptanalysis

At the core of algebraic cryptanalysis, as well as multivariate public-key cryptography is the problem of solving a multivariate polynomial system, which is

Algorithm 3. Function INFER_REPRESENTATIVE(ul, tv, F) : Function that applies the second inference rule to the EC structure.

Input: Propositional variable ul, truth value tv, the propositional formula F
Output: The EC structure and the $XG\_propagation\_stack$ are modified.

1: $new\_r \leftarrow$ CHOOSE_NEW_REPRESENTATIVE($EC[ul]$).
2: add new_r to R.
3: $EC[new\_r] \leftarrow EC[new\_r] \oplus EC[ul]$.
4: RESET_VECTOR($EC[ul]$).
5: **if** $tv = \top$ **then**
6:      FLIP_CONSTANT($EC[ul]$).
7:      FLIP_CONSTANT($EC[new\_r]$).
8: **end if**
9: **for each** r in R **do**
10:      **if** new_r is set to 1 in $EC[r]$ **then**
11:          $EC[r] \leftarrow EC[r] \oplus EC[new\_r]$.
12:          **if** all variable bits in $EC[r]$ are set to 0 **then**
13:              **if** the constant bit in $EC[r]$ is set to 1 **then**
14:                  add r to $XG\_propagation\_stack$.
15:              **else**
16:                  add $\neg r$ to $XG\_propagation\_stack$.
17:              **end if**
18:          **end if**
19:      **end if**
20: **end for**
21: set new_r to 0 in $EC[new\_r]$.
22: **if** all variable bits in $EC[new\_r]$ are set to 0 **then**
23:      **if** the constant bit in $EC[new\_r]$ is set to 1 **then**
24:          add new_r to $XG\_propagation\_stack$.
25:      **else**
26:          add $\neg new\_r$ to $XG\_propagation\_stack$.
27:      **end if**
28: **end if**

considered to be NP-hard. The crucial parameters in evaluating the hardness of a multivariate polynomial system are the number of variables, denoted by n, the number of equations, denoted by m and their ratio. The case of $m = n$ is considered to be the hardest, whereas overdetermined systems are easier to solve.

For our experimental work, we generate instances with parameters $m = 2n$ and with (pseudo)random solutions, where all coefficients are randomly generated following the uniform distribution. The process of generating one random instance follows these steps: (i) Fix parameters m and n. (ii) Choose randomly an n-bit solution vector. (iii) For each equation, choose randomly all coefficients except the 0/1 constant, and then compute the constant according to the solution vector chosen in the previous step. This generation approach results in dense polynomial systems, as each monomial has probability $1/2$ to appear in each equation. Heuristically, we expect most instances obtained in this way to

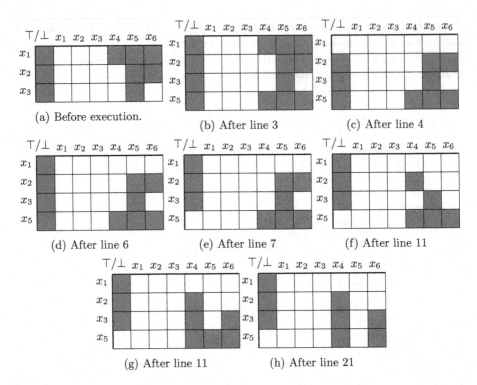

Fig. 3. Setting x_1 to TRUE (x_5 is chosen as the new representative). Stream of changes on the EC structure after execution of the respective lines of Algorithm 3.

be hard and to have no underlying structure. For MQ systems, currently the best solving tools are algebraic tools, such as the Joux-Vitse hybrid algorithm [13] and the libFes library [4] based on Bouillaguet *et al.*'s algorithm [5]. According to experimental results reported in [13], WDSat does not outperform algebraic solving tools for MQ instances.

Complexity Analysis. The complexity analysis in this section concerns MQ systems, but it can be extended for systems of higher degree. Let v denote the number of variables in a SAT instance. Since WDSAT is DPLL-based, we consider that the worst-case time complexity is, in general, $\mathcal{O}(2^v)$. However, as explained in Sect. 3, WDSAT has an advantage over generic SAT solvers when it reads a formula in ANF, as it decides to branch only on variables that are present in the initial Boolean polynomial system. Thus, the complexity is $\mathcal{O}(2^n)$ where $n \leq v$ (with equality only in the case where the initial Boolean system is linear). Moreover, for instances derived from the MQ problem, we can make a more precise estimation. The following analysis concerns the WDSAT XG-EXT variant, as this variant was found to be the most efficient for MQ systems. Our complexity analysis is based on estimating the DPLL-tree level on which conflicts are found.

Algorithm 4. Function SET_IN_XG(to_set, F) : Function that sets a list of literals to TRUE.

Input: A list of literals that need to be set to TRUE, the propositional formula F
Output: FALSE if unsatisfiability is detected with unit propagation, TRUE otherwise.

1: $XG\_propagation\_stack \leftarrow to\_set$.
2: **while** $XG\_propagation\_stack$ is not empty **do**
3:    $l \leftarrow$ top element from $XG\_propagation\_stack$.
4:    **if** $assignment[l] \neq$ TRUE **then**
5:        **if** $assignment[l] =$ FALSE **then**
6:            **return** FALSE.
7:        **end if**
8:        $assignment[l] \leftarrow$ TRUE.
9:        $ul \leftarrow$ GET_PROPOSITIONAL_VARIABLE(l).
10:        $tv \leftarrow$ GET_TRUTH_VALUE(l).
11:        **if** $x_1 \in R$ **then**
12:            INFER_REPRESENTATIVE(ul, tv, F).
13:        **else**
14:            INFER_NON_REPRESENTATIVE(ul, tv, F).
15:        **end if**
16:    **end if**
17: **end while**
18: **return** TRUE.

Recall that the EC structure in the XORGAUSS module of the WDSAT solver can be viewed as a matrix whose columns are all monomials and unary variables in the system, and the lines are linear XOR-clauses, similar to the Macaulay matrix [16]. Thus, this matrix holds a linearized system that will have a unique solution when the number of lines is equal to the number of columns. This is true because the GE that is performed on each step ensures that all remaining XOR-clauses represent linearly independent equations. For an MQ system, the number of columns in the EC structure, supposing that all monomials have at least one occurrence, is $n(n+1)/2$. It is well-known that overdetermined systems where $m \geq n(n+1)/2$ are solvable in polynomial time. Let n' be the number of remaining variables in the system after the solving process has started. Then, at level h of the binary search tree, we have that $n' = n - h$. As per our previous analysis, the system is solved or a conflict is met when $m \approx n'(n'+1)/2$, i.e. at level $h \approx n - \sqrt{2m}$. We conclude that the complexity of WDSAT with XG-EXT for solving instances derived from the MQ problem is

$$\mathcal{O}(2^{n-\sqrt{2m}}). \tag{3}$$

Even though this analysis is strongly linked to the GE, it does not necessarily hold for other SAT solvers that perform GE, such as CRYPTOMINISAT. If a solver does not apply the XG-EXT technique, it can not be guaranteed that the number of remaining columns in the EC matrix with entries different from 0 will be $n'(n'+1)/2$ on level h.

Experimental Results. Table 4 shows a comparison between different approaches for solving MQ systems. These experiments were performed on a 2.40 GHz Intel Xeon E5-2640 processor, all results are an average of 100 runs and running times are in seconds. The first four entries show the performance of non XOR-enabled SAT solvers, namely MINISAT [8], GLUCOSE [1], KISSAT [3], which

Table 4. Comparing different approaches for solving the MQ problem.

n	m	Input form	#Vars	#Clauses	Solver	Runtime	#Conflicts
25	50	CNF	8301	33006	MINISAT	11525.24	40718489
					GLUCOSE	2384.99	10982657
					KISSAT	2118.52	6622284
					RELAXED	3014.22	10353009
		CNF-XOR	325	920	CRYPTOMINISAT 5.6.5	2598.66	9806242
					CRYPTOMINISAT 5.6.5 + GE	383.06	2007847
					CRYPTOMINISAT 5.8.0	2870.81	9197978
					CRYPTOMINISAT 5.8.0 + GE	594.48	2407635
					WDSAT	57.85	14177200
					WDSAT + GE	23.77	1046328
		ANF	25	50	WDSAT + XG-EXT	**0.82**	**21140**
30	60	CNF-XOR	465	1365	CRYPTOMINISAT 5.6.5 + GE	28954.14	116013784
					WDSAT	2774.44	483437900
					WDSAT + GE	1223.16	34718415
		ANF	30	60	WDSAT + XG-EXT	**17.71**	**379346**

is the winner in the main track of the latest SAT competition [15] in 2020, and RELAXED_LCMDCBDL_NEWTECH [24], the winner in the main track on satisfiable instances. These solvers take as input a CNF and the number of variables and clauses shown in the table are an average of the 100 instances for the chosen parameters. We note that, for these specific instances, KISSAT has the best performance among the non XOR-enabled solvers.

For the XOR-enabled solvers, CRYPTOMINISAT and WDSAT, we tested different versions, specifically to see whether performing GE results in better running times for solving instances derived from the MQ problem. First, we conclude that the best version of WDSAT is the one with the XG-EXT technique. Then, we can see that CRYPTOMINISAT gives better results when the GE is turned on, however, CRYPTOMINISAT 5.8.0, which is the most recent version seems slower for these instances than CRYPTOMINISAT 5.6.5. For this reason, we report results for both versions. Note that in CRYPTOMINISAT 5.8.0 GE is used by default and it is automatically disabled if the solver detects that it performs badly. This version is denoted CRYPTOMINISAT 5.8.0 in Table 4, whereas CRYPTOMINISAT 5.8.0 + GE denotes experiments where CRYPTOMINISAT 5.8.0 is executed with the option **-autodisablegauss 0**, which ensures that GE is used throughout the entire solving process.

For versions of the solvers that have good performances (namely approaches with GE, plus the simplest version of WDSAT) we were able to increase the parameters and results are shown at the end of Table 4. We conclude that WDSAT outperforms all other solvers for these instances. Finally, to confirm our complexity analysis for the XG-EXT version of WDSAT, we checked the level at which conflicts occur, and found that it is either $\lfloor n - \sqrt{2m} \rfloor$ or $\lceil n - \sqrt{2m} \rceil$, with no exceptions.

Table 5 shows running time comparisons between WDSAT XG-EXT using the original CNF module and WDSAT XG-EXT using the compressed CNF module that we propose in Sect. 3.1. We conclude that running times are comparable and that replacing the CNF module in WDSAT by our proposed CNF module does not impair the performance of the solver, while allowing us to solve higher degree polynomial systems. For instance, we used the compressed CNF module to solve systems of degree (d) four and the results are shown at the end of Table 5.

Table 5. Comparing WDSAT's original CNF module with our compressed CNF module for solving multivariate polynomial systems.

d	OR-clause size	n	m	#Vars CNF	#Clauses CNF	CNF module	Runtime	#Conflicts
2	3	25	50	325	920	Original	0.82	21140
						Compressed	0.98	
		30	60	465	1365	Original	17.71	379346
						Compressed	21.26	
3	4	20	40	1350	5130	Original	30.65	57597
						Compressed	30.54	
		25	50	2625	10100	Original	3413.09	2095437
						Compressed	3529.71	
4	5	15	30	1940	8960	Compressed	4.86	4333
		18	36	4047	19023	Compressed	180.52	39204

5   Conclusion

In this paper, we gave implementation details of the WDSAT solver and showed that it has a broader range of cryptographic applications than the one it was initially designed for. Several cryptographic attacks can be reduced to the problem of solving a Boolean multivariate polynomial system, and when the derived systems are dense, experimental results suggest that WDSAT gives the best performance among state-of-the-art SAT solvers. In addition, our novel CNF module completes WDSAT, so that it can tackle Boolean polynomial systems of any degree. This paper does not alter the overall state-of-the-art, as for MQ instances, algebraic tools are still faster than XOR -enabled SAT solvers.

References

1. Audemard, G., Simon, L.: Predicting learnt clauses quality in modern SAT solvers. In: IJCAI 2009, Proceedings of the 21st International Joint Conference on Artificial Intelligence, Pasadena, California, USA, July 11–17, 2009, pp. 399–404 (2009)
2. Bettale, L., Faugère, J., Perret, L.: Hybrid approach for solving multivariate systems over finite fields. J. Math. Cryptol. **3**(3), 177–197 (2009)
3. Biere, A., Fazekas, K., Fleury, M., Heisinger, M.: CaDiCaL, Kissat, Paracooba, Plingeling and Treengeling entering the SAT competition 2020. In: Balyo, T., Froleyks, N., Heule, M., Iser, M., Järvisalo, M., Suda, M. (eds.) Proceedings of SAT Competition 2020 - Solver and Benchmark Descriptions. Department of Computer Science Report Series B, vol. B-2020-1, pp. 51–53. University of Helsinki (2020)
4. Bouillaguet, C.: LibFES-lite. https://github.com/cbouilla/libfes-lite (2016)
5. Bouillaguet, C., Cheng, C.-M., Chou, T., Niederhagen, R., Yang, B.-Y.: Fast exhaustive search for quadratic systems in $\mathbb{F}_2$ on FPGAs. In: Lange, T., Lauter, K., Lisoněk, P. (eds.) SAC 2013. LNCS, vol. 8282, pp. 205–222. Springer, Heidelberg (2014). https://doi.org/10.1007/978-3-662-43414-7_11
6. Courtois, N., Klimov, A., Patarin, J., Shamir, A.: Efficient algorithms for solving overdefined systems of multivariate polynomial equations. In: Preneel, B. (ed.) EUROCRYPT 2000. LNCS, vol. 1807, pp. 392–407. Springer, Heidelberg (2000). https://doi.org/10.1007/3-540-45539-6_27
7. Davis, M., Logemann, G., Loveland, D.W.: A machine program for theorem-proving. Commun. ACM **5**(7), 394–397 (1962)
8. Eén, N., Sörensson, N.: An extensible SAT-solver. In: Giunchiglia, E., Tacchella, A. (eds.) SAT 2003. LNCS, vol. 2919, pp. 502–518. Springer, Heidelberg (2004). https://doi.org/10.1007/978-3-540-24605-3_37
9. Faugère, J.C.: A new efficient algorithm for computing Gröbner basis (F4). J. Pure Appl. Algebra **139**(1–3), 61–88 (1999)
10. Galbraith, S.D., Gebregiyorgis, S.W.: Summation polynomial algorithms for elliptic curves in characteristic two. In: Meier, W., Mukhopadhyay, D. (eds.) INDOCRYPT 2014. LNCS, vol. 8885, pp. 409–427. Springer, Cham (2014). https://doi.org/10.1007/978-3-319-13039-2_24
11. Han, C.-S., Jiang, J.-H.R.: When Boolean satisfiability meets Gaussian elimination in a simplex way. In: Madhusudan, P., Seshia, S.A. (eds.) CAV 2012. LNCS, vol. 7358, pp. 410–426. Springer, Heidelberg (2012). https://doi.org/10.1007/978-3-642-31424-7_31
12. Heule, M., Dufour, M., van Zwieten, J., van Maaren, H.: March_eq: implementing additional reasoning into an efficient look-ahead SAT solver. In: Hoos, H.H., Mitchell, D.G. (eds.) SAT 2004. LNCS, vol. 3542, pp. 345–359. Springer, Heidelberg (2005). https://doi.org/10.1007/11527695_26
13. Joux, A., Vitse, V.: A crossbred algorithm for solving Boolean polynomial systems. In: Kaczorowski, J., Pieprzyk, J., Pomykała, J. (eds.) NuTMiC 2017. LNCS, vol. 10737, pp. 3–21. Springer, Cham (2018). https://doi.org/10.1007/978-3-319-76620-1_1
14. Laitinen, T., Junttila, T., Niemelä, I.: Conflict-driven XOR-clause learning. In: Cimatti, A., Sebastiani, R. (eds.) SAT 2012. LNCS, vol. 7317, pp. 383–396. Springer, Heidelberg (2012). https://doi.org/10.1007/978-3-642-31612-8_29
15. van Maaren, H., Franco, J.: The International SAT Competition Web Page. http://www.satcompetition.org/. Accessed 27 May 2020

16. Macaulay, F.S.: The Algebraic Theory of Modular Systems. Cambridge Tracts in Mathematics and Mathematical Physics, University Press (1916). https://books.google.fr/books?id=uA7vAAAAMAAJ
17. Massacci, F., Marraro, L.: Logical cryptanalysis as a SAT problem. J. Autom. Reasoning 24(1/2), 165–203 (2000). http://dblp.uni-trier.de/db/journals/jar/jar24.html#MassacciM00
18. McDonald, C., Charnes, C., Pieprzyk, J.: An algebraic analysis of Trivium ciphers based on the Boolean satisfiability problem. IACR Cryptol. ePrint Arch. 2007, 129 (2007). http://eprint.iacr.org/2007/129
19. Soos, M.: Enhanced Gaussian elimination in DPLL-based SAT solvers. In: POS-10. Pragmatics of SAT, Edinburgh, UK, July 10, 2010. EPiC Series in Computing, vol. 8, pp. 2–14. EasyChair (2010)
20. Soos, M., Meel, K.S.: BIRD: engineering an efficient CNF-XOR SAT solver and its applications to approximate model counting. In: The Thirty-Third AAAI Conference on Artificial Intelligence, AAAI 2019, The Thirty-First Innovative Applications of Artificial Intelligence Conference, IAAI 2019, The Ninth AAAI Symposium on Educational Advances in Artificial Intelligence, EAAI 2019, Honolulu, Hawaii, USA, 27 January–1 February 2019, pp. 1592–1599. AAAI Press (2019)
21. Soos, M., Nohl, K., Castelluccia, C.: Extending SAT solvers to cryptographic problems. In: Kullmann, O. (ed.) SAT 2009. LNCS, vol. 5584, pp. 244–257. Springer, Heidelberg (2009). https://doi.org/10.1007/978-3-642-02777-2_24
22. Trimoska, M., Ionica, S., Dequen, G.: Parity (XOR) reasoning for the index calculus attack. In: Simonis, H. (ed.) CP 2020. LNCS, vol. 12333, pp. 774–790. Springer, Cham (2020). https://doi.org/10.1007/978-3-030-58475-7_45
23. Trimoska, M., Ionica, S., Dequen, G.: A SAT-based approach for index calculus on binary elliptic curves. In: Nitaj, A., Youssef, A. (eds.) AFRICACRYPT 2020. LNCS, vol. 12174, pp. 214–235. Springer, Cham (2020). https://doi.org/10.1007/978-3-030-51938-4_11
24. Zhang, X., Cai, S.: Relaxed backtracking with Rephasing. In: Balyo, T., Froleyks, N., Heule, M., Iser, M., Järvisalo, M., Suda, M. (eds.) Proceedings of SAT Competition 2020 - Solver and Benchmark Descriptions. Department of Computer Science Report Series B, vol. B-2020-1, pp. 16–17. University of Helsinki (2020)

Author Index

Printed in the United States
by Baker & Taylor Publisher Services

Printed in the United States
by Baker & Taylor Publisher Services